POPULAR
MUSIC,
1920-1979

Popular Music, 1920-1979 is a revised cumulation of and supersedes Volumes 1 through 8 of the *Popular Music* series, all of which are still in print:

Volume 1, 2nd ed., 1950-59
Volume 2, 1940-49
Volume 3, 1960-64
Volume 4, 1930-39

Volume 5, 1920-29
Volume 6, 1965-69
Volume 7, 1970-74
Volume 8, 1975-79

Published 1986:

Volume 9, 1980-1984

POPULAR MUSIC, 1920-1979

An Annotated Index of over 18,000 American Popular Songs, Cumulating and Updating Eight Volumes of *Popular Music* and Including Introductory Essays, Lyricists and Composers Index, Important Performances Index, Awards Index, and List of Publishers

A Revised Cumulation

In Three Volumes

VOLUME 3:

Song Listings U-Z
Indexes
List of Publishers

Nat Shapiro and Bruce Pollock,
Editors

GALE RESEARCH COMPANY
BOOK TOWER ● *DETROIT, MICHIGAN 48226*

Nat Shapiro and Bruce Pollock, *Editors*
Linda S. Hubbard, *Managing Editor of Revised Cumulation*
Meta E. Jaenike, *Assistant Editor*
Diane S. Aronson, Thomas M. Bachmann, *Editorial Assistants*

Carol Blanchard, *Production Director*
Mary Beth Trimper, *Senior Production Associate*
Arthur Chartow, *Art Director*

Dennis LaBeau, *Editorial Data Systems Director*
Marie Evans, Theresa Rocklin, *Program Design*
Doris D. Goulart, *Editorial Data Entry Supervisor*
Jean Portfolio, *Editorial Data Entry Associate*
Sue Lynch, Joyce M. Stone, Anna Marie Woolard, *Senior Data Entry Assistants*
Patricia Smith, *Data Entry Assistant*

Frederick G. Ruffner, *Publisher*
James M. Ethridge, *Executive Vice-President/Editorial*
Dedria Bryfonski, *Editorial Director*
Ellen T. Crowley, *Director, Indexes and Dictionaries Division*

Library of Congress Cataloging in Publication Data

Shapiro, Nat.

Popular music, 1920-1979.

"An annotated index of over 18,000 American popular
songs, cumulating and updating eight volumes of
Popular music . . ."
    Includes indexes.
    1. Music, Popular (Songs, etc.)—United States—
Bibliography. I. Pollock, Bruce. II. Shapiro, Nat.
Popular music. III. Title.
ML120.U5S5   1985   784.5'00973   85-6749
ISBN 0-8103-0847-9

Computerized photocomposition by Automatech Graphics, New York, New York
Printed in the United States of America

Contents

POPULAR MUSIC, 1920-1979

Song Listings U-Z
Indexes
List of Publishers

U

U Need Some Loving Blues
Words and music by Perry Bradford.
Perry Bradford Music Publishing Co., 1921.
First recording by Mamie Smith and her Jazz Hounds (Okeh).

Uh! Oh! (The Nutty Squirrels)
Words and music by Granville "Sascha" Burland and Don Elliott.
Little Hurry Music, Inc., 1959.
Best-selling record by The Nutty Squirrels (Hanover).

Uh-Oh!
Words by Anne Croswell, music by Lee Pockriss.
Piedmont Music Co., Inc., 1963.
Introduced by Margery Gray and Byron Mitchell in *Tovarich* (musical).

Ukulele Lady
Words by Gus Kahn, music by Richard A. Whiting.
Bourne Co., 1925/Whiting Music Corp., 1925.
Popularized by Vaughn De Leath and by Nick Lucas. Sung by the
  chorus in *I'll See You in My Dreams* (film, 1951).

Um Um Um Um Um Um, also known as **Unh Unh Unh**
Words and music by Curtis Mayfield.
Warner-Tamerlane Publishing Corp., 1963.
Best-selling record in 1964 by Major Lance (Okeh).

The Umbrella Man
Words by James Cavanaugh, music by Vincent Rose and Larry
  Stock.
Harms, Inc., 1938/Larry Stock Music, Inc., 1938.
Introduced in United States by Guy Lombardo and his Royal Canadians.
  Introduced in London by Flanagan and Allen in *These Foolish Things*
  (revue).

Umbriago
Words and music by Irving Caesar and Jimmy Durante.
Robbins Music Corp., 1944.
Introduced by Jimmy Durante in *Music for Millions* (film).

Un Poquito de Tu Amor (Cuban)
Spanish words and music by Julio Gutierrez.
Peer International Corp., 1948.
Popularized in Latin America by Pedro Vargas and in the United States
  by Machito and his Orchestra.

Unbirthday Song
Words and music by Mack David, Al Hoffman, and Jerry
  Livingston.
Walt Disney Music Co., 1948, 1951.
Introduced in *Alice in Wonderland* (cartoon film, 1951).

Unborn Child
Words and music by Louise Bogan and James Seals.
Dawnbreaker Music Co., 1974.
Best-selling record by Seals & Crofts (Warner Brothers, 1974).

Unchain My Heart
Words and music by Agnes Jones (pseudonym for Bobby Sharp) and
  Freddy James (pseudonym for Teddy Powell).
Tee Pee Music Co., Inc., 1960.
Best-selling record in 1962 by Ray Charles (ABC-Paramount).

Unchained Melody
Words by Hy Zaret, music by Alex North.
Frank Music Co., 1955.
Theme from *Unchained* (film). Best-selling instrumental record by Les
  Baxter and his Orchestra (Capitol). Best-selling vocal record by Al
  Hibbler (Decca). Revived in 1965, with best-selling record by The
  Righteous Brothers (Philles). Nominated for an Academy Award,
  1955.

Uncle Albert/Admiral Halsey (English)
Words and music by Paul McCartney and Linda McCartney.
MPL Communications Inc., 1971.
Best-selling record by Paul McCartney & Wings (Apple, 1971).

Uncle John's Band
Words and music by Robert Hunter and Jerry Garcia.
Ice Nine Publishing Co., Inc., 1970.
Best-selling record by The Grateful Dead (Warner Brothers, 1970).

Uncle Pen
Words and music by Bill Monroe.
Kentucky Music, Inc., 1951.
Best-selling record in 1956 by Porter Wagoner (RCA Victor).

Uncle Remus Said
Words and music by Johnny Lange, Hy Heath, and Eliot Daniel.
Walt Disney Music Co., 1946.
Introduced by The Hall Johnson Choir in *Song of the South* (film).

Uncle Sam Blues
Words and music by Sara Martin and Clarence Williams.
MCA, Inc., 1923.
First recording by Sara Martin (Okeh).

Undecided
Words by Sid Robin, music by Charles Shavers.
MCA, Inc., 1939.
Introduced by Chick Webb and his Orchestra, vocal by Ella Fitzgerald.
  Revived in 1951 with best-selling record by The Ames Brothers
  (Coral).

Under a Blanket of Blue
Words by Marty Symes and Al J. Neiburg, music by Jerry
  Livingston.
World Music, Inc., 1933/Hallmark Music Co., 1933.
Introduced by Glen Gray and The Casa Loma Orchestra.

Under a Texas Moon
English words by Ray Perkins, Spanish words by Jimenez Gonzalez,
  music by Ray Perkins.
Remick Music Corp., 1929.
Introduced by Frank Fay, George E. Stone, and George Cooper in
  Under a Texas Moon (film, 1930).

Under My Thumb (English)
Words and music by Mick Jagger and Keith Richard.
Mirage Music, Ltd., London, England, 1966/ABKCO Music Inc.,
  1966.
Introduced by The Rolling Stones in their album, *Aftermath* (London).

Under Paris Skies (French)
English words by Kim Gannon, French words by Jean Drejac, music
  by Hubert Giraud.
Editions Choudens, Paris, France/MCA, Inc., 1951.
Original French title, "Sous le Ciel de Paris."

Under the Boardwalk
Words and music by Artie Resnick and Kenny Young.
The Hudson Bay Music Co., 1964.
Best-selling record by The Drifters (Atlantic).

Under the Bridges of Paris (French)
English words by Dorcas Cochran, French words by J. Rodor, music
   by Vincent Scotto.
Editions Fortin, Paris, France/Unichappell Music Inc., 1953.
Original title, "Sous les Ponts de Paris."

Under the Influence of Love
Words by Buck Owens, music by Harlan Howard.
Central Songs, 1961.
Best-selling record by Buck Owens (Capitol).

Under the Moon
Words by Ev. E. Lyn and Francis Wheeler, music by Ted Snyder.
Mills Music Inc., 1927.

Under the Yum-Yum Tree
Words by Sammy Cahn, music by James Van Heusen.
Colgems-EMI Music Inc., 1963/T. B. Harms Co., 1963.
From *Under the Yum-Yum Tree* (film). Introduced on records by Rob-
   ert Goulet (Columbia).

Under Your Spell
Words by Howard Dietz, music by Arthur Schwartz.
Harms, Inc., 1934/Movietone Music Corp., 1934.
Introduced on radio by Conrad Thibault. Sung by Lawrence Tibbett in
   Under Your Spell (film, 1936).

Under Your Spell Again
Words and music by Dusty Rhodes and Buck Owens.
Central Songs, 1959.
Best-selling records by Buck Owens (Capitol) and Ray Price (Columbia).

Under Your Spell Again
Words and music by Buck Owens.
Central Songs, 1960.
Best-selling record in 1965 by Johnny Rivers (Imperial).

Undercover Angel
Words and music by Alan O'Day.
WB Music Corp., 1977.
Best-selling record by Alan O'Day (Pacific, 1977).

Underneath the Arches (English)
Words and music by Reginald Connelly, Bud Flanagan, and Joseph McCarthy.
Campbell-Connelly Co., Ltd., London, England, 1952/Robbins Music Corp., 1933.
Introduced in England by Flanagan and Allen, comedy team. Additional lyrics written in United States by McCarthy. Best-selling record in 1948 by Primo Scala's Banjo and Accordion Orchestra (London) and The Andrews Sisters (Decca).

Underneath the Harlem Moon
Words by Mack Gordon, music by Harry Revel.
DeSylva, Brown & Henderson, Inc., 1932.

Underneath the Linden Tree (Swiss)
English words by Dick Manning, German words and music by Arthur Beul.
Edifo S.A., Zurich, Switzerland, 1947/La Salle Music Publishers, Inc., 1948, 1949.
Original title, "Regenpfeiffer Sing Dein Lied."

Underneath the Russian Moon
Words by James Kendis and Frank Samuels, music by Meyer Gusman.
Shapiro, Bernstein & Co., Inc., 1929.

Understand Your Man
Words and music by Johnny Cash.
Johnny Cash Music, Inc., 1964.
Best-selling record by Johnny Cash (Columbia).

Understanding (Is the Best Thing in the World)
Words and music by Jimmy Holiday and Ray Charles.
Unart Music Corp., 1967/Unart-Unart, 1967.
Best-selling record in 1968 by Ray Charles (ABC).

Underworld Blues
Words by Sippie Wallace and George W. Thomas, music by George W. Thomas.
Unpublished, copyright held by George W. Thomas. First recording by Sippie Wallace (Okeh).

Undun (Canadian)
Words and music by Randall C. Bachman.
Shillelagh Music Co., 1969.
Best-selling record by The Guess Who (RCA).

Uneasy Rider
Words and music by Charlie Daniels.
Kama Sutra Music Inc., 1973/Rada Dara Music, 1973.
Best-selling record by Charlie Daniels (Kama Sutra, 1973).

Unforgettable
Words and music by Irving Gordon.
Bourne Co., 1951.
Best-selling records by Nat "King" Cole (Capitol) and in 1959 by Dinah
  Washington (Mercury).

The Unforgiven (The Need for Love)
Words by Ned Washington, music by Dimitri Tiomkin.
Colby Music, Inc., 1960/Anne-Rachel Music Corp., 1960.
Adapted from theme from *The Unforgiven* (film). Best-selling record,
  instrumental, by Don Costa and his Orchestra (United Artists). First
  vocal recording by The McGuire Sisters (Coral).

Unh Unh Unh, see **Um Um Um Um Um Um.**

The Unicorn
Words and music by Shel Silverstein.
TRO-Hollis Music, Inc., 1962.
Best-selling record in 1968 by The Irish Rovers (Decca).

Union City Blue
Words and music by Nigel Harrison and Deborah Harry.
Rare Blue Music Inc., 1979.
Introduced by Blondie on *Eat to the Beat* (Chrysalis, 1979).

Union Man
Words and music by Earl Cate and Ernie Cate.
The Times Square Music Publications Co., 1976.
Best-selling record by The Cate Brothers (Asylum, 1976).

United
Words and music by Kenny Gamble and Leon Huff.
Razor Sharp Music, Inc., 1968/Blockbuster Music, Inc., 1968.
Best-selling record by Peaches and Herb (Date).

United Nations on the March (Soviet)
English words by Harold Rome, music by Dmitri Shostakovich.
Leo Feist Inc., 1943/MCA, Inc., 1943.
Adapted from Shostakovich song entitled, "Joy of Morning." English-
  language version introduced by Kathryn Grayson, accompanied by
  Jose Iturbi, in *Thousands Cheer* (film).

United We Stand (English)
Words and music by Tony Hiller and Peter Simons.
Belwin-Mills Publishing Corp., 1970.
Best-selling record by Brotherhood of Man (Deram, 1970).

The Universal Soldier
Words and music by Buffy Sainte-Marie.
Woodmere Music, 1963.
Introduced by Buffy Sainte-Marie (Vanguard). Revived in 1965 with
    best-selling records by Glen Campbell (Capitol) and Donovan (Hick-
    ory).

Unknown Soldier
Words and music by The Doors (Robert Krieger, James Morrison,
    John Densmore, and Raymond Manzarek.
Doors Music Co., 1968.
Best-selling record by The Doors (Elektra).

Unless (English)
Words and music by Robert Hargreaves, Stanley J. Damerell,
    Tolchard Evans, and Henry B. Tilsley.
Francis, Day & Hunter, Ltd., London, England, 1934/Bourne Co.,
    1934.
Introduced in England by Henry Hall and the BBC Orchestra. Revived
    in 1951 with best-selling record by Guy Mitchell (Columbia).

Unless You Care
Words and music by Philip Sloan and Steve Barri.
Trousdale Music Publishers, Inc., 1964.
Best-selling record by Terry Black (Tollie).

Unloved and Unclaimed
Words and music by Roy Acuff and Vito Pellettieri.
Acuff-Rose Publications Inc., 1948.
Best-selling record Roy Acuff (Columbia).

Unloved, Unwanted
Words and music by Wayne P. Walker and Irene Stanton.
Cedarwood Publishing Co., Inc., 1962.
Best-selling record by Kitty Wells (Decca).

Unlucky Blues, see **Unlucky Woman.**

Unlucky Woman, also known as **Unlucky Blues**
Words and music by Leonard Feather and Carol Feather.
Michael H. Goldsen, Inc., 1944.
Introduced by Helen Humes. Sung by Lena Horne in *Boogie Woogie*
    Dream (film).

Unmitigated Gall
Words and music by Mel Tillis.
Cedarwood Publishing Co., Inc., 1966.
Best-selling record by Faron Young (Mercury).

Unsquare Dance
Music by Dave Brubeck.
Derry Music Co., 1961.
Best-selling record by The Dave Brubeck Quartet (Columbia).

Unsuspecting Heart
Words by Freddy James, music by Joe Beal, Bob Singer, and Joe
   Shank.
Tee Pee Music Co., Inc., 1955.
Best-selling record by George Shaw (Decca).

Until
Words and music by Jack Fulton, Bob Crosby, and Hunter Kahler.
Music Sales Corp., 1945.
Best-selling record in 1948 by Tommy Dorsey and his Orchestra (Vic-
   tor).

Until It's Time for You to Go
Words and music by Buffy Sainte-Marie.
Gypsy Boy Music Inc., 1965.
Introduced by Buffy Sainte-Marie in her album, *Many a Mile* (Van-
   guard); best-selling record in 1967 by Buffy Sainte-Marie (Vanguard).
   Revived in 1970 by Neil Diamond (Uni) and in 1972 by Elvis Presley
   (RCA).

Until My Dreams Come True
Words and music by Dallas Frazier.
Acuff-Rose Publications Inc., 1967.
Best-selling record in 1969 by Jack Greene (Decca).

Until Sunrise
Words by Jack Wolf Fine, music by Marie Moss and Will Collins.
MCA, Inc., 1946/Colgems-EMI Music Inc., 1946.

(It Will Have To Do) Until the Real Thing Comes Along
Words and music by Sammy Cahn, Saul Chaplin, L. E. Freeman,
   Mann Holiner, and Alberta Nichols.
Chappell & Co., Inc., 1936/Anne-Rachel Music Corp., 1936/Cahn
   Music Co., 1936.
Sometimes called "The Slave Song." An earlier version, entitled "Till the
   Real Thing Comes Along," published by Shapiro, Bernstein & Co.,
   Inc. in 1931, credited to Mann Holiner and Alberta Nichols and
   introduced in Lew Leslie's *Rhapsody in Black* (revue). Best-selling

record of revised version by Andy Kirk and his Clouds of Joy, vocal by Pha Terrell (Decca).

Until Today
Words by Benny Davis, music by J. Fred Coots and Oscar Levant.
Marlo Music Corp., 1936.

Until Tomorrow
Words and music by Sammy Kaye.
World Music, Inc., 1940.
Best-selling record in 1941 by Sammy Kaye and his Orchestra (Blue-bird).

Until You Come Back to Me
Words and music by Clarence Paul, Stevie Wonder, and Morris Broadnax.
Jobete Music Co., Inc., 1967/Stone Agate Music Corp., 1967.
Best-selling record by Aretha Franklin (Atlantic, 1974).

The Untouchables
Music by Nelson Riddle.
Desilu Music Corp., 1959.
From *The Untouchables* (television series).

Unwanted Sign upon Your Heart
Words and music by Hank Snow.
Unichappell Music Inc., 1950.
Best-selling record in 1951 by Hank Snow (RCA Victor).

Up Above My Head, I Hear Music in the Air
Words and music by Sister Rosetta Tharpe.
Montauk Music, Inc., 1949.
Introduced and best-selling record by Sister Rosetta Tharpe (Decca).

Up and Down
Words and music by Dennis Lambert and Louis Pegues.
Fling Music, Inc., 1966/Grand Canyon Music, Inc., 1966/Shelby Singleton Music Inc., 1966.
Best-selling record by The McCoys (Bang).

Up Around the Bend
Words and music by John C. Fogerty.
Jondora Music, 1970.
Best-selling record by Creedence Clearwater Revival (Fantasy, 1970).

Up in a Puff of Smoke (English)
Words and music by Gerald Shury and Philip Swern.

Rondor Music Inc., 1974.
Best-selling record by Polly Brown (GTO, 1975).

Up in the Clouds
Words by Bert Kalmar, music by Harry Ruby.
Harms, Inc., 1927.
Introduced by Mary Eaton and Oscar Shaw in *The 5 o'Clock Girl* (musical). Sung by the chorus in *Three Little Words* (film, 1950).

Up on Cripple Creek
Words and music by Jaime Robbie Robertson.
Canaan Music Inc., 1969.
Best-selling record in 1969-70 by The Band (Capitol).

Up on the Roof
Words and music by Gerry Goffin and Carole King.
Screen Gems-EMI Music Inc., 1962.
Best-selling record in 1963 by The Drifters (Atlantic).

Up the Ladder to the Roof
Words and music by Vincent Dimirco and Frank Wilson.
Stone Agate Music Corp., 1970.
Best-selling record by The Supremes (Motown, 1970).

Up to Abergavenny, see **Abergavenny.**

Up-Up and Away
Words and music by Jim Webb.
The EMP Co., 1967.
Best-selling record by The 5th Dimension (Soul City). Won National Academy of Recording Arts and Sciences Awards, Song of the Year, 1967, and Record of the Year, 1967.

Up with the Lark
Words by Leo Robin, music by Jerome Kern.
T. B. Harms Co., 1946.
Introduced by Dorothy Gish, Buddy Swan, Constance Bennett, and voice of Louanne Hogan, dubbed for Jeanne Crain, in *Centennial Summer* (film).

Upon the Mountain
Words and music by Nathaniel Montague and Ewart G. Abner, Jr.
Conrad Music, 1956.
Best-selling record by The Magnificents (Vee Jay).

Ups-A-Daisy!
Words by Robert A. Simon, music by Lewis E. Gensler.
Harms, Inc., 1928.

Introduced by Joan Carter-Waddell and Russ Brown in *Ups-a-Daisy* (musical).

Ups and Downs
Words and music by Mark Lindsay and Terry Melcher.
Daywin Music, Inc., 1967.
Best-selling record by Paul Revere and The Raiders (Columbia).

Uptight (Everything's Alright)
Words and music by Sylvia Moy, Stevie Wonder, and Henry Cosby.
Jobete Music Co., Inc., 1965/Stone Agate Music Corp., 1965/Black Bull Music, 1965.
Best-selling records in 1965-66 by Stevie Wonder (Tamla) and in 1966 by The Ramsey Lewis Trio (Cadet).

Uptown
Words and music by Barry Mann and Cynthia Weil.
Screen Gems-EMI Music Inc., 1962.
Best-selling record by The Crystals (Philles).

Uptown Saturday Night
Words and music by Tom Scott and Morgan Ames.
WB Music Corp., 1974/Warner-Tamerlane Publishing Corp., 1974.
Performed by the voice of Dobie Gray in *Uptown Saturday Night* (film, 1974).

Urge for Going
Words and music by Joni Mitchell.
Siquomb Publishing Corp., 1966.
Best-selling record in 1967 by George Hamilton IV (RCA Victor).

The U.S. Air Force (The Wild Blue Yonder)
Words and music by Robert M. Crawford.
Carl Fischer, Inc., 1939.
Official Air Force song. Known earlier under titles, "Army Air Corps" and "Nothing'll Stop the Air Corps Now." Featured in Air Corps-sponsored *Winged Victory* (revue, 1943).

U.S. Male
Words and music by Jerry Reed (pseudonym for Jerry Reid Hubbard).
Vector Music, 1966.
Best-selling record in 1968 by Elvis Presley (RCA).

Use Me
Words and music by Bill Withers.
Interior Music Corp., 1972.
Best-selling record by Bill Withers (Sussex, 1972).

Use ta Be My Girl
Words and music by Kenny Gamble and Leon Huff.
Mighty Three Music, 1977.
Best-selling record by O'Jays (Philadelphia International, 1978). Nominated for a National Academy of Recording Arts and Sciences Award, Rhythm & Blues Song of the Year, 1978.

Use Your Head
Words and music by Wade Flemons, Chuck Barksdale, and Barrett Strong.
Shakewell Music, Inc., 1964.
Best-selling record by Mary Wells (20th Century-Fox).

Use Your Imagination
Words and music by Cole Porter.
Buxton Hill Music Corp., 1950.
Introduced by William Redfield and Patricia Gillette in *Out of This World* (musical).

Use Your Noggin'
Words by Sammy Cahn, music by James Van Heusen.
Shapiro, Bernstein & Co., Inc., 1964, 1966/Cahn Music Co., 1964/ Van Heusen Music Corp., 1964.
Introduced by Louise Troy, Sharon Dierking, and Gretchen Van Aken in *Walking Happy* (musical, 1966).

Uska Dara (Turkish)
English words and music by Stella Lee.
Screen Gems-EMI Music Inc., 1953.
Adapted from a Turkish popular song. First recorded by Eydie Gorme (Coral) in Turkish and English. Best-selling record, in Turkish, by Eartha Kitt (RCA Victor).

Utopia
Words by Aaron Schroeder, Wally Gold, and Martin Kalmanoff.
Dandy Dittys, 1960.
Introduced by Frank Gary (Crusade).

V

V-A-C-A-T-I-O-N
Words and music by Gary Weston, Hank Hunter, and Connie
   Francis.
Big Seven Music Corp., 1962.
Best-selling record by Connie Francis (MGM).

Vagabond Dreams
Words by Jack Lawrence, music by Hoagy Carmichael.
Paramount Music Corp., 1939.

Vahevela
Words and music by Danny Loggins and Daniel Lottermoser.
Gnossos Music, 1971.
Best-selling record by Loggins & Messina (Columbia, 1972).

Valencia (French-Spanish)
English words by Clifford Grey, French words by Lucien Jean Boyer
   and Jacques-Charles, music by Jose Padilla.
Editions Salabert S.A., Paris, France, 1925/Harms, Inc., 1926.
Introduced by Mistinguett at the Moulin Rouge in Paris in *Revue Mis-
   tinguett* (nightclub revue, 1925). Introduced in the United States by
   Hazel Dawn, Halfred Young, and Charlotte Woodruff in *The Great
   Temptations* (revue). Sung by Grace Bowman in *A Night in Spain*
   (revue, 1927). Another English-language version, with lyrics by Eric
   Valentine, published in 1926 by B. Feldman & Co., Ltd., London,
   England.

Valentine (French)
English words by Herbert Reynolds (pseudonym for M. E. Rourke),
   French words by Albert Willemetz, music by H. Christine.
Harms, Inc., 1926.
Introduced by Maurice Chevalier in Paris in *Paris Qui Chante* (revue).

The Valentino Tango, also known as **Noche de Amor**
Words by Jack Lawrence, music by Heinz Roemheld.

Leeds Music Corp., 1950.
From *Valentino* (film).

Valleri
Words and music by Tommy Boyce and Bobby Hart.
Screen Gems-EMI Music Inc., 1967.
Best-selling record in 1968 by The Monkees (Colgems).

Valley of Tears
Words and music by Antoine "Fats" Domino and Dave
    Bartholomew.
Unart Music Corp., 1957/Unart-Unart, 1957.
Best-selling record by Fats Domino (Imperial).

Vanessa
Music by Bernie Wayne.
Bernie Wayne Music Co., 1952.
Dedicated to film and television actress Vanessa Brown. Best-selling
    record, instrumental, by Hugo Winterhalter and his Orchestra (RCA
    Victor).

Vanity
Words by Jack Manus and Bernard Bierman, music by Guy Wood.
Jefferson Music Co., Inc., 1951.
Best-selling record by Don Cherry (Decca).

The Varsity Drag
Words and music by B. G. De Sylva, Lew Brown, and Ray
    Henderson.
Chappell & Co., Inc., 1927/Anne-Rachel Music Corp., 1927.
Introduced by Zelma O'Neal, Ruth Mayon, Don Tomkins, Wally Coyle,
    and the chorus in *Good News* (musical). Sung by Dorothy McNulty
    (Penny Singleton) and Billy Taft, with Abe Lyman and his Orchestra,
    in the first film version, 1930; and by June Allyson and Peter Lawford
    in the second film version, 1947.

Vaudeville Man
Words and music by Wendy Waldman.
Big Kitty Music, 1973.
Introduced by Maria Muldaur on *Maria Muldaur* (Warner Brothers,
    1973).

Vaya con Dios (May God Be with You)
Words and music by Larry Russell, Inez James, and Buddy Pepper.
Jarest Music Co., 1953/Beachhaven Music.
Introduced by Anita O'Day (Mercury). Best-selling record by Les Paul
    and Mary Ford (Capitol).

Vehicle
Words and music by James M. Peterik.
Bald Medusa Co., 1969.
Best-selling record in 1970 by The Ides of March (Warner Bros.).

The Velvet Glove
Words and music by Harold Spina.
Edwin H. Morris Co., 1953.
Best-selling record by Hugo Winterhalter and Henri Rene and their
    Orchestra (RCA Victor).

Velvet Moon
Words by Edgar De Lange, music by Josef Myrow.
M. Witmark & Sons, 1943/Scarsdale Music Corp., 1943.
Best-selling record by Harry James and his Orchestra (Columbia).

Vengeance
Words and music by Carly Simon.
C'est Music, 1979.
Best-selling record by Carly Simon (Elektra, 1979).

Venice Blue (French)
English words by Gene Lees, French words by Francoise Dorin,
    music by Charles Aznavour.
Editions Musicales Charles Aznavour, Paris, France, 1964, 1965/
    Ludlow Music Inc., 1964.
Original French title, "Que C'est Triste Venises." Introduced in French
    and English by Charles Aznavour.

Venice USA
Words and music by Van Morrison.
Essential Music, 1978.
Introduced by Van Morrison on *Wavelength* (Warner Brothers, 1978).

Ventura Highway
Words and music by Lee Bunnell.
WB Music Corp., 1972.
Best-selling record by America (Warner Brothers, 1972).

Venus
Words and music by Ed Marshall.
Rambed Publishing Co., Inc., 1959/Lansdale Music Corp., 1959.
Best-selling record by Frankie Avalon (Chancellor).

Venus (Netherlands)
English words and music by R. V. Leeuwen.
Fat Zach Music, Inc., 1969.
Best-selling record in 1970 by Shocking Blue (Colossus).

Venus and Mars/Rock Show (English)
Words and music by Paul McCartney.
MPL Communications Inc., 1975.
Best-selling record by Wings (Capitol, 1975).

Venus in Blue Jeans
Words and music by Howard Greenfield and Jack Keller.
Screen Gems-EMI Music Inc., 1961.
Best-selling record in 1962 by Jimmy Clanton (Ace).

Vera Cruz
Words by Sammy Cahn, music by Hugo Friedhofer.
Leo Feist Inc., 1954.
Recorded by Tony Martin for use behind the opening titles of *Vera Cruz*
(film). Vocal version deleted from the film prior to its premiere.

Verboten!, also known as **Forbidden**
Words by Mack David, music by Harry Sukman.
Leo Feist Inc., 1958.
Introduced by Paul Anka on the soundtrack of *Verboten!* (film).

The Verdict
Words by Glen Moore, music by Alan Freed.
Nom Music, Inc., 1955.
Best-selling record by The Five Keys (Capitol).

Vertigo
Words and music by Jay Livingston and Ray Evans.
Famous Music Co., 1958.
"Inspired by" *Vertigo* (film).

The Very Necessary You
Words by Johnny Burke, music by James Van Heusen.
Bourne Co., 1953/Music Sales Corp., 1953.
Introduced by Kevin Scott and Pat Stanley in *Carnival in Flanders*
(musical).

The Very Next Man
Words by Sheldon Harnick, music by Jerry Bock.
Sunbeam Music Corp., 1959.
Introduced by Patricia Wilson in *Fiorello!* (musical).

A Very Precious Love
Words by Paul Francis Webster, music by Sammy Fain.
M. Witmark & Sons, 1958.
Introduced in *Marjorie Morningstar* (film). Best-selling record by Doris
Day (Columbia). Nominated for an Academy Award, 1958.

A Very Special Day
Words by Oscar Hammerstein, II, music by Richard Rodgers.
Williamson Music Inc., 1953.
Introduced by Isabel Bigley in *Me and Juliet* (musical).

A Very Special Love
Words and music by Robert Allen.
Korwin Music, Inc., 1957.
Best-selling record by Johnny Nash (ABC Paramount).

A Very Special Love Song
Words and music by Billy Sherrill and Norro Wilson.
Algee Music Corp., 1974.
Best-selling record by Charlie Rich (Epic, 1974). Nominated for a National Academy of Recording Arts and Sciences Award, Country Song of the Year, 1974.

The Very Thought of You (English)
Words and music by Ray Noble.
Campbell-Connelly Co., Ltd., London, England/M. Witmark & Sons, 1934.
Introduced in United States by The Casa Loma Orchestra. Sung by Doris Day in *Young Man with a Horn* (film, 1950).

The Vespa Song
Words by Dusty Negulesco, music by Mario Nascimbene.
Unart Music Corp., 1962.
Introduced by Maurice Chevalier in *Jessica* (film).

Via Galactica
Words by Christopher Gore, music by Galt MacDermott.
Morkay Music, 1972.
Introduced by Irene Cara in *Via Galactica* (musical, 1972).

Victoria (English)
Words and music by Ray Davies.
Unichappell Music Inc., 1969/ABKCO Music Inc., 1969.
Best-selling record by The Kinks (Reprise, 1970).

Vict'ry Polka
Words by Samuel Cahn, music by Jule Styne.
Chappell & Co., Inc., 1943.
Best-selling record by Bing Crosby and The Andrews Sisters (Decca).

Video Killed the Radio Star (English)
Words and music by Geoffrey Downs, Trevor Horn, and Bruce Woolley.
Carbert Music Inc., 1979.

Best-selling records by The Buggles (Island, 1979) and Bruce Woolley & the Camera Club (Columbia, 1979).

Video Tape
Words and music by Steve Goodman.
Big Ears Music Inc., 1977/Red Pajamas Music, 1977.
Introduced by Steve Goodman on *Say It in Private* (Asylum, 1977).

Vieni Su (Icelandic)
English words and music by Johnny Cola.
Algonquin Music, Inc., 1949.
Best-selling record by Vaughn Monroe (Victor).

Vieni, Vieni (French)
English words by Rudy Vallee, French words by George Koger, Italian words by George Koger, music by Vincent Scotto.
M. Witmark & Sons, 1937, 1934/Soc. Fortin, 1934.
New arrangement, with added part-English chorus, popularized by Rudy Vallee.

The Viet Nam Blues
Words and music by Kris Kristofferson.
Buckhorn Music Publishing Co., Inc., 1965.
Best-selling record in 1966 by Dave Dudley (Mercury).

The Village of St. Bernadette (English)
Words and music by Eula Parker.
Francis, Day & Hunter, Ltd., London, England, 1959/Ludlow Music Inc., 1959.
Introduced in England by Anne Shelton. Best-selling United States record by Andy Williams (Cadence).

Vincent
Words and music by Don McLean.
Mayday Music, 1971.
Best-selling record by Don McLean (United Artists, 1972).

The Violet and a Rose
Words and music by Mel Tillis, Bud Augue, and John Reinfield.
Cedarwood Publishing Co., Inc., 1958.
Best-selling record in 1962 by "Little" Jimmy Dickens (Columbia).

Violets for Your Furs
Words by Tom Adair, music by Matt Dennis.
Music Sales Corp., 1941.
Introduced by Tommy Dorsey and his Orchestra, vocal by Frank Sinatra (Victor).

Violins from Nowhere
Words by Herb Magidson, music by Sammy Fain.
Bregman, Vocco & Conn, Inc., 1950/Magidson Music Co., Inc.,
1950.
Introduced by Art Carroll in *Michael Todd's Peep Show* (revue).

Viper's Drag
Music by Thomas "Fats" Waller.
Anne-Rachel Music Corp., 1934/Mayfair Music Corp., 1934.
Solo jazz piano composition, introduced by Fats Waller.

Virgin Man
Words and music by William "Smokey" Robinson, Jr. and Rose Ella
Jones.
Bertam Music Co., 1974.
Best-selling record by Smokey Robinson (Tamla, 1974).

Virginia
Words by B. G. De Sylva, music by George Gershwin.
New World Music Corp., 1923/Anne-Rachel Music Corp., 1923.
Introduced by Constance Binney and the chorus in *Sweet Little Devil*
(musical, 1924).

Visions of Johanna
Words and music by Bob Dylan.
Dwarf Music Co., Inc., 1966.
Introduced by Bob Dylan in his album, *Blonde on Blonde* (Columbia).

Visit Panama
Words and music by Cole Porter.
Chappell & Co., Inc., 1940.
Introduced by Ethel Merman in *Panama Hattie* (musical).

Viva Las Vegas
Words and music by Doc Pomus and Mort Shuman.
Elvis Presley Music, Inc., 1964.
Introduced by Elvis Presley in *Viva Las Vegas* (film).

Viva Tirado
Music by Gerald Wilson, words by Norman Gimbel.
Coast Music, 1962/Ludlow Music Inc., 1962.
Best-selling record by El Chicano (Kapp, 1970).

Vodka
Words by Otto Harbach and Oscar Hammerstein, II, music by
Herbert Stothart and George Gershwin.
New World Music Corp., 1926/Bill/Bob Publishing Co., 1926/WB

Music Corp., 1926.
Introduced by Dorothy Mackaye in *Song of the Flame* (operetta, 1925).

The Voice in My Heart
Words and music by Dave Franklyn.
Summit Music Corp., 1958.
Best-selling record by Eydie Gorme (ABC Paramount).

Voices
Words and music by Jim Webb.
Variety Music Inc., 1979/Porchester Music Inc., 1979.
Introduced in *Voices* (film, 1979).

Vol Vist Du Gaily Star
Words and music by Bulee "Slim" Gaillard and Bud Green.
Jewel Music Publishing Co., Inc., 1938.
Introduced by "Slim and Slam" (Slim Gaillard and Slam Stewart).

Volare, also known as **Nel Blu, Dipinto di Blu** (Italian)
English words by Mitchell Parish, Italian words by Domenico
   Modugno and F. Migliacci, music by Domenico Modugno.
Robbins Music Corp., 1958.
Introduced by Domenico Modugno. Awarded First Prize, San Remo
   (Italy) Song Festival. Best-selling record by Domenico Modugno
   (Decca). Revived in 1960 with best-selling record by Bobby Rydell
   (Cameo). Won a National Academy of Recording Arts and Sciences
   Award, Song of the Year, 1958.

Volcano
Words and music by Jimmy Buffett, Keith Sykes, and H. Dailey.
Coral Reefer Music, 1979/Keith Sykes Music, 1979.
Best-selling record by Jimmy Buffett (MCA, 1979).

The Volunteer
Words and music by Autry Inman.
Big Bopper Music Co., 1963.
Best-selling record by Autry Inman (Sims).

Volunteers
Words and music by Marty Balin and Paul Kantner.
Icebag Corp., 1969.
Best-selling record by Jefferson Airplane (RCA).

Voo-It! Voo-It!
Words and music by Ulysses Banks and Frosty Pyles.
Edwin H. Morris Co., 1946.
Best-selling record by The Blues Woman (Juke Box).

Voodoo Woman
Words and music by Bobby Goldsboro.
Unart Music Corp., 1965.
Best-selling record by Bobby Goldsboro (United Artists).

W

W-O-L-D
Words and music by Harry Chapin.
Story Songs Ltd., 1973.
Best-selling record by Harry Chapin (Elektra, 1974).

Wabash Blues
Words by Dave Ringle, music by Fred Meinken.
Leo Feist Inc., 1921/Dave Ringle, 1921.
Introduced by Isham Jones and his Orchestra, featuring Louis Panico on
    trumpet.

Wabash Moon
Words and music by Dave Dreyer, Morton Downey, and Billy
    McKenny.
Bourne Co., 1931.
Introduced by and theme song of Morton Downey.

Wack Wack
Words and music by Eldee Young, Isaac Holt, Hysear Walker, and
    Donald Storball.
McLaughlin Publishing Co., 1966/Yo-Ho Publishing Co., 1966.
Best-selling record in 1967 by Young-Holt Unlimited (Brunswick).

Wacky Dust
Words by Stanley Adams, music by Oscar Levant.
Robbins Music Corp., 1938/Stanley Adams Music, Inc., 1938/Largo
    Music, Inc., 1938.
Best-selling record by Ella Fitzgerald (Decca).

Wade in the Water
Music by Ramsey E. Lewis, Jr.
Ramsel Publishing Co., 1966.
Lewis's arrangement based on a pre-Civil War slave song. Best-selling
    record, instrumental, by The Ramsey Lewis Trio (Cadet).

Wade in the Water
Music by Dave Alpert, Bob Edmondson, and John Pisano.
Almo Music Corp., 1967.
Adapted from a pre-Civil War Slave song. Best-selling record by Herb
  Alpert and The Tijuana Brass (A&M).

Wagon Train
Words and music by Henri Rene and Bob Russell.
Gordon Music Co., Inc., 1957.
Title theme from *Wagon Train* (television series).

Wagon Wheels
Words and music by Billy Hill and Peter De Rose.
Shapiro, Bernstein & Co., Inc., 1933/Anne-Rachel Music Corp.,
  1933.
Introduced by Everett Marshall in *Ziegfeld Follies of 1934* (revue). Best-
  selling record by George Olsen and his Orchestra (Columbia).

Wah-Hoo!
Words and music by Cliff Friend.
DeSylva, Brown & Henderson, Inc., 1936.
Sung by The Andrews Sisters in *Moonlight and Cactus* (film, 1944).

The Wah-Watusi
Words by Kal Mann, music by Dave Appell.
Kalmann Music, Inc., 1962/Lowe Music Publishing Corp., 1962.
Best-selling record by The Orlons (Cameo).

The Wail of the Reefer Man
Words by Ted Koehler, music by Harold Arlen.
Arko Music Corp., 1932.
Introduced by Cab Calloway at Cotton Club (New York nightclub) in
  Cotton Club Parade (nightclub revue).

Wail of the Winds
Music by Harry Warren.
M. Witmark & Sons, 1935.
Theme song of Red Nichols and his Orchestra.

Waist Deep in the Big Muddy
Words and music by Pete Seeger.
TRO-Melody Trails, Inc., 1967.
Introduced by Pete Seeger.

Wait (English)
Words and music by John Lennon and Paul McCartney.
Northern Songs, Ltd., England, 1965/Maclen Music Inc., 1965.
Introduced by The Beatles in their album, *Rubber Soul* (Capitol).

Wait and See
Words by Johnny Mercer, music by Harry Warren.
Leo Feist Inc., 1945.
Introduced by Kenny Baker in *The Harvey Girls* (film, 1946).

Wait for Me, see **Johnny Concho's Theme.**

Wait for Me
Words and music by Daryl Hall.
Hot Cha Music Co., 1979/Six Continents Music Publishing Inc.,
   1979.
Best-selling record by Hall & Oates (RCA, 1979).

Wait for Me Baby
Words and music by Charlie Tobias, Nat Simon, and Harry Tobias.
Remick Music Corp., 1943.
Best-selling record by Dick Haymes (Decca).

Wait for Me, Mary
Words and music by Charles Tobias, Nat Simon, and Harry Tobias.
Remick Music Corp., 1942/Tobey Music Corp., 1942.
Best-selling record in 1943 by Dick Haymes (Decca).

Wait 'Til You See "Ma Cherie"
Words by Leo Robin, music by Richard A. Whiting.
Famous Music Co., 1929.
Introduced by Maurice Chevalier in *Innocents of Paris* (film).

Wait Till My Bobby Gets Home
Words and music by Phil Spector, Ellie Greenwich, and Jeff Barry.
Mother Bertha Music, Inc., 1963/Trio Music Co., Inc., 1963.
Best-selling record by Darlene Love (Philles).

Wait Till We're Sixty-Five
Words by Alan Jay Lerner, music by Burton Lane.
Chappell & Co., Inc., 1965.
Introduced by William Daniels and Barbara Harris in *On a Clear Day
   You Can See Forever* (musical). Sung by Barbra Streisand and Larry
   Blyden in the film version, 1970, but deleted before release of the film.

Wait Till You See Her, also known as **Wait Till You See Him**
Words by Lorenz Hart, music by Richard Rodgers.
Chappell & Co., Inc., 1942.
Introduced by Ronald Graham in *By Jupiter* (musical).

Wait Till You See Him, see **Wait Till You See Her.**

The Waiter and the Porter and the Upstairs Maid
Words and music by Johnny Mercer.
Famous Music Co., 1941.
Introduced by Bing Crosby, Mary Martin, and Jack Teagarden in *Birth of the Blues* (film).

Waitin' at the Gate for Katy
Words by Gus Kahn, music by Richard A. Whiting.
Movietone Music Corp., 1934.
Introduced by John Boles and chorus in *Bottoms Up* (film). Lyrics unrelated to lyrics of 1927 song, "Waitin' for Katy," also written by Gus Kahn, with music by Ted Shapiro.

Waitin' for My Dearie
Words by Alan Jay Lerner, music by Frederick Loewe.
United Artists Music Co., Inc., 1947.
Introduced by Marion Bell in *Brigadoon* (musical). Sung by voice of Carol Richards, dubbed for Cyd Charisse, in film version (1954).

Waitin' for the Evening Train
Words and music by Howard Dietz and Arthur Schwartz.
Harms, Inc., 1963.
Introduced by Mary Martin and George Wallace in *Jennie* (musical).

Waitin' for the Train To Come In
Words and music by Sunny Skylar and Martin Block.
MCA, Inc., 1945/Music Sales Corp., 1945.
Best-selling record by Peggy Lee (Capitol).

Waitin' in School
Words and music by Johnny Burnette and Dorsey Burnette.
Unart Music Corp., 1957/Unart-Unart, 1957.
Best-selling record in 1958 by Ricky Nelson (Imperial).

Waitin' in Your Welfare Line
Words by Nat Stuckey, music by Don Rich and Buck Owens.
Blue Book Music, 1966.
Best-selling record by Buck Owens (Capitol).

Waiting
Words and music by Harry Nilsson.
Six Continents Music Publishing Inc., 1970/Duchess Music Corp., 1970.
Performed by the voice of Nilsson in *Jenny* (film, 1970).

Waiting at the End of the Road
Words and music by Irving Berlin.
Irving Berlin Music Corp., 1929.

Introduced by Daniel Haynes and the Dixie Jubilee Singers in *Hallelujah* (film).

Waiting for the Moving Van
Words and music by David Ackles.
Warner-Tamerlane Publishing Corp., 1972.
Performed by David Ackles on *American Gothic* (Elektra, 1972).

Waiting for the Sun To Come Out
Words by Arthur Francis (pseudonym for Ira Gershwin), music by George Gershwin.
New World Music Corp., 1920.
Introduced by Helen Ford and Joseph Lertora in *The Sweetheart Shop* (musical).

The Waiting Game
Words by Bob Hilliard, music by Robert Allen.
International Korwin Corp., 1958/Better Half Music Co., 1958.
Best-selling record by Harry Belafonte (RCA Victor).

Waiting in the Lobby of Your Heart
Words and music by Hank Thompson and Billy Gray.
Unichappell Music Inc., 1952.
Best-selling record by Hank Thompson (Capitol).

Wake Me When It's Over
Words by Sammy Cahn, music by James Van Heusen.
Robbins Music Corp., 1960.
From *Wake Me When It's Over* (film).

Wake the Town and Tell the People
Words and music by Sammy Gallop, music by Jerry Livingston.
Anne-Rachel Music Corp., 1954.
Best-selling record in 1955 by Les Baxter and his Orchestra (Capitol).

Wake Up and Live
Words by Mack Gordon, music by Harry Revel.
Robbins Music Corp., 1937.
Introduced by Alice Faye in *Wake Up and Live* (film).

Wake Up and Sing
Words and music by Cliff Friend, Carmen Lombardo, and Charles Tobias.
Shapiro, Bernstein & Co., Inc., 1936/Ched Music Co., 1936.
Introduced by Guy Lombardo and his Royal Canadians.

Wake Up, Brother, and Dance, also known as **Sophia**
Words by Ira Gershwin, music by George Gershwin.

1947

Gershwin Publishing Corp., 1937/Chappell & Co., Inc., 1937.
Written for, but not used in, *Shall We Dance?* (film). With new title, "Sophia," and new lyrics copyrighted by Ira Gershwin in 1964, song introduced by Dean Martin in *Kiss Me Stupid* (film, 1964).

Wake Up, Everybody (Part 1)
Words and music by Gene McFadden, John Whitehead, and Vic Carstarphen.
Mighty Three Music, 1976.
Best-selling record by Harold Melvin & the Blue Notes (Phila. International, 1976).

Wake Up Irene
Words and music by Weldon Allard and Johnny Hatchcock.
Hall-Clement Publications, 1953.
Best-selling record in 1954 by Hank Thompson (Capitol).

Wake Up, Little Susie
Words and music by Boudleaux Bryant and Felice Bryant.
Acuff-Rose Publications Inc., 1957/House of Bryant Publications, 1957.
Best-selling record by The Everly Brothers (Cadence).

Walk a Mile in My Shoes
Words and music by Joe South (pseudonym for Joe Souter).
Lowery Music Co., Inc., 1969.
Best-selling record in 1970 by Joe South (Capitol).

Walk Away from Love
Words and music by Charles Kipps, Jr.
Charles Kipps Music Inc., 1974.
Best-selling record by David Ruffin (Motown, 1975).

Walk Away Renee
Words and music by Mike Brown (pseudonym for Mike Lookofsky), Tony Sansone, and Bob Calilli.
The Times Square Music Publications Co., 1966.
Best-selling records by The Left Banke (Smash) and in 1968 by The Four Tops (Motown).

Walk, Don't Run
Words and music by John H. Smith, Jr.
Forshay Music, 1960.
Best-selling record by The Ventures (Dolton). Best-selling record in 1964 of updated version entitled "Walk-Don't Run '64," by The Ventures (Dolton).

Walk Hand in Hand
Words and music by Johnny Cowell.
Republic Music Corp., 1956.
Introduced by Canadian singer Denny Vaughan (Kapp). Best-selling record by Tony Martin (RCA Victor).

A Walk in the Black Forest (West German)
Music by Horst Jankowski.
MRC Music Corp., 1962.
Original German title, "Eine Schwarzwaldfahrt." Best-selling record in 1965 by Horst Jankowski and his Orchestra (Mercury).

A Walk in the Spring Rain
Words and music by Don Black and Elmer Bernstein.
Colgems-EMI Music Inc., 1970.
Performed by the voice of Michael Dees in *A Walk in the Spring Rain* (film, 1970).

Walk, Jenny, Walk
Words by Henry Creamer, music by Bob Schafer and Sam Wooding.
Goodman Music Co., Inc., 1923.
Introduced by Sam Wooding's Orchestra at the Nest Club (Harlem). First recording by the Original Memphis Five (Columbia).

Walk Like a Man
Words and music by Bob Crewe and Bob Gaudio.
Claridge Music, 1963.
Best-selling record by The Four Seasons (Vee Jay). Revived in 1974 by Grand Funk (Capitol).

Walk Me Out in the Morning Dew, see Morning Dew.

Walk Me to the Door
Words and music by Conway Twitty.
Twitty Bird Music Publishing Co., 1962/Tree Publishing Co., Inc., 1962/Tree-Twitty Bird, 1962.
Best-selling record in 1963 by Ray Price (Columbia).

Walk On
Words and music by Neil Young.
Silver Fiddle, 1974.
Best-selling record by Neil Young (Reprise, 1974).

Walk On, Boy
Words and music by Mel Tillis and Wayne P. Walker.
Cedarwood Publishing Co., Inc., 1960.
Best-selling records by Mel Tillis (Columbia) and Jimmy Dean (Columbia).

Walk On By
Words and music by Kendall Hayes.
Lowery Music Co., Inc., 1961.
Best-selling record by Leroy Van Dyke (Mercury).

Walk on By
Words and music by Hal David, music by Burt F. Bacharach.
Blue Seas Music Inc., 1963/Jac Music Co., Inc., 1963.
Best-selling record in 1964 by Dionne Warwick (Scepter). Revived in
    1969 with best-selling record by Isaac Hayes (Enterprise).

Walk On Out of My Mind
Words and music by Red Lane (pseudonym for Hollis DeLaughter).
Tree Publishing Co., Inc., 1967.
Best-selling record in 1968 by Waylon Jennings (RCA).

Walk on the Wild Side
Words by Mack David, music by Elmer Bernstein.
Columbia Pictures Publications, 1961, 1962.
From *Walk on the Wild Side* (film, 1962). Best-selling record by Jimmy
    Smith (Verve). Nominated for an Academy Award, 1962.

Walk on the Wild Side
Words and music by Lou Reed.
Unichappell Music Inc., 1972.
Best-selling record by Lou Reed (RCA, 1973).

Walk on Water
Words and music by Neil Diamond.
Prophet Music Inc., 1972.
Best-selling record by Neil Diamond (Uni, 1972).

Walk Out Backwards
Words and music by Bill Anderson.
Tree Publishing Co., Inc., 1960/Champion Music Corp., 1960.
Best-selling record in 1961 by Bill Anderson (Decca).

Walk Right Back
Words and music by Sonny Curtis.
Warner-Tamerlane Publishing Corp., 1960.
Best-selling record in 1961 by The Everly Brothers (Warner Bros).

Walk Right In
Words by Gus Cannon, music by H. Woods.
Peer International Corp., 1930.
Introduced in 1929 by Gus Cannon's Jug Stompers (Victor). Revived in
    1963 with best-selling record by The Rooftop Singers (Vanguard).

Walk Right In, see **Open the Door to Your Heart.**

Walk Tall (Walk Straight)
Words and music by Don Wayne.
Painted Desert Music Corp., 1964.
Best-selling record in 1965 by Faron Young (Mercury).

Walk This Way
Words and music by Joe Perry and Steven Tyler.
Daksel Music Corp., 1975.
Best-selling record by Aerosmith (Columbia, 1977).

Walk through This World with Me
Words and music by Sandra Seamons and Kay Savage.
Glad Music Co., 1965.
Best-selling record in 1967 by George Jones (Musicor).

Walk Up
Words and music by Bart Howard.
Almanac Music, Inc., 1956.
Introduced by Mabel Mercer.

Walkin' after Midnight
Words by Don Hecht, music by Alan Block.
Acuff-Rose Publications Inc., 1956.
Best-selling record in 1957 and 1958 by Patsy Cline (Decca).

Walkin' Back to Happiness (English)
Words by John Schroeder, music by Mike Hawker.
Bourne Filmusic, Inc., London, England, 1961.
From *Look at Life* (British film). Best-selling record in England by
   Helen Shapiro (English Columbia).

Walkin' by the River
Words by Robert Sour, music by Una Mae Carlisle.
Unichappell Music Inc., 1940/Screen Gems-EMI Music Inc., 1940.
Introduced and best-selling record by Una Mae Carlisle (Bluebird).

Walkin' Down to Washington
Words and music by Dick Sanford and Sammy Mysels.
Valiant Music Co., Inc., 1960.
Introduced and best-selling record by Mitch Miller and his Orchestra
   and Chorus (Columbia).

Walkin' in the Rain, see **Just Walking in the Rain.**

Walkin' in the Rain with the One I Love
Words and music by Barry White.

Unichappell Music Inc., 1972/Sa-Vette Music, 1972.
Best-selling record by Love Unlimited (Uni, 1972).

Walkin' My Baby Back Home
Words and music by Roy Turk and Fred E. Ahlert.
DeSylva, Brown & Henderson, Inc., 1930/Cromwell Music, Inc.,
    1930.
Introduced by Harry Richman. Revived in 1952 with best-selling record
    by Johnnie Ray (Columbia). Sung by Donald O'Connor in *Walkin'*
    My Baby Back Home (film, 1953).

Walkin', Talkin', Cryin', Barely Beatin' Broken Heart
Words and music by Justin Tubb and Roger Miller.
Tree Publishing Co., Inc., 1963.
Introduced by Johnny Wright (Decca).

Walkin' to Missouri
Words and music by Bob Merrill.
Anne-Rachel Music Corp., 1952.
Best-selling record by Sammy Kaye and his Orchestra (Columbia).

(I'll Be) Walkin' with My Honey (Soon, Soon, Soon)
Words by Buddy Kaye, music by Sam Medoff.
Republic Music Corp., 1945.
Best-selling record by Sammy Kaye and his Orchestra (Victor).

Walkin' with Peninnah
Words by Earl Shuman, music by Leon Carr.
April Music Inc., 1964.
Introduced by Marc London and Christopher Norris in *The Secret Life*
    of Walter Mitty (musical).

Walking Away Whistling
Words and music by Frank Loesser.
Frank Music Co., 1959.
Introduced by Ellen McCown in 1960 in *Greenwillow* (musical).

Walking Happy
Words by Sammy Cahn, music by James Van Heusen.
Shapiro, Bernstein & Co., Inc., 1962, 1966/Cahn Music Co., 1962/
    Van Heusen Music Corp., 1962.
Introduced by Louise Troy, Norman Wisdom, and chorus in *Walking*
    Happy (musical, 1966).

Walking in Rhythm
Words and music by Barney Perry.
Black Byrd Music, 1974.
Best-selling record by Blackbyrds (Fantasy, 1975).

Walking in Space
Words by Gerome Ragni and James Rado, music by Galt MacDermot.
United Artists Music Co., Inc., 1967.
Introduced by the company in the Off Broadway version of *Hair* (musical); sung by the company in the Broadway version, 1968. Best-selling recording, instrumental, in 1969 by Quincy Jones in his album, *Walking in Space* (A&M).

Walking in the Rain
Words and music by Barry Mann, Cynthia Weil, and Phil Spector.
Screen Gems-EMI Music Inc., 1964.
Best-selling record by The Ronettes (Philles). Revived in 1969-70 with best-selling record by Jay and The Americans (United Artists).

Walking in the Sunshine, also known as **Sing a Little Sunshine Song**
Words and music by Roger Miller.
Tree Publishing Co., Inc., 1967.
Best-selling record by Roger Miller (Smash).

Walking My Cat Named Dog
Words and music by Norma Tanega.
Saturday Music Inc., 1966.
Best-selling record by Norma Tanega (New Voice).

Walking on New Grass
Words and music by Ray Pennington.
Tree Publishing Co., Inc., 1966.
Best-selling record by Kenny Price (Boone).

Walking on the Moon (English)
Words and music by Gordon Sumner.
Virgin Music Ltd., 1979.
Introduced by The Police on *Regatta Du Blanc* (A&M, 1979).

Walking Proud
Words and music by Gerry Goffin and Carole King.
Screen Gems-EMI Music Inc., 1963.
Best-selling record by Steve Lawrence (Columbia).

Walking Song
Words and music by Kate McGarrigle.
Garden Court Music Co., 1977.
Introduced by Kate & Anna McGarrigle on *Dancer with Bruised Knees* (Warner Brothers, 1977).

Walking Tall
Words and music by Walter Scharf and Don Black.
Asco Music, 1972.
Performed by the voice of Johnny Mathis in *Walking Tall* (film, 1973).

Walking the Dog
Words and music by Rufus Thomas.
East Publications, 1963.
Best-selling record by Rufus Thomas (Stax).

Walking the Floor over You
Words and music by Ernest Tubb.
Unichappell Music Inc., 1941.
Introduced by and theme song of Ernest Tubb. Best-selling records by Ernest Tubb (Decca) and Bing Crosby, with Bob Crosby and his Orchestra (Decca).

Walking the Streets
Words and music by Gene Evans, Jimmy Fields, and Jimmy Littlejohn.
Cherio Corp., 1955.
Best-selling record in 1961 by Webb Pierce (Decca).

Walking to New Orleans
Words and music by Antoine Domino, Dave Bartholomew, and Robert Guidry.
Unart Music Corp., 1960/Unart-Unart, 1960.
Best-selling record by Fats Domino (Imperial).

Walking with Susie
Words by Sidney D. Mitchell and Archie Gottler, music by Con Conrad.
DeSylva, Brown & Henderson, Inc., 1929.
Introduced by Frank Richardson and the chorus in *William Fox Movietone Follies of 1929* (film).

Wall to Wall Love
Words and music by Helen Carter and June Carter.
Acuff-Rose Publications Inc., 1962/Milene Music Co., 1962.
Best-selling record by Bob Gallion (Hickory).

The Wallflower, see **Dance with Me Henry.**

Walter Winchell Rhumba
Words by Carl Sigman, music by Noro Morales.
Robbins Music Corp., 1944.
Introduced by Xavier Cugat and his Orchestra in *Holiday in Mexico* (film, 1946).

Waltz at Maxim's
Words by Alan Jay Lerner, music by Frederick Loewe.
Mara-Lane Music Corp., 1958.
Introduced in *Gigi* (film).

Waltz de Funk
Music by Patti Bown.
Duchess Music Corp., 1960, 1963.
Introduced by Patti Bown (Columbia).

Waltz down the Aisle
Words and music by Cole Porter.
Harms, Inc., 1934.
Dropped from *Anything Goes* (musical) and *Jubilee* (musical, 1935).

Waltz for a Ball
Words and music by Richard Rodgers.
Williamson Music Inc., 1957.
Introduced in *Cinderella* (television musical).

Waltz for Debby
Words by Gene Lees, music by Bill Evans.
Acorn Music Corp., 1964, 1965.
Adapted from jazz composition by Evans. First vocal recording by Tony
   Bennett (Columbia).

Waltz from *The Cardinal*
Music by Jerome Moross.
Chappell & Co., Inc., 1963.
From *The Cardinal* (film).

Waltz in Swingtime
Words by Dorothy Fields, music by Jerome Kern.
T. B. Harms Co., 1936.
Danced to by Fred Astaire and Ginger Rogers in *Swing Time* (film).

The Waltz of Long Ago
Words and music by Irving Berlin.
Irving Berlin Music Corp., 1923.
Introduced by Grace Moore in *Music Box Revue of 1923* (revue).

The Waltz of the Bells, see **Ting-a-Ling.**

Waltz of the Wind
Words and music by Fred Rose.
Milene Music Co., 1947.
Best-selling record by Roy Acuff (Columbia).

Waltz Theme (English)
Music by Richard Addinsell.
Keith Prowse Music Publishing Co., Ltd., London, England/Sam
 Fox Publishing Co., Inc., 1945.
Waltz theme from *Blithe Spirit* (film). Introduced on records by Henri
 Rene and his Orchestra (Victor).

A Waltz Was Born in Vienna
Words by Earle Crooker, music by Frederick Loewe.
Chappell & Co., Inc., 1936.
Introduced in *The Illustrator's Show* (revue). Sung in *Salute to Spring*
 (musical, 1937), summer production of St. Louis Municipal Opera
 Company.

The Waltz You Saved for Me
Words by Gus Kahn, music by Emil Flindt and Wayne King.
Leo Feist Inc., 1930.
Introduced by and theme song of Wayne King and his Orchestra. Theme
 of *Lady Esther Serenade* (radio musical series).

Waltzing in a Dream
Words by Bing Crosby and Ned Washington, music by Victor
 Young.
MCA, Inc., 1932/Victor Young Publications, Inc., 1932.
Introduced by Bing Crosby.

Waltzing in the Clouds
Words by Gus Kahn, music by Robert Stolz.
Universal Music Corp., 1940.
Introduced by Deanna Durbin in *Spring Parade* (film). Nominated for
 an Academy Award, 1940.

Waltzing Matilda (Australian)
Words by A. B. "The Banjo" Paterson, music by Marie Cowan.
Allan & Co., Melbourne, Australia, 1936/Ascherberg, Hopwood &
 Crew, Ltd., London, England, 1941/Carl Fischer, Inc., 1941.
Australian bush song adopted as marching song by Australian Army
 during World War II. Text reputedly written by Paterson in 1895.
 Popular arrangement by Orrie Lee. Music resembles another folk
 song, "Bonny Wood of Craigielea," which may, in turn, stem from the
 seventeenth-century English song, "The Bold Fusilier."

The Wanderer
Words and music by Ernest Maresca.
Schwartz Music Co., Inc., 1960/Rust Enterprises, Inc., 1960.
Best-selling record in 1962 by Dion (Laurie).

Wanderin'
Words and music by Sammy Kaye.
Republic Music Corp., 1950.
Based on an American folk song discovered in Minnesota by Carl Sandburg. Best-selling record by Sammy Kaye and his Orchestra (Columbia).

Wanderlust
Music by Edward Kennedy "Duke" Ellington and Johnny Hodges.
American Academy of Music, Inc., 1939.
Introduced by Duke Ellington and his Orchestra.

Wand'rin Star
Words by Alan Jay Lerner, music by Frederick Loewe.
Chappell & Co., Inc., 1951.
Introduced by Rufus Smith, Robert Penn, and Jared Reed in *Paint Your Wagon* (musical).

Wang-Dang-Doodle
Words and music by Willie Dixon.
Arc Music Corp., 1962.
Best-selling record in 1966 by Ko Ko Taylor (Checker).

The Wang Wang Blues
Words by Leo Wood, music by Gus Muller, "Buster" Johnson, and Henry Busse.
Leo Feist Inc., 1921.
Introduced by Paul Whiteman and his Orchestra, featuring Henry Busse on trumpet. Interpolated by Van and Schenck in *Ziegfeld Follies of 1921* (revue).

Want-Ads
Words and music by General Johnson, Barney Perkins, and Greg S. Perry.
Gold Forever Music Inc., 1970.
Best-selling record by Honey Cone (Hot Wax, 1971).

Wanted
Words and music by Jack Fulton and Lois Steele.
M. Witmark & Sons, 1954.
Best-selling record by Perry Como (RCA Victor).

Wanted Man
Words and music by Bob Dylan.
Big Sky Music, 1969.
Sung by Johnny Cash in his album, *Johnny Cash at San Quentin* (Columbia). Revived in 1975 by Jerry Wallace (MGM).

Wanting You
Words by Oscar Hammerstein, II, music by Sigmund Romberg.
Harms, Inc., 1928.
Introduced by Evelyn Herbert and Robert Halliday in *The New Moon*
  (operetta). Sung by Lawrence Tibbett and Grace Moore in the first
  film version, 1930; and by Jeanette MacDonald and Nelson Eddy in
  the second film version, 1940.

War
Words and music by Norman Whitfield and Barrett Strong.
Stone Agate Music Corp., 1970.
Best-selling record by Edwin Starr (Gordy, 1970).

War and Peace
Words by Wilson Stone, music by Nino Rota.
Famous Music Co., 1956.
Adapted from a theme from *War and Peace* (film). Best-selling record
  by Vic Damone (Mercury).

War Dance for Wooden Indians
Music by Raymond Scott.
Advanced Music Corp., 1938.
Introduced by The Raymond Scott Quintet. Performed by The Ray-
  mond Scott Quintet and The Condos Brothers in *Happy Landing*
  (film).

The War Is Over
Words and music by Phil Ochs.
Barricade Music Inc., 1968.
Sung by Phil Ochs in his album, *Tape from California* (A&M).

War Song
Words and music by Neil Young.
Silver Fiddle, 1972.
Best-selling record by Neil Young and Graham Nash (Reprise, 1972).

Warm
Words by Sid Jacobson, music by Jimmy Krondes.
Fred Fisher Music Co., 1956.
Introduced by Johnny Mathis (Columbia).

Warm All Over
Words and music by Frank Loesser.
Frank Music Co., 1956.
Introduced by Jo Sullivan in *The Most Happy Fella* (musical).

Warm and Tender Love, also known as **Wrap Me in Your Warm
  and Tender Love**

1958

Words and music by Bobby Robinson and Ida Irral Berger.
Duane Music, Inc., 1966/Cotillion Music Inc., 1966/Quinvy Music
  Publishing Co., 1966.
Best-selling record by Percy Sledge (Atlantic).

Warm and Willing
Words and music by Jimmy McHugh, Jay Livingston, and Ray
  Evans.
Miller Music Corp., 1959.
From *A Private's Affair* (film).

The Warm Red Wine
Words and music by Cindy Walker.
Unichappell Music Inc., 1949.
Best-selling record by Ernest Tubb (Decca).

Warm Valley
Words by Bob Russell, music by Duke Ellington.
Robbins Music Corp., 1943.
Song version of instrumental composition introduced by Duke Ellington
  and his Orchestra in 1940 (Victor).

Warmer Than a Whisper
Words and music by Sammy Cahn, music by James Van Heusen.
Chappell & Co., Inc., 1962.
Introduced by Dorothy Lamour in *The Road to Hong Kong* (film).

Warsaw Concerto (English)
Music by Richard Addinsell.
Keith Prowse Music Publishing Co., Ltd., London, England/
  Chappell & Co., Inc., 1942.
Introduced by pianist Louis Kentner and the London Symphony Or-
  chestra, conducted by Muir Mathieson, in *Suicide Squadron* (film).
  Lyrics by Carl Sigman added in 1958. Song version entitled "The
  World Outside."

Was I To Blame for Falling in Love with You
Words and music by Chester Conn, Victor Young, and Gus Kahn.
Leo Feist Inc., 1930.
Theme song of The Casa Loma Orchestra.

Was It Rain?
Words by Walter Hirsch, music by Lou Handman.
Anne-Rachel Music Corp., 1937.
Introduced by Frances Langford in *The Hit Parade* (film).

Was She Prettier Than I?
Words and music by Hugh Martin and Timothy Gray.

Cromwell Music, Inc., 1964.
Introduced by Louise Troy in *High Spirits* (musical).

Was That the Human Thing To Do
Words by Joe Young, music by Sammy Fain.
Warock Music, Inc., 1931/M. Witmark & Sons, 1931.
Introduced by Guy Lombardo and his Royal Canadians.

Washboard Blues
Words and music by Hoagy Carmichael, Fred B. Callahan, and
    Irving Mills.
Mills Music Inc., 1926.
First recording in 1925 by Curtis Hitch's Happy Harmonists, with Car-
    michael at the piano (Gennett). Best-selling records in 1926 by Red
    Nichols and his Five Pennies (Brunswick), in 1927 by Paul Whiteman
    and his Orchestra (Victor), and in 1938 by Mildred Bailey and her
    Orchestra (Vocalion).

Washington Square
Words and music by Bob Goldstein and David Shire.
Chappell & Co., Inc., 1963/Intersong, USA Inc., 1963.
Best-selling instrumental recording by The Village Stompers (Epic).
    First vocal version by Marilyn May (RCA Victor).

The Washington Twist
Words and music by Irving Berlin.
Irving Berlin Music Corp., 1962.
Introduced by Anita Gillette in *Mr. President* (musical). Introduced on
    records by Andre Kostelanetz (Columbia).

Wasn't It Beautiful While It Lasted
Words by B. G. De Sylva and Lew Brown, music by Ray
    Henderson.
DeSylva, Brown & Henderson, Inc., 1930/Anne-Rachel Music Corp.,
    1930.
Introduced by Grace Brinkley and Oscar Shaw in *Flying High* (musical).

Wasted Days and Wasted Nights
Words and music by Freddy Fender and Wayne Duncan.
Unart Music Corp., 1975.
Best-selling record by Freddy Fender (ABC/Dot, 1975).

Wasted Words
Words and music by Don Gibson.
Acuff-Rose Publications Inc., 1956.
Best-selling record in 1956 and 1957 by Ray Price (Columbia).

Watch Closely Now
Words and music by Kenny Ascher and Paul Williams.
WB Music Corp., 1976.
Introduced by Kris Kristofferson in *A Star Is Born* (film, 1976). Best-selling record by Kris Kristofferson (Columbia, 1977).

Watch Her Ride
Words and music by Paul Kantner.
Icebag Corp., 1968.
Best-selling record by Jefferson Airplane (RCA).

Watch Me Rock, I'm over Thirty
Words and music by Loudon Wainwright.
Snowden Music, 1978.
Introduced by Loudon Wainwright on *Final Exam* (Arista, 1978).

Watch Out for Lucy (English)
Words and music by Eric Clapton.
Stigwood Music Inc., 1978.
Best-selling record by Eric Clapton (RSO, 1979).

Watch the Flowers Grow
Words and music by L. Russell Brown and Raymond Bloodworth.
Saturday Music Inc., 1967.
Best-selling record by The Four Seasons (Philips).

Watch What Happens (French)
English words by Norman Gimbel, French words by Jacques Demy, music by Michel Legrand.
Productions Michel Legrand, Paris, France, 1964, 1965/Jonware Music Corp., 1964, 1965/Vogue Music, 1964, 1965.
"Lola's Theme," introduced in French by voice of Georges Blanes (dubbed for Marc Michel) in *The Umbrellas of Cherbourg* (French film). Used earlier as a theme in Jacques Demy's *Lola* (French film, 1960). Introduced in English by Jean-Paul Vignon (Columbia).

Watch Where You're Going
Words and music by Don Gibson.
Acuff-Rose Publications Inc., 1965.
Best-selling record by Don Gibson (RCA Victor).

Watchin' Scotty Grow
Words and music by Mac Davis.
Screen Gems-EMI Music Inc., 1970.
Best-selling record by Bobby Goldsboro (United Artists, 1971).

Watching My Dreams Go By
Words by Al Dubin, music by Joe Burke.

M. Witmark & Sons, 1929.
Introduced by Winnie Lightner in *She Couldn't Say No* (film, 1930).

Watching the Clouds Roll By
Words and music by Bert Kalmar and Harry Ruby.
Harms, Inc., 1928.
Introduced by Bernice Ackerman and Milton Watson in *Animal Crackers* (musical).

Watching the Detectives (English)
Words and music by Elvis Costello.
Plangent Visions Music, Inc., London, England, 1977.
Introduced by Elvis Costello on *My Aim Is True* (Columbia, 1977).

Watching the River Flow
Words and music by Bob Dylan.
Big Sky Music, 1971.
Best-selling record by Bob Dylan (Columbia, 1971).

Watching the River Run
Words and music by Kenny Loggins and Jim Messina.
Gnossos Music, 1973/Jasperilla Music Co., 1973/Portofino Music, 1973.
Best-selling record by Loggins & Messina (Columbia, 1974).

Water Boy
Words and music by Avery Robinson.
Boosey & Hawkes Inc., 1922.
Concert song, part of which is an adaptation of the folk song, "Jack o'Diamonds."

Water under the Bridge
Words by E. Y. Harburg, music by Vernon Duke.
Harms, Inc., 1933.
Introduced by Everett Marshall, and danced to by Patricia Bowman, in *Ziegfeld Follies of 1934* (revue).

Water with the Wine (English)
Words and music by Joan Armatrading.
Cheshire Music Inc., 1976.
Introduced by Joan Armatrading on *Joan Armatrading* (A&M, 1976).

Watercolors
Words and music by Janis Ian.
April Music Inc., 1975.
Performed by the voice of Janis Ian in *Between the Lines* (film, 1975).

Waterloo
Words and music by John Loudermilk and Marijohn Wilkin.
Cedarwood Publishing Co., Inc., 1959.
Best-selling record by Stonewall Jackson (Columbia).

Waterloo (Swiss)
English words and music by Benny Anderson, Bjorn Ulvaeus, and
    Stig Anderson.
Countless Songs Ltd., 1974.
Best-selling record by Abba (Atlantic, 1974).

Watermelon Man
Words and music by Oscar Brown, Jr.
Kicks Music, 1962/Edward B. Marks Music Corp., 1962.
Introduced by Oscar Brown, Jr. Revived in in 1965 with best-selling
    record by Gloria Lynn (Fontana).

Watermelon Man
Music by Herb Hancock.
Hancock Music Co., 1962.
Best-selling record, instrumental, in 1963 by Mongo Santamaria (Battle).

Watermelon Weather
Words by Paul Francis Webster, music by Hoagy Carmichael.
Morley Music Co., Inc., 1952.
Best-selling record by Perry Como and Eddie Fisher (RCA Victor).

Waters of the Perkiomen
Words by Al Dubin, music by F. Henri Klickmann.
Mills Music Inc., 1925.

Watertown
Words and music by Bob Gaudio and Jake Holmes.
Sergeant Music Co., 1970/DeValbo Music, 1970.
Best-selling record by Frank Sinatra (Reprise, 1970).

Wave
Words and music by Patti Smith.
Ninja Music Co., 1979.
Introduced by Patti Smith on *Wave* (Arista, 1979).

Wave to Me, My Lady
Words and music by William Stein and Frank Loesser.
Frank Music Co., 1945.
Introduced by Guy Lombardo and his Royal Canadians. Best-selling
    record in 1946 by Elton Britt (Victor).

Wavelength
Words and music by Van Morrison.
Essential Music, 1978.
Best-selling record by Van Morrison (Warner Brothers, 1978).

The Waves Roll Out
Words and music by Shel Silverstein and Bob Gibson.
Hollis Music, Inc., 1963.
Introduced by Shel Silverstein.

'Way Back Home
Words and music by Al Lewis and Tom Waring.
Bregman, Vocco & Conn, Inc., 1935/Sovereign Music Corp., 1935.
Introduced by Fred Waring and his Pennsylvanians.

'Way Back When
Words and music by Henri A. Keates, Harry I. Robinson, and Louis
   Robinson.
Will Rossiter, 1927.

Way Down
Words and music by Layng Martine.
Ray Stevens Music, 1977.
Best-selling record by Elvis Presley (RCA, 1977).

Way Down East
Music by Larry Adler.
Saunders Publications, Inc., 1960, 1962, 1963.
Theme from *The Great Chase* (film, 1962), introduced on soundtrack by
   Larry Adler.

'Way Down Yonder in New Orleans
Words and music by Henry Creamer and Turner Layton.
Shapiro, Bernstein & Co., Inc., 1922.
Introduced by Creamer and Layton. Sung by the chorus, and danced to
   by Fred Astaire and Ginger Rogers, in *The Story of Vernon and Irene
   Castle* (film, 1939); and by Betty Hutton in *Somebody Loves Me* (film,
   1952). Best-selling record in 1960 by Freddie Cannon (Swan).

The Way I Feel Today
Words by Andy Razaf, music by Don Redman and Howard
   Quicksell.
Mayfair Music Corp., 1929, 1930.
First recording by McKinney's Cotton Pickers (Victor). Not copy-
   righted until 1930.

The Way I Feel Tonight
Words and music by Harvey Shields.

Rosewater Music, 1977/Careers Music Inc., 1977.
Best-selling record by Bay City Rollers (Arista, 1977).

The Way I Want to Touch You
Words and music by Toni Tennille.
I Love Music, 1974/Temanja Music, 1974/Moonlight & Magnolias
  Music Publishing, 1974.
Best-selling record by The Captain & Tennille (A & M, 1975).

The Way It Used to Be (Italian)
English words by Roger Cook and Roger Greenaway, Italian words
  by Gianni Argenio, music by Franco Cassano and Corrado Conti.
Durium Edizioni Musicali, Milan, Italy, 1969/Maribus Music Inc.,
  1969.
Original Italian title, "Melodia." Best-selling record of English version by
  Engelbert Humperdinck (Parrot).

The Way of a Clown
Words and music by Barry Mann and Howard Greenfield.
Screen Gems-EMI Music Inc., 1960.
Introduced by Teddy Randazzo and Barry Mann (Am-Par).

The Way of Love (J'ai le Mal de Toi) (French)
French words and music by Jacques Dieval, English words by Al
  Stillman.
Chappell & Co., Inc., 1965.
Best-selling records by Kathy Kirby (Parrot, 1965) and Cher (Kapp,
  1972).

Way Out West (on West End Avenue)
Words by Lorenz Hart, music by Richard Rodgers.
Chappell & Co., Inc., 1937.
Introduced by Wynn Murray, Alex Courtney, Clifton Darling, James
  Gillis, and Robert Rounseville in *Babes in Arms* (musical).

A Way to Survive
Words and music by Moneen Carpenter and Hank Cochran.
Tree Publishing Co., Inc., 1964.
Best-selling record in 1966 by Ray Price (Columbia).

The Way We Were
Words by Marilyn Bergman and Alan Bergman, music by Marvin
  Hamlisch.
Colgems-EMI Music Inc., 1973.
Performed by the voice of Barbra Streisand in *The Way We Were* (film,
  1973). Best-selling record by Barbra Streisand (Columbia, 1974).
  Revived in 1975 by Gladys Knight and The Pips, in medley with "Try
  To Remember." Won an Academy Award, Song of the Year, 1973; a

National Academy of Recording Arts and Sciences Award, Song of the Year, 1974.

The Way You Do Things
Words and music by William Robinson and Bobby Rogers.
Jobete Music Co., Inc., 1964.
Best-selling record by The Temptations (Gordy). Revived in 1978 by Rita Coolidge (A & M).

The Way You Look Tonight
Words by Dorothy Fields, music by Jerome Kern.
T. B. Harms Co., 1936.
Introduced by Fred Astaire in *Swing Time* (film). Won an Academy Award, 1936.

The Ways of a Woman in Love
Words and music by Charlie Rich and Bill Justis.
Hi-Lo Music Inc., 1958.
Best-selling record by Johnny Cash (Sun).

The Ways to Love a Man
Words and music by Billy Sherrill, Glenn Sutton, and Tammy Wynette.
Al Gallico Music Corp., 1969/Algee Music Corp., 1969.
Best-selling record by Tammy Wynette (Epic).

Wayward Wind
Words and music by Stan Lebowsky and Herb Newman.
Hillary Music, Inc., 1956/Bamboo Music, Inc., 1956.
Best-selling record by Gogi Grant (Era).

We Ain't Got Nothing Yet
Words and music by Emil Thielhelm, Michael Esposito, Ralph Scala, and Ronald Gilbert.
Ananga-Ranga Music Corp., 1966.
Best-selling record in 1966-67 by The Blues Magoos (Mercury).

We Almost Lost Detroit
Words and music by Gil Scott-Heron.
Brouhaha Music, 1977.
Introduced by Gil Scott-Heron on *Bridges* (Arista, 1977).

We Are Family
Words and music by Bernard Edwards and Nile Rodgers.
Chic Music Inc., 1979.
Best-selling record by Sister Sledge (Cotillion, 1979). Nominated for a National Academy of Recording Arts and Sciences Award, Rhythm & Blues Song of the Year, 1979.

We Are Not Strangers
Words and music by Elizabeth Swados.
Blackwood Music Inc., 1978.
Introduced by Evan Miranda and Company of Runaways in *Runaways*
  (musical, 1978).

We Are the Champions (English)
Words and music by Freddie Mercury.
Regline Music Co., 1977.
Best-selling record by Queen (Electra, 1978).

We Are the Future
Words and music by Mel Bolton, James Holiday, Troy Laws, and
  Friendly Womack.
Derglenn Publishing, 1978/Old Brompton Road Pub, 1978.
Introduced by High Inergy in *Almost Summer* (film, 1978).

We Belong Together
Words and music by Robert Carr and Johnny Mitchell.
Maureen Music, Inc., 1956.
Best-selling record by Robert and Johnny (Old Town).

We Belong Together
Words and music by Johnny Mitchell, Robert Carr, and Sam Weiss.
Maureen Music, Inc., 1958/Big Seven Music Corp., 1958.
Best-selling record in 1968 by Robert and Johnny (Old Town).

We Can Fly
Words and music by Bob Cowsill, Artie Kornfeld, Steve Duboff, and
  Bill Cowsill.
Akbestal Music, Inc., 1968/Luvlin Music Inc., 1968.

We Can Talk
Words and music by Richard Manuel.
Dwarf Music Co., Inc., 1968.
Introduced by The Band in their album, *Music from Big Pink* (Capitol).

We Can Work It Out (English)
Words and music by John Lennon and Paul McCartney.
Northern Songs, Ltd., England, 1965/Maclen Music Inc., 1965.
Best-selling record in 1966 by The Beatles (Capitol). Revived in 1971 by
  Stevie Wonder (Tamla).

We Can't Hide It Anymore
Words and music by Barry Murphy.
Groovesville Music Inc., 1975.
Best-selling record by Larry Santos (Casablanca, 1976).

We Could Be Close
Music by Jule Styne, words by Bob Merrill.
Chappell & Co., Inc., 1972/Merrill Music Corp., 1972.
Introduced by Robert Morse and Elaine Joyce in *Sugar* (musical, 1972).

We Could Make Such Beautiful Music
Words by Robert Sour, music by Henry Manners.
Unichappell Music Inc., 1940.
Best-selling record in 1947 by Vaughn Monroe and his Orchestra (Victor).

We Did It
Words and music by Charles E. McCormick.
The Crystal Jukebox Inc., 1973.
Best-selling record by Syl Johnson (Hi, 1973).

We Did It Before (And We Can Do It Again)
Words and music by Cliff Friend and Charlie Tobias.
Ched Music Co., 1941/M. Witmark & Sons, 1941.
Interpolated into score and introduced by Eddie Cantor in *Banjo Eyes* (musical). Featured in *Sweet of the Fleet* (film, 1942).

We Don't Talk Anymore (English)
Words and music by Al Tarney.
ATV Music Corp., 1979.
Best-selling record by Cliff Richard (EMI America, 1979).

We Got Latin Soul, see **We Got More Soul.**

We Got Love
Words by Kal Mann, music by Bernie Lowe.
Kalmann Music, Inc., 1959/Lowe Music Publishing Corp., 1959.
Best-selling record by Bobby Rydell (Cameo).

We Got More Soul, also known as **We Got Latin Soul**
Words and music by Arlester Christian.
Drive-In Music Co., Inc., 1969.
Best-selling record by Dyke and The Blazers (Original Sound).

We Got to Get You a Woman
Words and music by Todd Rundgren.
Screen Gems-EMI Music Inc., 1970/Earmark Music Inc., 1970.
Best-selling record by Runt (Ampex, 1971).

We Got Us
Words by Chuck Sweeney, music by Moose Charlap.
Maxana Music Corp., 1960.
Introduced by Eydie Gorme and Steve Lawrence (United Artists).

We Gotta Get Out of This Place
Words and music by Barry Mann and Cynthia Weil.
Screen Gems-EMI Music Inc., 1965.
Best-selling record by The Animals (MGM).

We Had It All
Words and music by Troy Seals and Donnie Fritts.
Danor Music Inc., 1973.
Performed by Bonnie Koloc on *Close Up* (Epic, 1976).

We Just Couldn't Say Good-bye
Words and music by Harry Woods.
Words & Music, Inc., 1932/Essex Music, Inc., 1932.

We Just Disagree (English)
Words and music by Jim Krueger.
Blackwood Music Inc., 1977/Bruiser Music, Div. of Scoop
  Enterprises, 1977.
Best-selling record by Dave Mason (Columbia, 1977).

We Kiss in a Shadow
Words by Oscar Hammerstein, II, music by Richard Rodgers.
Williamson Music Inc., 1951.
Introduced by Doretta Morrow and Larry Douglas in *The King and I*
  (musical).

We Live in Two Different Worlds
Words and music by Fred Rose.
Milene Music Co., 1943.
Best-selling record in 1945 by Tex Ritter (Capitol).

We Love You (English)
Words and music by Mick Jagger and Keith Richard.
ABKCO Music Inc., 1967.
Best-selling record by The Rolling Stones (London).

We Love You Beatles
Words by Lee Adams, music by Charles Strouse.
Edwin H. Morris Co., 1964.
Based on "We Love You Conrad" from *Bye Bye Birdie* (musical, 1960).
  Best-selling record by The Carefrees (London International).

We Love You, Call Collect
Words by Martin Wark, music by Ralph Carmichael.
Lexicon Music Inc., 1969.
Best-selling record by Art Linkletter (Capitol).

1969

We May Never Love Like This Again
Words and music by Joel Hirschhorn and Al Kasha.
WB Music Corp., 1974/Warner-Tamerlane Publishing Corp., 1974/
Twentieth Century Fox Music Corp., 1974/Fox Fanfare Music
Inc., 1974.
Performed by the voice of Maureen McGovern in *The Towering Inferno*
(film, 1974). Best-selling record by Maureen McGovern (20th Cen-
tury, 1975). Won an Academy Award, 1974.

We May Never Pass This Way (Again)
Words and music by James Seals and Darrell Crofts.
Dawnbreaker Music Co., 1973.
Best-selling record by Seals & Crofts (Warner Brothers, 1973).

We Meet Again, see **The Song from** *Desiree.*

We Might As Well Forget It
Words and music by Johnny Bond.
Peer International Corp., 1944.
Best-selling record by Bob Wills and his Texas Playboys (Okeh).

We Missed You
Words and music by Bill Anderson.
Tree Publishing Co., Inc., 1962/Champion Music Corp., 1962.
Best-selling record by Kitty Wells (Decca).

We Must Be Vigilant
Words by Edgar Leslie, music by Joe Burke.
Ahlert-Burke Corp., 1942/Joe Burke Music Co., 1942/Edgar Leslie,
1942.
Based on melody of the 1891 E. H. Meacham march, "American Patrol."
Identified with Phil Spitalny's All-Girl Orchestra. Featured in *When
Johnny Comes Marching Home* (film).

We Must Have Been Out of Our Minds
Words and music by Melba Montgomery.
Glad Music Co., 1963.
Best-selling record by George Jones and Melba Montgomery (United
Artists).

We Mustn't Say Goodbye
Words by Al Dubin, music by James Monaco.
Morley Music Co., Inc., 1943.
Introduced by Vaughn Monroe and his Orchestra. Featured in *Stage
Door Canteen* (film). Nominated for an Academy Award, 1943.

We Never Talk Much
Words by Sammy Cahn, music by Nicholas Brodszky.

Robbins Music Corp., 1950.
Introduced by Fernanco Lamas and Jane Powell in *Rich, Young and Pretty* (film).

We Open in Venice
Words and music by Cole Porter.
Chappell & Co., Inc., 1948.
Introduced by Alfred Drake, Patricia Morison, Lisa Kirk, and Harold Lang in *Kiss Me Kate* (musical). Sung by Kathryn Grayson, Howard Keel, Ann Miller, and Tommy Rall in film version (1953).

We Saw the Sea
Words and music by Irving Berlin.
Irving Berlin Music Corp., 1936.
Introduced by Fred Astaire and male chorus in *Follow the Fleet* (film).

We Shall Overcome
Words and music by Zilphia Horton, Frank Hamilton, Guy Carawan, and Pete Seeger.
Ludlow Music Inc., 1960, 1963.
Believed to have originated as religious folk song later turned into a formal Baptist hymn, entitled "I'll Overcome Some Day," by C. Albert Tindley, copyrighted in 1901.

We Sure Can Love Each Other
Words and music by Billy Sherrill and Tammy Wynette.
Altam Music Corp., 1971.
Best-selling record by Tammy Wynette (Epic, 1971).

We Three (My Echo, My Shadow and Me)
Words and music by Dick Robertson, Nelson Cogane, and Sammy Mysels.
Edwin H. Morris Co., 1940/Penn Music Co., 1940.
Best-selling record The Ink Spots (Decca).

We Two Shall Meet Again (Austrian)
English words by Harry B. Smith, German words by Julius Brammer and Alfred Gruenwald, music by Emmerich Kalman.
Harms, Inc., 1927.
Introduced in *The Circus Princess* (operetta).

We Will Always Be Sweethearts
Words by Leo Robin, music by Oscar Straus.
Famous Music Co., 1932.
Introduced by Maurice Chevalier and Jeanette MacDonald in *One Hour with You* (film).

Wear It on Our Face
Words and music by Bobby Miller.
Chevis Publishing Corp., 1968.
Best-selling record by The Dells (Cadet).

Wear My Ring around Your Neck
Words and music by Bert Carroll and Russell Moody.
Elvis Presley Music, Inc., 1958/Tideland Music Publishing Corp.,
    1958/Pinelawn Music Publishing Co., Inc., 1958.
Best-selling record by Elvis Presley (RCA Victor).

Wear Your Love Like Heaven (English)
Words and music by Donovan Leitch.
Donovan Music, Ltd., London, England, 1967/Peer International
    Corp., 1967.
Best-selling record by Donovan (Epic).

Weary Blues from Waitin'
Words and music by Hank Williams.
Fred Rose Music, Inc., 1951.
Best-selling record in 1953 by Hank Williams (M-G-M).

Weary River
Words by Grant Clarke, music by Louis Silvers.
Bourne Co., 1929/Fred Fisher Music Co., 1929.
Introduced by the voice of an unidentified vocalist, dubbed for Richard
    Barthelmess, in *Weary River* (film).

Weary Way Blues
Words by Ida Cox, music by Lovie Austin.
Mills Music Inc., 1923.
Introduced by Ida Cox.

Weave Me the Sunshine
Words and music by Peter Yarrow.
Marybeth Music, 1972.
Introduced by Peter Yarrow on *Peter* (Warner Brothers, 1972). Best-
    selling record by Perry Como (RCA, 1974).

Weaver of Dreams
Words by Jack Elliott, music by Victor Young.
Chappell & Co., Inc., 1951/Edwin H. Morris Co., 1951/Larry
    Shayne Music Inc., 1951.
Best-selling record by Nat "King" Cole (Capitol).

The Wedding
Words and music by Pat Gaston, Bobby Williams, and Jacqueline
    McCoy.

Unichappell Music Inc., 1955/Maureen Music, Inc., 1955.
Best-selling record by The Solitaires (Old Town).

The Wedding
Words and music by Albert A. Beach and Guy Wood.
Criterion Music Corp., 1958.
Best-selling record by June Valli (Mercury).

The Wedding (La Novia) (Argentinian)
English words by Fred Jay, Spanish words and music by Joaquin
    Prieto.
Ediciones Internacionales Fermata, Buenos Aires, Argentina, 1961/
    Regent Music.
Original Spanish-language version introduced in Argentina by Joaquin
    Prieto. Introduced on records in United States by Anita Bryant (Co-
    lumbia). Best-selling record in England and United States in 1964 by
    Julie Rogers (Mercury).

Wedding Bell Blues
Words and music by Laura Nyro.
Blackwood Music Inc., 1966.
Introduced in 1967 by Laura Nyro in her album, *More Than a New
    Discovery* (Verve Forecast); best-selling record in 1969 by The 5th
    Dimension (Soul City). Revived in 1973 by Nyro on her album *The
    First Songs* (Columbia), a re-issue of *More Than a New Discovery.*

Wedding Bells
Words and music by Claude Boone.
Edwin H. Morris Co., 1947.
Best-selling record in 1949 by Hank Williams (MGM).

Wedding Bells Are Breaking Up That Old Gang of Mine
Words by Irving Kahal and Willie Raskin, music by Sammy Fain.
Rytvoc, Inc., 1929.

The Wedding of Lilli Marlene (English)
Words and music by Tommie Connor and Johnny Reine (pseudonym
    for John Harold Johnson).
Box & Cox Publications, Inc., 1949/MCA, Inc., 1949.
Best-selling record in the United States by The Andrews Sister (Decca).

The Wedding of the Painted Doll
Words by Arthur Freed, music by Nacio Herb Brown.
Miller Music Corp., 1929.
Introduced by James Burrows in *The Broadway Melody* (film).

The Wedding Rhumba, see **The Wedding Samba.**

The Wedding Samba, also known as **The Wedding Rhumba**
Words and music by Abraham Ellstein, Allan Small, and Joseph
 Liebowitz.
Duchess Music Corp., 1940, 1947.
Original Yiddish title, "Der Nayer Sher." Introduced in 1940 as "The
 Wedding Rhuma." Best-selling records in 1949-50 by The Andrews
 Sisters (Decca) and Edmundo Ros and his Orchestra (London).

The Wedding Song
Words by Martin Kalmanoff and Aaron Schroeder, music by Irving
 Fields.
Venus Music Corp., 1948.
Adapted from Yiddish folk song, "Rosinkes and Mandeln" ("Raisins and
 Almonds"). Introduced by Irving Fields and the Campos Trio (Vic-
 tor).

Wedding Song, also known as **There is Love**
Words and music by Noel Paul Stookey.
Public Domain Foundation, 1971.
Best-selling record by Paul Stookey (Warner Brothers, 1971).

Wee Baby Blues
Words and music by Pete Johnson and Joe Turner.
MCA, Inc., 1944.
Introduced by Johnson and Turner in Kansas City during the 1930's.
 Best-known record by Joe Turner and Art Tatum (Decca).

(In the) Wee Small Hours (Of the Morning)
Words by Bob Hilliard, music by David Mann.
Redd Evans Music Co., 1955.
Best-selling record by Frank Sinatra (Capitol).

The Week-End
Words and music by Lou Stallman, Bobby Weinstein, and Teddy
 Randazzo.
Vogue Music, 1964.
Introduced in 1966 by Jack Jones (Kapp) and Steve Lawrence (Co-
 lumbia).

A Week-End in Havana
Words by Mack Gordon, music by Harry Warren.
Bregman, Vocco & Conn, Inc., 1941.
Introduced by Carmen Miranda in *Week-End in Havana* (film).

A Week in a Country Jail
Words and music by Tom T. Hall.
Unichappell Music Inc., 1969.
Best-selling record in 1970 by Tom T. Hall (Mercury).

A Week in the Country
Words and music by Baker Knight.
Acuff-Rose Publications Inc., 1963.
Best-selling record in 1964 by Ernest Ashworth (Hickory).

Weekend in New England
Words and music by Randy Edelman.
Unart Music Corp., 1976.
Best-selling record by Barry Manilow (Arista, 1977).

The Weekend of a Private Secretary
Words by Johnny Mercer, music by Bernie Hanighen.
Remick Music Corp., 1938/Commander Publications, 1938.
Introduced by Mildred Bailey, with Red Norvo and his Orchestra.

Weepin' and Cryin'
Words and music by Tommy Brown.
Canadiana-Ensign, 1951/Ensign Music Corp., 1951.
Best-selling record in 1952 by The Griffin Brothers (Dot).

Weeping Blues
Music by James P. Johnson.
Perry Bradford Music Publishing Co., 1923.
Jazz instrumental. First recording by James P. Johnson (Columbia).

Weeping Willow Blues
Words and music by Paul Carter.
C.R. Publishing Co., 1924.
First recording by Bessie Smith (Columbia).

Weeping Woman Blues
Words by Bessie Smith, music by Gertrude "Ma" Rainey.
Northern Music Corp., 1928.
First recording by Ma Rainey (Paramount).

The Weight
Words and music by Jaime Robbie Robertson.
Dwarf Music Co., Inc., 1968.
Best-sellings records by Jackie DeShannon (Imperial), The Band (Capitol), and in 1969 by Aretha Franklin (Atlantic) and Diana Ross and The Supremes and The Temptations (Motown).

Welcome Back
Words and music by John Sebastian.
John Sebastian Music, 1976.
Performed by the voice of John Sebastian in *Welcome Back, Kotter* (television show, 1976). Best-selling record by John Sebastian (Reprise, 1976).

Welcome Home
Words and music by Harold Rome.
Chappell & Co., Inc., 1954/Florence Music Co., Inc., 1954.
Introduced by Ezio Pinza in *Fanny* (musical).

Welcome Me, Love
Words and music by Tony Romeo.
Big Apple Music Co., 1969.
Best-selling record by Brooklyn Bridge (Buddah).

Welcome to Kanagawa
Words and music by Stephen Sondheim.
Revelation Music Publishing Corp., 1976/Rilting Music Inc., 1976.
Introduced by Ernest Harada in *Pacific Overtures* (musical, 1976).

Welcome to L. A.
Words and music by Richard Baskin.
United Artists Music Co., Inc., 1976.
Performed by the voice of Richard Baskin in *Welcome to L. A.* (film, 1977).

Welcome to My Dream
Words by Johnny Burke, music by James Van Heusen.
Bourne Co., 1945/Music Sales Corp., 1945.
Introduced by Bing Crosby in *Road to Utopia* (film).

Welcome to My World
Words and music by Ray Winkler and John Hathcock.
Neillrae Music, 1961/Tuckahoe Music, Inc., 1961.
Best-selling record in 1964 by Jim Reeves (RCA Victor).

Welcome to the Theatre
Words by Lee Adams, music by Charles Strouse.
Strada Music Co., 1970.
Introduced by Lauren Bacall in *Applause* (musical, 1970).

Welfare Cadillac
Words and music by Guy Drake.
Bull Fighter Music, 1969.
Best-selling record by Guy Drake (Royal American, 1970).

Welfare Mothers
Words and music by Neil Young.
Silver Fiddle, 1979.
Introduced by Neil Young on *Rust Never Sleeps* (Reprise, 1979).

Well All Right! (Tonight's the Night)
Words and music by Frances Faye, Don Raye, and Dan Howell

(pseudonym for David Kapp).
Leeds Music Corp., 1939.
Best-selling record by The Andrews Sisters (Decca).

We'll Be the Same
Words by Lorenz Hart, music by Richard Rodgers.
Harms, Inc., 1931.
Introduced by Harriette Lake (Ann Sothern) and Jack Whiting, and
   reprised by Jack Whiting and Gus Shy, in *America's Sweetheart*
   (musical).

We'll Be Together Again
Words and music by Frankie Laine and Carl Fischer.
Cares Music Co., 1945/Carey Fisher Music Co., 1945.
Introduced and best-selling record by Frankie Laine (Mercury).

Well, Did You Evah?
Words and music by Cole Porter.
Chappell & Co., Inc., 1939.
Introduced in 1939 by Betty Grable and Charles Walters in *Du Barry
   Was a Lady* (musical). Reintroduced by Frank Sinatra and Bing
   Crosby in *High Society* (film, 1956).

We'll Gather Lilacs (Now That You're Home Once More)
   (English)
Words and music by Ivor Novello.
Chappell & Co., Ltd., London, England/Chappell & Co., Inc., 1945.
Introduced by Muriel Barron and Olive Gilbert in London in *Perchance
   To Dream* (musical).

Well, Git It
Music by Sy Oliver.
Embassy Music Corp., 1942.
Introduced by Tommy Dorsey and his Orchestra (Victor).

We'll Go Away Together
Words by Langston Hughes, music by Kurt Weill.
Chappell & Co., Inc., 1946/Hampshire House Publishing Corp.,
   1946.
Introduced by Brian Sullivan and Anne Jeffreys in *Street Scene* (musical,
   1947).

We'll Have a Kingdom
Words by Otto Harbach and Oscar Hammerstein, II, music by
   Rudolf Friml.
Warner Brothers-Seven Arts Music, 1926.
Introduced by Desiree Ellinger and Joseph Santley in *The Wild Rose*
   (musical).

We'll Have a New Home in the Mornin'
Words and music by Gene Buck, J. Russel Robinson, and Willard
   Robison.
Bourne Co., 1927.
Introduced by Kitty O'Connor in *Take the Air* (musical).

We'll Make Hay While the Sun Shines
Words by Arthur Freed, music by Nacio Herb Brown.
Robbins Music Corp., 1933.
Introduced by Bing Crosby and Marion Davies in *Going Hollywood*
   (film).

We'll Meet Again (English)
Words and music by Ross Parker and Hughie Charles.
Irwin Dash Music Co., Ltd., London, England/World Music, Inc.,
   1939.
Introduced by and identified with Vera Lynn. Sung by Miss Lynn on
   soundtrack of *Dr. Strangelove or: How I Learned To Stop Worrying
   and Love the Bomb* (film, 1964).

We'll Never Have to Say Goodbye Again, see **Never Have to Say
Goodbye Again.**

Well, Oh, Well
Words and music by Tiny Bradshaw, Lois Mann, and Henry
   Bernard.
Fort Knox Music Co., 1950/Yellow Dog Music Inc., 1950.
Best-selling record by Tiny Bradshaw (King).

A Well Respected Man (English)
Words and music by Ray Davies.
Edward Kassner Music Co., Ltd., London, England, 1965/American
   Metropolitan Enterprises of New York, Inc.
Best-selling record in 1965-66 by The Kinks (Reprise).

We'll Sing in the Sunshine
Words and music by Gale Garnett.
Lupercalia Music Publishing Co., 1963.
Best-selling record in 1964-65 by Gale Garnett (RCA Victor). Won a
   National Academy of Recording Arts and Sciences Award, Best Folk
   Recording, 1964.

Well, There It Is!
Words by Irving Taylor, music by Vic Mizzy.
Kiss Music Co., 1940/Unison Music Co., 1940.
Introduced by Barry Wood.

Well, You Needn't
Music by Thelonious Monk.
Regent Music, 1947.
First recording, jazz instrumental, by Thelonious Monk (Blue Note).

Wendy
Words by Betty Comden and Adolph Green, music by Jule Styne.
Edwin H. Morris Co., 1954.
Introduced by Mary Martin in *Peter Pan* (musical).

Went to See the Gypsy
Words and music by Bob Dylan.
Big Sky Music, 1970.
Performed by Bob Dylan on *New Morning* (Columbia, 1970).

We're a Winner
Words and music by Curtis Mayfield.
Warner-Tamerlane Publishing Corp., 1967.
Best-selling record in 1968 by The Impressions (ABC).

We're All Alone
Words and music by William Scaggs.
Boz Scaggs Music, 1976.
Best-selling record by Rita Coolidge (A & M, 1977).

We're All Playing in the Same Band
Words and music by Bert Sommer.
Luvlin Music Inc., 1970/Sommersongs, 1970.
Best-selling record by Bert Sommer (Eleuthera, 1970).

We're an American Band
Words and music by Don Brewer.
Brew Music Co., 1973.
Best-selling record by Grand Funk Railroad (Capitol, 1973).

We're Getting Careless with Our Love
Words and music by Frank Johnson and Donald David.
Groovesville Music Inc., 1973.
Best-selling record by Johnnie Taylor (Stax, 1974).

We're Gonna Be in High Society
Words and music by Dan Swan, Allan Copeland, and Mort Green.
Leeds Music Corp., 1955.

Adapted from the traditional New Orleans jazz band marching tune, "High Society." Vocal version introduced by Jo Stafford (Columbia).

We're Gonna Make It
Words and music by Raynard Miner, Billy Davis, Carl William Smith, and Gene Barge.
Chevis Publishing Corp., 1965.
Best-selling record by Little Milton (Checker).

We're Having a Baby
Words by Harold Adamson, music by Vernon Duke.
Robbins Music Corp., 1942.
Introduced by Eddie Cantor and June Clyde in *Banjo Eyes* (musical, 1941).

We're in the Money (The Gold Digger's Song)
Words by Al Dubin, music by Harry Warren.
Remick Music Corp., 1933.
Introduced by Ginger Rogers in *Gold Diggers of 1933* (film).

We're Not Children
Words and music by Jay Livingston and Ray Evans.
Livingston & Evans, Inc., 1958.
Introduced by Jacquelyn McKeever and Paul Valentine in *Oh Captain!* (musical).

We're Off To See the Wizard
Words by E. Y. Harburg, music by Harold Arlen.
Leo Feist Inc., 1939.
Introduced by Judy Garland, Bert Lahr, Jack Haley, and Ray Bolger in *The Wizard of Oz* (film).

We're the Couple in the Castle
Words by Frank Loesser, music by Hoagy Carmichael.
Famous Music Co., 1941.
Introduced in *Mr. Bug Goes to Town* (cartoon film).

We're the Talk of the Town
Words by Buck Owens, music by Rollie Weber.
Blue Book Music, 1963.
Best-selling record by Buck Owens and Rose Maddox (Capitol).

Were Thine That Special Face
Words and music by Cole Porter.
Chappell & Co., Inc., 1948.
Introduced by Alfred Drake in *Kiss Me Kate* (musical). Sung by Howard Keel in film version (1953).

We're Working Our Way through College
Words by Johnny Mercer, music by Richard A. Whiting.
Harms, Inc., 1937.
Introduced by Dick Powell and chorus in *Varsity Show* (film).

Were You Foolin'?
Words by Edgar Leslie, music by Fred E. Ahlert.
T. B. Harms Co., 1934.
Introduced by Grace Hayes and Newell Chase.

Were Your Ears Burning, Baby?
Words and music by Mack Gordon and Harry Revel.
DeSylva, Brown & Henderson, Inc., 1934.
Introduced by Ben Bernie and his Orchestra in *Shoot the Works* (film).

Weren't We Fools?
Words and music by Cole Porter.
Harms, Inc., 1927.

Werewolf
Words and music by Les Emmerson.
Unichappell Music Inc., 1974/Galeneye Music, 1974.
Best-selling record by Five Man Electrical Band (Polydor, 1974).

Werewolves of London
Words and music by Leroy Marinell, Robert Wachtel, and Warren
    Zevon.
Polite Music, 1978/Zevon Music, 1978.
Best-selling record by Warren Zevon (Asylum, 1978).

West End Avenue
Words and music by Stephen Schwartz.
Belwin-Mills Publishing Corp., 1974/Grey Dog Music, 1974.
Introduced by Dale Soules in *The Magic Show* (musical, 1974).

West End Blues
Words by Clarence Williams, music by Joe Oliver.
MCA, Inc., 1928.
First recording by King Oliver and his Dixie Syncopators (Vocalion).
    Most famous and best-selling version by Louis Armstrong and his Hot
    Five (Okeh).

West Indies Blues
Words and music by Edgar Dowell, Spencer Williams, and Clarence
    Williams.
MCA, Inc., 1923.

West of the Great Divide
Words by George Whiting, music by Ernest R. Ball.
Anne-Rachel Music Corp., 1924/M. Witmark & Sons, 1924.

West Side Baby
Words and music by Dallas Bartley and John Cameron.
Cherio Corp., 1947.
Best-selling record by Dinah Washington (Mercury).

Western Movies
Words by Cliff Goldsmith, music by Fred Smith.
Elizabeth Music, 1958/Aries Music Co., 1958.
Best-selling record by The Olympics (Liberty).

Western Union
Words and music by Mike Rabon, Norman Ezell, and John Durrill.
Best-selling record by The Five Americans (Abnak).

Western Union Blues
Words and music by Ida Cox.
Northern Music Corp., 1928.
First recording by Ida Cox (Paramount).

Westward Ho!—The Covered Wagon March
Words by R. A. Barnes, music by Hugo Riesenfeld.
Warner Brothers-Seven Arts Music, 1923.
"Exploitation song" for *The Covered Wagon* (film).

Westwind
Words by Ogden Nash, music by Kurt Weill.
Chappell & Co., Inc., 1943/Hampshire House Publishing Corp.,
    1943.
Introduced by John Boles in *One Touch of Venus* (musical). Another
    lyric to this Weill melody, entitled "My Week," written by Ann Ronell
    for, but never used in, film version (1948). See "My Week".

We've Come Too Far to End It Now
Words and music by David Jones, Wade Brown, Jr., and Johnny
    Bristol.
Jobete Music Co., Inc., 1972.
Best-selling record by The Miracles (Tamla, 1972).

We've Gone Too Far
Words and music by Hank Thompson and Billy Gray.
Morning Music, Ltd., 1954/Hall-Clement Publications, 1954.
Best-selling record by Hank Thompson (Capitol).

We've Got Tonight
Words and music by Bob Seger.
Hideout Records/Distributing Co., 1976.
Best-selling record by Bob Seger (Capitol, 1979).

We've Only Just Begun
Words and music by Paul Williams and Roger Nichols.
Irving Music Inc., 1970.
Best-selling record by The Carpenters (A & M, 1970). Nominated for a
   National Academy of Recording Arts and Sciences Award, Song of
   the Year, 1970.

A Whale of a Tale
Words and music by Al Hoffman and Norman Gimbel.
Wonderland Music Co., Inc., 1953.
Introduced by Kirk Douglas in *20,000 Leagues under the Sea* (film).

Wham Bam (Shang a Lang)
Words and music by Richard Giles.
Colgems-EMI Music Inc., 1975.
Best-selling record by Silver (Arista, 1976).

What a Beautiful Beginning
Words by Sidney Clare, music by Harry Akst.
Movietone Music Corp., 1937.
Introduced by Anthony (Tony) Martin In *Sing and Be Happy* (film).

What a Bringdown (English)
Words and music by Ginger Baker.
Unichappell Music Inc., 1969.
Sung in 1968 by Cream in their album, *Wheels of Fire* (Atco).

What a Country!
Words by Lee Adams, music by Charles Strouse.
Strada Music Co., 1962.
Introduced by Ray Bolger and chorus in *All American* (musical).

What a Day
Words and music by Harry Woods.
Shapiro, Bernstein & Co., Inc., 1929.

What a Deal
Words and music by Jay Livingston and Ray Evans.
Vanguard Songs, 1945.
Introduced by Martha Tilton (Capitol).

What a Difference a Day Makes, see **What a Diff'rence a Day Made.**

What a Difference You've Made in My Life
Words and music by Archie Jordan.
T. B. Harms Co., 1977.
Best-selling record by Ronnie Milsap (RCA, 1977).

What a Diff'rence a Day Made, also known as **What a Difference a Day Makes** (Mexican)
English words by Stanley Adams, Spanish words and music by Maria Grever.
Edward B. Marks Music Corp., 1934/Stanley Adams Music, Inc., 1934.
Original Spanish title, "Cuando Vuelva a Tu Lado." Revived in 1959 with best-selling record by Dinah Washington (Mercury) and in 1975 by Esther Phillips (Kudu).

What a Dream, also known as **Oh What a Dream**
Words and music by Chuck Willis.
Berkshire Music, Inc., 1954/Chuck Willis Music Co., 1954.
Best-selling record by Ruth Brown (Atlantic).

What a Fool Believes
Words and music by Kenny Loggins and Michael McDonald.
Milk Money Music, 1978/Snug Music, 1978.
Best-selling record by The Doobie Brothers (Warner Brothers, 1979).
Won National Academy of Recording Arts and Sciences Awards, Record of the Year, 1979, and Song of the Year, 1979.

What a Life Trying To Live without You
Words by Charlotte Kent, music by Louis Alter.
Harms, Inc., 1932.
Introduced by Helen Morgan.

What a Little Moonlight Can Do
Words and music by Harry Woods.
Campbell-Connelly Co., Ltd., London, England/Harms, Inc., 1934.
Introduced in *Roadhouse Nights* (British film). Identified with Billie Holiday.

What a Night This Is Going To Be!
Words and music by Marian Grudeff and Raymond Jessel.
Edward B. Marks Music Corp., 1964, 1965.
Introduced by Fritz Weaver, Inga Swenson, Peter Sallis, and Virginia Vestoff in *Baker Street* (musical, 1965).

What a Perfect Combination
Words by Bert Kalmar and Irving Caesar, music by Harry Ruby and
    Harry Akst.
Harms, Inc., 1932.
Introduced by Eddie Cantor in *The Kid from Spain* (film).

What a Piece of Work Is Man
Words by William Shakespeare, music by Galt MacDermot.
United Artists Music Co., Inc., 1967.
Words are from *Hamlet*. Introduced by Ronald Dyson and Walter Har-
    ris in the Broadway version, 1968, of *Hair* (musical).

What a Sweet Thing That Was
Words and music by Gerry Goffin and Carole King.
Screen Gems-EMI Music Inc., 1961.
Best-selling record by The Shirelles (Scepter).

What a Way to Go
Words by Betty Comden and Adolph Green, music by Jule Styne.
Miller Music Corp., 1964.
"Inspired" by *What a Way To Go!"* (film).

What a Woman in Love Won't Do
Words and music by John D. Loudermilk.
Acuff-Rose Publications Inc., 1966.
Best-selling record in 1967 by Sandy Posey (MGM).

What a Wonderful World
Words by Howard Dietz, music by Arthur Schwartz.
Chappell & Co., Inc., 1935.
Introduced by Eleanor Powell, Woods Miller, and The Continentals in
    At Home Abroad (revue).

What a Wonderful World, see **Wonderful World.**

What a Wonderful World
Words and music by George David Weiss and George Douglas.
Valando Music, Inc., 1967.
Introduced by Louis Armstrong (ABC).

What Am I Going to Do without Your Love?
Words and music by William Stevenson and Sylvia Moy.
Stone Agate Music Corp., 1966.
Best-selling record by Martha and The Vandellas (Gordy).

What Am I Gonna Do about You?
Words by Sammy Cahn, music by Jule Styne.
Paramount Music Corp., 1946, 1947.

Introduced by Eddie Bracken and Virginia Welles in *Ladies' Man* (film, 1947).

What Am I Gonna Do with You
Words and music by Barry White.
Six Continents Music Publishing Inc., 1975/Sa-Vette Music, 1975.
Best-selling record by Barry White (20th Century, 1975).

What Am I Here For
Music by Edward Kennedy "Duke" Ellington.
Robbins Music Corp., 1942.
Introduced by Duke Ellington and his Orchestra (Victor).

What Am I Living For?
Words and music by Fred Jay and Art Harris.
Unichappell Music Inc., 1958/Tideland Music Publishing Corp., 1958.
Best-selling record by Chuck Willis (Atlantic).

What Am I Worth
Words and music by Darrell Edwards and George Jones.
Starrite Publishing Co., 1955.
Best-selling record in 1956 by George Jones (Starday).

What Are They Doing to Us Now?
Words and music by Harold Rome.
Florence Music Co., Inc., 1962.
Introduced by Barbra Streisand, Kelly Brown, James Hickman, Luba Lisa, Wilma Curley, Pat Turner, and chorus in *I Can Get It for You Wholesale* (musical).

What Are You Doing New Year's Eve
Words and music by Frank Loesser.
Frank Music Co., 1947.
Introduced by Margaret Whiting (Capitol).

What Are You Doing the Rest of Your Life?
Words by Alan Bergman and Marilyn Bergman, music by Michel Legrand.
United Artists Music Co., Inc., 1969.
Performed by the voice of Michael Dees in *The Happy Ending* (film, 1970). Best-selling record by J. P. Morgan (Beverly Hills, 1970). Nominated for an Academy Award, 1969.

What Became of the People We Were
Words by Michael Weller, words and music by Jim Steinman.
Casserole Music Inc., 1974.
Introduced by Kimberly Farr and Terry Kiser in *More Than You Deserve* (musical, 1974).

What Becomes of the Brokenhearted?
Words and music by James Dean, Paul Riser, and William
    Weatherspoon.
Jobete Music Co., Inc., 1966/Stone Agate Music Corp., 1966.
Best-selling record by Jimmy Ruffin (Soul).

What Can I Do? (French)
English words by Harold Rome, French words by Edith Piaf, music
    by Henri Betti.
Arpege Editions Musicales, Paris, France, 1947, 1949/Leeds Music
    Corp., 1949.
Original French title, "Mais Qu'est-ce que J'ai." Introduced in France by
    Edith Piaf. Identified with Piaf and Yves Montand.

What Can I Say After I Say I'm Sorry?
Words and music by Walter Donaldson and Abe Lyman.
Miller Music Corp., 1926/Donaldson Publishing Co., 1926.
Introduced by Abe Lyman and his Orchestra. Sung by Doris Day in
    Love Me or Leave Me (film, 1955).

What Can You Do with a Man?
Words by Lorenz Hart, music by Richard Rodgers.
Chappell & Co., Inc., 1938.
Introduced by Wynn Murray and Teddy Hart in *The Boys from Syracuse* (musical).

What Can You Say in a Love Song?
Words by Ira Gershwin and E. Y. Harburg, music by Harold Arlen.
New World Music Corp., 1934.
Introduced by Josephine Houston and Bartlett Simmons in *Life Begins
    at 8:40* (revue).

What-Cha Gonna Do Now
Words and music by Tommy Collins.
Central Songs, 1954.
Best-selling record by Tommy Collins (Capitol).

What Cha Gonna Do with My Lovin'
Words and music by Reggie Lucas and James Mtube.

Scarab Publishing Corp., 1979/Ensign Music Corp., 1979.
Best-selling record by Stephanie Mills (20th Century, 1979).

What Color (Is a Man)
Words and music by Marge Barton.
Screen Gems-EMI Music Inc., 1965.
Best-selling record by Bobby Vinton (Epic).

What Did I Do To Be So Black and Blue, also known as **Black and Blue**
Words by Andy Razaf, music by Thomas "Fats" Waller and Harry Brooks.
Mills Music Inc., 1929/Anne-Rachel Music Corp., 1929.
Introduced by Edith Wilson in *Connie's Hot Chocolates* (revue). Popularized by Ethel Waters.

What Did I Do?
Words by Mack Gordon, music by Josef Myrow.
Bregman, Vocco & Conn, Inc., 1947.
Introduced in *When My Baby Smiles at Me* (film, 1948).

What Did I Ever See in Him?
Words by Lee Adams, music by Charles Strouse.
Edwin H. Morris Co., 1960.
Introduced by Chita Rivera and Susan Watson in *Bye Bye Birdie* (musical).

What Did You Learn in School Today?
Words and music by Tom Paxton.
Teena Music Corp., 1962.
Introduced by Tom Paxton.

What Do I Care
Words by Al Stillman, music by Max Steiner.
M. Witmark & Sons, 1959.
Adapted from the theme from *The FBI Story* (film).

What Do I Care—What Do I Care, My Sweetie Turned Me Down, also known as **My Sweetie Turned Me Down**
Words by Gus Kahn, music by Walter Donaldson.
Bourne Co., 1925/Donaldson Publishing Co., 1925.

What Do I Care?
Words and music by Johnny Cash.
Johnny Cash Music, Inc., 1958.
Best-selling record by Johnny Cash (Columbia).

What Do I Have To Do To Make You Love Me?
Words and music by Inez James and Sidney Miller.
Bregman, Vocco & Conn, Inc., 1948.
Introduced in *Are You with It?* (film). Best-selling record by Vaughn
  Monroe and his Orchestra (Victor).

What Do the Simple Folks Do?
Words by Alan Jay Lerner, music by Frederick Loewe.
Chappell & Co., Inc., 1960.
Introduced by Julie Andrews and Richard Burton in *Camelot* (musical).

What Do We Do on a Dew Dew Dewy Day, also known as
  (What Do We Do on a) Dew Dew Dewy Day
Words and music by Howard Johnson, Charles Tobias, and Al
  Sherman.
Bourne Co., 1927.

What Do You Care, Honey, What I Do
Words and music by Perry Bradford.
Perry Bradford Music Publishing Co., 1922.
Introduced by Edith Wilson.

What Do You Do in the Infantry
Words and music by Frank Loesser.
Frank Music Co., 1943.
Unofficial song of United States Infantry. Introduced by Bing Crosby.

What Do You Do Sunday, Mary?, also known as **Mary**
Words by Irving Caesar, music by Stephen Jones.
Warner Brothers-Seven Arts Music, 1923.
Introduced by Luella Gear and Robert Woolsey in *Poppy* (musical).

What Do You Give to a Man Who's Had Everything
Music by Jule Styne, words by Bob Merrill.
Chappell & Co., Inc., 1972/Merrill Music Corp., 1972.
Introduced by Tony Roberts and Elaine Joyce in *Sugar* (musical, 1972).

What Do You Think I Am?
Words and music by Hugh Martin and Ralph Blane.
Chappell & Co., Inc., 1941.
Introduced by June Allyson and Kenneth Bowers in *Best Foot Forward*
  (musical).

What Do You Want with Me
Words and music by Chad Stuart and Jeremy Clyde.
Unichappell Music Inc., 1964.
Best-selling record by Chad and Jeremy (World Artists).

What Does It Matter?
Words and music by Irving Berlin.
Irving Berlin Music Corp., 1927.
Introduced on radio by Lucrezia Bori.

What Does It Take (to Keep a Man Like You Satisified?)
Words and music by James Glaser.
Canadiana-Glaser, 1966/Ensign Music Corp., 1966.
Best-selling record in 1967 by Skeeter Davis (RCA Victor).

What Does It Take (to Win Your Love)?
Words and music by Johnny Bristol, Harvey Fuqua, and Vernon
  Bullock.
Jobete Music Co., Inc., 1968.
Best-selling record in 1969 by Jr. Walker and The All Stars (Soul).

What D'Ya Say?
Words and music by B. G. De Sylva, Lew Brown, and Ray
  Henderson.
Anne-Rachel Music Corp., 1928/DeSylva, Brown & Henderson, Inc.,
  1928.
Introduced by Frances Williams and Harry Richman in *George White's
  Scandals of 1928* (revue).

What Ever Happened to Saturday Night
Words and music by Richard O'Brian.
Hallenbeck Music Co., 1974.
Introduced by Ray Kennedy in *The Rocky Horror Show* (musical,
  1975).

What Ev'ry Girl Should Know
Words by Robert Wells, music by David Holt.
Daywin Music, Inc., 1954.
Best-selling record by Doris Day (Columbia).

What Goes On (English)
Words and music by John Lennon and Paul McCartney.
Northern Songs, Ltd., England, 1966/Maclen Music Inc., 1966.
Best-selling record by The Beatles (Capitol).

What Goes On Here in My Heart
Words and music by Leo Robin and Ralph Rainger.
Paramount Music Corp., 1938.
Introduced by Betty Grable and Jack Whiting in *Give Me a Sailor* (film).

What Goes on When the Sun Goes Down
Words and music by John Schweers.

Hall-Clement Publications, 1976.
Best-selling record by Ronnie Milsap (RCA, 1976).

What Good Does It Do?
Words by E. Y. Harburg, music by Harold Arlen.
Harwin Music Corp., 1957.
Introduced by Ricardo Montalban, Ossie Davis, and Augustine Rios in
    Jamaica (musical).

What Good Is Love
Words and music by Harold Rome.
Florence Music Co., Inc., 1937.
Introduced by Nettie Harary in *Pins and Needles* (revue).

What Good Would the Moon Be?
Words by Langston Hughes, music by Kurt Weill.
Chappell & Co., Inc., 1946.
Introduced by Anne Jeffreys in *Street Scene* (musical, 1947).

What Happened to Me Tonight?
Words and music by Richard Adler.
Sahara Music, Inc., 1961.
Introduced by Sally Ann Howes in *Kwamina* (musical).

What Happened?
Words by Howard Dietz, music by Vernon Duke.
T. B. Harms Co., 1944.
Introduced by Nanette Fabray and Allan Jones in *Jackpot* (musical).

What Has Become of Hinky Dinky Parlay Voo
Words and music by Al Dubin, Irving Mills, Jimmy McHugh, and
    Irwin Dash.
Mills Music Inc., 1924/Al Dubin Music Co., 1924/Ireneadele
    Publishing, 1924.
Popularized by the Happiness Boys (Billie Jones and Ernie Hare).

What Have They Done to My Song, Ma, also known as **Look
    What They've Done to My Song, Ma**
Words and music by Melanie Safka.
Yellow Dog Music Inc., 1970.
Best-selling records by The New Seekers (Elektra, 1970) and Ray
    Charles (ABC, 1972).

What Have They Done to the Rain?
Words and music by Malvina Reynolds.
Schroder Music Co., 1962, 1964.
Introduced by Malvina Reynolds. Best-selling record in 1964-65 by The
    Searchers (Kapp).

What Have You Got That Gets Me?
Words and music by Leo Robin and Ralph Rainger.
Famous Music Co., 1938.
Introduced by The Yacht Club Boys, Joyce Comptom, Joan Bennett, and Jack Benny in *Artists and Models Abroad* (film).

What I Did for Love
Words by Edward Kleban, music by Marvin Hamlisch.
American Compass Music Corp., 1975.
Introduced by Priscilla Lopez (and Company) in *A Chorus Line* (musical, 1975). Best-selling record by Jack Jones (RCA, 1975).

(How Can I Write on Paper) What I Feel in My Heart
Words and music by Danny Harrison, Don Carter, George Kent, and Jim Reeves.
Tuckahoe Music, Inc., 1961.
Best-selling record in 1962 by Jim Reeves (RCA Victor).

What I Need Most
Words and music by Hugh X. Lewis.
Cedarwood Publishing Co., Inc., 1964.
Best-selling record by Hugh X. Lewis (Kapp).

What in the World's Come Over You
Words and music by Jack Scott.
Unart Music Corp., 1959/Unart-Unart, 1959.
Best-selling record by Jack Scott (Top Rank).

What Is a Husband? (What Is a Wife?)
Words and music by Bill Katz, Ruth Roberts, and Gene Piller.
Vernon Music Corp., 1955.
Introduced on *The Garry Moore Show* (television program). Best-selling record by Steve Allen (Coral).

What Is a Man
Words by Lorenz Hart, music by Richard Rodgers.
Chappell & Co., Inc., 1940.
Initially introduced by Vivienne Segal in 1940 production of *Pal Joey* (musical) with different lyrics and entitled "Love Is My Friend." During the run of the show, song was rewritten and introduced under the title, "What Is a Man," but not copyrighted until 1952.

What Is Hip
Words and music by Emilio Castillo, John Garibaldi, and Stephen Kupka.
Kuptillo Music, 1972.
Best-selling record by Tower of Power (Warner Brothers, 1974).

What Is Life (English)
Words and music by George Harrison.
Zero Productions, 1970.
Best-selling record by George Harrison (Apple, 1971).

What Is Life without Love?
Words and music by Eddy Arnold, Vernice McAlpin, and Owen
    Bradley.
Adams-Vee & Abbott, Inc., 1946.
Best-selling record by Eddy Arnold (Victor).

What Is Love?
Words and music by Lee Pockriss and Paul Vance.
Planetary Music Publishing Corp., 1959.
Best-selling record by The Playmates (Roulette).

What Is Success
Words and music by Allan Toussaint.
Marsaint Music Inc., 1970.
Performed by Bonnie Raitt on *Streetlights* (Warner Brothers, 1974).

What Is That Tune?
Words and music by Cole Porter.
Chappell & Co., Inc., 1938.
Introduced by Libby Holman in *You Never Know* (musical).

What Is There To Say
Words by E. Y. Harburg, music by Vernon Duke.
T. B. Harms Co., 1933.
Introduced by Jane Froman and Everett Marshall in *Ziegfeld Follies of
    1934* (revue).

What Is This Feeling in the Air?
Words by Betty Comden and Adolph Green, music by Jule Styne.
Stratford Music Corp., 1961.
Introduced by Carol Lawrence and company in *Subways Are for Sleep-
    ing* (musical).

What Is This Thing Called Love?
Words and music by Cole Porter.
Harms, Inc., 1929.
Introduced by Elsie Carlisle, and danced to by Tilly Losch, Toni Birk-
    mayer, Alanova, and William Cavanagh, in the London production
    and sung by Frances Shelley, and danced to by Miss Losch and Mr.
    Birkmayer, in the New York production of *Wake Up and Dream*
    (musical). Sung by Ginny Simms in *Night and Day* (film, 1946);
    performed by Harry James and his Orchestra in *Young Man with a*

Horn (film, 1950); and sung by Lucille Norman and Gordon MacRae, and danced to by Janice Rule and GeneNelson, in *Starlift* (film, 1951).

What Is Truth
Words and music by Johnny Cash.
Song of Cash Inc., 1970.
Best-selling record by Johnny Cash (Columbia, 1970).

What It Was, Was Football
Words and music by Andy Griffith.
Bentley Music Co., 1954.
A comedy monologue. Best-selling record by Andy Griffith (Capitol).

What Kind of Fool Am I? (English)
Words and music by Leslie Bricusse and Anthony Newley.
Essex Music International, Ltd., London, England, 1961/Ludlow
    Music Inc., 1961.
Introduced by Anthony Newley in London and New York (1962) pro-
    ductions of *Stop the World—I Want To Get Off* (musical). Best-
    selling record in 1962 by Sammy Davis, Jr. (Reprise). Won a National
    Academy of Recording Arts and Sciences Award, Song of the Year,
    1962.

What Kind of Fool Do You Think I Am?
Words and music by Ray Whitley.
Low-Twi Music, Inc., 1963.
Best-selling record in 1964 by The Tams (ABC-Paramount). Revived in
    1969 with best-selling record by Bill Deal and The Rhondels (Herit-
    age).

What Kind of Love Is This?
Words and music by Johnny Nash.
Planetary Music Publishing Corp., 1962.
Best-selling record by Joey Dee (Roulette).

What Kinda Deal Is This?
Words and music by Wayne Gilbreath.
Lair Music Publishing Co., 1965.
Best-selling record in 1966 by Bill Carlisle (Hickory).

What Makes a Man Wander?
Words and music by Harlan Howard.
Bramble Music Publishing Co., Inc., 1964.
Best-selling record by Jan Howard (Decca).

What Makes the Sunset
Words by Sammy Cahn, music by Jule Styne.

Miller Music Corp., 1944.
Introduced by Frank Sinatra in *Anchors Aweigh* (film, 1945).

What More Can a Woman Do?
Words and music by Peggy Lee and Dave Barbour.
Michael H. Goldsen, Inc., 1945.
Introduced by Peggy Lee (Capitol).

What More Can I Ask? (English)
Words by A. E. Wilkins, music by Ray Noble.
Lawrence Wright Music Co., Ltd., London, England, 1932/T. B.
    Harms Co., 1933.
Introduced by Ray Noble and his Orchestra.

What! No Spinach?
Words and music by William Tracey, Hugh Aitkin, and Dinty
    Moore.
Skidmore Music, Ltd., London, England, 1926.

What Now My Love (French)
English words by Carl Sigman, French words by P. Dalanoe, music
    by Gilbert Becaud.
Editions le Rideau Rouge, Paris, France, 1962/Remick Music Corp.,
    1962.
Original French title, "Et Maintenant." Introduced in France by Gilbert
    Becaud. Best-selling record by Jane Morgan (Kapp) and in 1966 by
    Sonny and Cher (Atco), Herb Alpert and The Tijuana Brass (A & M),
    and Mitch Ryder and The Detroit Wheels (New Voice).

What Shall I Do?
Words and music by Cole Porter.
Chappell & Co., Inc., 1938.
Introduced by Lupe Velez in *You Never Know* (musical).

What the World Needs Now Is Love
Words by Hal David, music by Burt Bacharach.
Blue Seas Music Inc., 1965/Jac Music Co., Inc., 1965.
Best-selling record by Jackie DeShannon (Imperial). Revived in 1965 by
    Tom Clay, in medley with "Abraham, Martin, and John."

What To Do
Words and music by Sid Robin.
MCA, Inc., 1942.
Introduced by The Andrews Sisters in *What's Cookin' Soldier* (film).

What Was
Music by Ken Wannberg, words by Stephen Lehner.

Warner-Tamerlane Publishing Corp., 1977.
Performed by the voice of Bev Kelly in *The Late Show* (film, 1977).

What We're Fighting For
Words and music by Tom T. Hall.
Unichappell-Newkeys, 1965/Canadiana-New Keys, 1965.
Best-selling record by Dave Dudley (Mercury).

What Will I Tell My Heart
Words and music by Peter Tinturin, Jack Lawrence, and Irving
    Gordon.
DeSylva, Brown & Henderson, Inc., 1937/MPL Communications
    Inc., 1937.

What Will My Mary Say?
Words and music by Paul Vance and Eddie Snyder.
Andrew Scott Inc., 1961.
Best-selling record in 1963 by Johnny Mathis (Columbia).

What Would I Do without You
Words and music by Ray Charles.
Unichappell Music Inc., 1956.
Best-selling record by Ray Charles (Atlantic).

What Would You Do (If You Were Me)
Words and music by Fred Rose and Johnny Bond.
Southern Music Publishing Co., Inc., 1949/Milene Music Co., 1949.
Introduced by Johnny Bond.

What Would You Do (If You Were in My Place)
Words and music by Richard Adler and Jerry Ross.
J & J Ross Co., 1952/Richard Adler Music, 1952.
Best-selling record by Rosemary Clooney (Columbia).

What Would You Do (If Jesus Came to Your House)
Words and music by Hugh Ashley and Lois Blanchard.
Earl Barton Music, Inc., 1956.
Best-selling record by Porter Wagoner (RCA Victor).

What Wouldn't I Do for That Man!
Words by E. Y Harburg, music by Jay Gorney.
Famous Music Co., 1929.
Introduced by Helen Morgan in *Applause* (film) and *Glorifying the
    American Girl* (film).

What You Gave Me
Words and music by Nicholas Ashford and Valerie Simpson.

Jobete Music Co., Inc., 1969.
Best-selling record by Marvin Gaye and Tammi Terrell (Tamla).

What You Won't Do for Love
Words and music by Robert Caldwell and Alfons Kettner.
Lindseyanne Music Co., Inc., 1978/Sherlyn Publishing Co., Inc.,
   1978.
Best-selling record by Bobby Caldwell (Clouds, 1979).

What You're Doing (English)
Words and music by John Lennon and Paul McCartney.
Northern Songs, Ltd., England, 1964/Maclen Music Inc., 1964.
Best-selling record by The Beatles (Capitol).

Whatcha' Gonna Do When Your Baby Leaves You
Words and music by Chuck Willis.
Tideland Music Publishing Corp., 1956/Chuck Willis Music Co.,
   1956.
Best-selling record by Fats Domino (Imperial).

What'cha Gonna Do?
Words and music by Ahmet Ertegun.
Unichappell Music Inc., 1955.
Best-selling record by The Drifters (Atlantic).

Whatcha Gonna Do?
Words and music by Cory Lerios and David Jenkins.
Irving Music Inc., 1977/Pablo Cruise Music, 1977.
Best-selling record by Pablo Cruise (A & M, 1977).

Whatcha Know Joe
Words and music by James "Trummy" Young.
New Era Music Corp., 1940.
Introduced by Jimmie Lunceford and his Orchestra (Columbia).

Whatcha Say
Words by Ted Koehler, music by Burton Lane.
Harms, Inc., 1945.
Introduced by Louis Armstrong in *Pillow to Post* (film).

Whatcha See Is What You Get
Words and music by Tony Hester.
Groovesville Music Inc., 1971.
Best-selling record by The Dramatics (Volt, 1971).

What'd I Say
Words and music by Ray Charles.

Unichappell Music Inc., 1959.
Best-selling record by Ray Charles (Atlantic).

Whatever Gets You Thru the Night (English)
Words and music by John Lennon.
ATV Music Corp., 1974/Lennon Music, 1974.
Best-selling record by John Lennon & Plastic Ono Band (Apple, 1974).

Whatever Happened to Baby Jane?
Words and music by Lukas Heller and Frank De Vol.
Warner-Tamerlane Publishing Corp., 1963.
Introduced by Debbie Burton, with narration by Bette Davis (MGM).

Whatever Happened to Randolph Scott
Words and music by Harold Reid and Don Reid.
American Cowboy Music Co., 1973.
Best-selling record by The Statler Brothers (Mercury, 1974).

Whatever Happened to Us
Words and music by Loudon Wainwright.
Snowden Music, 1974.
Performed by Loudon Wainwright on *Unrequited* (Columbia, 1974).

Whatever It Is I'm Against It
Words by Bert Kalmar, music by Harry Ruby.
Famous Music Co., 1933.
Introduced by Groucho Marx in *Horse Feathers* (film, 1932).

Whatever Lola Wants (Lola Gets)
Words and music by Richard Adler and Jerry Ross.
Frank Music Co., 1955.
Introduced by Gwen Verdon in *Damn Yankees* (musical).

Whatever Will Be, Will Be, see **Que Sera, Sera.**

What'll I Do?
Words and music by Irving Berlin.
Irving Berlin Music Corp., 1924.
Introduced by Grace Moore and John Steel during the run of *Music Box Revue of 1923* (revue, 1923). Sung by the chorus in *Alexander's Ragtime Band* (film, 1938); and by Danny Thomas in *Big City* (film, 1948).

What's Easy for Two Is So Hard for One
Words and music by William Robinson.
Jobete Music Co., Inc., 1963.
Best-selling record by Mary Wells (Motown).

What's Going On
Words and music by Al Cleveland, Marvin Gaye, and Renauldo Benson.
Jobete Music Co., Inc., 1970/Stone Agate Music Corp., 1970.
Best-selling record by Marvin Gaye (Tamla, 1971).

What's Good about Goodbye?
Words by Leo Robin, music by Harold Arlen.
Harwin Music Corp., 1948.
Introduced by Tony Martin in *Casbah* (film).

What's Good about Goodnight?
Words by Dorothy Fields, music by Jerome Kern.
T. B. Harms Co., 1938.
Introduced by Irene Dunne in *Joy of Living* (film).

What's He Doin' in My World?
Words and music by Carl Belew, Eddie Bush, and B. J. Moore.
Acuff-Rose Publications Inc., 1965.
Best-selling record by Eddy Arnold (RCA Victor).

What's in It for Me?
Words and music by Harold Rome.
Florence Music Co., Inc., 1962.
Introduced by Harold Lang and Sheree North in *I Can Get It for You Wholesale* (musical).

What's It Gonna Be?
Words and music by Mort Shuman and Jerry Ragovoy.
Unichappell Music Inc., 1967/Canadiana-Unichappell, 1967.
Best-selling record by Dusty Springfield (Philips).

What's Made Milwaukee Famous (Has Made a Loser Out of Me)
Words and music by Glenn Sutton.
Al Gallico Music Corp., 1968.
Best-selling record by Jerry Lee Lewis (Smash).

What's New at the Zoo?
Words by Betty Comden and Adolph Green, music by Jule Styne.
Stratford Music Corp., 1960.
Introduced by Nancy Dussault and chorus in *Do Re Mi* (musical).

What's New, Pussycat?
Words by Hal David, music by Burt Bacharach.
United Artists Music Co., Inc., 1965.
Introduced in *What's New, Pussycat?* (film). Best-selling record by Tom Jones (Parrot). Nominated for an Academy Award, 1965.

What's New?
Words by Johnny Burke, music by Bob Haggart.
M. Witmark & Sons, 1939/Limerick Music Corp., 1939/Marke
  Music Publishing Co., Inc., 1939/Reganesque Music Co., 1939.
Introduced in 1938 as instrumental, entitled "I'm Free," by Bob Crosby
  and his Orchestra. Theme song of Billy Butterfield and his Orchestra.

What's That I Hear
Words and music by Phil Ochs.
Appleseed Music, Inc., 1963.
Introduced by Phil Ochs (Elektra).

What's the Good Word, Mister Bluebird
Words and music by Al Hoffman, Allan Roberts, and Jerry
  Livingston.
Bourne Co., 1943.

What's the Matter Now
Words and music by Spencer Williams and Clarence Williams.
MCA, Inc., 1926.
First recording by Clarence Williams' Stompers (Okeh).

What's the Reason (I'm Not Pleasin' You)?
Words by Coy Poe and Jimmie Grier, music by Truman "Pinky"
  Tomlin and Earl Hatch.
Bourne Co., 1935.
Introduced by Pinky Tomlin in *Times Square Lady* (film).

What's the Use of Breaking Up?
Words and music by Kenny Gamble, Jerry Butler, and Theresa Bell.
Parabut Music Corp., 1969/Assorted Music, 1969.
Best-selling record by Jerry Butler (Mercury).

What's the Use of Getting Sober
Words and music by Bubsy Meyers.
MCA, Inc., 1938.
Best-selling record in 1943 by Louis Jordan and his Tympany Five
  (Decca).

What's the Use of Talking
Words by Lorenz Hart, music by Richard Rodgers.
Warner Brothers-Seven Arts Music, 1926.
Introduced by Betty Starbuck and Sterling Holloway in *The Garrick
  Gaieties of 1926* (revue).

What's the Use of Wond'rin'
Words by Oscar Hammerstein, II, music by Richard Rodgers.
Williamson Music Inc., 1945.

Introduced by Jan Clayton in *Carousel* (musical). Sung by Shirley Jones and chorus in film version (1957).

What's This
Words and music by Dave Lambert.
Robbins Music Corp., 1945.
Introduced by Dave Lambert and Buddy Stewart, with Gene Krupa and his Orchestra (Columbia). First bop vocal recording, according to jazz historian Leonard Feather.

What's Wrong with Me?
Words by Edward Heyman, music by Nacio Herb Brown.
Leo Feist Inc., 1948.
Introduced by Kathryn Grayson in *The Kissing Bandit* (film).

What's Wrong with Me?
Words and music by Richard Adler.
Sahara Music, Inc., 1961.
Introduced by Sally Ann Howes in *Kwamina* (musical).

What's Your Mama's Name Child
Words and music by Dallas Frazier and Earl Montgomery.
Acuff-Rose Publications Inc., 1972/Altam Music Corp., 1972.
Best-selling record by Tanya Tucker (Columbia, 1973).

What's Your Name
Words and music by Claude Johnson.
Unichappell Music Inc., 1961.
Best-selling record in 1962 by Don and Juan (Big Top). Revived in 1974 by Andy Williams (Barnaby).

What's Your Name
Words and music by Gary Rossington and Ronnie Van Zant.
Duchess Music Corp., 1977/Get Loose Music Inc., 1977.
Best-selling record by Lynyrd Skynyrd (MCA, 1978).

What's Your Story, Morning Glory?
Words and music by Jack Lawrence, Paul Francis Webster, and Mary Lou Williams.
Advanced Music Corp., 1938, 1940/Cecilia Music Publishing Co., 1938/MPL Communications Inc., 1938.
Introduced by Andy Kirk and his Clouds of Joy, featuring Mary Lou Williams, pianist and arranger. Best-selling record by Jimmie Lunceford and his Orchestra (Columbia); also by Andy Kirk and his Clouds of Joy (Decca).

Wheel in the Sky
Words and music by Neal Schon, Robert Fleischman, and Diane

Valory.
Weed High Nightmare Music, 1978.
Best-selling record by Journey (Columbia, 1978).

Wheel of Fortune
Words and music by Bennie Benjamin and George Weiss.
Claude A. Music, 1952/Abilene Music Inc., 1952.
Best-selling records by Kay Starr (Capitol) and Sunny Gale (Derby).

The Wheel of Hurt
Words and music by Charles Singleton and Eddie Snyder.
Screen Gems-EMI Music Inc., 1966.
Best-selling records by Al Martino (Capitol) and Margaret Whiting (London).

The Wheeler Dealers
Words and music by Randy Sparks.
Miller Music Corp., 1963.
From *The Wheeler Dealers* (film). Introduced by The New Christy Minstrels.

Wheels, also known as **Tell the World**
Words and music by Jimmy Torres and Richard Stephens.
Dundee Music, 1960.
Best-selling records in 1961 by The String-A-Longs (Warwick) and in 1962 by Billy Vaughn and his Orchestra (Dot).

When
Words and music by Paul Evans and Jack Reardon.
Sounds Music Co., 1958/Big Hurry Music, Inc., 1958.
Best-selling record by The Kalin Twins (Decca).

When a Gypsy Makes His Violin Cry
Words by Dick Smith, Frank Wine-Gar, and Jimmy Rogan, music by Emery Deutsch.
Bregman, Vocco & Conn, Inc., 1935.
Introduced by and theme song of Emery Deutsch and his Orchestra.

When a Kid from the East Side (Found a Sweet Society Rose)
Words and music by Al Dubin and Jimmy McHugh.
Mills Music Inc., 1926.
"Inspired" by Irving Berlin's marriage to Ellen Mackay.

When a Man Loves a Woman
Words and music by Calvin H. Lewis and Andrew Wright.
Quinvy Music Publishing Co., 1966/Cotillion Music Inc., 1966.
Best-selling record by Percy Sledge (Atlantic).

When a Soldier Knocks and Finds Nobody Home
Words and music by Ernest Tubb, Moon Mullican, and Lou Wayne.
Noma Music, Inc., 1947.

When a Woman Loves a Man
Words by Billy Rose, music by Ralph Rainger.
Robbins Music Corp., 1930.
Introduced by Fanny Brice in *Be Yourself* (film).

When a Woman Loves a Man
Words by Johnny Mercer, music by Bernard Hanighen and Gordon
  Jenkins.
Anne-Rachel Music Corp., 1934.

When Banana Skins Are Falling, I'll Come Sliding Back to You
Words and music by Al Frazzini, Paul De Frank, and Irving Mills.
Mills Music Inc., 1926.

When Big Profundo Sang Low C
Words by Marion T. Bohannon, music by George Botsford.
Remick Music Corp., 1921.

When Buddha Smiles
Words by Arthur Freed, music by Nacio Herb Brown and King
  Zany (pseudonym for Jack Dill).
Warner Brothers-Seven Arts Music, 1921.
Best-selling record by Paul Whiteman and his Orchestra (Victor).

When Day Is Done (Austrian)
English words by B. G. De Sylva, German words and music by
  Robert Katscher.
Wiener Boheme Verlag, Vienna, Austria, 1924/Warner Brothers-
  Seven Arts Music, 1926/Anne-Rachel Music Corp., 1926.
Original German title, "Madonna, Du Bist Schoener als der Sonnen-
  schein!" From *Kuesse um Mitternacht* (Austrian revue, 1924). Intro-
  duced in the United States by Paul Whiteman and his Orchestra.

When Did I Fall in Love?
Words by Sheldon Harnick, music by Jerry Bock.
Sunbeam Music Corp., 1959.
Introduced by Ellen Hanley in *Fiorello!* (musical).

When Did You Leave Heaven
Words by Walter Bullock, music by Richard A. Whiting.
Robbins Music Corp., 1936/Whiting Music Corp., 1936.
Introduced by Tony Martin in *Sing, Baby, Sing* (film). Nominated for
  an Academy Award, 1936.

When Do We Dance?
Words by Ira Gershwin, music by George Gershwin.
WB Music Corp., 1925.
Introduced by Allen Kearns, Gertrude McDonald, and Lovey Lee in
Tip-Toes (musical).

When Everything Was Green
Words by Robert Colby, music by Ettore Stratta.
Croma Music Co., Inc., 1964.
Introduced in 1965 by The Brothers Four (Columbia).

When Francis Dances with Me
Words by Benny Ryan, music by Violinsky (pseudonym for Sol
Ginsberg).
Leo Feist Inc., 1921.

When He Comes Home to Me
Words and music by Leo Robin and Sam Coslow.
Famous Music Co., 1934.
Introduced by Helen Morgan in *You Belong to Me* (film).

When He Touches Me (Nothing Else Matters), also known as
When She Touches Me (Nothing Else Matters)
Words and music by Carolyn Varga.
Painted Desert Music Corp., 1966.
Best-selling record in 1969 by Peaches and Herb (Date).

When Hearts Are Young
Words by Cyrus Wood, music by Sigmund Romberg and Alfred
Goodman.
Harms, Inc., 1922.
Introduced by Wilda Bennett in *The Lady in Ermine* (operetta).

When I Been Drinkin'
Words and music by Big Bill Broonzy.
Duchess Music Corp., 1947, 1948.
First recorded in 1941 by Big Bill Broonzy (Okeh).

When I Die
Words and music by Steve Kennedy and William Smith.
Cliffdweller Music, 1969.
Best-selling record by Motherlode (Buddah).

When I Die Just Let Me Go to Texas
Words and music by Ed Bruce, Bobby Borchers, and Patsy Bruce.
Tree Publishing Co., Inc., 1977/Sugarplum Music Co., 1977.
Best-selling record by Ed Bruce (Epic, 1977).

When I Dream
Words and music by V. Stephenson.
House of Gold Music Inc., 1979.
Best-selling record by Crystal Gayle (United Artists, 1979).

When I Dream of the Last Waltz with You
Words by Gus Kahn, music by Ted Fiorito.
Leo Feist Inc., 1925.
Introduced by Ted Fiorito and his Orchestra.

When I Fall in Love
Words and music by Albert Selden.
Chappell & Co., Inc., 1948.
Introduced by Marilyn Day in *Small Wonder* (revue).

When I Fall in Love
Words by Edward Heyman, music by Victor Young.
Victor Young Publications, Inc., 1952/Intersong, USA Inc., 1952.
Introduced in *One Minute to Zero* (film). Best-selling record by Nat
   "King" Cole (Capitol). Revived in 1962 with best-selling record by The
   Lettermen (Capitol).

When I Get Home (English)
Words and music by John Lennon and Paul McCartney.
Northern Songs, Ltd., England, 1964/Maclen Music Inc., 1964.
Best-selling record by The Beatles (Capitol).

When I Get Thru with You, You'll Love Me Too
Words and music by Harlan Howard.
Tree Publishing Co., Inc., 1962.
Best-selling record by Patsy Cline (Decca).

When I Grow Too Old To Dream
Words by Oscar Hammerstein, II, music by Sigmund Romberg.
Robbins Music Corp., 1935.
Introduced by Evelyn Laye and Ramon Novarro in *The Night Is Young*
   (film). Sung by Jose Ferrer in *Deep in My Heart* (film, 1954).

When I Grow Up
Words by Edward Heyman, music by Ray Henderson.
Movietone Music Corp., 1935.
Introduced by Shirley Temple in *Curly Top* (film).

When I Grow Up, also known as **G-Man Song**
Words and music by Harold Rome.
Florence Music Co., Inc., 1942.
Introduced by Berni Gould in *Pins and Needles* (revue).

When I Grow Up To Be a Man
Words and music by Brian Wilson.
Irving Music Inc., 1964.
Best-selling record by The Beach Boys (Capitol).

When I Look at You
Words by Paul Francis Webster, music by Walter Jurmann.
Leo Feist Inc., 1942.
Introduced by Judy Garland in *Presenting Lily Mars* (film, 1943).

When I Look in Your Eyes
Words and music by Leslie Bricusse.
Hastings Music Corp., 1967.
Introduced by Rex Harrison in *Doctor Dolittle* (film).

When I Need You (American-English)
Words by Carole Bayer Sager, music by Albert Hammond.
Unichappell Music Inc., 1977/Begonia Melodies Inc., 1977/April
    Music Inc., 1977/R & M Music Productions Inc., 1977.
Best-selling record by Leo Sayer (Warner Brothers, 1977).

When I Needed You Most of All
Words and music by David Buskin.
Lou Levy Music Co., Inc., 1972.
Performed by Tracy Nelson on *Poor Man's Paradise* (Columbia, 1973).

When I Paint My Masterpiece, also known as **Masterpiece**
Words and music by Bob Dylan.
Big Sky Music, 1971.
Performed by Bob Dylan on *Bob Dylan's Greatest Hits, Volume II*
    (Columbia, 1971).

When I See an Elephant Fly
Words by Ned Washington, music by Oliver Wallace.
Bourne Co., 1941.
Introduced by Cliff Edwards, as voice of the crow, in *Dumbo* (cartoon
    film).

When I Take My Sugar to Tea
Words and music by Sammy Fain, Irving Kahal, and Pierre Norman
    Connor.
Famous Music Co., 1931.
Interpolated in *Monkey Business* (film) and *The Mating Season* (film,
    1951).

When I Walk with You
Words by John Latouche, music by Duke Ellington.
Chappell & Co., Inc., 1947/Fisher Music Corp., 1947.

Introduced by Jet MacDonald and Alfred Drake in *Beggar's Holiday* (musical).

When I Wanted You
Words and music by Gino Cunico.
Home Grown Music Inc., 1976.
Best-selling record by Barry Manilow (Arista, 1979).

When I Was a Little Cuckoo
Words and music by Cole Porter.
Chappell & Co., Inc., 1944.
Introduced by Beatrice Lillie in *Seven Lively Arts* (revue).

When I Was Young (English)
Words and music by Eric Burdon, Victor Brigs, Barry Jenkins, Danny McCulloch, and John Weider.
Slamina Music, Ltd., England, 1967/Carbert Music Inc., 1967/ Canadiana-Six Continents, 1967/Yameta Co., Ltd., 1967/ Unichappell Music Inc., 1967/Unichappell Music-Six Continents, 1967.
Best-selling record by Eric Burdon and The Animals (MGM).

When I'm Gone
Words and music by William Robinson, Jr.
Jobete Music Co., Inc., 1964, 1965.
Best-selling record in 1965 by Brenda Holloway (Tamla).

When I'm Looking at You
Words by Clifford Grey, music by Herbert Stothart.
Robbins Music Corp., 1929.
Introduced by Lawrence Tibbett in *The Rogue Song* (film, 1930).

When I'm Not Near the Girl I Love
Words by E. Y. Harburg, music by Burton Lane.
Chappell & Co., Inc., 1946.
Introduced by David Wayne in *Finian's Rainbow* (musical, 1947).

When I'm Sixty-four (English)
Words and music by John Lennon and Paul McCartney.
Northern Songs, Ltd., England, 1967/Maclen Music Inc., 1967.
Introduced by The Beatles in their album, *Sgt. Pepper's Lonely Hearts Club Band* (Capitol); sung by the Beatles in *Yellow Submarine* (film, 1968).

When I'm the President
Words and music by Al Lewis and Al Sherman.
Al Sherman Music Co., 1931/Sovereign Music Corp., 1931.
Introduced by Eddie Cantor.

When I'm with You
Words by Mack Gordon, music by Harry Revel.
Robbins Music Corp., 1936.
Introduced by Shirley Temple and Tony Martin, and reprised by Alice
   Faye, in *Poor Little Rich Girl* (film).

When I'm Wrong
Words and music by B. B. King.
Duchess Music Corp., 1975/King Guitar Inc., 1975.
Best-selling record by B. B. King (ABC, 1976).

When in Rome (I Do As the Romans Do)
Words by Carolyn Leigh, music by Cy Coleman.
Edwin H. Morris Co., 1964.
Introduced by Barbra Streisand (Columbia).

When Is Sometime?
Words by Johnny Burke, music by James Van Heusen.
Bourne Co., 1948/Music Sales Corp., 1948.
Introduced by Bing Crosby in *A Connecticut Yankee* (film, 1949).

When It's Harvest Time in Peaceful Valley
Words and music by Robert Martin and Raymond McKee.
MCA, Inc., 1930.
Sung in *Swing in the Saddle* (film, 1944).

When It's Lamp Lightin' Time in the Valley
Words and music by Joe Lyons, Sam C. Hart, Herald Goodman,
   Dean Upoon, and Curt Poulton.
Shapiro, Bernstein & Co., Inc., 1933.

When It's Night-time in Italy, It's Wednesday Over Here
Words and music by James Kendis and Lew Brown.
Shapiro, Bernstein & Co., Inc., 1923.
Introduced on radio by James "Jimmy" Kendis.

When It's Round-up Time in Heaven
Words and music by Jimmie Davis.
Peer International Corp., 1936.
Best-selling record by Gene Autry (Columbia).

When It's Sleepy Time down South
Words and music by Leon Rene, Otis Rene, and Clarence Muse.
Mills Music Inc., 1931/Leon Rene Publications, 1931/Otis Rene
   Publications, 1931.
Introduced by Clarence Muse. Theme of Louis Armstrong and his Or-
   chestra.

When It's Springtime in Alaska
Words and music by Tillman Franks.
Cedarwood Publishing Co., Inc., 1959.
Best-selling record by Johnny Horton (Columbia).

When It's Springtime in the Rockies
Words by Mary Hale Woolsey, music by Robert Sauer.
Robbins Music Corp., 1923.
Popularized by Rudy Vallee and his Connecticut Yankees.

When Joey Comes Around, see **When Julie Comes Around.**

When Julie Comes Around, also known as **When Joey Comes Around**
Words and music by Lee Pockriss and Paul Vance.
Emily Music Corp., 1969/Paul J. Vance Publishing Co., 1969.
Best-selling record in 1969-70 by The Cliff Links (Decca).

When Lights Are Low
Words and music by Gus Kahn, Ted Koehler, and Ted Fiorito.
Leo Feist Inc., 1923/Gilbert Keyes Music Co., 1923.
Introduced by by Ted Fiorito and his Orchestra.

When Lights Are Low
Words by Spencer Williams, music by Benny Carter.
Mills Music Inc., 1936/Colgems-EMI Music Inc., 1936.
Introduced in England by Benny Carter and his Orchestra, vocal by
    Elizabeth Welch (English Decca).

When Liking Turns to Loving
Words and music by Kenny Young and Jay Fishman.
Unart Music Corp., 1965/Unart-Unart, 1965/Morris Music, Inc.,
    1965/Canadiana-Morris, 1965.
Best-selling record in 1966 by Ronnie Dove (Diamond).

When Lindy Comes Home
Words and music by George M. Cohan.
New York American, Inc., 1927.
Introduced by George M. Cohan.

When Love Comes Your Way
Words and music by Cole Porter.
Chappell & Co., Ltd., London, England, 1933/Harms, Inc., 1933.
Written for, but not used in, *Nymph Errant* (British musical). Intro-
    duced by Derek Williams and Margaret Adams in *Jubilee* (musical,
    1935).

When Love Goes Wrong
Words by Harold Adamson, music by Hoagy Carmichael.
Twentieth Century Fox Music Corp., 1953.
Introduced by Marilyn Monroe and the voice of Eileen Wilson in *Gentlemen Prefer Blondes* (film).

When Love Has Turned to Hate
Words and music by Ernest Tubb and Pete Pyle.
Unichappell Music Inc., 1947.

When Love Is Young
Words by Harold Adamson, music by Jimmy McHugh.
Universal Music Corp., 1937.
Introduced by Virginia Bruce in *When Love Is Young* (film).

When Mexican Joe Met Jole Blon
Words and music by Sheb Wooley.
Aberbach, Inc., 1953/Brenner Music, Inc., 1953.
Best-selling record by Hank Snow (RCA Victor).

When My Baby Smiles at Me
Words by Andrew B. Sterling and Ted Lewis, music by Bill Munro.
T. B. Harms Co., 1920.
Introduced by and theme song of Ted Lewis. Interpolated by Lewis in *Greenwich Village Follies of 1920* (revue). Sung by the Ritz Brothers in *Sing, Baby, Sing* (film, 1936).

When My Blue Moon Turns to Gold Again
Words and music by Wiley Walker and Gene Sullivan.
Peer International Corp., 1941.
Best-selling record by Gene Autry (Okeh).

When My Dreamboat Comes Home
Words and music by Cliff Friend and Dave Franklin.
M. Witmark & Sons, 1936.
Introduced by Guy Lombardo and his Royal Canadians.

When My Dreams Come True
Words and music by Irving Berlin.
Irving Berlin Music Corp., 1929.
Introduced by Oscar Shaw and Mary Eaton in *The Cocoanuts* (film).

When My Little Girl Is Smiling
Words and music by Gerry Goffin and Carole King.
Screen Gems-EMI Music Inc., 1961.
Best-selling record by The Drifters (Atlantic) and Jimmy Justice (Kapp).

When My Man Comes Home
Words by J. Mayo Williams, music by Buddy Johnson.
Northern Music Corp., 1944.
Introduced and best-selling record by Buddy Johnson and his Orchestra
(Decca).

When My Ship Comes In
Words by Gus Kahn, music by Walter Donaldson.
Robbins Music Corp., 1934.
Introduced by Eddie Cantor in *Kid Millions* (film).

**When My Sugar Walks Down the Street, All the Little Birdies
Go Tweet-Tweet-Tweet**
Words and music by Gene Austin, Jimmy McHugh, and Irving
Mills.
Mills Music Inc., 1924/Ireneadele Publishing, 1924.
Introduced by Gene Austin. Featured by and identified with Phil Harris
and his Orchestra.

When Shall We Meet Again?
Words by Raymond B. Egan, music by Richard A. Whiting.
Remick Music Corp., 1921.
Introduced by the Duncan Sisters in *Tip Top* (musical, 1920).

When She Touches Me (Nothing Else Matters), see **When He
Touches Me (Nothing Else Matters).**

When She Wants Good Lovin', My Baby Comes to Me, see
(When She Needs Good Lovin') She Comes to Me.

When Something Is Wrong with My Baby
Words and music by David Porter and Isaac Hayes.
Irving Music Inc., 1966.
Best-selling record in 1967 by Sam and Dave (Stax).

(Oh, How I'll Miss You) When Summer Is Gone
Words and music by Hal Kemp.
Morley Music Co., Inc., 1937.
Theme song of Hal Kemp and his Orchestra.

When Sunny Gets Blue
Words by Jack Segal, music by Marvin Fisher.
Marvin Music Co., 1956.
Best-selling record by Johnny Mathis (Columbia).

When the Autumn Leaves Begin To Fall
Words by Neville Fleeson, music by Albert Von Tilzer.
Broadway Music Corp., 1920/Jerry Vogel Music Co., Inc., 1920.

When the Bloom Is on the Sage
Words and music by Fred Howard and Nat Vincent.
Southern Music Publishing Co., Inc., 1930.
Theme of *Tom Mix and His Straight-Shooters* (radio series).

When the Boy in Your Arms Is the Boy in Your Heart, also
known as **When the Girl in Your Arms Is the Girl in your
Heart**
Words and music by Sid Tepper and Roy C. Bennett.
Pickwick Music, Ltd., London, England/MCA, Inc., 1961.
From *The Young Ones* (British film, 1962). Best-selling record record
in 1962 by Connie Francis (MGM).

When the Boys Come Home
Words by E. Y. Harburg, music by Harold Arlen.
Chappell & Co., Inc., 1944.
Introduced by "The Five Daughters" in *Bloomer Girl* (musical).

When the Boys Talk about the Girls
Words and music by Bob Merrill.
Boca Music Inc., 1958/Golden Bell Songs, 1958/Planetary Music
Publishing Corp., 1958.
Best-selling record by Valerie Carr (Roulette).

When the Children Are Asleep
Words by Oscar Hammerstein, II, music by Richard Rodgers.
Williamson Music Inc., 1945.
Introduced by Eric Mattson and Jan Clayton in *Carousel* (musical).
Sung by Robert Rounseville and Barbara Ruick in film version (1957).

When the Girl in Your Arms Is the Girl in your Heart, see
When the Boy in Your Arms Is the Boy in Your Heart.

When the Grass Grows Over Me
Words and music by Don Chapel.
Glad Music Co., 1968.
Best-selling record in 1969 by George Jones (Musicor).

When the Honeymoon Was Over
Words and music by Fred Fisher.
Fred Fisher Music Co., 1921.

When the Idle Poor Become the Idle Rich
Words by E. Y. Harburg, music by Burton Lane.

Chappell & Co., Inc., 1946.
Introduced by Ella Logan and chorus in *Finian's Rainbow* (musical, 1947).

When the Leaves Come Tumbling Down
Words and music by Richard Howard.
Leo Feist Inc., 1922.

When the Lights Go On Again (All over the World)
Words and music by Eddie Seiler, Sol Marcus, and Bennie Benjamin.
Porgie Music Corp., 1942.
Best-selling records by Vaughn Monroe and his Orchestra (Victor) and
   Lucky Millinder and his Orchestra (Decca). Featured in *When the
   Lights Go On Again* (film, 1944).

**When the Moon Comes over Madison Square (The Love Lament
   of a Western Gent)**
Words by Johnny Burke, music by James V. Monaco.
Anne-Rachel Music Corp., 1940.
Introduced by Bing Crosby in *Rhythm on the River* (film).

When the Moon Comes over the Mountain
Words and music by Kate Smith, Harry Woods, and Harold
   Johnson.
Robbins Music Corp., 1931.
Introduced by and theme song of Kate Smith. Sung by Miss Smith in
   The Big Broadcast (film, 1932).

When the Morning Comes
Words and music by Hoyt Axton.
Lady Jane Music, 1971.
Best-selling record by Hoyt Axton (A & M, 1971).

When the Morning Glories Wake Up in the Morning
Words by Billy Rose, music by Fred Fisher.
Fred Fisher Music Co., 1927/Double-A Music Corp., 1927.

When the One You Love, Loves You
Words and music by Paul Whiteman, Cliff Friend, and Abel Baer.
Leo Feist Inc., 1924.
Introduced by Paul Whiteman and his Orchestra.

**When the Organ Played at Twilight, the Song That Reached My
   Heart** (English)
Words by Raymond Wallace, music by Jimmy Campbell and Reg
   Connelly.
Campbell-Connelly Co., Ltd., London, England/Campbell-Connelly,
   Inc., 1929/Anne-Rachel Music Corp., 1929.

Not copyrighted in the United States. Introduced in the United States and featured by organist Jesse Crawford.

When the Red, Red Robin Comes Bob, Bobbin' Along
Words and music by Harry Woods.
Bourne Co., 1926.
Introduction claimed by both Sophie Tucker and Lillian Roth.

When the Sea Is All around Us
Words by Sheldon Harnick, music by David Baker.
MCA, Inc., 1955.
Introduced by James Harwood in *Shoestring Revue* (revue). Later associated with Dorothy Loudon.

When the Ship Comes In
Words and music by Bob Dylan.
M. Witmark & Sons, 1963.
Introduced by Bob Dylan (Columbia).

When the Snow Is on the Roses (West German)
English words by Larry Kusik and Eddie Snyder, German words by Ernst Bader, music by James Last.
Francis, Day & Hunter, Inc., 1967/Miller Music Corp., 1967.
Original German title, "Der Weg ins Land der Liebe." Best-selling record of English version by Ed Ames (RCA Victor). Revived in 1972 by Sonny James (Columbia).

When the Spring Is in the Air
Words by Oscar Hammerstein, II, music by Jerome Kern.
T. B. Harms Co., 1932.
Introduced by Katherine Carrington and ensemble in *Music in the Air* (musical).

When the Sun Comes Out
Words by Ted Koehler, music by Harold Arlen.
Bregman, Vocco & Conn, Inc., 1941.
Best-selling record by Jimmy Dorsey and his Orchestra (Decca).

When the Sun Goes Down
Words and music by Leroy Carr.
Leeds Music Corp., 1935.
Traditional blues, introduced by Leroy Carr.

When the Swallows Come Back to Capistrano
Words and music by Leon Rene.
M. Witmark & Sons, 1940.
Best-selling record by The Ink Spots (Decca).

When the Wind Was Green
Words and music by Don Hunt.
Don Hunt, 1949.
Best-selling record by Bobby Wayne (London).

(Ah, the Apple Trees) When the World Was Young (French)
English words by Johnny Mercer, French words by Angela Vannier,
    music by M. Philippe-Gerard.
Enoch & Cie, Paris, France/Criterion Music Corp., 1950.
Original French title "Le Chevalier de Paris (Les Pommiers Doux)."
    Introduced in the United States by Peggy Lee.

When There's a Breeze on Lake Louise
Words by Mort Greene, music by Harry Revel.
MCA, Inc., 1942/Harry Revel Music Corp., 1942.
Introduced by Joan Merrill in *The Mayor of 44th Street* (film). Nomi-
    nated for an Academy Award, 1942.

When There's No You (English)
Words and music by Les Reed and Jackie Rae.
Donna Music Publishing Co., 1970/Drummer Boy Music Corp.,
    1970.
Best-selling record by Englebert Humperdinck (Parrot, 1971). Based on
    "Vesti La Giubba" from *Pagliacci*, by Ruggiero Leoncavallo.

When They Ask about You
Words and music by Sam H. Stept.
Bourne Co., 1943.
Best-selling record in 1944 by Jimmy Dorsey and his Orchestra, vocal
    by Kitty Kallen (Decca).

When They Played the Polka
Words by Lou Holzer, music by Fabian Andre.
Robbins Music Corp., 1938.
Introduced by Horace Heidt and his Brigadiers.

When Tomorrow Comes
Words by Irving Kahal, music by Sammy Fain.
M. Witmark & Sons, 1933.
Introduced by Kay Francis in *Mandalay* (film, 1934).

When Two Worlds Collide
Words and music by Roger Miller and Bill Anderson.
Tree Publishing Co., Inc., 1961.
Best-selling record by Roger Miller (RCA Victor). Revived in 1969 best-
    selling record by Jim Reeves (RCA).

When We Get Married
Words and music by Donald Hogan.
Big Seven Music Corp., 1961.
Best-selling record by The Dreamlovers (Heritage). Revived in 1970 by
    The Intruders (Gamble).

When Will I Be Loved
Words and music by Phil Everly.
Acuff-Rose Publications Inc., 1960.
Best-selling record by The Everly Brothers (Cadence). Revived in 1975
    by Linda Ronstadt (Capitol).

When Will I Find Love (West German)
English words by Marcel Stellman, German words by Johannes
    Brandt, music by Nikolaus Brodszky.
Beboton Verlag-Hans Sikorski, GmbH, Hamburg, Federal Republic
    of Germany, 1932, 1956/Fred Fisher Music Co., 1961, 1964.
Original German title, "Was Kann So Schoen Sein Wie Deine Liebe."

When Will I See You Again
Words and music by Kenny Gamble and Leon Huff.
Mighty Three Music, 1974.
Best-selling record by The Three Degrees (Philadelphia International,
    1974).

When Winter Comes
Words and music by Irving Berlin.
Irving Berlin Music Corp., 1939.
Introduced by Rudy Vallee in *Second Fiddle* (film).

When You and I Were Seventeen
Words by Gus Kahn, music by Charles Rosoff.
Bourne Co., 1924.
Popularized by Ruth Etting.

When You and I Were Young Maggie Blues
Words and music by Jack Frost and Jimmy McHugh.
Mills Music Inc., 1922/Ireneadele Publishing, 1922.
Popularized by Van and Schenck. Best-selling record in 1951 by Bing
    and Gary Crosby (Decca).

When You Are Dancing the Waltz
Words by Lorenz Hart, music by Richard Rodgers.
Chappell & Co., Inc., 1936.
Introduced by Charles Collins and Steffi Duna in *Dancing Pirate* (film).

When You Come to the End of the Day
Words by Gus Kahn, music by Frank Westphal.
Bourne Co., 1929.

When You Cry (You Cry Alone)
Words and music by Merle Travis, Tex Atchison, and Wesley Tuttle.
Elvis Presley Music, Inc., 1946/Unichappell Music Inc., 1946.

When You Dance
Words and music by Andrew Jones and L. Kirkland.
Angel Music, Inc., 1955.
Best-selling record in 1956 by The Turbans (Herald).

When You Gonna Wake Up
Words and music by Bob Dylan.
Special Rider Music, 1979.
Introduced by Bob Dylan on *Slow Train Coming* (Columbia, 1979).

When You Hear the Time Signal
Words by Johnny Mercer, music by Victor Schertzinger.
Paramount Music Corp., 1942.
Introduced by Dorothy Lamour in *The Fleet's In* (film).

When You Leave, Don't Slam the Door
Words and music by Joe Allison.
Tex Ritter Music Publications, Inc., 1946.
Best-selling record by Tex Ritter (Capitol).

When You Walked Out Someone Else Walked Right In
Words and music by Irving Berlin.
Irving Berlin Music Corp., 1923.

When You Want Me (English)
Words and music by Noel Coward.
Operating Co. Salina, Ltd., Jamaica/Chappell & Co., Inc., 1961.
Introduced by Grover Dale and Patricia Hary in *Sail Away* (musical).

When You Were a Smile on Your Mother's Lips (and a Twinkle in Your Daddy's Eye)
Words by Irving Kahal, music by Sammy Fain.
Remick Music Corp., 1934.
Introduced in *Dames* (film).

When You Wish upon a Star
Words by Ned Washington, music by Leigh Harline.
Bourne Co., 1940.
Introduced by voice of Cliff Edwards as "Jiminy Cricket" on soundtrack
    of *Pinocchio* (cartoon film). Won an Academy Award, 1940.

When Your Hair Has Turned to Silver (I Will Love You Just the Same)
Words by Charles Tobias, music by Peter De Rose.
Edwin H. Morris Co., 1930/Ched Music Co., 1930.
First recording by Russ Morgan and his Orchestra. Popularized by Rudy Vallee.

When Your Lover Has Gone
Words and music by E. A. Swan.
Remick Music Corp., 1931.
Sung on soundtrack of *Blonde Crazy* (film).

When You're Gone I Won't Forget
Words by Ivan Reid, music by Peter De Rose.
Jerry Vogel Music Co., Inc., 1920.

When You're Hot, You're Hot
Words and music by Jerry Reed.
Vector Music, 1971.
Best-selling record by Jerry Reed (RCA, 1971).

When You're in Love
Words by Johnny Mercer, music by Gene de Paul.
Robbins Music Corp., 1954/Hub Music Co., 1954.
Introduced by Jane Powell and Howard Keel in *Seven Brides for Seven Brothers* (film).

When You're in Love (The Whole World Is Jewish)
Words and music by Mark Bucci.
62 Revue Publishers, Inc., 1961.
Introduced in *New Faces of '62* (revue, 1962).

When You're in Love with a Beautiful Woman
Words and music by Even Stevens.
Debdave Music Inc., 1979.
Best-selling record by Dr. Hook (Capitol, 1979).

When You're Smiling (the Whole World Smiles at You)
Words and music by Mark Fisher, Joe Goodwin, and Larry Shay.
Mills Music Inc., 1928.
First recording by Louis Armstrong and his Orchestra.

When You're with Somebody Else
Words by L. Wolfe Gilbert, music by Ruth Etting and Abel Baer.
Leo Feist Inc., 1927.
Introduced by Ruth Etting.

When You're Young and in Love
Words and music by Van McCoy.
Morris Music, Inc., 1964/Canadiana-Morris, 1964.
Introduced by Ruby and The Romantics (Kapp). Best-selling record in
    1967 by The Marvelettes (Tamla).

When Yuba Plays the Rhumba on the Tuba
Words and music by Herman Hupfeld.
Harms, Inc., 1931.
Introduced by Walter O'Keefe in *The Third Little Show* (revue). Best-
    selling record by Rudy Vallee.

Whenever a Teenager Cries
Words and music by Ernie Maresca.
S & J Music Publishing Corp., 1964, 1965.
Best-selling record by Reparata and The Delrons (World Artists).

Whenever He Holds You
Words and music by Bobby Goldsboro.
Unart Music Corp., 1964.
Introduced by Bobby Goldsboro (United Artists).

Whenever I Call You "Friend"
Words and music by Melissa Manchester and Kenny Loggins.
Rumanian Pickleworks Co., 1978/Milk Money Music, 1978.
Best-selling record by Kenny Loggins (Columbia, 1978).

Whenever Mabel Comes in the Room
Words and music by Jerry Herman.
Jericho Music Corp., 1975/Edwin H. Morris Co., 1975.
Introduced by Stanley Simmonds in *Mack and Mabel* (musical, 1975).

Where Am I Going?
Words by Dorothy Fields, music by Cy Coleman.
Notable Music Co., Inc., 1965/Lida Enterprises, Inc., 1965.
Introduced by Gwen Verdon in *Sweet Charity* (musical). Sung by Shirley
    MacLaine in the film version, 1969. Best-selling record in 1966 by
    Barbra Streisand (Columbia).

Where Am I? (Am I in Heaven?)
Words by Al Dubin, music by Harry Warren.
Harms, Inc., 1935.
Introduced by James Melton in *Stars over Broadway* (film).

Where Are the Songs We Sung? (English)
Words and music by Noel Coward.
Chappell & Co., Ltd., London, England/Keith Prowse Music
    Publishing Co., Ltd., London, England/Chappell & Co., Inc.,

1938.
Introduced in London by Peggy Wood in *Operette* (musical).

Where Are You Going
Words by Danny Meehan, music by Bobby Scott.
Cannonball Music, 1970.
Performed by the voice of Jerry Butler in *Joe* (film, 1970).

Where Are You Now (Mexican)
English words by Marion B. Yarnall, Spanish words by Ernesto B.
 Yarnall, music by Luis Arcaraz and Don Marcotte.
Peer International Corp., 1941, 1943.
Mexican title, "Prisionero del Mar." Introduced by Xavier Cugat and his
 Orchestra.

Where Are You?
Words by Harold Adamson, music by Jimmy McHugh.
Leo Feist Inc., 1936.
Introduced by Gertrude Niesen in *Top of the Town* (film, 1937).

Where Can He Be?
Words by Howard Dietz, music by Arthur Schwartz.
Harms, Inc., 1931.
Introduced by Helen Broderick and chorus in *The Band Wagon* (revue).

Where Can I Go without You
Words by Peggy Lee, music by Victor Young.
Ivan Mogull Music Corp., 1952/Chappell & Co., Inc., 1952.
Introduced by Nat "King" Cole.

Where Can I Go? (English)
Words by Sonny Miller and Leo Fuld, music by Sigmunt Berland.
G. Ricordi & C., SpA, Milan, Italy, 1948/B. Feldman & Co., Ltd.,
 1949/Shapiro, Bernstein & Co., Inc., 1949.
Song about Jewish refugees. According to Fuld, melody was adapted
 from a tango originally written in 1928 by East European composer
 Oscar Struck, who died in the Warsaw ghetto. Under the Yiddish title,
 "Wi Ahyn Soll Ich Gehn," published in France in 1948. English version
 written in 1949 and introduced and recorded by Fuld in England
 (English Decca). Best-selling record in the United States in 1950 by
 Fuld (London).

Where Did Our Love Go
Words and music by Eddie Holland, Lamont Dozier, and Brian
 Holland.
Stone Agate Music Corp., 1964.
Best-selling record by The Supremes (Motown). Revived in 1971 by
 Donnie Elbert (All Platinum).

Where Did the Good Go
Words and music by Richard M. Sherman and Robert B. Sherman.
The Times Square Music Publications Co., 1974.
Introduced by Patty Andrews in *Over Here* (musical, 1974).

Where Did the Night Go?
Words and music by Harold Rome.
Florence Music Co., Inc., 1952.
Introduced by Patricia Marand and Jack Cassidy in *Wish You Were Here* (musical).

Where Did They Go, Lord
Words and music by Dallas Frazier and A. L. (Doodle) Owens.
Acuff-Rose Publications Inc., 1970/Elvis Music Inc., 1970.
Best-selling record by Elvis Presley (RCA, 1971).

Where Did You Learn To Love?
Words and music by Jule Styne, Sammy Cahn, and Harry Harris.
Edwin H. Morris Co., 1946/Cahn Music Co., 1946.

Where Do I Begin, see **Theme from *Love Story*.**

Where Do I Go from Here
Words and music by Brook Benton and James Shaw.
Benday Music Corp., 1969.
Best-selling record in 1970 by Brook Benton (Cotillion).

Where Do I Go?
Words by Gerome Ragni and James Rado, music by Galt MacDermot.
United Artists Music Co., Inc., 1967.
Introduced by Walker Daniels and the company in the Off Broadway version of *Hair* (musical); sung by James Rado and the company in the Broadway version, 1968. Best-selling record in 1968 by Carla Thomas (Stax).

Where Do I Put Her Memory
Words and music by James Weatherly.
Keca Music Inc., 1974.
Best-selling record by Charley Pride (RCA, 1979).

Where Do They Go When They Row, Row, Row?
Words by Bert Kalmar and George Jessel, music by Harry Ruby.
Mills Music Inc., 1920.
Introduced by George Jessel.

Where Do You Come From?
Words and music by Ruth Batchelor and Bob Roberts.

Elvis Presley Music, Inc., 1962.
Introduced by Elvis Presley in *Girls! Girls! Girls!* (film).

Where Do You Go?
Words and music by Sonny Bono (pseudonym for Salvatore Bono).
Cotillion Music Inc., 1965/Chris-Marc Music, 1965.
Best-selling record by Cher (Imperial).

Where Do You Work-a John? (Push-a Push-a Push)
Words and music by Mortimer Weinberg, Charley Marks, and Harry
   Warren.
Shapiro, Bernstein & Co., Inc., 1926.
Popularized by (Fred) Waring's Pennsylvanians.

Where Does a Little Tear Come From
Words and music by Marge Barton and Fred A. MacRae.
Mimosa Publishing Co., 1964.
Best-selling record by George Jones (United Artists).

Where Does the Good Times Go?
Words and music by Buck Owens.
Blue Book Music, 1966.
Best-selling records in 1967 by Buck Owens (Capitol) and Sonny James
   (Capitol).

Where Flamingos Fly (English)
Words by Jimmy Kennedy, music by Mischa Spoliansky.
Colgems-EMI Music Inc., 1948.
Best-selling record by Martha Tilton (Capitol).

Where Have All the Flowers Gone?
Words and music by Peter Seeger.
Fall River Music Inc., 1961.
Inspired by passage from Mikhail Sholokhov's novel, *And Quiet Flows
   the Don*. Additional verses by Jod Hickerson. Best selling records by
   The Kingston Trio (Capitol) and in 1965 by Johnny Rivers (Imperial).

Where Have We Met Before?
Words by E. Y. Harburg, music by Vernon Duke.
Harms, Inc., 1932.
Introduced by John Hundley, Sue Hicks, Donald Burr, and Patricia
   Dorn in *Walk a Little Faster* (revue).

Where Have You Been All My Life
Words by Herb Magidson, music by Ben Oakland.
Magidson Music Co., Inc., 1936/Claude Rivaux, 1936.
Introduced by Mae Clarke and John Payne in *Hats Off* (film).

Where Have You Been?
Words and music by Cole Porter.
Harms, Inc., 1930.
Introduced by Charles King and Hope Williams in *The New Yorkers* (musical).

Where I Oughta Be
Words and music by Harlan Howard.
Red River Songs, Inc., 1962.
Best-selling record by Skeeter Davis (RCA Victor).

Where in the World
Words and music by Mack Gordon and Harry Revel.
Leo Feist Inc., 1938.
Introduced by Don Ameche in *Josette* (film).

Where Is Love? (English)
Words and music by Lionel Bart.
Lakeview Music Co., Ltd., London, England, 1960/Hollis Music, Inc., 1960.
Introduced by Keith Hamshere, and reprised by Madeleine Newbury, in London production, and sung by Paul O'Keefe, and reprised by Dortha Duckworth, in New York production (1963) of *Oliver!* (musical).

Where Is My Meyer? (Where's Himalaya?) (East German)
English words by L. Wolfe Gilbert, German words by Fritz Rotter and Otto Stransky, music by Anton Profes.
Drei Masken Verlag, A-G, Berlin, Federal Republic of Germany, 1926/Leo Feist Inc., 1927.
Original German title, "Was Macht der Maier am Himalaya?" Introduced during the run of *Balieff's Chauve-Souris* (revue, 1922).

Where Is That Someone for Me
Words by Stella Unger, music by Victor Young.
Chappell & Co., Inc., 1955.
Introduced by Gloria De Haven in *Seventh Heaven* (musical).

Where Is the Life That Late I Led?
Words and music by Cole Porter.
Chappell & Co., Inc., 1948.
Introduced by Alfred Drake in *Kiss Me Kate* (musical). Sung by Howard Keel in film version (1953).

Where Is the Love
Words and music by Ralph MacDonald and William Salter.
Antisia Music Inc., 1971.
Best-selling record by Roberta Flack and Donnie Hathaway (Atlantic, 1972). Revived in 1975 with best-selling record by Betty Wright (Al-

ston). Won a National Academy of Recording Arts and Sciences Award, Rhythm & Blues Song of the Year, 1975.

Where Is the Man of My Dreams?
Words by B. G. De Sylva, music by George Gershwin.
New World Music Corp., 1922.
Introduced by Winnie Lightner and the Original Piano Trio (George Delworth, Edgar Fairchild, and Herbert Clair) in *George White's Scandals of 1922* (revue).

Where Is the One
Words and music by Alec Wilder and Eddie Finckel.
Famous Music Co., 1948.
First recording by Frank Sinatra (Columbia).

Where Is the Song of Songs for Me?
Words and music by Irving Berlin.
Irving Berlin Music Corp., 1928.
Introduced by Lupe Velez in *Lady of the Pavements* (film, 1929).

Where Is the Wonder?
Words by Dion McGregor, music by Michael Barr.
Emanuel Music Corp., 1965.
Introduced by Barbra Streisand.

Where Is Your Heart, see **The Song from Moulin Rouge.**

Where Love Has Gone
Words by Sammy Cahn, music by James Van Heusen.
Famous Music Co., 1964.
Introduced by Jack Jones in *Where Love Has Gone* (film). Nominated for an Academy Award, 1964.

Where, Oh Where?
Words and music by Cole Porter.
Buxton Hill Music Corp., 1950.
Introduced by Barbara Ashley in *Out of This World* (musical).

Where or When
Words by Lorenz Hart, music by Richard Rodgers.
Chappell & Co., Inc., 1937.
Introduced by Mitzi Green and Ray Heatherton in *Babes in Arms* (musical). Sung by Judy Garland in film version, 1939. Sung by Lena Horne in *Words and Music* (film, 1948). Used as theme in *Gaby* (film, 1956). Best-selling record in 1960 by Dion and The Belmonts (Laurie).

Where Peaceful Waters Flow
Words and music by Jim Weatherly.

Keca Music Inc., 1972.
Best-selling record by Gladys Knight & the Pips (Buddah, 1973).

Where Shall I Find Him? (English)
Words and music by Noel Coward.
Operating Co. Salina, Ltd., Jamaica/Chappell & Co., Inc., 1961.
Introduced by Patricia Harty in *Sail Away* (musical).

Where Shall I Go?, see **Song of the Wanderer.**

Where the Black-Eyed Susans Grow
Words by Dave Radford, music by Richard A. Whiting.
Remick Music Corp., 1940.

Where the Blue and Lonely Go
Words and music by James Warren, Alvaro Verissimo, William
    Silva, and Charles Sagle.
Sands Music Corp., 1966.
Best-selling record in 1969 by Roy Drusky (Mercury).

Where the Blue of the Night (Meets the Gold of the Day)
Words and music by Roy Turk, Bing Crosby, and Fred E. Ahlert.
DeSylva, Brown & Henderson, Inc., 1931/Fred Ahlert Music Corp.,
    1931/Cromwell Music, Inc., 1931.
Introduced by Bing Crosby in *The Big Broadcast* (film, 1932). Also used
    by Crosby as his theme song.

Where the Blues Were Born in New Orleans
Words by Cliff Dixon, music by Bob Carleton.
Edwin H. Morris Co., 1946.
Introduced by Louis Armstrong and his All-Stars in *New Orleans* (film,
    1947).

Where the Boys Are
Words by Howard Greenfield, music by Neil Sedaka.
Screen Gems-EMI Music Inc., 1960/Big Seven Music Corp., 1960.
Introduced by Connie Francis in *Where the Boys Are* (film). Best-selling
    record in 1961 by Connie Francis (MGM).

Where the Hot Wind Blows
Words by Buddy Kaye, music by Jimmy McHugh.
Boca Music Inc., 1960.
Introduced by The Ames Brothers on soundtrack over credits of *Where
    the Hot Wind Blows* (French-Italian film).

Where the Lazy Daisies Grow
Words and music by Cliff Friend.
Warner Brothers-Seven Arts Music, 1924.

Where the Lazy River Goes By
Words by Harold Adamson, music by Jimmy McHugh.
Robbins Music Corp., 1936.
Introduced by Barbara Stanwyck and Tony Martin in *Banjo on My Knee* (film).

(I'm Headin' for the Blue Horizon) Where the Mountains Meet the Sky
Words and music by Aston "Deacon" Williams.
Republic Music Corp., 1942.
Introduced and best-selling record by Sammy Kaye and his Orchestra, vocal by Billy Williams (Victor).

Where the Music's Playing, see I'll Take You Where the Music's Playing.

Where the Shy Little Violets Grow
Words and music by Gus Kahn and Harry Warren.
Remick Music Corp., 1928.

Where the Sweet Forget-Me-Nots Remember
Words by Mort Dixon, music by Harry Warren.
Remick Music Corp., 1929.

Where Was I?
Words by Al Dubin, music by W. Franke Harling.
Remick Music Corp., 1939.
Introduced in *'Til We Meet Again* (film, 1940). Best-selling records in 1940 by Charlie Barnet and his Orchestra (Bluebird) and Jan Savitt and his Orchestra (Decca).

Where Were You on Our Wedding Day
Words and music by Harold Logan, Lloyd Price, and John Patton.
Duchess Music Corp., 1959/Manitou-Duchess, 1959.
Best-selling record by Lloyd Price (ABC Paramount).

Where Were You When I Needed You?
Words by Marvin Moore, music by Bernie Wayne.
Edward B. Marks Music Corp., 1965.
Best-selling record in 1966 by Grass Roots (Dunhill).

Where Were You When I Was Falling in Love
Words and music by Steve Jobe, Jeff Silbar, and John Samuel Lorber.

House of Gold Music Inc., 1979/Bobby Goldsboro Music, 1979.
Best-selling record by Lobo (MCA, 1979).

Where Were You-Where Was I?
Words and music by George M. Cohan.
George M. Cohan Music Publishing Co., 1928.
Introduced by Joseph Wagstaff and Polly Walker in *Billie* (musical).

Where Will the Dimple Be?
Words and music by Bob Merrill and Al Hoffman.
Roger Music, Inc., 1955.
Best-selling record by Rosemary Clooney (Columbia).

Where Will the Words Come From?
Words and music by Glen D. Hardin and Sonny Curtis.
Best-selling record in 1966-67 by Gary Lewis and The Playboys (Liberty).

Where You Are
Words by Mack Gordon, music by Harry Warren.
Leo Feist Inc., 1941.
Introduced by Alice Faye, The Ink Spots, and John Payne in *The Great American Broadcast* (film).

Where You Go, I Go
Words by Ira Gershwin, music by George Gershwin.
New World Music Corp., 1932.
Introduced by Lyda Roberti and Jack Pearl in *Pardon My English* (musical, 1933).

Where You Lead
Words and music by Carole King and Toni Stern.
Colgems-EMI Music Inc., 1971.
Best-selling record by Barbra Streisand (Columbia, 1971, 1972). Medley with "Sweet Inspiration", 1972.

Where'd You Get Those Eyes?
Words and music by Walter Donaldson.
Leo Feist Inc., 1926.

Where's That Rainbow?
Words by Lorenz Hart, music by Richard Rodgers.
Warner Brothers-Seven Arts Music, 1926.
Introduced by Helen Ford and Margaret Breen in *Peggy-Ann* (musical).
Sung by Ann Sothern in *Words and Music* (film, 1948).

Where's the Playground Susie
Words and music by Jimmy Webb.

Jobete Music Co., Inc., 1967.
Best-selling record in 1969 by Glen Campbell (Capitol).

Wherever Love Takes Me
Words by Don Black, music by Elmer Bernstein.
MCA Music, 1974.
Performed by the voice of Maureen McGovern in *Gold* (film, 1974).
  Nominated for an Academy Award, 1974.

Wherever There's Me—There's You
Words and music by Sunny Skylar and Pat Lewis (pseudonym for
  Eli Oberstein).
Music Sales Corp., 1946.
Introduced by Betty Hutton (Victor).

Which Hazel?
Words and music by Ned Norworth and Abner Silver.
Warner Brothers-Seven Arts Music, 1921.

Which One Is To Blame
Words and music by Redd Stewart and Sunny Dull.
Ridgeway Music Co., 1959.
Best-selling record by The Wilburn Brothers (Decca).

Which Side Are You On
Words by Mrs. Sam Reece.
Public Domain Foundation, 1932.
Written by wife of Sam Reece, union organizer, during coal strike in
  Harlan County, Kentucky in 1932. Music adapted from traditional
  Baptist hymn. First recorded by The Almanac Singers in early 1940's.

Which Way You Goin' Billy (Canadian)
Words and music by Terry Jacks.
E. B. Marks Music Corp., 1969/Rockfish Music, 1969.
Best-selling record by The Poppy Family (London, 1970).

The Whiffenpoof Song
Words and music by Meade Minnigerode, George S. Pomeroy, Tod
  B. Galloway, and Rudy Vallee.
Miller Music Corp., 1936.
Members of Yale University Glee Club adapted Rudyard Kipling's poem
  "Gentleman Rankers" and adopted it as theme of The Whiffenpoof
  Society in 1909. First published version in *The New Yale Song Book*
  (G. Schirmer, Inc., 1918). Rudy Vallee brought his slightly revised
  version to attention of general public in 1935.

While a Cigarette Was Burning
Words and music by Charles Kenny and Nick Kenny.

Bourne Co., 1938.

Introduced by Joan Edwards. Used as a theme for the Fred Waring Chesterfield radio show.

While Hearts Are Singing
Words by Clifford Grey, music by Oscar Straus.
Famous Music Co., 1931.
Introduced by Claudette Colbert in *The Smiling Lieutenant* (film).

While My Guitar Gently Weeps (English)
Words and music by George Harrison.
Zero Productions, 1969.
Introduced by The Beatles in their album, *The Beatles* (Apple).

While the City Sleeps
Words by Lee Adams, music by Charles Strouse.
Strada Music Co., 1964.
Introduced by Billy Daniels in *Golden Boy* (musical).

While We're Young
Words by Bill Engvick, music by Alec Wilder and Morty Palitz.
Ludlow Music Inc., 1943.
Introduced by Mabel Mercer. First recording by Fred Waring and his Pennsylvanians (Decca).

While You Danced, Danced, Danced
Words and music by Stephan Weiss.
Cromwell Music, Inc., 1951.
Best-selling record by Georgia Gibbs (Mercury).

The Whip
Words by Otto Harbach and Oscar Hammerstein, II, music by Emmerich Kalman and Herbert Stothart.
Warner Brothers-Seven Arts Music, 1927/Charles Emmerich Kalman, Inc., 1927.
Introduced by Robert Chisholm in *Golden Dawn* (operetta).

Whip-poor-will
Words by Clifford Grey, music by Jerome Kern.
T. B. Harms Co., 1920.
Introduced by Marilyn Miller and Irving Fisher in *Sally* (musical).

Whipped Cream
Music by Naomi Neville.
Marsaint Music Inc., 1964.
Introduced in 1965 by Herb Alpert's Tijuana Brass (A&M).

Whirlwind
Words and music by Stan Jones.
Edwin H. Morris Co., 1949.
Best-selling record by Margaret Whiting (Capitol).

Whiskey and Gin
Words and music by Johnnie Ray.
Carlyle Music Publishing Corp., 1951.
First recording, coupled with "Tell the Lady I Said Goodbye," made by
  Johnnie Ray (Okeh).

Whiskey Bent and Hell Bound
Words and music by Hank Williams, Jr.
Bocephus Music Inc., 1979.
Best-selling record by Hank Williams, Jr. (Elektra, 1979).

Whispering
Words and music by John Schonberger, Richard Coburn, and
  Vincent Rose.
Miller Music Corp., 1920/Fred Fisher Music Co., 1920.
Best-selling record by Paul Whiteman and his Orchestra (Victor). Sung
  by Vivian Blaine in *Greenwich Village* (film, 1944).

Whispering Bells
Words and music by C. E. Quick.
Gil Music Corp., 1957/Fee Bee Music, 1957.
Best-selling record by The Del Vikings (Dot).

Whispering Grass (Don't Tell the Trees)
Words by Fred Fisher, music by Doris Fisher.
Mills Music Inc., 1940/Fisher Music Corp., 1940.
Best-selling record by The Ink Spots (Decca).

Whispering Winds
Words and music by Corky Robbins.
Lear Music, Inc., 1952.
Best-selling record by Patti Page (Mercury).

Whispers, see **The Whisper's Getting Louder.**

The Whisper's Getting Louder, also known as **Whispers**
Words and music by Barbara Acklin and David Scott.
Warner-Tamerlane Publishing Corp., 1966/Unichappell Music Inc.,
  1966.
Best-selling record by Jackie Wilson (Brunswick).

Whispers in the Dark
Words by Leo Robin, music by Frederick Hollander.

Famous Music Co., 1937.
Introduced by Connee Boswell, with Andre Kostelanetz and his Orchestra, in *Artists and Models* (film). Nominated for an Academy Award, 1937.

Whistle While You Work
Words by Larry Morey, music by Frank Churchill.
Bourne Co., 1937.
Introduced by voice of Adrienne Caselotti, as Snow White, in *Snow White and the Seven Dwarfs* (cartoon film).

Whistling Away the Dark
Words by Johnny Mercer, music by Henry Mancini.
Famous Music Co., 1970/Holmby Music Corp., 1970.
Introduced by Julie Andrews in *Darling Lili* (film, 1970). Nominated for an Academy Award, 1970.

The Whistling Boy
Words by Dorothy Fields, music by Jerome Kern.
T. B. Harms Co., 1937.
Introduced by Grace Moore in *When You're in Love* (film).

Whistling in the Dark
Words by Allen Boretz, music by Dana Suesse.
MCA, Inc., 1931.

White Bird
Words and music by David La Flamme and Linda La Flamme.
Davlin Music, 1969.
Best-selling record by David La Flamme (Amherst, 1976).

White Christmas
Words and music by Irving Berlin.
Irving Berlin Music Corp., 1942.
Introduced by Bing Crosby and Marjorie Reynolds in *Holiday Inn* (film). First public performance by Crosby in wartime show for United States armed forces in the Philippine Islands. Sung by Crosby in *White Christmas* (film, 1953). Estimated to be world's "most valuable popular song," with more than 45,000,000 records sold by end of 1963. Won an Academy Award, 1942.

The White Dove (Austrian)
English words by Clifford Grey, German words by Alfred Maria Willner and Robert Bodanzky, music by Franz Lehar.
Glocken Verlag, Inc., Frankfurt, Federal Republic of Germany, 1930/Chappell & Co., Inc., 1911, 1930.
Introduced under original German title, "Ich Weiss Ein Rezept," in 1910 Viennese operetta, *Zigeunerliebe (Gypsy Love)*. First English-lan-

guage version, with lyrics by Harry B. Smith and Robert B. Smith and entitled "The Melody of Love," presented in 1911 American production of *Gypsy Love*. Clifford Grey's English-language version introduced by Lawrence Tibbett in *The Rogue Song* (film).

White Heat
Music by Will Hudson.
American Academy of Music, Inc., 1934.
Introduced by Jimmie Lunceford and his Orchestra.

White Jazz
Music by H. Eugene Gifford.
American Academy of Music, Inc., 1933.
Best-selling record by the Casa Loma Orchestra.

The White Knight
Words and music by Jay Huguely.
Unichappell Music Inc., 1976.
Best-selling record by Cletus Maggard & The Citizen's Band (Mercury, 1978).

White Lightning
Words and music by Jape Richardson.
Glad Music Co., 1959.
Best-selling record by George Jones (Mercury).

White on White
Words by Bernice Ross, music by Lor Crane.
Painted Desert Music Corp., 1963, 1964.
Best-selling record in 1964 by Danny Williams (United Artists).

White Orchids
Words by Charles Tobias, music by Peter De Rose.
Robbins Music Corp., 1945/Ched Music Co., 1945.

White Rabbit
Words and music by Grace Slick.
Irving Music Inc., 1967.
Best-selling record by Jefferson Airplane (RCA Victor).

White Rhythm and Blues
Words and music by John David Souther.
Ice Age Music, 1979.
Best-selling record by J. D. Souther (Columbia, 1980).

White Riot (English)
Words and music by Mick Jones and Joe Strummer (pseudonym for John Mellor).

Riva Music Ltd., 1976.
Introduced by The Clash on *The Clash* (Epic, 1979).

White Room (English)
Words and music by Jack Bruce and Pete Brown.
Unichappell Music Inc., 1968.
Best-selling record by Cream (Atco).

White Silver Sands
Words and music by Charles G. "Red" Matthews.
Sharina Music Co., 1957.
First recorded by Dave Gardner (O-J). Best-selling record by Don
   Rondo (Jubilee). Revived in 1960 with best-selling record, instrumen-
   tal, by Bill Black's Combo (Hi).

A White Sport Coat (And a Pink Carnation)
Words and music by Marty Robbins.
Fred Rose Music, Inc., 1957.
Best-selling record by Marty Robbins (Columbia).

Whiteman Stomp
Words and music by Jo Trent and Thomas "Fats" Waller.
Robbins Music Corp., 1928/Anne-Rachel Music Corp., 1928.
First recording in 1927 by Fletcher Henderson and his Orchestra, featur-
   ing Fats Waller at the piano (Columbia).

A Whiter Shade of Pale (English)
Words and music by Keith Reid and Gary Brooker.
Essex Music International, Ltd., London, England, 1967/TRO-Essex
   Music, Inc., 1967.
Best-selling record by Procol Harum (Deram).

Who Am I That You Should Care for Me?
Words by Gus Kahn, music by Vincent Youmans.
Vincent Music Co., Inc., 1929/Gus Kahn Music Co., 1929.
Written for *Rainbow* (musical, 1928), but dropped before the New York
   opening.

Who Am I?
Words by Walter Bullock, music by Jule Styne.
Mills Music Inc., 1940.
Introduced by Frances Langford and Kenny Baker in *Hit Parade of 1941*
   (film). Nominated for an Academy Award, 1940.

Who Am I? (English)
Words and music by Tony Hatch and Jackie Trent.
Welbeck Music Ltd., London, England, 1966/ATV Music Corp.,
   1966/Manitou-Duchess, 1966/Duchess Music Corp., 1966/ATV

Music Publishing of Canada, Ltd., 1966.
Best-selling record by Petula Clark (Warner Bros.).

Who Are We To Say (Obey Your Heart)
Words by Gus Kahn, music by Sigmund Romberg.
Leo Feist Inc., 1939.
Introduced by Nelson Eddy in *Girl of the Golden West* (film, 1938).

Who Are You
Words by Lorenz Hart, music by Richard Rodgers.
Chappell & Co., Inc., 1940.
Introduced by Allan Jones in *The Boys from Syracuse* (film).

Who Are You (English)
Words and music by Peter Townsend.
Towser Tunes Inc., 1978.
Best-selling record by The Who (MCA, 1978).

Who Are You Now?
Words by Bob Merrill, music by Jule Styne.
Chappell & Co., Inc., 1964.
Introduced by Barbra Streisand in *Funny Girl* (musical).

Who Ate Napoleons with Josephine When Bonaparte Was Away?
Words by Alfred Bryan, music by E. Ray Goetz.
Remick Music Corp., 1920.
Introduced by in *As You Were* (musical).

Who Can I Turn To (When Nobody Needs Me) (English)
Words and music by Leslie Bricusse and Anthony Newley.
Concord Music, Ltd., London, England/Musical Comedy
   Productions Inc., 1964.
Introduced by Anthony Newley in *The Roar of the Greasepaint—The Smell of the Crowd* (musical). First and best-selling record by Tony Bennett (Columbia). Best-selling record in 1965 by Dionne Warwick (Scepter).

Who Can I Turn To?
Words and music by Alec Wilder and Bill Engvick.
Ludlow Music Inc., 1941.
Best-selling record by Tommy Dorsey and his Orchestra, vocal by Jo Stafford (Victor).

Who Cares (For Me)
Words and music by Don Gibson.
Acuff-Rose Publications Inc., 1959.
Best-selling record by Don Gibson (RCA Victor).

Who Cares What People Say?
Words by Jack Scholl, music by M. K. Jerome.
Harms, Inc., 1947.
Introduced by Ann Sheridan in *Nora Prentiss* (film).

Who Cares What You Have Been?
Words by L. Wolfe Gilbert, music by Martin Freed.
Leo Feist Inc., 1929.
Introduced by Helen Morgan in *Ziegfeld Midnight Frolic of 1928* (revue, 1928).

Who Cares?
Words and music by Jack Yellen, music by Milton Ager.
Warner Brothers, Inc., 1922/Advanced Music Corp., 1922.
Interpolated by Al Jolson in *Bombo* (musical, 1921), after the New York opening.

Who Cares? (So Long As You Care for Me)
Words by Ira Gershwin, music by George Gershwin.
New World Music Corp., 1931, 1952.
Introduced by William Gaxton and Lois Moran in *Of Thee I Sing* (musical). Slightly revised version sung by Jack Carson and Betty Oakes in 1952 revival.

Who Do You Know in Heaven (That Made You the Angel You Are?)
Words by Al Stillman, music by Peter De Rose.
Robbins Music Corp., 1949.
Best-selling record by The Ink Spots (Decca).

Who Do You Love, I Hope
Words and music by Irving Berlin.
Irving Berlin Music Corp., 1946.
Introduced by Betty Nyman and Kenny Bowers in *Annie Get Your Gun* (musical).

Who Do You Think You Are (English)
Words and music by Desmond Dyer and C. K. Scott.
Belsize Music, London, England, 1974/American Dream Music Co., 1974.
Best-selling record by Bo Donaldson (ABC, 1974).

Who Is Gonna Love Me?
Words by Hal David, music by Burt Bacharach.
Blue Seas Music Inc., 1967/Jac Music Co., Inc., 1967.
Best-selling record in 1968 by Dionne Warwick (Scepter).

Who Killed Norma Jean?
Words by Norman Rosten, music by Pete Seeger.
Ludlow Music Inc., 1963.
Dedicated to Marilyn Monroe. Introduced by Pete Seeger.

Who Knows What Might Have Been?
Words and music by Betty Comden and Adolph Green, music by
    Jule Styne.
Stratford Music Corp., 1961.
Introduced by Sydney Chaplin and Carol Lawrence in *Subways Are for
    Sleeping* (musical).

Who Knows Where the Time Goes? (English)
Words and music by Sandy Denny.
Winckler Music, Copenhagen, Denmark/Irving Music Inc., 1969.
Sung by Judy Collins in her album, *Who Knows Where the Time Goes*
    (Elektra) and by Fairport Convention in their album, *Unhalfbricking*
    (A&M). Featured in *The Subject Was Roses* (film, 1968).

Who Knows?
Words and music by Cole Porter.
Chappell & Co., Inc., 1937.
Introduced by Nelson Eddy in *Rosalie* (film).

Who Knows?
Words and music by Harold Rome.
Florence Music Co., Inc., 1962.
Introduced by Marilyn Cooper in *I Can Get It for You Wholesale*
    (musical).

Who Loves You
Words and music by Bob Gaudio and Judy Parker.
Jobete Music Co., Inc., 1975/Seasons Music Co., 1975.
Best-selling record by The Four Seasons (Warner Brothers/Curb, 1975).

Who Minds about Me?
Words by Walter Bullock, music by Victor Schertzinger.
Sam Fox Publishing Co., Inc., 1936.
Introduced by Clarence Muse, with The Hall Johnson Choir, in *Follow
    Your Heart* (film).

Who Needs You
Words by Al Stillman, music by Robert Allen.
International Korwin Corp., 1956.
Best-selling record in 1956 and 1957 by The Four Lads (Columbia).

Who Put the Bomp (In the Bomp Ba Bomp Ba Bomp)
Words and music by Barry Mann and Gerry Goffin.

Screen Gems-EMI Music Inc., 1961.
Best-selling record by Barry Mann (ABC-Paramount).

Who Shot Sam
Words and music by Darrell Edwards, Ray Jackson, and George
   Jones.
Glad Music Co., 1959/Fort Knox Music Co., 1959.
Best-selling record by George Jones (Mercury).

Who Shot the Hole in My Sombrero?
Words and music by Milton Leeds and Billy Hayes.
Elvis Presley Music, Inc., 1949/Unichappell Music Inc., 1949.

Who Takes Care of the Caretaker's Daughter
Words and music by Paul Revere and Chick Endor.
Shapiro, Bernstein & Co., Inc., 1924.
Interpolated by Cliff "Ukulele Ike" Edwards in *Lady, Be Good!* (musi-
   cal). Also known as "Who Takes Care of the Caretaker's Daughter
   While the Caretaker's Busy Taking Care."

Who Threw the Whiskey in the Well?
Words and music by Lucky Millinder, Eddie De Lange, and Johnny
   Brooks.
Advanced Music Corp., 1945.
Best-selling record of uncopyrighted song with same title (but with only
   De Lange and Brooks listed as writers) in 1942 by Doc Wheeler and
   his Orchestra (Bluebird). Best-selling record in 1945 by Lucky Millin-
   der and his Orchestra (Decca).

Who Was That Lady?
Words by Sammy Cahn, music by James Van Heusen.
Frank Music Co., 1959.
Introduced by Dean Martin. From *Who Was That Lady?* (film).

Who Will Answer (Spanish)
English words by Sheila Davis, Spanish words and music by L. E.
   Aute (pseudonym for Luis Eduardo Aute Gutierrez).
Blue Network Music, Inc., 1967.
Original Spanish title, "Aleluya #1." Best-selling record of English ver-
   sion in 1968 by Ed Ames (RCA).

(It All Depends) Who Will Buy the Wine, see **Who'll Buy the
   Wine.**

Who Will Buy? (English)
Words and music by Lionel Bart.
Lakeview Music Co., Ltd., London, England/Hollis Music, Inc.,
   1960.

Introduced by Keith Hamshere and chorus in London production and sung by Paul O'Keefe and chorus in New York production (1963) of *Oliver!* (musical).

Who Would Have Dreamed?
Words and music by Cole Porter.
Chappell & Co., Inc., 1940.
Introduced by Larry Douglas and Janis Carter in *Panama Hattie* (musical).

Who Wouldn't Be Blue?
Words by Benny Davis, music by Joe Burke.
Mills Music Inc., 1928/Ahlert-Burke Corp., 1928/Joe Burke Music Co., 1928.

Who Wouldn't Love You
Words by Bill Carey, music by Carl Fischer.
Maestro Music, Inc., 1942.
Best-selling record by Kay Kyser and his Orchestra (Columbia).

Who?
Words by Otto Harbach and Oscar Hammerstein, II, music by Jerome Kern.
T. B. Harms Co., 1925.
Introduced by Marilyn Miller and Paul Frawley in *Sunny* (musical). Sung by Miss Miller and Lawrence Gray in the first film version, 1930; by Anna Neagle and John Carroll in the second film version, 1941; by Judy Garland in *Till the Clouds Roll By* (film, 1946); and by Ray Bolger in *Look for the Silver Lining* (film, 1949).

Who? Me?
Words and music by Riley Shepard.
Elvis Presley Music, Inc., 1948/Unichappell Music Inc., 1948.
Best-selling record by Tex Williams (Capitol).

Whoa! Sailor!
Words and music by Hank Thompson.
Ernest Tubb Music, Inc., 1948.
Best-selling record by Hank Thompson (Capitol).

Who'd She Coo
Words and music by William Beck, Jim Williams, Marshall Jones, Marvin Pierce, Ronald Middlebrooks, Clarence Satchell, and Leroy Bonner.
Rick's Music Inc., 1976.
Best-selling record by The Ohio Players (Mercury, 1976).

Whodunit
Words and music by Kenny St. Lewis and Freddy Perren.
Bull Pen Music Co., 1977/Perren Vibes Music Inc., 1977.
Best-selling record by Tavares (Capitol, 1977).

The Whole Darned Thing's for You
Words by Roy Turk, music by Fred E. Ahlert.
Robbins Music Corp., 1930.
Introduced by Lawrence Gray in *Children of Pleasure* (film).

Whole Lot of Shakin' in My Heart (Since I Met You)
Words and music by Frank Wilson.
Stone Agate Music Corp., 1966.
Best-selling record by The Miracles (Tamla).

Whole Lot-ta Shakin' Goin' On
Words and music by Dave Williams and Sunny David.
Valley Publishers, Inc., 1957/Cherio Corp., 1957.
Best-selling record by Jerry Lee Lewis (Sun).

Whole Lotta Love (English)
Words and music by James Page, Robert Plant, John Paul Jones
    (pseudonym for John Baldwin), and John Bonham.
Superhype Publishing, 1969.
Best-selling record by Led Zeppelin (Atlantic).

Whole Lotta Loving
Words and music by Antoine "Fats" Domino and Dave
    Bartholomew.
Unart Music Corp., 1958/Unart-Unart, 1958.
Best-selling record by Fats Domino (Imperial).

The Whole World Is a Stage
Words and music by Al Kent (pseudonym for Albert Hamilton),
    Ronnie Savoy (pseudonym for Eugene Hamilton), and Eddie
    Wingate.
Stone Agate Music Corp., 1967.
Best-selling record by The Fantastic Four (Ric Tic).

The Whole World Is Singing My Song
Words by Mann Curtis, music by Vic Mizzy.
Robbins Music Corp., 1946/Unison Music Co., 1946.
Best-selling record by Les Brown and his Orchestra, vocal by Doris Day
    (Columbia).

Who'll Be the Next in Line? (English)
Words and music by Ray Davies.
Edward Kassner Music Co., Ltd., London, England, 1965/American

Metropolitan Enterprises of New York, Inc.
Best-selling record by The Kinks (Reprise).

Who'll Be the Next One To Cry over You
Words and music by Johnny Black.
E. B. Marks Music Corp., 1921.

Who'll Buy My Violets? (La Violetera) (French-Spanish)
English words by E. Ray Goetz, Spanish words by Eduardo
    Montesinos, French words by Albert Willemetz and Saint-
    Graniere, music by Jose Padilla.
Harms, Inc., 1923.
Original Spanish title, "La Violetera." Introduced by and identified with
    Raquel Meller. English-language version introduced in the United
    States by Irene Bordoni in *Little Miss Bluebeard* (play with songs).
    Performed on the soundtrack of Charlie Chaplin's *City Lights* (film,
    1931); and sung by Sarita Montiel in *La Violetera* (Spanish film, 1957).

Who'll Buy the Wine, also known as **(It All Depends) Who Will
    Buy the Wine**
Words and music by Billy Mize.
Penny Music Co., 1960/Unichappell Music Inc., 1960.
Best-selling record in 1960 by Charlie Walker (Columbia). Apparently
    not copyrighted, but cleared by BMI in 1965.

Who'll Stop the Rain
Words and music by John C. Fogerty.
Jando Music Inc., 1970.
Best-selling record by Creedence Clearwater Revival (Fantasy, 1970).
    Subsequently had a film named after it.

Who'll Take My Place When I'm Gone
Words by Raymond Klages, music by Billy Fazioli.
Broadway Music Corp., 1922.

Who's Afraid of Love
Words by Sidney D. Mitchell, music by Lew Pollack.
Movietone Music Corp., 1936.
Introduced by Don Ameche and Leah Ray in *One in a Million* (film).

Who's Afraid of the Big Bad Wolf
Words and music by Frank E. Churchill, words by Ann Ronell.
Bourne Co., 1933.
From *The Three Little Pigs* (cartoon film short).

Who's Been Cheatin' Who
Words and music by Ned Miller and Sue Miller.

Central Songs, 1962.
Best-selling record by Johnny and Jonie Mosley (Columbia).

Who's Been Sleeping in My Bed?
Words by Hal David, music by Burt F. Bacharach.
Famous Music Co., 1963.
"Inspired" by *Who's Been Sleeping in My Bed?* (film, 1964).

Who's Cheating Who?
Words and music by Carl Smith, Billy Davis, and Raynard Miner.
Chevis Publishing Corp., 1965.
Best-selling record by Little Milton (Checker).

Who's Gonna Mow Your Grass?
Words and music by Buck Owens.
Blue Book Music, 1969.
Best-selling record by Buck Owens and His Buckaroos (Capitol).

Who's Gonna Play This Old Piano
Words and music by Ray Griff.
Blue Echo Music, 1972.
Best-selling record by Jerry Lee Lewis (Mercury, 1972).

Who's Gonna Take the Blame
Words and music by Nick Ashford and Valerie Simpson.
Jobete Music Co., Inc., 1970.
Best-selling record by The Miracles (Tamla, 1970).

Who's Got the Pain?
Words and music by Richard Adler and Jerry Ross.
Frank Music Co., 1955.
Introduced by Gwen Verdon in *Damn Yankees* (musical).

Who's Julie?
Words and music by Wayne Carson Thompson.
Earl Barton Music, Inc., 1968.
Best-selling record in 1969 by Mel Tillis (Kapp).

Who's Making Love?
Words and music by Homer Banks, Bettye Crutcher, Don Davis,
   and Raymond Jackson.
Irving Music Inc., 1968.
Best-selling records by Johnnie Taylor (Stax) and in 1969 by Young-Holt
   Unlimited (Brunswick).

Who's Sorry Now?
Words by Bert Kalmar and Harry Ruby, music by Ted Snyder.
Mills Music Inc., 1923/Harry Ruby Music Co., 1923/Ted Snyder

Music Publishing Co., 1923.
Introduced by Van and Schenck. Sung by Gloria De Haven in *Three Little Words* (film, 1950). Best-selling record in 1957 by Connie Francis (M-G-M).

Who's Wonderful, Who's Marvelous? Miss Annabelle Lee, also known as **Miss Annabelle Lee**
Words by Sidney Clare and Harry Richman, music by Lew Pollack and Harry Richman.
Bourne Co., 1927.
Introduced by Harry Richman.

Who's Yehoodi
Words by Bill Seckler, music by Matt Dennis.
Saunders Publications, Inc., 1940.
Title derived from catch-line used by comedian Jerry Colonna. Best-selling record by Kay Kyser and his Orchestra (Columbia).

Who's Your Little Whoozis?
Words and music by Ben Bernie, Al Goering, and Walter Hirsch.
Famous Music Co., 1931/World Music, Inc., 1931.
Introduced by Ben Bernie and his Orchestra.

Whose Baby Are You?
Words by Anne Caldwell, music by Jerome Kern.
T. B. Harms Co., 1920.
Introduced by Louise Groody and Hal Skelly in *The Night Boat* (musical).

Whose Baby Are You?
Words by Sammy Cahn, music by Jule Styne.
Sands Music Corp., 1947.
Introduced by Peter Lawford in *It Happened in Brooklyn* (film).

Whose Big Baby Are You
Words by Ted Koehler, music by Jimmy McHugh.
Robbins Music Corp., 1935.
Introduced by Alice Faye in *King of Burlesque* (film).

Whose Garden Was This
Words and music by Tom Paxton.
United Artists Music Co., Inc., 1970.
Performed by John Denver on *Whose Garden Was This* (RCA, 1970).

Whose Heart Are You Breaking Tonight?
Words and music by Benny Davis and Ted Murray.
Planetary Music Publishing Corp., 1964.
Best-selling record in 1965 by Connie Francis (MGM).

Why
Words by Bob Marcucci, music by Peter De Angelis.
Debmar Publishing Co., Inc., 1960.
Best-selling record by Frankie Avalon (Chancellor). Revived in 1972 by
 Donny Osmond (MGM).

Why (English)
Words and music by Bill Crompton and Tony Sheridan.
Pan Musik, Ltd., London, England/Al Gallico Music Corp., 1964.
Best-selling record by The Beatles with Tony Sheridan (MGM).

Why
Words and music by Cindy Walker.
Tree Publishing Co., Inc., 1964.
Introduced by Eddy Arnold (RCA Victor).

Why, Baby, Why
Words and music by George Jones and Darrell Edwards.
Fort Knox Music Co., 1955.
Best-selling records in 1956 by Webb Pierce (Decca) and George Jones
 (Starday).

Why Baby Why
Words and music by Luther Dixon and Larry Harrison.
Paxwin Music Corp., 1957.
Best-selling record by Pat Boone (Dot).

Why Begin Again, also known as **Pastel Blue**
Words by Don Raye, music by Artie Shaw and Charlie Shavers.
MCA, Inc., 1943/Music Sales Corp., 1943.
Lyric version of jazz instrumental composition, "Pastel Blue," which was
 introduced by John Kirby and his Band in 1939.

Why Can't I Be Like You?
Words by Sidney D. Mitchell and Archie Gottler, music by Con
 Conrad.
Chappell & Co., Inc., 1929.
Introduced by Dixie Lee in *William Fox Movietone Follies of 1929*
 (film).

**(If You Let Me Make Love to You Then) Why Can't I Touch
 You?,** also known as **If You Let Me Make Love to You Then
 Why Can't I Touch You?**
Words by C.C. Courtney, music by Peter Link.
Chappell & Co., Inc., 1969.
Introduced by the company in *Salvation* (Off Broadway musical). Best-
 selling record in 1970 by Ronnie Dyson (Columbia).

2043

Why Can't I?
Words by Lorenz Hart, music by Richard Rodgers.
Harms, Inc., 1929.
Introduced by Lillian Taiz and Inez Courtney in *Spring Is Here* (musical). Sung by Doris Day and Martha Raye in *Billy Rose's Jumbo* (film, 1962).

Why Can't the English
Words by Alan Jay Lerner, music by Frederick Loewe.
Chappell & Co., Inc., 1956.
Introduced by Rex Harrison in *My Fair Lady* (musical).

Why Can't This Night Go On Forever
Words by Charles Newman, music by Isham Jones.
World Music, Inc., 1933.
Introduced by Jane Froman.

Why Can't We Be Friends
Words and music by Sylvester Allen, Harold Ray Brown, Morris Dickerson, Gerald Goldstein, Leroy "Lonnie" Jordan, Lee Oskar Levitin, Charles Miller, and Howard Scott.
Far Out Music, 1975.
Best-selling record by War (United Artists, 1975).

Why Can't We Live Together
Words and music by Tim Thomas.
Sherlyn Publishing Co., Inc., 1972.
Best-selling record by Timmy Thomas (Glades, 1973).

(Birdies Sing in Cages Too) Why Can't You
Words and music by B. G. De Sylva, Lew Brown, Ray Henderson, and Al Jolson.
Anne-Rachel Music Corp., 1929/DeSylva, Brown & Henderson, Inc., 1929.
Introduced by Al Jolson in *Say It with Songs* (film).

Why Can't You Behave
Words and music by Cole Porter.
Chappell & Co., Inc., 1948.
Introduced by Lisa Kirk and Harold Lang in *Kiss Me Kate* (musical). Sung by Ann Miller in film version (1953).

Why Can't You Feel Sorry for Me
Words and music by Merle Kilgore and Marvin Rainwater.
Al Gallico Music Corp., 1964.
Introduced by Carl Smith (Columbia).

Why Dance?
Words by Roy Turk, music by Fred E. Ahlert.
Fred Ahlert Music Corp., 1931/Cromwell Music, Inc., 1931/Pencil Mark Music, Inc., 1931.

Why Did I Kiss That Girl?
Words by Lew Brown, music by Robert King and Ray Henderson.
Shapiro, Bernstein & Co., Inc., 1924.

Why Did You Do It to Me, Babe?
Words by Andrew B. Sterling, music by Harry Von Tilzer.
Bibo Music Publishers, 1920.

Why Did You Do It?
Words by Howard Dietz, music by Arthur Schwartz.
DeSylva, Brown & Henderson, Inc., 1937.
Introduced by Evelyn Laye and ensemble in *Between the Devil* (musical).

Why Do Fools Fall in Love
Words and music by Frank Lymon and George Goldner.
Patricia Music Publishing Corp., 1956.
Best-selling record by Frankie Lymon and The Teenagers (Gee) and Gale Storm (Dot). Revived in 1967 with best-selling record by The Happenings (B. T. Puppy).

Why Do I Dream Those Dreams
Words by Al Dubin, music by Harry Warren.
M. Witmark & Sons, 1934.
Introduced by Dick Powell in *Wonder Bar* (film).

Why Do I Love You?
Words by B. G. De Sylva and Ira Gershwin, music by George Gershwin.
New World Music Corp., 1925/Anne-Rachel Music Corp., 1925.
Introduced in *Tell Me More!* (musical).

Why Do I Love You?
Words by Oscar II Hammerstein, music by Jerome Kern.
T. B. Harms Co., 1927.
Introduced by Norma Terris, Howard Marsh, Charles Winninger, and Edna May Oliver in *Show Boat* (musical). Sung by Kathryn Grayson and Howard Keel in the third film version, 1951.

Why Do I?
Words by Lorenz Hart, music by Richard Rodgers.
Warner Brothers-Seven Arts Music, 1926.

Introduced by June Cochrane and Francis X. Donegan in *The Girl Friend* (musical).

Why Do Lovers Break Each Other's Hearts?
Words and music by Ellie Greenwich, Tony Powers, and Phil Spector.
Six Continents Music Publishing Inc., 1962.
Best-selling record by Bob B. Soxx and The Blue Jeans (Philles).

Why Do the Wrong People Travel? (English)
Words and music by Noel Coward.
Operating Co. Salina, Ltd., Jamaica/Chappell & Co., Inc., 1961.
Introduced by Elaine Stritch in *Sail Away* (musical).

Why Do Things Happen to Me
Words and music by Roy Hawkins.
Modern Music Publishing Co., Inc., 1950.
Best-selling record by Roy Hawkins (Modern).

Why Do Ya Roll Those Eyes?
Words by Morrie Ryskind, music by Philip Charig.
Warner Brothers-Seven Arts Music, 1926.
Introduced by Helen Morgan, Lyman Byck, Evelyn Bennett, and Betty Compton in *Americana of 1926* (revue).

Why Do You Have To Go
Words and music by Verne Allison and Ewart G. Abner, Jr.
Conrad Music, 1957.
Best-selling record by The Dells (Vee Jay).

Why Do You Pass Me By (French)
English words by Desmond Carter, French words by Charles Trenet, music by John Hess and Paul Misraki.
Editions Vianelly, Paris, France/DeSylva, Brown & Henderson, Inc., 1936.
Original French title, "Vous Qui Passes Sans Me Voir." Introduced by Charles Trenet.

Why Do You Suppose?
Words by Lorenz Hart, music by Richard Rodgers.
Harms, Inc., 1929.
Introduced by Barbara Newberry and Jack Whiting in *Heads Up!* (musical).

Why Does It Get So Late So Early?
Words and music by Allie Wrubel, words by John Lehmann.
Harms, Inc., 1946/Allison's Music, Inc., 1946.

Why Does It Have To Rain on Sunday
Words and music by Bob Merrill and Vi Ott.
Duchess Music Corp., 1947.
Best-selling record by Freddy Martin and his Orchestra (Victor).

Why Don't They Understand
Words and music by Jack Fishman and Joe Henderson.
Henderson Music, Ltd., London, England/Hollis Music, Inc., 1957.
Best-selling record in 1958 by George Hamilton IV (ABC Paramount).

Why Don't We Do It in the Road (English)
Words and music by John Lennon and Paul McCartney.
Northern Songs, Ltd., England, 1969/Maclen Music Inc., 1969.
Introduced by The Beatles in their album, *The Beatles* (Apple).

Why Don't We Do This More Often
Words by Charles Newman, music by Allie Wrubel.
Allison's Music, Inc., 1941/World Music, Inc., 1941.
Introduced by Freddy Martin and his Orchestra, vocal by Eddie Stone
    (Victor) and Kay Kyser and his College of Musical Knowledge, vocal
    by Harry Babbitt and Ginny Simms (Columbia).

Why Don't You Believe Me
Words and music by Lew Douglas, King Laney, and Roy Rodde.
Brandom Music Co., 1952/T. B. Harms Co., 1952.
Best-selling record in 1952 and 1953 by Joni James (M-G-M).

Why Don't You Do Right (Get Me Some Money, Too!)
Words and music by Joe McCoy.
Mayfair Music Corp., 1942.
Introduced by Lil Green. Performed by Benny Goodman and his Or-
    chestra, with Peggy Lee, in *Stage Door Canteen* (film, 1943). Best-
    selling record by Benny Goodman and his Orchestra, vocal by Peggy
    Lee (Columbia).

Why Don't You Fall in Love with Me
Words by Al Lewis, music by Mabel Wayne.
Harms, Inc., 1942.
Best-selling records by Johnny Long and his Orchestra (Decca) and
    Dinah Shore (Victor). Also known as "As Long As You're Not in Love
    with Anyone Else, Why Don't You Fall in Love with Me."

Why Don't You Haul Off and Love Me?
Words and music by Wayne Raney and Lonnie Glosson.
Fort Knox Music Co., 1949.
Best-selling record by Wayne Raney (King).

Why Don't You Love Me
Words and music by Hank Williams.
Fred Rose Music, Inc., 1950/Hiriam Music, 1950.
Best-selling record by Hank Williams (M-G-M).

Why Don't You Spend the Night
Words and music by Bob McDill.
Hall-Clement Publications, 1979.
Best-selling record by Ronnie Milsap (RCA, 1980).

Why Don't You Write Me
Words and music by Laura Hollins.
Fort Knox Music Co., 1955.
Best-selling record by The Jacks (RPM).

Why Don't You?
Words by Joseph McCarthy, music by Harry Tierney.
Leo Feist Inc., 1920.
Sung by Alice Delysia in *Afgar* (musical).

Why Dream?
Words and music by Ralph Rainger, Leo Robin, and Richard A.
   Whiting.
Famous Music Co., 1935.
Introduced by Henry Wadsworth in *Big Broadcast of 1936* (film).

Why Fight the Feeling
Words and music by Frank Loesser.
Paramount Music Corp., 1950.
Introduced by Betty Hutton in *Let's Dance* (film).

Why Have You Left the One You Left Me For
Words and music by Christopher True.
Mother Tongue Music, 1978.
Best-selling record by Crystal Gayle (United Artists, 1978).

Why Him
Music by Burton Lane, words by Alan Jay Lerner.
Chappell & Co., Inc., 1979.
Introduced by Georgia Brown in *Carmelina* (musical, 1979).

Why I Sing the Blues
Words and music by B.B. King and Dave Clark.
Sounds of Lucille Inc., 1969/Duchess Music Corp., 1969.
Best-selling record by B.B. King (Blues Way).

Why I'm Walkin'
Words and music by Stonewall Jackson and Melvin Endsley.

Ernest Tubb Music, Inc., 1960/Acuff-Rose Publications Inc., 1960.
Best-selling record by Stonewall Jackson (Columbia).

Why Me
Words and music by Kris Kristofferson.
Resaca Music Publishing Co., 1972.
Best-selling record by Kris Kristofferson (Monument, 1973). Nominated
    for a National Academy of Recording Arts and Sciences Award,
    Country Song of the Year, 1973.

Why Not String Along with Me?
Words by Lew Brown, music by Lew Pollack.
Twentieth Century Fox Music Corp., 1938.
Introduced by Ethel Merman in *Straight, Place and Show* (film).

Why Not Tonight?
Words and music by Jimmy Gilreath.
Fame Publishing Co., Inc., 1966.
Best-selling record in 1967 by Jimmy Hughes (Fame).

Why Should I Care?
Words and music by Cole Porter.
Chappell & Co., Inc., 1937.
Introduced in *Rosalie* (film).

Why Should I Cry
Words and music by Zeke Clements.
Unichappell Music Inc., 1950.
Best-selling record by Eddy Arnold (RCA Victor).

Why Should I Cry over You?
Words and music by Ned Miller and Chester Conn.
Leo Feist Inc., 1922.

Why Should We Try Anymore
Words and music by Hank Williams.
Fred Rose Music, Inc., 1950/Hiriam Music, 1950.
Best-selling record by Hank Williams (M-G-M).

Why Shouldn't I
Words and music by Cole Porter.
Harms, Inc., 1935.
Introduced by Margaret Adams in *Jubilee* (musical).

Why Stars Come Out at Night
Words and music by Ray Noble.
Famous Music Co., 1935.
Introduced by Ray Noble and his Orchestra.

Why Try To Change Me Now
Words and music by Cy Coleman and Joseph A. McCarthy.
Notable Music Co., Inc., 1952.
Introduced by Frank Sinatra.

Why Was I Born?
Words by Oscar II Hammerstein, music by Jerome Kern.
T. B. Harms Co., 1929.
Introduced by Helen Morgan in *Sweet Adeline* (musical). Sung by Wini
    Shaw, and reprised by Irene Dunne, in the film version, 1934; by Lena
    Horne in *Till the Clouds Roll By* (film, 1946); and by the voice of Gogi
    Grant, dubbed for Ann Blyth, in *The Helen Morgan Story* (film,
    1957).

Why Why
Words and music by Wayne P. Walker, Mel Tillis, and George
    Sherry.
Cedarwood Publishing Co., Inc., 1957.
Best-selling record by Carl Smith (Columbia).

Why Worry?
Words and music by Seymour Simons.
Warner Brothers-Seven Arts Music, 1920/Marlong Music Corp.,
    1920.
Introduced by Nora Bayes in *Her Family Tree* (musical).

Why?
Words by Arthur Swanstrom and Benny Davis, music by J. Fred
    Coots.
Words & Music, Inc., 1929/Essex Music, Inc., 1929.
Introduced by Lily Damita and Jack Donahue in *Sons o' Guns* (musical).

Wichita Lineman
Words and music by Jim Webb.
Canopy Music Inc., 1968.
Best-selling record in 1968-69 by Glen Campbell (Capitol).

Wicked Blues
Words and music by Perry Bradford.
Perry Bradford Music Publishing Co., 1922.
First recording by Lizzie Miles (Okeh).

The Wicked Messenger
Words and music by Bob Dylan.
Dwarf Music Co., Inc., 1968.
Introduced by Bob Dylan in his album, *John Wesley Harding* (Co-
    lumbia).

Wiederseh'n (West German)
English words and music by Bert Kaempfert, Herbert Rehbein, and
 Milt Gabler.
Edition Doma Bert Kaempfert, Zug, Switzerland, 1965/Screen
 Gems-EMI Music Inc., 1965.
Best-selling record in 1966 by Al Martino (Capitol).

Wigwam
Words and music by Bob Dylan.
Big Sky Music, 1970.
Best-selling record by Bob Dylan (Columbia, 1970).

Wild As a Wildcat
Words and music by Carmol Taylor.
Tree Publishing Co., Inc., 1965.
Best-selling record by Charlie Walker (Epic).

Wild Billy's Circus Story
Words and music by Bruce Springsteen.
Laurel Canyon Music Ltd., 1973/Bruce Springsteen Publishing, 1973.
Performed by Bruce Springsteen on *The Wild, the Innocent, and the E
 Street Shuffle* (Columbia, 1973).

Wild Bird
Words and music by Wendy Waldman.
Irving Music Inc., 1975.
Introduced by Wendy Waldman on *Wendy Waldman* (Warner Brothers,
 1975). Also performed by Maria Muldaur on LP *Sweet Harmony*
 (Reprise) 1976.

Wild Cat Blues
Music by Thomas "Fats" Waller and Clarence Williams.
MCA, Inc., 1923.
Jazz instrumental. First recording by Clarence Williams' Blue Five
 (Okeh).

Wild Flower Rag
Music by Clarence Williams.
MCA, Inc., 1929.
Jazz instrumental. Introduced by Clarence Williams.

Wild Honey
Words and music by George Hamilton, Harry Tobias, and Neil
 Moret (pseudonym for Charles N. Daniels).
Robbins Music Corp., 1934.
Introduced by and theme song of George Hamilton and his Orchestra.

Wild Honey
Words and music by Brian Wilson and Mike Love.
Irving Music Inc., 1967.
Best-selling record by The Beach Boys (Capitol).

Wild Honey Pie (English)
Music by John Lennon and Paul McCartney.
Northern Songs, Ltd., England, 1969/Maclen Music Inc., 1969.
Introduced by The Beatles in their album, *The Beatles* (Apple).

Wild Horses
Words and music by K. C. Rogan (pseudonym for Johnny Burke).
George Simon, Inc., 1953.
Adapted from Robert Schumann's "Wild Horseman." Best-selling record
by Perry Como (RCA Victor).

Wild Horses (English)
Words and music by Mick Jagger and Keith Richards.
ABKCO Music Inc., 1970.
Performed by The Rolling Stones on *Sticky Fingers* (Rolling Stones,
1971).

Wild in the Country
Words and music by George Weiss, Hugo Peretti, and Luigi
Creatore.
Gladys Music, 1961.
Best-selling record by Elvis Presley (RCA Victor).

Wild in the Streets
Words and music by Garland Jeffreys.
Sheepshead Bay Music, 1973/Castle Music, 1973.
Revived by Garland Jeffreys on *Ghostwriter* (A & M, 1977). Best-selling
record by Garland Jeffreys (Atlantic, 1974).

Wild Is the Wind
Words by Ned Washington, music by Dimitri Tiomkin.
Anne-Rachel Music Corp., 1957.
Introduced in *Wild Is the Wind* (film). Best-selling record by Johnny
Mathis (Columbia). Nominated for an Academy Award, 1957.

Wild Man Blues
Music by Louis Armstrong and Ferdinand "Jelly Roll" Morton.
Edwin H. Morris Co., 1927/International Music, Inc., 1927.
Jazz instrumental. First recording by Johnny Dodds' Black Bottom
Stompers (Brunswick). Best-selling records by Louis Armstrong and
his Hot Seven (Okeh) and Jelly Roll Morton's Red Hot Peppers
(Victor).

Wild Night
Words and music by Van Morrison.
WB Music Corp., 1971/Caledonia Productions, 1971.
Best-selling record by Van Morrison (Warner Brothers, 1971).

Wild One
Words and music by Lowe Bernie, Kal Mann, and Dave Appell.
Lowe Music Publishing Corp., 1960/Kalmann Music, Inc., 1960.
Best-selling record by Bobby Rydell (Cameo).

Wild One
Words and music by William Stevenson and Ivy Hunter.
Jobete Music Co., Inc., 1964.
Best-selling record by Martha and The Vandellas (Gordy).

The Wild Rose
Words by Clifford Grey, music by Jerome Kern.
T. B. Harms Co., 1920.
Introduced by Marilyn Miller in *Sally* (musical). Sung by June Haver in
   Look for the Silver Lining (film, 1949).

The Wild Side of Life
Words and music by W. Warren and A. A. Carter.
Unart Music Corp., 1952/Unart-Unart, 1952.
Best-selling record by Hank Thompson (Capitol). Revived in 1976 by
   Rod Stewart on A Night on the Town (Warner Bros.).

Wild Thing
Words and music by Chip Taylor.
Blackwood Music Inc., 1965.
Best-selling records in 1966 by The Troggs (Atco, Fontana) and in 1967
   by Senator Bobby (Parkway). Revived in 1974 by Fancy (Big Tree).

Wild Week-end
Words and music by Bill Anderson.
Stallion Music Inc., 1967.
Best-selling record in 1968 by Bill Anderson (Decca).

Wild Weekend, also known as **Wild Weekend Cha Cha**
Words and music by Tom Shannon and Phil Todaro.
Tupper Publishing Co., 1960/Embassy Music Corp., 1960.
Best-selling record in 1963 by The Rebels (Swan).

Wild Weekend Cha Cha, see **Wild Weekend.**

The Wild, Wild West
Words by Johnny Mercer, music by Harry Warren.

Leo Feist Inc., 1945.
Introduced by Virginia O'Brien in *The Harvey Girls* (film, 1946).

Wild, Wild Young Men
Words and music by Ahmet Ertegun.
Unichappell Music Inc., 1955.
Best-selling record in 1953 by Ruth Brown (Atlantic).

Wild World (English)
Words and music by Cat Stevens.
Island Music, 1970.
Best-selling record by Cat Stevens (A & M, 1971).

The Wildest Gal in Town
Words by Jack Yellen, music by Sammy Fain.
Yellen & Fain, 1947.
Best-selling record by Billy Eckstine (MGM).

Wildfire
Words and music by Michael Murphey and Larry Cansler.
Warner-Tamerlane Publishing Corp., 1975.
Best-selling record by Michael Murphey (Epic, 1975).

Wildflower
Words by Otto Harbach and Oscar Hammerstein, II, music by
    Vincent Youmans and Herbert Stothart.
Warner Brothers-Seven Arts Music, 1923.
Introduced by Guy Robertson in *Wildflower* (musical).

Wildflower (Canadian)
Words and music by David Richardson and Doug Edwards.
Edsel Music, 1972.
Best-selling record by Skylark (Capitol, 1973).

Wildwood Days
Words by Kal Mann, music by Dave Appell.
Kalmann Music, Inc., 1963.
Best-selling record by Bobby Rydell (Cameo).

Wildwood Flower
Words and music by Hank Thompson.
Hall-Clement Publications, 1955.
Best-selling record by Hank Thompson (Capitol).

Wildwood Weed
Words and music by Dan Bowman and Jim Stafford.
Famous Music Co., 1974/Ensign Music Corp., 1974/Parody

Publishing, 1974.
Best-selling record by Jim Stafford (MGM, 1974).

Wilhelmina
Words by Mack Gordon, music by Josef Myrow.
Twentieth Century Fox Music Corp., 1950.
Introduced in *Wabash Avenue* (film). Nominated for an Academy Award, 1950.

Wilkes-Barre, Pa.
Words by Anne Croswell, music by Lee Pockriss.
Piedmont Music Co., Inc., 1963.
Introduced by Vivien Leigh and Byron Mitchell in *Tovarich* (musical).

Will He Like Me?
Words by Sheldon Harnick, music by Jerry Bock.
The Times Square Music Publications Co., 1963.
Introduced by Barbara Cook in *She Loves Me* (musical).

Will I Ever Tell You
Words and music by Meredith Willson.
Frank Music Co., 1957/Rinimer Corp., 1957.
Introduced by Barbara Cook in *The Music Man* (musical).

Will It Go Round in Circles
Words and music by Billy Preston and Bruce Fisher.
Irving Music Inc., 1973.
Best-selling record by Billy Preston (A&M, 1973).

Will Santy Come to Shanty Town?
Words and music by Eddy Arnold, Steve Nelson, and Ed Nelson, Jr.
Unichappell Music Inc., 1949/Chappell & Co., Inc., 1949.
Best-selling record by Eddy Arnold (Victor).

Will She Come from the East? (East-North-West or South)
Words and music by Irving Berlin.
Irving Berlin Music Corp., 1922.
Introduced by John Steel in *Music Box Revue of 1922* (revue).

Will You Be Staying after Sunday?
Words and music by Al Kasha and Joel Hirschhorn.
Screen Gems-EMI Music Inc., 1968.
Best-selling record in 1969 by The Peppermint Rainbow (Decca).

Will You Love Me Tomorrow?
Words and music by Gerry Goffin and Carole King.
Screen Gems-EMI Music Inc., 1960, 1961.

Best-selling record in 1961 by The Shirelles (Scepter). Revived in 1968 with best-selling record by The Four Seasons (Philips).

Will You Marry Me Tomorrow, Maria?
Words by Oscar Hammerstein, II, music by Jerome Kern.
T. B. Harms Co., 1937.
Introduced by William Frawley in *High, Wide and Handsome* (film).

Will You Remember
Words by Dusty Negulesco, music by Marqueritte Monnot.
Unart Music Corp., 1962.
Introduced by Maurice Chevalier in *Jessica* (film).

Will You Remember Me?
Words by Maxwell Anderson, music by Kurt Weill.
DeSylva, Brown & Henderson, Inc., 1938.
Introduced by Richard Kollmar in *Knickerbocker Holiday* (musical).

Will You Remember? Will You Forget?
Words by Robert A. Simon and Clifford Grey, music by Lewis E.
   Gensler.
Warner Brothers-Seven Arts Music, 1928.
Introduced by Marie Saxon and Roy Royston in *Ups-a-Daisy* (musical).

Will You Still Be Mine?
Words by Tom Adair, music by Matt Dennis.
Music Sales Corp., 1941.
Introduced by Tommy Dorsey and his Orchestra, vocal by Connie
   Haines (Victor).

Will Your Lawyer Talk to God
Words and music by Harlan Howard and Richard Johnson.
Tree Publishing Co., Inc., 1961.
Best-selling record in 1962 by Kitty Wells (Decca).

Willa, Willa
Words by Earl Shuman, music by Leon Carr.
April Music Inc., 1964.
Introduced by Charles Rydell in *The Secret Life of Walter Mitty* (musical).

Willie the Weeper
Words and music by Billy Walker and Freddie Hart.
Tree Publishing Co., Inc., 1962.
Best-selling record by Billy Walker (Decca).

Willie the Whistling Giraffe
Words by Rube Golberg, music by Ruth Cleary Patterson.
Ben Bloom Music Corp., 1951.

Willing
Words and music by Lowell George.
Abraham Music, 1970/Naked Snake Publishing, 1970.
Performed by Little Feat on *Little Feat* (Warner Brothers, 1970).

Willing and Eager
Words and music by Richard Rodgers.
Williamson Music Inc., 1962.
Introduced by Pat Boone and Ann-Margret in *State Fair* (film).

Willingly, also known as **Melodie Perdue** (French)
English words by Carl Signam, French words by Jean Broussole,
   music by Hubert Giraud.
Editions Do Re Mi, Paris, France/Nouvelles Editions Meridian,
   Paris, France/Shapiro, Bernstein & Co., Inc., 1958.
Best-selling record, in French, by Les Compagnons de la Chanson (Capitol).

Willingly
Words and music by Hank Cochran.
Tree Publishing Co., Inc., 1961.
Best-selling record in 1962 by Shirley Collie and Willie Nelson (Liberty).

Willkommen
Words by Fred Ebb, music by John Kander.
The Times Square Music Publications Co., 1966.
Introduced by Joel Grey and the company in *Cabaret* (musical). Sung
   by Grey in the film version, 1972.

Willow in the Wind
Words by E. Y. Harburg, music by Harold Arlen.
Leo Feist Inc., 1944.
Introduced in *Kismet* (film).

Willow Tree
Words by Andy Razaf, music by Thomas "Fats" Waller.
Anne-Rachel Music Corp., 1928/Harms, Inc., 1928.
Introduced by Fats Waller and James P. Johnson in *Keep Shufflin'*
   (revue).

Willow Weep for Me
Words and music by Ann Ronell.
Bourne Co., 1932.
Introduced by Paul Whiteman and his Orchestra, vocal by Irene Taylor.

Willow, Willow, Willow
Words and music by Robert Wright and George Forrest.
Empress Music, Inc., 1961.
Introduced by Lee Venora in *Kean* (musical).

Wimoweh, also known as **The Lion Sleeps Tonight** (South African)
English words and music by Paul Campbell (pseudonym for The
    Weavers), English words by Roy Ilene.
Folkways Music Publishers, Inc., 1951.
Words and music adapted and arranged by Paul Campbell (collective
    pseudonym for The Weavers— Pete Seeger, Fred Hellerman, Lee
    Hays, and Ronnie Gilbert). New lyrics by Roy Ilene added in 1952.
    Adapted from the South African (Zulu) song, "Mbube," first recorded
    in South Africa in the 1930's by Solomon Linda. Best-selling record
    by The Weavers and Gordon Jenkins (Decca). Adapted in 1961 as
    "The Lion Sleeps Tonight," with new words and music by Hugo
    Peretti, Luigi Creatore, George Weiss, and Albert Stanton. Best-sell-
    ing record in 1961 by The Tokens (RCA Victor). Revived in 1972 by
    Robert John (Atlantic).

Win Your Love for Me
Words and music by L. C. Cook.
ABKCO Music Inc., 1958.
Best-selling record by Sam Cooke (Keen).

Winchester Cathedral (English)
Words and music by Geoff Stevens.
Meteor Music Publishing Co., Ltd., London, England/Southern
    Music Publishing Co., Inc., 1966.
Best-selling record by The New Vaudeville Band (Fontana).

The Wind Cries Mary
Words and music by Jimi Hendrix.
Canadiana-Six Continents, 1967/Super Songs Unlimited-Sealark,
    1967/Unichappell Music-Six Continents, 1967.
Introduced by The Jimi Hendrix Experience in their album, *Are You
    Experienced?* (Reprise).

Windmill under the Stars
Words by Johnny Mercer, music by Jerome Kern.
T. B. Harms Co., 1942.

**The Windmills of Your Mind (Theme from *The Thomas Crown
    Affair*)**
Words by Marilyn Bergman and Alan Bergman, music by Michel
    Legrand.
United Artists Music Co., Inc., 1968.

Introduced by the voice of Noel Harrison on the soundtrack of *The Thomas Crown Affair* (film). Best-selling record in 1969 by Dusty Springfield (Atlantic). Won an Academy Award, 1968.

The Window Up Above
Words and music by George Jones.
Glad Music Co., 1961/Fort Knox Music Co., 1961.
Best-selling record by George Jones (Mercury). Revived in 1975 by Mickey Gilley (Playboy).

The Windows of the World
Words by Hal David, music by Burt Bacharach.
Blue Seas Music Inc., 1967/Jac Music Co., Inc., 1967.
Best-selling record by Dionne Warwick (Scepter).

The Winds of Chance, see *Airport* **Love Theme.**

Windy
Words and music by Ruthann Friedman.
Irving Music Inc., 1967.
Best-selling records by The Association (Warner Bros.) and Wes Montgomery (A&M).

Wine and Roses, see **I Threw Away the Rose.**

Wine Me Up
Words and music by Faron Young and Billy Beaton.
Acuff-Rose Publications Inc., 1969.
Best-selling record by Faron Young (Mercury).

Wine, Women and Song
Words and music by Al Dexter and Aubrey Gass.
Al Dexter Songs, 1946.
Best-selling record by Al Dexter (Columbia).

Wine, Women, and Song
Words and music by Betty Sue Perry.
Sure Fire Music Co., Inc., 1963.
Best-selling record in 1964 by Loretta Lynn (Decca).

Wings
Words by Ballard Macdonald, music by J. S. Zamecnik.
Sam Fox Publishing Co., Inc., 1927.
Love theme from *Wings* (film).

Wings of a Dove, also known as **(On the) Wings of a Dove**

(On the) Wings of a Dove, see also **Wings of a Dove.**
Words and music by Robert B. Ferguson.
Larrick Music Co., 1959/Husky Music Co., Inc., 1959.
Best-selling record in 1960 by Ferlin Husky (Capitol).

Winners
Words and music by Joe Raposo.
Jonico Music Inc., 1973/Sergeant Music Co., 1973.
Best-selling record by Frank Sinatra (Reprise, 1974).

Winners and Losers
Words and music by Danny Hamilton and Ann Hamilton.
Spitfire Music Inc., 1976.
Best-selling record by Hamilton, Joe Frank & Reynolds (Playboy, 1976).

Winter Lady
Words and music by Leonard Cohen.
Stranger Music Inc., 1967.
Introduced in 1968 by Leonard Cohen in his album, *Songs of Leonard Cohen* (Columbia); sung by the voice of Leonard Cohen on the soundtrack of *McCabe and Mrs. Miller* (film, 1971).

Winter of My Discontent
Words by Ben Ross Berenberg, music by Alec Wilder.
Ludlow Music Inc., 1955.
Introduced by Mabel Mercer.

The Winter Waltz
Words and music by Larry Neill.
Gale & Gayles, Inc., 1950.
Adapted from Waldteufel's "Skater's Waltz." Best-selling record by Mitch Miller and his Orchestra (Columbia).

Winter Weather
Words and music by Ted Shapiro.
Leo Feist Inc., 1941.
Best-selling record in 1942 by Benny Goodman and his Orchestra, vocal by Peggy Lee (Okeh).

Winter Wonderland
Words by Richard B. Smith, music by Felix Bernard.
Bregman, Vocco & Conn, Inc., 1934.
Best-selling record in 1950 by The Andrews Sisters (Decca).

Winter World of Love (English)
Words and music by Les Reed and Barry Mason.
Glenwood Music Corp., 1969.
Best-selling record by Engelbert Humperdinck (Parrot).

Wintergreen for President
Words by Ira Gershwin, music by George Gershwin.
New World Music Corp., 1931.
Introduced by ensemble in *Of Thee I Sing* (musical).

Wipe Out
Music by Robert Berryhill, Patrick Connolly, James Fuller, and Ron Wilson.
Miraleste Music, 1963/Robin Hood Music Co., 1963.
Best-selling instrumental by The Surfaris (Dot). Revived in 1966 with best-selling record by the same group.

Wise Old Owl
Words and music by Joe Ricardel.
Screen Gems-EMI Music Inc., 1940.
Best-selling record in 1941 by Al Donahue and his Orchestra (Vocalion).

Wish Me a Rainbow
Words and music by Jerry Livingston and Ray Evans.
Famous Music Co., 1966.
Introduced by Mary Badham in *This Property Is Condemned* (film). Best-selling record in 1967 by The Gunter Kallman Chorus (4 Corners of the World).

Wish You Didn't Have to Go
Words and music by Dan Pennington and Lindon Oldham.
Fame Publishing Co., Inc., 1965.
Best-selling record in 1967 by James and Bobby Purify (Bell).

Wish You Were Here
Words and music by Harold Rome.
Florence Music Co., Inc., 1952.
Introduced by Jack Cassidy in *Wish You Were Here* (musical). Best-selling record by Eddie Fisher (RCA Victor).

Wish You Were Here, Buddy
Words and music by Pat Boone (pseudonym for Charles E. Boone).
Spoone Music Corp., 1966.
Best-selling record by Pat Boone (Dot).

Wishful, Sinful
Words and music by The Doors (James Morrison, John Densmore, Robert Krieger, and Raymond Manzarek.
Doors Music Co., 1968.
Best-selling record in 1969 by The Doors (Elektra).

Wishful Thinking
Words by Leo Robin, music by Ralph Rainger.

Robbins Music Corp., 1940.
Introduced by Virginia Gilmore in *Tall, Dark and Handsome* (film).

Wishful Thinking
Words and music by Wynn Stewart.
Jat Music, Inc., 1959.
Best-selling record in 1960 by Wynn Stewart (Challenge).

Wishin' and Hopin'
Words by Hal David, music by Burt Bacharach.
Blue Seas Music Inc., 1963/Jac Music Co., Inc., 1963.
Best-selling record in 1964 by Dusty Springfield (Philips).

Wishing (Will Make It So)
Words and music by B. G. De Sylva.
DeSylva, Brown & Henderson, Inc., 1939/Anne-Rachel Music Corp., 1939.
Introduced by Irene Dunne in *Love Affair* (film). Best-selling record by Glenn Miller and his Orchestra. Nominated for an Academy Award, 1939.

Wishing and Waiting for Love
Words by Grant Clarke, music by Harry Akst.
M. Witmark & Sons, 1929.
Introduced by Alice White in *Broadway Babies* (film).

The Wishing Doll
Words by Mack David, music by Elmer Bernstein.
United Artists Music Co., Inc., 1966.
Introduced in *Hawaii* (film). Nominated for an Academy Award, 1966.

Wishing for Your Love
Words and music by Sampson Horton.
Rightsong Music Inc., 1958.
Best-selling record by The Voxpoppers (Mercury).

Wishing Ring
Words and music by Al Britt and Pete Maddux.
Acuff-Rose Publications Inc., 1952.
Best-selling record in 1953 by Joni James (M-G-M).

The Wishing Star, see **Theme from *Taras Bulba*.**

The Wishing Well (Down in the Well) (Australian)
Words and music by Peter Hiscock.
Woomera Music, Pty., Ltd., Reservoir Victoria, Australia, 1964/Jaspar Music, 1964/Hanks Music, Inc., 1964.
Best-selling record in 1965 by Hank Snow (RCA Victor).

Wishing You Were Here
Words and music by Peter Cetera.
Big Elk Music, 1974/Polish Prince Music, 1974.
Best-selling record by Chicago (Columbia, 1974).

Witch Doctor
Words and music by Ross Bagdasarian.
Armen Bagdasarian, 1958.
Best-selling record by David Seville (pseudonym for Bagdasarian) (Liberty).

Witch Queen of New Orleans
Words and music by Patrick Vegas and Lolly Vegas.
Blackwood Music Inc., 1971/Novalene Music, 1971.
Best-selling record by Redbone (Epic, 1972).

Witchcraft
Words and music by Dave Bartholomew and Pearl King.
Unart Music Corp., 1955/Unart-Unart, 1955/Elvis Presley Music, Inc., 1955.
Best-selling record by Elvis Presley (RCA Victor).

Witchcraft
Words by Carolyn Leigh, music by Cy Coleman.
Morley Music Co., Inc., 1957.
Introduced by Gerry Matthews in Julius Monk's *Take Five* (nightclub revue). Best-selling record by Frank Sinatra (Capitol).

With a Banjo on My Knee
Words by Harold Adamson, music by Jimmy McHugh.
Robbins Music Corp., 1936.
Introduced by Buddy Ebsen and Walter Brennan in *Banjo on My Knee* (film).

With a Feather in Your Cap
Words by Dorothy Fields, music by Jimmy McHugh.
Robbins Music Corp., 1933.
Introduced by Jeanie Lang on opening program at Radio City Music Hall (New York, December 27, 1932).

With a Girl Like You (English)
Words and music by Reg Presley.
Dick James Music Ltd., London, England/Dick James Music Inc., 1966.
Best-selling record by The Troggs (Atco, Fontana).

With a Hey and a Hi and a Ho Ho Ho!
Words by Mann Curtis, music by Vic Mizzy.

2063

Bourne Co., 1947/Unison Music Co., 1947.
Introduced by Louis Prima and his Orchestra (Victor).

With a Little Bit of Luck
Words by Alan Jay Lerner, music by Frederick Loewe.
Chappell & Co., Inc., 1956.
Introduced by Stanley Holloway in *My Fair Lady* (musical).

With a Little Help from My Friends (English)
Words and music by John Lennon and Paul McCartney.
Northern Songs, Ltd., England, 1967/Maclen Music Inc., 1967.
Introduced by The Beatles in their album, *Sgt. Pepper's Lonely Hearts Club Band* (Capitol); sung by The Beatles in *Yellow Submarine* (film, 1968); best-selling record in 1968 by Joe Cocker (A&M).

With a Little Luck (English)
Words and music by Paul McCartney.
MPL Communications Inc., 1978.
Best-selling record by Wings (Capitol, 1978).

With a Smile and a Song
Words by Larry Morey, music by Frank Churchill.
Bourne Co., 1937.
Introduced by voice of Adrienne Caselotti, as Snow White, in *Snow White and the Seven Dwarfs* (cartoon film).

With a Song in My Heart
Words by Lorenz Hart, music by Richard Rodgers.
Harms, Inc., 1929.
Introduced by Lillian Taiz and John Hundley in *Spring Is Here* (musical). Sung by Alexander Gray in *Spring Is Here* (film, 1930); by Susanna Foster in *This Is the Life* (film, 1944); by Tom Drake in *Words and Music* (film, 1948); by Doris Day, with Harry James and his Orchestra, in *Young Man with a Horn* (film, 1950); and by the voice of Jane Froman, dubbed for Susan Hayward, in *With a Song in My Heart* (film, 1952). Theme song of *Major Bowes' Capitol Theatre Family* (radio variety show).

With All My Heart
Words by Gus Kahn, music by Jimmy McHugh.
Leo Feist Inc., 1935.
Introduced by Peggy Conklin in *Her Master's Voice* (film, 1936).

With All My Heart
English words by Bob Marcucci and Pete De Angelis, Italian words by Bob Marcucci and Pete De Angelis, music by Pete De Angelis.
Debmar Publishing Co., Inc., 1957.
Best-selling record by Jodie Sands (Chancellor).

With All My Heart and Soul, see **Anema e Core.**

With Every Breath I Take
Words and music by Leo Robin and Ralph Rainger.
Famous Music Co., 1934.
Introduced by Bing Crosby in *Here Is My Heart* (film).

With God on Our Side
Words and music by Bob Dylan.
M. Witmark & Sons, 1963.
Music based on melody of "Patriot Game," by Dominic Behan. Introduced by Bob Dylan (Columbia).

With My Eyes Wide Open, I'm Dreaming
Words by Mack Gordon, music by Harry Revel.
DeSylva, Brown & Henderson, Inc., 1934.
Introduced by Dorothy Dell and Jack Oakie in *Shoot the Works* (film). Sung by Dean Martin in *The Stooge* (film, 1952).

With My Head in the Clouds
Words and music by Irving Berlin.
Irving Berlin Music Corp., 1942.
Introduced by Private Robert Shanley in *This Is the Army* (revue).

With One Exception
Words and music by Billy Sherrill and Glenn Sutton.
Al Gallico Music Corp., 1967.
Best-selling record by David Houston (Epic).

With Pen in Hand
Words and music by Bobby Goldsboro.
Detail Music, Inc., 1968.
Best-selling records by Billy Vera (Atlantic) and Johnny Darrell (United Artists) and in 1969 by Vikki Carr (Liberty).

With Plenty of Money and You
Words by Al Dubin, music by Harry Warren.
Harms, Inc., 1936.
Introduced by Dick Powell in *Gold Diggers of 1937* (film). Sung by Doris Day in *My Dream Is Yours* (film, 1949).

With So Little To Be Sure Of
Words and music by Stephen Sondheim.
Burthen Music Co., Inc., 1964.
Introduced by Lee Remick and Harry Guardino in *Anyone Can Whistle* (musical).

(I'm Still without a Sweetheart) With Summer Coming On
Words by Roy Turk, music by Fred E. Ahlert.
Fred Ahlert Music Corp., 1932/Cromwell Music, Inc., 1932.

With the Wind and the Rain in Your Hair
Words and music by Jack Lawrence and Clara Edwards.
G. Schirmer Inc., 1930/Paramount Music Corp., 1940.
Revised by Jack Lawrence from an art song written by Clara Edwards
    and published by G. Schirmer, Inc. in 1930. Introduced and best-
    selling record by Kay Kyser and his College of Musical Knowledge,
    vocal by Ginny Sims (Columbia).

With These Hands
Words by Benny David, music by Abner Silver.
Cromwell Music, Inc., 1950.
Introduced by Nelson Eddy and Jo Stafford in 1951. Best-selling record
    in 1953 by Eddie Fisher (RCA Victor). Revived in 1965 with best-
    selling record by Tom Jones (Parrot).

With This Ring
Words and music by Luther Dixon, Richard Wylie, and Anthony
    Hester.
Vee Ve Music Corp., 1967.
Best-selling record by The Platters (Musicor).

With You
Words by Jo Trent, music by Edward Kennedy "Duke" Ellington.
Robbins Music Corp., 1925.
Written for *Chocolate Kiddies* (revue), which toured Europe with a
    Negro cast, headed by Lottie Gee.

With You
Words and music by Irving Berlin.
Irving Berlin Music Corp., 1929.
Introduced by Harry Richman in *Puttin' on the Ritz* (film, 1930).

With You I'm Born Again
Music by David Shire, words by Carol Connors.
Check Out Music, 1979.
Performed by the voice of Billy Preston and Syreeta in *Fast Break* (film,
    1979). Best-selling record by Billy Preston and Syreeta (Motown,
    1979).

With You on My Mind
Words by Lew Brown, music by Lew Pollack.
Twentieth Century Fox Music Corp., 1938.
Introduced by Ethel Merman in *Straight, Place and Show* (film).

With You on My Mind
Words by Charlotte Hawkins, music by Nat "King" Cole.
Ivan Mogull Music Corp., 1957.
Best-selling record by Nat "King" Cole (Capitol).

With Your Love
Words and music by Martyn Buchwald, Joey Covington, and Victor
    Smith.
Diamondback Music Co., 1976.
Best-selling record by The Jefferson Starship (Grunt, 1976).

Wither Thou Goest
Words and music by Guy Singer.
Kavelin Music, 1954/Unichappell Music Inc., 1954.
Best-selling record by Les Paul and Mary Ford (Capitol).

Within You, without You (English)
Words and music by George Harrison.
Northern Songs, Ltd., England, 1967/Maclen Music Inc., 1967.
Introduced by The Beatles in their album, *Sgt. Pepper's Lonely Hearts
    Club Band* (Capitol).

Without a Song
Words by Billy Rose and Edward Eliscu, music by Vincent
    Youmans.
Miller Music Corp., 1929/Anne-Rachel Music Corp., 1929.
Introduced by Lois Deppe and Russell Wooding's Jubilee Singers in
    Great Day (musical).

Without a Word of Warning
Words and music by Mack Gordon and Harry Revel.
DeSylva, Brown & Henderson, Inc., 1935.
Introduced by Bing Crosby in *Two for Tonight* (film).

Without Her
Words and music by Harry Nilsson.
Rock Music, 1965.
Performed in 1968 by Blood, Sweat and Tears in their album, *Child Is
    Father to the Man* (Columbia); best-selling record in 1969 by Herb
    Alpert (A&M).

Without Love
Words by B. G. De Sylva and Lew Brown, music by Ray
    Henderson.
DeSylva, Brown & Henderson, Inc., 1930/Anne-Rachel Music Corp.,
    1930.
Introduced by Grace Brinkley, and reprised by Oscar Shaw and Kate

Smith, in *Flying High* (musical). Sung by Sheree North in *The Best Things in Life Are Free* (film, 1956).

Without Love
Words and music by Cole Porter.
Buxton Hill Music Corp., 1954.
Introduced by Hildegarde Neff in 1955 in *Silk Stockings* (musical).

Without Love (There Is Nothing)
Words and music by Danny Small.
Gomace Music, Inc., 1956/Unichappell Music Inc., 1956.
Best-selling record in 1957 by Clyde McPhatter (Atlantic). Revived in
    1970 by Tom Jones (Parrot). Original foreign title was "Buen Viage
    (Bon Voyage)."

Without That Certain Thing (English)
Words and music by Max Nesbitt and Harry Nesbitt.
T. B. Harms Co., 1933.

Without You, also known as **Tres Palabras** (Mexican)
English words by Ray Gilbert, Spanish words and music by Osvaldo
    Farres.
Peer International Corp., 1942, 1945.
Introduced by voice of Andy Russell in *Make Mine Music* (cartoon film,
    1946).

Without You
Words and music by J. D. Miller.
Acuff-Rose Publications Inc., 1956.
Best-selling record by Eddie Fisher (RCA Victor).

Without You
Words and music by Johnny Tillotson.
Ridge Music Corp., 1961.
Best-selling record by Johnny Tillotson (Cadence).

Without You (English)
Words and music by Thomas Evans and William Peter Ham.
Apple Music, Ltd., London, England, 1970.
Best-selling record by Nilsson (RCA, 1972). Nominated for a National
    Academy of Recording Arts and Sciences Award, Record of the Year,
    1972.

Without Your Love
Words by Johnny Lange, music by Fred Stryker.
John Lange Music Co., 1937.
Introduced in *Pick a Star* (film).

Wives and Lovers
Words by Hal David, music by Burt F. Bacharach.
Famous Music Co., 1963.
"Inspired" by *Wives and Lovers* (film). Best-selling record by Jack Jones (Kapp). Won a National Academy of Recording Arts and Sciences Award, Solo Vocal Performance/Male, 1963.

WKRP in Cincinnati
Words and music by James Thomas Wells and Hugh Wilson.
Fast Fade Music, 1978/MTM Enterprises Inc., 1978.
Performed by the voice of Steve Carlisle in *WKRP in Cincinnati* (television series, 1978).

Woke Up This Morning
Words and music by Riley King and Jules Taub.
Modern Music Publishing Co., Inc., 1953/Sounds of Lucille Inc., 1953.
Best-selling record by B. B. King (RPM).

Wolverine Blues
Words and music by John Spikes, Benjamin Spikes, and Ferdinand "Jelly Roll" Morton.
Edwin H. Morris Co., 1923.
Introduced by King Oliver's Creole Jazz Band. First recording by Jelly Roll Morton (Gennett).

Wolverton Mountain
Words and music by Merle Kilgore and Claude King.
Painted Desert Music Corp., 1962.
Adapted from traditional American mountain song. Best-selling record by Claude King (Columbia).

Woman
Words and music by Dick Gleason.
Regent Music, 1953.
Introduced by Johnny Desmond (Coral). Best-selling record by Jose Ferrer and Rosemary Clooney (Columbia). Released on a single record along with its sequel, entitled "Man."

Woman (English)
Words and music by Bernard Webb.
Northern Songs, Ltd., England, 1966/Maclen Music Inc., 1966.
Best-selling record by Peter and Gordon (Capitol).

Woman (Sensuous Woman)
Words and music by Gary S. Paxton.
Acoustic Music Inc., 1972.
Best-selling record by Don Gibson (Hickory, 1972). Nominated for a

National Academy of Recording Arts and Sciences Award, Country Song of the Year, 1972.

A Woman, a Lover, a Friend
Words and music by Sid Wyche.
Regent Music, 1959/Lena Music, Inc., 1959.
Best-selling record in 1960 by Jackie Wilson (Brunswick).

Woman Alone with the Blues
Words and music by Willard Robison.
Edwin H. Morris Co., 1955.
Identified with Peggy Lee.

A Woman Always Knows
Words and music by Billy Sherrill.
Algee Music Corp., 1971.
Best-selling record by David Houston (Epic, 1971).

A Woman Always Understands
Words by Roy Alfred, music by Marvin Fisher.
Fred Rose Music, Inc., 1948.
Introduced by Tex Beneke and his Orchestra (Victor).

Woman Disputed, I Love You
Words by Bernie Grossman, music by Edward Ward.
Warner Brothers-Seven Arts Music, 1928.
Theme song of *Woman Disputed* (film).

Woman Don't Go Astray
Words and music by King Floyd.
Malaco Music Co., 1971/Roffignac Music Co., 1971.
Best-selling record by King Floyd (Chimmeyville, 1971).

Woman from Tokyo (English)
Words and music by Jon Lord, Ian Gillian, Richard Blackmore, Roger Glover, and Ian Paice.
Mauve Music Inc., 1973.
Best-selling record by Deep Purple (Warner Brothers, 1973).

Woman Helping Man
Words and music by Mark Charron.
Warner-Tamerlane Publishing Corp., 1968.
Best-selling record in 1969 by The Vogues (Reprise).

A Woman in Love
Words and music by Frank Loesser.
Frank Music Co., 1955.

Introduced by Frank Sinatra in the film version of *Guys and Dolls*. Best-selling record by Frankie Laine (Columbia).

A Woman in Love
Words and music by Charles Anderson.
Ring a Ding Music Co./Lencal Music Co.
Copyright year unknown; composition registered with BMI in 1967.
    Best-selling record by Bonnie Guitar (Dot).

The Woman in the Moon
Words and music by Kenny Ascher and Paul Williams.
First Artists Music Co., 1976.
Introduced by Barbra Streisand in *A Star Is Born* (film, 1976).

The Woman in the Shoe
Words by Arthur Freed, music by Nacio Herb Brown.
Robbins Music Corp., 1929.
Introduced by Ethelind Terry in *Lord Byron of Broadway* (film, 1930).

A Woman Is a Sometime Thing
Words by Du Bose Heyward, music by George Gershwin.
Gershwin Publishing Corp., 1935/Chappell & Co., Inc., 1935.
Introduced by Edward Matthews in *Porgy and Bess* (opera). Sung by
    Leslie Scott in film version, 1959.

A Woman Lives for Love
Words and music by George Richey, Norris Wilson, and Glenn
    Sutton.
Al Gallico Music Corp., 1970.
Best-selling record by Wanda Jackson (Capitol, 1970).

Woman of the River, also known as **Mambo Bacan** (Italian)
Italian words by Franco Giordano, music by Roman Vatro.
R. P. D. Industri e Musicali, Milan, Italy/Hollis Music, Inc., 1955.
Introduced in *Woman of the River* (Italian film).

Woman of the World
Words and music by Sharon Higgins.
Sure Fire Music Co., Inc., 1968.
Best-selling record in 1969 by Loretta Lynn (Decca).

Woman, Woman
Words and music by James W. Glaser and James O. Payne.
Ensign Music Corp., 1967.
Best-selling record in 1967-68 by Gary Puckett and The Union Gap
    (Columbia).

2071

Woman's Got Soul
Words and music by Curtis Mayfield.
Warner-Tamerlane Publishing Corp., 1963.
Best-selling record in 1965 by The Impressions (ABC-Paramount).

Woman's Got to Have It
Words and music by Bobby Womack, Linda Cooke, and Darryl
 Carter.
Unart Music Corp., 1969.
Best-selling record by Bobby Womack (United Artists, 1972).

A Woman's Intuition
Words and music by Madeline Burroughs.
Sure Fire Music Co., Inc., 1959.
Best-selling record by The Wilburn Brothers (Decca).

A Woman's Prerogative
Words by Johnny Mercer, music by Harold Arlen.
A-M Music Corp., 1946.
Introduced by Pearl Bailey in *St. Louis Woman* (musical).

Women Do Funny Things, see **Women Do Funny Things to Me.**

Women Do Funny Things to Me, also known as **Women Do
 Funny Things**
Words and music by Larry Kingston.
Fort Knox Music Co., 1965/Window Music Publishing Inc., 1965.
Best-selling record in 1966 by Del Reeves (United Artists).

Women I've Never Had
Words and music by Hank Williams, Jr.
Bocephus Music Inc., 1979.
Best-selling record by Hank Williams, Jr. (Elektra, 1980).

Women's Love Rights
Words and music by William Weatherspoon and Angelo Bond.
Gold Forever Music Inc., 1971.
Best-selling record by Laura Lee (Hot Wax, 1971).

Wonder Bar
Words by Al Dubin, music by Harry Warren.
M. Witmark & Sons, 1934.
Introduced by Al Jolson in *Wonder Bar* (film).

Wonder Could I Live There Anymore, also known as **I Wouldn't
 Want to Live There Anymore**
Words and music by Bill Rice.
T. B. Harms Co., 1969.

Best-selling record by Charley Pride (RCA, 1970). Nominated for a National Academy of Recording Arts and Sciences Award, Country Song of the Year, 1970.

Wonder of You
Words and music by Baker Knight.
Duchess Music Corp., 1958, 1970.
Best-selling record in 1964 by Ray Peterson (RCA Victor). Revived in 1970 with best-selling record, in medley with "Mama Liked the Roses," under the title, "The Wonder of You/Mama Liked the Roses," by Elvis Presley (RCA Victor).

Wonder Why
Words by Sammy Cahn, music by Nicholas Brodszky.
Robbins Music Corp., 1950.
Introduced by Jane Powell in *Rich, Young and Pretty* (film). Nominated for an Academy Award, 1951.

Wonderful Baby
Words and music by Don McLean.
Unart Music Corp., 1975.
Best-selling record by Don McLean (United Artists, 1975).

Wonderful Copenhagen
Words and music by Frank Loesser.
Frank Music Co., 1951.
Introduced by Danny Kaye in *Hans Christian Andersen* (film).

A Wonderful Day Like Today (English)
Words and music by Leslie Bricusse and Anthony Newley.
Concord Music, Ltd., London, England/Musical Comedy
   Productions Inc., 1964.
Introduced by Cyril Ritchard and The Urchins in *The Roar of the Greasepaint—The Smell of the Crowd* (musical).

A Wonderful Guy
Words by Oscar Hammerstein, II, music by Richard Rodgers.
Williamson Music Inc., 1949.
Introduced by Mary Martin in *South Pacific* (musical). Sung by Mitzi Gaynor in film version (1958).

Wonderful One
Words by Dorothy Terriss (pseudonym for Theodora Morse), music

by Paul Whiteman and Ferde Grofe.
Leo Feist Inc., 1922.
Music adapted from a theme by film director Marshall Neilan. Introduced and best-selling record by Paul Whiteman and his Orchestra (Victor).

Wonderful Summer
Words and music by Gil Garfield and Perry Botkin, Jr.
Rock Music, 1963.
Introduced by Robin Ward (Dot).

Wonderful To Be Young
Words and music by Hal David, music by Burt F. Bacharach.
Famous Music Co., 1962.
Introduced by Cliff Richard in *Wonderful To Be Young* (film).

Wonderful Tonight (English)
Words and music by Eric Clapton.
Stigwood Music Inc., 1977.
Best-selling record by Eric Clapton (RSO, 1978).

Wonderful! Wonderful!
Words by Ben Raleigh, music by Sherman Edwards.
Edward B. Marks Music Corp., 1956.
Best-selling record by Johnny Mathis (Columbia). Revived in 1963 with best-selling record by The Tymes (Parkway).

Wonderful, Wonderful Day
Words by Johnny Mercer, music by Gene de Paul.
Robbins Music Corp., 1954.
Introduced by Jane Powell in *Seven Brides for Seven Brothers* (film).

Wonderful World, also known as **What a Wonderful World**
Words and music by Barbara Campbell, Lou Adler, and Herb Alpert.
ABKCO Music Inc., 1960.
Best-selling record by Sam Cooke (Keen). Revived in 1965 with best-selling record by Herman's Hermits (MGM) and in 1978 by Art Garfunkel (Columbia).

Wonderful World, Beautiful People
Words and music by Jimmy Cliff.
Island Music, 1969.
Best-selling record in 1969-70 by Jimmy Cliff (A&M).

Wonderful World of Love
Words and music by Jack Brooks and Sid Ramin.

Chesnick Music, Inc., 1963.
Introduced by Robert Goulet (Columbia).

The Wonderful World of the Young
Words and music by Sid Tepper and Roy C. Bennet.
MCA, Inc., 1962.
Best-selling record by Andy Williams (Columbia).

Wonderful You
Words by Jack Meskill and Max Rich, music by Pete Wendling.
Mills Music Inc., 1929.

Wondering
Words and music by Joe Werner.
Aberbach, Inc., 1952/Hill & Range Songs Inc., 1952.
Best-selling record by Webb Pierce (Decca).

Wondering
Words and music by Jack Schafer.
Egap Music, Inc., 1957.
Best-selling record by Patti Page (Mercury).

Wondering Where the Lions Are (Canadian)
Words and music by Bruce Cockburn.
Golden Mountain Music Inc., 1979.
Best-selling record by Bruce Cockburn (Millennium, 1980).

Wonderland
Words and music by Milan Williams.
Jobete Music Co., Inc., 1979/Old Fashion Music, 1979.
Best-selling record by The Commodores (Motown, 1979).

Wonderland by Night (West German)
German words by Lincoln Chase, music by Klauss-Gunter Neuman.
Screen Gems-EMI Music Inc., 1960.
Original German title, "Wunderland bei Nacht." Best-selling instrumen-
    tal recording by Bert Kaempfert (Decca); best-selling vocal recording
    by Anita Bryant (Carlton).

Won't Get Fooled Again (English)
Words and music by Peter Townshend.
ABKCO Music Inc., 1971/Suolubaf Music, 1971/Towser Tunes Inc.,
    1971.
Performed by The Who on *Who's Next* (MCA, 1971).

Woo-Hoo
Words and music by George Donald McGraw.

Skidmore Music Co., Inc., 1959/Wrights Music Co., 1959.
Best-selling record by The Rock-a-Teens (Roulette).

Woodchopper's Ball
Music by Woody Herman and Joe Bishop.
MCA, Inc., 1939.
Introduced by Woody Herman and his Orchestra.

Wooden Heart (West German)
English words and music by Fred Wise, Ben Weisman, Kay
    Twomey, and Berthold Kaempfert.
Gladys Music, 1960.
Music adapted from German folk song, "Muss I Denn zum Staedtele
    Hinaus." Introduced by Elvis Presley in *G.I. Blues* (film). Best-selling
    record by Elvis Presley (RCA Victor) and in 1961 by Joe Dowell
    (Smash).

Wooden Ships
Words and music by David Crosby, Stephen Stills, and Paul
    Kantner.
Guerrilla Music, 1969/Gold Hill Music Inc., 1969/Icebag Corp.,
    1969.
Introduced by Crosby, Stills and Nash in their album, *Crosby, Stills and
    Nash* (Atlantic).

The Wooden Soldier and the China Doll
Words by Charles Newman, music by Isham Jones.
Leo Feist Inc., 1932.

The Woodpecker Song (Italian)
English words by Harold Adamson, Italian words by C. Bruno-Di
    Lazzaro, music by Eldo di Lazzaro.
Edizioni EMI, Milan, Italy, 1939/Robbins Music Corp., 1940.
Original title, "Reginella Campagnola." Introduced on records in the
    United States by Will Glahe and his Musette Orchestra (Victor). Sung
    by Gene Autry and Mary Lee in *Ride Tenderfoot Ride* (film). Best-
    selling record by Kay Kyser and his College of Musical Knowledge
    (Columbia).

Woodstock
Words and music by Joni Mitchell.
Siquomb Publishing Corp., 1969.
Best-selling record by Crosby, Stills, Nash and Young (Atlantic); sung
    in 1970 by Joni Mitchell in her album, *Ladies of the Canyon* (Reprise);
    best-selling record in 1971 by Matthew's Southern Comfort (Decca).

Woody Woodpecker
Words and music by George Tibbles and Ramey Idress.

MCA, Inc., 1947.
Based on Walter Lantz film cartoon character, Woody Woodpecker, featured in *Wet Blanket Policy* (cartoon film, 1948). Best-selling records in 1948 by Kay Kyser and his Orchestra (Columbia) and Mel Blanc and The Sportsmen (Capitol). Nominated for an Academy Award, 1948.

The Wooing of the Violin
Words by Robert B. Smith, music by Victor Herbert.
Harms, Inc., 1920.
Introduced in *Oui Madame* (musical).

Wooly Bully
Words and music by Domingo Samudio.
Beckie Publishing Co., Inc., 1964.
Best-selling record in 1965 by Sam the Sham and The Pharoahs (MGM).

The Word (English)
Words and music by John Lennon and Paul McCartney.
Northern Songs, Ltd., England, 1965/Maclen Music Inc., 1965.
Introduced by The Beatles in their album, *Rubber Soul* (Capitol).

Word Games
Words and music by Bill Graham.
Show Biz Music, 1974.
Best-selling record by Billy Walker (RCA, 1975).

Words
Words and music by Johnny Horton.
Vogue Music, 1952, 1957, 1962.
Best-selling record in 1962 by Johnny Horton (Columbia), released posthumously.

Words
Words and music by Tommy Boyce and Bobby Hart.
Screen Gems-EMI Music Inc., 1966.
Best-selling record in 1967 by The Monkees (Colgems).

Words (English)
Words and music by Barry Gibb, Robin Gibb, and Maurice Gibb.
Gibb Brothers Music, 1968.
Best-selling record by The Bee Gees (Atco).

The Words Are in My Heart
Words by Al Dubin, music by Harry Warren.
M. Witmark & Sons, 1935.
Introduced by Dick Powell in *Gold Diggers of 1935* (film).

The Words I'm Gonna Have to Eat
Words and music by Liz Anderson.
Acuff-Rose Publications Inc., 1965.
Best-selling record in 1967 by Bill Phillips (Decca).

Words of Love
Words and music by John Phillips.
Best-selling record in 1966-67 by The Mamas and The Papas (Dunhill).

Words without Music
Words by Ira Gershwin, music by Vernon Duke.
Chappell & Co., Inc., 1936.
Introduced by Gertrude Niesen in *Ziegfeld Follies of 1936* (revue).

Work Song
Words by Oscar Jr. Brown, music by Nat Adderley.
Upam Music Co., 1960.
Adapted from jazz instrumental. Vocal version introduced by Oscar
    Brown, Jr. (Columbia). Best-selling record in 1966 by Herb Alpert and
    The Tijuana Brass (A&M).

The Work Song
Words and music by Catherine McGarrigle Wainwright.
Garden Court Music Co., 1973.
Performed by Maria Muldaur on *Maria Muldaur* (Warner Brothers,
    1973).

Work with Me Annie
Words and music by Henry "Hank" Ballard.
Fort Knox Music Co., 1954.
Best-selling record by The Midnighters (Federal).

Workin' at the Car Wash Blues
Words and music by Jim Croce.
MCA Music, 1974/Blendingwell Music, 1974.
Best-selling record by Jim Croce (ABC, 1974).

Workin' My Way Back to You
Words and music by Sandy Linzer and Denny Randell.
Seasons Four Music Corp., 1965/Screen Gems-EMI Music Inc.,
    1965.
Best-selling record in 1966 by The Four Seasons (Philips).

Workin' on a Groovy Thing
Words and music by Neil Sedaka and Roger Atkins.
Screen Gems-EMI Music Inc., 1968.
Best-selling record in 1969 by The 5th Dimension (Soul City).

Working Class Hero (English)
Words and music by John Lennon.
Maclen Music Inc., 1970.
Performed by John Lennon on *Plastic Ono Band* (Apple, 1970). Revived
  in 1979 by Maryanne Faithfull on *Broken English* (Island).

Working for the Man
Words and music by Roy Orbison.
Acuff-Rose Publications Inc., 1962.
Best-selling record by Roy Orbison (Monument).

Working in the Coal Mine
Words and music by Allen Toussaint.
Marsaint Music Inc., 1966.
Best-selling record by Lee Dorsey (Amy).

Working' Man Blues
Words and music by Merle Haggard.
Blue Book Music, 1969.
Best-selling record by Merle Haggard and The Strangers (Capitol).

World
Words and music by James Brown.
Dynatone Publishing Co., 1969.
Best-selling record by James Brown (King).

A World I Can't Live In
Words and music by Roger Miller.
Tree Publishing Co., Inc., 1960.
Introduced by Jaye P. Morgan (MGM).

The World I Used To Know
Words and music by Rod McKuen.
In Music Co., 1963, 1964.
Introduced by Rod McKuen. Best-selling record in 1964 by Jimmie
  Rodgers (Dot).

The World Is a Circle
Words by Hal David, music by Burt Bacharach.
Colgems-EMI Music Inc., 1972/New Hidden Valley Music Co.,
  1972/JC Music Co., 1972.
Performed by the voice of Shawn Phillips in *Lost Horizon* (film, 1973).

The World Is a Ghetto
Words and music by Sylvester Allen, Harold R. Brown, Morris
  Dickerson, Leroy "Lonnie" Jordan, Charles Miller, Lee Oscar
  Levitin, and Howard Scott.

Far Out Music, 1972.
Best-selling record by War (United Artists, 1973).

The World Is in My Arms
Words by E. Y. Harburg, music by Burton Lane.
Chappell & Co., Inc., 1940.
Introduced by Jack Whiting, Eunice Healey, The Ranchettes, The Tanner Sisters, The Radio Aces, and chorus in *Hold On to Your Hats* (musical).

The World Is Mine (Tonight) (English)
Words by Holt Marvell (pseudonym for Eric Maschwitz), music by George Posford.
Keith Prowse Music Publishing Co., Ltd., London, England/Sam Fox Publishing Co., Inc., 1935.
Introduced by Nino Martini in *The Gay Desperado* (film, 1936).

The World Is Round
Words and music by Tony Senn, Tommy Stough, and Henry Paul Johnson.
Acuff-Rose Publications Inc., 1966.
Best-selling record by Roy Drusky (Mercury).

World of Fantasy
Words and music by Clarence N. Burke and Gregory K. Fowler.
Warner-Tamerlane Publishing Corp., 1966.
Best-selling record by The Five Stairsteps and Cubie (Windy C).

A World of Love, also known as **Caesar and Cleopatra Theme**
Words by Sid Wayne, music by Alex North.
Robbins Music Corp., 1963.
Adapted from a theme from *Cleopatra* (film).

World of Make Believe
Words and music by Pete McCord, Marion Carpenter, and Pee Wee Maddux.
Gulf Stream Music, 1974/Singing River Publishing Co., Inc., 1974.
Best-selling record by Bill Anderson (Decca, 1974).

A World of Our Own (English)
Words and music by Tom Springfield.
Chappell & Co., Inc., 1965.
Best-selling records by The Seekers (Capitol) and in 1968 by Sonny James (Capitol).

The World Outside (English)
Words by Carl Sigman, music by Richard Addinsell.
Keith Prowse Music Publishing Co., Ltd., London, England, 1958/

Chappell & Co., Inc., 1958.
Adapted from the theme from Addinsell's "Warsaw Concerto." Introduced by The Four Aces (Decca).

The World Owes Me a Living
Words by Larry Morey, music by Leigh Harline.
Bourne Co., 1934.
From *The Grasshopper and the Ant* (Silly Symphony cartoon film).

A World So Full of Love
Words and music by Roger Miller and Faron Young.
Tree Publishing Co., Inc., 1960.
Introduced by Faron Young (Capitol).

World That We Dreamed Of
Words and music by Joe McDonald.
McDonald Music Co., 1970.
Introduced by Country Joe McDonald in *Gas! or It Became Necessary to Destroy the World* (film, 1970).

The World We Knew (Over and Over) (West German)
English words by Carl Sigman, music by Bert Kaempfert and Herbert Rehbein.
Screen Gems-EMI Music Inc., 1967.
Best-selling record by Frank Sinatra (Reprise).

World Weary (English)
Words and music by Noel Coward.
Chappell & Co., Ltd., London, England, 1928/Chappell & Co., Inc., 1928.
Introduced by Beatrice Lillie in the New York production of *This Year of Grace* (revue).

World without Love (English)
Words and music by John Lennon and Paul McCartney.
Northern Songs, Ltd., England, 1964/Maclen Music Inc., 1964.
Best-selling record by Peter and Gordon (Capitol) and Bobby Rydell (Cameo).

Worlds Apart
Words by Sheldon Harnick, music by Jerry Bock.
The Times Square Music Publications Co., 1963.
From *Man in the Moon* (Bil and Cora Baird marionette play with music).

Worried, see **I'm Worried over You.**

Worried and Lonesome Blues
Music by James P. Johnson.
Perry Bradford Music Publishing Co., 1923.
Jazz instrumental. First recording by James P. Johnson (Columbia).

Worried Guy
Words and music by Jack Reardon and Paul Evans.
B. F. Wood Music Co., Inc., 1964.
Best-selling record by Johnny Tillotson (MGM).

Worried Life Blues
Words and music by Maceo Merriweather.
Duchess Music Corp., 1941, 1960/Wabash Music Co.
Introduced by Big Maceo (Merriweather) (Bluebird).

A Worried Man
Words and music by Dave Guard and Tom Glazer.
Unichappell Music Inc., 1959.
Adapted from a traditional American folk song. Part of the standard repertoire of The Carter Family, country and western artists. Best-selling record by The Kingston Trio (Capitol).

Worried Man Blues
Words and music by A. P. Carter.
Peer International Corp., 1935.
Introduced by The Carter Family.

Worried Mind
Words and music by Jimmie Davis and Ted Daffan.
Peer International Corp., 1941.
Best-selling record by Jimmie Davis (Decca).

Worry, Worry, Worry
Words and music by Ramez Idriss and George Tibbles.
Colgems-EMI Music Inc., 1948.
Best-selling record by Kay Kyser and his Orchestra (Columbia).

The Worst That Could Happen
Words and music by Jim Webb.
The EMP Co., 1967.
Best-selling record in 1969 by Brooklyn Bridge (Buddah).

Would I Love You (Love You, Love You)
Words by Bob Russell, music by Harold Spina.
Spina Music, 1951/Harrison Music Corp., 1951.
Best-selling record by Patti Page (Mercury).

Would Ya?
Words and music by Bob Fellows.
Atlantic Music Corp., 1949.
Best-selling record by Johnny Mercer (Capitol).

Would You
Words by Arthur Freed, music by Nacio Herb Brown.
Robbins Music Corp., 1936.
Introduced by Jeanette MacDonald in *San Francisco* (film). Sung by
  Debbie Reynolds in *Singin' in the Rain* (film, 1952).

Would You
Words by Johnny Burke, music by James Van Heusen.
Bourne Co., 1945/Music Sales Corp., 1945.
Introduced by Bing Crosby in *Road to Utopia* (film).

Would You Believe Me?
Words by Charles Tobias, music by M. K. Jerome.
Remick Music Corp., 1947.
Introduced by Trudy Erwin in *Love and Learn* (film).

Would You Hold It against Me?
Words and music by Dottie West and Bill West.
Tree Publishing Co., Inc., 1965.
Best-selling record in 1966 by Dottie West (RCA Victor).

Would You Lay with Me (in a Field of Stone)
Words and music by David Allen Coe.
Window Music Publishing Inc., 1974/Captive Music, 1974.
Best-selling record by Tanya Tucker (Columbia, 1974).

**Would You Like To Take a Walk? (Sump'n Good'll Come from
  That)**
Words by Mort Dixon and Billy Rose, music by Harry Warren.
Remick Music Corp., 1930.
Introduced by Hannah Williams and Hal Thompson in *Sweet and Low*
  (revue).

Would You Take Another Chance on Me
Words and music by Jerry Foster and Bill Rice.
T. B. Harms Co., 1971/Jack & Bill Music Co., 1971.
Best-selling record by Jerry Lee Lewis (Mercury, 1971).

Wouldja for a Big Red Apple, see **Red Apple.**

Wouldn't It Be Loverly?
Words by Alan Jay Lerner, music by Frederick Loewe.

Chappell & Co., Inc., 1956.
Introduced by Julie Andrews in *My Fair Lady* (musical).

Wouldn't It Be Nice?
Words by Tony Asher, words and music by Brian Wilson.
Irving Music Inc., 1966.
Best-selling record by The Beach Boys (Capitol).

A Wound Time Can't Erase
Words and music by William D. Johnson.
Harbor Hills Music, 1957.
Best-selling record in 1962 by Stonewall Jackson (Columbia).

W.P.A. Blues
Words and music by Lester Melrose and Casey Bill
   (pseudonym for William Weldon).
MCA, Inc., 1936.
Introduced by Casey Bill (pseudonym for William Weldon).

Wrap Me in Your Warm and Tender Love, see **Warm and Tender
   Love.**

Wrap Your Arms Around Me
Words and music by Harry Casey and Richard Finch.
Sherlyn Publishing Co., Inc., 1977/Harrick Music Inc., 1977.
Best-selling record by K.C. & the Sunshine Band (TK, 1977).

**Wrap Your Troubles in Dreams (and Dream Your Troubles
   Away)**
Words by Ted Koehler and Billy Moll, music by Harry Barris.
Shapiro, Bernstein & Co., Inc., 1931.
Introduced by Bing Crosby.

Wrapped Up in a Dream
Words and music by William Best and Irving Berman.
MCA, Inc., 1948.
Best-selling record by Do, Ray, and Me (Commodore).

Wrappin' It Up (The Lindy Glide)
Music by Fletcher Henderson.
American Academy of Music, Inc., 1934.
Introduced by Fletcher Henderson and his Orchestra. Best-selling record
   in 1938 by Benny Goodman and his Orchestra.

The Wreck of the Edmund Fitzgerald (Canadian)
Words and music by Gordon Lightfoot.
Moose Music Ltd., 1976.
Best-selling record by Gordon Lightfoot (Reprise, 1976). Based on an

actual event. Nominated for a National Academy of Recording Arts and Sciences Award, Song of the Year, 1976.

The Wreck of the "Julie Plante"
Words by William Henry Drummond, music by Geoffrey O'Hara.
Oliver Ditson Co., 1920.
Based on a traditional French-Canadian song.

The Wreck of the Old 97
Words by, music by Henry C. Work.
Unpublished. A ballad about a 1903 train wreck in Danville, Virginia. Based on the nineteenth century song, "The Ship That Never Returned," by Henry C. Work. Best-selling record by Vernon Dalhart (Victor). Another version, published in 1924 by Shapiro, Bernstein & Co., Inc., had lyrics by Charles W. Noell and Fred J. Lewey and music adapted by Henry Whitter and the alternate title, "The Wreck on the Southern Old 97."

The Wreck of the Shenandoah
Words and music by Maggie Andrews (pseudonym for Carson Robison).
Shapiro, Bernstein & Co., Inc., 1925.
Introduced by Carson Robison. Inspired by the wreck of a United States Army dirigible in Ohio.

Wreck on the Highway
Words and music by Dorsey Dixon.
Acuff-Rose Publications Inc., 1946.
Best-selling record in 1946 by Roy Acuff (Okeh). Revived in 1961 with best-selling record by Wilma Lee and Stoney Cooper (Hickery).

Wringin' and Twistin'
Words by Jo Trent, music by Frank Trumbauer and Thomas "Fats" Waller.
Robbins Music Corp., 1927/World Music, Inc., 1927.
Jazz instrumental. First recording by Tram, Bix, and Lang (Frankie Trumbauer, Bix Beiderbecke, and Eddie Lang) (Okeh).

Wringle Wrangle
Words and music by Stan Jones.
Walt Disney Music Co., 1956.
Introduced by Fess Parker in *Westward Ho the Wagons!* (film).

Write Me a Letter
Words and music by Howard Biggs.
Bee Music Corp., 1947.
Best-selling record by The Ravens (National).

Write Me Sweetheart
Words and music by Roy Acuff.
Acuff-Rose Publications Inc., 1943.
Best-selling record by Roy Acuff (Okeh).

Writing on the Wall
Words and music by Sandy Baron, Mark Barkan, and George Eddy
(pseudonym for George Paxton).
Paxwin Music Corp., 1961.
Best-selling record by Adam Wade (Co-ed).

Written on the Wind
Words by Sammy Cahn, music by Victor Young.
Northern Music Corp., 1956.
Introduced by The Four Aces, behind the opening titles, on the sound-
track of *Written on the Wind* (film). Nominated for an Academy
Award, 1956.

Wrong for Each Other
Words and music by Doc Pomus and Mort Shuman.
S. J. W. Music, Inc., 1964.
Best-selling record by Andy Williams (Columbia).

Wrong Note Rag
Words by Betty Comden and Adolph Green, music by Leonard
Bernstein.
Chappell & Co., Inc., 1953/Amberson Enterprises Inc., 1953/G.
Schirmer Inc., 1953.
Introduced by Rosalind Russell and Edith Adams in *Wonderful Town*
(musical).

Wrong Side of the Road
Words and music by Tom Waits.
Fifth Floor Music Inc., 1978.
Introduced by Tom Waits on *Blue Valentine* (Asylum, 1978).

Wunderbar
Words and music by Cole Porter.
Chappell & Co., Inc., 1948.
Introduced by Alfred Drake and Patricia Morison in *Kiss Me Kate*
(musical). Sung by Kathryn Grayson and Howard Keel in film version
(1953).

The Wurlitzer Prize (I Don't Want to Get over You)
Words and music by Bobby Emmons and Chips Moman.
Baby Chick Music Inc., 1977.
Best-selling record by Waylon Jennings (RCA, 1977).

Wuthering Heights (English)
Words and music by Kate Bush.
EMI Music Publishing, Ltd., London, England, 1977/Glenwood
  Music Corp., 1977.
Best-selling record by Kate Bush (EMI-America, 1978).

Wynken, Blynken and Nod
Words by Eugene Field, music by Leigh Harline.
G. Schirmer Inc., 1938.
Introduced in *Wynken, Blynken and Nod* (*Silly Symphony* cartoon
  film).

X

X-Ray Blues
Music by Ray Charles.
Unichappell Music Inc., 1962.
Introduced by Ray Charles and Milt Jackson (Atlantic).

Y

Ya Got Me
Words by Betty Comden and Adolph Green, music by Leonard
Bernstein.
M. Witmark & Sons, 1945.
Introduced by Nancy Walker, Betty Comden, Adolph Green, and Cris
Alexander in *On the Town* (musical, 1944).

Ya Wanna Buy a Bunny?
Words and music by Carl Hoefle and Del Porter.
Tune Towne Tunes, Inc., 1949.
Introduced by Spike Jones and his City Slickers (Victor).

Ya Ya
Words and music by Lee Dorsey, Clarence Lewis, and Morgan
Robinson.
Frost Music Corp., 1961.
Best-selling record by Lee Dorsey (Fury).

Yah-ta-ta, Yah-ta-ta (Talk, Talk, Talk)
Words by Johnny Burke, music by Jimmy Van Heusen.
Bourne Co., 1945/Music Sales Corp., 1945.
Best-selling record by Bing Crosby and Judy Garland (Decca).

Yakety Axe, see **Yakety Sax.**

Yakety Sax, also known as **Yakety Axe**
Words and music by Randy Randolph and James Rich.
Tree Publishing Co., Inc., 1963.
Introduced, as "Yakety Sax," by Boots Randolph (Monument). Best-
selling record, as "Yakety Axe," in 1965 by Chet Atkins (RCA Victor).

Yakety Yak
Words and music by Jerry Leiber and Mike Stoller.
Tiger Music, Inc., 1958.
Best-selling record by The Coasters (Atco).

Y'All Come, see **You All Come.**

Y'All Come Back Saloon
Words and music by Sharon Vaughan.
Jack & Bill Music Co., 1977.
Best-selling record by The Oak Ridge Boys (ABC/DOT, 1977).

Yaller Yaller Gold
Words by Tom Blackburn, music by George Bruns.
Wonderland Music Co., Inc., 1955.
Introduced by Fess Parker in *Davy Crockett and Mike Fink* (television show).

The Yam
Words and music by Irving Berlin.
Irving Berlin Music Corp., 1938.
Introduced by Fred Astaire and Ginger Rogers in *Carefree* (film).

Yancey Special
Words by Andy Razaf, music by Meade "Lux" Lewis.
Shapiro, Bernstein & Co., Inc., 1938.
Introduced by pianist Meade "Lux" Lewis. Dedicated to Jimmy Yancey, boogie-woogie pianist and composer. Featured by Bob Crosby and his Orchestra, with Bob Zurke on piano.

Yank Me, Crank Me
Words and music by Ted Nugent.
Magicland Music, 1978.
Best-selling record by Ted Nugent (Epic, 1978).

The Yankee Doodle Blues
Words by Irving Caesar and B. G. De Sylva, music by George Gershwin.
New World Music Corp., 1922/Irving Caesar Music Corp., 1922.
Interpolated in *Spice of 1922* (revue). Interpolated theme of John Howard Lawson's *Processional* (play, 1925). Performed by pianist Hazel Scott in *Rhapsody in Blue* (film, 1945); and sung by June Haver and Gloria De Haven in *I'll Get By* (film, 1950).

Yankee Rose
Words by Sidney Holden, music by Abe Frankl.
Bourne Co., 1926.

The Yard Went On Forever
Words and music by Jim Webb.
Canopy Music Inc., 1968.
Best-selling record by Richard Harris (Dunhill).

Yardbird Suite
Music by Charlie Parker.
Atlantic Music Corp., 1946.
First recording by Charlie Parker, with Miles Davis, Dodo Marmarosa, Arv Garrison, Vic McMillan, and Roy Porter (Dial).

Yassu
Words by Ned Washington, music by Dimitri Tiomkin.
Columbia Pictures Publications, 1961.
Based on traditional Greek song. Wedding song from *The Guns of Navarone* (film).

Year after Year
Words and music by Bart Howard.
Almanac Music, Inc., 1955.
Introduced by Mabel Mercer.

A Year from Today
Words and music by Al Jolson, Ballard Macdonald, and Dave Dreyer.
Bourne Co., 1929.
Featured by Norma Talmadge in *New York Nights* (film).

Year of the Cat (English)
Words and music by Peter Wood and Al Stewart.
Dick James Music Inc., 1977/Unichappell Music Inc., 1977.
Best-selling record by Al Stewart (Janus, 1977).

The Year That Clayton Delaney Died
Words and music by Tom T. Hall.
Unichappell Music Inc., 1971/New Keys Music Inc., 1971.
Best-selling record by Tom T. Hall (Mercury, 1971).

Yearning (Just for You)
Words and music by Benny Davis and Joe Burke.
Bourne Co., 1925/World Music, Inc., 1925.
Best-selling record by Gene Austin (Victor).

Yearning for Love
Words by Mitchell Parish and Irving Mills, music by Edward Kennedy "Duke" Ellington.
Mills Music Inc., 1936/Everbright Music Co., 1936.
Introduced by Duke Ellington and his Orchestra.

Years
Words and music by Kye Fleming and Dennis Morgan.
Hall-Clement Publications, 1979.

Best-selling records by Barbara Mandrell (ABC, 1979) and Wayne Newton (Aries, 1980).

Yeh Yeh
Words and music by Rodgers Grant, Pat Patrick, and Jon
  Hendricks.
Mongo Music, 1963.
Introduced instrumentally by Mongo Santamaria (Battle). Best-selling
  record in England in 1964 by Georgie Fame with The Blue Flames
  (Imperial).

Yeh! Yeh!
Words by Jon Hendricks, music by Rodgers Grant and Pat Patrick.
Mongo Music, 1965.
Best-selling record by Georgie Fame (Imperial).

Yellow Balloon
Words by Dick St. John (pseudonym for Richard Frank Gosting),
  words and music by Gary Zekley and Jay Lee.
Colgems-EMI Music Inc., 1967.
Best-selling record by The Yellow Balloon (Canterbury).

The Yellow Bandana
Words and music by Al Gorgoni, Steve Karliski, and Larry Kolber.
Screen Gems-EMI Music Inc., 1960, 1963.
Best-selling record in 1963 by Faron Young (Mercury).

Yellow Bird
Words and music by Norman Luboff, Marilyn Keith, and Alan
  Bergman.
Frank Music Co., 1957.
Adapted from a West Indian folk song. Introduced by The Norman
  Luboff Choir. Best-selling record, instrumental, in 1961 by Arthur
  Lyman (Hi-Fi).

Yellow River
Words and music by Jeff Christie.
Unichappell Music Inc., 1970.
Best-selling record by Christie (Epic, 1970).

The Yellow Rose of Texas
Words and music by Don George.
Planetary Music Publishing Corp., 1955.
From an anonymous minstrel song of the 1860's. First revived by conductor Richard Bales in his album, *The Confederacy* (Columbia). Best-selling records by Mitch Miller and his Orchestra and Chorus (Columbia) and Johnny Desmond (Coral).

Yellow Roses
Words and music by Kenny Devine and Sam Nichols.
Travis Music Co., Inc., 1953.
Best-selling record in 1955 by Hank Snow (RCA Victor).

Yellow Roses on Her Gown
Words and music by Michael Moore.
MCA Music, 1976.
Best-selling record by Johnny Mathis (Columbia, 1976).

Yellow Submarine (English)
Words and music by John Lennon and Paul McCartney.
Northern Songs, Ltd., England, 1966/Maclen Music Inc., 1966.
Best-selling record by The Beatles (Capitol); sung by The Beatles in
  Yellow Submarine (film, 1968).

Yer Blues (English)
Words and music by John Lennon and Paul McCartney.
Northern Songs, Ltd., England, 1968/Maclen Music Inc., 1968.
Introduced by The Beatles in their album, *The Beatles* (Apple).

Yes, I Know Why
Words and music by Webb Pierce.
Cedarwood Publishing Co., Inc., 1956.
Best-selling record by Webb Pierce (Decca).

Yes, I'm Ready
Words and music by Barbara Mason.
Dandelion Music Co., 1965/Jamie Music Publishing Co., 1965.
Best-selling record by Barbara Mason (Arctic). Revived in 1979 by Teri
  DeSario and K.C. (Casablanca).

Yes Indeed! (A Jive Spiritual)
Words and music by Sy Oliver.
Embassy Music Corp., 1941.
Introduced by Tommy Dorsey and his Orchestra, vocal by Sy Oliver and
  Jo Stafford (Victor).

Yes It Is (English)
Words and music by John Lennon and Paul McCartney.
Northern Songs, Ltd., England, 1965/Maclen Music Inc., 1965.
Best-selling record by The Beatles (Capitol).

Yes, Mr. Peters
Words and music by Steve Karliski and Larry Kolber.
Screen Gems-EMI Music Inc., 1964.
Best-selling record in 1965 by Roy Drusky and Priscilla Mitchell (Mercury).

Yes, My Darling Daughter
Words and music by Jack Lawrence.
MPL Communications Inc., 1939.
Adapted from Ukrainian folk song. Introduced by Gracie Barrie in *Crazy with the Heat* (revue, 1941). Best-selling record by Dinah Shore (Bluebird).

Yes, My Heart
Words and music by Bob Merrill.
Robbins Music Corp., 1961.
Introduced by Anna Maria Alberghetti and Roustabouts in *Carnival!* (musical).

Yes Sir, That's My Baby
Words by Gus Kahn, music by Walter Donaldson.
Bourne Co., 1925/Donaldson Publishing Co., 1925.
Introduced by Eddie Cantor. Best-selling record by Gene Austin (Victor). Sung by Donald O'Connor, Gloria De Haven, Charles Coburn, Barbara Brown, and Joshua Shelley in *Yes Sir, That's My Baby* (film, 1949); by Doris Day, Danny Thomas, and two children in *I'll See You in My Dreams* (film, 1951); and by the voice of Cantor, dubbed for Keefe Brasselle, in *The Eddie Cantor Story* (film, 1953).

Yes Tonight, Josephine
Words and music by Roy Irwin.
Screen Gems-EMI Music Inc., 1957.
Best-selling record by Johnnie Ray (Columbia).

Yes We Can Can
Words and music by Allan Toussaint.
Marsaint Music Inc., 1970.
Best-selling record by The Pointer Sisters (Blue Thumb, 1973).

Yes! We Have No Bananas
Words and music by Frank Silver and Irving Cohn.
Shapiro, Bernstein & Co., Inc., 1923.
Introduced by Frank Silver's Music Masters. Interpolated by Eddie Cantor in *Make It Snappy* (revue, 1922), after the New York opening. Sung by the Pied Pipers in *Luxury Liner* (film, 1948); and by the voice of Cantor on the soundtrack of *The Eddie Cantor Story* (film, 1954).

Yes, Yes, Yes
Words and music by Michael Hazlewood.
April Music Inc., 1975.
Best-selling record by Bill Cosby (Capitol, 1976).

Yester Love
Words and music by William Robinson and Alfred Cleveland.

Jobete Music Co., Inc., 1968.
Best-selling record by Smokey Robinson and The Miracles (Tamla).

Yester-me Yester-you Yesterday
Words by Ronald Miller, music by Bryan Wells.
Stein & Van Stock, Inc., 1966.
Best-selling record in 1969 by Stevie Wonder (Tamla).

Yesterday (English)
Words and music by John Lennon and Paul McCartney.
Northern Songs, Ltd., England, 1965/Maclen Music Inc., 1965.
Best-selling records by The Beatles (Capitol) and in 1967 by Ray Charles (ABC).

Yesterday and You, see **Armen's Theme.**

Yesterday Once More
Words and music by John Bettis and Richard Carpenter.
Almo Music Corp., 1973/Hammer & Nails Music, 1973/Sweet Harmony Music Inc., 1973.
Best-selling record by The Carpenters (A&M, 1973).

Yesterday When I Was Young (French)
English words by Herbert Kretzmer, French words and music by Charles Aznavour.
Editions Musicales Charles Aznavour, Paris, France/TRO-Hampshire House Publishing Corp., 1966.
Original French title, "Hier encore." Introduced in France by Charles Aznavour. Best-selling record of English version in 1969 by Roy Clark (Dot).

Yesterdays
Words by Otto Harbach, music by Jerome Kern.
T. B. Harms Co., 1933.
Introduced by Fay Templeton in *Roberta* (musical).

Yesterday's Dreams
Words and music by Pamela Sawyer, Ivy Hunter, Vernon Bullock, and Jack Goga.
Jobete Music Co., Inc., 1968.
Best-selling record by The Four Tops (Motown).

Yesterday's Gardenias
Words and music by Dick Robertson, Nelson Cogane, and Sammy Mysels.
Morley Music Co., Inc., 1942.
Best-selling record by Glenn Miller and his Orchestra, vocal by Ray Eberle and The Modernaires (Victor).

Yesterday's Girl
Words and music by Hank Thompson and Billy Gray.
Brazos Valley Music, Inc., 1952.
Best-selling record in 1953 by Hank Thompson (Capitol).

Yesterday's Hero (Australian)
Words and music by Harry Vanda and George Young.
Best-selling records by John Paul Young (Ariola America, 1976) and
   The Bay City Rollers (Arista, 1976).

Yesterday's Memories
Words and music by Hank Cochran.
Tree Publishing Co., Inc., 1962.
Best-selling record by Eddy Arnold (RCA Victor).

Yesterday's Papers (English)
Words and music by Mick Jagger and Keith Richard.
ABKCO Music Inc., 1967.
Introduced by The Rolling Stones in their album, *Between the Buttons*
   (London).

Yesterday's Roses
Words and music by Gene Autry and Fred Rose.
Western Music Publishing Co., 1942/Milene Music Co., 1942.
Best-selling record by Gene Autry (Columbia).

Yesterday's Tears
Words and music by Ernest Tubb.
Unichappell Music Inc., 1943.
Best-selling record by Ernest Tubb (Decca).

Yesterthoughts
Words by Stanley Adams, music by Victor Herbert.
M. Witmark & Sons, 1940.
Adaptation of Herbert's instrumental composition of same name, origi-
   nally published in 1900. Best-selling record by Glenn Miller and his
   Orchestra, vocal by Ray Eberle (Bluebird).

Yet...I Know (French)
English words by Don Raye, French words by Charles Aznavour,
   music by Georges Garvarentz.
Les Editions French Music, Paris, France, 1963, 1964/Editions
   Musicales Charles Aznavour, Paris, France, 1963, 1964/MCA
   Music, 1963.
Original French title, "Et Pourtant." Introduced by Charles Aznavour.
   Introduced in English by Steve Lawrence (Columbia).

A Yiddishe Momme, see **My Yiddishe Momme.**

Y.M.C.A. (French-American)
English words and music by Henri Belolo, Jacques Morali, and
 Victor Willis.
Can't Stop Music, 1978.
Best-selling record by Village People (Casablanca, 1979).

Yo San
Words by May Tully, music by Jean Hazard.
R. L. Huntzinger, Inc., 1920.

Yo Te Amo Means I Love You
Words by Alfred Bryan, music by Richard A. Whiting.
Famous Music Co., 1928.
Introduced by Lupe Velez in *The Wolf Song* (film, 1929).

Yo Yo
Words and music by Joe South.
Lowery Music Co., Inc., 1966.
Best-selling record by The Osmonds (MGM, 1971).

The Yodel Blues
Words by Johnny Mercer, music by Robert Emmett Dolan.
Chappell & Co., Inc., 1949.
Introduced in *Texas, Li'l Darlin'* (musical).

Yogi
Words and music by Lou Stallman, Sid Jacobson, and Charles
 Koppelman.
Saxon Music Corp., 1960.
Best-selling record by Bill Black (Hi) and Ivy Three (Shell).

Yolanda
Words by Arthur Freed, music by Harry Warren.
Miller Music Corp., 1945.
Introduced by Fred Astaire in *Yolanda and the Thief* (film).

Yonder Comes a Sucker
Words and music by Jim Reeves.
Tree Publishing Co., Inc., 1955.
Best-selling record by Jim Reeves (RCA Victor).

Yoo-Hoo
Words by B. G. De Sylva, music by Al Jolson.
Remick Music Corp., 1921.
Interpolated by Al Jolson in *Bombo* (musical).

You
Words by Al Wohlman, music by Bud Cooper.
Bourne Co., 1923.

You
Words by Harold Adamson, music by Walter Donaldson.
Leo Feist Inc., 1936.
Introduced by The Ziegfeld Brides and Grooms in *The Great Ziegfeld*
(film).

You
Words by Sunny Skylar, music by Morton Frank.
Republic Music Corp., 1952.
Adapted from "Musetta's Waltz" from Puccini's *La Boheme.* Best-selling
record by Sammy Kaye and his Orchestra (Columbia).

You
Words and music by Ivy Hunter, Jack Goga, and Jeffrey Bowen.
Jobete Music Co., Inc., 1968.
Best-selling record by Marvin Gaye (Tamla).

You (English)
Words and music by George Harrison.
Zero Productions, 1975.
Best-selling record by George Harrison (Apple, 1975).

You
Words and music by Tom Snow.
Beechwood Music Corp., 1975/Snow Music, 1975.
Best-selling record by Rita Coolidge (A & M, 1978).

You Ain't Goin' Nowhere
Words and music by Bob Dylan.
Dwarf Music Co., Inc., 1967.
Introduced in 1968 by The Byrds (Columbia); sung in 1969 by Joan Baez
in her album, *Any Day Now* (Vanguard) and in 1972 by Bob Dylan
in his album, *Bob Dylan's Greatest Hits, Vol. II* (Columbia).

You Ain't Heard Nothing Yet
Words by Al Jolson and Gus Kahn, music by B. G. De Sylva.
Remick Music Corp., 1929.
Introduced by Al Jolson. Copyright in dispute August, 1983.

You Ain't Seen Nothin' Yet (Canadian)
Words and music by Randy Bachman.
Top Soil Music, 1974.
Best-selling record by Bachman-Turner Overdrive (Mercury, 1974).

You Ain't Woman Enough
Words and music by Loretta Lynn.
Sure Fire Music Co., Inc., 1965.
Best-selling record in 1966 by Loretta Lynn (Decca).

You All Come, also known as **Y'All Come**
Words and music by Arlie Duff.
Fort Knox Music Co., 1953.
Best-selling record by Arlie Duff (Starday).

You Alone (Solo Tu)
Words by Al Stillman, music by Robert Allen.
Roncom Music Co., 1953.
Best-selling record by Perry Como (RCA Victor).

You Always Come Back (to Hurting Me)
Words and music by Tom T. Hall and Johnny Rodriguez.
Hallnote Music, 1973.
Best-selling record by Johnny Rodriguez (Mercury, 1973).

You Always Hurt the One You Love
Words and music by Allan Roberts and Doris Fisher.
Doris Fisher Music Corp., 1944/Allan Roberts Music Co., 1944.
Best-selling record by The Mills Brothers (Decca).

You and I
Words and music by Meredith Willson.
Bourne Co., 1941.
Theme of *Maxwell House Coffee-Time* (radio program). Best-selling
    record by Glenn Miller and his Orchestra, vocal by Ray Eberle (Blue-
    bird).

You and I
Words by Arthur Freed, music by Nacio Herb Brown.
Leo Feist Inc., 1945.
Introduced by Leon Ames (with dubbed voice of Arthur Freed) and
    Mary Astor in *Meet Me in St. Louis* (film).

You and I
Words and music by James Johnson, Jr.
Jobete Music Co., Inc., 1978.
Best-selling record by Rick James (Gordy, 1978).

You and I Know
Words by Albert Stillman and Laurence Stallings, music by Arthur
    Schwartz.
Robbins Music Corp., 1937.
Introduced by Anne Booth and Ronald Graham in *Virginia* (musical).

You and Me
Words and music by Johnny Wright, Jack Anglin, and Jim Anglin.
Unichappell Music Inc., 1955.
Best-selling record in 1956 by Red Foley and Kitty Wells (Decca).

You and Me
Words and music by George Richey and Billy Sherrill.
Algee Music Corp., 1976.
Best-selling record by Tammy Wynette (Epic, 1976).

You and Me
Words and music by Alice Cooper and Dick Wagner.
Early Frost Music Corp., 1977/Ezra Music Corp., 1977.
Best-selling record by Alice Cooper (Warner Brother, 1977).

You and Me Against the World
Words and music by Kenny Ascher and Paul Williams.
Almo Music Corp., 1974.
Best-selling record by Helen Reddy (Capitol, 1974). Nominated for a
    National Academy of Recording Arts and Sciences Award, Song of
    the Year, 1974.

You and Me and Rain on the Roof, see **Rain on the Roof.**

You and the Night and the Music
Words by Howard Dietz, music by Arthur Schwartz.
Harms, Inc., 1934.
Introduced on radio by Conrad Thibault. Sung by Libby Holman and
    Georges Metaxa in *Revenge with Music* (musical).

You and the Waltz and I
Words by Paul Francis Webster, music by Walter Jurmann.
Leo Feist Inc., 1942.
Introduced by Kathryn Grayson in *Seven Sweethearts* (film).

You and Your Beautiful Eyes
Words by Mack David, music by Jerry Livingston.
Hallmark Music Co., 1950/T. B. Harms Co., 1950.
Introduced by Dean Martin in *At War with the Army* (film).

You Are a Song
Words and music by James Weatherly.
Keca Music Inc., 1974.
Best-selling record by Batdorf & Rodney (Arista, 1975).

You Are Beautiful
Words by Oscar Hammerstein, II, music by Richard Rodgers.
Williamson Music Inc., 1958.

Introduced by Ed Kenny and Juanita Hall in *Flower Drum Song* (musical).

You Are Everything
Words and music by Thom Bell and Linda Creed.
Assorted Music, 1971/Bell Boy Music, 1971.
Best-selling record by The Stylistics (Avco, 1972).

You Are Love
Words by Oscar Hammerstein II, music by Jerome Kern.
T. B. Harms Co., 1927.
Introduced by Norma Terris and Howard Marsh in *Show Boat* (musical). Sung by Allan Jones and Irene Dunne in the second film version, 1936; and by Kathryn Grayson and Howard Keel in the third film version, 1951.

You Are Mine Evermore (Austrian)
English words by Harry B. Smith, German words by Julius Brammer and Alfred Gruenwald, music by Emmerich Kalman.
Harms, Inc., 1927.
Introduced in *The Circus Princess* (operetta).

You Are My Destiny
Words and music by Paul Anka.
Management Agency & Music Publishing, 1958/Duchess Music Corp., 1958/Manitou-Management Music Publishing, 1958.
Best-selling record by Paul Anka (ABC Paramount).

You Are My Flower
Words and music by A. P. Carter.
Peer International Corp., 1939.
Introduced by The Carter Family. Revived in 1964 with best-selling record by Lester Flatt and Earl Scruggs (Columbia).

You Are My Love
Words and music by Jimmie Nabbie.
Jubilee Music Inc., 1955.
Best-selling record by Joni James (MGM).

You Are My Lucky Star
Words by Arthur Freed, music by Nacio Herb Brown.
Robbins Music Corp., 1935.
Introduced by Frances Langford in *Broadway Melody of 1936* (film). Sung by Gene Kelly and Debbie Reynolds in *Singin' in the Rain* (film, 1953). Theme song of Enoch Light and his Orchestra.

You Are My Miracle (English)
Words and music by Roger Whittaker.

Tembo Music, Ltd., London, England, 1979/Tembo Music, 1979.
Best-selling record by Roger Whittaker (RCA, 1979).

You Are My Sunshine
Words and music by Jimmie Davis and Charles Mitchell.
Peer International Corp., 1940.
Theme song of composer Davis during his successful campaign for election as Governor of Louisiana. Featured by Tex Ritter in *Take Me Back to Oklahoma* (film). Best-selling records by Bing Crosby (Decca) and Bob Atcher (Columbia). Revived in 1962 with best-selling record by Ray Charles (ABC-Paramount).

You Are My Treasure
Words and music by Cindy Walker.
Forrest Hills Music Inc., 1968.
Best-selling record by Jack Greene (Decca).

You Are Never Away
Words by Oscar Hammerstein, II, music by Richard Rodgers.
Williamson Music Inc., 1947.
Introduced by John Battles, Roberta Jonay, and chorus in *Allegro* (musical).

You Are Not My First Love
Words and music by Bart Howard and Peter Windsor.
Walden Music Inc., 1953.
Introduced by Mabel Mercer.

You Are So Beautiful
Words and music by Billy Preston and Bruce Fischer.
Irving Music Inc., 1974/Almo Music Corp., 1974/Preston Songs, 1974.
Best-selling record by Joe Cocker (A & M, 1975).

You Are So Lovely and I'm So Lonely
Words by Lorenz Hart, music by Richard Rodgers.
Harms, Inc., 1935.
Introduced by Walter Pidgeon in *Something Gay* (play).

You Are the One
Words and music by Pat Patterson.
Fort Knox Music Co., 1956.
Best-selling record by Carl Smith (Columbia).

You Are the Sunshine of My Life
Words and music by Stevie Wonder.
Jobete Music Co., Inc., 1972/Black Bull Music, 1972.
Best-selling record by Stevie Wonder (Tamla, 1973). Nominated for

National Academy of Recording Arts and Sciences Awards, Record of the Year, 1973, and Song of the Year, 1973.

You Are the Woman
Words and music by Rick Roberts.
Stephen Stills Music, 1976.
Best-selling record by Firefall (Atlantic, 1976).

You Are Too Beautiful
Words by Lorenz Hart, music by Richard Rodgers.
Harms, Inc., 1932.
Introduced by Al Jolson in *Hallelujah, I'm a Bum* (film, 1933).

You Are Woman, I Am Man, also known as **I Am Woman, You Are Man**
Words by Bob Merrill, music by Jule Styne.
Chappell & Co., Inc., 1964.
Introduced by Barbra Streisand and Sydney Chaplin in *Funny Girl* (musical).

You, Baby (Nobody but You)
Words and music by P. F. Sloan and Steve Barri.
MCA, Inc., 1965.
Best-selling record in 1966 by The Turtles (White Whale).

You Beat Me to the Punch
Words and music by William Robinson and Ronald White.
Jobete Music Co., Inc., 1962.
Best-selling record by Mary Wells (Motown).

You Belong to Me
Words and music by Pee Wee King, Redd Stewart, and Chilton Price.
Ridgeway Music Co., 1952/Regent Music, 1952/Dunbar-Ridgeway, 1952.
First recording by, and recording debut of, Joni James (Smash). Best-selling records by Jo Stafford (Columbia) and Patti Page (Mercury). Revived in 1962 with best-selling record by The Duprees (Coed).

You Belong to Me
Music by Michael McDonald, words by Carly Simon.
Snug Music, 1977/C'est Music, 1977.
Best-selling record by Carly Simon (Electra, 1978).

You Belong to My Heart, also known as **Solamente Una Vez** (Mexican)
English words by Ray Gilbert, Spanish words and music by Agustin Lara.

Promotora Hispano Americana de Musica, Mexico City, Mexico, 1941, 1943/Peer International Corp., 1943.
Introduced by Dora Luz in *The Three Caballeros* (cartoon film, 1944). Best-selling record in 1945 by Bing Crosby, with Xavier Cugat and his Orchestra (Decca). Sung in *Mr. Imperium* (film, 1951).

You Better. . ., see You'd Better Sit Down Kids.

You Better Get It
Words and music by Joe Tex (pseudonym for Joseph Arrington, Jr.).
Tree Publishing Co., Inc., 1965.
Best-selling record by Joe Tex (Dial).

You Better Go Now
Words by Bickley Reichner, music by Irvin Graham.
Chappell & Co., Inc., 1936/Malvern Music Co., 1936.
Introduced by Nancy Nolan and Tom Rutherford in *New Faces of 1936* (revue). First recording by Fairchild and Carroll and Orchestra, vocal by Rae Giersdorf (Liberty Music Shop). Revived in 1945 by Billie Holiday (Decca). Best-selling record by Jeri Southern (Decca).

You Better Know It
Words and music by Jackie Wilson and Norm Henry.
Lena Music, Inc., 1959/Regent Music, 1959.
Best-selling record by Jackie Wilson (Brunswick).

You Better Not Do That
Words and music by Tommy Collins.
Central Songs, 1953.
Best-selling record in 1954 by Tommy Collins (Capitol).

You Better Run
Words and music by Felix Cavaliere and Eddie Brigati.
Downtown Music, 1966.
Best-selling record by The Rascals (Atlantic).

You Better Think Twice
Words and music by Jim Messina.
Little Dickens Music Publishers, 1970.
Best-selling record by Poco (Epic, 1970).

You Better Watch Yourself
Words and music by Walter Jacobs.
Arc Music Corp., 1959.
Best-selling record in 1954 by Little Walter (Checker).

You Broke Your Promise
Words and music by Irving Taylor, George Wyle, and Eddie Pola.
Rytvoc, Inc., 1949.

You Brought a New Kind of Love to Me
Words and music by Sammy Fain, Irving Kahal, and Pierre Norman
Connor.
Famous Music Co., 1930.
Introduced by Maurice Chevalier in *The Big Pond* (film). Used as a
theme for *A New Kind of Love* (film, 1963).

You Call Everybody Darling
Words and music by Sam Martin, Ben Trace, and Clem Watts.
Edwin H. Morris Co., 1946.
Best-selling record in 1948 by Al Trace and his Orchestra (Regent).

You Call It Madness (but I Call It Love)
Words and music by Gladys Du Bois, Paul Gregory, Con Conrad,
and Russ Columbo.
Edwin H. Morris Co., 1931/Colgems-EMI Music Inc., 1931.

You Came a Long Way from St. Louis
Words by Bob Russell, music by John Benson Brooks.
Jewel Music Publishing Co., Inc., 1948/Harrison Music Corp., 1948.
Introduced by Ray McKinley and his Orchestra.

You Came Along (from Out of Nowhere), see Out of Nowhere.

You Can All Join In (English)
Words and music by David Mason.
Island Music, Ltd., London, England, 1968/Island Music, 1968.
Introduced in 1969 by Traffic in their album, *Traffic* (United Artists).

You Can Dance with Any Girl At All
Words by Irving Caesar, music by Vincent Youmans.
Warner Brothers-Seven Arts Music, 1924.
Introduced by Josephine Whittell and Wellington Cross in *No, No,
Nanette* (musical, 1925).

You Can Depend on Me
Words and music by Charles Carpenter, Louis Dunlap, and Earl
Hines.
Peer International Corp., 1932.
First recording by Louis Armstrong and his Orchestra (Columbia).
Revived in 1961 with best-selling record by Brenda Lee (Decca).

You Can Do No Wrong
Words and music by Cole Porter.

Chappell & Co., Inc., 1948.
Introduced by Judy Garland in *The Pirate* (film).

You Can Fly! You Can Fly! You Can Fly!
Words by Sammy Cahn, music by Sammy Fain.
Walt Disney Music Co., 1951.
Introduced in *Peter Pan* (cartoon film).

You Can Get It If You Really Want (Jamaican)
Words and music by Jimmy Cliff.
Island Music, 1970.
Performed by Jimmy Cliff in *The Harder They Come* (film, 1973).

You Can Have Her
Words and music by Bill Cook.
Big Billy Music, Co., 1960/Harvard Music, Inc., 1960.
Best-selling record in 1961 by Roy Hamilton (Epic).

You Can Have Him
Words and music by Irving Berlin.
Irving Berlin Music Corp., 1949.
Introduced by Mary McCarty and Allyn McLerie in *Miss Liberty* (musical).

You Can Have Him, I Don't Want Him, Didn't Love Him Anyhow Blues!
Words by William Tracey, music by Dan Dougherty.
Goodman Music Co., Inc., 1922.

You Can Leave Your Hat On
Words and music by Randy Newman.
Unpublished. Performed by Randy Newman on *Sail Away* (Warner Brothers, 1972).

You Can Make My Life a Bed of Roses
Words and music by Lew Brown and Ray Henderson.
DeSylva, Brown & Henderson, Inc., 1932.
Introduced by Buddy Rogers and June Knight in *Hot-cha!* (musical).

You Cannot Win If You Do Not Play
Words and music by Steve Forbert.
Rolling Tide Music, 1978.
Introduced by Steve Forbert on *Alive on Arrival* (Nemperor, 1978).

You Can't Always Get What You Want (English)
Words and music by Mick Jagger and Keith Richard.
Mirage Music, Ltd., London, England, 1969/ABKCO Music Inc.,

1969.
Introduced by The Rolling Stones in their album, *Let It Bleed* (London).

You Can't Be a Beacon (If Your Light Don't Shine)
Words and music by Martin Cooper.
Martin Cooper Music, 1974/Fargo House Inc., 1974.
Best-selling record by Donna Fargo (ABC, 1974).

You Can't Be Too Strong (English)
Words and music by Graham Parker.
Participation Music Inc., 1979.
Introduced by Graham Parker on *Shooting Out Sparks* (Arista, 1979).

You Can't Be True, Dear (West German)
English words by Hal Cotton, German words by Gerhard Ebeler,
  music by Ken Griffin.
Gerhard Ebeler Verlag, Cologne, Federal Republic of Germany,
  1935/Bristol Music Corp., 1948.
Original German title, "Du Kannst Nicht Treu Sein." Best-selling record
  by Ken Griffin and Jerry Wayne (Rondo). Adaptation of music by
  Ken Griffin from the original by Hans Otten.

You Can't Break My Heart ('Cause It's Already Broken)
Words and music by Henry Sweesy and Gary Garett.
Peer International Corp., 1946.
Best-selling record by Spade Cooley (Columbia).

You Can't Brush Me Off
Words and music by Irving Berlin.
Irving Berlin Music Corp., 1940.
Introduced by April Ames, Nick Long, Jr., and The Martins in *Louisiana Purchase* (musical).

You Can't Change That
Words and music by Ray Parker, Jr.
Raydiola Music, 1979.
Best-selling record by Raydio (Arista, 1979).

You Can't Do That (English)
Words and music by John Lennon and Paul McCartney.
Northern Songs, Ltd., England, 1964/Maclen Music Inc., 1964.
Best-selling record by The Beatles (Capitol). Sung by The Beatles in
  Help! (film).

You Can't Do What My Last Man Did
Words and music by J. C. Johnson and Allie Moore.
Record Music Publishing Co., 1923.

Introduced and first recording by Ethel Waters, accompanied by J. C. Johnson (Black Swan).

You Can't Get a Man with a Gun
Words and music by Irving Berlin.
Irving Berlin Music Corp., 1946.
Introduced by Ethel Merman in *Annie Get Your Gun* (musical). Sung by Betty Hutton in film version (1950).

You Can't Get That No More
Words and music by Louis Jordan and Sam Theard.
Leeds Music Corp., 1944.
Best-selling record by Louis Jordan and his Tympany Five (Decca).

You Can't Have Everything
Words and music by Mack Gordon and Harry Revel.
Miller Music Corp., 1937.
Introduced by Alice Faye in *You Can't Have Everything* (film).

You Can't Have My Love
Words and music by Chuck Harding, Marty Roberts, Hank Thompson, and Billy Gray.
Hall-Clement Publications, 1954.
Best-selling record by Wanda Jackson and Billy Gray (Decca).

You Can't Hold a Memory in Your Arms
Words by Hy Zaret, music by Arthur Altman.
Leeds Music Corp., 1942.
Introduced by Jane Frazee, with Woody Herman and his Orchestra, in *What's Cookin' Soldier* (film). Popularized by Frances Langford. Title by Thekla Hollingsworth.

You Can't Hurry Love
Words and music by Eddie Holland, Lamont Dozier, and Brian Holland.
Stone Agate Music Corp., 1965.
Best-selling record in 1966 by The Supremes (Motown).

You Can't Keep a Good Man Down
Words and music by Perry Bradford.
Perry Bradford Music Publishing Co., 1920.
Introduced and first recording by Mamie Smith and her Jazz Hounds (Okeh).

You Can't Pick a Rose in December
Words and music by Leon Payne.
Fred Rose Music, Inc., 1949.
Best-selling record in 1960 by Ernest Ashworth (Decca).

You Can't Pull the Wool over My Eyes
Words and music by Milton Ager, Charles Newman, and Murray Mencher.
Advanced Music Corp., 1936/World Music, Inc., 1936.

You Can't Roller Skate in a Buffalo Herd
Words and music by Roger Miller.
Tree Publishing Co., Inc., 1964.
Introduced by Roger Miller (Smash).

You Can't Run Away from It
Words by Johnny Mercer, music by Gene de Paul.
Columbia Pictures Publications, 1956.
From *You Can't Run Away from It* (film). Best-selling record by The Four Aces (Decca).

You Can't Say No to a Soldier
Words by Mack Gordon, music by Harry Warren.
Mayfair Music Corp., 1942.
Introduced by Joan Merrill in *Iceland* (film).

You Can't See the Sun When You're Cryin'
Words and music by Allan Roberts and Doris Fisher.
George Simon, Inc., 1946.
Best-selling record by Vaughn Monroe and his Orchestra (Victor).

You Can't Sit Down
Words and music by Dee Clark, Cornell Muldrow, and Kal Mann.
Conrad Music, 1960.
Best-selling record in 1963 by The Dovells (Parkway).

You Can't Stop Me from Dreaming
Words and music by Cliff Friend and Dave Franklin.
Remick Music Corp., 1937.
Introduced by Guy Lombardo and his Royal Canadians.

You Can't Stop Me from Lovin' You
Words by Mann Holiner, music by Alberta Nichols.
Anne-Rachel Music Corp., 1931.
Interpolated by Ethel Waters and Blue McAllister in Lew Leslie's *Rhapsody in Black* (revue).

You Can't Take a Dream from a Dreamer
Words and music by Redd Evans, Jack Perry, and Harry Sims.
Valiant Music Co., Inc., 1961.
Introduced by Tony Bennett (Columbia).

You Can't Turn Me Off
Words and music by Marilyn McLeod and Pam Sawyer.
Jobete Music Co., Inc., 1977.
Best-selling record by High Inergy (Gordy, 1977).

You Cheated
Words and music by Don Burch.
Balcones Publishing Co., 1958.
Best-selling record by The Shields (Dot).

You Comb Her Hair
Words and music by Harlan Howard and Hank Cochran.
Tree Publishing Co., Inc., 1963.
Best-selling record by George Jones (United Artists).

You Could Drive a Person Crazy
Words and music by Stephen Sondheim.
Herald Square Music Co., 1970/Rilting Music Inc., 1970.
Introduced by Donna McKechnie, Pamela Myers and Company in
    Company (musical, 1970).

You Couldn't Be Cuter
Words by Dorothy Fields, music by Jerome Kern.
T. B. Harms Co., 1938.
Introduced by Irene Dunne in *Joy of Living* (film).

You Decorated My Life
Words and music by Deborah Kay Hupp and Robert Morrison.
Music City Music Inc., 1978.
Best-selling record by Kenny Rogers (United Artists, 1979). Won a
    National Academy of Recording Arts and Sciences Award, Country
    Song of the Year, 1979.

You Didn't Have to Be So Nice
Words and music by John Sebastian and Steve Boone (pseudonym
    for John Stephen Boone).
The Hudson Bay Music Co., 1965.
Best-selling record in 1965-66 by The Lovin' Spoonful (Kama Sutra).

You Didn't Have To Tell Me—I Knew It All the Time
Words and music by Walter Donaldson.
Bregman, Vocco & Conn, Inc., 1931.

You Do
Words by Mack Gordon, music by Josef Myrow.
Bregman, Vocco & Conn, Inc., 1947.
Introduced by Dan Dailey in *Mother Wore Tights* (film). Best-selling
    records by Bing Crosby with Carmen Cavallaro and his Orchestra

(Decca), Vaughn Monroe (Victor), and Margaret Whiting (Capitol). Nominated for an Academy Award, 1947.

You Do Something to Me
Words and music by Cole Porter.
Harms, Inc., 1929.
Introduced by William Gaxton and Genevieve Tobin in *Fifty Million Frenchmen* (musical). Sung by Jane Wyman in *Night and Day* (film, 1946); by Doris Day in *Starlift* (film, 1951); by the voice of Gogi Grant, dubbed for Ann Blyth, in *The Helen Morgan Story* (film, 1957); and by Louis Jourdan in *Can-Can* (film, 1960).

You Do the Darndest Things, Baby
Words by Sidney D. Mitchell, music by Lew Pollack.
Movietone Music Corp., 1936.
Introduced by Jack Haley in *Pigskin Parade* (film).

You Done Me Wrong
Words and music by Ray Price and Shirley Jones.
Cedarwood Publishing Co., Inc., 1956/Fort Knox Music Co., 1956/ Starrite Publishing Co., 1956.
Best-selling record by Ray Price (Columbia).

You Don't Bring Me Flowers
Words by Alan Bergman and Marilyn Bergman, words and music by Neil Diamond.
Stonebridge Music, 1977/Threesome Music, 1977.
Best-selling record by Barbra Streisand and Neil Diamond (Columbia, 1978). Originally written as theme for TV show *All That Glitters* but never used. Nominated for National Academy of Recording Arts and Sciences Awards, Record of the Year, 1979, and Song of the Year, 1978.

You Don't Care What Happens to Me
Words and music by Fred Rose.
Milene Music Co., 1945.
Best-selling record by Bob Wills and his Texas Playboys (Columbia).

You Don't Have to Be a Star (to Be in My Show)
Words and music by James Dean and John Henry Glover.
Groovesville Music Inc., 1976.
Best-selling record by Marilyn McCoo & Billy Davis, Jr. (ABC, 1976).

You Don't Have To Go
Words and music by Matcher James Reed.
Conrad Music, 1954.
Best-selling record in 1955 by Jimmy Reed (Vee-Jay).

You Don't Have To Know the Language
Words by Johnny Burke, music by James Van Heusen.
Bourne Co., 1947/Music Sales Corp., 1947.
Introduced by Bing Crosby and The Andrews Sisters in *Road to Rio* (film).

You Don't Have to Paint Me a Picture, also known as **Paint Me a Picture**
Words and music by Roger Carroll Tillison, Leon Russell, and Thomas Garrett.
Warner-Tamerlane Publishing Corp., 1966.
Best-selling record by Gary Lewis and The Playboys (Liberty).

You Don't Have to Say You Love Me (Italian)
English words by Vicki Wickham and Simon Napier-Bell, Italian words by V. Pallavicini, music by P. Donaggio.
Accordo Edizioni Musicali, Milan, Italy/Robbins Music Corp., 1966.
Original Italian title, "Io che non vivo (senza te)." Best-selling record of English version by Dusty Springfield (Philips). Revived in 1966 by Elvis Presley (RCA).

You Don't Hear
Words and music by Jerry Huffman and Tom Cash.
House of Cash-Southwind Music, 1965/Unichappell Music Inc., 1965.
Best-selling record by Kitty Wells (Decca).

You Don't Know (English)
Words and music by John Schroeder and Michael Hawker.
Lorna Music Co., London, England, 1961/Edward B. Marks Music Corp., 1961.
Best-selling record in England by Helen Shapiro (English Columbia).

You Don't Know
Words and music by Meredith Willson.
Frank Music Co., 1963/Rinimer Corp., 1963.
Introduced by Janis Paige in *Here's Love* (musical).

You Don't Know Him
Words and music by Jay Livingston and Ray Evans.
Livingston & Evans, Inc., 1958.
Introduced by Jacquelyn McKeever and Abbe Lane in *Oh Captain!* (musical).

You Don't Know Like I Know
Words and music by David Porter and Isaac Hayes.
Irving Music Inc.-East Memphis, 1965/Cotillion Music Inc., 1965.
Best-selling record in 1966 by Sam and Dave (Stax).

You Don't Know Me
Words and music by Cindy Walker and Eddy Arnold.
Unichappell Music Inc., 1955.
Best-selling record in 1956 by Eddy Arnold (RCA Victor). Revived in
    1962 with best-selling record by Ray Charles (ABC Paramount) and
    in 1967 with best-selling record by Elvis Presley (RCA Victor).

You Don't Know My Mind
Words by Sam H. Gray and Virginia Liston, music by Clarence
    Williams.
MCA, Inc., 1923.
Introduced and first recording by Virginia Liston (Okeh).

You Don't Know Paree
Words and music by Cole Porter.
Harms, Inc., 1929.
Introduced by William Gaxton in *Fifty Million Frenchmen* (musical).

You Don't Know What Love Is
Words and music by Don Raye and Gene de Paul.
MCA, Inc., 1941.
Introduced by Carol Bruce in *Keep 'em Flying* (film).

You Don't Know What You Mean to Me
Words and music by Eddie Floyd and Steve Cropper.
Cotillion Music Inc., 1968/Irving Music Inc., 1968.
Best-selling record by Sam and Dave (Atlantic).

You Don't Know What You've Got
Words and music by Paul Hampton and George Burton.
Post Music, Inc., 1961.
Best-selling record by Ral Donner (Gone).

You Don't Like It—Not Much
Words and music by Ned Miller, Art Kahn, and Chester Conn.
Leo Feist Inc., 1927.
Introduced by Art Kahn and his Orchestra.

You Don't Love Me
Words and music by Gay Crosse.
Cherio Corp., 1948.
Best-selling record by Camille Howard (Specialty).

You Don't Love Me Anymore
Words and music by Alan Ray and Jeffrey Raymond.
Briarpatch Music, 1977/Debdave Music Inc., 1977.
Best-selling record by Eddie Rabbitt (Elektra, 1978).

You Don't Love Me When I Cry
Words and music by Laura Nyro.
Blackwood Music Inc., 1969.
Introduced by Laura Nyro in her album, *New York Tendaberry* (Columbia).

You Don't Mess Around with Jim
Words and music by Jim Croce.
MCA Music, 1972/Blendingwell Music, 1972.
Best-selling record by Jim Croce (ABC, 1972).

You Don't Owe Me a Thing
Words and music by Marty Robbins.
Fred Rose Music, Inc., 1956.
Introduced by Marty Robbins. Best-selling record in 1957 by Johnnie Ray (Columbia).

You Don't Own Me
Words and music by John Madara and David White.
Merjoda Music, Inc., 1963.
Best-selling record in 1964 by Lesley Gore (Mercury).

You Don't Remind Me
Words and music by Cole Porter.
Buxton Hill Music Corp., 1950.
Written for, but deleted from, *Out of This World* (musical).

(In the Summer Time) You Don't Want My Love
Words and music by Roger Miller.
Tree Publishing Co., Inc., 1960.
Best-selling records by Andy Williams (Cadence) and Roger Miller (RCA Victor).

You Dropped Me Like a Red Hot Penny
Words by Joe Young, music by Fred E. Ahlert.
Fred Ahlert Music Corp., 1936/Pencil Mark Music, Inc., 1936/ Warock Music, Inc., 1936.

You Fascinate Me So
Words by Carolyn Leigh, music by Cy Coleman.
Edwin H. Morris Co., 1958.
Introduced by Jean Arnold in *Julius Monk's Demi-Dozen* (nightclub revue).

You Forgot about Me
Words and music by Dick Robertson, James F. Hanley, and Sammy Mysels.
Morley Music Co., Inc., 1940/Penn Music Co., 1940.

You Forgot Your Gloves
Words by Edward Eliscu, music by Ned Lehac.
Robbins Music Corp., 1931.
Introduced by Constance Carpenter and Jerry Norris in *The Third Little Show* (revue).

You Gave Me a Mountain
Words and music by Marty Robbins.
Mojave Music, Inc., 1968/Elvis Presley Music, Inc., 1968/Noma Music, Inc., 1968.
Best-selling records in 1969 by Johnny Bush (Stop) and Frankie Laine (ABC).

You Go to My Head
Words by Haven Gillespie, music by J. Fred Coots.
Remick Music Corp., 1938.
Introduced by Glen Gray and The Casa Loma Orchestra. First recording by Larry Clinton and his Orchestra, vocal by Bea Wain (Victor). Theme song of Mitchell Ayres and his Orchestra.

You Got Me Dizzy
Words and music by Jimmy Reed and Ewart Abner, Jr.
Conrad Music, 1956.
Best-selling record in 1957 by Jimmy Reed (Vee Jay).

You Got the Love
Words and music by Chaha Khan and Ray Parker, Jr.
MCA Music, 1974.
Best-selling record by Rufus (ABC, 1974).

You Got to Me
Words and music by Neil Diamond.
Tallyrand Music, 1967.
Best-selling record by Neil Diamond (Bang).

You Got What It Takes, also known as **You've Got What It Takes**
Words and music by Berry Gordy, Jr., Gwen Gordy, and Tyran Carlo.
Jobete Music Co., Inc., 1959.
Best-selling record in 1960 by Marv Johnson (United Artists). Revived in 1965 with best-selling record by Joe Tex (Dial) and in 1967 with best-selling record by The Dave Clark Five (Epic).

You Gotta Be a Football Hero (To Get Along with the Beautiful Girls)
Words and music by Al Lewis, Al Sherman, and Buddy Fields.
Leo Feist Inc., 1933/Sovereign Music Corp., 1933/Colgems-EMI

Music Inc., 1933.
Popularized by Ben Bernie and his Orchestra.

You Gotta Be My Baby
Words and music by George Jones.
Starrite Publishing Co., 1956.
Best-selling record by George Jones (Starday).

You Gotta Love Everybody
Words and music by Bill Norvas and Kay Thompson.
Edwin H. Morris Co., 1956.
Best-selling record by Della Reese (Jubilee).

You Gotta S-M-I-L-E To Be H-A-Double P-Y
Words and music by Mack Gordon and Harry Revel.
Robbins Music Corp., 1936.
Introduced by Shirley Temple in *Stowaway* (film).

You Have Cast Your Shadow on the Sea
Words by Lorenz Hart, music by Richard Rodgers.
Chappell & Co., Inc., 1938.
Introduced by Marcy Westcott and Eddie Albert in *The Boys from Syracuse* (musical).

You Have Everything
Words by Howard Dietz, music by Arthur Schwartz.
DeSylva, Brown & Henderson, Inc., 1937.
Introduced by Charles Walters and Vilma Ebsen in *Between the Devil* (musical).

You Have Taken My Heart
Words by Johnny Mercer, music by Gordon Jenkins.
Anne-Rachel Music Corp., 1933.
Introduced by Lanny Ross.

You Have the Choice
Words and music by Maurice Jarre and Harold Pinter.
Famous Music Co., 1976.
Performed by the voice of Jeanne Mareau in *The Last Tycoon* (film, 1976).

You Haven't Changed at All
Words by Alan Jay Lerner, music by Frederick Loewe.
Leo Feist Inc., 1945.
Introduced by Irene Manning and Bill Johnson in *The Day before Spring* (musical).

You Haven't Done Nothin'
Words and music by Stevie Wonder.
Jobete Music Co., Inc., 1974/Black Bull Music, 1974.
Best-selling record by Stevie Wonder (Tamla, 1974).

You Hit the Spot
Words and music by Mack Gordon and Harry Revel.
Famous Music Co., 1935.
Introduced by Mack Gordon, Frances Langford, and Jack Oakie in
Collegiate (film, 1936).

You, I
Words and music by Steve McNicol.
Shelby Singleton Music Inc., 1968.
Best-selling record in 1969 by The Rugbys (Amazon).

You Irritate Me So
Words and music by Cole Porter.
Chappell & Co., Inc., 1941.
Introduced by Jack Williams and Nanette Fabray in *Let's Face It* (musical).

You Keep Coming Back Like a Song
Words and music by Irving Berlin.
Irving Berlin Music Corp., 1943, 1945.
Introduced by Bing Crosby in *Blue Skies* (film, 1946). Nominated for an
Academy Award, 1946.

You Keep Me Hangin' On
Words and music by Eddie Holland, Lamont Dozier, and Brian
Holland.
Stone Agate Music Corp., 1966.
Best-selling records by The Supremes (Motown) and in 1968 by Joe
Simon (Sound Stage 7) and Vanilla Fudge (Atco).

You Keep Running Away
Words and music by Eddie Holland, Lamont Dozier, and Brian
Holland.
Stone Agate Music Corp., 1967.
Best-selling record by The Four Tops (Motown).

You Know—I Know Ev'rything's Made for Love, also known as
Everything's Made for Love
Words and music by Howard Johnson, Charles Tobias, and Al
Sherman.
Shapiro, Bernstein & Co., Inc., 1926.

You Know I Love You
Words by Riley King, music by Jules Taub.
Modern Music Publishing Co., Inc., 1952/Sounds of Lucille Inc., 1952.
Best-selling record by B. B. King (RPM).

You Know What I Mean
Words and music by Garry Bonner and Alan Gordon.
The Hudson Bay Music Co., 1967.
Best-selling record by The Turtles (White Whale).

You Know You Belong to Somebody Else So Why Don't You Leave Me Alone
Words by Eugene West, music by James V. Monaco and Ira Schuster.
Fred Fisher Music Co., 1922/Edwin H. Morris Co., 1922.

You Leave Me Breathless
Words by Ralph Freed, music by Frederick Hollander.
Famous Music Co., 1938.
Introduced by Fred MacMurray in *Cocoanut Grove* (film).

You Let Me Down
Words by Al Dubin, music by Harry Warren.
Harms, Inc., 1935.
Introduced by Jane Froman in *Stars over Broadway* (film).

You Light Up My Life
Words and music by Joe Brooks.
Big Hill Music Corp., 1977.
Performed by the voice of Kasey Ciszk in *You Light Up My Life* (film, 1977). Best-selling record by Debby Boone (Warner Bros., 1977). Nominated for a National Academy of Recording Arts and Sciences Award, Record of the Year, 1977. Won an Academy Award, 1977.

You Like Me Too Much (English)
Words and music by George Harrison.
Northern Songs, Ltd., England, 1965/Maclen Music Inc., 1965.
Introduced by The Beatles in their album, *Beatles VI* (Capitol).

You Little Trustmaker
Words and music by Christopher Jackson.
The EMP Co., 1973/Bacon Fat Music Co., 1973.
Best-selling record by The Tymes (RCA, 1974).

You Love Me
Words by Anne Croswell, music by Lee Pockriss.
Piedmont Music Co., Inc., 1963.

Introduced by Vivien Leigh and Jean Pierre Aumont in *Tovarich* (musical).

You Love the Thunder
Words and music by Jackson Browne.
Swallow Turn Music, 1977/WB Music Corp., 1977.
Introduced by Jackson Browne on *Running on Empty* (Asylum, 1978).
  Best-selling record by Jackson Browne (Asylum, 1978).

You Lucky People You
Words by Johnny Burke, music by Jimmy Van Heusen.
Anne-Rachel Music Corp., 1941.
Introduced by Bing Crosby in *Road to Zanzibar* (film).

You Made Me Believe in Magic
Words and music by Leonard Boone.
Rare Blue Music Inc., 1977.
Best-selling record by The Bay City Rollers (Arista, 1977).

You Make It Easy
Words and music by James Taylor.
Country Road Music Inc., 1975.
Introduced by James Taylor on *Gorilla* (Warner Brothers, 1975).

You Make Loving Fun (English)
Words and music by Christine McVie.
Gentoo Music Inc., 1977.
Best-selling record by Fleetwood Mac (Warner Brothers, 1977).

You Make Me Dream Too Much
Words by Sammy Cahn, music by Jule Styne.
Skidmore Music Co., Inc., 1944.
Introduced by Georgia Carroll, with Kay Kyser and his Orchestra, in *Carolina Blues* (film).

You Make Me Feel Brand New
Words and music by Linda Creed and Thom Bell.
Mighty Three Music, 1974.
Best-selling record by The Stylistics (Avco, 1974).

You Make Me Feel Like Dancing (American-English)
Words and music by Vini Poncia and Leo Sayer.
Braintree Music, 1976/Chrysalis Music Corp., 1976.
Best-selling record by Leo Sayer (Warner Bros., 1977). Won a National Academy of Recording Arts and Sciences Award, Rhythm & Blues Song of the Year, 1977.

You Make Me Feel So Young
Words by Mack Gordon, music by Josef Myrow.
Bregman, Vocco & Conn, Inc., 1946.
Introduced by Vera-Ellen and Frank Lattimore in *Three Little Girls in Blue* (film).

You Make Me Real
Words and music by Jim Morrison.
Doors Music Co., 1970.
Best-selling record by The Doors (Elektra, 1970).

You May Be Right
Words and music by Billy Joel.
April Music Inc., 1979/Impulsive Music, 1979.
Best-selling record by Billy Joel (Columbia, 1980).

You Mean Everything to Me
Words and music by Neil Sedaka and Howard Greenfield.
Screen Gems-EMI Music Inc., 1960.
Introduced by Neil Sedaka (RCA Victor).

You Mean So Much to Me
Words and music by Bruce Springsteen.
Laurel Canyon Music Ltd., 1976/Bruce Springsteen Publishing, 1976.
Introduced by Southside Johnny and the Asbury Jukes on *I Don't Want to Go Home*(Epic, 1976).

You Mean the World to Me
Words and music by Billy Sherrill and Glenn Sutton.
Al Gallico Music Corp., 1967.
Best-selling record by David Houston (Epic).

You Met Your Match...
Words and music by Don Hunter, Stevie Wonder, and Lula Hardaway.
Jobete Music Co., Inc., 1968/Stone Agate Music Corp., 1968/Black Bull Music, 1968.
Best-selling record by Stevie Wonder (Tamla).

You Moved Right In
Words by Harold Adamson, music by Jimmy McHugh.
Famous Music Co., 1945.
Introduced by Marjorie Reynolds in *Bring on the Girls* (film).

You Must Believe in Spring (French)
English words by Marilyn Bergman and Alan Bergman, French words by Jacques Demy, music by Michel Legrand.
Productions Michel Legrand, Paris, France, 1967/N. S. Beaujolais

Music, Inc., 1968.
Original French title, "Chanson de Maxence." Introduced in *Les Demoiselles de Rochefort* (French film).

You Must Have Been a Beautiful Baby
Words by Johnny Mercer, music by Harry Warren.
Remick Music Corp., 1938.
Introduced by Dick Powell in *Hard To Get* (film). Sung by Doris Day in *My Dream Is Yours* (film, 1949). Revived in 1961 with best-selling record by Bobby Darin (Atco) and in 1967 with best-selling record by The Dave Clark Five (Epic).

You Mustn't Feel Discouraged
Words by Betty Comden, words and music by Adolph Green, music by Jule Styne.
Stratford Music Corp., 1964/Chappell & Co., Inc., 1964.
Introduced by Carol Burnett and Tiger Haynes in *Fade Out—Fade In* (musical).

You Mustn't Kick It Around
Words by Lorenz Hart, music by Richard Rodgers.
Chappell & Co., Inc., 1940.
Introduced by Gene Kelly, June Havoc, Diane Sinclair, Sondra Barrett, and chorus in *Pal Joey* (musical).

You Nearly Lose Your Mind
Words and music by Ernest Tubb.
Unichappell Music Inc., 1943.
Best-selling record by Ernest Tubb (Decca).

You Need Hands (English)
Words and music by Roy Irwin.
Lakeview Music Corp., 1957/Leeds Music Corp., 1957.
Best-selling record by Eydie Gorme (ABC Paramount).

You Need Someone, Someone Needs You
Words by Oscar Hammerstein, II, music by Lewis E. Gensler.
Harms, Inc., 1922.
Introduced by Nora Bayes and Arthur Uttry in *Queen o'Hearts* (musical).

You Needed Me
Words and music by Randy Goodrum.
Chappell & Co., Inc., 1975/Ironside Music, 1975.
Best-selling record by Anne Murray (Capitol, 1978). Nominated for National Academy of Recording Arts and Sciences Awards, Record of the Year, 1978, and Song of the Year, 1978.

You Never Done It Like That
Words and music by Howard Greenfield and Neil Sedaka.
Kiddio Music Co., 1977/Don Kirshner Music Inc., 1977.
Best-selling record by The Captain & Tennille (A & M, 1978).

You Never Even Called Me by My Name
Words and music by Steve Goodman.
Kama Rippa Music, 1973.
Best-selling record by David Allen Coe (Columbia, 1975).

You Never Give Me Your Money (English)
Words and music by John Lennon and Paul McCartney.
Northern Songs, Ltd., England, 1969/Maclen Music Inc., 1969.
Introduced by The Beatles in their album, *Abbey Road* (Apple).

You Never Know
Words and music by Cole Porter.
Chappell & Co., Inc., 1938.
Introduced by Libby Holman in *You Never Know* (musical).

You Never Miss a Real Good Thing (Till He Says Goodbye)
Words and music by Bob McDill.
Hall-Clement Publications, 1976.
Best-selling record by Crystal Gayle (United Artists, 1976).

You Never Miss the Water Till the Well Runs Dry
Words by Paul Secon, music by Arthur Kent.
Arthur Kent Music Co., 1946.
Best-selling record by The Mills Brothers (Decca).

You Only Live Twice (English)
Words and music by Leslie Bricusse and John Barry.
United Artists Music Co., Inc., 1967/Unart Music Corp., 1967.
Title song of *You Only Live Twice* (British film). Best-selling record by
    Nancy Sinatra (Reprise).

You Oughta Be in Pictures
Words by Edward Heyman, music by Dana Suesse.
Harms, Inc., 1934.
Interpolated by Jane Froman in *Ziegfeld Follies of 1934* (revue). Sung
    by Doris Day in *Starlift* (film, 1951).

You Oughta Be with Me
Words and music by Al Green, Willie Mitchell, and Al Jackson.
JEC Publishing, 1972/Al Green Music Inc., 1972.
Best-selling record by Al Green (Hi, 1972).

You Oughta See My Baby
Words by Roy Turk, music by Fred E. Ahlert.
Fred Fisher Music Co., 1920/Fred Ahlert Music Corp., 1920.

You Really Got Me (English)
Words and music by Ray Davies.
Edward Kassner Music Co., Ltd., London, England/Jay-Boy Music
  Corp., 1964.
Best-selling record in England and United States by The Kinks (Re-
prise).

You Really Know How to Hurt a Guy
Words and music by Roger Christian, Jan Berry, and Jill Gibson.
Screen Gems-EMI Music Inc., 1965.
Best-selling record by Jan and Dean (Liberty).

You Remind Me of My Mother
Words and music by George M. Cohan.
George M. Cohan Music Publishing Co., 1922.
Introduced by Charles King and Elizabeth Hines in *Little Nellie Kelly*
  (musical).

You Said a Bad Word
Words and music by Joe Tex.
Tree Publishing Co., Inc., 1972.
Best-selling record by Joe Tex (Dial, 1972).

You Said It
Words by Jack Yellen, music by Harold Arlen.
Advanced Music Corp., 1931.
Introduced by Mary Lawler and Stanley Smith in *You Said it* (musical).
  Recorded by Harold Arlen, with Red Nichols and his Orchestra
  (Brunswick).

You Say the Nicest Things, Baby
Words by Harold Adamson, music by Jimmy McHugh.
Sam Fox Publishing Co., Inc., 1948.
Introduced by Betty Jane Watson and Bill Callahan, and reprised by
  Bobby Clark and Irene Rich, in *As the Girls Go* (musical).

You Say the Sweetest Things, Baby
Words by Mack Gordon, music by Harry Warren.
Twentieth Century Fox Music Corp., 1940.
Introduced by Alice Faye in *Tin Pan Alley* (film).

You Send Me
Words and music by L. C. Cooke.

ABKCO Music Inc., 1957.
Best-selling record by Sam Cooke (Keen).

You Sexy Thing (English)
Words and music by Errol Brown and Anthony Wilson.
Finchley Music Corp., 1975.
Best-selling record by Hot Chocolate (Big Tree, 1975).

You Should Be Dancing (English)
Words and music by Barry Gibb, Maurice Gibb, and Robin Gibb.
Gibb Brothers Music, 1976.
Best-selling record by The Bee Gees (RSO, 1976).

You Should See Yourself
Words by Dorothy Fields, music by Cy Coleman.
Notable Music Co., Inc., 1965/Lida Enterprises, Inc., 1965.
Introduced by Gwen Verdon in *Sweet Charity* (musical).

You Showed Me
Words and music by Gene Clark (pseudonym for Harold E. Clark)
    and Jim McGuinn.
Tickson Music, 1965.
Best-selling record in 1969 by The Turtles (White Whale).

You Showed Me the Way
Words and music by Bud Green, Ella Fitzgerald, Teddy McRae, and
    Chick Webb.
Robbins Music Corp., 1937/Rytvoc, Inc., 1937.
Introduced by Chick Webb and his Orchestra, vocal by Ella Fitzgerald.

You Started Something
Words by Leo Robin, music by Ralph Rainger.
Twentieth Century Fox Music Corp., 1941.
Introduced by Betty Grable, Don Ameche, and Robert Cummings in
    Moon over Miami (film).

You Started Something
Words and music by Al Rinker and Floyd Huddleston.
Screen Gems-EMI Music Inc., 1947.
Best-selling record by Tony Pastor and his Orchestra (Columbia).

You Stayed Away Too Long
Words by George Whiting and Nat Schwartz, music by J. C.
    Johnson.
Record Music Publishing Co., 1936.
Introduced by Fats Waller.

You Stepped into My Life (English)
Words and music by Barry Gibb, Robin Gibb, and Maurice Gibb.
Gibb Brothers Music, 1976.
Best-selling records by Wayne Newton (Aries, 1979) and Melba Moore
(Epic, 1979).

You Stepped Out of a Dream
Words by Gus Kahn, music by Nacio Herb Brown.
Leo Feist Inc., 1940.
Introduced by Tony Martin in *Ziegfeld Girl* (film, 1941).

You Take My Breath Away
Words by Bruce Hart, music by Stephen Lawrence.
SJL Music Co., 1978.
Introduced by Rex Smith in *Sooner or Later* (film). Best-selling record
by Rex Smith (Columbia, 1979).

You Talk Too Much
Words and music by Joe Jones and Reginald Hall.
Ben-Ghazi Enterprises, Inc., 1960/Big Seven Music Corp., 1960.
Best-selling record by Joe Jones (Roulette).

You Taught Me To Love Again
Words by Charles Carpenter, music by Tommy Dorsey and Henri
Woode.
Larry Spier, Inc., 1939/Fisher Music Corp., 1939.
Introduced by Tommy Dorsey and his Orchestra, vocal by Jack Leon-
ard.

You Tell Her, I S-t-u-t-t-e-r
Words and music by Billy Rose and Cliff Friend.
Bourne Co., 1922.

You Tell Me, see **You Tell Me Why.**

You Tell Me Why, also known as **You Tell Me**
Words and music by Ronald Elliott.
Clears Music, 1965.
Best-selling record by The Beau Brummels (Autumn).

You Think of Ev'rything
Words by Joseph McCarthy and Billy Rose, music by Jimmy Van
Heusen.
Robbins Music Corp., 1940/Van Heusen Music Corp., 1940.
Introduced in Billy Rose's *New Aquacade* (New York World's Fair
revue).

You Told a Lie (I Believed You)
Words and music by Teepee Mitchell and Lew Porter.
Bourne Co., 1949/Murbo Music Publishing Inc., 1949.
Best-selling record by Marjorie Hughes (Columbia).

You Took Advantage of Me
Words by Lorenz Hart, music by Richard Rodgers.
Harms, Inc., 1928.
Introduced by Joyce Barbour and Busby Berkeley in *Present Arms*
(musical). Popularized by Morton Downey.

**You Took Her off My Hands (Now Please Take Her off My
Mind)**
Words and music by Wynn Stewart, Skeets McDonald, and Harlan
Howard.
Central Songs, 1956.
Best-selling record in 1963 by Ray Price (Columbia).

You Took Me by Surprise
Words by John Latouche, music by Vernon Duke.
Miller Music Corp., 1941.
Introduced in *The Lady Comes Across* (musical).

You Took the Words Right Out of My Heart
Words and music by Leo Robin and Ralph Rainger.
Paramount Music Corp., 1937.
Introduced by Dorothy Lamour and Leif Erickson in *Big Broadcast of
1938* (film).

You Took the Words Right Out of My Mouth
Words by Harold Adamson, music by Burton Lane.
Robbins Music Corp., 1935.
Introduced by Maurice Chevalier in *Folies Bergere* (film).

You Took the Words Right Out of My Mouth
Words and music by Jim Steinman.
E. B. Marks Music Corp., 1977/Neverland Music Publishing Co.,
1977/Peg Music Co., 1977.
Best-selling record by Meat Loaf (Epic, 1978).

You Try Somebody Else (We'll Be Back Together Again)
Words and music by B. G. De Sylva, Lew Brown, and Ray
Henderson.
DeSylva, Brown & Henderson, Inc., 1931/Anne-Rachel Music Corp.,
1931.
Popularized by Russ Columbo. Sung by Sheree North in *The Best
Things in Life Are Free* (film, 1956).

You Turn Me On, also known as **The Turn On Song**
Words and music by Ian Whitcomb.
Burdette Music Co., 1965.
Best-selling record by Ian Whitcomb (Tower).

You Turn Me on, I'm a Radio
Words and music by Joni Mitchell.
Crazy Crow Music, 1972.
Best-selling record by Joni Mitchell (Asylum, 1973).

You Turned My World Around (West German)
Music by Burt Kampfert and Herbert Rehbein, English words by
   Kim Carnes Ellingson and Dave Ellingson.
Screen Gems-EMI Music Inc., 1973.
Best-selling record by Frank Sinatra (Reprise, 1974).

You Turned the Tables on Me
Words by Sidney D. Mitchell, music by Louis Alter.
Movietone Music Corp., 1936/Anne-Rachel Music Corp., 1936/
   Gladys Music, 1936.
Introduced by Alice Faye in *Sing, Baby, Sing* (film).

You Two-Timed Me Once Too Often
Words and music by Jenny Lou Carson.
Acuff-Rose Publications Inc., 1945.
Best-selling record by Tex Ritter (Capitol).

You Upset Me, Baby
Words by Maxwell Davis, music by Joe Josea.
Modern Music Publishing Co., Inc., 1954.
Best-selling record by B. B. King (RPM).

You Walk By
Words by Ben Raleigh, music by Bernie Wayne.
Bernie Wayne Music Co., 1940/Benral Music Co., 1940.
Introduced by Guy Lombardo and his Royal Canadians. Best-selling
   record by Eddy Duchin and his Orchestra (Columbia).

You Wanna Give Me a Lift
Words and music by Loretta Lynn.
Sure Fire Music Co., Inc., 1969.
Best-selling record in 1970 by Loretta Lynn (Decca).

You Wanted Someone to Play with (I Wanted Someone to Love)
Words by Frank Capano and Margie Morris, music by George B.
   McConnell and Nat Osborne.
Edwin H. Morris Co., 1928/Capano Music, 1928.
Revived in 1967 with best-selling record by Frankie Laine (ABC).

You Was
Words by Paul Francis Webster, music by Sonny Burke.
Crystal Music Publishers, Inc., 1949/Webster Music Corp., 1949.
Best-selling record by Doris Day and Buddy Clark (Columbia).

You Wear It Well
Words and music by Rod Stewart and Martin Quittenton.
Three Bridges Music Corp., 1972.
Best-selling record by Rod Stewart (Mercury, 1972).

(Jeannie Marie) You Were a Lady
Words and music by Ricci Mareno, Charlie Black, and Jerry
    Gillespie.
Ricci Mareno Music, 1974.
Best-selling record by Tommy Overstreet (ABC, 1974).

You Were Made for Me (English)
Words and music by Mitch Murray.
B. Feldman & Co., Ltd., 1963/Edward B. Marks Music Corp., 1963.
Best-selling record in 1965 by Freddie and The Dreamers (Tower).

You Were Meant for Me
Words and music by Noble Sissle and Eubie Blake.
Robbins Music Corp., 1924.
Introduced by Gertrude Lawrence and Noel Coward in London in *London Calling!* (revue, 1923). Introduced in the United States by Miss Lawrence and Jack Buchanan in *Andre Charlot's Revue of 1924* (revue).

You Were Meant for Me
Words by Arthur Freed, music by Nacio Herb Brown.
Robbins Music Corp., 1929.
Introduced by Charles King in *The Broadway Melody* (film, 1929). Sung by the voice of Charles King, dubbed for Conrad Nagel, in *Hollywood Revue of 1929* (film, 1929); by Bull Montana and Winnie Lightner in *The Show of Shows* (film, 1929); by Frank Morgan in *Hullabaloo* (film, 1940); and by Dan Dailey in *You Were Meant for Me* (film, 1948).

You Were Mine
Words and music by Paul Giacalone.
Patsy Ann Music, 1959/Unart Music Corp., 1959.
Best-selling record by The Fireflies (Ribbon).

You Were Never Lovelier
Words by Johnny Mercer, music by Jerome Kern.
T. B. Harms Co., 1942.
Introduced by Fred Astaire in *You Were Never Lovelier* (film).

You Were on My Mind
Words and music by Sylvia Fricker.
M. Witmark & Sons, 1964, 1965.
Introduced by Ian and Sylvia (Vanguard). Best-selling record in 1965 by
    We Five (A&M). Revived in 1967 with best-selling record by Crispian
    St. Peters (Jamie).

You Were Only Fooling
Words by William E. Faber and Fred Meadows, music by Larry
    Fotine.
Bregman, Vocco & Conn, Inc., 1946.
Best-selling record by Blue Barron and his Orchestra (MGM). Revived
    in 1965 with best-selling record by Vic Damone (Warner Bros.).

You Were Only Teasing Me
Words and music by Ernest Tubb and T. Texas Tyler.
Unichappell Music Inc., 1946.
Best-selling record by T. Texas Tyler (4 Star).

You Were There (English)
Words and music by Noel Coward.
Chappell & Co., Ltd., London, England/Chappell & Co., Inc., 1935.
Introduced by Gertrude Lawrence and Noel Coward in *Shadow Play*,
    one of ten short plays in *Tonight at 8:30* (plays with music), presented
    in London in 1935 and in New York in 1936.

You Will Find Your Love in Paris (French)
English words by Mack Gordon, French words by Flavien Monod,
    French words and music by Guy La Farge.
Editions Musicales, Paris, France, 1948/Remick Music Corp., 1953,
    1958.
Second English-language version of "La Seine." Best-selling record Patti
    Page (Mercury).

You Will Have To Pay for Your Yesterday
Words by Bonnie Dodd and Sarah Jane Cooper, music by Tex
    Ritter.
Criterion Music Corp., 1945.
Best-selling record by Tex Ritter (Capitol).

You Will Remember Vienna
Words by Oscar Hammerstein, II, music by Sigmund Romberg.
Harms, Inc., 1930.
Introduced by Vivienne Segal and Alexander Gray in *Viennese Nights*
    (film). Sung by Helen Traubel in *Deep in My Heart* (film, 1954).

You Will Wear Velvet
Words by Douglass Cross, music by George Cory.

General Music Publishing Co., Inc., 1954.
Introduced by Mabel Mercer.

You Will, Won't You?
Words by Anne Caldwell and Otto Harbach, music by Jerome Kern.
T. B. Harms Co., 1926.
Introduced by Dorothy Stone and Roy Hoyer in *Criss Cross* (musical).

You Wonderful You
Words by Jack Brooks and Saul Chaplin, music by Harry Warren.
Four Jays Music Co., 1950.
Introduced by Gene Kelly and Judy Garland in *Summer Stock* (film).

You Won't Be Satisfied (Until You Break My Heart)
Words and music by Freddy James and Larry Stock.
Mutual Music Society, Inc., 1945.
Best-selling record by Les Brown and his Orchestra, vocal by Doris Day
  (Columbia).

You Won't See Me (English)
Words and music by John Lennon and Paul McCartney.
Northern Songs, Ltd., England, 1966/Maclen Music Inc., 1966.
Introduced by The Beatles in their album, *Rubber Soul* (Capitol).
  Revived in 1974 by Anne Murray (Capitol).

You Wouldn't Fool Me, Would You?
Words and music by B. G. De Sylva, Lew Brown, and Ray
  Henderson.
Anne-Rachel Music Corp., 1928/DeSylva, Brown & Henderson, Inc.,
  1928.
Introduced by John Barker and Irene Delroy in *Follow Thru* (musical,
  1929).

You Wouldn't Listen
Words and music by Millas, Peterik, and Borch.
Junik Music, Inc., 1966.
Best-selling record by The Ides of March (Parrot).

You You You (West German)
English words by Robert Mellin, German words by Walter
  Rothenberg, music by Lotar Olias.
Screen Gems-EMI Music Inc., 1953.
Best-selling record by The Ames Brothers (RCA Victor). Revived in
  1966 with best-selling record by Mel Carter (Imperial).

You, You, You Are the One (West German)
English words by Fred Wise and Milton Leeds, music by Tetos
  Demey.

Misirlou Music, Inc., 1948.

Based on German folk song, "Du, Du Liegst Mir im Herzen." Introduced by Johnny Eager (Grand). Best-selling record by The Ames Brothers (Coral).

You'd Be So Nice To Come Home To
Words and music by Cole Porter.
Chappell & Co., Inc., 1942.
Introduced by Janet Blair and Don Ameche in *Something To Shout About* (film, 1943). Nominated for an Academy Award, 1943.

You'd Better Come Home (English)
Words and music by Tony Hatch.
Manitou-Duchess, 1965/Welbeck Music, 1965/Duchess Music Corp., 1965/ATV Music Corp., 1965/ATV Music Publishing of Canada, Ltd., 1965.
Best-selling record by Petula Clark (Warner Bros.).

You'd Better Go
Words and music by Art Kornfield and Ted Daryll.
Big Seven Music Corp., 1964.
Best-selling record by Chance Eden (Roulette).

You'd Better Love Me
Words and music by Hugh Martin and Timothy Gray.
Cromwell Music, Inc., 1964.
Introduced by Tammy Grimes in *High Spirits* (musical).

You'd Better Sit Down Kids, also known as **You Better...**
Words and music by Sonny Bono (pseudonym for Salvatore Bono).
Cotillion Music Inc., 1967/Chris-Marc Music, 1967.
Best-selling record in 1967-68 by Cher (Imperial).

You'd Never Know the Old Place Now
Words by Marve Fisher, music by Matt Dennis.
Dorsey Brothers' Music, Inc., 1941.

You'll Always Be the One I Love
Words by Sunny Skylar, music by Ticker Freeman.
Music Sales Corp., 1947.
Introduced by Frank Sinatra. Revived in 1964 with best-selling record by Dean Martin (Reprise).

You'll Answer to Me
Words by Hal David, music by Sherman Edwards.
Shapiro, Bernstein & Co., Inc., 1961.
Best-selling record by Patti Page (Mercury).

You'll Be Mine in Apple Blossom Time
Words by Charles Tobias, music by Peter De Rose.
Edwin H. Morris Co., 1931.

You'll Be Sorry
Words and music by Fred Rose and Gene Autry.
Western Music Publishing Co., 1942.
Best-selling record by Gene Autry (Columbia).

You'll Drive Me Back (Into Her Arms Again)
Words and music by Merle Kilgore and Miriam Lewis.
Al Gallico Music Corp., 1963.
Best-selling record in 1964 by Faron Young (Mercury).

(If You Can't Sing It) You'll Have To Swing It, also known as
   Mr. Paganini
Words and music by Sam Coslow.
Famous Music Co., 1936.
Introduced by Martha Raye in *Rhythm on the Range* (film).

You'll Lose a Good Thing
Words and music by Barbara Lynn Ozen.
Jamie Music Publishing Co., 1962/Crazy Cajun Music, 1962.
Best-selling record by Barbara Lynn (Jamie). Revived in 1976 by Freddy
   Fender (ABC/Dot).

You'll Never Find Another Love Like Mine
Words and music by Kenny Gamble and Leon Huff.
Mighty Three Music, 1976.
Best-selling record by Lou Rawls (Philadelphia International, 1976).

You'll Never Get a Better Chance Than This
Words and music by Justin Tubb.
Tree Publishing Co., Inc., 1962.
Introduced by Johnny and Jack (Decca).

You'll Never Get Away
Words and music by Joan Whitney, Alex Kramer, and Hy Zaret.
Bourne Co., 1952.
Introduced by The Paulette Sisters. Best-selling record by Teresa Brewer
   and Don Cornell (Coral).

You'll Never Get Away from Me
Words by Stephen Sondheim, music by Jule Styne.
Chappell & Co., Inc., 1959.
Introduced by Ethel Merman and Jack Klugman in *Gypsy* (musical).

You'll Never Get to Heaven (If You Don't Stop Hurting Me)
Words and music by Jim McBride.
Berwill Publishing Co., 1973.
Best-selling record by The Stylistics (Avco, 1973).

You'll Never Know
Words by Mack Gordon, music by Harry Warren.
Bregman, Vocco & Conn, Inc., 1943.
Introduced by Alice Faye in *Hello, Frisco, Hello* (film). Also sung by
Alice Faye in *Four Jills in a Jeep* (film, 1944). Best-selling record by
Dick Haymes (Decca). Won an Academy Award, 1943.

You'll Never Walk Alone
Words by Oscar Hammerstein, II, music by Richard Rodgers.
Williamson Music Inc., 1945.
Introduced by Christine Johnson in *Carousel* (musical). Sung by Clara-
mae Turner in film version (1957). Revived in 1965 with best-selling
record by Gerry and The Pacemakers (Laurie) and in 1969 with best-
selling record by Brooklyn Bridge (Buddah).

Young American (English)
Words and music by David Bowie.
Mainman Music, 1974/Chrysalis Music Corp., 1974.
Best-selling record by David Bowie (RCA, 1975).

Young and Foolish
Words by Arnold B. Horwitt, music by Albert Hague.
Chappell & Co., Inc., 1954.
Introduced by David Daniels and Gloria Marlowe in *Plain and Fancy*
(musical).

Young and Healthy
Words by Al Dubin, music by Harry Warren.
M. Witmark & Sons, 1932.
Introduced by Dick Powell in *Forty-Second Street* (film, 1933).

Young and Warm and Wonderful
Words by Hy Zaret, music by Lou Singer.
Frank Music Co., 1958.
Best-selling record by Tony Bennett (Columbia).

Young at Heart
Words by Carolyn Leigh, music by Johnny Richards.
Cherio Corp., 1954/June S. Tune, 1954.
From the melody of a song called "Moonbeam," written by Richards in
1939. Introduced and best-selling record by Frank Sinatra (Capitol).
Subsequently used as title song of *Young at Heart* (film).

Young Blood
Words and music by Jerry Leiber, Mike Stoller, and Doc Pomus.
Freddy Bienstock Music Co., 1957/Unichappell Music Inc., 1957/
  The Hudson Bay Music Co., 1957.
Best-selling record by The Coasters (Atco). Revived in 1976 by Bad
  Company (Swan Song).

Young Emotions
Words by Mack David, music by Jerry Livingston.
Nelson Music Publishing Co., 1962.
Best-selling record in 1960 Ricky Nelson (Imperial).

A Young Girl (French)
English words by Oscar Brown, Jr., French words by Charles
  Aznavour, music by Charles Aznavour and R. Chauvigny.
Editions Vianelly, Paris, France/Edward B. Marks Music Corp.,
  1964/France Music Co., 1964.
Original French title, "Une Enfant." Introduced by Charles Aznavour.
  Best-selling record of English version in 1965 by Noel Harrison (Lon-
  don).

Young Girl
Words and music by Jerry Fuller.
Warner-Tamerlane Publishing Corp., 1968.
Best-selling record by Gary Puckett and The Union Gap (Columbia).

Young Hearts Run Free
Words and music by Dave Crawford.
Da Ann Music, 1976.
Best-selling record by Candi Staton (Warner Brothers, 1976).

Young Ideas
Words by Chuck Sweeney, music by Moose Charlap.
Harms, Inc., 1955.
Introduced in *The King and Mrs. Candle* (television musical). Intro-
  duced on records by Tony Martin (RCA Victor).

Young Love
Words and music by Ric Cartey and Carole Joyner.
Lowery Music Co., Inc., 1956.
Introduced by Ric Cartey. Subsequently used as title song for *Young
  Love* (film). Best-selling records in 1957 by Tab Hunter (Dot) and
  Sonny James (Capitol). Revived in 1966 with best-selling record by
  Lesley Gore (Mercury).

Young Lovers
Words and music by Ray Hildebrand and Jill Jackson.

Le Bill Music, Inc., 1963/Marbill Music, 1963.
Best-selling record by Paul and Paula (Philips).

The Young Man with a Horn
Words by Ralph Freed, music by George Stoll.
Leo Feist Inc., 1944.
Introduced by June Allyson with Harry James in *Two Girls and a Sailor*
(film). Sung by Miss Allyson, again with James, in *The Opposite Sex*
(film, 1956).

A Young Man's Fancy
Words by John Murray Anderson and Jack Yellen, music by Milton
Ager.
Leo Feist Inc., 1920/Jack Yellen Music, 1920/Warner Brothers, Inc.,
1920.
Introduced by Rosalind Fuller in *What's in a Name* (revue).

The Young New Mexican Puppeteer
Words by Earl Shuman, music by Leon Carr.
George Pincus & Sons Music Corp., 1972.
Best-selling record by Tom Jones (Parrot, 1972).

The Young Ones
Words and music by Sid Tepper and Roy C. Bennett.
Harms-Whitmark, Ltd., London, England/M. Witmark & Sons,
1961.
Introduced by Cliff Richard with The Shadows in *The Young Ones*
(Britisn film, 1962).

Young Only Yesterday
Words and music by Bob Perper and Yvette Ball.
Gil Music Corp., 1963.

Young Woman's Blues
Words and music by Bessie Smith.
Frank Music Co., 1927.
First recording by Bessie Smith (Columbia).

Young World
Words and music by Jerry Fuller.
Matragun Music Inc., 1962/Acuff-Rose Publications Inc., 1962.
Best-selling record by Ricky Nelson (Imperial).

Youngblood
Words and music by Rickie Lee Jones.
Easy Money Music, 1979.
Best-selling record by Rickie Lee Jones (Warner Brothers, 1979).

Younger Girl
Words and music by John Sebastian.
The Hudson Bay Music Co., 1965.
Best-selling records in 1966 by The Critters (Kapp) and The Hondells
(Mercury).

Younger Than Springtime
Words by Oscar Hammerstein, II, music by Richard Rodgers.
Williamson Music Inc., 1949.
Introduced by William Tabbart in *South Pacific* (musical). Sung by voice
of Bill Lee, dubbed for John Kerr, in film version (1958).

Your Bulldog Drinks Champagne
Words and music by David Bellamy and Jim Stafford.
Famous Music Co., 1975.
Best-selling record by Jim Stafford (MGM, 1975).

Your Cash Ain't Nothin' but Trash
Words and music by Charles Calhoun.
Unichappell Music Inc., 1954.
Best-selling record by The Clovers (Atlantic). Revived in 1974 by Steve
Miller (Capitol).

Your Cheatin' Heart
Words and music by Hank Williams.
Fred Rose Music, Inc., 1952/Hiriam Music, 1952.
Best-selling records in 1953 by Hank Williams (M-G-M) and Joni James
(M-G-M).

Your Father's Moustache
Words and music by Bill Harris and Woody Herman.
Edwin H. Morris Co., 1945.
Introduced by Woody Herman and his Orchestra (Columbia).

Your Feet's Too Big
Words and music by Ada Benson and Fred Fisher.
Fisher Music Corp., 1936/Morley Music Co., Inc., 1936.
Popularized by Fats Waller.

Your Good Girl's Gonna Go Bad
Words and music by Billy Sherrill and Glenn Sutton.
Al Gallico Music Corp., 1967.
Best-selling record by Tammy Wynette (Epic).

Your Good Thing (Is About to End)
Words and music by David Porter and Isaac Hayes.
Irving Music Inc., 1966.

Best-selling record in 1969 by Lou Rawls (Capitol). Revived in 1979 by Bonnie Raitt (Warner Bros.) Featured on the album *The Glow*.

Your Head on My Shoulder
Words by Harold Adamson, music by Burton Lane.
Robbins Music Corp., 1934.
Introduced by Ann Sothern and George Murphy in *Kid Millions* (film).

Your Heart Turned Left (And I Was on the Right)
Words and music by Harlan Howard.
Glad Music Co., 1964.
Best-selling record by George Jones (United Artists).

Your Husband, My Wife
Words and music by Toni Wine and Irwin Levine.
Big Apple Music Co., 1969.
Best-selling record by Brooklyn Bridge (Buddah).

Your Land and My Land
Words by Dorothy Donnelly, music by Sigmund Romberg.
Harms, Inc., 1927.
Introduced by Nathaniel Wagner and the chorus in *My Maryland* (operetta).

Your Letter (English)
Words and music by Joan Armatrading.
Irving Music Inc., 1977.
Introduced by Joan Armatrading on *To the Limit* (A&M, 1977).

Your Love
Words and music by Walter Johnson and H. B. Barnum.
El Patricio Music, 1975.
Best-selling record by Marilyn McCoo & Billy Davis, Jr. (ABC, 1977).

Your Love Is All That I Crave
Words and music by Al Dubin, Perry Bradford, and Jimmy Johnson.
M. Witmark & Sons, 1929.
Introduced by Frank Fay, with Harry Akst at the piano, in *The Show of Shows* (film).

Your Love Keeps Lifting Me (Higher and Higher), see **(Your Love Has Lifted Me) Higher and Higher.**

Your Mama Don't Dance
Words and music by Kenny Loggins and Jim Messina.
MCA Music, 1972/Jasperilla Music Co., 1972.
Best-selling record by Loggins & Messina (Columbia, 1973).

Your Mother and Mine
Words by Joe Goodwin, music by Gus Edwards.
Robbins Music Corp., 1929.
Introduced by Charles King in *Hollywood Revue of 1929* (film). Sung
by Beatrice Lillie, Frank Fay, Louise Fazenda, and Lloyd Hamilton
in *The Show of Shows* (film).

Your Mother Should Know (English)
Words and music by John Lennon and Paul McCartney.
Comet Music Corp., 1967.
Introduced by The Beatles in their album, *Magical Mystery Tour* (Capitol).

Your Mother's Son-in-Law
Words by Mann Holiner, music by Alberta Nichols.
Anne-Rachel Music Corp., 1933.
Introduced by John Mason, Edith Wilson, Toni Ellis, Martha Thomas,
Worthy and Thompson, and chorus in Lew Leslie's *Blackbirds of
1933-34* (revue). Debut recording of Billie Holiday, with Benny Goodman and his Orchestra (Columbia).

Your Name Is Beautiful
Words and music by Diana Lampert and John Gluck.
Denny Music, Inc., 1958.
Best-selling record by Carl Smith (Columbia).

Your Old Love Letters
Words and music by Johnny Bond.
Red River Songs, Inc., 1955.
Best-selling record in 1961 by Porter Wagoner (RCA Victor).

Your Old Standby
Words and music by Janie Bradford and William Robinson, Jr.
Jobete Music Co., Inc., 1963.
Best-selling record by Mary Wells (Motown).

Your Old Used To Be
Words and music by Hilda M. Young and Faron Young.
Johnny Bienstock Music, 1960.
Best-selling record by Johnny Burnette (Liberty).

Your Other Love
Words by Ben Raleigh, music by Claus Ogerman.
Helios Music Corp., 1963/Big Seven Music Corp., 1963.
Introduced by Connie Francis (MGM).

Your Own Back Yard
Words and music by Dion Di Mucci and Tony Fasce.

Wedge Music, 1970/Aliben Music, 1970.
Best-selling record by Dion (Warner Brothers, 1970).

Your Own Special Way (English)
Words and music by Mike Rutherford.
Hidden Music, 1977.
Best-selling record by Genesis (Atco, 1977).

Your Precious Love
Words and music by Valerie Simpson and Nicholas Ashford.
Jobete Music Co., Inc., 1967.
Best-selling record by Marvin Gaye and Tammi Terrell (Tamla).

Your Red Wagon
Words by Don Raye, music by Gene de Paul and Richard M. Jones.
Leeds Music Corp., 1940, 1946, 1948.
Based on an instrumental blues composition by Richard M. Jones. Best-
   selling record in 1947 by The Andrews Sisters (Decca).

Your Smiles, Your Tears
Words by Irving Caesar, music by Sigmund Romberg.
Shubert Music Publishing Corp., 1930.
Introduced by Guy Robertson and Ethelind Terry in *Nina Rosa* (musi-
   cal).

Your Smiling Face
Words and music by James Taylor.
Country Road Music Inc., 1977.
Best-selling record by James Taylor (Columbia, 1977).

Your Socks Don't Match
Words and music by Leon Carr and Leo Corday.
Duchess Music Corp., 1941.
Introduced by Fats Waller, Best-selling record by Bing Crosby and Louis
   Jordan (Decca).

Your Song (English)
Words and music by Elton John and Bernie Taupin.
Dick James Music Inc., 1970.
Best-selling record by Elton John (MCA, 1971).

Your Tender Loving Care
Words and music by Buck Owens.
Blue Book Music, 1967.
Best-selling record by Buck Owens (Capitol).

Your Time Is Gonna Come (English)
Words and music by Jimmy Page and John Paul Jones (pseudonym

for John Baldwin).
Superhype Publishing, 1969.
Introduced by Led Zeppelin in their album, *Led Zeppelin* (Atlantic).

Your Time to Cry
Words and music by Joe Simon, Raeford Gerald, and Dock Price, Jr.
Unichappell Music Inc., 1970/Gaucho Music, 1970.
Best-selling record by Joe Simon (Spring, 1970).

Your True Love
Words and music by Carl Lee Perkins.
Knox Music, Inc., 1957.
Best-selling record by Carl Perkins (Sun).

Your Unchanging Love
Words and music by Brian Holland, Lamont Dozier, and Eddie
    Holland.
Stone Agate Music Corp., 1965.
Best-selling record in 1967 by Marvin Gaye (Tamla).

Your Used To Be
Words and music by Howard Greenfield and Jack Keller.
Screen Gems-EMI Music Inc., 1962.
Best-selling record by Brenda Lee (Decca).

You're a Builder-Upper
Words by Ira Gershwin and E. Y. Harburg, music by Harold Arlen.
New World Music Corp., 1934.
Introduced by Ray Bolger and Dixie Dunbar in *Life Begins at 8:40*
    (revue).

You're a Heavenly Thing
Words and music by Joe Young and Little Jack Little.
World Music, Inc., 1935/Warock Music, Inc., 1935.
Introduced by Little Jack Little.

You're a Lucky Guy
Words by Sammy Cahn, music by Saul Chaplin.
M. Witmark & Sons, 1939.

You're a Natural
Words by Frank Loesser, music by Manning Sherwin.
Famous Music Co., 1938.
Introduced by Gracie Allen in *College Swing* (film).

You're a Part of Me
Words and music by Kim Carnes.
Chappell & Co., Inc., 1975.

Best-selling records by Susan Jacks (Mercury, 1975), Kim Carnes (A & M, 1976), and Charlie McLain (Epic, 1979).

You're a Queer One, Julie Jordan
Words by Oscar Hammerstein, II, music by Richard Rodgers.
Williamson Music Inc., 1945.
Introduced by Jean Darling and Jan Clayton in *Carousel* (musical). Sung by Barbara Ruick and Shirley Jones in film version (1957).

You're a Special Part of Me
Words and music by Gregory Wright, Harold Johnson, and Andrew Porter.
Jobete Music Co., Inc., 1973.
Best-selling record by Diana Ross and Marvin Gaye (Motown, 1973).

You're a Sweet Little Headache
Words and music by Leo Robin and Ralph Rainger.
Paramount Music Corp., 1938.
Introduced by Bing Crosby in *Paris Honeymoon* (film, 1939).

You're a Sweetheart
Words by Harold Adamson, music by Jimmy McHugh.
Universal Music Corp., 1937.
Introduced by Alice Faye in *You're a Sweetheart* (film). Sung by Frank Sinatra in *Meet Danny Wilson* (film, 1952).

You're a Wonderful One
Words and music by Eddie Holland, Brian Holland, and Dozier Lamont.
Jobete Music Co., Inc., 1964.
Best-selling record by Marvin Gaye (Tamla).

You're All I Need
Words by Gus Kahn, music by Bronislaw Kaper and Walter Jurmann.
Robbins Music Corp., 1935.
Introduced by Lorraine Bridges in *Escapade* (film).

You're All I Need to Get By
Words and music by Nicholas Ashford and Valerie Simpson.
Jobete Music Co., Inc., 1968.
Best-selling record by Marvin Gaye and Tammi Terrell (Tamla). Revived in 1971 with best-selling record by Aretha Franklin (Atlantic).

You're All I Want for Christmas
Words and music by Glen Moore and Seger Ellis.

Duchess Music Corp., 1948.
Introduced by Frank Gallagher (Dana).

You're All I've Got Tonight
Words and music by Ric Ocasek.
Lido Music Inc., 1978.
Introduced by The Cars on *Cars* (Elektra, 1978).

You're Always in My Arms (but Only in My Dreams)
Words by Joseph McCarthy, music by Harry Tierney.
Leo Feist Inc., 1929.
Introduced by Bebe Daniels and John Boles in *Rio Rita* (film).

You're an Angel
Words by Dorothy Fields, music by Jimmy McHugh.
Bourne Co., 1935.
Introduced by Ann Sothern and Gene Raymond in *Hooray for Love*
    (film).

You're an Old Smoothie
Words and music by B. G. De Sylva, Richard A. Whiting, and
    Nacio Herb Brown.
Harms, Inc., 1932/Anne-Rachel Music Corp., 1932.
Introduced by Ethel Merman and Jack Haley in *Take a Chance* (musi-
    cal). Theme song of Del Courtney and his Orchestra.

You're As Pretty As a Picture
Words by Harold Adamson, music by Jimmy McHugh.
Universal Music Corp., 1938.
Introduced by Deanna Durbin in *That Certain Age* (film).

You're Blase (English)
Words by Bruce Sievier, music by Ord Hamilton.
Chappell & Co., Ltd., London, England, 1931/Chappell & Co., Inc.,
    1932.
Introduced in London by Binnie Hale in *Bow Bells* (musical).

You're Breaking My Heart (Italian)
Italian words and music by Pat Genaro and Sunny Skylar.
Screen Gems-EMI Music Inc., 1948.
Adapted from Leoncavallo's "La Mattinata." Best-selling records in 1949
    by Vic Damone (Mercury) and Buddy Clark (Columbia).

You're Dangerous
Words by Johnny Burke, music by Jimmy Van Heusen.
Famous Music Co., 1941.
Introduced by Bing Crosby in *Road to Zanzibar* (film).

You're Devastating
Words by Otto Harbach, music by Jerome Kern.
T. B. Harms Co., 1933.
Introduced by Bob Hope and Tamara in *Roberta* (musical).

You're Driving Me Crazy (What Did I Do?)
Words and music by Walter Donaldson.
Anne-Rachel Music Corp., 1930/Donaldson Publishing Co., 1930/
Tobago Music Co.
Introduced by Guy Lombardo and his Royal Canadians. Sung by Adele
Astaire, Eddie Foy, Jr., and chorus in *Smiles* (musical).

You're Easy To Dance With
Words and music by Irving Berlin.
Irving Berlin Music Corp., 1942.
Introduced by Fred Astaire in *Holiday Inn* (film).

You're Everywhere
Words by Edward Heyman, music by Vincent Youmans.
Miller Music Corp., 1932/Vincent Youmans Co., Inc., 1932.
Introduced by Natalie Hall and Michael Bartlett in *Through the Years*
(musical).

You're Everywhere
Words by Paul Francis Webster, music by Harry Revel.
Chappell & Co., Inc., 1947.
Introduced in *It Happened on 5th Avenue* (film).

You're Far Too Near to Me
Words by Ira Gershwin, music by Kurt Weill.
Chappell & Co., Inc., 1945/Hampshire House Publishing Corp.,
1945.
Introduced by Earl Wrightson in *The Firebrand of Florence* (musical).

You're for Me
Words and music by Tommy Collins and E. A. Owens, Jr.
Central Songs, 1954.
Best-selling record in 1963 by Buck Owens (Capitol).

You're Free To Go
Words and music by Don Robertson and Lou Herscher.
Anne-Rachel Music Corp., 1955.
Best-selling record in 1956 by Carl Smith (Columbia).

You're Getting To Be a Habit with Me
Words by Al Dubin, music by Harry Warren.
M. Witmark & Sons, 1932.
Introduced by Bebe Daniels in *Forty-Second Street* (film, 1933).

You're Gone (French)
English words by Mort Goode, French words by Agnes Varda, music by Michel Legrand.
Productions Michel Legrand, Paris, France/Editions Hortensia, Paris, France/N. S. Beaujolais Music, Inc., 1965.
Original French title, "Sans Toi." French version introduced by Corinne Marchand in *Cleo de 5 a 7* (French film, 1962). English version introduced by Grady Tate (Skye).

You're Gonna Change (Or I'm Gonna Leave)
Words and music by Hank Williams.
Fred Rose Music, Inc., 1949.
Best-selling record by Hank Williams (MGM).

You're Gonna Get What's Comin (English)
Words and music by Robert Palmer.
Bungalow Music, 1978.
Best-selling record by Bonnie Raitt (Warner Brothers, 1979).

You're Gonna Hear from Me
Words by Dory Previn, music by Andre Previn.
Remick Music Corp., 1965.
Introduced by the voice of Jackie Ward, dubbed for Natalie Wood, in *Inside Daisy Clover* (film, 1966). Best-selling record in 1966 by Andy Williams (Columbia).

You're Gonna Hurt Yourself
Words and music by Bob Crewe and Charles Calello.
Saturday Music Inc., 1965/Seasons Four Music Corp., 1965.
Best-selling record in 1966 by Frankie Valli (Smash).

You're Gonna Kill That Girl
Words and music by Douglas Colvin, John Cummings, Thomas Erdelyi, and Jeff Hyman.
Taco Tunes Inc., 1977/Bleu Disque Music, 1977.
Introduced by The Ramones on *Leave Home* (Sire, 1977).

You're Gonna Lose That Girl (English)
Words and music by John Lennon and Paul McCartney.
Maclen Music Inc., 1965/Unart Music Corp., 1965.
Sung by The Beatles in *Help!* (film) and in their album, *Help!* (Capitol).

You're Gonna Lose Your Gal
Words by Joe Young, music by James V. Monaco.
International Pauline Corp., 1933.
Sung by Doris Day and Gordon MacRae in *Starlift* (film, 1951).

You're Gonna Make Me Cry
Words and music by Deadric Malone.
Duchess Music Corp., 1964/Manitou-Duchess, 1964.
Best-selling record in 1965 by O.V. Wright (Back Beat).

You're Gonna Miss Me
Words and music by Eddie Curtis.
Anne-Rachel Music Corp., 1959/Planetary Music Publishing Corp.,
1959.
Best-selling record by Connie Francis (M-G-M).

You're in Love
Words and music by Cole Porter.
Harms, Inc., 1932.
Introduced by Fred Astaire, Claire Luce, and Erik Rhodes in *Gay
Divorce* (musical).

**You're in Love with Everyone but the One Who's in Love with
You**
Words by Mort Dixon, music by Ray Henderson.
Mills Music Inc., 1924/Olde Clover Leaf Music, 1924.

You're in Love with Someone
Words by Johnny Burke, music by James Van Heusen.
Bourne Co., 1949/Music Sales Corp., 1949.
Introduced by Bing Crosby in *Top o' the Morning* (film).

You're in My Heart (The Final Acclaim) (English)
Words and music by Rod Stewart.
Riva Music Ltd., 1977.
Best-selling record by Rod Stewart (Warner Brothers, 1978).

You're Irish and You're Beautiful
Words and music by Charlie Tobias and Al Lewis.
Sovereign Music Corp., 1943.

You're Just a Dream Come True
Words by Charles Newman, music by Isham Jones.
Leo Feist Inc., 1931.
Theme song of Isham Jones and his Orchestra.

You're Just in Love
Words and music by Irving Berlin.
Irving Berlin Music Corp., 1950.
Introduced by Ethel Merman and Russell Nype in *Call Me Madam*
(musical). Best-selling record by Perry Como (RCA Victor).

You're Just the Kind
Words by Bill Carey, music by Carl Fischer.
Boca Music Inc., 1949.
Introduced by Frankie Laine (Mercury).

You're Laughing at Me
Words and music by Irving Berlin.
Irving Berlin Music Corp., 1937.
Introduced by Dick Powell in *On the Avenue* (film).

You're Lonely and I'm Lonely
Words and music by Irving Berlin.
Irving Berlin Music Corp., 1940.
Introduced by Zorina and Victor Moore in *Louisiana Purchase* (musical).

You're Lookin' at Country
Words and music by Loretta Lynn.
Sure Fire Music Co., Inc., 1970.
Best-selling record by Loretta Lynn (Decca, 1971).

You're Lucky to Me
Words by Andy Razaf, music by Eubie Blake.
Shapiro, Bernstein & Co., Inc., 1930.
Introduced by Neeka Shaw and John Bubbles, and reprised by Ethel Waters and Eubie Blake, in Lew Leslie's *Blackbirds of 1930* (revue).

You're Making a Fool out of Me
Words and music by Tompall Glaser.
Canadiana-Glaser, 1958/Ensign Music Corp., 1958.
Best-selling record by Jimmy Newman (M-G-M).

You're Mine
Words and music by Robert Carr and Johnny Mitchell.
Maureen Music, Inc., 1956.
Best-selling record by Robert and Johnny (Old Town).

You're Mine, You!
Words by Edward Heyman, music by John Green.
Famous Music Co., 1933.

You're Moving Out Today
Words and music by Carole Bayer Sager, Bruce Roberts, and Bette Midler.
Unichappell Music Inc., 1977/Fedora Music, 1977/Devine's Music Ltd., 1977.
Best-selling records by Bette Midler (Atlantic, 1977) and Carole Bayer Sager (Elektra, 1977).

You're My Best Friend
Words and music by Wayland Holyfield.
Vogue Music, 1975.
Best-selling record by Don Williams (ABC/Dot, 1975).

You're My Best Friend (English)
Words and music by John Deacon.
Trident Music, 1975/Glenwood Music Corp., 1975.
Best-selling record by Queen (Elektra, 1976).

You're My Everything
Words by Mort Dixon and Joe Young, music by Harry Warren.
Harms, Inc., 1931/Warock Music, Inc., 1931.
Introduced by Jeanne Aubert and Lawrence Gray in *The Laugh Parade*
   (revue). Sung by Dan Dailey in *You're My Everything* (film, 1949).

You're My Everything
Words and music by Norman Whitfield, Roger Penzabene, and
   Cornelius Grant.
Stone Agate Music Corp., 1967.
Best-selling record by The Temptations (Gordy).

You're My Girl
Words by Sammy Cahn, music by Jule Styne.
Cahn Music Co., 1947/Producers Music Publishing Co., Inc., 1947.
Introduced by Mark Dawson and Lois Lee in *High Button Shoes*.

(Say) You're My Girl
Words and music by Roy Orbison and Bill Dees.
Acuff-Rose Publications Inc., 1965.
Best-selling record by Roy Orbison (Monument).

You're My Home
Words and music by Billy Joel.
Blackwood Music Inc., 1973.
Performed by Billy Joel on *Billy Joel* (Columbia, 1973).

You're My Jamaica
Words and music by Kent Robbins.
Hall-Clement Publications, 1978.
Best-selling record by Charley Pride (RCA, 1979).

You're My Man
Words and music by Glenn Sutton.
Flagship Music Inc., 1971.
Best-selling record by Lynn Anderson (Columbia, 1971).

You're My Past, Present and Future
Words by Mack Gordon, music by Harry Revel.
DeSylva, Brown & Henderson, Inc., 1933.
Introduced by Russ Columbo in *Broadway thru a Keyhole* (film).

You're My Thrill
Words by Ned Washington, music by Burton Lane.
Robbins Music Corp., 1935.
Introduced by Ted Lewis in *Here Comes the Band* (film).

You're My World (Italian)
English words by Carl Sigman, Italian words by Gino Paoli, music
   by Umberto Bindi.
Edizioni Musicali M.E.C., Italy, 1963, 1964/Plan Two Music, Inc.,
   1963.
Original title, "Il Mio Mondo." Best-selling record by Cilla Black (Capitol). Revived in 1977 by Helen Reddy (Capitol).

You're Nearer
Words by Lorenz Hart, music by Richard Rodgers.
Chappell & Co., Inc., 1940.
New song written especially for film version of the musical, *Too Many
   Girls*. Introduced in film by Richard Carlson.

You're Next
Music by Lillian Hardin Armstrong.
MCA, Inc., 1926.
First recording by Louis Armstrong and his Hot Five (Okeh).

You're No Good
Words and music by Clint Ballard, Jr.
Blue Seas Music Inc., 1963/Jac Music Co., Inc., 1963/Edwin H.
   Morris Co., 1963/U.S. Songs, 1963.
Best-selling record by Linda Ronstadt (Capitol, 1975).

You're Nobody 'til Somebody Loves You
Words and music by Russ Morgan, Larry Stock, and James
   Cavanaugh.
Shapiro, Bernstein & Co., Inc., 1944/Southern Music Publishing Co.,
   Inc., 1944.
Introduced by Russ Morgan and his Orchestra (Decca).

You're Not Mine Anymore
Words and music by Webb Pierce and The Wilburn Brothers.
Cedarwood Publishing Co., Inc., 1954.
Best-selling record by Webb Pierce (Decca).

You're Not So Easy To Forget
Words by Herb Magidson, music by Ben Oakland.
Leo Feist Inc., 1947/Magidson Music Co., Inc., 1947.
Introduced in *Song of the Thin Man* (film).

You're Not the Kind
Words and music by Will Hudson and Irving Mills.
Mills Music Inc., 1936.

You're Not the Only Oyster in the Stew
Words by Johnny Burke, music by Harold Spina.
Bourne Co., 1934.
Best-selling record by Fats Waller and his Rhythm.

You're Only Lonely
Words and music by John David Souther.
Ice Age Music, 1979.
Best-selling record by J. D. Souther (Columbia, 1979).

You're Running Wild
Words and music by Ray Edenton and Don Winters.
Acuff-Rose Publications Inc., 1956.
Best-selling record by The Louvin Brothers (Capitol).

You're Sensational
Words and music by Cole Porter.
Buxton Hill Music Corp., 1956.
Introduced by Frank Sinatra in *High Society* (film).

You're Simply Delish
Words by Arthur Freed, music by Joseph Meyer.
Robbins Music Corp., 1930.
Introduced by Cliff Edwards and Fifi D'Orsay in *Those Three French
    Girls* (film).

You're Sixteen, You're Beautiful and You're Mine
Words and music by Dick Sherman and Bob Sherman.
Warner-Tamerlane Publishing Corp., 1960.
Best-selling record by Johnny Burnette (Liberty). Revived in 1974 by
    Ringo Starr (Apple).

You're Slightly Terrific
Words by Sidney D. Mitchell, music by Lew Pollack.
Movietone Music Corp., 1936.
Introduced by Tony Martin and Dixie Dunbar in *Pigskin Parade* (film).

You're So Desirable
Words and music by Ray Noble.
Bregman, Vocco & Conn, Inc., 1938.
Introduced by Ray Noble and his Orchestra.

You're So Fine
Words and music by Lance Finney, Bob West, and Willie Schofield.
C. & B. West Publishing Co., 1959.
Best-selling record by The Falcons (Unart).

You're So Much a Part of Me
Words and music by Richard Adler and Jerry Ross.
J & J Ross Co., 1953/Richard Adler Music, 1953.
Introduced by Carleton Carpenter and Elaine Dunn in *John Murray Anderson's Almanac* (revue).

You're So Right for Me
Words and music by Jay Livingston and Ray Evans.
Livingston & Evans, Inc., 1958.
Introduced by Edward Platt and Abbe Lane in *Oh Captain!* (musical).

You're So Understanding
Words and music by Bernie Wayne and Ben Raleigh.
Unichappell Music Inc., 1949/Benral Music Co.
Introduced and best-selling record by Blue Barron and his Orchestra (M-G-M).

You're So Vain
Words and music by Carly Simon.
Quackenbush Music Ltd., 1972.
Best-selling record by Carly Simon (Elektra, 1973). Nominated for National Academy of Recording Arts and Sciences Awards, Record of the Year, 1973, and Song of the Year, 1973.

You're Still a Young Man
Words and music by Emilio Castillo and Stephen Kupka.
Kuptillo Music, 1972.
Best-selling record by Tower of Power (Warner Brothers, 1972).

You're Still Mine
Words by Eddie Thorpe, music by Faron Young.
Johnny Bienstock Music, 1956.
Best-selling record by Faron Young (Capitol).

You're Still My Baby
Words and music by Chuck Willis.
Berkshire Music, Inc., 1954/Chuck Willis Music Co., 1954.
Best-selling record by Chuck Willis (Okeh).

You're Such a Comfort to Me
Words by Mack Gordon, music by Harry Revel.
DeSylva, Brown & Henderson, Inc., 1933.
Introduced by Ginger Rogers, Jack Oakie, Thelma Todd, and Jack
    Haley in *Sitting Pretty* (film).

You're the Best Thing That Ever Happened to Me, also known as
    Best Thing That Ever Happened to Me
Words and music by Jim Weatherly.
Keca Music Inc., 1972.
Best-selling record by Ray Price (Columbia, 1973) and Gladys Knight
    & the Pips (Buddah, 1974).

You're the Cause of It All
Words by Sammy Cahn, music by Jule Styne.
Chappell & Co., Inc., 1946.
Introduced in *The Kid from Brooklyn* (film).

You're the Cream in My Coffee
Words and music by B. G. De Sylva, Lew Brown, and Ray
    Henderson.
Anne-Rachel Music Corp., 1928/DeSylva, Brown & Henderson, Inc.,
    1928.
Introduced by Ona Munson and Jack Whiting in *Hold Everything!*
    (musical).

You're the Cure for What Ails Me
Words by E. Y. Harburg, music by Harold Arlen.
Remick Music Corp., 1936.
Introduced by Al Jolson, Sybil Jason, Edward Everett Horton, and Allen
    Jenkins in *The Singing Kid* (film).

You're the Devil in Disguise
Words and music by Bill Giant, Bernie Baum, and Florence Kaye.
Elvis Presley Music, Inc., 1963.
Best-selling record by Elvis Presley (RCA Victor).

You're the First, the Last, My Everything
Words and music by Barry White, Tony Sepe, and Peter Radcliffe.
Unichappell Music Inc., 1974/Sa-Vette Music, 1974/My Baby's
    Music, 1974.
Best-selling record by Barry White (20th Century, 1974).

You're the Love
Words and music by Louie Shelton and David Batteau.
Blue Harbor Music Co., 1978/David Batteau Music, 1978.
Best-selling record by Seals & Crofts (Warner Brothers, 1978).

You're the Nearest Thing to Heaven
Words by Johnny Cash, music by Hoydt Johnson and Jim Atkins.
Hi-Lo Music Inc., 1958/E & M Publishing Co., 1958.
Best-selling record by Johnny Cash (Sun).

You're the One
Words by J. Russel Robinson and George Waggner, music by
   Vincent Youmans.
J. Russel Robinson, Inc., 1930.
Introduced by Gloria Swanson in *What a Widow!* (film). First recording
   in 1966 by Nolan Van Way (Evergreen).

You're the One (For Me)
Words by Johnny Mercer, music by Jimmy McHugh.
Paramount Music Corp., 1940.
Introduced by Orrin Tucker and Bonnie Baker in *You're the One* (film).

You're the One (English)
Words and music by Petula Clark and Tony Hatch.
Welbeck Music, 1965/Northern Music Corp., 1965.
Best-selling record by The Vogues (Co&Ce).

You're the One, also known as **You're the One I Need**
Words and music by William Robinson.
MCA, Inc., 1966.
Best-selling record by The Marvelettes (Tamla).

You're the One I Care For
Words by Harry Link, music by Bert Lown and Chauncey Gray.
Anne-Rachel Music Corp., 1930.
Introduced by Bert Lown and his Orchestra.

You're the One I Need, see **You're the One.**

You're the One That I Want
Words and music by John Farrar.
Stigwood Music Inc., 1978/John Farrar Music, 1978/Ensign Music
   Corp., 1978.
Introduced by Olivia Newton-John and John Travolta in *Grease* (film,
   1978). Best-selling record by Olivia Newton-John and John Travolta
   (RSO, 1978).

You're the Only Good Thing (That's Happened to Me)
Words and music by Chuck Gregory.
Golden West Melodies, Inc., 1954, 1959.
Introduced in 1954 by Gene Autry. Best-selling record in 1960 by
   George Morgan (Columbia).

You're the Only One
Words and music by Seth Justman and Peter Wolf.
Murray Productions, 1977.
Best-selling record by J. Geils Band (Atlantic, 1977).

You're the Only One
Words and music by Bruce Roberts and Carole Bayer Sager.
Unichappell Music Inc., 1979/Begonia Melodies Inc., 1979/Fedora
   Music, 1979.
Best-selling record by Dolly Parton (RCA, 1979).

You're the Only Star (in My Blue Heaven)
Words and music by Gene Autry.
Shapiro, Bernstein & Co., Inc., 1938.
Introduced by Gene Autry in *The Old Barn Dance* (film).

You're the Only World I Know
Words and music by Sonny Jones and Robert F. Tubert.
Marson Inc., 1964.
Best-selling record by Sonny James (Capitol).

You're the Rainbow
Words and music by Ralph Rainger and Leo Robin.
Paramount Music Corp., 1943.
Introduced in *Melody Inn* (film).

You're the Reason
Words and music by Bobby Edwards, Mildred Imes, Fred Henley,
   and Terry Fell.
Vogue Music, 1960.
Best-selling record in 1961 by Bobby Edwards (Crest).

You're the Reason I'm in Love
Words and music by Jack Morrow.
Beechwood Music Corp., 1956.
Best-selling record in 1957 by Sonny James (Capitol).

You're the Reason I'm Living
Words and music by Bobby Darin.
The Hudson Bay Music Co., 1962.
Best-selling record in 1963 by Bobby Darin (Capitol).

You're the Reason Our Kids Are Ugly
Words and music by L. E. White and Lola Jean Dillon.
Twitty Bird Music Publishing Co., 1977/Coal Miner's Music Inc.,
    1977.
Best-selling record by Conway Twitty and Loretta Lynn (MCA, 1978).

You're the Top
Words and music by Cole Porter.
Harms, Inc., 1934.
Introduced by Ethel Merman and William Gaxton in *Anything Goes*
    (musical). Sung by Miss Merman and Bing Crosby in first film version,
    1936 and by Crosby, Mitzi Gaynor, Donald O'Connor and Jeanmaire
    in second film version, 1956. Sung by Ginny Simms and Cary Grant
    in *Night and Day* (film, 1946).

You're Too Dangerous, Cherie (La Vie en Rose) (French)
English words by Mack David, French words by Edith Piaf, music
    by Louiguy.
Arpege Editions Musicales, Paris, France, 1946/Harms, Inc., 1948,
    1950/T. B. Harms Co., 1948.
Original French title, "La Vie en Rose." First English-language version
    featured in *To the Victor* (film). Reintroduced in 1950, under original
    French title and with new lyrics by Mack David, with best-selling
    record by Tony Martin (Victor).

Yours (Cuban)
English words by Jack Sherr and Albert Gamse, Spanish words by
    Augustin Rodriguez, music by Gonzalo Roig.
E. B. Marks Music Corp., 1931, 1932, 1937.
Original Spanish title, "Quierme Mucho." First recording in Spanish by
    Tito Schipa (Victor). First English-language version, with lyrics by
    Carol Raven and entitled "Love Me Tonight," copyrighted in 1932.
    Present version sung by Gene Autry in *Sioux City Sue* (film, 1946).
    Best-selling record in 1941 by Jimmy Dorsey and his Orchestra
    (Decca) and in 1952 by Vera Lynn (London).

Yours and Mine
Words by Arthur Freed, music by Nacio Herb Brown.
Robbins Music Corp., 1937.
Introduced by Judy Garland, and reprised by Eleanor Powell, in *Broad-
    way Melody of 1938* (film).

Yours for a Song
Words by Billy Rose and Ted Fetter, music by Dana Suesse.
Robbins Music Corp., 1939.
Introduced by Morton Downey at New York World's Fair in *Billy
    Rose's Aquacade* (revue).

Yours Is My Heart Alone (Austrian)

English words by Harry Bache Smith, German words by Ludwig Herzer and Fritz Loehner, music by Franz Lehar.

W. Karczag, Vienna, Austria, 1929/Shubert Music Publishing Corp., 1931.

Original German title, "Dein Ist Mein Ganzes Herz." Introduced by Richard Tauber in Berlin in *Das Land des Laechelns (The Land of Smiles)* (operetta).

Yours, Love

Words and music by Harlan Howard.

Tree Publishing Co., Inc., 1968/Harlan Howard Songs, 1968.

Best-selling record in 1969 by Dolly Parton and Porter Wagoner (RCA).

Yours Sincerely

Words by Lorenz Hart, music by Richard Rodgers.

Harms, Inc., 1929.

Introduced by Glenn Hunter and Lillian Taiz in *Spring Is Here* (musical). Sung by Alexander Gray and Bernice Claire in *Spring Is Here* (film, 1930).

You've Been a Good Ole Wagon

Words and music by John Henry (pseudonym for Perry Bradford).

MCA, Inc., 1925.

First recording by Bessie Smith (Columbia).

You've Been Cheatin'

Words and music by Curtis Mayfield.

Warner-Tamerlane Publishing Corp., 1965.

Best-selling record in 1965-66 by The Impressions (ABC).

You've Been Doing Wrong for So Long

Words and music by Frank Johnson and Terry Woodford.

Stone Diamond Music Corp., 1974/Song Tailors Music Co., 1974.

Best-selling record by Thelma Houston (Motown, 1974).

You've Been in Love Too Long

Words and music by Ivy Hunter, Clarence Paul, and William Stevenson.

Jobete Music Co., Inc., 1965/Stone Agate Music Corp., 1965.

Best-selling record by Martha and The Vandellas (Gordy).

You've Broken a Fine Woman's Heart

Words and music by Stan Freeman and Franklin Underwood.

Hampshire House Publishing Corp., 1970/East Gate Music, 1970.

Introduced by David Burns in *Lovely Ladies, Kind Gentlemen* (musical, 1970).

You've Changed
Words by Bill Carey, music by Carl Fischer.
Melody Lane, Inc., 1942, 1943, 1947.
Best-selling record by Harry James and his Orchestra, vocal by Dick Haymes (Columbia).

You've Changed
Words and music by Edward Heyman, Tony Martin, and Victor Young.
Victor Young Publications, Inc., 1952.
Introduced in *The Fabulous Senorita* (film).

You've Come Home
Words by Carolyn Leigh, music by Cy Coleman.
Edwin H. Morris Co., 1960, 1961.
Introduced by Keith Andes in *Wildcat* (musical).

You've Got a Friend
Words and music by Carole King.
Colgems-EMI Music Inc., 1971.
Performed by Carole King on *Tapestry* (Ode, 1971). Best-selling records by James Taylor (Warner Brothers, 1971), Roberta Flack and Donnie Hathaway (Atlantic, 1971). Won a National Academy of Recording Arts and Sciences Award, Song of the Year, 1971.

You've Got Everything
Words by Gus Kahn, music by Walter Donaldson.
Robbins Music Corp., 1933.

You've Got Me Crying Again
Words by Charles Newman, music by Isham Jones.
World Music, Inc., 1933.
Popularized by Ruth Etting.

You've Got Me Dangling on a String
Words and music by Ronald Dunbar and Edythe Wayne.
Gold Forever Music Inc., 1970.
Best-selling record by The Chairmen of the Board (Invictus, 1970).

You've Got Me in the Palm of Your Hand!
Words by Cliff Friend and Edgar Leslie, music by James V. Monaco.
Bregman, Vocco & Conn, Inc., 1932/Edwin H. Morris Co., 1932.

You've Got Me This Way (Whatta-Ya-Gonna Do about It)
Words by Johnny Mercer, music by Jimmy McHugh.
Bregman, Vocco & Conn, Inc., 1940.
Introduced by Kay Kyser and his College of Musical Knowledge in *You'll Find Out* (film).

You've Got Personality
Words and music by Harold Logan and Lloyd Price.
Lloyd and Logan, Inc., 1959.
Best-selling record by Lloyd Price (ABC Paramount).

You've Got Something
Words and music by Cole Porter.
Chappell & Co., Inc., 1936.
Introduced by Bob Hope and Ethel Merman in *Red, Hot and Blue!*
  (musical).

You've Got Something There
Words by Johnny Mercer, music by Richard A. Whiting.
Harms, Inc., 1937.
Introduced by Rosemary Lane and Dick Powell in *Varsity Show* (film).

You've Got That Thing
Words and music by Cole Porter.
Harms, Inc., 1929.
Introduced by Jack Thompson and Betty Compton in *Fifty Million
  Frenchmen* (musical).

You've Got the Best of Me
Words by Lorenz Hart, music by Richard Rodgers.
Chappell & Co., Inc., 1941.
Introduced by Buddy Ebsen and Diosa Costello in *They Met in Argen-
  tina* (film).

You've Got To Be Carefully Taught
Words by Oscar Hammerstein, II, music by Richard Rodgers.
Williamson Music Inc., 1949.
Introduced by William Tabbart in *South Pacific* (musical). Sung by voice
  of Bill Lee, dubbed for John Kerr, in film version (1958).

You've Got to Hide Your Love Away (English)
Words and music by John Lennon and Paul McCartney.
Northern Songs, Ltd., England, 1965/Unart-Unart, 1965/Maclen
  Music Inc., 1965/Unart Music Corp., 1965/Maclen Music of
  Canada, 1965.
Sung by The Beatles in *Help!* (film) and in their album, *Help!* (Capitol).
  Best-selling record by Silkie (Fontana).

**You've Got To See Mamma Ev'ry Night or You Can't See
Mamma At All**
Words and music by Billy Rose and Con Conrad.
Leo Feist Inc., 1923/Conrad Music, 1923.
Popularized by Sophie Tucker.

You've Got What Gets Me
Words by Ira Gershwin, music by George Gershwin.
New World Music Corp., 1932.
Introduced by Dorothy Lee and Bert Wheeler in *Girl Crazy* (film). First
  recording in 1959 by Ella Fitzgerald (Verve).

You've Got What It Takes, see **You Got What It Takes.**

You've Got Your Troubles (English)
Words and music by Roger Greenaway and Roger Cook.
Mills Music Ltd., London, England/Mills Music Inc., 1965.
Best-selling record by The Fortunes (Press).

You've Got Yours and I'll Get Mine
Words and music by William Hart and Thomas R. Bell.
Nickel Shoe Music Co., Inc., 1969/Bell Boy Music, 1969.
Best-selling record by The Delfonics (Philly Groove).

You've Gotta Eat Your Spinach, Baby
Words and music by Mack Gordon and Harry Revel.
Robbins Music Corp., 1936.
Introduced by Shirley Temple, Alice Faye, and Jack Haley in *Poor Little
  Rich Girl* (film).

You've Gotta Pay the Price
Words and music by Al Kent (pseudonym for Albert Hamilton) and
  Hermon L. Weems.
Stone Agate Music Corp., 1967.
Best-selling records by Al Kent (Ric Tic) and in 1969 by Gloria Taylor
  (Silver Fox).

You've Just Stepped In (from Stepping Out on Me)
Words and music by Don Trowbridge.
Sure Fire Music Co., Inc.
Copyright year unknown; composition registered with BMI in 1968.
  Best-selling record by Loretta Lynn (Decca).

You've Lost That Lovin' Feelin'
Words and music by Phil Spector, Barry Mann, and Cynthia Weil.
Screen Gems-EMI Music Inc., 1964.
Best-selling record in 1964-65 by The Righteous Brothers (Philles).
  Revived in 1969 with best-selling record by Dionne Warwick (Scep-
  ter).

You've Made Me So Very Happy
Words and music by Berry Gordy, Jr., Patrice Holloway, Frank
  Wilson, and Brenda Holloway.
Jobete Music Co., Inc., 1967/Stone Agate Music Corp., 1967.

Best-selling records by Brenda Holloway (Tamla) and in 1969 by Blood, Sweat and Tears (Columbia).

You've Never Been This Far Before
Words and music by Conway Twitty (pseudonym for Harold Jenkins).
Twitty Bird Music Publishing Co., 1973.
Best-selling record by Conway Twitty (MCA, 1973).

You've Really Got a Hold on Me
Words and music by William Robinson.
Jobete Music Co., Inc., 1963.
Best-selling record by The Miracles (Tamla).

You've Still Got a Place in My Heart
Words and music by Leon Payne.
Fred Rose Music, Inc.
Copyright year unknown; composition registered with BMI in 1950.
   Best-selling record in 1968 by Dean Martin (Reprise).

Yummy, Yummy, Yummy
Words and music by Arthur Resnick and Joe Levine.
The Hudson Bay Music Co., 1968.
Best-selling record by Ohio Express (Buddah).

Z

Zabadak (English)
Words and music by Howard Blaikley.
Lynn Music, Ltd., London, England, 1967/Al Gallico Music Corp., 1967.
Best-selling record in 1968 by Dave, Dozy, Beaky, Mick, and Tich Dee (Imperial).

Zambezi, also known as **Sweet African** (South African)
Afrikaans words by Bob Hilliard, music by Nico Carstens and Anton De Waal.
Carstens-De Waal Publications, Johannesburg, South Africa, 1954/ Shapiro, Bernstein & Co., Inc., 1955.
Best-selling record by Lou Busch and his Orchestra (Capitol).

Zigeuner (English)
Words and music by Noel Coward.
Harms, Inc., 1929.
Introduced by Peggy Wood in the London production and sung by Evelyn Laye in the New York production of *Bitter Sweet* (operetta). Sung by Anna Neagle in the first film version (British), 1933; and by Jeanette MacDonald in the second film version, 1940.

Zing a Little Zong
Words by Leo Robin, music by Harry Warren.
Famous Music Co., 1952/Four Jays Music Co., 1952.
Introduced by Bing Crosby and Jane Wyman in *Just for You* (film). Nominated for an Academy Award, 1952.

Zing Went the Strings of My Heart
Words and music by James Hanley.
Harms, Inc., 1935.
Introduced by Hal Le Roy and Eunice Healy in *Thumbs Up* (revue, 1934). Sung by Judy Garland in *Listen, Darling* (film, 1938) and by Gene Nelson in *Lullaby of Broadway* (film, 1951).

Zing Zing - Zoom Zoom
Words by Charles Tobias, music by Sigmund Romberg.
Robbins Music Corp., 1950.
Best-selling record by Perry Como (RCA Victor).

Zip
Words by Lorenz Hart, music by Richard Rodgers.
Chappell & Co., Inc., 1940, 1951, 1962.
Introduced by Jean Casto in *Pal Joey* (musical).

Zip-a-Dee-Doo-Dah
Words by Ray Gilbert, music by Allie Wrubel.
Walt Disney Music Co., 1945.
Introduced by James Baskett in *Song of the South* (film, 1946). Best-selling record by Johnny Mercer with The Pied Pipers (Capitol). Revived in 1962 with best-selling record by Bob B. Soxx and The Blue Jeans (Philles). Won an Academy Award, 1947.

Zip Code
Words and music by Mike Rabon, Norman Ezell, and John Durrill.
Jetstar Publishers, Inc., 1967.
Best-selling record by The Five Americans (Abnak).

Zonky
Words by Andy Razaf, music by Thomas "Fats" Waller.
Anne-Rachel Music Corp., 1929.
Introduced at Connie's Inn (New York nightclub) in *Load of Coal* (nightclub revue).

A Zoot Suit (For My Sunday Gal)
Words and music by Ray Gilbert and Bob O'Brien.
Screen Gems-EMI Music Inc., 1941.
Best-selling record by Kay Kyser and his Orchestra, vocal by Harry Babbitt (Columbia).

Zorba, the Greek, see **Theme from *Zorba, the Greek*.**

Zsa Zsa
Music by Bernie Wayne.
Times Square Music Publication, 1953 / Bernie Wayne Music Co., 1953.
Dedicated to Zsa Zsa Gabor. Best-selling record by Bernie Wayne and his Orchestra (Coral).

Indexes and List of
Publishers

Lyricists & Composers Index

Lyricists & Composers Index

2170

Travelin' Light
What a Beautiful Beginning
What a Perfect Combination
Wishing and Waiting for Love
Alaimo, Stephen
Melissa
Alan, Charles
Mile after Mile
Albeniz, Isaac
Moonlight Masquerade
Albert, Morris
Feelings
Albertano, Linda
Molly and Tenbrooks
Albertine, Charles
The Sound of Surf
Alberts, Al
Tell Me Why
Albrecht, Elmer
Elmer's Tune
Alden, John
Le Veeda
Alden, Joseph R.
Sleepy Time Gal
Alderidge, Ava
Sharing the Night Together
Alen, Dick
Here Comes the Judge
Alencar, Paulo
The Baion
Alexander, Arthur
Anna (Go to Him)
Alexander, Edna
Sugar (That Sugar Baby o' Mine)
Alexander, Fitzroy, see Melody, Lord
Alexander, Gary
Pandora's Golden Heebie Jeebies
Alexander, J.
Shake Your Rump to the Funk
Alexander, James
Lookin' for a Love
Soul Finger
Alexander, Jeff
Theme from The Lieutenant (Like March)
Alexander, Van, see Feldman, Al
Alfred, Roy
The Best Man
Captain Kidd
Congratulations to Someone

Destination Moon
Fla-Ga-La-Pa
A Fool Was I
Here Comes That Heartache Again
The Huckle Buck
It's the Sentimental Thing To Do
I've Got News for You
The Late, Late Show
Lean Baby
Let's Lock the Door (And Throw Away the Key)
Promise Her Anything (But Give Her Love)
Rock and Roll Waltz
She Can't Find Her Keys
Show Must Go On
A Woman Always Understands
Alguero, Augusto
If She Should Come to You (La Montana)
Allan, Gene
Comin' Home Soldier
Mr. Lonely
Allan, Lewis
Strange Fruit
Allard, Weldon
I Guess I'll Never Learn
Wake Up Irene
Allbritten, Dub
Anybody but Me
Eventually
I'm Sorry
Allen, Barclay
The New Look
Allen, Bud
One o'Clock Blues
Allen, Budd
I Know What You're Puttin' Down
Allen, C.
Shake Your Rump to the Funk
Allen, Charlie
Are You Ready
Allen, Henry "Red", Jr.
Biffy Blues
Feeling Drowsy
Swing Out
Allen, Joe
Should I Come Home (or Should I Go Crazy)

Lyricists & Composers Index

Anderson, Frank
  Love Me! Love Me! Love Me! (Or
    Leave Me Alone)
Anderson, Gary
  Not Me
  Quarter to Three
  School Is Out
Anderson, Ian
  Bungle in the Jungle
  Living in the Past
  Minstrel in the Gallery
  My Sunday Feeling
  A Song for Jeffrey
Anderson, John Murray
  Nightingale, Bring Me a Rose
  Sixty Seconds Every Minute, I Think
    of You
  A Young Man's Fancy
Anderson, Jon
  And You and I
  Roundabout
Anderson, Leroy
  Belle of the Ball
  Blue Tango
  Fiddle Faddle
  Forgotten Dreams
  Jazz Pizzicato
  Sleigh Ride
  The Syncopated Clock
  The Typewriter
Anderson, Liz
  Be Quiet, Mind
  From Now On All My Friends Are
    Gonna Be Strangers
  If I Kiss You (Will You Go Away?)
  I'm a Lonesome Fugitive
  Mama Spank
  Pick of the Week
  Ride, Ride, Ride
  The Words I'm Gonna Have to Eat
Anderson, Maxwell
  Apple Jack
  Big Mole
  Catfish Song
  Come In, Mornin'
  How Can You Tell an American?
  It Never Was You
  The Little Gray House
  Lost in the Stars

River Chanty
September Song
Stay Well
There's Nowhere To Go but Up
This Time Next Year
Thousands of Miles
Trouble Man
Will You Remember Me?
Anderson, Melvin
  I Wonder Why
Anderson, R. Alex
  Cockeyed Mayor of Kaunakakai
Anderson, Stig
  Dancing Queen
  Fernando
  I Do, I Do, I Do, I Do, I Do
  Knowing Me, Knowing You
  Mamma Mia
  The Name of the Game
  S.O.S.
  Waterloo
Andre, Fabian
  Dream a Little Dream of Me
  When They Played the Polka
Andreoli, Pete
  New York Is a Lonely Town
Andreolli, John
  Hi Mom
Andrew, S.
  Combination of the Two
Andrews, Chris
  Girl Don't Come
  It's Alright
Andrews, Lee
  Long Lonely Nights
Andrews, Maggie
  The Wreck of the Shenandoah
Angelos, Bill
  One More Time
Anglin, Jack
  One by One
  You and Me
Anglin, Jim
  One by One
  You and Me
Angulo, Hector
  Guantanamera
Angulo, Rafael
  Cuban Mambo

Gate Mouth
Gully Low Blues
Gut Bucket Blues
I Want a Big Butter and Egg Man
Ol' Man Mose
Potato Head Blues
Wild Man Blues
Armstrong, William
Slip Away
Arnheim, Gus
After All Is Said and Done
I Cried for You (Now It's Your Turn
To Cry over Me)
It Must Be True (You Are Mine, All
Mine)
Mandalay
Put Your Little Arms around Me
Sweet and Lovely
Arnold, Bruce
Can't Find the Time
Arnold, Buddy
"I"
Arnold, Chris
Can't Smile Without You
Arnold, Eddy
C-H-R-I-S-T-M-A-S
Easy on the Eyes
Enclosed, One Broken Heart
A Heart Full of Love (For a Handful
of Kisses)
I'll Hold You in My Heart (Till I
Can Hold You in My Arms)
I'm Throwing Rice (At the Girl That
I Love)
Just a Little Lovin' (Will Go a Long
Way)
Molly Darling
One Kiss Too Many
Show Me the Way Back to Your
Heart
That Do Make It Nice
That's How Much I Love You
Then I Turned and Walked Slowly
Away
There's No Wings on My Angel
What Is Life without Love?
Will Santy Come to Shanty Town?
You Don't Know Me
Arnold, Kay
Cross the Brazos at Waco

Matamoros
Arnold, Kokomo
Milk Cow Blues
Arnold, Malcolm
The Children's Marching Song
Madrigal
The River Kwai March
Arnold, Polly
Slap 'er Down Agin, Paw
Arodin, Sidney
Lazy River
Arrington, Joseph, Jr., see Tex, Joe
Arthur, Bobb
There's That Lonely Feeling Again
Ascher, Kenny
Rainbow Connection
Watch Closely Now
The Woman in the Moon
You and Me Against the World
Ascher, Robert
Hop, Skip, Jump
Tracy's Theme
Ash, Frances
I'm Gonna Love That Gal
Ash, Paul
I'm Knee Deep in Daisies
Just Once Again
Thinking of You
Ashcroft, Johnny
Little Boy Lost
Asher, Tony
Caroline, No
God Only Knows
Wouldn't It Be Nice?
Asherman, Eddie
All That Glitters Is Not Gold
Slap 'er Down Agin, Paw
Ashford, Nicholas
Ain't No Mountain High Enough
Ain't Nothing Like the Real Thing
California Soul
Good Lovin' Ain't Easy to Come By
Keep on Lovin' Me Honey
Let's Go Get Stoned
Some Things You Never Get Used
To
What You Gave Me
Your Precious Love
You're All I Need to Get By

Ashford, Nick
  The Boss
  I Don't Need No Doctor
  I'm Every Woman
  Reach Out and Touch (Somebody's Hand)
  Remember Me
  Stuff Like That
  Who's Gonna Take the Blame
Ashley, Hugh
  What Would You Do (If Jesus Came to Your House)
Ashley, Leon
  Flower of Love
  Laura (What's He Got That I Ain't Got)?
Ashworth, Ernest, *see* Worth, Billy
Astaire, Fred
  I'm Building Up to an Awful Let-Down
Astor, Bob
  Here Comes the Judge
Astore, L.
  Botch-a-Me
Atcher, Bob
  Crying Myself to Sleep
  I Want To Be Wanted
Atcheson, Tex
  Sleepy-Eyed John
Atchinson, Tex
  Sick, Sober and Sorry
Atchison, Tex
  When You Cry (You Cry Alone)
Atchley, Sam
  Coca Cola Cowboy
Atkins, Boyd
  Heebie Jeebies
Atkins, Chet
  Midnight
  Teen Scene
Atkins, Jim
  You're the Nearest Thing to Heaven
Atkins, Roger
  Getting Together
  Green Grass
  It's My Life
  Make Me Your Baby
  Princess in Rags
  Workin' on a Groovy Thing

Atkinson, Craig
  Psychotic Reaction
Atteridge, Harold
  Don't Send Your Wife to the Country
  Give Your Heart in June Time
  Tell Me What's the Matter, Lovable Eyes
  That Barber in Seville
Atwood, Hub
  No One Ever Tells You
Audinot, Rafael
  Rhumba Rhapsody
Augue, Bud
  The Violet and a Rose
Augustus, Frank
  Come Tomorrow
Auletti, Leonard
  The Bunny Hop
Auric, Georges
  Bonjour Tristesse
  Heart of Paris
  O Willow Waly
  The Song from Moulin Rouge
  Theme from *Goodbye Again*
Austin, Billy
  Is You Is, or Is You Ain't (Ma' Baby)
Austin, Bobby Allen
  Try a Little Kindness
Austin, Gene
  How Come You Do Me Like You Do?
  The Lonesome Road
  Mister Deep Blue Sea
  Occidental Woman
  Ridin' Around in the Rain
  When My Sugar Walks Down the Street, All the Little Birdies Go Tweet-Tweet-Tweet
Austin, Lovie
  Chirpin' the Blues
  Down Hearted Blues
  I've Got the Blues for Rampart Street
  Weary Way Blues
Austin, Ray
  I Look at Heaven (When I Look at You)
  Tonight We Love

A Lifetime of Loneliness
Living Together, Growing Together
Long Ago Tomorrow
The Look of Love
Lost Horizon
Message to Michael
My Little Red Book (All I Do Is Talk about You)
Odds and Ends (of a Beautiful Love Affair)
One Less Bell to Answer
Only Love Can Break a Heart
Paper Mache
Please Make Him Love Me
Promises, Promises
Raindrops Keep Fallin' on My Head
Send Me No Flowers
This Guy's in Love with You
Trains and Boats and Planes
Twenty-four Hours from Tulsa
What the World Needs Now Is Love
What's New, Pussycat?
Who Is Gonna Love Me?
The Windows of the World
Wishin' and Hopin'
The World Is a Circle
Bacharach, Burt F.
Anonymous Phone Call
Another Night
Any Day Now
Are You There (with Another Girl)?
Baby, It's You
The Blob
Don't You Believe It
Forever My Love
Heavenly
Hot Spell
I Say a Little Prayer
Magic Moments
Make It Easy on Yourself
The Man Who Shot Liberty Valance
(Don't Go) Please Stay
The Story of My Life
Tower of Strength
Walk on By
Who's Been Sleeping in My Bed?
Wives and Lovers
Wonderful To Be Young
Bachman, Randall
No Time

Bachman, Randall C.
Laughing
These Eyes
Undun
Bachman, Randy
Hey You
Let It Ride
Roll on Down the Highway
Takin' Care of Business
You Ain't Seen Nothin' Yet
Backer, William
I'd Like to Teach the World to Sing
Badale, Andy
Face It Girl, It's Over
Badazz, Randy
Rise
Bader, Ernst
When the Snow Is on the Roses
Badger, Ronald
I Want To Know
Baer, Abel
Don't Wake Me Up
Gee! but You're Swell
Harriet
Hello, Aloha! How Are You?
High Up on a Hill Top
I Miss My Swiss, My Swiss Miss Misses Me
I'll Love You in My Dreams
I'm Sitting Pretty in a Pretty Little City
It's the Girl
Just Give Me a June Night, the Moonlight, and You
Let Me Linger in Your Arms
Lonesome in the Moonlight
Lucky Lindy!
Mamma Loves Papa, Papa Loves Mamma
My Mother's Eyes
Right Kind of Man
There Are Such Things
When the One You Love, Loves You
When You're with Somebody Else
Baer, Barbara
Respectable
Sweet Talkin' Guy
Baez, Joan
Diamonds and Rust

Lyricists & Composers Index

Bagdasarian, Ross
  Alvin's Harmonica
  Alvin's Orchestra
  Armen's Theme
  The Chipmunk Song (Christmas
    Don't Be Late)
  Come On-a My House
  Witch Doctor
Baham, Roy
  Charlie's Shoes
Bahler, Tom
  Julie, Do Ya Love Me
  Living in a House Divided
  She's Out of My Life
Bailey, Jim
  Everybody Plays the Fool
Bailey, Philip
  Saturday Nite
  Shining Star
  That's the Way of the World
Bailey, Red
  Softly and Tenderly (I'll Hold You in
    My Arms)
Bainbridge, Margie
  This White Circle on My Finger
Baird, Tom
  Born to Wander
  Does Your Mama Know about Me
Baker, David
  Someone's Been Sending Me Flowers
  When the Sea Is All around Us
Baker, Ginger
  What a Bringdown
Baker, Jack
  I Hear a Rhapsody
Baker, James
  It's Been a Long Time
Baker, Josephine
  Black Bottom Ball
  Lonesome Lovesick Blues
Baker, LaVern
  I Can't Love You Enough
Baker, Mickey
  Love Is Strange
  Two Shadows on Your Window
Baker, Norman Buddy
  The Shaggy D. A.
Baker, Phil
  Did You Mean It?
  A Hundred Years from Now

  Invitation to a Broken Heart
  Love and Kisses (from Baby to You)
  Strange Interlude
Baker, Yvonne
  Let Me In
Balderrana, Robert
  I Need Somebody
Baldridge, Fanny
  Let's Dance
Baldwin, Donald
  Happy People
Baldwin, John, see also Jones, John
    Paul
  D'Yer Maker
Balfe, David William
  Beautiful Sunday
Balin, Marty
  Volunteers
Balin, Martyn
  Comin' Back to Me
Ball, Dave
  Set Me Free
Ball, Dennis
  Set Me Free
Ball, Ernest R.
  Down the Winding Road of Dreams
  Hollywood Rose
  I'll Forget You
  Out There in the Sunshine with You
  Ten Thousand Years from Now
  West of the Great Divide
Ball, Kenny
  Midnight in Moscow
Ball, Noel
  Oh Julie
Ball, Roger
  Cut the Cake
  Pick Up the Pieces
Ball, Ronnie
  How Do You Do? (Let Echols
    Check)
Ball, Yvette
  Young Only Yesterday
Ballan, Paula
  Chicken Corden Blues
Ballard, Clint
  The Game of Love
Ballard, Clint, Jr.
  Ginger Bread
  Good Timin'

2184

It's Just a Little Bit Too Late
Litty Bitty Girl
One of Us (Will Weep Tonight)
You're No Good
Ballard, F. D. "Pat"
Please Handle with Care
Ballard, Hank
Dance with Me Henry
Finger Poppin' Time
Let's Go, Let's Go, Let's Go
The Twist
Ballard, Henry
Sexy' Ways
Ballard, Henry "Hank"
Work with Me Annie
Ballard, Pat
Any Ice To-day, Lady?
Mister Sandman
Oh, Baby Mine (I Get So Lonely)
So Beats My Heart for You
Ballard, Russ
Liar
New York Groove
Ballman, Wanda
If You're Not Gone Too Long
Balthrop, J. A.
Family Man
Bandini, Al
A Girl! a Girl!
Banks, Anthony
Follow You Follow Me
Banks, Darrell
Open the Door to Your Heart
Banks, Homer
I Could Never Be President
I Like What You're Doing to Me
If Loving You Is Wrong I Don't
Want to Be Right
If You're Ready (Come Go with Me)
Take Care of Your Homework
Who's Making Love?
Banks, Larry
Go Now
Banks, Marian
Malaguena
Banks, Ulysses
Voo-It! Voo-It!
Bannon, Royal C.
Only One Love in My Life

Barans, Peter
Ahead of the Game
Barbarin, Paul
Bourbon Street Parade
Come Back Sweet Papa
Don't Forget To Mess Around When
You're Doing the Charleston
Every Tub
Freakish Light Blues
Tack Annie
Barbata, John
Elenor
Barberis, Billy
Big Wide World
Have You Looked into Your Heart
Sinner Man
Barbieri, Gato
Last Tango in Paris
Barbour, Dave
Blum Blum
Don't Be So Mean to Baby ('Cause
Baby's So Good to You)
I Don't Know Enough about You
It's a Good Day
Manana (Is Soon Enough for Me)
What More Can a Woman Do?
Barcelata, Lorenzo
Bells of San Raquel
Maria Elena
Barclay, Eddie
Once upon a Summertime
Bare, Bobby
500 Miles Away from Home
Happy To Be Unhappy
Barefoot, Carl
Danger! Heartbreak Ahead
Barer, Marshall
The Bigger the Figure
I Want To Love You
I'm Just a Country Boy
Summer Is A-Comin' In
Thunder and Lightning (Lightning
and Thunder)
Barge, Gene
Quarter to Three
School Is Out
Twist, Twist Senora
We're Gonna Make It
Barge, M.
Leaving Me

Lyricists & Composers Index

Lyricists & Composers Index

You're Lonely and I'm Lonely
Berlin, Milton
  I Wuv a Wabbit
Berlin, Murray
  The Late, Late Show
Berline, Byron
  The Apple Dumpling Gang
Berman, Irving
  Daddy, Daddy
  Time Out for Tears
  Wrapped Up in a Dream
Bernard, Andrew
  Judy in Disguise
Bernard, Felix
  $21 a Day—Once a Month
  Winter Wonderland
Bernard, Henry
  I'll Sail My Ship Alone
  Sittin' on It All the Time
  Well, Oh, Well
Bernie, Ben, *see also* Green, Ben
  I Can't Believe It's True
  Strange Interlude
  Sweet Georgia Brown
  Who's Your Little Whoozis?
Bernie, Lowe
  Wild One
Bernie, Saul
  Don't Cry Baby
Bernier, Buddy
  Bamboo
  The Big Apple
  Hear My Song, Violetta
  Hurry Home
  Mile after Mile
  The Night Has a Thousand Eyes
  Our Love
  Poinciana (Song of the Tree)
Berns, Bert
  Are You Lonely for Me (Baby)?
  Everybody Needs Somebody to Love
  Here Comes the Night
  I Want Candy
  I'll Take Good Care of You
  Piece of My Heart
  Twenty-five Miles
Bernstein, Abe
  This Girl Is a Woman Now
Bernstein, Alan
  After the Lovin'

Bernstein, Elmer
  Baby, the Rain Must Fall
  The Bird Man
  By Love Possessed
  From the Terrace (Love Theme)
  A Girl Named Tamiko
  The Great Escape March
  Hawaii
  Love Theme from *The Rat Race*
  Love with the Proper Stranger
  The Magnificent Seven
  Main Title Theme from *The Rat Race*
  Meatballs
  Molly-O
  Monica
  Somewhere in the Used To Be
  The Sons of Katie Elder
  Theme from *By Love Possessed*
  Theme from *Summer and Smoke*
  To Kill a Mockingbird
  True Grit
  A Walk in the Spring Rain
  Walk on the Wild Side
  Wherever Love Takes Me
  The Wishing Doll
Bernstein, Leonard
  America
  Come Up to My Place
  Cool
  Duet for One (the First Lady of the Land)
  Gee, Officer Krupke
  I Can Cook Too
  I Feel Pretty
  I Get Carried Away
  It's Love
  A Little Bit in Love
  Lonely Town
  Lucky To Be Me
  Maria
  My Name Is Barbara
  New York, New York
  Ohio
  On the Waterfront
  One Hand, One Heart
  A Quiet Girl
  Some Other Time
  Something's Coming
  Somewhere

Take Care of This House
Tonight
Wrong Note Rag
Ya Got Me
Bernstein, Roger
Symphony
Berrios, Pedro
Aurora
Cae Cae
My Shawl (Ombo)
Berry, Chuck
Almost Grown
Bye Bye Johnny
Carol
Johnny B. Goode
Mabelline
Memphis
My Ding-a-Ling
Nadine (Is It You?)
No Money Down
No Particular Place To Go
The Promised Land
Reelin' and Rockin'
Rock and Roll Music
Roll Over Beethoven
School Day (Ring! Ring! Goes the Bell)
Surfin' U.S.A.
Sweet Little Sixteen
Too Much Monkey Business
Berry, J.
Pony Time
Berry, Jan
The Anaheim, Azusa and Cucamonga Sewing Circle, Book Review and Timing Assoc.
Come On, Let Yourself Go
Dead Man's Curve
Drag City
Honolulu Lulu
I Adore Him
Jenny-Lee
Surf City
Three Window Coupe
You Really Know How to Hurt a Guy
Berry, Leon
Christopher Columbus
Berry, Richard
Louie Louie

Berryhill, Robert
Wipe Out
Bertal-Maubon
Titina
Bertini, U.
Chella Lla
On an Evening in Roma
Tell Me You're Mine
Besoyan, Rick
Do You Ever Dream of Vienna?
Look for a Sky of Blue
Once in a Blue Moon
Bessinger, Frank Wright
Oh! Boy, What a Girl
Best, Denzil
Bemsha Swing
Best, Pat
I Understand Just How You Feel
Best, William
(I Love You) For Sentimental Reasons
Wrapped Up in a Dream
Bestor, Don
Contented
Down by the Winegar Works
Betti, Henri
C'est Si Bon
What Can I Do?
Bettis, John
Goodbye to Love
I Need to Be in Love
Only One Love in My Life
Only Yesterday
Top of the World
Yesterday Once More
Betts, Richard
Blue Sky
Jessica
Ramblin Man
Beul, Arthur
Toolie Oolie Doolie (The Yodel Polka)
Underneath the Linden Tree
Biberman, Herbert
Slaves (Don't You Know My Name?)
Bibo, Irving
Am I Wasting My Time on You?
Cherie
Old Man Atom (Talking Atomic Blues)

Lyricists & Composers Index

Oriental Eyes
  Play That Song of India Again
Bickel, Jack
  Heart Broken
Bickerton, Wayne
  Can't Stop Loving You
  Nothing but a Heartache
Bideu, Lou
  Percolator
Bierman, Arthur
  Midnight Masquerade
Bierman, Bernard
  Forgiving You
  Hills of Colorado
  Midnight Masquerade
  My Cousin Louella
  Vanity
Biese, Paul
  Teasin'
Bigard, Albany "Barney"
  Beggar's Blues
  Double Check Stomp
  Mood Indigo
  Saratoga Swing
  Saturday Night Function
  Sloppy Joe
Bigard, Barney
  Clarinet Lament
Bigelow, Bob
  Hard Hearted Hannah, the Vamp of
    Savannah
Bigeou, Esther
  Panama Limited Blues
Biggs, Howard
  Got You on My Mind
  Melancholy Me
  Write Me a Letter
Bilk, Acker
  Stranger on the Shore
Bill, Casey, *see* Weldon, William
Billings, Hal
  Love Is Just a Flower
Bindi, Umberto
  Our Concerto
  You're My World
Binnick, Bernard
  Keem-o-Sabe
Binton, Bobby
  Comin' Home Soldier

Biondi, Ray
  Bolero at the Savoy
  Boogie Blues
Bird, Bill
  Broadway
Birdsong, Larry
  Pleadin' for Love
Birtles, Beeb
  Happy Anniversary
Bishop, Elvin
  Fooled Around and Fell in Love
  Travelin' Shoes
Bishop, Joe
  Blue Evening
  Blue Flame
  Blue Lament (Cry for Me)
  Blue Prelude
  Out of Space
  Woodchopper's Ball
Bishop, Stephen
  Animal House
  Dream Girl
  On and On
  Save It for a Rainy Day
  Somewhere in Between
Bishop, Walter
  Bop! Goes My Heart
  Harlem Drag
  Jack, You're Dead
  Mad about You
  One o'Clock Blues
  Shhh, It's a Military Secret
  The Stuff Is Here (and It's Mellow)
  Swing, Brother, Swing
Bivens, Bruce
  Josephine
Bivins, Burke
  Don't Let Julia Fool Ya
Bivins, Edward
  There's No Me Without You
Bixio, C. A.
  Mama
Bixio, Cesare A.
  Serenade in the Night
  Tell Me That You Love Me
Bizet, Georges
  Beat Out That Rhythm on a Drum
  Dat's Love
  My Joe
  Stan' Up an' Fight

2198

Bloom, Bobby
  Indian Giver
  Montego Bay
  Mony Mony
  Special Delivery
Bloom, Marty
  Cannon Ball Blues
  Does the Spearmint Lose Its Flavor on the Bedpost Over Night?
  Melancholy
Bloom, Rube
  Day In—Day Out
  Don't Worry 'bout Me
  Fools Rush In (Where Angels Fear To Tread)
  Give Me the Simple Life
  Here's to My Lady
  I Can't Face the Music (without Singing the Blues)
  I Wish I Could Tell You
  Lost in a Dream
  The Man from the South (with a Big Cigar in His Mouth)
  Maybe You'll Be There
  Out in the Cold Again
  Soliloquy
  Song of the Bayou
  Spring Fever
  Stay on the Right Side, Sister
  Take Me
  Truckin'
Bloom, Vera
  Jealousy
Blue, David
  Outlaw Man
Blume, David
  A Turn Down Day
Blythe, James
  Block and Tackle Blues
  Fade Away Blues
  Mecca Flat Blues
  Oriental Man
Bobbit, Charles
  How Long Can I Keep It Up
Bocage, E.
  My Dearest Darling
Bocage, Edwin
  Slippin' and Slidin'
Bocage, Peter
  Bouncing Around

  Lou'siana Swing
  Mama's Gone, Goodbye
  New Orleans Wiggle
  Sud Bustin' Blues
Bock, Jerry
  All of These and More
  Artificial Flowers
  Days Gone By
  Dear Friend
  Do You Love Me?
  Far from the Home I Love
  Fiddler on the Roof
  Gentlemen Jimmy
  Good Clean Fun
  Grand Knowing You
  He Tossed a Coin
  I Wonder What It's Like
  If I Were a Rich Man
  Ilona
  I'm Available
  Just My Luck
  Little Old New York
  Lovely Laurie
  Matchmaker, Matchmaker
  Miracle of Miracles
  Mr. Wonderful
  My Gentle Young Johnny
  My Miss Mary
  Never Mind
  Never Too Late
  Now I Have Everything
  Politics and Poker
  Popsicles in Paris
  Sabbath Prayer
  Sea-Shell
  She Loves Me
  Sunrise, Sunset
  'Til Tomorrow
  To Life
  Tommy, Tommy
  Tonight at Eight
  Too Close for Comfort
  Tradition
  The Very Next Man
  When Did I Fall in Love?
  Will He Like Me?
  Worlds Apart
Bodanzky, Robert
  The White Dove

Boutelje, Philip
  She Wouldn't Do What I Asked Her
    To
Bovington, Jay
  Heart, Be Careful
Bowen, James
  I'm Stickin' with You
Bowen, Jeffrey
  Happy People
  Shakey Ground
  You
Bowen, Jimmy
  Party Doll
Bowens, Johannes
  Paloma Blanca
Bower, "Bugs"
  Caterina
  The Closing Credits
  Las Vegas
Bowers, Robert Hood
  The Moon Shines on the
    Moonshine
Bowers, William
  Oh Love, Hast Thou Forsaken Me
Bowie, David
  All the Young Dudes
  Changes
  Fame
  Golden Years
  Move On
  Space Oddity
  Starman
  Stay
  Suffragette City
  TVC 15
  Young American
Bowles, George
  I Call You Sugar
Bowling, Roger
  Blanket on the Ground
  Coward of the County
  Lucille
Bowman, Brooks
  East of the Sun (and West of the
    Moon)
  Love and a Dime
Bowman, Don
  Anita, You're Dreaming
  Wildwood Weed

Bowman, Priscilla
  Hands Off
Bown, Patti
  G'Won Train
  Waltz de Funk
Bowne, Jerry
  Friendly Tavern Polka
Box, Betty
  I Feel Love
  Sunshine Smiles
Box, Elton
  Just a Little Fond Affection
Box, Euel
  I Feel Love
Box, Evel
  Sunshine Smiles
Boyce, Donald
  Jungle Boogie
  Spirit of the Boogie
Boyce, Tommy
  Action
  Alice Long (You're Still My Favorite
    Girlfriend)
  Be My Guest
  Come a Little Bit Closer
  Green Grass
  I Wonder What She's Doing
    Tonight?
  Last Train to Clarksville
  Out and About
  Peaches 'n' Cream
  Pretty Little Angel Eyes
  (I'm Not Your) Steppin' Stone
  Valleri
  Words
Boyd, Alphonso
  Shakey Ground
Boyd, Eddie
  Five Long Years
Boyd, Elisse
  Guess Who I Saw Today
Boyd, Walter
  5-10-15-20 (25-30 Years of Love)
Boyer, Lucien
  Paree!
Boyer, Lucien Jean
  Valencia
Boylan, Terence
  Shake It

2207

Now! Baby, Now!
One Is a Lonely Number
Only Trust Your Heart
We Never Talk Much
Wonder Why
Brodszky, Nikolaus
When Will I Find Love
Bronson, George
Kitty from Kansas City
Brooker, Gary
Homburg
In Held 'Twas in I
A Salty Dog
Shine On Brightly
A Whiter Shade of Pale
Brooks, Arthur
For Your Precious Love
Brooks, Fred
I'm Just a Country Boy
Brooks, George
Dying by the Hour
Jazzbo Brown
One and Two Blues
Send Me to the 'Lectric Chair
Trombone Cholly
Brooks, Hadda
Jump Back Honey
Brooks, Harry
Ain't Misbehavin'
Saturday
Sweet Savannah Sue
What Did I Do To Be So Black and
Blue
Brooks, Harvey O.
I Want You—I Need You
I'm No Angel
A Little Bird Told Me
They Call Me Sister Honky Tonk
Brooks, Jack
Am I in Love
Innamorata (Sweetheart)
It's Dreamtime
Ole Buttermilk Sky
Rose Tattoo
Saturday Date
Somebody
That's Amore
Wonderful World of Love
You Wonderful You

Brooks, Joe
If Ever I See You Again
You Light Up My Life
Brooks, Joey
Seein' the Right Love Go Wrong
Brooks, John Benson
A Boy from Texas, a Girl from
Tennessee
Just As Though You Were Here
Ninety Nine Years (Dead or Alive)
One Lonely Night
You Came a Long Way from St.
Louis
Brooks, Johnny
Who Threw the Whiskey in the
Well?
Brooks, Mel
Blazing Saddles
Brooks, Richard
For Your Precious Love
Brooks, Ruth
In Shadowland
Brooks, Shelton
Darktown Has a Gay White Way
House Rent Ball
Broomer, Bernie
Oh, How It Hurts
Broones, Martin
At the Close of Day
Bring Back Those Minstrel Days
I Can't Get Over a Girl Like You
I Don't Want Your Kisses
Ich Liebe Dich (I Love You)
Broonzy, Big Bill
Baby, I Done Got Wise
Just a Dream
Keep Your Hand on Your Heart
Key to the Highway
Sun Gonna Shine in My Door
When I Been Drinkin'
Broonzy, Willie Lee "Big Bill"
Big Bill Blues
House Rent Stomp
Broughton, Philip
Funny (Not Much)
Broussard, Joe
Mr. Big Stuff
Broussole, Jean
Willingly

Browd, Wade, Jr.
  Love Me for a Reason
Brown, A. W.
  Lonesome Mama
Brown, Al W.
  Ain't It a Shame
Brown, Alfred
  In a Moment
Brown, Arthur
  Fire!
Brown, Billie
  Lonesome Mama
Brown, Billie Jean
  Here Comes the Judge
Brown, Boots
  Cerveza
Brown, Charles
  Please Come Home for Christmas
  Tell Me You'll Wait for Me
Brown, Charles Mose
  Drifting Blues
Brown, Chuck
  Bustin' Loose Part 1
Brown, Elkin
  Blues Plus Booze (Means I Lose)
Brown, Errol
  Brother Louie
  Disco Queen
  Emma
  Every 1's a Winner
  You Sexy Thing
Brown, Fleta Jan
  East of the Moon, West of the Stars
Brown, Forman
  Two Hearts That Pass in the Night
Brown, Frankie
  Born To Lose
  No Letter Today
Brown, Gayle Candis
  It's Too Late (Baby, Too Late)
Brown, George
  Have You Ever Been Lonely (Have
    You Ever Been Blue?)
  Ladies Night
  Open Sesame
  Spirit of the Boogie
  That's When Your Heartaches Begin
  Too Hot
Brown, George H.
  Tahiti Honey

Brown, George M.
  Hollywood Swinging
  Jungle Boogie
Brown, Harold R.
  Cisco Kid
  Gypsy Man
  Me and Baby Brother
  Spill the Wine
  The World Is a Ghetto
Brown, Harold Ray
  L.A. Sunshine
  Low Rider
  Summer
  Why Can't We Be Friends
Brown, J.
  Cryin' Heart Blues
Brown, James
  Ain't It Funky Now?
  Ain't That a Groove?
  America Is My Home
  Baby, You're Right
  Bring It Up
  Brother Rapp
  Cold Sweat
  Don't Be a Drop-out
  Get It Together
  Get on the Good Foot
  Goodbye, My Love
  Hot Pants
  How Long Can I Keep It Up
  I Can't Stand Myself (When You
    Touch Me)
  I Don't Mind
  I Don't Want Nobody to Give Me
    Nothing (Open Up the Door, I'll
    Get It Myself)
  I Got the Feelin'
  I Got You (I Feel Good)
  It's a Man's, Man's, Man's World
    (But It Wouldn't Be Nothing
    without a Woman. . .)
  Let Yourself Go
  Licking Stick—Licking Stick
  Lost Someone
  Lowdown Popcorn
  Mother Popcorn (You Got to Have a
    Mother for Me) (Part 1)
  Papa's Got a Brand New Bag
  The Payback
  Please, Please, Please

Lyricists & Composers Index

Buckingham, Lindsay
  Go Your Own Way
  Tusk
Buckins, Mickey
  Double Lovin'
Buckner, Milt
  Hamp's Boogie Woogie
Budd, Roy
  My Little Friend
Buff, Wade
  It's Almost Tomorrow
Buffano, Jules
  Thanks for the Buggy Ride
Buffett, Jimmy
  Changes in Lattitudes, Changes in
    Attitudes
  Cheeseburger in Paradise
  Come Monday
  Death of an Unpopular Poet
  Door Number Three
  Fins
  Great Filling Station Holdup
  Havana Daydreamin'
  Livingston Saturday Night
  Manana
  Margaritaville
  Peanut Butter Conspiracy
  A Pirate Looks at Forty
  Volcano
Bugatti, Dominic
  Heaven on the Seventh Floor
  Married Men
Buie, Buddy
  Champagne Jam
  Change of Heart
  Do It or Die
  Everyday with You Girl
  I'm Not Gonna Let It Bother Me
    Tonight
  Imaginary Lover
  Party Girl
  So into You
  Stormy
  Traces
Buie, Perry C., *see also* Buie, Buddy
  I Take It Back
Bulhoes, Max
  Come to the Mardi Gras

Bullock, Vernon
  If I Could Build My Whole World
    around You
  What Does It Take (to Win Your
    Love)?
  Yesterday's Dreams
Bullock, Walter
  Half Moon on the Hudson
  I Could Use a Dream
  I Love To Walk in the Rain
  I Still Love To Kiss You
    Goodnight
  Magnolias in the Moonlight
  Swing Low Sweet Rhythm
  Swing Me an Old Fashioned Song
  When Did You Leave Heaven
  Who Am I?
  Who Minds about Me?
Bunch, Boyd
  The Broken Record
Bunnell, Lee
  A Horse with No Name
  Tin Man
  Ventura Highway
Burch, Don
  You Cheated
Burch, Fred
  Dream On Little Dreamer
  Old Showboat
  P.T. 109
  (Love Is Like a) Ramblin' Rose
Burch, Fred B.
  Tragedy
Burdge, Gordon
  Portrait of Jennie
Burdon, Eric
  I'm Crying
  Inside—Looking Out
  Monterey
  San Franciscan Nights
  Sky Pilot
  When I Was Young
Burello, Tony
  God Bless Us All
Burgers, Jan
  Midnight in Moscow
Burgess, Dave
  Everlovin'
  Everybody but Me
  I'm Available

Byron, Al
  Happy Go Lucky Me
  Roses Are Red (My Love)
Cacavas, John
  Black Is Beatuiful
  The Gallant Men
Caddigan, Jack J.
  Blue Diamonds
Cadena, Ozzie
  The Right Time
Cadman, Charles Wakefield
  The Builder
Caesar, Irving
  Animal Crackers in My Soup
  Chansonette
  Count Your Blessings
  Crazy Rhythm
  (Oh Suzanna) Dust Off That Old
    Pianna
  Elizabeth
  Gigolette
  Good Evening Friends
  The Hen and the Cow, (It's Only a
    Dream of the Past)
  I Love Her, She Loves Me
  I Want To Be Happy
  If I Forget You
  Imagination
  Is It True What They Say about
    Dixie?
  It Goes Like This (That Funny
    Melody)
  Just a Gigolo
  Lady, Play Your Mandolin
  My Blackbirds Are Bluebirds Now
  Nashville Nightingale
  Nasty Man
  Nightingale, Bring Me a Rose
  Nina Rosa
  Oh, Donna Clara
  Saskatchewan
  Satisfied!
  Sixty Seconds Every Minute, I Think
    of You
  Someone Will Make You Smile
  Sous les Toits de Paris (Under a
    Roof in Paree)
  South American Joe
  Stonewall Moskowitz March
  Sweethearts Forever

  Tea for Two
  That's What I Want for Christmas
  There's Nothing Wrong in a Kiss
  Too Many Rings around Rosie
  Umbriago
  What a Perfect Combination
  What Do You Do Sunday, Mary?
  The Yankee Doodle Blues
  You Can Dance with Any Girl At
    All
  Your Smiles, Your Tears
Caesar, William F.
  Crooning (Crooning Lullabies)
Cafra, Catherine
  Skinny Minnie
Cage, Earl, Jr.
  Mini-Skirt Minnie
Cahn, Sammy
  All That Love Went to Waste
  All the Way
  And Then You Kissed Me
  Anywhere
  As Long As There's Music
  Autumn in Rome
  Be My Love
  Because You're Mine
  Bei Mir Bist Du Schon (Means That
    You're Grand)
  The Best of Everything
  The Boys' Night Out
  The Brooklyn Bridge
  By Love Possessed
  Call Me Irresponsible
  Can't You Just See Yourself
  Can't You Read between the Lines?
  The Charm of You
  Closer Than a Kiss
  Dark Is the Night
  Day by Day
  Dedicated to You
  Doggie, Take Your Time
  Dormi, Dormi, Dormi
  Everything Makes Music When
    You're in Love
  Ev'ry Day I Love You (Just a Little
    Bit More)
  Face to Face
  Five Minutes More
  Forever Darling

2221

Lyricists & Composers Index

Lyricists & Composers Index

Lyricists & Composers Index

2233

She's Everybody's Sweetheart but
  Nobody's Gal
Since Ma Is Playing Mah Jong
Singin' the Blues (Till My Daddy
  Comes Home)
Skippy
The Song I Love
Steppin' Out
That Barber in Seville
That's You, Baby
Walking with Susie
Why Can't I Be Like You?
You Call It Madness (but I Call It
  Love)
You've Got To See Mamma Ev'ry
  Night or You Can't See Mamma
  At All
Conrad, Jack
  Every Time I Think of You
  Isn't It Time
Conrad, Jack S.
  Family of Man
Conrad, Robin
  She's My Girl
Conselman, William
  Roses in the Rain
Constantin, Jean
  Love Is Like Champagne
Contet, Henri
  All My Love
  Embrasse
  Love Me Some More
  Mademoiselle de Paree
  Padam...Padam...(How It Echoes
    the Beat of My Heart)
Conti, Bill
  Gonna Fly Now (Theme from
    Rocky)
  Too Close to Paradise
Conti, Corrado
  To the Door of the Sun (Alle Porte
    Del Sole)
  The Way It Used to Be
Conway, Jim
  Tomboy
Cooder, Ry
  Hard Working Man
Cook, Bill
  Forgive This Fool
  You Can Have Her

Cook, Don
  Lady Lay Down
Cook, Joe
  Peanuts
Cook, L. C.
  Win Your Love for Me
Cook, Mercer
  Is I in Love? I Is
Cook, Robert
  Are These Really Mine
  There Must Be a Way
Cook, Roger
  Doctor's Orders
  Here Comes That Rainy Day Feeling
    Again
  Home Lovin' Man
  I Was Kaiser Bill's Batman
  I'd Like to Teach the World to Sing
  Long Cool Woman (in a Black
    Dress)
  My Baby Loves Lovin'
  Talking in Your Sleep
  The Way It Used to Be
  You've Got Your Troubles
Cook, Will Marion
  I'm Coming Virginia
Cooke, C. L.
  Messin' Around
Cooke, L. C.
  You Send Me
Cooke, Linda
  Woman's Got to Have It
Cooke, Sam
  Another Saturday Night
  Bring It On Home to Me
  A Change Is Gonna Come
  Cupid
  Frankie and Johnnie
  Good News
  Having a Party
  It's Got the Whole World Shakin'
  Shake
  Sugar Dumpling
  Sweet Soul Music
  Twistin' the Night Away
Cooley, Eddie
  Fever
Cooley, Spade
  Mama and Daddy Broke My Heart
  Shame on You

Lyricists & Composers Index

Lyricists & Composers Index

Cox, Roy E., Jr.
  Hot Smoke and Sassafras
Crafer, Art
  No Arms Can Ever Hold You (Like
    These Arms of Mine)
Craft, Morton
  Alone
Craft, Morty
  Tell Her for Me
Craft, Morty and The Willows
  Church Bells May Ring
Craft, Paul
  Dropkick Me, Jesus
  Hank Williams, You Wrote My Life
Craft, Selma
  Alone
  Tell Her for Me
Craig, Francis
  Beg Your Pardon
  Near You
Crain, Tommy
  The Devil Went down to
    Georgia
Cramer, Floyd
  Fancy Pants
  Last Date
  My Last Date With You
  On the Rebound
Crandall, Bill
  Short Shorts
Crane, Jimmie
  Every Day of My Life
  Hurt
  I Can't Get You out of My Heart (Ti
    Amo—Ti Voglio Amor)
  I Need You Now
  If I Give My Heart to You
  My Believing Heart
Crane, Lor
  Don't Just Stand There (What's on
    Your Mind?)
  Say Something Funny
  White on White
Crane, Vincent
  Fire!
Crawford, Blackie
  Always Late (With Your Kisses)
Crawford, Cliff
  Chip Chip

Crawford, Dave
  Philadelphia
  Young Hearts Run Free
Crawford, Robert M.
  The U.S. Air Force (The Wild Blue
    Yonder)
Crayton, Pee Wee
  Blues after Hours
Creamer, Henry
  Dear Old Southland
  Down by the River
  If I Could Be with You One Hour
    To-Night
  Jersey Walk
  Strut Miss Lizzie
  Walk, Jenny, Walk
  'Way Down Yonder in New Orleans
Creath, Charles
  Market Street Blues
Creatore, Luigi, see also Markwell,
    Mark
  Bimbombey
  Can't Help Falling in Love
  The Crazy Otto Rag
  Experience Unnecessary
  Hello Heartache, Goodbye, Love
  Let's Put It All Together
  Wild in the Country
Creed, Linda
  Betcha by Golly, Wow
  Break Up to Make Up
  The Greatest Love of All
  I'm Coming Home
  I'm Stone in Love with You
  Rockin' Roll Baby
  The Rubberband Man
  You Are Everything
  You Make Me Feel Brand New
Creme, Lawrence
  Rubber Bullets
Cretecos, Jimmy
  Doesn't Somebody Want to Be
    Wanted
Crewe, Bob
  Big Girls Don't Cry
  Bye Bye Baby (Baby Goodbye)
  Can't Take My Eyes Off You
  Get Dancin'
  Girl Come Running
  I Make a Fool of Myself

I've Got Five Dollars and It's
  Saturday Night
The Last Ride
Look Who's Talkin'
Shadow on My Heart
Shut That Cake
Tangled Mind
Truck Drivers (Blues)
Worried Mind
Dahl, Steve
  Do You Think I'm Disco
Dahlstrom, Patti
  Emotion (Amoreuse)
Dailey, H.
  Volcano
Dain, Irving
  Coca Cola Cowboy
Dain, Sharon Lee, *see* DeShannon,
  Jackie
Dalanoe, P.
  What Now My Love
Dale, Jim
  Georgy Girl
Dale, Jimmy
  Just Say I Love Her (Dicitencello
  Vuie)
Dallas, Dick
  I Wish I Knew How It Would Feel
  to Be Free
Dalton, Bill
  Short Shorts
Daly, William
  Every Day
  Oh Gee, Oh Gosh, I Love You
Damato, Pete
  Just Ask Your Heart
Damerell, Stanley J.
  If
  Lady of Spain
  Let's All Sing Like the Birdies Sing
  Lights of Paris
  Unless
Dameron, Tadd
  Good Bait
  If You Could See Me Now
Damon, Russ
  Cotton Candy
D'Amour, Jodi
  No Chemise, Please!

Dana, Walter
  Helen Polka
  Longing for You
Dance, Leo
  My Time Is Your Time
Daniderff, Leo
  Titina
Daniel, Eliot
  Blue Shadows on the Trail
  Casey at the Bat
  Disco Lucy (I Love Lucy Theme)
  Lavender Blue (Dilly Dilly)
  Never
  Pecos Bill
  Uncle Remus Said
Daniel, Marcus
  Slip Away
  Tell Mama
Daniels, Charles N., *see also* Moret,
  Neil
  Put Your Little Arms around Me
Daniels, Charlie
  The Devil Went down to Georgia
  Long Haired Country Boy
  The South's Gonna Do It
  Uneasy Rider
Daniels, Dorothy
  My Heart Belongs to Only You
Daniels, Frank
  My Heart Belongs to Only You
Daniels, Jack
  It's a Man Down There
  Turn Back the Hands of Time
Daniels, Lee
  Dansero
Danko, Rick
  Life Is a Carnival
  This Wheel's On Fire
Dankworth, Johnny
  Let's Slip Away
Danoff, Bill
  Afternoon Delight
  Boulder to Birmingham
  Friends with You
  Take Me Home, Country Road
Danoff, Sid
  Dance, Everyone, Dance
Danpa
  Autumn Concerto

Lyricists & Composers Index

Lyricists & Composers Index

Sailor Boys Have Talk to Me in
  English
Send My Baby Back tò Me
(Why Did I Tell You I Was Going
  to) Shanghai
Summertime Lies
De Metruis, Claude
  Hard Headed Woman
  I Was the One
De Moraes, Vinicius
  No More Blues
de Nascimento, Alfredo Ricardo
  The Bandit
De Nota, Diane
  Just Ask Your Heart
de Oliveira, Milton
  Come to the Mardi Gras
de Paul, Gene
  Ain't That Just Like a Man
  Bless Your Beautiful Hide
  Cow-Cow Boogie (Cuma-Ti-Yi-Yi-
    Ay)
  Daddy-O (I'm Gonna Teach You
    Some Blues)
  (Nobody Knows Better Than I) He's
    My Guy
  If I Had My Druthers
  I'll Remember April
  Irresistible You
  It's Whatcha Do with Whatcha Got
  Jubilation T. Cornpone
  Lonesome Polecat
  Love in a Home
  Love That Boy
  Milkman, Keep Those Bottles Quiet
  Mister Five by Five
  Namely You
  Pig Foot Pete
  Sobbin' Women
  A Song Was Born
  Spring Spring Spring
  Star Eyes
  Starlight, Starbright
  Teach Me Tonight
  When You're in Love
  Wonderful, Wonderful Day
  You Can't Run Away from It
  You Don't Know What Love Is
  Your Red Wagon

De Rosa, Francis D.
  The Big Guitar
De Rose, Peter
  All I Need Is You
  Angel
  As Years Go By
  Autumn Serenade
  Blue September
  Close to Me
  Deep Purple
  Gretchen
  Have You Ever Been Lonely (Have
    You Ever Been Blue?)
  I Got Worry (Love Is on My Mind)
  I Just Roll Along, Havin' My Ups
    and Downs
  If You Turn Me Down (Dee-Own-
    Down-Down)
  The Lamp Is Low
  Lilacs in the Rain
  Love Ya
  Manhattan Mood
  A Marshmallow World
  Moonlight Mood
  Muddy Waters
  Now or Never
  On a Little Street in Singapore
  Orchids for Remembrance
  The Oregon Trail
  Rain
  Somebody Loves You
  Somewhere in Old Wyoming
  Song of the Blacksmith, Clang,
    Clang, Clang
  Spring Has Sprung
  The Starlit Hour
  Suez
  That's Life I Guess
  That's Where I Came In
  There's a Home in Wyomin'
  Twenty-four Hours of Sunshine
  Wagon Wheels
  When Your Hair Has Turned to
    Silver (I Will Love You Just the
    Same)
  When You're Gone I Won't Forget
  White Orchids
  Who Do You Know in Heaven (That
    Made You the Angel You Are?)

Chickery Chick
The End of the World
A House with Love in It
Laroo, Laroo, Lilli Bolero
Moonlight Swim
My Sugar Is So Refined
That's the Chance You Take
Too Young
Dee, Tommy
Three Stars
Deen, Dixie
Truck Drivin' Son-of-a-Gun
Dees, Bill
Breakin' Up Is Breakin' My Heart
Communication Breakdown
Crawling Back
Goodnight
It's Over
Oh, Pretty Woman
Ride Away
Twinkle Toes
(Say) You're My Girl
Dees, Rick
Disco Duck (Part 1)
Dehn, Paul
O Willow Waly
Dehr, Richard
Green Fields
Love Is a Golden Ring
Marianne
Memories Are Made of This
Mister Tap Toe
Del Rio, Venita
Mountain of Love
Delaney, Pearl
Nobody Knows the Way I Feel This
Mornin'
Delaney, Tom
Alabama Blues
The Down Home Blues
Follow the Deal On Down
The Jazz Me Blues
The Louisiana Mess Around
Nobody Knows the Way I Feel This
Mornin'
Slow and Steady
Delanoe, Pierre
Back Track!
The Day the Rains Came
Let It Be Me

DeLaughter, Hollis, see Lane, Red
DeLaughter, Hollis R., see Lane, Red
Delecluse, Claude
The Left Bank
Delerue, Georges
The Theme from *Jules and Jim*
Delettre, Jean
Hands across the Table
Delgado, Pepe
The Dream Peddler
Dello, Carmen
The Picnic Song
Dello, Theresa
The Picnic Song
Dellon, Harold A.
Colorado
Delmore, Alton
Beautiful Brown Eyes
Blues, Stay Away from Me
Delmore, Rabon
Blues, Stay Away from Me
DeLorme, Gaye
Earache My Eye
DeLory, Al
Mister Custer
Demarais, H. G.
Good Morning, Little School Girl
Demetrius, Claude
Ain't That Just Like a Woman
Demey, Tetos
You, You, You Are the One
Dempsey, Greg
Boogie Bands and One Night Stands
Demy, Jacques
I Will Wait for You
Watch What Happens
You Must Believe in Spring
Deni'
Canto D'Amore (Song of Love)
Denniker, Paul
Beside an Open Fireplace
The Milkmen's Matinee
Rhythm Lullaby
S'posin'
Dennis, Blandflo
Substitute
Dennis, Matt
Angel Eyes
Everything Happens to Me
Let's Get Away from It All

Lyricists & Composers Index

Lyricists & Composers Index

Domino, Antoine
  Don't Come Knockin'
  Let The Four Winds Blow
  My Girl Josephine
  Three Nights a Week
  Walking to New Orleans
Domino, Antoine "Fats"
  Ain't That a Shame
  All by Myself
  Be My Guest
  Blue Monday
  Bo Weevil
  The Fat Man
  Goin' Home
  Going to the River
  I Want To Walk You Home
  I'm Gonna Be a Wheel Someday
  I'm in Love Again
  I'm Ready
  I'm Walkin'
  It's You I Love
  Please Don't Leave Me
  Poor Me
  So Long
  Valley of Tears
  Whole Lotta Loving
Donaggio, P.
  You Don't Have to Say You Love
    Me
Donahue, Al
  Do You Wanna Jump, Children?
  Don't Cross Your Fingers, Cross
    Your Heart
  Low Down Rhythm in a Top Hat
Donaldson, Walter
  At Sundown
  Beside a Babbling Brook
  Carolina in the Morning
  Chili Bom Bom
  Clouds
  Come West, Little Girl, Come West
  Could Be
  Cuckoo in the Clock
  Did I Remember?
  Down South
  An Earful of Music
  Feelin' High
  For My Sweetheart
  Georgia
  Give Me My Mammy

Hello! Beautiful!
He's the Last Word
The Horse with the Dreamy Eyes
I Love the Land of Old Black Joe
I Wonder Where My Baby Is To-
  Night
I'd Be Lost Without You
I'm Bringing a Red, Red Rose
I'm Telling You
I'm with You!
In the Middle of the Night
Isn't She the Sweetest Thing
I've Had My Moments
Jungle Fever
Just Like a Melody Out of the Sky
Just Once Again
Kansas City Kitty
Lazy Lou'siana Moon
Let It Rain! Let It Pour! I'll Be in
  Virginia in the Morning
Let's Talk About My Sweetie
Little White Lies
Love Me or Leave Me
Makin' Whoopee
The Midnight Waltz
Mindin' My Business
Mister Meadowlark
My Baby Just Cares for Me
My Best Girl
My Blue Heaven
My Buddy
My Little Bimbo Down on the
  Bamboo Isle
My Mammy
My Mom
Nevada
Oh, Baby! Don't Say No, Say Maybe
Okay Toots
On Behalf of the Visiting Firemen
On the 'Gin, 'Gin, 'Ginny Shore
Once in a Lifetime
Reaching for Some-one and Not
  Finding Anyone There
Riptide
Romance
Sam, the Old Accordion Man
Seven or Eleven—My Dixie Pair
  o'Dice
Sing Me a Baby Song
Sioux City Sue

2266

Just a Girl That Men Forget
Keep Young and Beautiful
The Kiss Waltz
A Latin Tune, a Manhattan Moon
  and You
The Little Things You Used To Do
Living on Velvet
Lonesomest Girl in Town
Love Is Where You Find It
Love Will Find a Way
Lullaby of Broadway
Lulu's Back in Town
Many Happy Returns of the Day
Memories of France
Muchacha
My Dream of the Big Parade
My Kingdom for a Kiss
No More Love
Outside of You
Page Miss Glory
Painting the Clouds with Sunshine
Pettin' in the Park
Ping Pongo
Remember Me?
Remember My Forgotten Man
The Rose in Her Hair
Sally
September in the Rain
Shadow Waltz
Shanghai Lil
She's a Latin from Manhattan
Shuffle Off to Buffalo
The Song of the Marines (We're
  Shovin' Right Off Again)
South American Way
Stranger in Paree
Summer Night
Three's a Crowd
Tip Toe through the Tulips with Me
Tripoli—On the Shores of Tripoli
Watching My Dreams Go By
Waters of the Perkiomen
We Mustn't Say Goodbye
We're in the Money (The Gold
  Digger's Song)
What Has Become of Hinky Dinky
  Parlay Voo
When a Kid from the East Side
  (Found a Sweet Society Rose)
Where Am I? (Am I in Heaven?)

Where Was I?
Why Do I Dream Those Dreams
With Plenty of Money and You
Wonder Bar
The Words Are in My Heart
You Let Me Down
Young and Healthy
Your Love Is All That I Crave
You're Getting To Be a Habit with
  Me
Duboff, Steve
  The Pied Piper
  The Rain, the Park and Other Things
  We Can Fly
DuBois, Geraldine
  Pal-ing Around with You
Dubois, Ja'net
  Movin' on Up
Duchin, Eddy
  My Twilight Dream
Duchow, Lawrence
  The Swiss Boy (Schweizer Bub')
Duckworth, Willie Lee
  Sound Off
Dudan, Pierre
  Comme Ci, Comme Ca
Duddy, Lyn
  Darn It Baby, That's Love
  Johnny Angel
  Let It Ring
Dudley, Dave
  There Ain't No Easy Runs
Duff, Arlie
  You All Come
Duffy, Steve
  She Thinks I Still Care
Duke, Billy
  I Cried
Duke, Vernon
  April in Paris
  Autumn in New York
  Cabin in the Sky
  Do What You Wanna Do
  Got a Bran' New Daddy
  He Hasn't a Thing except Me
  Honey in the Honeycomb
  I Am Only Human After All
  I Can't Get Started
  I Like the Likes of You

Lyricists & Composers Index

Lyricists & Composers Index

Tulip or Turnip (Tell Me, Tell Me,
Dream Face)
Warm Valley
When I Walk with You

Ellington, E. A.
The Petite Waltz

Ellington, Edward Kennedy "Duke"
Alabamy Home
Awful Sad
Azure
Baby When You Ain't There
Best Wishes
Birmingham Breakdown
Black and Tan Fantasy
Black Beauty
Black Butterfly
Blind Man's Buff
Blue Feeling
Blue Light
The Blues with a Feeling
Boy Meets Horn
Caravan
Choo-Choo (I Gotta Hurry
Home)
Clarinet Lament
The Creeper
Creole Rhapsody
Crescendo in Blue
Daybreak Express
The Dicty Glide
Diminuendo in Blue
Doin' the Voom Voom
Down in Our Alley Blues
Drop Me Off in Harlem
The Duke Steps Out
Dusk on the Desert
East St. Louis Toodle-o
Echoes of Harlem
Flaming Youth
The Gal from Joe's
Goin' to Town
Grievin'
Gypsy without a Song
Harlem Flat Blues
Harlem Speaks
Harmony in Harlem
Haunted Nights
High Life
Hot and Bothered

I Let a Song Go Out of My
Heart
If You Were in My Place (What
Would You Do?)
I'm Checking Out Goombye
I'm Satisfied
Immigration Blues
In a Sentimental Mood
It Don't Mean a Thing (If It Ain't
Got That Swing)
I've Got To Be a Rug Cutter
Jeep's Blues
Jig Walk
Jim Dandy
Lazy Rhapsody
Lost in Meditation
Merry-Go-Round
Mississippi Moan
Misty Mornin'
The Mooch
Mood Indigo
Move Over
Please Forgive Me
Portrait of the Lion
Prelude to a Kiss
Pretty Soft for You
Pyramid
Reminiscing in Tempo
Rent Party Blues
Rhapsody, Jr.
Ring Dem Bells
Rockin' in Rhythm
Saddest Tale
Saturday Night Function
Scattin' at the Kit Kat
Serenade to Sweden
Showboat Shuffle
Skrontch
Slippery Horn
Solitude
Something To Live For
Sophisticated Lady
Steppin' into Swing Society
Stompy Jones
Take It Easy
Tootin' through the Roof
Wanderlust
What Am I Here For
With You
Yearning for Love

Lyricists & Composers Index

Evans, Tolchard
He Is Here
If
Lady of Spain
Let's All Sing Like the Birdies Sing
Lights of Paris
Unless
Evans, Willie
Metro Polka
Evelyn, Alicia
I Get the Sweetest Feeling
Pepper-Hot Baby
Everette, Bill
Gitarzan
Everly, Don
Cathy's Clown
So Sad (To Watch Good Love Go Bad)
'Til I Kissed You
Everly, Phil
Cathy's Clown
Gee, but It's Lonely
(Girls, Girls, Girls Were) Made To Love
When Will I Be Loved
Evoy, Lawrence Wayne
Last Song
Ewald, Marnie
Revenge
Eyton, Frank
Body and Soul
Ezell, Norman
I See the Light
Sound of Love
Western Union
Zip Code
Ezrin, Bob
Beth
Detroit Rock City
Faber, Billy
If I Live To Be a Hundred
I'm a Lonely Little Petunia (In an Onion Patch)
Faber, William E.
You Were Only Fooling
Fagan, Donald
Deacon Blues
Dr. Wu
Fagen, Donald
Any World (That I'm Welcome To)

Bad Sneakers
Black Friday
Daddy Don't Live in That New York City No More
Dirty Work
Do It Again
The Fez
F.M. (No Static at All)
Josie
Kid Charlemagne
My Old School
Peg
Pretzel Logic
Reeling in the Years
Rikki Don't Lose That Number
Show Biz Kids
Faile, Tommy
Phantom 309
Fain, Sammy
Ah, the Moon Is Here
Alice in Wonderland
All the Time
Am I Gonna Have Trouble with You?
And There You Are
April Love
Are You Havin' Any Fun?
By a Waterfall
A Certain Smile
Dear Hearts and Gentle People
The Dickey-Bird Song
Ev'ry Day
Face to Face
The Gift of Love
G'wan Home, Your Mudder's Callin'
Happy in Love
Here Comes the Banana Man, We've Got Bananas Now
Home Is Where the Heart Is
I Can Dream, Can't I?
I Can See You
I Speak to the Stars
I'll Be Seeing You
I'm Late
Imitation of Life
Joy in the Morning
Kiss Me and Kill Me with Love
Let a Smile Be Your Umbrella (on a Rainy Day)

2282

Lyricists & Composers Index

Lyricists & Composers Index

Fitzgerald, Ella
  Chew-Chew-Chew (Chew Your
    Bubble Gum)
  Oh, but I Do
  A-Tisket A-Tasket
  You Showed Me the Way
Fitzgerald, Tyrone
  Funky Nassau
Fitzsimmons, Dale
  California Polka
Flanagan, Bud
  Underneath the Arches
Flanagan, Ralph
  Hot Toddy
Flatow, Leon
  I'm Telling You
Flatt, Lester
  Fireball
Fleeson, Neville
  I'll Be with You in Apple Blossom
    Time
  When the Autumn Leaves Begin To
    Fall
Fleetwood, Ansley
  Just Good Ol' Boys
Fleischman, Robert
  Wheel in the Sky
Fleming, Kye
  Sleeping Single in a Double Bed
  Years
Fleming, Phil
  How Do You Do
Flemons, Wade
  Stay in My Corner
  Use Your Head
Flender, Harold
  Paris Blues
Fletcher, Donald
  Dancing Machine
Fletcher, "Dusty"
  Open the Door, Richard!
Fletcher, Lucy
  Sugar Blues
Flindt, Emil
  The Waltz You Saved for Me
Flint, Shelby
  I Will Love You
Flood, Dick
  Trouble's Back in Town

Flores, Jose Asuncion
  I Live for Only You
Flowers, Danny
  Tulsa Time
Floyd, Eddie
  I've Never Found a Girl (to Love Me
    Like You Do)
  Knock on Wood
  6345789 (634-5789)
  You Don't Know What You Mean
    to Me
Floyd, King
  Groove Me Baby
  Woman Don't Go Astray
Fluri, Edward, see Rambeau, Eddie
Flynn, Allan
  Be Still, My Heart!
  Maybe
Flynn, Jimmy
  Georgia Rose
Fogarty, J. Paul
  Betty Co-Ed
  Charlie Cadet
  Joe College
Fogel, Marty
  Disco Mystic
Fogelberg, Dan
  Heart Hotels
  Longer
  Part of the Plan
  The Power of Gold
Fogerty, John
  Rockin' All over the World
Fogerty, John C.
  Almost Saturday Night
  Bad Moon Rising
  Commotion
  Down on the Corner
  Fortunate Son
  Green River
  Have You Ever Seen the Rain
  Lodi
  Long as I Can See the Light
  Lookin' Out My Back Door
  Proud Mary
  Run Through the Jungle
  Someday Never Comes
  Sweet Hitch-Hiker
  Travelin' Band
  Up Around the Bend

Freeman, Ernie
  Jivin' Around
  Percolator
Freeman, Everett
  How Do I Love Thee
Freeman, James
  Our Anniversary
Freeman, John C.
  Just Don't Want to Be Lonely
    Tonight
Freeman, L. E.
  (It Will Have To Do) Until the Real
    Thing Comes Along
Freeman, Lawrence "Bud"
  Craze-ology
Freeman, Myrna
  The Last Waltz
Freeman, Stan
  Faith
  I Got Everything I Want
  I Had a Ball
  I've Got Everything I Want
  The Other Half of Me
  You've Broken a Fine Woman's
    Heart
Freeman, Ticker
  So Dear to My Heart
  (I Don't Care) That's All I Want To
    Know
  You'll Always Be the One I Love
Frey, Glen
  Best of My Love
  Desperado
  Heartache Tonight
  Hotel California
  I Can't Tell You Why
  James Dean
  Life in the Fast Lane
  Lyin' Eyes
  New Kid in Town
  One of These Nights
  Take It Easy
  Tequila Sunrise
Fricker, Sylvia
  You Were on My Mind
Friday, Freddy
  Java
Fridie, Langdon
  Troglodyte (Cave Man)

Fried, Gerald
  One Potato, Two Potato
  Roots Medley
Fried, Martin
  Broadway Rose
Friedhofer, Hugo
  Lights of Paris
  Vera Cruz
Friedhofer, Hugo W.
  Love Theme from *One-Eyed Jacks*
Friedland, Stephen
  Nobody Knows What's Goin' On (In
    My Mind but Me)
Friedman, Charles
  Kiss Me Another
  One Finger Piano
Friedman, Dean
  Ariel
Friedman, Gary William
  Dream Babies
  How I Feel
  Light Sings All over the World
  Sounds
Friedman, Jim
  Hey Nelly Nelly
Friedman, Ruthann
  Windy
Friend, Cliff
  Below the Equator
  The Broken Record
  Chili Bom Bom
  Concert in the Park
  Don't Sweetheart Me
  Give Me a Night in June
  Gonna Build a Big Fence around
    Texas
  (I'm Tellin' the Birds, Tellin' the
    Bees) How I Love You
  I Must See Annie Tonight
  I Wanna Go Where You Go, Do
    What You Do, Then I'll Be Happy
  It Goes Like This (That Funny
    Melody)
  Just Because You're You
  Just Give Me a June Night, the
    Moonlight, and You
  Let It Rain! Let It Pour! I'll Be in
    Virginia in the Morning
  Let Me Linger in Your Arms

Lyricists & Composers Index

Gabler, Milt
  Danke Schoen
  Love
  Skinny Minnie
  Stay Here with Me
  Sweet Maria
  Tell Me Why
  Wiederseh'n
Gabler, Milton
  Choo Choo Ch' Boogie
  Now and Forever
Gadd, Steve
  Stuff Like That
Gade, Jacob
  Jealousy
Gaillard, Bulee "Slim"
  Vol Vist Du Gaily Star
Gaillard, Slim
  Cement Mixer (Put-ti, Put-ti)
  Down by the Station
  The Flat Foot Floogie
  Tutti-Frutti
Gaines, Lee
  Just A-Sittin' and A-Rockin'
  Just Squeeze Me (But Don't Tease
    Me)
Gainsbourg, Serge
  Je T'Aime Moi Non Plus
Galbraith, Gordon
  I Got You
Galdieri, M.
  Love Theme from *La Strada*
Galdieri, Michele
  Non Dimenticar
Gale, Eric
  Stuff Like That
Galhardo, Jose
  April in Portugal
  Lisbon Antigua
Gall, Robert
  Charlemagne
  For Mama
Gallagher, Benny
  Breakaway
Gallagher, Ed
  Mister Gallagher and Mister Shean
Gallagher, Michael
  Do You Feel Like We Do
Gallagher, S. T.
  Illusion

Gallop, Sammy
  Autumn Serenade
  The Blossoms on the Bough
  A Bluebird Singing in My Heart
    (The La, La, La Song)
  Boogie Woogie Maxixe
  Count Every Star
  Don't Let Me Stand in Your Way
  Elmer's Tune
  Forgive My Heart
  Free
  Holiday for Strings
  How Can I Replace You
  Joey's Song
  Make Her Mine
  Maybe You'll Be There
  My Lady Loves To Dance
  Night Lights
  Outside of Heaven
  Serenade to a Lemonade
  Shoo-Fly Pie and Apple Pan Dowdy
  Somewhere along the Way
  That Wonderful Girl of Mine
  There Must Be a Way
  Wake the Town and Tell the People
Galloway, Tod B.
  The Whiffenpoof Song
Gamble, Ken
  I'm Gonna Make You Love Me
Gamble, Kenneth
  Explosion in My Soul
  Expressway to Your Heart
Gamble, Kenny
  Are You Happy?
  (Love Is Like a) Baseball Game
  A Brand New Me
  Brand New Me
  Break Up to Make Up
  Close the Door
  Cowboys to Girls
  Darlin' Darlin' Baby (Sweet, Tender
    Love)
  Do the Choo Choo
  Don't Leave Me This Way
  Don't Let Love Hang You Up
  Drowning in the Sea of Love
  Enjoy Yourself
  For the Love of Money
  Give the People What They Want
  Hey, Western Union Man

Hooked on You
If
It Don't Matter to Me
Lost Without Your Love
Make It with You
Part-Time Love
Popsicles and Icicles
Sweet Surrender
Gathers, Helen
  Mr. Lee
Gatlin, Larry
  All the Gold in California
  Broken Lady
  I Just Can't Get Her Out of My
    Mind
  I Just Wish You Were Someone I
    Love
  Penny Annie
Gatsos, Nikos
  Adios, My Love (The Song of
    Athens)
  Athina (White Rose of Athens)
Gaudio, Bob
  Beggin'
  Big Girls Don't Cry
  Big Man in Town
  Bye Bye Baby (Baby Goodbye)
  Can't Take My Eyes Off You
  Dawn (Go Away)
  December 1963 (Oh What a Night)
  Girl Come Running
  I Make a Fool of Myself
  I Would Be in Love (Anyway)
  Marlena
  The Proud One
  Rag Doll
  Ronnie
  Save It For Me
  Sherry
  Short Shorts
  Silence Is Golden
  Soon (I'll Be Home Again)
  The Sun Ain't Gonna Shine
    Anymore
  To Give (the Reason I Live)
  Walk Like a Man
  Watertown
  Who Loves You
Gay, Byron
  Four or Five Times

Horses
Sittin' on a Log (Pettin' My Dog)
Toodle-oo, So Long, Good-Bye
Gay, Noel
  The King's Horses (and the King's
    Men)
  Lambeth Walk
  Leaning on the Lamp Post
  Run, Rabbit, Run
Gayden, Mac
  Everlasting Love
  It's All Right
Gaye, Anna
  Baby, I'm for Real
  The Bells
Gaye, Marvin
  Baby, I'm for Real
  Beechwood 4-5789
  The Bells
  Come Get to This
  Dancing in the Street
  Got to Give It Up (Part 1)
  Inner City Blues (Make Me Wanna
    Holler)
  Let's Get It On
  Mercy Mercy Me (the Ecology)
  Pretty Little Baby
  Pride and Joy
  Stubborn Kind of Fellow
  Theme from *Trouble Man*
  What's Going On
Gayle, Tim
  It's Too Late Now
Gaylord, Ronnie
  Cuddle Me
Gayten, Paul
  But I Do
  For You My Love
  My Dearest Darling
Gaze, Heino
  Ask Me
  The Berlin Melody
  Calcutta
  Rainy Day Refrain (Dadim,
    Dadom)
Geddins, Robert
  Haunted House
  I Want To Know
Gee, Jack
  Cold in Hand Blues

Lyricists & Composers Index

Gerhard, Ake
  Lay Down Your Arms
Gerlach, Horace
  Daddy's Little Girl
Gerlach, Nick, *see* Kincaid, Jesse Lee
Gernhard, Phil
  The Return of the Red Baron
  Snoopy versus the Red Baron
Gershwin, Arthur
  Invitation to the Blues
Gershwin, George
  Aren't You Kind of Glad We Did?
  The Babbitt and the Bromide
  Back Bay Polka
  Because, Because
  (I've Got) Beginner's Luck
  Bess, You Is My Woman
  Bidin' My Time
  Blah-Blah-Blah
  Boy! What Love Has Done to Me
  But Not for Me
  By Strauss
  Changing My Tune
  Clap Yo' Hands
  Cossack Love Song (Don't Forget
    Me)
  Could You Use Me
  Dear Little Girl
  Delishious
  Do Do Do
  Do It Again
  Do What You Do!
  Drifting Along with the Tide
  Embraceable You
  Far Away
  Fascinating Rhythm
  Feeling I'm Falling
  Fidgety Feet
  A Foggy Day
  For You, for Me, for Evermore
  Funny Face
  Got a Rainbow
  The Half of It Dearie Blues
  Hang On to Me
  Hangin' Around with You
  He Loves and She Loves
  High Hat
  How Long Has This Been Going On?
  I Can't Be Bothered Now
  I Found a Four Leaf Clover

I Got Plenty o' Nuttin'
I Got Rhythm
I Love To Rhyme
I Loves You Porgy
I Mean To Say
I Was Doing All Right
I Won't Say I Will but I Won't Say I
  Won't
If I Became the President
I'll Build a Stairway to Paradise
The Illegitimate Daughter
Isn't It a Pity?
It Ain't Necessarily So
I've Got a Crush on You
I've Got To Be There
The Jolly Tar and the Milkmaid
Just Another Rhumba
K-ra-zy for You
Katinkitschka
Let 'Em Eat Cake
Let's Call the Whole Thing Off
Let's Kiss and Make Up
The Life of a Rose
Little Jazz Bird
Liza (All the Clouds'll Roll Away)
Looking for a Boy
Lorelei
Love Is Here To Stay
Love Is Sweeping the Country
Love Walked In
Luckiest Man in the World
Mademoiselle in New Rochelle
The Man I Love
Maybe
Mine
Mischa, Jascha, Toscha, Sascha
My Cousin in Milwaukee
My Man's Gone Now
My One and Only
Nashville Nightingale
Nice Work If You Can Get It
Nightie-Night
Of Thee I Sing
Oh Bess, Oh Where's My Bess
Oh Gee! Oh Joy!
Oh Lady, Be Good
On and On and On
On My Mind the Whole Night Long
Once

Lyricists & Composers Index

Gluck, John, Jr.
  Blue Winter
  It's My Party
  Mecca
Gmeiner, Tom
  Heart Healer
Goble, Graham
  Lady
  Reminiscing
Godley, Kevin
  I'm Mandy, Fly Me
  Rubber Bullets
Godwin, Mable
  Ling Ting Tong
Godwin, Ron
  Murder, She Said
Goehring, George
  Lipstick on Your Collar
Goell, Kermit
  How Wonderful To Know
  Huggin' and Chalkin'
  I Thought It Was Over
  Luna Rossa
  Near You
  One Finger Melody
  The Right Kind of Love
  Rose Ann of Charing Cross
  Shepherd Serenade
  Slowly
Goering, Al
  Stockholm Stomp
  Who's Your Little Whoozis?
Goetschius, Marjorie
  I Dream of You (More Than You
    Dream I Do)
Goetz, Coleman
  Congratulations
Goetz, E. Ray
  The Bamboula
  Do I Love You? (When There's
    Nothing but Yes in My Eyes)
  If You Could Care
  The Land of Going To Be
  So This Is Love
  Who Ate Napoleons with Josephine
    When Bonaparte Was Away?
  Who'll Buy My Violets? (La
    Violetera)
Goff, Duke
  Run Woman Run

Goffin, Gerry
  At the Club
  Do You Know Where You're Going
    To
  Does Goodnight Mean Goodbye
  Don't Ask Me To Be Friends
  Don't Bring Me Down
  Don't Say Nothin' Bad (About My
    Baby)
  Don't Try To Fight It, Baby
  Every Breath I Take
  Everything and Nothing
  Go Away, Little Girl
  Goin' Back
  Halfway to Paradise
  Happy Times (Are Here To Stay)
  Her Royal Majesty
  He's a Bad Boy
  Hey, Girl
  Hi-De-Ho
  How Can I Meet Her?
  How Many Tears
  Hung on You
  I Can't Hear You No More
  I Can't Stay Mad at You
  I Want To Stay Here
  I Wasn't Born to Follow
  I'll Meet You Halfway
  I'm Into Something Good
  It Might As Well Rain until
    September
  It's Gonna Be All Right
  It's Not the Spotlight
  I've Got Bonnie
  I've Got to Use My Imagination
  Just Once in My Life
  Keep Your Hands off My Baby
  Let's Turkey Trot
  The Loco-Motion
  (You Make Me Feel Like) A Natural
    Woman
  Oh! No, Not My Baby
  Oh! Oh! (It Started All Over Again)
  Old Smokey Locomotion
  On This Side of Goodbye
  One Fine Day
  Pleasant Valley Sunday
  Point of No Return
  Poor Little Rich Girl
  Run to Him

2311

Lyricists & Composers Index

Lyricists & Composers Index

Money Isn't Everything
The Mounties
Music in the Night (and Laughter in the Air)
My Favorite Things
My Girl Back Home
My Joe
The Next Time It Happens
No Other Love
Nobody Else but Me
Oh, What a Beautiful Mornin'
Oklahoma
Ol'Man River
One Alone
One Flower Grows Alone in Your Garden
The One Girl
One Kiss
One More Dance
Out of My Dreams
People Will Say We're In Love
Pore Jud
A Puzzlement
A Real Nice Clambake
Reckless
The Riff Song
Romance
Rose-Marie
Shall We Dance?
Sixteen Going on Seventeen
So Far
Softly, As in a Morning Sunrise
Soliloquy
Some Enchanted Evening
Somebody Ought To Be Told
Something New Is in My Heart
Something Wonderful
The Song Is You
Song of the Flame
The Sound of Music
Stan' Up an' Fight
Stouthearted Men
Sunday
Sunny
The Surrey with the Fringe on Top
Sweet Thursday

Tennessee Fish Fry
That Lucky Fellow
That Week in Paris
That's for Me
Then You Will Know
There Is Nothin' Like a Dame
The Things I Want
This Nearly Was Mine
Totem Tom Tom
'Twas Not So Long Ago
Two Little Bluebirds
A Very Special Day
Vodka
Wanting You
We Kiss in a Shadow
We'll Have a Kingdom
What's the Use of Wond'rin'
When I Grow Too Old To Dream
When the Children Are Asleep
When the Spring Is in the Air
The Whip
Who?
Why Do I Love You?
Why Was I Born?
Wildflower
Will You Marry Me Tomorrow, Maria?
A Wonderful Guy
You Are Beautiful
You Are Love
You Are Never Away
You Need Someone, Someone Needs You
You Will Remember Vienna
You'll Never Walk Alone
Younger Than Springtime
You're a Queer One, Julie Jordan
You've Got To Be Carefully Taught
Hammond, Albert
Gimme Dat Ding
I Need to Be in Love
It Never Rains in Southern California
Little Arrows
99 Miles from L.A.
When I Need You

Lyricists & Composers Index

The Eagle and Me
Evelina
Fancy Meeting You
Freedom Is the Word
Fun To Be Fooled
God's Country
The Great Come-and-Get-It Day
Happiness Is a Thing Called Joe
How Are Things in Glocca Morra?
I Am Only Human After All
I Could Go On Singing
I Got a Song
I Like the Likes of You
I Love To Sing-a
If I Only Had a Brain
If This Isn't Love
I'll Take Tallulah
I'm Yours
In the Shade of the New Apple
    Tree
In Your Own Quiet Way
It's Only a Paper Moon
It's Smart To Be People
I've Gone Romantic on You
The Jitterbug
Last Call for Love
Last Night When We Were Young
Let's Hit the Nail on the Head
Let's Put Our Heads Together
Let's Take a Walk around the
    Block
Life's a Dance
Life's Full of Consequence
Little Biscuit
Little Drops of Rain
Long Before You Came Along
Look to the Rainbow
Lydia, the Tattooed Lady
The Merry Old Land of Oz
Mewsette
Moanin' in the Mornin'
Moonlight and Pretzels
More and More
Napoleon
Necessity
New Deal Rhythm
Old Devil Moon
Over the Rainbow
Paris Is a Lonely Town
Poor You

Pretty To Walk With
Push the Button
Right As the Rain
Said I to My Heart, Said I
Satan's L'il Lamb
Savannah
Save Me, Sister
Shoein' the Mare
Something Sort of Grandish
Song of the Woodman
Speaking of Love
Speaking of the Weather
Suddenly
Take It Slow, Joe
Take My Hand, Paree
Tell Me, Tell Me Evening Star
That Great Come-and-Get-It Day
Then I'll Be Tired of You
There's a Great Day Coming
    Manana
There's a Little Bit of You in Every
    Love Song
T'morra', T'morra'
Two Blind Loves
Water under the Bridge
We're Off To See the Wizard
What Can You Say in a Love Song?
What Good Does It Do?
What Is There To Say
What Wouldn't I Do for That
    Man!
When I'm Not Near the Girl I
    Love
When the Boys Come Home
When the Idle Poor Become the Idle
    Rich
Where Have We Met Before?
Willow in the Wind
The World Is in My Arms
You're a Builder-Upper
You're the Cure for What Ails Me
Hardaway, Lila Mae
    Signed, Sealed, Delivered I'm Yours
Hardaway, Lula
    I Don't Know Why
    I Was Made to Love Her
    You Met Your Match...
Harden, Bobby
    Tippy Toeing

2331

Harden, Melvin
  Backfield in Motion
Hardin, Charles
  Not Fade Away
Hardin, Glen D.
  Count Me In
  My Heart's Symphony
  Where Will the Words Come From?
Hardin (Armstrong), Lillian
  I'm Gonna Get Cha
Hardin, Lillian
  My Sweet Lovin' Man
Hardin, Tim
  Don't Make Promises
  If I Were a Carpenter
  Lady Came from Baltimore
  Misty Roses
  Reason to Believe
Harding, Chuck
  You Can't Have My Love
Harding, Gladwyn E. "Chuck"
  Honky Tonk Girl
Hardwick, Otto
  Down in Our Alley Blues
Hardy, Bill
  Amen (Yea-Man)
Harford, Frank
  I'm Wastin' My Time on You
  Long Time Gone
  Rock 'n Rye
Hargis, Reginald
  Dazz
  Dusic
Hargrave, Ron
  High School Confidential
Hargreaves, Robert
  If
  Lady of Spain
  Let's All Sing Like the Birdies Sing
  Unless
Hargrove, Linda
  Just Get Up and Close the Door
  Let It Shine
Harlen, Jack
  Alley Cat
Harline, Leigh
  Give a Little Whistle
  Hi-Diddle-Dee-Dee (An Actor's Life
    for Me)
  I've Got No Strings

Jiminy Cricket
Theme from *The Travels of Jaimie
  McPheeters*
Three Cheers for Anything
Turn On the Old Music Box
When You Wish upon a Star
The World Owes Me a Living
Wynken, Blynken and Nod
Harling, W. Franke
  Always in All Ways
  Beyond the Blue Horizon
  Give Me a Moment Please
  She'll Love Me and Like It
  Sing You Sinners
  Tabu
  Tonight Is Mine
  Where Was I?
Harmati, Sandor
  Bluebird of Happiness
Harmon, Jean
  Evolution Blues
Harnick, Sheldon
  All of These and More
  Artificial Flowers
  Away from You
  Days Gone By
  Dear Friend
  Do You Love Me?
  Far from the Home I Love
  Fiddler on the Roof
  Freddy
  Gentlemen Jimmy
  Good Clean Fun
  Grand Knowing You
  He Tossed a Coin
  I Wonder What It's Like
  If I Were a Rich Man
  Ilona
  Just My Luck
  Little Old New York
  Lovely Laurie
  Matchmaker, Matchmaker
  Merry Little Minuet
  Miracle of Miracles
  My Gentle Young Johnny
  My Miss Mary
  Never Too Late
  Now I Have Everything
  Politics and Poker
  Popsicles in Paris

A Tree in the Park
Try Again Tomorrow
A Twinkle in Your Eyes
Wait Till You See Her
Way Out West (on West End
    Avenue)
We'll Be the Same
What Can You Do with a Man?
What Is a Man
What's the Use of Talking
When You Are Dancing the Waltz
Where or When
Where's That Rainbow?
Who Are You
Why Can't I?
Why Do I?
Why Do You Suppose?
With a Song in My Heart
You Are So Lovely and I'm So
    Lonely
You Are Too Beautiful
You Have Cast Your Shadow on the
    Sea
You Mustn't Kick It Around
You Took Advantage of Me
You're Nearer
Yours Sincerely
You've Got the Best of Me
Zip
Hart, Mickey
    Playing in the Band
Hart, Roger
    Just Like Me
Hart, Sadie N.
    Enclosed, One Broken Heart
Hart, Sam C.
    When It's Lamp Lightin' Time in the
        Valley
Hart, William
    Break Your Promise
    Didn't I (Blow Your Mind This
        Time)
    I'm Sorry
    La La La (Means I Love You)
    Ready or Not (Here I Come)
    You've Got Yours and I'll Get Mine
Hartford, John
    Gentle on My Mind
Hartman, Dan
    Free Ride

Hartman, Don
    I Found a Dream
Hartmann, Maurie
    I'm a Lonely Little Petunia (In an
        Onion Patch)
    Tell Me Why
Harvey, Alex
    Baby, Baby (I Know You're a Lady)
    Delta Dawn
    Reuben James
    Rings
    Tell It All Brother
Harvey, Bill
    Next Time You See Me
Harvey, Sarah
    Here Comes the Judge
Haskins, Will R.
    Abie's Wild Irish Rose
Hatch, Earl
    What's the Reason (I'm Not Pleasin'
        You)?
Hatch, Tony, see also Anthony, Hatch
    Call Me
    Color My World
    Crazy Downtown
    Don't Give Up
    Don't Sleep in the Subway
    Downtown
    I Couldn't Live without Your Love
    I Know a Place
    My Love
    The Other Man's Grass Is Always
        Greener
    Round Every Corner
    A Sign of the Times
    Who Am I?
    You'd Better Come Home
    You're the One
Hatchcock, Johnny
    Wake Up Irene
Hatcher, Charles
    Agent Double-O-Soul
    Oh How Happy
    Stop Her on Sight (SOS)
Hatcher, Harley
    All for the Love of Sunshine
Hathaway, Donnie
    Come Back Charleston Blue
Hathcock, John
    I Guess I'll Never Learn

Lyricists & Composers Index

Haymes, Bob
  Lipstick and Candy and Rubber Sole
    Shoes
  My Love, My Love
  That's All
Haynes, Walter
  Eight-by-Ten
  Girl on the Billboard
  (It's) Time to Pay the Fiddler
Hays, Barry
  Radar Love
Hays, Billy
  Every Day of My Life
  Goodness Knows How I Love You
Hays, Lee
  Badman's Blunder
  Gotta Travel On
  If I Had a Hammer
Hayward, Charles
  The Devil Went down to Georgia
Hayward, Justin
  I Dreamed Last Night
  Nights in White Satin
  Question
  Story in Your Eyes
  Tuesday Afternoon (Forever
    Afternoon)
Haywood, Leon
  I Want'a Do Something Freaky to
    You
Hazan, Al
  Daydreams
Hazard, Jean
  Yo San
Hazel, Edward
  Shakey Ground
Hazelwood, Albert
  The Air That I Breathe
Hazelwood, Eddie
  Sick, Sober and Sorry
Hazelwood, Lee
  The Lonely One
Hazelwood, Mike
  The Air That I Breathe
  Gimme Dat Ding
  It Never Rains in Southern California
Hazlewood, Lee
  Bonnie Come Back
  Boss Guitar
  Cannon Ball

Friday's Child
Houston
How Does That Grab You Darlin'?
In Our Time
Ladybird
Lightning's Girl
Love Eyes
Not the Lovin' Kind
Rebel-Rouser
Some Velvet Morning
Sugar Town
Summer Wine
These Boots Are Made for Walking
This Town
Hazlewood, Michael
  Yes, Yes, Yes
Hazlewood, Mike
  Little Arrows
Hazzard, Anthony
  Ha, Ha Said the Clown
Head, Roy
  Apple of My Eye
  Treat Her Right
Heagney, Billy
  Cross-Words between Sweetie and
    Me
  Mama, Let Rosie Alone
Heard, Dick
  Kentucky Rain
Heath, Hy
  Deacon Jones
  I'll Never Stand in Your Way
  The Little Red Fox (N'ya N'ya Ya
    Can't Catch Me)
  Mule Train
  Run Boy
  Sombody Bigger Than You and I
  Take These Chains from My Heart
  Uncle Remus Said
Heatherton, Fred
  I've Got a Lovely Bunch of
    Cocoanuts (Roll or Bowl a Ball—
    A Penny a Pitch)
Hebb, Bobby
  A Natural Man
  Sunny
Hecht, Don
  Walkin' after Midnight
Hecht, Ken
  No One Knows

2338

Lyricists & Composers Index

The Birth of the Blues
Black Bottom
Broadway
Button Up Your Overcoat!
Bye Bye Blackbird
Come to Me
Counterfeit Bill from Louisville
Curly Top
Don't Bring Lulu
Don't Hold Everything
Don't Tell Her What's Happened to Me
Dummy Song (I'll Take the Legs from Some Old Table)
Five Foot Two, Eyes of Blue; Has Anybody Seen My Girl
Follow the Swallow
For Old Times' Sake
Georgette
The Girl Is You and the Boy Is Me
Good for You, Bad for Me
Good News
Here Am I—Broken Hearted
Here I Am
He's a Ladies Man
I Thought I'd Die
I Want a Lovable Baby
I Want To Be Bad
I Wonder How I Look When I'm Asleep
I Wonder Who's Dancing with You Tonight
If I Had a Girl Like You
If I Had a Talking Picture of You
I'm a Dreamer, Aren't We All?
I'm in Love with You, That's Why
I'm in Seventh Heaven
I'm on the Crest of a Wave
I'm Sitting on Top of the World
It All Depends on You
I've Got To Get Hot
Just a Memory
Just Imagine
Keep Your Skirts Down, Mary Ann
Let's Call It a Day
Life Is Just a Bowl of Cherries
Little Pal
Lucky Day
Lucky in Love
Magnolia

My Lucky Star
My Sin
My Song
My Tonia
Nasty Man
(There's Something about an) Old Fashioned Girl
An Old Sombrero
Peter Pan, I Love You
Pickin' Cotton
Pompanola
Say When
The Simple Things in Life
So Blue
The Song I Love
Sonny Boy
Sunny Side Up
Thank Your Father
That Old Gang of Mine
That's Why Darkies Were Born
This Is the Missus
The Thrill Is Gone
Together
Turn on the Heat
The Varsity Drag
Wasn't It Beautiful While It Lasted
What D'Ya Say?
When I Grow Up
(Birdies Sing in Cages Too) Why Can't You
Why Did I Kiss That Girl?
Without Love
(I Am the Words), You Are the Melody
You Can Make My Life a Bed of Roses
You Try Somebody Else (We'll Be Back Together Again)
You Wouldn't Fool Me, Would You?
You're in Love with Everyone but the One Who's in Love with You
You're the Cream in My Coffee
Hendler, Herb
  Hot Toddy
Hendra, Tony
  Colorado
  Deteriorata
Hendricks, Belford
  I'm Too Far Gone to Turn Around
  It's Just a Matter of Time

Lyricists & Composers Index

Be My Life's Companion
Big Brass Band from Brazil
Bouquet of Roses
Boutonniere
Careless Hands
Castanets and Lace
Civilization (Bongo, Bongo, Bongo)
The Coffee Song (They've Got an
  Awful Lot of Coffee in Brazil)
Dear Hearts and Gentle People
Dearie
Don't Ever Be Afraid To Go Home
Don't You Believe It
Downhearted
English Muffins and Irish Stew
Ev'ry Street's a Boulevard in Old
  New York
From the Candy Store on the Corner
  (To the Chapel on the Hill)
How Do You Speak to an Angel?
I Feel Like I'm Gonna Live Forever
I'm Late
In the Middle of the House
The King of Holiday Island
A Kookie Little Paradise
Mention My Name in Sheboygan
Money Burns a Hole in My Pocket
Moonlight Gambler
My Fair Lady
My Little Corner of the World
My Summer Love
The Only Man on the Island
Our Day Will Come
Pancho Maximilian Hernandeez (The
  Best President We Ever Had)
Passing Fancy
(Don't Go) Please Stay
A Poor Man's Roses (Or a Rich
  Man's Gold)
Red Silk Stockings and Green
  Perfume
Sailor Boys Have Talk to Me in
  English
Send My Baby Back to Me
(Why Did I Tell You I Was Going
  to) Shanghai
Sitting in the Back Seat
Somebody Bad Stole de Wedding Bell
  (Who's Got de Ding Dong?)
Song and Dance Man

Stay with the Happy People
Summertime Lies
That's What I Like
The Thousand Islands Song
Tower of Strength
The Waiting Game
(In the) Wee Small Hours (Of the
  Morning)
Zambezi
Hilliard, Jimmy
  That Chick's Too Young To Fry
Hillman, Chris
  Christine's Tune
  Sin City
  So You Want to Be a Rock 'n Roll
    Star
Hillman, Marcia
  Now
Hillman, Roc
  My Devotion
  The New Look
Hilton, Eddie
  Cover Me
Himber, Richard
  Actions Speak Louder Than Words
  It Isn't Fair
Hines, Earl
  Apex Blues
  Cavernism
  Deep Forest
  Grand Piano Blues
  My Monday Date
  Rosetta
  Stormy Monday Blues
  You Can Depend on Me
Hinton, Eddie
  Choo-Choo Train
Hinton, Edward, see Hilton, Eddie
Hinton, Joe
  Gotta Hold on to This Feeling
Hippard, Bob
  Don't Write Her Off
Hirsch, Louis A.
  It's Getting Dark on Old Broadway
  Learn To Smile
  The Love Nest
  Mary
  My Rambler Rose
  'Neath the South Sea Moon
  Nightingale, Bring Me a Rose

Lyricists & Composers Index

Holland, Brian
  Baby, I Need Your Loving
  Baby Love
  Back in My Arms Again
  Bernadette
  Can I Get a Witness
  Come and Get These Memories
  Come See about Me
  Darling Baby
  Forever Came Today
  Give Me Just a Little More Time
  The Happening
  Heat Wave
  Heaven Must Have Sent You
  How Sweet It It (To Be Loved by
    You)
  I Can't Help Myself (Sugar Pie,
    Honey Bunch)
  I Guess I'll Always Love You
  I Hear a Symphony
  I'm Ready for Love
  (Come 'round Here) I'm the One
    You Need
  In and Out of Love
  In My Lonely Room
  It's the Same Old Song
  Jimmy Mack
  Just a Little Bit of You
  La La La La La
  Little Darling (I Need You)
  Live Wire
  Locking Up My Heart
  Love Is Here and Now You're Gone
  Love Is Like a Heat Wave
  Love Is Like an Itching in My Heart
  Mickey's Monkey
  My World Is Empty without You
  Nothing but Heartaches
  Nowhere to Run
  One, Two, Three (1-2-3)
  Playboy
  Please Mr. Postman
  Quicksand
  Reach Out I'll Be There
  Reflections
  (I'm a) Road Runner
  7 Rooms of Gloom
  Shake Me, Wake Me (When It's
    Over)
  Something about You

Standing in the Shadows of Love
Stop! In the Name of Love
Strange I Know
Take Me in Your Arms (Rock Me a
  Little While)
This Old Heart of Mine (Is Weak for
  You)
Where Did Our Love Go
You Can't Hurry Love
You Keep Me Hangin' On
You Keep Running Away
Your Unchanging Love
You're a Wonderful One
Holland, Eddie
  Ain't Too Proud to Beg
  All I Need
  Baby, I Need Your Loving
  Baby Love
  Back in My Arms Again
  Beauty Is Only Skin Deep
  Bernadette
  Can I Get a Witness
  Come and Get These Memories
  Come See about Me
  Darling Baby
  Everybody Needs Love
  Forever Came Today
  The Happening
  Heat Wave
  Heaven Must Have Sent You
  How Sweet It It (To Be Loved by
    You)
  I Can't Help Myself (Sugar Pie,
    Honey Bunch)
  I Guess I'll Always Love You
  I Hear a Symphony
  (I Know) I'm Losing You
  I'm Ready for Love
  (Come 'round Here) I'm the One
    You Need
  In and Out of Love
  In My Lonely Room
  It's the Same Old Song
  (Loneliness Made Me Realize) It's
    You That I Need
  Jimmy Mack
  Just a Little Bit of You
  La La La La La
  Little Darling (I Need You)
  Live Wire

Lyricists & Composers Index

Lyricists & Composers Index

John, Robert
  Sad Eyes
Johns, Brooke
  Tessie, Stop Teasin' Me
Johns, Leo
  Melodie d'Amour
Johns, Sammy
  Chevy Van
Johnsen, Cliff
  Stars and Stripes on Iwo Jima Isle
Johnson, Arnold
  Does Your Heart Beat for Me?
  Good-Bye Blues
Johnson, Bruce
  Beach Girl
Johnson, Buddy
  Did You See Jackie Robinson Hit
    That Ball
  Hittin' on Me
  I'm Just Your Fool
  Since I Fell for You
  When My Man Comes Home
Johnson, "Buster"
  The Wang Wang Blues
Johnson, Charles
  The Charleston Is the Best Dance
    After All
  Hot Bones and Rice
  Hot Tempered Blues
  Rubber Biscuit
Johnson, Chick
  Oh! Gee, Oh! Gosh, Oh! Golly, I'm
    in Love
Johnson, Clarence
  Achin' Hearted Blues
  I'm Goin' Away To Wear You Off
    My Mind
  Kansas City Man Blues
  Love Jones
Johnson, Claude
  What's Your Name
Johnson, E.
  Jenny, Take a Ride
Johnson, Earl King
  Teasing You
Johnson, Edith
  Good Chib Blues
  Honeydripper Blues
  Nickle's Worth of Liver

Johnson, Edward
  Jersey Bounce
Johnson, Emanuel
  Gloria
Johnson, Enotris
  Jenny, Jenny
  Long Tall Sally
  Miss Ann
Johnson, Frank
  We're Getting Careless with Our
    Love
  You've Been Doing Wrong for So
    Long
Johnson, Fred
  All in My Mind
Johnson, Freddie
  Birmingham Black Bottom
  Don't You Leave Me Here
Johnson, Freddy
  It Ain't Like That No More
Johnson, General
  Bring the Boys Home
  One Monkey Don't Stop No Show
  Patches (I'm Depending on You)
  Pay to the Piper
  Somebody's Been Sleeping in My Bed
  Stick-Up
  Want-Ads
Johnson, George
  I'll Be Good to You
  Stomp
Johnson, Harold
  G'bye Now
  Smoke from Your Cigarette
  When the Moon Comes over the
    Mountain
  You're a Special Part of Me
Johnson, Haven
  My Last Affair
Johnson, Hazel
  It's Too Late (Baby, Too Late)
Johnson, Henry Paul
  The World Is Round
Johnson, Hiram
  Could This Be Magic
Johnson, Howard
  Am I Wasting My Time on You?
  At the Moving Picture Ball
  Feather Your Nest
  Georgia

2363

Lyricists & Composers Index

Lyricists & Composers Index

Jones, Sonny
  You're the Only World I Know
Jones, Stan
  Cheyenne
  Riders in the Sky
  Searchers (Ride Away)
  Whirlwind
  Wringle Wrangle
Jones, Stephen
  What Do You Do Sunday, Mary?
Jones, Tom
  Everything Beautiful Happens at
    Night
  Gonna Be Another Hot Day
  I Can See It
  Is It Really Me?
  Love, Don't Turn Away
  A Man and a Woman
  Much More
  My Cup Runneth Over
  Raunchy
  Simple Little Things
  Soon It's Gonna Rain
  They Were You
Jones, Walter
  I Don't Want to Do Wrong
Jones, Willie
  Even Tho'
Joplin, Janis
  Down on Me
  Kozmic Blues
Joplin, Scott
  The Entertainer
  Magnetic Rag
Jordan, Archie
  It Was Almost Like a Song
  Let's Take the Long Way Around
    the World
  What a Difference You've Made in
    My Life
Jordan, Fred
  Belle
Jordan, Joe
  Love for a Day
  Morocco Blues
Jordan, Leroy "Lonnie"
  Cisco Kid
  Gypsy Man
  L.A. Sunshine
  Low Rider

Me and Baby Brother
Slipping into Darkness
Spill the Wine
Summer
Why Can't We Be Friends
The World Is a Ghetto
Jordan, Louis
  Barnyard Boogie
  Blue Light Boogie
  Don't Burn the Candle at Both Ends
  Early in the Mornin'
  I Know What You're Puttin' Down
  Is You Is, or Is You Ain't (Ma'
    Baby)
  Ration Blues
  Reet, Petite and Gone
  Run Joe
  Saturday Night Fish Fry
  You Can't Get That No More
Jordan, Robert
  (My Heart Goes) Ka-Ding-Dong
Jordan, Roy
  I'll Never Know
  My Love's a Gentle Man
Jorge Lima Menezes, *see* Ben, Jorge
Josea, Joe
  Cherry Pie
  Oop Shoop
  Partin' Time
  Peace of Mind
  Sweet Sixteen
  You Upset Me, Baby
Josefovits, Teri
  Au Revoir Again
Joseph, N. E.
  Ethiopia
Joseph, Ray
  Kathy-O
  A Sinner Kissed an Angel
Josie, Lou
  Midnight Confessions
Jouannest, Gerard
  Marieke
  Sons of
Jourdan, Michel
  Free Again
  Let Me Try Again (Laisse Moi Le
    Temps)
  Time, Time

2368

The Night Is Young and You're So
  Beautiful
Now I'm a Lady
Roam On, My Little Gypsy
  Sweetheart
Sittin' on a Backyard Fence
There's Something about a Rose That
  Reminds Me of You
Three's a Crowd
Wedding Bells Are Breaking Up That
  Old Gang of Mine
When I Take My Sugar to Tea
When Tomorrow Comes
When You Were a Smile on Your
  Mother's Lips (and a Twinkle in
  Your Daddy's Eye)
You Brought a New Kind of Love to
  Me
Kahan, Stanley
  The Girl with the Golden Braids
  Talk to Me
Kahaneck, Elroy
  Tryin' to Beat the Morning Home
Kahler, Hunter
  Until
Kahn, Art
  You Don't Like It—Not Much
Kahn, Donald
  Dream on a Summer Night
Kahn, Gus, *see also* Keyes, Gilbert
  Ain't We Got Fun?
  All God's Chillun Got Rhythm
  Around the Corner
  Baby Feet Go Pitter Patter
  Bashful
  Beloved
  Beside a Babbling Brook
  Bimini Bay
  Blue Lovebird
  Blue Venetian Waters
  Broken Hearted Melody
  Carioca
  Carolina in the Morning
  Charley, My Boy
  Chloe
  Clouds
  Come West, Little Girl, Come West
  Coquette
  Day Dreaming
  Do What You Do!

Dream a Little Dream of Me
An Earful of Music
Falling in Love with You
Farewell to Dreams
Flying Down to Rio
For My Sweetheart
Gone
Goofus
Guilty
Ha-cha-cha
Hangin' on the Garden Gate (Sayin'
  Good Night)
Happy, I Am Happy
Here We Are
He's the Last Word
Honolulu
Hour of Parting
How Strange
I Never Knew That Roses Grew
I Wonder Where My Baby Is To-
  Night
I'll Never Be the Same
I'll See You in My Dreams
I'm Bringing a Red, Red Rose
I'm Sitting High on a Hilltop
I'm Sorry, Sally
I'm Thru with Love
I'm Worried over You
Isn't She the Sweetest Thing
It Had To Be You
I've Got a Pocketful of Sunshine
I've Had My Moments
Josephine
Let's Talk About My Sweetie
The Little Old Clock on the Mantel
A Little Street Where Old Friends
  Meet
Liza (All the Clouds'll Roll Away)
Love Me Forever
Love Me or Leave Me
Makin' Whoopee
A Message from the Man in the
  Moon
The Midnight Waltz
Mindin' My Business
Music Makes Me
My Baby Just Cares for Me
My Buddy
My Heart Is Singing
New O'leans

No, No, Nora
Nobody's Sweetheart
Now That You've Gone
Oh! What a Pal Was "Whoozis"
Okay Toots
Once in a Lifetime
The One I Love Belongs to
    Somebody Else
One Night of Love
Orchids in the Moonlight
Persian Rug
Rhythm of the Raindrops
Riptide
San Francisco
Sing Me a Baby Song
Sittin' in a Corner
Sleepy Head
So At Last It's Come to This
Someone To Care For
Sometime
Spain
Sugar Plum
Sweetheart Darlin'
Swingin' Down the Lane
Thanks a Million
That Certain Party
This Night (Will Be My Souvenir)
Tomorrow Is Another Day
Tonight Is Mine
Toot, Toot, Tootsie! (Goo'Bye)
Two Together
Ukulele Lady
Waitin' at the Gate for Katy
The Waltz You Saved for Me
Waltzing in the Clouds
Was I To Blame for Falling in Love
    with You
What Do I Care—What Do I Care,
    My Sweetie Turned Me Down
When I Dream of the Last Waltz
    with You
When Lights Are Low
When My Ship Comes In
When You and I Were Seventeen
When You Come to the End of the
    Day
Where the Shy Little Violets Grow
Who Am I That You Should Care
    for Me?

Who Are We To Say (Obey Your
    Heart)
With All My Heart
Yes Sir, That's My Baby
You Ain't Heard Nothing Yet
You Stepped Out of a Dream
You're All I Need
You've Got Everything
Kahn, Keene
    Charming Little Faker
Kahn, Murl
    Petticoats of Portugal
Kahn, Roger Wolfe
    Crazy Rhythm
    Imagination
Kaihan, Maewa
    Now Is the Hour (Maori Farewell
        Song)
Kaiserman, Mauricio
    Feelings
Kalman, Emmerich
    Dear Eyes That Haunt Me
    Like You
    My Bajadere
    The One I'm Looking For
    Play Gypsies—Dance Gypsies
    We Two Shall Meet Again
    The Whip
    You Are Mine Evermore
Kalmanoff, Martin
    At a Sidewalk Penny Arcade
    First Name Initial
    Just Say I Love Her (Dicitencello
        Vuie)
    Utopia
    The Wedding Song
Kalmar, Bert
    All Alone Monday
    Dancing the Devil Away
    The Egg and I
    Ev'ryone Says "I Love You"
    Hooray for Captain Spaulding
    I Gave You Up Just Before You
        Threw Me Down
    I Love You So Much
    I Wanna Be Loved by You
    I'm a Vamp from East Broadway
    Keep On Doin' What You're Doin'
    Keep Romance Alive
    A Kiss To Build a Dream On

Lyricists & Composers Index

Mandy 'n' Me
My Sunny Tennessee
Nevertheless
Over and Over Again
The Same Old Moon
She's Mine, All Mine!
So Long! Oh-Long (How Long You Gonna Be Gone?)
Thinking of You
Three Little Words
Timbuctoo
Tired of It All
Up in the Clouds
Watching the Clouds Roll By
What a Perfect Combination
Whatever It Is I'm Against It
Where Do They Go When They Row, Row, Row?
Who's Sorry Now?

Kamano, Johnny
I'm a Lonely Little Petunia (In an Onion Patch)

Kamen, Michael
I Do the Rock

Kampfert, Bert
You Turned My World Around

Kander, John
And All That Jazz
Beautiful
Cabaret
A Family Affair
Happy Ending
Harmony
How Lucky Can You Get
I Don't Care Much
If You Could See Her (The Gorilla Song)
It's the Strangest Thing
Lucky Lady
Married (Heiraten)
Maybe This Time
Meeskite
The Money Song
My Coloring Book
My Own Best Friend
My Own Space
Shine It On
Theme from *New York, New York*
There's a Room in My House
The Thing of It Is

Tomorrow Belongs to Me
Willkommen

Kane, Artie
Don't Ask to Stay Until Tomorrow

Kane, John
Cuz You're So Sweet

Kanner, Hal
I Guess I'll Get the Papers and Go Home

Kanter, Hal
Move Over, Darling

Kantner, Paul
The Ballad of You and Me and Pooneil
Volunteers
Watch Her Ride
Wooden Ships

Kaper, Bronislaw
Ada
All God's Chillun Got Rhythm
Blue Lovebird
Blue Venetian Waters
Cosi Cosa
Drifting
Forever Darling
Gloria
Hi-Lili, Hi-Lo
Invitation
Just for Tonight
Love Song from *Mutiny on the Bounty*
Love Theme from *The Brothers Karamazov*
A Message from the Man in the Moon
My Heart Is Singing
The Next Time I Care (I'll Be Careful)
On Green Dolphin Street
The Prodigal (Love Theme)
San Francisco
Somebody Up There Likes Me
Take My Love
Theme from *Auntie Mame*
Theme from *Mutiny on the Bounty*
Theme from *The Swan*
Tomorrow Is Another Day
You're All I Need

Ring of Fire
She Understands Me
She Went a Little Bit Farther
Tiger Woman
Why Can't You Feel Sorry for Me
Wolverton Mountain
You'll Drive Me Back (Into Her
  Arms Again)
Killen, Buddy
Ballad of Two Brothers
Forever
I May Never Get to Heaven
Lady Bird
Losing Your Love
Sugar Lips
The Twelfth Rose
Killen, William
Ain't Gonna Bump No More (with
  No Big Fat Woman)
Killen, William D., see Killen, Buddy
Killette, Ronald B., see Trail, Buck
Killion, Leo V.
By-U, By-O (The Lou'siana
  Lullaby)
Hut Sut Song
Kilmer, Joyce
Trees
Kim, Andy
How'd We Ever Get This Way?
Jingle Jangle
Rainbow Ride
Rock Me Gently
Shoot 'em Up, Baby
So Good Together
Sugar, Sugar
Sunshine
Kincaid, Jesse Lee
Baby, You Come Rollin' cross My
  Mind
King, B. B.
Partin' Time
Paying the Cost to Be the Boss
When I'm Wrong
Why I Sing the Blues
King, Ben E.
Stand by Me
King, Bob
Tighter Tighter
King, Carole
At the Club

Beautiful
Been to Canaan
Believe in Humanity
Chicken Soup with Rice
Corazon
Crying in the Rain
Don't Bring Me Down
Don't Say Nothin' Bad (About My
  Baby)
Every Breath I Take
Go Away, Little Girl
Goin' Back
Halfway to Paradise
Happy Times (Are Here To Stay)
Her Royal Majesty
He's a Bad Boy
Hey, Girl
Hi-De-Ho
How Many Tears
Hung on You
I Can't Hear You No More
I Can't Stay Mad at You
I Feel the Earth Move
I Want To Stay Here
I Wasn't Born to Follow
I'm Into Something Good
It Might As Well Rain until
  September
It's Going to Take Some Time
It's Gonna Be All Right
It's Too Late
I've Got Bonnie
Jazzman
Just Once in My Life
Keep Your Hands off My Baby
The Loco-Motion
(You Make Me Feel Like) A Natural
  Woman
Nightingale
Oh! No, Not My Baby
Old Smokey Locomotion
On This Side of Goodbye
One Fine Day
Only Love Is Real
Pierre
Pleasant Valley Sunday
Point of No Return
Poor Little Rich Girl
Really Rosie
Smackwater Jack

Lyricists & Composers Index

So Far Away
Some Kind-a Wonderful
Sweet Seasons
Take Good Care of My Baby
Tapestry
This Little Girl
Up on the Roof
Walking Proud
What a Sweet Thing That Was
When My Little Girl Is Smiling
Where You Lead
Will You Love Me Tomorrow?
You've Got a Friend
King, Charles E.
The Hawaiian Wedding Song
King, Claude
Little Bitty Heart
Tiger Woman
Wolverton Mountain
King, Edward
Saturday Night Special
Sweet Home Alabama
King, Edward C.
Tomorrow
King, Erwin
Tennessee Polka
Tennessee Tears
King, Freddy
Hide Away—1962
San-Ho-Zay
King, Irving
Show Me the Way To Go Home
King, J.
Reveille Rock
King, Jack
How Am I To Know?
King, Jimmy
Soul Finger
King, Jon
Anthrax
I Found That Essence Rare
King, Kenneth
Everyone's Gone to the Moon
It's Good News Week
King, Nelson
There'll Be No Teardrops Tonight
King, Pearl
I Hear You Knocking
One Night
Witchcraft

King, Pee Wee
Bonaparte's Retreat
I'll Forgive You, but I Can't
Forget
Slow Poke
Tennessee Tango
Tennessee Waltz
You Belong to Me
King, Ray
Truck Drivin' Son-of-a-Gun
King, Riley
Peace of Mind
Please Love Me
Sweet Sixteen
Three O'Clock Blues
Woke Up This Morning
You Know I Love You
King, Riley B.
Ask Me No Questions
Ghetto Woman
So Excited
King, Robert
(I Scream, You Scream, We All
Scream for) Ice Cream
I've Got the Yes! We Have No
Banana Blues
Peter Pan, I Love You
Why Did I Kiss That Girl?
King, Robert A.
I Ain't Nobody's Darling
Keep Your Skirts Down, Mary
Ann
Moonlight on the Colorado
Toot, Toot, Tootsie! (Goo'Bye)
King, Robert L.
Draggin' the Line
King, Roy
I'll Pray for You
King, Tom
Beatnik Fly
Crossfire
Girl in Love
Red River Rock
Time Won't Let Me
King, Wayne
Beautiful Love
Blue Hours
Corn Silk
Goofus
Josephine

2380

Lyricists & Composers Index

Knape, S.
God, Love and Rock 'n' Roll (We Believe)

Knight, Baker
Big City Girls
Cowboy Boots
Don't the Girls All Get Prettier at Closing Time
I Got a Feeling
Lonesome Town
Never Be Anyone Else but You
Nobody's Baby Again
Not Enough Indians
Somewhere There's a Someone
Sweeter Than You
A Week in the Country
Wonder of You
The Wonder of You

Knight, Frederick
Ring My Bell

Knight, Gary
The River Is Wide

Knight, Gladys
Daddy Could Swear, I Declare
I Don't Want to Do Wrong

Knight, Merald, Jr.
Daddy Could Swear, I Declare
I Don't Want to Do Wrong

Knipper, Lev
Meadowland

Kniss, Richard L.
The Song Is Love
Sunshine on My Shoulders

Knopfler, Mark
Down to the Waterline
Lady Writer
Sultans of Swing

Knott, Joe
Add Some Music to Your Day

Knox, Buddy
Hula Love
I'm Stickin' with You
Party Doll
Rock Your Little Baby To Sleep

Koch, John
I Want You All to Myself

Koehler, Charles
Leave Me with a Smile

Koehler, Ted
And There You Are
Animal Crackers in My Soup
As Long As I Live
Best Wishes
Between the Devil and the Deep Blue Sea
Breakfast Ball
Calico Days
Curly Top
Don't Worry 'bout Me
Dreamy Melody
Ev'ry Night about This Time
Get Happy
Gladly
Happy As the Day Is Long
Here Goes (a Fool)
Hey, What Did the Bluebird Say?
Hittin' the Bottle
I Can't Face the Music (without Singing the Blues)
I Gotta Right To Sing the Blues
I Love a Parade
Ill Wind (You're Blowin' Me No Good)
I'm Shooting High
I've Got My Fingers Crossed
I've Got the World on a String
Kickin' the Gong Around
Let's Fall in Love
Linda
Lovely Lady
The March of Time
Me and the Blues
Minnie the Moocher's Wedding Day
Music, Music Everywhere (but Not a Song in My Heart)
Now I Know
Out in the Cold Again
Picture Me without You
Public Melody Number One
Raisin' the Rent
Say When
The Simple Things in Life
Sing My Heart
Some Sunday Morning
Spreadin' Rhythm Around
Stay on the Right Side, Sister
Stop! You're Breakin' My Heart
Stormy Weather

Sweet Dreams, Sweetheart
Tell Me with a Love Song
Tess's Torch Song (I Had a Man)
That's What I Hate about Love
There's No Two Ways about Love
Truckin'
The Wail of the Reefer Man
Whatcha Say
When Lights Are Low
When the Sun Comes Out
Whose Big Baby Are You
Wrap Your Troubles in Dreams (and
  Dream Your Troubles Away)
Koetscher, Edmund
  Liechtensteiner Polka
Koffman, Moe
  The Swingin' Shepherd Blues
Kogen, Harry
  Swiss Lullaby
Koger, George
  Vieni, Vieni
Koger, Georges
  Pigalle
  Two Loves Have I
Kohan, Buz
  One More Time
Kohler, Donna
  The Hula Hoop Song
Kohlman, Churchill
  Cry
Koki, Sam
  Paradise Isle
Kolber, Larry
  Forget Me Not
  Forty Winks Away
  I Love How You Love Me
  Little Things Like That
  Maybe He'll Come Back to Me
  Patches
  Sweet Little You
  The Yellow Bandana
  Yes, Mr. Peters
Kollo, Walter
  The Land of Going To Be
Kong, Leslie
  Israelites
Konte, Frank
  Ride Captain Ride
Koogmans, George
  Radar Love

Kooper, Al
  House in the Country
  I Can't Quit Her
  I Love You More Than You'll Ever
    Know
  I Must Be Seeing Things (and
    Hearing Things)
  The Modern Adventures of Plato,
    Diogenes, and Freud
  Somethin' Goin' On
  This Diamond Ring
Koplow, Don Howard
  Oh, Happy Day
Koppelman, Charles
  Yogi
Korb, Arthur
  Go On with the Wedding
  It Takes Time
Kornfeld, Art
  Come On, Let Yourself Go
  I Adore Him
  You'd Better Go
Kornfeld, Artie
  Dead Man's Curve
  The Pied Piper
  We Can Fly
  The Rain, the Park and Other
    Things
Korngold, Erich Wolfgang
  Music in the Night (and Laughter in
    the Air)
Kortchmar, Danny
  Honey, Don't Leave L.A.
Kosloff, Ira
  I Want You, I Need You, I Love
    You
Kosma, Joseph
  Autumn Leaves
Kostelanetz, Andre
  Moon Love
  On the Isle of May
Kountz, Richard
  Lady Divine
Kraemer, Peter
  Hello, Hello
Kramer, Alex
  Ain't Nobody Here but Us
    Chickens
  Candy
  Comme Ci, Comme Ca

Lyricists & Composers Index

Lyricists & Composers Index

Lehman, Kenny
  Dance, Dance, Dance (Yowsah, Yowsah, Yowsah)
Lehmann, John
  Why Does It Get So Late So Early?
Lehmann, Johnny
  Alone at Last
  The Man from the Diners' Club
  T.L.C.
Lehner, Stephen
  What Was
Lehrman, Ted
  The Mighty Sons of Hercules
Leib, Bell
  The Blond Sailor
Leib, Joseph, *see* Parish, Mitchell
Leiber, Jerry, *see also* Glick, Elmo
  Along Came Jones
  Bernie's Tune
  Black Denim Trousers and Motorcycle Boots
  Bossa Nova Baby
  Charlie Brown
  Don't
  Down in Mexico
  Drip Drop
  D.W. Washburn
  Hound Dog
  I Need Your Lovin'
  I Want To Do More
  I Who Have Nothing
  I'm a Woman
  Is That All There Is?
  Jailhouse Rock
  Just Tell Her Jim Said Hello
  Kansas City
  Love Me
  Love Potion Number Nine
  Loving You
  Lucky Lips
  The Man Who Robbed the Bank at Santa Fe
  On Broadway
  Only in America
  Poison Ivy
  Ruby Baby
  Searchin'
  (When She Needs Good Lovin') She Comes to Me
  She's Not You

Spanish Harlem
Stand by Me
Treat Me Nice
Yakety Yak
Young Blood
Leibert, Dick
  Come and Dance with Me
Leigh, Carolyn
  Be a Performer
  The Best Is Yet To Come
  Deep Down Inside
  Firefly
  Give a Little Whistle
  Good Intentions
  Here's to Us
  Hey, Look Me Over
  Hibiscus
  How Little We Know (How Little It Matters How Little We Know)
  I Walk a Little Faster
  I Won't Grow Up
  I'm Flying
  I'm Waiting Just for You
  It Amazes Me
  I've Got To Crow
  I've Got Your Number
  Just Because You're You
  Little Me
  Marry Young
  My, How the Time Goes By
  Now I Lay Me Down To Sleep
  The Other Side of the Tracks
  Pass Me By
  Playboy's Theme
  Poor Little Hollywood Star
  Positively No Dancing
  Real Live Girl
  The Rules of the Road
  Spring in Maine
  Stay with Me
  Tall Hope
  The Tempo of the Times
  Tender Shepherd
  When in Rome (I Do As the Romans Do)
  Witchcraft
  You Fascinate Me So
  Young at Heart
  You've Come Home

2392

Lyricists & Composers Index

Lewis, Stan
  I'll Be Home
Lewis, Stanley
  Susie Q
Lewis, Steve
  Day by Day You're Going To Miss
    Me
  Sud Bustin' Blues
Lewis, Steve J.
  Kiss Me Sweet
Lewis, Ted
  Bee's Knees
  Show Me the Way
  When My Baby Smiles at Me
Libbey, Dee
  Mangos
Liberace
  Sincerely Yours
Lichty, Katherine
  Almost Always
Liebert, Billy
  A Dear John Letter
Liebling, Howard
  California Nights
  Sunshine, Lollipops and Rainbows
Liebman, Joseph
  The Blues I Got Comin' Tomorrow
  Strange Feeling
Liebowitz, Joseph
  The Wedding Samba
Lief, Max
  How Long Will It Last?
Liferman, Georges
  Charlemagne
Liggins, Joe
  The Honeydripper
  I've Got a Right To Cry
  Pink Champagne
Lightfoot, Gordon
  Carefree Highway
  Cotton Jenny
  Early Mornin' Rain
  (That's What You Get) For Lovin'
    Me
  If You Could Read My Mind
  Rainy Day People
  Ribbon of Darkness
  Steel Rail Blues
  Sundown
  The Wreck of the Edmund Fitzgerald

Lilley, Joseph J.
  Jingle Jangle Jingle
Lincke, Paul
  The Glow-Worm
Lincoln, Philamore
  Temma Harbour
Lincoln, Shedrick
  Rubber Biscuit
Lind, Bob
  Elusive Butterfly
Lind, Jonathan
  Boogie Wonderland
Linde, Dennis
  Burning Love
  Mornin' Mornin'
Lindeman, Edith
  Little Things Mean a Lot
Linden, Dave
  Love Is a Hurtin' Thing
Lindley, Donald
  Rhythm of the Day
Lindsay, Mark
  Don't Take It So Hard
  Good Thing
  The Great Airplane Strike of 1966
  Him or Me, What's It Gonna Be?
  I Had a Dream
  Let Me!
  Mr. Sun, Mr. Moon
  Peace of Mind
  Steppin' Out
  Too Much Talk (and Not Enough
    Action)
  Ups and Downs
Lindsay, Mort
  The Stolen Hours
Lindt, R.
  Liechtensteiner Polka
Ling, Sam
  Bad Luck
  Eddie, My Love
Linhart, Buzzy
  Friends
Link, Harry
  Don't Take That Black Bottom
    Away
  I'm Just Wild About Animal
    Crackers
  I've Got a Feeling I'm Falling

Lyricists & Composers Index

Luban, Francia
  A Gay Ranchero
  Say Si Si
Lubin, Joe
  Cha-hua-hua
  Inspiration
  It Happened to Jane
  Midnight Lace
  Move Over, Darling
  Please Don't Eat the Daisies
  The Secret
  Show Time
  Teacher's Pet
  Tutti Frutti
  Twinkle Lullaby
Luboff, Norman
  Yellow Bird
Lucas, Ann
  Loose Talk
Lucas, Buddy
  Steamboat
Lucas, Carroll
  How Soon (Will I Be Seeing You)
Lucas, Nick
  I'm 'Way Ahead of You
Lucas, Reggie
  The Closer I Get to You
  What Cha Gonna Do with My
    Lovin'
Lucchesi, Roger
  The Portuguese Washerwomen
Luccisano, Joe
  There's a Moon Out Tonight
Lucia, Peter
  Crimson and Clover
Luckesch, Rudolf
  Hear My Song, Violetta
Lugo, Francisco
  I Need Somebody
Luke, Robin
  Susie Darlin
Luna, Gabriel
  Time Was
Lunceford, Jimmie
  Dream of You
  (If I Had) Rhythm in My Nursery
    Rhymes
Lunsford, Orville
  The All-American Boy

Lurie, Elliot
  Brandy (You're a Fine Girl)
Lutcher, Nellie
  He's a Real Gone Guy
  Hurry On Down
Luther, Frank
  Barnacle Bill the Sailor
Luttazzi, L.
  Souvenir d'Italie
Lutz, Michael
  Smokin' in the Boys Room
Lyall, William
  Magic
Lyle, Graham
  Breakaway
Lyle, Lessie
  Forever and Always
Lyman, Abe
  Did You Mean It?
  I Cried for You (Now It's Your Turn
    To Cry over Me)
  Love Is Just a Flower
  Mandalay
  Mary Lou
  What Can I Say After I Say I'm
    Sorry?
Lyman, Tommy
  Montmartre Rose
Lymon, Frank
  Why Do Fools Fall in Love
Lyn, Ev. E.
  Under the Moon
Lyn, Merril
  I Give You My Word
Lyn, Shirley
  I Overlooked an Orchid
  Mister Moon
Lynes, Gary
  Love Me Forever
Lynn, Cheryl
  Got to Be Real
Lynn, Loretta
  Coal Miner's Daughter
  Dear Uncle Sam
  Don't Come Home a-Drinkin' (with
    Lovin' on Your Mind)
  Fist City
  I Wanna Be Free
  Rated X
  To Make a Man (Feel Like a Man)

Lyricists & Composers Index

I Can't Love You Any More (Any
  More Than I Do)
I'll Buy That Dream
I'll Dance at Your Wedding
I'm Stepping Out with a Memory
  Tonight
Linger in My Arms a Little Longer,
  Baby
(I'm Afraid) The Masquerade Is Over
Midnight in Paris
Music, Maestro, Please!
A Needle in a Haystack
The Organ Grinder
Say a Pray'r for the Boys over There
Singin' in the Bathtub
Something I Dreamed Last Night
Twinkle, Twinkle, Little Star
Violins from Nowhere
Where Have You Been All My Life
You're Not So Easy To Forget
Magill, Jacqueline
  Mary Lou
Magine, Frank
  Dreamy Melody
  Save the Last Dance for Me
Maher, L. Brent
  A Lesson in Leavin'
Mahoney, Edward
  Baby Hold On
  Maybe I'm a Fool
  Two Tickets to Paradise
Mahoney, Jack
  Titina
Maiden, Tony
  At Midnight (My Love Will Lift You
    Up)
  Sweet Thing
Mainegra, Richard
  Here's Some Love
  Separate Ways
Makeba, Miriam
  Pata Pata (Phatha Phatha)
Malcolm, Calum
  The Shape of Things to Come
Malcolm, Horace
  If You're a Viper
Malie, Tommy
  Jealous
  Looking at the World thru Rose
    Colored Glasses

Stars Are the Windows of Heaven
Malkin, Norman
  Hey, Mr. Banjo
Malloy, David
  Gone Too Far
  I Just Want to Love You
  Suspicions
Malneck, Matt
  Eeny, Meeny, Meiny, Mo
  Figety Joe
  Goody-Goody
  Gypsy
  Hey, Good Looking
  I Go for That
  I Saw Her at Eight o'Clock
  If You Were Mine
  I'm Thru with Love
  Meet Miss America
  Shangri-La
  So At Last It's Come to This
  Stairway to the Stars
Malneck, Matty
  Ariane
  If I Had a Million Dollars
  I'll Never Be the Same
  Love in the Afternoon
  Pardon My Southern Accent
Malone, Deadric
  Ain't Nothing You Can Do
  Ain't That Loving You
  Annie Get Your Yo-Yo
  Blind Man
  Call on Me
  Don't Cry No More
  Eight Men and Four Women
  I Pity the Fool
  Share Your Love with Me
  That's the Way Love Is
  Turn On Your Love Light
  You're Gonna Make Me Cry
Malone, George
  Book of Love
Malone, Johnny
  Please Love Me Forever
Malotte, Albert Hay
  Ferdinand the Bull
  Song of the Open Road
Maltby, Richard
  Having Myself a Fine Time

Lyricists & Composers Index

Maltby, Richard, Jr.
Autumn
No More Songs for Me
Mana-Zucca, Mme.
I Love Life
Nichavo!
Manascalco, John
Goodnight My Love (Pleasant
Dreams)
Manchester, Melissa
Better Days
Come in from the Rain
Just Too Many People
Midnight Blue
Whenever I Call You "Friend"
Mancini, Henry
All His Children
Baby Elephant Walk
Bachelor in Paradise
Charade
Come to Me
Days of Wine and Roses
Dear Heart
Don't You Forget It
Hatari!
In the Arms of Love
It's Easy to Say
Joanna
Mr. Lucky
Moon River
Move 'em Out
Peter Gunn Theme
Pink Panther Theme
Send a Little Love My Way
The Sweetheart Tree
Toy Tiger
Whistling Away the Dark
Mandel, Johnny
Close Enough for Love
Emily
The Shadow of Your Smile
Song from M*A*S*H (Suicide Is
Painless)
A Time for Love
Mandell, Toni
Chicken Corden Blues
Mangione, Chuck
Feels So Good
Give It All You Got
Hill Where the Lord Hides

Manigault, Robert
Troglodyte (Cave Man)
Manilow, Barry
Copacabana (at the Copa)
Could It Be Magic
Daybreak
Even Now
It's a Miracle
This One's for You
Manker, Sidney
Raunchy
Manlio, Tito
Anema e Core
How Wonderful To Know
Mann, Barry
Amy
Blame It on the Bossa Nova
Bless You
Brown Eyed Woman
Come On Over to My Place
Conscience
Don't Be Afraid, Little Darlin'
Don't Make My Baby Blue
The Farmer's Daughter
Footsteps
Forty Winks Away
The Grass Is Greener
Heart (I Hear You Beating)
Here You Come Again
He's Sure the Boy I Love
Home of the Brave
How Can I Tell Her It's Over
How Much Love
Hungry
I Just Can't Help Believing
I Love How You Love Me
I Want You To Meet My Baby
If a Woman Answers
I'll Never Dance Again
I'll Take You Home
I'm Gonna Be Strong
It's Getting Better
Johnny Loves Me
Kicks
Looking through the Eyes of Love
Magic Town
Make Your Own Kind of Music
Mary's Little Lamb
My Dad
New World Coming

Lyricists & Composers Index

Are You Really Mine?
Chella Lla
Dennis the Menace
Don't Stay Away Too Long
Fascination
Gilly Gilly Ossenfeffer Katzenellen
    Bogen by the Sea
The Hawaiian Wedding Song
The Horse with the Easter Bonnet
Hot Diggity
I Can't Tell a Waltz from a Tango
I Still Feel the Same About You
The Island of Forgotten Lovers
Ivy Rose
Jilted
La Plume de Ma Tante
Mama, Teach Me To Dance
Mi Casa, Su Casa (My House Is
    Your House)
Moon-Talk
The Morningside of the Mountain
O Dio Mio
Oh, Oh, I'm Falling in Love Again
Papa Loves Mambo
The Pussy Cat Song (Nyow! Nyot
    Nyow!)
Rosanne
Santo Natale
Secretly
Takes Two To Tango
Torero
The Treasure of Sierra Madre
Underneath the Linden Tree
Manning, Kathleen Lockhart
    In the Luxembourg Gardens
Manning, Paul
    The Blue Train
Manone, Joe "Wingy"
    Downright Disgusted
Manson, Eddy
    Joey's Theme
Manston, Frere
    Abergavenny
Mantz, Nancie
    Green Light
    I Had Too Much to Dream (Last
        Night)
Manuel, Richard
    In a Station
    Tears of Rage

We Can Talk
Manus, Jack
    Am I Wasting My Time?
    Forgiving You
    Hills of Colorado
    Midnight Masquerade
    My Cousin Louella
    Vanity
Manzanero, Armando
    It's Impossible
Manzarek, Ray
    Love Her Madly
    Riders on the Storm
    Roadhouse Blues
    20th Century Fox
Manzarek, Raymond, *see also*
        Manzarek, Ray
    Love Me Two Times
    People Are Strange
    Wishful, Sinful
The Mar-Keys
    Last Night
Marais, Dee
    Poor Man's Riches
Marais, Josef
    A-round the Corner (Beneath the
        Berry Tree)
    Ma Says, Pa Says
    Sugarbush
Marascalco, John
    Be My Guest
    Good Golly Miss Molly
    Ready Teddy
    Rip It Up
Marascalco, John S.
    Send Me Some Lovin'
Marbot, Rolf
    Call Me Darling (Call Me
        Sweetheart, Call Me Dear)
Marcellino, Gerald
    I Am Love (Parts 1&2)
    Sad Tomorrows
Marchan, Bobby
    I Got a Thing Going On
Marchetti, F. D.
    Fascination
Marco, Sano
    May I Never Love Again
Marcotte, Don
    Dormi, Dormi (Sleep, Sleep)

Lyricists & Composers Index

Martin, Tony
You've Changed
Martin, Trade
Take Me for a Little While
Martine, Layng
Way Down
Martine, Layng, Jr.
Rub It In
Martinez, Rudy
I Need Somebody
96 Tears
Martins, David
Steel Men
Martins, Roberto
Cae Cae
Martita
My Jealous Eyes (That Turned from Blue to Green)
Marvell, Holt
These Foolish Things (Remind Me of You)
The World Is Mine (Tonight)
Marvin, Frankie
Honey, Do You Think It's Wrong
Marvin, Hank
Sam
Marvin, Johnny
At the Close of a Long, Long Day
Dust
Goodbye, Little Darlin', Goodbye
(Listen to the) Rhythm of the Range
There Ain't No Use in Cryin' Now
Marzano, Norman
Do Something to Me
Mas, Carolyne
Stillsane
Mascari, Eddie
I Got a Wife
Mascheroni, Vittorio
Jealous of You
Maschwitz, Eric, *see also* Marvell, Holt
At the Balalaika
He Wears a Pair of Silver Wings
A Nightingale Sang in Berkeley Square
Rainy Day Refrain (Dadim, Dadom)
Maser, Mort
Somehow
Mason, Barbara
Oh, How It Hurts

Sad, Sad Girl
Yes, I'm Ready
Mason, Barry
Delilah
Here It Comes Again
I Never Said Goodbye
Kiss Me Goodbye
The Last Waltz
Les Bicyclettes de Belsize
Love Grows (Where My Rosemary Goes)
Love Me Tonight
A Man without Love
My Marie
Say You'll Stay Until Tomorrow
Winter World of Love
Mason, Dave
Let It Go, Let It Flow
Only You Know and I Know
Mason, David
Feelin' Alright?
You Can All Join In
Mason, James
I Dig Rock and Roll Music
Mason, John
Open the Door, Richard!
Mason, Marilyn
Love Takes Time
Mason, Melvin
I Do
Mason, Nikki
Au Revoir Again
Masser, Michael
Do You Know Where You're Going To
The Greatest Love of All
Last Time I Saw Him
So Sad the Song
Touch Me in the Morning
Massey, Curt
Petticoat Junction
Massey, Guy
The Prisoner's Song
Massey, Louise
My Adobe Hacienda
Masters, Frankie
Charming Little Faker
Scatterbrain
Masters, Johnnie
Honeymoon on a Rocket Ship

Lyricists & Composers Index

My Shining Hour
Namely You
Not Mine
Old King Cole
The Old Music Master
On Behalf of the Visiting Firemen
On the Atchison, Topeka and the
  Santa Fe
On with the Dance
Once upon a Summertime
One for My Baby (And One More
  for the Road)
Ooh! What You Said
Out of This World
Pardon My Southern Accent
Peter Piper
Pink Panther Theme
P.S. I Love You
Red Apple
Ride, Tenderfoot, Ride
Ridin' on the Moon
The Rumba Jumps
Satin Doll
Say It with a Kiss
Says Who, Says You, Says I?
Sentimental and Melancholy
Silhouetted in the Moonlight
Skylark
Sluefoot
Sobbin' Women
Somebody Else's Moon (Not Mine)
Something's Gotta Give
Spring Spring Spring
Strip Polka (Take It Off!-Take It
  Off!)
Summer Wind
The Sweetheart Tree
Swing Your Partner Round and
  Round
Talk to Me Baby
Tangerine
Thanksgivin'
That Old Black Magic
There's a Fella Waitin' in
  Poughkeepsie
This Time the Dream's on Me
Too Marvelous for Words
Trav'lin' Light
Two of a Kind
Wait and See

The Waiter and the Porter and the
  Upstairs Maid
The Weekend of a Private Secretary
We're Working Our Way through
  College
When a Woman Loves a Man
(Ah, the Apple Trees) When the
  World Was Young
When You Hear the Time Signal
When You're in Love
Whistling Away the Dark
The Wild, Wild West
Windmill under the Stars
A Woman's Prerogative
Wonderful, Wonderful Day
The Yodel Blues
You Can't Run Away from It
You Have Taken My Heart
You Must Have Been a Beautiful
  Baby
You Were Never Lovelier
You're the One (For Me)
You've Got Me This Way (Whatta-
  Ya-Gonna Do about It)
You've Got Something There
Merchant, Michael Dee
  Time
Mercury, Freddie
  Bicycle Race
  Bohemian Rhapsody
  Crazy Little Thing Called Love
  Death on Two Legs
  Killer Queen
  Somebody to Love
  We Are the Champions
Mernit, Billy
  Special Delivery
Meroff, Benny
  Lonely Melody
Merrell, Wandra
  Pepino, the Italian Mouse
Merrick, Bob
  New Girl in Town
Merrick, Walt
  Run Joe
Merrill, Blanche
  I'm an Indian
Merrill, Bob
  Above the Stars
  Absent Minded Me

Lyricists & Composers Index

Beautiful Candy
Belle, Belle (My Liberty Belle)
Butterflies
Candy and Cake
The Chicken Song (I Ain't Gonna
Take It Settin' Down)
Cornet Man
Did You Close Your Eyes When We
Kissed
Don't Rain on My Parade
Feet Up (Pat Him on the Po-Po)
Find Yourself a Man
Fool's Paradise
Funny (Not Much)
Funny Girl
Honeycomb
If I Knew You Were Comin' I'd've
Baked a Cake
I'm Bashful
I'm the Greatest Star
It Was Always You
It's Good To Be Alive
Let Me In
Let's Always Love
Look at 'er
Lover's Gold
Make Yourself Comfortable
Mambo Italiano
Mira (Can You Imagine That?)
Miracle of Love
The Music That Makes Me Dance
My Truly, Truly Fair
Oh, Oh, Rosie
People
Pittsburgh, Pennsylvania
Sadie, Sadie
The Sheik of Chicago (Mustafa)
She's My Love
Sparrow in the Treetop
A Sweet Old-Fashioned Girl
That Doggie in the Window
That Hound Dog in the Window
('Cause I Love Ya) That's A-Why
Theme from *Carnival!*
Theme from *The Wonderful World
of the Brothers Grimm*
Tina Marie
Toys
Walkin' to Missouri
We Could Be Close

What Do You Give to a Man Who's
Had Everything
When the Boys Talk about the Girls
Where Will the Dimple Be?
Who Are You Now?
Why Does It Have To Rain on
Sunday
Yes, My Heart
You Are Woman, I Am Man
Merrill, Robert
Staying Young
Take Me Along
Merritt, Leon
Mama, Come Get Your Baby Boy
Merritt, Neal
May the Bird of Paradise Fly Up
Your Nose
Merritt, O. O.
That's Why I Was Born
Merriweather, Maceo
Worried Life Blues
Mertis, John, Jr.
Take My Love, I Want To Give It
All to You
Mescoli, Gino
My Love, Forgive Me (Amore,
Scusami)
Meshel, Wilbur
L. David Sloane
Meskill, Jack
Au Revoir, Pleasant Dreams
Burning Sands
Here Comes the Banana Man, We've
Got Bananas Now
I Was Lucky (C'etait Ecrit)
On the Beach at Bali-Bali
Rhythm of the Rain
Smile, Darn Ya, Smile
So I Took the Fifty Thousand
Dollars
There's Danger in Your Eyes, Cherie!
Wonderful You
Messenheimer, Sam
Singing a Vagabond Song
Messina, James
Angry Eyes
Messina, Jim
My Music
Thinking of You
Watching the River Run

2432

You Better Think Twice
Your Mama Don't Dance
Metcalfe, Clive
  A Summer Song
Metis, Frank
  The Enchanted Sea
Metis, John, Jr.
  Need Your Love So Bad
Meyer, Chuck
  Suddenly There's a Valley
Meyer, Don
  For Heaven's Sake
Meyer, George
  In a Little Bookshop
Meyer, George W.
  Brown Eyes, Why Are You Blue?
  Cover Me Up with the Sunshine of
    Virginia
  Cry Baby Blues
  The Hen and the Cow, (It's Only a
    Dream of the Past)
  Hiawatha's Melody of Love
  I Believe in Miracles
  If I Can't Have You (If You Can't
    Have Me)
  If I Only Had a Match
  I'm a Little Blackbird Looking for a
    Bluebird
  Mandy, Make Up Your Mind
  My Song of the Nile
  Row! Row! Rosie
  Sittin' in a Corner
  There Are Such Things
  They'll Never Miss the Wine in
    Dixieland
  Tuck Me to Sleep in My Old 'tucky
    Home
Meyer, Joseph
  According to the Moonlight
  As Long As I've Got My Mammy
  Born and Bred in Old Kentucky
  But I Did
  California, Here I Come
  Clap Hands! Here Comes Charley!
  Crazy Rhythm
  A Cup of Coffee, a Sandwich, and
    You
  Fancy Our Meeting
  Golden Gate
  Happy Go Lucky Lane

Headin' for Louisville
Hello Tucky
How Long Will It Last?
Hurry Home
I Wish I Were Twins (So I Could
  Love You Twice As Much)
Idle Gossip
If You Knew Susie Like I Know
  Susie
Imagination
It's an Old Southern Custom
Ji-Ji-Boo
Junk Man
Just a Little Closer
Love Lies
The Meadows of Heaven
Mickey Mouse's Birthday Party
My Honey's Lovin' Arms
Passe
You're Simply Delish
Meyer, Sol
  Tahiti Honey
Meyers, Billy
  Bugle Call Rag
  Cotton Picker's Ball
  Everybody Stomp
  The House of David Blues
  Nobody's Sweetheart
  Oriental
  Railroad Man
  Spanish Shawl
Meyers, Bubsy
  What's the Use of Getting Sober
Meyers, Henry
  The Four Freedoms
  Four Rivers
  Hello, Mi Amigo
Michael, William
  Mission Bell
Michaels, Lee
  Do You Know What I Mean
Michaels, Sidney
  Half the Battle
  Look for Small Pleasures
  To Be Alone with You
Michaels, Steven
  Someone You Love
Michaels, Tony
  Happy

Lyricists & Composers Index

Michalski, John
  Psychotic Reaction
Michels, Walter
  San
Micheyl, Mick
  Le Gamin de Paris
Mickens, Robert
  Hollywood Swinging
  Jungle Boogie
  Spirit of the Boogie
Middlebrooks, Harry
  Spooky
Middlebrooks, Ralph
  Fire
  Funky Worm
  Love Rollercoaster
  Sweet Sticky Thing
Middlebrooks, Ronald
  Skin Tight
  Who'd She Coo
Midler, Bette
  You're Moving Out Today
Migliacci, F.
  Volare
Migliacci, Franco
  Pink Panther Theme
Mikaljohn
  I Love the Way You Love
Miketta, Bob
  Robin Hood
Mikolas, Joe
  Mexican Pearls
Milburn, Ken
  Stop the Start of Tears (in My Heart)
Miles, Dick
  The Coffee Song (They've Got an
    Awful Lot of Coffee in Brazil)
  I'll Remember Suzanne
Miles, Florence
  At Last! At Last!
Miles, Lizzie
  She Walked Right Up and Took My
    Man Away
Miles, Richard
  Jack, You're Dead
Miley, Bubber
  Black and Tan Fantasy
  Doin' the Voom Voom
  Down in the Mouth Blues
  East St. Louis Toodle-o

Goin' to Town
  Lenox Avenue Shuffle
Millas
  You Wouldn't Listen
Miller, Barbara
  Call Me Mister Brown
Miller, Bernard
  I Can't Stand the Rain
Miller, Bernie
  Bernie's Tune
Miller, Bob
  Chime Bells
  Seven Years with the Wrong Woman
  Things That Might Have Been
  Twenty One Years
Miller, Bobby
  Always Together
  Does Anybody Know I'm Here?
  Stay in My Corner
  There Is
  Wear It on Our Face
Miller, Charles
  L.A. Sunshine
  Low Rider
  Me and Baby Brother
  Summer
  Why Can't We Be Friends
  The World Is a Ghetto
Miller, Charles W.
  Cisco Kid
  Gypsy Man
  Spill the Wine
Miller, Ed E.
  Don't Let the Rain Come Down
    (Crooked Little Man)
Miller, Eddie
  After Loving You
  I'd Rather Drink Muddy Water
  I'll Release You
  (Love's Got Me in a) Lazy Mood
  Release Me
  Thanks a Lot
  There She Goes
Miller, Everett
  Red Apple
Miller, Francis
  Married But Not to Each Other
Miller, Frank
  Green Fields
  Love Is a Golden Ring

Mitchell, "Teepee"
Need You
You Told a Lie (I Believed You)

Mitchell, Willie
Call Me (Come Back Home)
Echoes of Love
I'm Still in Love with You
L-O-V-E (Love)
Let's Stay Together
Livin' for You
Look What You Done for Me
You Oughta Be with Me

Mitchum, Robert
Hey! Mister Cotton-Picker

Mize, Billy
My Baby Walks All over Me
Who'll Buy the Wine

Mize, Buddy
The Shoe Goes on the Other Foot
Tonight

Mize, Vernon
I've Run Out of Tomorrows

Mizell, Alphonso, see Mizell, Fonce

Mizell, Fonce
ABC
The Love You Save
Mama's Pearl
Sugar Daddy

Mizzy, Vic
Choo'n Gum
Didja Ever?
The Enchanted Melody
Hotta Chocolotta
I Had a Little Talk with the Lord
I Like It, I Like It
The Jones Boy
Kille Kille (Indian Love Talk)
Moment of Fear
My Dreams Are Getting Better All
the Time
Pretty Kitty Blue Eyes
Take It Easy
There's a Far Away Look in Your
Eye
Three Little Sisters
Well, There It Is!
The Whole World Is Singing My
Song

With a Hey and a Hi and a Ho Ho
Ho!

Mockridge, Cyril
It's a Woman's World

Modeliste, Joseph
Look-ka Py Py
Sophisticated Cissy

Modeliste, Joseph, Jr.
Cissy Strut

Modugno, Domenico
Addio, Addio
Ask Me
Ciao, Ciao, Bambina
Stay Here with Me
Volare

Modugno, Migliacci
Addio, Addio

Moeller, Edith
The Happy Wanderer (Val-de Ri—
Val-de Ra)

Moeller, Friedrich Wilhelm
The Happy Wanderer (Val-de Ri—
Val-de Ra)

Moeller, Tommy
Concrete and Clay

Moffatt, Hugh
Old Flames (Can't Hold a Candle to
You)

Moffett, Pamela
Baby Come Close

Moffitt, Kenneth R.
Oh Julie

Mogo
Al Di La

Mogol
Help Yourself
I Don't Know What He Told You
Let's Live for Today

Mogol, B.
I Who Have Nothing

Mogol, I.
Bella Linda

Mohr, Halsey K.
Good-bye, Dixie, Good-bye
It Will Never Be Dry Down in
Havana, No Matter What Happens
'round Here

Lyricists & Composers Index

Moishe
  Tonight My Heart She Is (Will Be)
    Crying
Molinare, Nicanor
  Chiu, Chiu
Molinary, Phyllis
  Everytime I Sing a Love Song
Moll, Billy
  At the Close of a Long, Long Day
  Gid-ap, Garibaldi
  I Want a Little Girl
  (I Scream, You Scream, We All
    Scream for) Ice Cream
  Moonlight on the Colorado
  So the Bluebirds and the Blackbirds
    Got Together
  Wrap Your Troubles in Dreams (and
    Dream Your Troubles Away)
Mollica, James J., III
  Atomic
Moman, Chips
  (Hey Won't You Play) Another
    Somebody Done Somebody Wrong
    Song
  Luckenbach, Texas (Back to the
    Basics of Love)
  This Time
  The Wurlitzer Prize (I Don't Want
    to Get over You)
Monaco, James
  Crazy People
  Six Lessons from Madame La Zonga
  We Mustn't Say Goodbye
Monaco, James V.
  All That I Want Is You
  An Apple for the Teacher
  April Played the Fiddle
  Caresses
  Cross-Word Mamma You Puzzle Me
    but Papa's Gonna Figure You Out
  Crying for Joy
  Dirty Hands, Dirty Face
  East Side of Heaven
  Ev'ry Night about This Time
  Hang Your Heart on a Hickory Limb
  I Can't Begin To Tell You
  I Haven't Time To Be a Millionaire
  I'm Making Believe
  Laugh and Call It Love
  A Man and His Dream

Masculine Women! Feminine Men!
Me and the Boy Friend
Me and the Man in the Moon
Meet the Sun Half-Way
On the Sentimental Side
Once Too Often
Only Forever
The Only Only One for Me
The Pessimistic Character (With the
  Crab Apple Face)
Red Lips Kiss My Blues Away
Rhythm on the River
Sing a Song of Sunbeams
Sweet Potato Piper
That Sly Old Gentleman (from
  Featherbed Lane)
That's for Me
This Is My Night To Dream
Through (How Can You Say We're
  Through?)
Time Alone Will Tell
Too Romantic
When the Moon Comes over
  Madison Square (The Love Lament
  of a Western Gent)
You Know You Belong to Somebody
  Else So Why Don't You Leave Me
  Alone
You're Gonna Lose Your Gal
You've Got Me in the Palm of Your
  Hand!
Monaco, Jimmy
  Don't Let That Moon Get Away
  I'll Take Care of Your Cares
  I've Got a Pocketful of Dreams
  My Heart Is Taking Lessons
Monk, Thelonious
  Bemsha Swing
  Blue Monk
  Criss-Cross
  Epistrophy
  In Walked Bud
  Misterioso
  'Round Midnight
  Ruby, My Dear
  Straight, No Chaser
  Well, You Needn't
Monnot, Marguerite
  Dis-Donc, Dis-Donc
  If You Love Me (Really Love Me)

Lyricists & Composers Index

Morton, Ferdinand "Jelly Roll"
Big Foot Ham
Black Bottom Stomp
Boogaboo Blues
Burnin' the Iceberg
Cannon Ball Blues
Dead Man Blues
Freakish
Froggie Moore
Georgia Swing
Grandpa's Spells
Jungle Blues
Kansas City Stomp
King Porter Stomp
London Blues
Midnight Mamma
Milenberg Joys
Mr. Jelly Lord
New Orleans Blues
New Orleans Bump
The Pearls
Seattle Hunch
Shoe Shiner's Drag
Shreveport Stomps
Sidewalk Blues
Tank Town Bump
Wild Man Blues
Wolverine Blues

Morton, George
Give Him a Great Big Kiss
I Can Never Go Home Anymore
Leader of the Pack

Morton, George F.
Remember (Walking in the Sand)

Mosel, I.
Merry Christmas Waltz

Moseley, Bob
AuReet

Mosely, Robert
Big, Cold Wind
Goodbye My Lover, Goodbye
Midnight Flyer
Since I Made You Cry

Mosher, Bob
Munster's Theme

Mosley, Leo "Snub"
Pretty Eyed Baby

Mosley, Robert
Sha-La-La

Moss, Jeffrey
Rubber Duckie
This Way to Sesame Street

Moss, Marie
Until Sunrise

Moss, Tyrone
Everybody's Everything

Mosser, Peter
Morgen

Mossman, Ted
Full Moon and Empty Arms
Silly Milly
Till the End of Time

Moten, Bennie
Ding Dong Blues
Harmony Blues
It Won't Be Long
It's Hard To Laugh or Smile
Kansas City Shuffle
Kansas City Squabble
Let's Get It
Moten Stomp
Moten Swing
Moten's Blues
Pass Out Lightly
South
Terrific Stomp
Tough Breaks Stomp

Moten, Buster
Let's Get It
Moten Swing

Moten, Mae
Mercy, Mr. Percy

Mothersbaugh, Mark
Devo Corporate Anthem

Motola, George
Goodnight My Love (Pleasant Dreams)

Motzan, Otto
Bright Eyes
Mandy 'n' Me

Moulton, Herb
Makin' Love, Mountain Style

Moustaki, G.
Milord

Moy, Melvin
Home Cookin'

Lyricists & Composers Index

Moy, Sylvia
  Honey Chile
  (We've Got) Honey Love
  I Was Made to Love Her
  I'm Wondering
  It Takes Two
  Little Ole Man (Uptight Everything's
    Alright)
  Love Bug Leave My Heart Alone
  My Baby Loves Me
  My Cherie Amour
  Nothing's Too Good for My Baby
  Shoo-Be-Doo-Be-Doo-Da-Day
  Uptight (Everything's Alright)
  What Am I Going to Do without
    Your Love?
Moyer, Penny
  Set Him Free
Mozian, Roger King
  Asia Minor
Msarurgwa, August
  Skokiaan
Mtube, James
  What Cha Gonna Do with My
    Lovin'
Mtume, James
  The Closer I Get to You
Muhammad, Meekaaeel Abdul
  Ladies Night
Muldrow, Cornell
  You Can't Sit Down
Mullan, Jack
  He
Muller, Gus
  The Wang Wang Blues
Muller, Randy
  Movin'
Mullican, Moon
  Cherokee Boogie
  New Pretty Blonde
  When a Soldier Knocks and Finds
    Nobody Home
Mulligan, Gerry
  Jeru
Mullins, Camerol
  I Won't Mehtion It Again
Mullins, Johnny
  Blue Kentucky Girl
  Success

Mundy, James
  Bolero at the Savoy
  Cavernism
Mundy, Jimmy
  Air Mail Special
  Don'cha Go 'way Mad
  So Far, So Good
  Solo Flight
  Swingtime in the Rockies
  Trav'lin' Light
Munnings, Ralph
  Funky Nassau
Munoz, Rafael
  Tropical Meringue
Munro, Bill
  When My Baby Smiles at Me
Munzo, Jose
  Moliendo Cafe
Murden, Orlando
  For Once in My Life
Murph, Randolph
  Love Jones
Murphey, Michael
  Carolina in the Pines
  Wildfire
Murphy, Audie
  Shutters and Boards
Murphy, Barry
  We Can't Hide It Anymore
Murphy, Jesse
  Our Anniversary
Murphy, Michael
  Geronimo's Cadillac
Murphy, Mike
  Airplane Song (My Airplane)
Murphy, Owen
  By Special Permission (of the
    Copyright Owners I Love You)
  Rhythm of the Day
Murphy, Ralph
  Half the Way
Murphy, Walter
  A Fifth of Beethoven
Murray, Fred
  I'm Henry VIII, I Am
Murray, Henry, Jr.
  She Blew a Good Thing
Murray, J. P.
  Do the New York
  Two Loves Have I

Lyricists & Composers Index

Mention My Name in Sheboygan
Red Silk Stockings and Green
  Perfume
The Singing Hills
There's a Chill on the Hill Tonight
Walkin' Down to Washington
We Three (My Echo, My Shadow
  and Me)
Yesterday's Gardenias
You Forgot about Me
Myx, James, Jr.
  Inner City Blues (Make Me Wanna
  Holler)
Nabbie, Jimmie
  You Are My Love
Nacho, Tata, *see* Esperon, Ignacio
  Fernandex
Nader, Neval
  Fly By Night
  Mecca
Nagle, Ron
  Don't Touch Me There
Nahan, Irv
  Dance with Me
Nakamura, Hachidai
  Sukiyaki (My First Lonely Night)
Nance, Dolores
  Endless Sleep
Nance, Jack
  It's Only Make Believe
  The Story of My Love
Napier-Bell, Simon
  You Don't Have to Say You Love
  Me
Napoleon, Phil
  The Great White Way Blues
  Just Hot
  Shufflin' Mose
  Sioux City Sue
Napton, Johnny
  My Devotion
Nardone, Belle
  Santo Natale
Nascimbene, M.
  Barabbas
Nascimbene, Mario
  Eve's Theme
  Happy Thieves Theme
  Love Theme from *A Farewell to
  Arms*

Song of the Barefoot Contessa
Theme from *Romanoff and Juliet*
Theme from *Sons and Lovers*
The Vespa Song
Naset, C.
  Dreamy Melody
Nash, Graham
  Carrie-Anne
  Chicago
  Dear Eloise
  Jennifer Eccles
  Just a Song Before I Go
  Marrakesh Express
  On a Carousel
  Our House
  Pay You Back with Interest
  Stop, Stop, Stop
  Teach Your Children
  Tell Me to My Face
Nash, Johnny
  Hold Me Tight
  I Can See Clearly Now
  What Kind of Love Is This?
Nash, Ogden
  Foolish Heart
  How Much I Love You
  I'm a Stranger Here Myself
  Just Like a Man
  Madly in Love
  Out of the Clear Blue Sky
  Round About
  Speak Low
  That's Him
  The Trouble with Women
  Westwind
Nash, Otha
  Spirit of the Boogie
Nathan, Charles
  Say You're Mine Again
  Somewhere (There Is Someone)
Nathan, N.
  Hold in the Wall
Nathan, Sidney
  New Pretty Blonde
Nathanson, Nat
  Blackin' Blues
Nauman, Paul
  Ball of Fire
Naumann, Paul
  Do Something to Me

Navarro, Esther
  Speedoo
Naylor, Charles
  Shake Me I Rattle (Squeeze Me I
    Cry)
Nazareth, Ernesto
  Blame It on the Samba
Nazelles, Rene
  C'est Pas Comme Ca (It's Not Like
    That)
  Sous les Toits de Paris (Under a
    Roof in Paree)
Nebb, Jimmy
  No Arms Can Ever Hold You (Like
    These Arms of Mine)
Neely, Henry M.
  Mem'ries
Neese, Chuck
  Rednecks, White Socks and Blue
    Ribbon Beer
Neff, Ricky
  John Riley
Negrette, George
  I Want My Mama
Negulesco, Dusty
  It Is Better To Love
  Jessica
  The Vespa Song
  Will You Remember
Neiburg, A. J.
  I'm Confessin' (That I Love You)
Neiburg, Al J.
  (When It's) Darkness on the Delta
  In a Blue and Pensive Mood
  It's Sunday Down in Caroline
  It's the Talk of the Town
  I've Got an Invitation to a Dance
  The Shag
  Sweet Slumber
  Under a Blanket of Blue
Neil, Fred
  Candy Man
  Everybody's Talkin' (Echoes)
  Tear Down the Walls
Neil, Marcia
  Funny (Not Much)
Neill, Larry
  The Winter Waltz
Nelson, Arnett
  Buddy's Habits

Nelson, Benjamin
  There Goes My Baby
Nelson, Betty
  Don't Play That Song (You Lied)
Nelson, D. C.
  Too Late
Nelson, Earl
  The Duck
Nelson, Ed. G.
  Auf Wiedersehn, My Dear
  (Don't Your Conscience Ever Bother
    You) Hang Your Head in Shame
  I Apologize
  Josephine Please No Lean on the Bell
  Oh! Mother I'm Wild!
  The Pal That I Loved Stole the Gal
    That I Loved
  Peggy O'Neil
  Pretty Kitty Kelly
  Sweet Promises and Good Intentions
  Ten Little Fingers and Ten Little
    Toes—Down in Tennessee
Nelson, Ed, Jr.
  I'm Throwing Rice (At the Girl That
    I Love)
  One Kiss Too Many
  Send Ten Pretty Flowers (To My
    Girl in Tennessee)
  Show Me the Way Back to Your
    Heart
  Will Santy Come to Shanty Town?
Nelson, Edward G.
  Settin' the Woods on Fire
Nelson, Gerald H.
  Tragedy
Nelson, Harrison
  I Got Loaded
Nelson, Jimmy
  "T" 99 Blues
Nelson, Oliver
  Hobo Flats
Nelson, Ozzie
  I'm Looking for a Guy Who Plays
    Alto and Baritone and Doubles on
    a Clarinet. . .
Nelson, Portia
  It's As Simple As That
  Sunday in New York
Nelson, Prince
  Soft and Wet

Newbury, Mickey
An American Trilogy
Funny, Familiar, Forgotten Feelings
Here Comes the Rain, Baby
Just Dropped In (to See What
Condition My Condition Was In)
She Even Woke Me Up to Say
Goodbye
Sweet Memories
Newell, Norman
Adios, My Love (The Song of
Athens)
Athina (White Rose of Athens)
The Melba Waltz
More (Theme from *Mondo Cane*)
Say Wonderful Things
To the Door of the Sun (Alle Porte
Del Sole)
Newley, Anthony
The Beautiful Land
The Candy Man
Feeling Good
Goldfinger
Gonna Build a Mountain
The Joker
Look at That Face
Lumbered
My First Love Song
Once in a Lifetime
Someone Nice Like You
Sweet Beginning
This Dream
Tribute
Typically English
What Kind of Fool Am I?
Who Can I Turn To (When Nobody
Needs Me)
A Wonderful Day Like Today
Newman, Alfred
Airport Love Theme
Anastasia
The Best of Everything
The Girl Upstairs
How Green Was My Valley
How the West Was Won
Love Theme from *The Robe*
The Moon of Manakoora
The Pleasure of His Company
Sentimental Rhapsody
The Song from *Desiree*

Street Scene
Through a Long and Sleepless Night
Newman, Charles
A Boy in Khaki—A Girl in Lace
Flowers for Madame
He's My Uncle
Honestly
I Can't Believe It's True
I Keep Remembering (Someone I
Should Forget)
I Met Her on Monday
I Wouldn't Change You for the
World
I'll Never Have To Dream Again
Pigalle
Private Buckaroo
Silver Shadows and Golden Dreams
Six Lessons from Madame La Zonga
Sweethearts on Parade
Tiny Little Fingerprints
Why Can't This Night Go On
Forever
Why Don't We Do This More Often
The Wooden Soldier and the China
Doll
You Can't Pull the Wool over My
Eyes
You're Just a Dream Come True
You've Got Me Crying Again
Newman, Emil
Lost April
Newman, Herb
The Birds and the Bees
Wayward Wind
Newman, Herbert
So This Is Love
Newman, Jimmy
Bayou Talk
Cry, Cry Darling
Pirogue (Pero)
Newman, Joel
Kisses Sweeter Than Wine
Newman, Lionel
Adventures in Paradise
Again
As If I Didn't Have Enough on My
Mind
The Cowboy and the Lady
Daniel Boone
Kiss Them for Me

Lyricists & Composers Index

2452

Lyricists & Composers Index

Torero
Nitzsche, Jack
  Hard Working Man
  Needles and Pins
Nivert, Taffy
  Friends with You
  Take Me Home, Country Road
Nix, Robert
  Champagne Jam
  Cherryhill Park
  I'm Not Gonna Let It Bother Me
    Tonight
  Imaginary Lover
  So into You
Nix, Sally
  All My Love Belongs to You
  I Can't Go On without You
  I Love You, Yes I Do
  I Want a Bow-Legged Woman
  Sneaky Pete
Nixon, Tom
  Do the Funky Penguin
Noack, Eddie
  These Hands
Noah, Peter
  San Antonio Stroll
Noble, Harry
  Hold Me, Thrill Me, Kiss Me
Noble, Jimmy
  Blue Flame
Noble, Johnny
  Hawaiian War Chant
  Little Brown Gal
Noble, Keith
  A Summer Song
Noble, Ray
  (In the Gloaming) By the Fireside
  Change Your Mind
  Cherokee
  Goodnight Sweetheart
  I Hadn't Anyone till You
  If You Love Me
  Love Is the Sweetest Thing
  Love Locked Out
  The Touch of Your Lips
  The Very Thought of You
  What More Can I Ask?
  Why Stars Come Out at Night
  You're So Desirable

Nocentelli, Leo
  Cissy Strut
  Look-ka Py Py
  Sophisticated Cissy
Noe, Dale
  It's Such a Pretty World Today
  Missing Angel
Noe, Dale E.
  Missing You
Nolan, Bob
  Blue Prairie
  Cool Water
  Ne-Hah-Nee (Clear Water)
  The Touch of God's Hand
  Tumbling Tumbleweeds
Noland, Andrew
  Funky Worm
Noonan, Steve
  Buy for Me the Rain
Noone, Jimmie
  Apex Blues
Norlind, Lloyd B.
  Out of the Silence
Norman, Jose
  Cuban Pete
Norman, Karyl
  I'm Through Shedding Tears over
    You
Norman, Monty
  Dis-Donc, Dis-Donc
  Irma la Douce
  The James Bond Theme
  Our Language of Love
  There Is Only Paris for That
Norman, Pierre
  The Miracle of the Bells
Norrell, Charles E.
  Those Lonely Hands of Mine
North, Alex
  Antony and Cleopatra Theme
  Humpty Dumpty
  I'll Cry Tomorrow
  The Long Hot Summer
  Spartacus—Love Theme
  Theme from *The Misfits*
  Unchained Melody
  A World of Love
North, Christopher
  Nice, Nice, Very Nice

2453

Goodnight
In Dreams
It's Over
Oh, Pretty Woman
Only the Lonely (Know the Way I
    Feel)
Ride Away
Running Scared
See Ruby Fall
So Young
Twinkle Toes
Working for the Man
(Say) You're My Girl
Orent, Milton
In the Land of Oo-Bla-Dee
Orlowski, Anne
Rubber Ball
Ormont, David
My Kingdom for a Kiss
Ornadel, Cyril
If I Ruled the World
Portrait of My Love
There's Something about You
Ornelas, Rene
Lo Mucho Que Te Quiero
Ornellos, Rene
Angelito
Orr, Charles
The Gal Who Invented Kissin'
The Guy Who Invented Kissin'
Orsborn, Victor
Dance (Disco Heat)
Ortolani, Riz
La Donna nel Mondo
More (Theme from *Mondo Cane*)
The Seventh Dawn
Till Love Touches Your Life
Ory, Edward "Kid"
Muskrat Ramble
Osborn, Jeffrey
Holding on (When Love Is Gone)
Osborn, Joe
Catch a Little Raindrop
Osborne, Gary
I'm Dreaming
Part-Time Love
Osborne, Jimmy
The Death of Little Kathy Fiscus

Osborne, Nat
You Wanted Someone to Play with (I
    Wanted Someone to Love)
Osborne, Will
Beside an Open Fireplace
Between 18th and 19th on Chestnut
    Street
Just Me and My Radio
Pompton Turnpike
Roses Are Forget-Me-Nots
Osmond, Alan
Crazy Horses
Hold Her Tight
Osmond, Alan R.
Down by the Lazy River
Osmond, Merrill
Crazy Horses
Down by the Lazy River
Hold Her Tight
Osmond, Wayne
Crazy Horses
Hold Her Tight
Osser, Abe
(Ah, Yes) There's Good Blues
    Tonight
Osser, Edna
I Dream of You (More Than You
    Dream I Do)
Rosanne
(Ah, Yes) There's Good Blues
    Tonight
Osser, Glenn
Rosanne
Osterman, Jack
Can't You Understand?
O'Sullivan, Raymond
Alone Again (Naturally)
Clair
Get Down
Out of the Question
Otis, Clyde
Baby (You've Got What It Takes)
Boll Weevil Song
Call Me
Doncha' Think It's Time
Endlessly
For My Baby
I'm Too Far Gone to Turn Around
It's Just a Matter of Time
Kiddio

Mademoiselle de Paree
Mr. Ghost Goes to Town
Moonlight Love
Moonlight Serenade
One Morning in May
Orchids for Remembrance
Organ Grinder's Swing
Riverboat Shuffle
Ruby
The Scat Song (Scat 'n' Skeet 'n' Hi De Hi)
Sentimental Gentleman from Georgia
Sidewalks of Cuba
The Sinner
Sleigh Ride
Sophisticated Lady
Sophisticated Swing
Stairway to the Stars
Star Dust
The Starlit Hour
Stars Fell on Alabama
Sweet Lorraine
Take Me in Your Arms
Tzena, Tzena, Tzena
Volare
Yearning for Love
Parissi, Robert
  Play That Funky Music
Parker, Barry
  The Sand and the Sea
Parker, Brian
  Concrete and Clay
Parker, Charles
  Hootie Blues
Parker, Charlie
  Ah-Leu-Cha
  Billie's Bounce
  Confirmation
  Donna Lee
  Now's the Time
  Ornithology
  Yardbird Suite
Parker, Dale
  As Far As I'm Concerned
  Little Angel with a Dirty Face
Parker, Dorothy
  How Am I To Know?
  I Wished on the Moon
Parker, Eula
  The Village of St. Bernadette

Parker, Graham
  Clear Head
  Don't Ask Me Questions
  Fool's Gold
  Heat Treatment
  Hold Back the Night
  Local Girls
  Pourin' It All Out
  Protection
  Soul on Ice
  (Let Me Get) Sweet on You
  Turned Up Too Late
  You Can't Be Too Strong
Parker, Johnny
  Baby Sittin' Boogie
  Tra La La
Parker, Judy
  December 1963 (Oh What a Night)
  Who Loves You
Parker, Jr.,Herman
  Mystery Train
Parker, Leroy
  'Round Her Neck She Wore a Yellow Ribbon
Parker, Ray, Jr.
  Jack and Jill
  You Can't Change That
  You Got the Love
Parker, Richard
  Ooo Wee Baby, I Love You
Parker, Robert
  Barefootin'
Parker, Rod
  Donde Esta Santa Claus? (Where Is Santa Claus?)
Parker, Ross
  Joy
  Monday, Tuesday, Wednesday
  There'll Always Be an England
  We'll Meet Again
Parker, Sol
  Dansero
  This Love of Mine
Parks, Carson
  Cab Driver
Parks, Carson C.
  Somethin' Stupid
Parks, Larry
  (The Bees Are for the Birds) The Birds Are for the Bees

Perkins, Carl Lee
  Blue Suede Shoes
  Boppin' the Blues
  Your True Love
Perkins, Frank
  Cabin in the Cotton
  Emaline
  Fandango
  The Scat Song (Scat 'n' Skeet 'n' Hi
    De Hi)
  Sentimental Gentleman from Georgia
  Stars Fell on Alabama
Perkins, Ray
  The End of the Lonesome Trail
  Lady Luck
  The Only Song I Know
  Smiling Irish Eyes
  Tessie, Stop Teasin' Me
  Under a Texas Moon
Perper, Bob
  Young Only Yesterday
Perren, Freddy
  ABC
  Boogie Fever
  Do It Baby
  Heaven Must Be Missing an Angel
    (Part 1)
  Hot Line
  I Pledge My Love
  I Will Survive
  The Love You Save
  Makin' It
  Mama's Pearl
  Reunited
  Shake Your Groove Thing
  Sugar Daddy
  That Once in a Lifetime
  Whodunit
Perren, Frederick, see Perren, Frederick
Perricone, Jack
  Run Joey Run
Perricone, Lawrence
  Call Me Back, Pal o' Mine
Perry, Barney
  Walking in Rhythm
Perry, Betty Sue
  Before I'm Over You
  The Home You're Tearin' Down
  Roll Muddy River
  Wine, Women, and Song

Perry, Greg S.
  Bring the Boys Home
  One Monkey Don't Stop No Show
  Pay to the Piper
  Somebody's Been Sleeping in My Bed
  Stick-Up
  Want-Ads
Perry, Herb
  I'm Never Satisfied
Perry, Jack
  You Can't Take a Dream from a
    Dreamer
Perry, Joe
  Walk This Way
Perry, Leonard
  One Love in My Lifetime
Perry, Roger
  A Kid Again
Perry, Steve
  Any Way You Want It
  Lovin', Touchin', Squeezin'
Perryman, Willie
  Bald Headed Lena
  Red's Boogie
Persons, Ted
  Things Ain't What They Used To Be
Peterik
  You Wouldn't Listen
Peterik, James M.
  Vehicle
Peters, Ben
  Before the Next Teardrop Falls
  Daytime Friends
  It's Gonna Take a Little Bit Longer
  Kiss an Angel Good Morning
  Love Put a Song in My Heart
  More to Me
  My Woman's Man
  Tell Me What It's Like
  Turn the World Around (the Other
    Way)
Peters, Ben James, Jr.
  That's a No No
Peters, Jerry
  Going in Circles
  Love Is
Peters, Mal
  The Poet's Dream
Petersburski, J.
  Oh, Donna Clara

2465

Here Comes the Show Boat
I'm Always Stuttering
I'm Feelin' Devilish
Is That Religion?
Jazz Babies' Ball
Livin' High, Sometimes
Love Me
Panama Limited Blues
Pile of Logs and Stone Called Home
Sugar (That Sugar Baby o' Mine)
Sweet Georgia Brown
Them There Eyes
Pinter, Harold
    You Have the Choice
Pinz, Shelley
    Green Tambourine
    Jelly Jungle (of Orange Marmalade)
    Rice Is Nice
Pippa, Salvatore
    Lonely Teenager
Pippin, Don
    Hold Me in Your Arms
Pippin, Steve
    Better Love Next Time
    This Time I'm in It for Love
Piron, A. J.
    Bouncing Around
    Day by Day You're Going To Miss
      Me
    Kiss Me Sweet
    Lou'siana Swing
    Mama's Gone, Goodbye
    New Orleans Wiggle
    Sud Bustin' Blues
Pirone, Harry
    I Want To Cry
Pisano, Gigi
    Pansy
Pisano, John
    Wade in the Water
Pistilli, Gene
    Medicine Man
    Sunday Will Never Be the Same
Pitman, Jack
    Beyond the Reef
Pitney, Gene
    Hello, Mary Lou
    He's a Rebel
    (I Wanna) Love My Life Away

Pitt, Eugene
    My True Story
Pitts, Clyde
    Sweetheart of the Year
Pitts, Tom
    I Never Knew I Could Love
      Anybody Like I'm Loving You
Place, Mary Kay
    Baby Boy
Plant, Robert
    Black Dog
    D'Yer Maker
    Heartbreaker
    Immigrant Song
    Living Loving Maid (She's Just a
      Woman)
    Stairway to Heaven
    Whole Lotta Love
Plante, Jacques
    Domino
    I Will Follow Him
    Mystery Street
Plater, Bobby
    Jersey Bounce
Plummer, Howard
    Still
Plummer, Howard, Jr.
    I Can't Love You Enough
Pober, Leon
    Pearly Shells (Pupa O Ewa)
    Tiny Bubbles (Hua li'i)
Pockriss, Lee
    All for You
    Big Daddy
    Calcutta
    Catch a Falling Star
    Dommage, Dommage (Too bad, too
      bad)
    A Handbag Is Not a Proper Mother
    I Go to Bed
    I Know the Feeling
    Itsy Bitsy Teenie Weenie Yellow
      Polkadot Bikini
    Jimmy's Girl
    Johnny Angel
    A Kookie Little Paradise
    Leader of the Laundromat
    My Heart Is an Open Book
    My Little Corner of the World
    Nitchevo

Lyricists & Composers Index

All of You
All through the Night
Allez-Vous-En, Go Away
Always True to You (In My Fashion)
Another Op'nin', Another Show
Anything Goes
At Long Last Love
Be a Clown
Begin the Beguine
Between You and Me
Bianca
Blow, Gabriel, Blow
Brush Up Your Shakespeare
Buddie, Beware
But in the Morning, No!
By the Mississinewah
Ca, C'est l'Amour
Can-Can
C'est Magnifique
Cherry Pies Ought To Be You
Close
Come Along with Me
Come On In
Come to the Supermarket (In Old Peking)
Could It Be You?
Count Your Blessings
Do I Love You?
Don't Fence Me In
Don't Look at Me That Way
Down in the Depths, on the Ninetieth Floor
Dream Dancing
Easy To Love
Ev'ry Day a Holiday
Ev'ry Time We Say Goodbye
Ev'rything I Love
Experiment
Far, Far Away
Farewell Amanda
Farming
Find Me a Primitive Man
For No Rhyme or Reason
Fresh As a Daisy
Friendship
From Alpha to Omega
From Now On
From This Moment On
Get Out of Town

Give Him the Oo-La-La
Goodbye, Little Dream, Goodbye
The Great Indoors
Gypsy in Me
The Heaven Hop
Hey, Babe, Hey! (I'm Nuts about You)
Hey, Good-Lookin'
How Could We Be Wrong
How's Your Romance?
I Adore You
I Always Knew
I Am Ashamed That Women Are So Simple
I Am in Love
I Am Loved
I Concentrate on You
I Get a Kick out of You
I Happen To Like New York
I Hate Men
I Hate You, Darling
I Love Paris
I Love You
I Love You, Samantha
I Want To Go Home
I Worship You
If You Loved Me Truly
If You Smile at Me
I'm a Gigolo
I'm Getting Myself Ready for You
I'm in Love
I'm in Love Again
I'm Unlucky at Gambling
In the Still of the Night
It Might Have Been
It Was Written in the Stars
It's a Chemical Reaction
It's All Right with Me
It's D'Lovely
I've a Strange New Rhythm in My Heart
I've Come to Wive It Wealthily in Padua
I've Got My Eyes on You
I've Got You on My Mind
I've Got You Under My Skin
I've Still Got My Health
Josephine
Just One of Those Things
Katie Went to Haiti

2471

Lyricists & Composers Index

Rand, Ande
  Only You
Rand, Ellery
  (There Was a) Night on the Water
Rand, Lionel
  Let There Be Love
Randall, Earl
  About to Make Me Leave Home
Randall, Lille
  I Want To Cry
Randazzo, Teddy
  Big Wide World
  Feels So Good to Be Loved So Bad
  Goin' Out of My Head
  Have You Looked into Your Heart
  Hurt So Bad
  I'm on the Outside (Looking In)
  In the Back of My Heart
  It's Gonna Take a Miracle
  Less Than Tomorrow
  Pretty Blue Eyes
  Rain in My Heart
  Sinner Man
  Take Me Back
  The Week-End
Randell, Buddy
  Lies (Are Breakin' My Heart)
Randell, Denny
  Attack
  Baby, Make Your Own Sweet Music
  I Wanna Dance Wit' Choo (Doo Dat
    Dance) Part I
  Keep the Ball Rollin'
  Let's Hang On (to What We've Got)
  A Lover's Concerto
  Native New Yorker
  Opus 17 (Don't Worry 'bout Me)
  Swearin' to God
  Workin' My Way Back to You
Randi, Don
  Mexican Pearls
Randle, Earl
  Echoes of Love
  I'll Be Around
  I'm Gonna Tear Your Playhouse
    Down
Randolph, Eugene
  A Tear Fell
Randolph, Randy
  Yakety Sax

Randolph, Zilner
  Ol' Man Mose
Raney, Wayne
  Blues, Stay Away from Me
  Why Don't You Haul Off and Love
    Me?
Rankin, Ken
  In the Name of Love
Rankin, Kenny
  Peaceful
Rans, Robert
  Dance with Me
  Do Ya Wanna Get Funky with Me
Ransom, R., Jr.
  Dusic
Ranson, R., Jr.
  Dazz
Ranucci, Renato, see Rascel, Renato
Rapee, Erno
  Angela Mia (My Angel)
  Charmaine
  (I'm in Heaven When I See You
    Smile) Diane
  Rippling Waters
  Someday, Somewhere (We'll Meet
    Again)
Raposo, Joe
  Bein' Green
  Sing
  This Way to Sesame Street
  Three's Company
  Winners
Rappaport, Robert Lawrence
  Martian Hop
Rappaport, Steve
  Martian Hop
Rappolo, Leon, see also Rappolo, Leon
  Farewell Blues
  Milenberg Joys
Rasbach, Oscar
  Trees
Rascel, Renato
  Arrivederci, Roma
Rashkow, Michael, see Lendell, Mike
Raskin, Gene
  Those Were the Days
Raskin, Milton
  Naked City Theme
Raskin, William
  That's When Your Heartaches Begin

Big Chief De Sota
Blue, Turning Gray over You
Christopher Columbus
Concentratin' (on You)
Deep Forest
Dip Your Brush in the Sunshine
Dusky Stevedore
Gee Baby, Ain't I Good to You
Havin' a Ball
Honeysuckle Rose
I'm Gonna Move on the Outskirts of Town
In the Mood
The Joint Is Jumpin'
Keeping Out of Mischief Now
Knock Me a Kiss
Lonesome Me
Lonesome Swallow
Louisiana
A Lover's Lullaby
Mama Stayed Out the Whole Night Long (but Mama Didn't Do No Wrong)
Massachusetts
Memories of You
The Milkmen's Matinee
My Baby Sure Knows How To Love
My Fate Is in Your Hands
My Handy Man
My Special Friend Is Back in Town
No One Can Toddle Like My Cousin Sue
Nobody but My Baby Is Gettin' My Love
On Revival Day
Patty Cake, Patty Cake (Baker Man)
A Porter's Love Song to a Chambermaid
Reefer Man
Rhythm Lullaby
S'posin'
Stealin' Apples
Stompin' at the Savoy
Strange As It Seems
Sweet Savannah Sue
Take Your Tomorrow (and Give Me Today)
That's What I Like about the South
The Way I Feel Today

What Did I Do To Be So Black and Blue
Willow Tree
Yancey Special
You're Lucky to Me
Zonky
Rea, Chris
    Fool (If You Think Its Over)
Rea, David
    For Yasgur's Farm
Read, John Dawson
    A Friend of Mine Is Going Blind
Reagan, Russ
    The Dedication Song
Reardon, Frank
    Same Old Saturday Night
Reardon, Jack
    The Good Life
    La Strada del' Amore
    When
    Worried Guy
Reaves, Erell
    Lights of Paris
Rebennack, Mac
    Right Place Wrong Time
    Something Special
    Such a Night
Rebennack, Malcolm
    Ship on a Stormy Sea
Record, Eugene
    Have You Seen Her
    Homely Girl
    Love Makes a Woman
    Oh Girl
    Soulful Strut (Am I the Same Girl?)
    Two Little Kids
Record, Eugene B.
    There'll Come a Time
Rector, Eddie
    Senorita Blues
Rector, Johnny
    Married by the Bible, Divorced by the Law
Redbird, William Chief
    Cherokee Boogie
Redd, Gene
    Please Come Home for Christmas
Redd, Henry J.
    Free

Lyricists & Composers Index

Shine On Brightly
A Whiter Shade of Pale
Reine, Johnnie
Red River Rose
Reine, Johnny
The Wedding of Lilli Marlene
Reiner, Peter
The Mighty Sons of Hercules
Reinfield, John
The Violet and a Rose
Reinhardt, Django
It's the Bluest Kind of Blues My
Baby Sings
Reisch, Walter
Don't Ask Me Why
Tell Me Why You Smile, Mona Lisa
Reisfeld, Bert
Call Me Darling (Call Me
Sweetheart, Call Me Dear)
Spring Magic
The Three Bells
Reisman, Joe
Joey's Song
Reizner, June
Barry's Boys
Relf, Keith
Happenings Ten Years Time Ago
Over Under Sideways Down
Shapes of Things
Remaily, Robin
Euphoria
Remigi, M.
Can I Trust You?
Renard, Jean
Losing You
Rendine, Furio
Pansy
Rene, Henri
Wagon Train
Rene, Leon
Convicted
Dusty Road
Gloria
I Lost My Sugar in Salt Lake City
Mexico Joe (The Jumpin' Jivin'
Caballero)
Someone's Rocking My Dreamboat
When It's Sleepy Time down South
When the Swallows Come Back to
Capistrano

Rene, Leon T.
I Sold My Heart to the Junk Man
Rene, Malou
One Track Mind
Tossin' and Turnin'
Rene, Otis
Dusty Road
I'm Lost
Someone's Rocking My Dreamboat
When It's Sleepy Time down South
Rene, Otis J., Jr.
I Sold My Heart to the Junk Man
Reneau, Bud
The Days of Sand and Shovels
Reneau, George, see Reneau, Bud
Renis, Tony
I Don't Know What He Told You
Quando, Quando, Quando (Tell Me
When)
Tonight I'll Say a Prayer
Renoir, Jean
Merry-Go-Round
Resnick, Art
Crabs Walk Sideways
Resnick, Arthur
Chip Chip
Good Lovin'
A Little Bit of Heaven
Quick Joey Small (Run, Joey, Run)
Yummy, Yummy, Yummy
Resnick, Artie
I've Got Sand in My Shoes
One Kiss for Old Times' Sake
Under the Boardwalk
Resnick, Kris
Chewy, Chewy
Down at Lulu's
Shake
Reuss, Alan
More and More
Revaux, Jacques
My Way
Revel, Harry
Afraid To Dream
Are You with It?
Be a Good Sport
Broadway's Gone Hawaii
But Definitely
Cigarettes, Cigars
College Rhythm

Danger—Love at Work
Did You Ever See a Dream Walking?
Doin' the Uptown Lowdown
Don't Let It Bother You
From the Top of Your Head to the Tip of Your Toes
A Full Moon and an Empty Heart
Good Morning Glory
Good Night Lovely Little Lady
Goodnight, My Love
Got My Mind on Music
Head over Heels in Love
Help Yourself to Happiness
Here I Go Again
I Feel Like a Feather in the Breeze
I Hum a Waltz
I Never Knew Heaven Could Speak
I Played Fiddle for the Czar
I Wanna Be in Winchell's Column
I Wanna Go to the Zoo
I Wish I Were Aladdin
I'd Like To Set You to Music
If I Had a Dozen Hearts
I'm Bubbling Over
I'm Hummin'—I'm Whistlin'—I'm Singin'
I'm Like a Fish out of Water
It Takes Two To Make a Bargain
It Was a Night in June
It's Swell of You
It's the Animal in Me
I've Got a Date with a Dream
Jet
Just beyond the Rainbow
Let's K-nock K-nees
Love Thy Neighbor
The Loveliness of You
May I?
May I Have the Next Romance with You?
Meet the Beat of My Heart
Never in a Million Years
Oh, My Goodness!
An Old Straw Hat
Once in a Blue Moon
One Never Knows, Does One?
An Orchid to You
Paris in the Spring
Please Pardon Us, We're in Love
Remember Me to Carolina

(She Walks Like You—She Talks Like You) She Reminds Me of You
The Slap Polka
Slightly Perfect
A Star Fell out of Heaven
Stay As Sweet As You Are
Straight from the Shoulder (Right from the Heart)
Such Is Life, Such Is Love
Sweet As a Song
Sweet Someone
Swing Is Here To Stay
Take a Number from One to Ten
Takes Two To Make a Bargain
Thanks for Ev'rything
There's a Bluebird at My Window
There's a Lull in My Life
There's That Look in Your Eyes
This Is My Beloved
Two for Tonight
Underneath the Harlem Moon
Wake Up and Live
Were Your Ears Burning, Baby?
When I'm with You
When There's a Breeze on Lake Louise
Where in the World
With My Eyes Wide Open, I'm Dreaming
Without a Word of Warning
You Can't Have Everything
You Gotta S-M-I-L-E To Be H-A-Double P-Y
You Hit the Spot
You're Everywhere
You're My Past, Present and Future
You're Such a Comfort to Me
You've Gotta Eat Your Spinach, Baby
Revere, Paul
Good Thing
The Great Airplane Strike of 1966
Steppin' Out
Who Takes Care of the Caretaker's Daughter
Revil, Rudi
The Little Shoemaker
Reyam, G.
Rivers of Babylon

2493

Lyricists & Composers Index

Lyricists & Composers Index

Stouthearted Men
Student Life
Students March Song
Tell Me Daisy
Then You Will Know
Three Little Maids
To the Inn We're Marching
Wanting You
When Hearts Are Young
When I Grow Too Old To Dream
Who Are We To Say (Obey Your
  Heart)
You Will Remember Vienna
Your Land and My Land
Your Smiles, Your Tears
Zing Zing - Zoom Zoom
Rome, Harold
  Along with Me
  Anyone Would Love You
  Be Kind to Your Parents
  Chain Store Daisy
  Doing the Reactionary
  The Face on the Dime
  Fair Warning
  Fanny
  F.D.R. Jones
  Four Little Angels of Peace
  A Funny Thing Happened
  A Gift Today
  Goodbye Darling, Hello Friend
  Have I Told You Lately?
  I Have To Tell You
  I Like You
  I Say Hello
  It's Better with a Union Man or
    (Bertha, the Sewing Machine Girl)
  Love Is a Very Light Thing
  Meadowland
  Mene, Mene, Tekel
  Miss Marmelstein
  Momma, Momma!
  The Money Song (Funny, Funny,
    Funny, What Money Can Do)
  My Heart Is Unemployed
  (All of a Sudden) My Heart Sings
  Nobody Makes a Pass at Me
  Once Knew a Fella
  One Big Union for Two
  The Red Ball Express
  Restless Heart

Sing Me a Song with Social
  Significance
The Sound of Money
South America, Take It Away
Sunday in the Park
United Nations on the March
Welcome Home
What Are They Doing to Us Now?
What Can I Do?
What Good Is Love
What's in It for Me?
When I Grow Up
Where Did the Night Go?
Who Knows?
Wish You Were Here
Rome, Richard
  The Best Disco in Town (Medley)
Romeo, Tony
  Blessed Is the Rain
  I Think I Love You
  I'm Gonna Make You Mine
  Indian Lake
  Poor Baby
  Welcome Me, Love
Ronell, Ann
  Baby's Birthday Party
  Linda
  (Don't Look Now, but) My Heart Is
    Showing
  My Week
  Rain on the Roof
  Who's Afraid of the Big Bad Wolf
  Willow Weep for Me
Ronn, E.
  Titina
Roppolo, Leon
  Make Love to Me
Rosa, Malia
  Forever and Ever
Rose, Billy
  Back in Your Own Back Yard
  Barney Google
  Cheerful Little Earful
  Clap Hands! Here Comes Charley!
  Come On, Spark Plug!
  Cooking Breakfast for the One I
    Love
  Crying for Joy
  A Cup of Coffee, a Sandwich, and
    You

Does the Spearmint Lose Its Flavor
on the Bedpost Over Night?
Don't Bring Lulu
Dummy Song (I'll Take the Legs
from Some Old Table)
Evangeline
Fifty Million Frenchmen Can't Be
Wrong
Follow the Swallow
Golden Gate
Got the Jitters
Great Day!
Happy Days and Lonely Nights
Here Comes the Show Boat
The House Is Haunted (by the Echo
of Your Last Goodbye)
I Can't Get the One I Want
I Found a Million Dollar Baby (in a
Five and Ten Cent Store)
I Got a "Code" in My "Doze"
I Wanna Be Loved
I Wonder Who's Dancing with You
Tonight
I'd Rather Be Blue over You (Than
Be Happy with Somebody Else)
If I Had a Girl Like You
If You Want the Rainbow (You
Must Have the Rain)
I'm Ka-razy for You
In the Merry Month of Maybe
In the Middle of the Night
It Happened in Monterey
It's Only a Paper Moon
I've Got a Feeling I'm Falling
Me and My Shadow
More Than You Know
The Night Is Young and You're So
Beautiful
Poor Papa (He's Got Nuthin' At All)
Right or Wrong I Love You
Say It with a Red, Red Rose
She's Everybody's Sweetheart but
Nobody's Gal
Since Ma Is Playing Mah Jong
Suddenly
Swanee Butterfly
That Old Gang of Mine
There's a Rainbow 'round My
Shoulder
To-night You Belong to Me

When a Woman Loves a Man
When the Morning Glories Wake Up
in the Morning
Without a Song
Would You Like To Take a Walk?
(Sump'n Good'll Come from That)
You Tell Her, I S-t-u-t-t-e-r
You Think of Ev'rything
Yours for a Song
You've Got To See Mamma Ev'ry
Night or You Can't See Mamma
At All
Rose, C. E.
My Filipino Rose
Rose, David
California Melodies
Dance of the Spanish Onion
Four-Twenty, A.M.
Holiday for Strings
Manhattan Square Dance
One Love
Our Waltz
Serenade to a Lemonade
So-o-o-o-o in Love
Stringopation
The Stripper
Rose, Ed.
Sudan
Rose, Fred
After Tomorrow
At Mail Call Today
Bartender's Blues
Be Honest with Me
Before You Call
Blue Eyes Crying in the Rain
Blues in My Mind
Charlestonette
Crazy Heart
'Deed I Do
Deep Henderson
Doo Dah Blues (Sweet Cryin' Babe)
End of the World
Flamin' Mamie
Foggy River
(Don't Your Conscience Ever Bother
You) Hang Your Head in Shame
Honest and Truly
I Hang My Head and Cry
I Talk to Myself about You

Lyricists & Composers Index

Lyricists & Composers Index

Safka, Melanie
  Bitter Bad
  Brand New Key
  Nickel Song
  Peace Will Come (According to Plan)
  Ring the Living Bell
  Stop! I Don't Wanna Hear It
    Anymore
  What Have They Done to My Song,
    Ma
Sager, Carole Bayer
  Better Days
  Better Than Ever
  Break It to Me Gently
  Come in from the Rain
  Don't Cry Out Loud
  Heartbreaker
  I Still Believe in Love
  I'd Rather Leave While I'm in Love
  If You Really Knew Me
  If You Remember Me
  Jennifer
  Just for Tonight
  Looking Through the Eyes of Love
  Midnight Blue
  Nobody Does It Better
  Quiet Please, There's a Lady on
    Stage
  Sweet Memory
  They're Playing My Song
  Too Close to Paradise
  When I Need You
  You're Moving Out Today
  You're the Only One
Sagle, Charles
  Where the Blue and Lonely Go
Sahm, Doug
  She's about a Mover
Sahm, Douglas
  Mendocino
Sain, Oliver
  Don't Mess Up a Good Thing
St. Clair, Robert
  Rose of Calvary
St. Cyr, John
  Messin' Around
Saint-Graniere
  Who'll Buy My Violets? (La
    Violetera)

St. Helier, Ivy
  Coal-Black Mammy
St. John, Dick
  Tell Me
  Yellow Balloon
St. Lewis, Kenny
  Boogie Fever
  Heaven Must Be Missing an Angel
    (Part 1)
  Hot Line
  Whodunit
St. Louis, Louis
  Sandy
St. Nicholas, Nick
  It's Never Too Late
Sainte-Marie, Buffy
  Cod'ine
  God Is Alive, Magic Is Afoot
  He's an Indian Cowboy in the Rodeo
  I'm Gonna Be a Country Girl Again
  Poppies
  Tall Trees in Georgia
  The Universal Soldier
  Until It's Time for You to Go
Salmirs-Bernstein
  Joey
Salt, Waldo
  O-He-O-Hi-O-Ho
  Rachel
  Summer Song
Salter, William
  Where Is the Love
Salvador, Henri
  I Will Live My Life for You
  Melodie d'Amour
Salvatore, Bono, see Bono, Sonny
Sam, Senora
  I'll Be Good to You
Samoht, Yennik
  Stoned Love
Sample, Joe
  Adventures in Paradise
Sampson, Edgar
  Blue Lou
  Don't Be That Way
  If Dreams Come True
  Lullaby in Rhythm
  Stompin' at the Savoy
Samudio, Domingo
  Ju Ju Hand

2506

Schumann, Walter
  Dragnet
  It's Dreamtime
  St. George and the Dragonet
Schuster, Ira, *see also* Siras, John
  Did You Ever Get That Feeling in
    the Moonlight
  Hold Me
  (Shout! Wherever You May Be) I
    Am an American
  Ten Little Fingers and Ten Little
    Toes—Down in Tennessee
  You Know You Belong to Somebody
    Else So Why Don't You Leave Me
    Alone
Schuster, Joe
  Dance of the Paper Dolls
Schwab, Charles M.
  Slow River
  Sugar Foot Strut
Schwabach, Kurt
  Danke Schoen
Schwandt, Wilbur
  Dream a Little Dream of Me
Schwartz, Arthur
  After All You're All I'm After
  Alone Together
  Alone Too Long
  Before I Kiss the World Goodbye
  Born Again
  By Myself
  Confession
  Dancing in the Dark
  Don't Be a Woman If You Can
  The Dreamer
  Farewell, My Lovely
  For the First Time
  A Gal in Calico
  Good-bye Jonah
  Got a Bran' New Suit
  Hang Up
  Happy Habit
  Haunted Heart
  High and Low (I've Been Looking
    for You)
  Hoops
  The Hottentot Potentate
  How Sweet You Are
  I Guess I'll Have to Change My Plan
  I Love Louisa

I See Your Face before Me
I Still Look at You That Way
If There Is Someone Lovelier Than
  You
I'll Buy You a Star
I'm Like a New Broom
I'm Ridin' for a Fall
Look Who's Dancing
Louisiana Hayride
Love Is a Dancing Thing
Love Is the Reason
Lucky Seven
Magic Moment
Make the Man Love Me
The Moment I Saw You
More Love Than Your Love
New Sun in the Sky
Oh, but I Do!
An Old Flame Never Dies
A Rainy Day
A Rainy Night in Rio
Relax-Ay-Voo
Rhode Island Is Famous for You
Seal It with a Kiss
She's Such a Comfort to Me
A Shine on Your Shoes
Smokin' Reefers
Something To Remember You By
Something You Never Had Before
Tennessee Fish Fry
Thank Your Lucky Stars
That's Entertainment
Then I'll Be Tired of You
There's No Holding Me
They're Either Too Young or Too
  Old
Thief in the Night
This Is It
Through a Thousand Dreams
Triplets
Under Your Spell
Waitin' for the Evening Train
What a Wonderful World
Where Can He Be?
Why Did You Do It?
You and I Know
You and the Night and the Music
You Have Everything
Schwartz, Jean
  Au Revoir, Pleasant Dreams

Lyricists & Composers Index

Lyricists & Composers Index

I'm Gonna Lock My Heart (and
  Throw Away the Key)
(I've Been So Wrong for So Long,
  but) I'm So Right Tonight
Low Down Rhythm in a Top Hat
(Give Me the) Moon over Brooklyn
My Extraordinary Gal
Shank, Joe
  Unsuspecting Heart
Shanklin, Wayne
  The Big Hurt
  Chanson d'Amour
  Jezebel
  The Little Boy and the Old Man
  Primrose Lane
Shannon, Del
  Hats Off to Larry
  I Go to Pieces
  Keep Searchin' (We'll Follow the
    Sun)
  Little Town Flirt
  Runaway
  Stranger in Town
Shannon, Ronnie
  I Can't See Myself Leaving You
Shannon, Ronny
  Baby, I Love You
  I Never Loved a Man (the Way I
    Love You)
Shannon, Tom
  Wild Weekend
Shaper, Hal
  Softly, As I Leave You
  The Theme from *The Go-Between*
Shapiro, Brad
  Don't Knock My Love
Shapiro, D.
  Let's Live for Today
Shapiro, Dan
  I Wanna Get Married
  Kiss Me and Kill Me with Love
Shapiro, Elliott
  Sierra Sue
Shapiro, Herb
  Dream Babies
Shapiro, J.
  Treasure of Love
Shapiro, Joe
  Round and Round
  Think Twice

Shapiro, Mike
  Spooky
Shapiro, Mrs. Ted
  Ask Anyone in Love
Shapiro, Ted
  Ask Anyone in Love
  A Handful of Stars
  If I Had You
  Winter Weather
Sharbutt, Del
  A Romantic Guy, I
  Silver and Gold
Sharp, Bobby, *see* Jones, Agnes
Sharp, Eric Clapton
  Tales of Brave Ulysses
Sharp, Martha
  Born a Woman
  Come Back When You Grow Up
  Maybe Just Today
  The Single Girl
Sharpe, Jack
  So Rare
Sharpley, Bill
  Agent Double-O-Soul
Shavers, Charles
  Undecided
Shavers, Charlie
  Why Begin Again
Shaw, Artie
  Back Bay Shuffle
  Concerto for Clarinet
  If It's You
  Love of My Life
  Nightmare
  Non-Stop Flight
  Summit Ridge Drive
  Traffic Jam
  Why Begin Again
Shaw, James
  Where Do I Go from Here
Shaw, Sydney
  Dreamy
  Heavenly
  Passing Through
Shaw, Tommy
  Blue Collar Man
  Renegade
  Sing for the Day
Shawn, Nelson
  Jim

2521

Put Another Log on the Fire
Queen of the Silver Dollar
Sunny Side of Life
Sylvia's Mother
The Taker
25 Minutes To Go
The Unicorn
The Waves Roll Out
Simeone, Harry
  The Little Drummer Boy
Simington, Lamar
  Goodbye My Lover, Goodbye
Simkins, Lewis
  Long Gone
Simmons, Billy
  M-i-s-s-i-s-s-i-p-p-i
Simmons, Charles
  Love Don't Love Nobody
  A Mighty Love
  They Just Can't Stop It (the Games People Play)
Simmons, Gene
  Calling Dr. Love
  Christine Sixteen
  Rock and Roll All Night
Simmons, Pat
  Black Water
  Dependin' on You
  Echoes of Love
Simmons, Rousseau
  Just Wait 'till You See My Baby Do the Charleston Dance
  Pleasure Mad
Simms, Alice D.
  Encore, Cherie
  Foolishly Yours
Simms, Earl
  Funky Street
Simms, Joseph
  Ain't It a Shame
Simon, Bill
  Time and Again
  Two Left Feet Polka
Simon, Carly
  Anticipation
  Attitude Dancing
  Cow Town
  Haven't Got Time for the Pain
  He Likes to Roll
  Long Term Physical Effects

Right Thing to Do
That's the Way I've Always Heard It Should Be
Tranquillo (Melt My Heart)
Vengeance
You Belong to Me
You're So Vain
Simon, Howard
  Sweet Child, I'm Wild about You
Simon, Joe
  Get Down, Get Down (Get on the Floor)
  Power of Love
  Theme from *Cleopatra Jones*
  Your Time to Cry
Simon, Nat
  And Mimi
  An Apple Blossom Wedding
  Bamboo
  Coax Me a Little Bit
  The Cocoanut Song
  Crosstown
  Down the Trail of Achin' Hearts
  The Gaucho Serenade
  Goody Goodbye
  Her Bathing Suit Never Got Wet
  I Wish That I Could Hide inside This Letter
  Is That the Way To Treat a Sweetheart?
  Istanbul, not Constantinople
  Little Curly Hair in a High Chair
  Little Lady Make Believe
  The Mama Doll Song
  My Bolero (When the Bolero Began)
  No Can Do
  The Old Lamp-Lighter
  Poinciana (Song of the Tree)
  A Rosewood Spinet
  Summer Green and Winter White
  Sweet Heartaches
  Wait for Me Baby
  Wait for Me, Mary
Simon, Paul
  America
  American Tune
  At the Zoo
  The Big, Bright Green Pleasure Machine
  Bleecker Street

Sinatra, Frank
  I'm a Fool To Want You
  This Love of Mine
Sinatra, Ray
  Lonely Love
Sinclair, Gordon
  The Americans (a Canadian's
    Opinion)
Sinfield, Peter
  Court of the Crimson King
Singer, A.
  At the Hop
Singer, Bob
  Unsuspecting Heart
Singer, Dolph
  Just Around the Corner
Singer, Guy
  Wither Thou Goest
Singer, Lou
  Gypsy without a Song
  Lost in Meditation
  One Meat Ball
  Sleepy Serenade
  Young and Warm and Wonderful
Singleton, Charles
  Don't Forbid Me
  For a Penny
  Hurts Me to My Heart
  If I May
  Just As Much As Ever
  Lady
  Light of Love
  Mambo Baby
  Moon over Naples
  My Personal Possession
  (My Heart Goes) Piddily Patter
    Patter
  Strangers in the Night
  The Wheel of Hurt
Singleton, Charlie
  Apple Green
Singleton, Margie
  Dum-De-Da
  Flower of Love
  Laura (What's He Got That I Ain't
    Got)?
  Lie to Me
  Love Has Laid Her Hands on Me
  Shake the Hand of a Fool
  She Understands Me

Singleton, Shelby
  Am I That Easy To Forget?
Sipes, Leonard, see Collins, Tommy
Siras, John
  Dance of the Paper Dolls
  In a Shanty in Old Shanty Town
Sissle, Noble
  Baltimore Buzz
  Bandana Days
  Gypsy Blues
  Honeysuckle Time
  I'm Craving for That Kind of Love
  I'm Just Wild about Harry
  Love Will Find a Way
  Manda
  Oriental Blues
  Shuffle Along
  You Were Meant for Me
Sizemore, Arthur
  Too Tired
Skidmore, W. E.
  Every Once in a While
Skilkret, Nathaniel
  Have You Forgotten?
Skinner, Albert
  Away All Boats
Skinner, Frank
  Away All Boats
  Back Street
  Head Low
  Interlude
Skinner, Jimmie
  I Found My Girl in the U.S.A.
  Let's Say Goodbye Like We Said
    Hello (In a Friendly Kind of Way)
Sklerov, Gloria
  Everytime I Sing a Love Song
  I Believe I'm Gonna Love You
  I Just Fall in Love Again
Skye, John
  I'm So in Love with You
Skylar, Sunny
  Amor
  And So to Sleep Again
  Are These Really Mine
  Ask Me
  Atlanta, G.A.
  Be Mine Tonight
  Besame Mucho (Kiss Me Much)
  Carina Marie

I Wonder If You Still Care for Me
Like You
The One I'm Looking For
Play Gypsies—Dance Gypsies
The Sheik of Araby
We Two Shall Meet Again
You Are Mine Evermore
Smith, Harry Bache
  Yours Is My Heart Alone
Smith, Howard Russell
  Third Rate Romance
Smith, Huey P.
  Rockin' Pneumonia and the Boogie
    Woogie Flu
Smith, Ike
  Mabel's Dream
Smith, J.
  Cryin', Prayin', Wishin', Waitin'
Smith, Jack
  Gimme a Little Kiss, Will Ya Huh?
Smith, James
  Battle Hymn of Lieutenant Calley
  Slippin' and Slidin'
Smith, Jerry Dean
  (Down at) Papa Joe's
Smith, Jesse
  I Do
Smith, Jimmy
  I Promise To Remember
Smith, John H., Jr.
  Walk, Don't Run
Smith, Kate
  When the Moon Comes over the
    Mountain
Smith, Kenneth Leslie
  On the Old Spanish Trail
Smith, L.
  Shake Your Rump to the Funk
Smith, Laura R.
  Little Sir Echo
Smith, Lloyd
  I'm Goin' Away To Wear You Off
    My Mind
  Sad Girl
Smith, Mamie
  Plain Old Blues
Smith, Marion
  Teardrops Will Fall
Smith, Mike
  Bits and Pieces

Can't You See That She's Mine?
Come Home
Glad All Over
Please Tell Me Why
Try Too Hard
Smith, Mira A.
  Soul Shake
Smith, Myra
  Buffalo Soldier
  The Girl Most Likely
  Reconsider Me
  There Never Was a Time
Smith, Myra Ann
  I Almost Called Your Name
Smith, Neal
  Eighteen
Smith, Patti
  Because the Night
  Frederick
  Hymn
  Rock and Roll Nigger
  Till Victory
  Wave
Smith, Paul J.
  Jing-A-Ling, Jing-A-Ling
Smith, Ray
  15 Years Ago
Smith, Raymond
  She Needs Someone to Hold Her
Smith, Rev. Guy
  The Great Speckled Bird
Smith, Richard B.
  Winter Wonderland
Smith, Robert B.
  The Wooing of the Violin
Smith, Sandra
  The Bridge Washed Out
Smith, "Stuff"
  Ise A-Muggin'
Smith, Tab
  Harvard Blues
Smith, Victor
  With Your Love
Smith, Walter
  Don't Sing Aloha When I Go
Smith, Warren
  I'm Goin' Away To Wear You Off
    My Mind
Smith, Whispering
  Mean Woman Blues

Spear, Eric
  Meet Mister Callaghan
Spector, Abner
  Smoky Places
Spector, Lona, *see* Stevens, Lona
Spector, Phil
  All Grown Up
  Baby, I Love You
  Be My Baby
  Black Pearl
  Chapel of Love
  Da Doo Ron Ron (When He Walked
    Me Home)
  A Fine, Fine Boy
  Hung on You
  I Can Hear Music
  If You Don't Want My Love
  Iodine
  Just Once in My Life
  Little Boy
  River Deep—Mountain High
  Second Hand Love
  Spanish Harlem
  Then He Kissed Me
  There's No Other
  To Know Him Is To Love Him
  True Love Leaves No Traces
  Wait Till My Bobby Gets Home
  Walking in the Rain
  Why Do Lovers Break Each Other's
    Hearts?
  You've Lost That Lovin' Feelin'
Spence, Lew
  The Marriage-Go-Round
  Nice 'n' Easy
  That Face
  That Old Song and Dance
Spencer, Carl
  Let Her Dance
Spencer, Casey
  I'm a Happy Man
Spencer, Glenn
  Roses
Spencer, Herb
  The Fishin' Hole
Spencer, Herbert
  East of the Moon, West of the Stars
  Lost April
Spencer, Judy
  Soft Summer Breeze

Spencer, Otis
  Broadway Rose
Spencer, Richard
  Color Him Father
Spencer, Tim
  Careless Kisses
  Cigareetes, Whusky and Wild, Wild
    Women
  Cowboy Camp Meetin'
  The Everlasting Hills of Oklahoma
  Room Full of Roses
  Roses
  The Timber Trail
Spencer, Vern (Tim)
  Blue Prairie
Spickard, Bob
  Pipeline
Spickol, Max
  Honestly
Spielman, Fred
  Go to Sleep, Go to Sleep, Go to
    Sleep
  I Thought It Was Over
  I'm Gonna See a Lot of You
  It Only Hurts for a Little While
  The Longest Walk
  One Finger Melody
  Paper Roses
  Shepherd Serenade
Spier, Larry
  Memory Lane
  One Summer Night
  Put Your Little Foot Right Out
Spikes, Benjamin
  Wolverine Blues
Spikes, Benjamin F.
  Froggie Moore
  (You'll Want My Love) Maybe
    Someday
Spikes, John
  Wolverine Blues
Spikes, John C.
  Froggie Moore
  (You'll Want My Love) Maybe
    Someday
Spilton, Alan
  Lover Come Back
Spina, Harold
  Annie Doesn't Live Here Anymore
  Be Mine

The Beat of My Heart
Half Moon on the Hudson
I Could Use a Dream
I Love To Walk in the Rain
I Still Love To Kiss You Goodnight
It's Dark on Observatory Hill
It's So Nice To Have a Man around
  the House
Lazy Summer Night
My Very Good Friend, the Milkman
Once
Swing Me an Old Fashioned Song
The Velvet Glove
Would I Love You (Love You, Love
  You)
You're Not the Only Oyster in the
  Stew
Spirit, John, *see* Shakespeare
Spiro, Harold
  Little Games
Spirt, John
  Martian Hop
Spitalny, Maurice
  Start the Day Right
Spitalny, Phil
  Save the Last Dance for Me
Spivery, William
  Operator
Spivey, Victoria
  T.B. Blues
Spolan, Gloria A.
  Hypotized
Spoliansky, Mischa
  Hour of Parting
  The Melba Waltz
  Where Flamingos Fly
Spotti, Pino
  I Want To Be Wanted
Spottswood, Willie
  Hold Tight—Hold Tight (Want Some
    Sea Food Mama)
Sprigato, Sylvester
  It Isn't Fair
Springer, George E.
  Lies
Springer, Joan
  Lovin' Spree
Springer, Phil
  Lovin' Spree
  Moonlight Gambler

  Never-Ending
  Santa Baby
Springer, Philip
  All Cried Out
  How Little We Know (How Little It
    Matters How Little We Know)
  Sweet William
  Teasin'
Springer, Tony
  Santa Baby
Springfield, Tom
  Georgy Girl
  I'll Never Find Another You
  A World of Our Own
Springsteen, Bruce
  Adam Raised a Cain
  Backstreets
  Badlands
  Because the Night
  Blinded by the Light
  Born to Run
  Darkness on the Edge of Town
  Fire
  For You
  4th of July, Asbury Park (Sandy)
  Growin' Up
  He's Got the Fever
  Independence Day
  Jungleland
  Lost in the Flood
  Prove It All Night
  Rosalita (Come Out Tonight)
  Spirit in the Night
  Tenth Avenue Freeze-Out
  Thunder Road
  Wild Billy's Circus Story
  You Mean So Much to Me
Springthorpe, Richard
  Speak to the Sky
Spunky
  Honolulu Lulu
Squire, Chris
  And You and I
Squires, Harry D.
  Make Me Know It (If You Mean
    What You Say)
Stafford, Jesse
  Oh Peter (You're So Nice)
Stafford, Jim
  My Girl Bill

So Many Ways
Start Movin'
Stevenson, John
  Rock 'n' Roll Heaven
Stevenson, W. S.
  Am I That Easy To Forget?
  Hot Rod Lincoln
  I'm Tired
  Let Me Be the One
  Lonely Street
  Release Me
  Stop the World (And Let Me Off)
  That's When I See the Blues (in
    Your Pretty Brown Eyes)
  There She Goes
Stevenson, William
  Ask the Lonely
  Beechwood 4-5789
  Can You Jerk Like Me
  Dancing in the Street
  Danger Heartbreak Dead Ahead
  Devil with the Blue Dress On
  I'll Always Love You
  I'll Keep Holding On
  It Should Have Been Me
  It Takes Two
  Jamie
  My Baby Loves Me
  Needle in a Haystack
  Nothing's Too Good for My Baby
  Playboy
  Pride and Joy
  Stubborn Kind of Fellow
  What Am I Going to Do without
    Your Love?
  Wild One
  You've Been in Love Too Long
Stewart, Al
  Come Closer to Me
  The Dream Peddler
  I'll Never Love Again
  On the Border
  Song on the Radio
  (Don't Telephone, Don't Telegraph)
    Tell a Woman
  Time Passages
  Year of the Cat
Stewart, Billy
  I Do Love You

Sitting in the Park
Stewart, C.
  Cryin', Prayin', Wishin', Waitin'
Stewart, Dorothy
  Give Me Your Hand
  Now Is the Hour (Maori Farewell
    Song)
Stewart, Eric
  Art for Art's Sake
  Dreadlock Holiday
  I'm Mandy, Fly Me
  I'm Not in Love
  People in Love
  The Things We Do for Love
Stewart, Harry
  I Just Go Nuts at Christmas
Stewart, Henry
  Soldier's Last Letter
Stewart, John
  Daydream Believer
  Gold
Stewart, Larry
  Please Play Our Song (Mister Record
    Man)
Stewart, Michael
  Hey There, Good Times
  I Love My Wife
Stewart, Redd
  Slow Poke
  Tennessee Tango
  Tennessee Waltz
  Which One Is To Blame
  You Belong to Me
Stewart, Rex
  Boy Meets Horn
  Mobile Bay
Stewart, Rod
  Ain't Love a Bitch
  Do You Think I'm Disco
  Do You Think I'm Sexy
  Every Picture Tells a Story
  Hot Legs
  I Was Only Joking
  Killing of Georgie (Part 1 & 2)
  Maggie May
  Stay with Me
  Three Time Loser
  Tonight's the Night (Gonna Be
    Alright)
  You Wear It Well

Lyricists & Composers Index

Terry, Johnny
  Please, Please, Please
Terry, Mike
  If Only Tomorrow (Could Be Like
    Today)
Terry, Robert Huntington
  The Answer
Testa, A.
  Can I Trust You?
  I Want To Be Wanted
Testa, Alberto
  I Don't Know What He Told You
  Tonight I'll Say a Prayer
Testa, Arturo
  Quando, Quando, Quando (Tell Me
    When)
Testoni, G. C.
  Barabbas
Tetteroo, Peter
  Ma Belle Amie
Tex, Joe
  Baby, You're Right
  Buying a Book
  Hold What You've Got
  I Gotcha
  I Want To (Do Everything for You)
  The Love You Save (May Be Your
    Own)
  Men Are Gettin' Scarce
  Papa Was Too
  Show Me
  Skinny Legs and All
  Someone To Take Your Place
  A Sweet Woman Like You
  S.Y.S.L.J.F.M. (The Letter Song)
  You Better Get It
  You Said a Bad Word
Tharp, Winston
  The Panic Is On
Tharp, Winston Collins
  Out of Space
Tharpe, Sister Rosetta
  Strange Things Are Happening Every
    Day
  Up Above My Head, I Hear Music
    in the Air
Theard, Sam
  Let the Good Times Roll
  You Can't Get That No More

(I'll Be Glad When Your're Dead),
  You Rascal You
Theodorakis, Mikis
  Beyond Tomorrow
  Love Theme from *Phaedra*
  Theme from *Zorba, the Greek*
Thibault, Gillis
  My Way
Thiele, Robert
  Duke's Place
Thielemans, Jean
  Bluesette
Thielhelm, Emil
  We Ain't Got Nothing Yet
Thomas, Arthur
  Old Records
  Signs
Thomas, Carla
  Gee Whiz! (Look at His Eyes)
Thomas, Clifton
  Lover's Holiday
  Pickin' Wild Mountain Berries
Thomas, David Clayton
  Go Down Gamblin'
  Spinning Wheel
Thomas, Dennis
  Hollywood Swinging
  Jungle Boogie
  Ladies Night
  Open Sesame
  Spirit of the Boogie
Thomas, Dick
  I Lost the Best Pal That I Had
  Sioux City Sue
Thomas, Don
  This Door Swings Both Ways
Thomas, Edward
  Pickin' Wild Mountain Berries
Thomas, Edward, Jr.
  Lover's Holiday
Thomas, F.
  Shake Your Rump to the Funk
Thomas, Gene
  Playboy
  Rings of Gold
Thomas, George W.
  Adam and Eve Had the Blues
  Bed Room Blues
  Fishtail Dance

Tillotson, Johnny
  It Keeps Right On A-Hurtin' Since I
    Left
  Without You
Tilmon, Abrim
  Baby Let Me Take You (in My
    Arms)
Tilsley, Harry
  I Never See Maggie Alone
Tilsley, Henry B.
  Lady of Spain
  Unless
Tilzer, Albert Von
  Roll Along Prairie Moon
Timbur, Dalton
  Timber, I'm Falling
Timm, W. A.
  Hot Pretzels
Timm, Wladimir A.
  Beer Barrel Polka (Roll Out the
    Barrel)
Timmons, Bobby
  Moanin'
Tinturin, Peter
  I'm Glad for Your Sake (but I'm
    Sorry for Mine)
  It's About Time
  What Will I Tell My Heart
Tiomkin, Dimitri
  Ballad of the Alamo
  Blowing Wild
  Circus World
  Duel in the Sun (A Duel of Two
    Hearts)
  The Fall of Love
  Friendly Persuasion
  Giant
  The Green Leaves of Summer
  The Guns of Navarone
  Hajji Baba
  The High and the Mighty
  High Noon
  Land of the Pharaohs
  The Old Man and the Sea
  Pretty Little Girl in the Yellow Dress
  Rawhide
  Return to Paradise
  Rio Bravo
  Search for Paradise
  So Little Time

Strange Are the Ways of Love
Strange Lady in Town
Theme from *The Sundowners*
Theme from *36 Hours* (A Heart
  Must Learn To Cry)
There's Never Been Anyone Else but
  You
Town without Pity
The Unforgiven (The Need for Love)
Wild Is the Wind
Yassu
Tipton, Bill
  Knock, Knock, Who's There?
Titelman, Russ
  Little Things Like That
  Sailor Boy
Titsworth, Paul
  I'm in Love with You
Titus, Libby
  Love Has No Pride
Tizol, Juan
  Caravan
  Gypsy without a Song
  Lost in Meditation
  Perdido
  Pyramid
Tobias, Charles
  After My Laughter Came Tears
  All Over the World
  Am I Gonna Have Trouble with
    You?
  As Years Go By
  Below the Equator
  The Broken Record
  Comes Love
  Don't Be Like That
  Ev'ry Day Away from You
  For the First Time (I've Fallen in
    Love)
  Get Out and Get Under the Moon
  Good Night Little Girl of My
    Dreams
  Gotta Big Date with a Little Girl
  Her Bathing Suit Never Got Wet
  He's Tall and Dark and Handsome
  Home Is Where the Heart Is
  I Came Here To Talk for Joe
  I Can Get It for You Wholesale
  I Remember Mama
  I Want You for Christmas

Lyricists & Composers Index

In the Valley of the Moon
Is That the Way To Treat a
Sweetheart?
It Seems Like Old Times
Just Another Day Wasted Away
(Waiting for You)
Kathy-O
Let's Make Memories Tonight
Little Curly Hair in a High Chair
Little Lady Make Believe
Love Ya
The Mama Doll Song
Me Too
Merry Christmas Waltz
Miss You
My First Impression of You
The Old Lamp-Lighter
An Old Water Mill
A Rosewood Spinet
Somebody Loves You
Spring Has Sprung
Start the Day Right
Summer Green and Winter White
Those Lazy-Hazy-Crazy Days of
Summer
Tiny Little Fingerprints
Trudy
Two Tickets to Georgia
Wait for Me, Mary
Wake Up and Sing
What Do We Do on a Dew Dew
Dewy Day
When Your Hair Has Turned to
Silver (I Will Love You Just the
Same)
White Orchids
Would You Believe Me?
You Know—I Know Ev'rything's
Made for Love
You'll Be Mine in Apple Blossom
Time
Zing Zing - Zoom Zoom

Tobias, Charlie
As Long As I Live
Coax Me a Little Bit
The Cocoanut Song
Don't Sit under the Apple Tree
(With Anyone Else but Me)
Don't Sweetheart Me
Flowers for Madame

Gee! but You're Swell
I Wish That I Could Hide inside
This Letter
Just a Prayer Away
Mickey Mouse's Birthday Party
Moon on My Pillow
No Can Do
Oh! Moytle
Rose O'Day (The Filla-Ga-Dusha
Song)
Somewhere in Old Wyoming
That's Where I Came In
Throw Another Log on the Fire
Time Waits for No One
Tomorrow Is Forever
Trade Winds
Wait for Me Baby
We Did It Before (And We Can Do
It Again)
You're Irish and You're Beautiful

Tobias, Elliott
Moon on My Pillow

Tobias, Fred
Born Too Late
Followed Closely by Teardrops
Good Timin'
Litty Bitty Girl
One of Us (Will Weep Tonight)
Quien Sabe? (Who Knows? Who
Knows?)

Tobias, Harry
At Your Command
Chimes of Arcady
The Daughter of Peggy O'Neil
Go to Sleepy, Little Baby
Gotta Big Date with a Little Girl
I'm Sorry Dear
It's a Lonesome Old Town When
You're Not Around
Lost and Found
Love Is All
Miss You
No Regrets
O-Oo Ernest, Are You Earnest with
Me
On the Sunny Side of the Rockies
Put Your Little Arms around Me
Sail Along, Silv'ry Moon
Sweet and Lovely
Wait for Me Baby

What Is Success
Yes We Can Can
Toussaint, Allen
Get Out of My Life Woman
Holy Cow
Java
Southern Nights
Working in the Coal Mine
Touzet, Rene
Let Me Love You Tonight
Made for Each Other
Towber, Chaim
I Love You Much Too Much
Towers, Leo
Bella Bella Marie
The Little Old Mill (Went Round and Round)
Silver Wings in the Moonlight
Towne, Billy
Never on Sunday
Towne, Charlie
Mambo Jambo
Townsend, Ed
For Your Love
The Love of My Man
Townsend, Edward
Sooner or Later (It Had to Happen)
Townsend, John
Smoke from a Distant Fire
Townshend, Edward
Finally Got Myself Together (I'm a Changed Man)
Let's Get It On
Townshend, Peter
Acid Queen
Bargain
Behind Blue Eyes
Blue, Red and Gray
Call Me Lightning
Champagne
5:15
Go to the Mirror, Boy
Goin' Mobile
Happy Jack
However Much I Booze
I Can See for Miles
I'm Free
It's a Boy
Join Together
Long Live Rock

Love, Reign O'er Me
The Magic Bus
Pictures of Lily
Pinball Wizard
Pure and Easy
The Real Me
The Seeker
Slip Kid
The Song Is Over
Squeeze Box
Street in the City
Substitute
Who Are You
Won't Get Fooled Again
Townsherd, Peter
Guitar and Pen
Trace, Al
Brush Those Tears from Your Eyes
Trace, Ben
You Call Everybody Darling
Tracey, William
Down by the Gas House
Good-bye, Dixie, Good-bye
Is My Baby Blue Tonight
It Will Never Be Dry Down in Havana, No Matter What Happens 'round Here
Them There Eyes
There's a Million Girlies Lonesome Tonight, and Still I'm Alone
What! No Spinach?
You Can Have Him, I Don't Want Him, Didn't Love Him Anyhow Blues!
Trader, Bill
A Fool Such As I
Trail, Buck
Girl Watcher
Trammel, Barbara
Don't Let the Stars Get in Your Eyes
Trapani, Tulio
Cara Mia
Travers, Mary
The Song Is Love
Travis, Merle
Cincinnati Lou
Dark As a Dungeon
Divorce Me C.O.D.
Fat Gal
I Want To Be Sure

Lyricists & Composers Index

Lyricists & Composers Index

2559

The Hard Way
Heaven Can Wait
High Hopes
His Rocking Horse Ran Away
How Long Did I Dream?
Humpty Dumpty Heart
I Thought about You
If You Please
Imagination
Isn't That Just Like Love
It Could Happen to You
It's Always You
It's Better in the Dark
It's the Dreamer in Me
Knockin' on Your Own Front Door
Life Is So Peculiar
Looking for Yesterday
Love Is a Bore
Love Is the Darndest Thing
Moonlight Becomes You
Nancy (With the Laughing Face)
Peace Brother
Personality
Polka Dots and Moonbeams (Around a Pug-Nosed Dream)
Road to Morocco
Romeo Smith and Juliet Jones
Shake Down the Stars
Sleighride in July
So Help Me (If I Don't Love You)
Star!
Suddenly It's Spring
Sunshine Cake
Swinging on a Star
That Little Dream Got Nowhere
Thoroughly Modern Millie
Yah-ta-ta, Yah-ta-ta (Talk, Talk, Talk)
You Lucky People You
You Think of Ev'rything
You're Dangerous
Van Hoy, Rafe
  Golden Ring
  Lady Lay Down
Van Leen, Theis
  Hocus Pocus
Van, Mel
  Hit and Run Affair
Van Ness, Clarke
  Filipino Baby

Van Parys, George
  Merry-Go-Round
Van Peebles, Melvin
  Ain't Love Grand
  Lily Done the Zampoughi Every Time I Pulled Her Coattail
  Quittin' Time
  Tenth and Greenwich (Women's House of Detention)
Van Warmer, Randy
  Just When I Needed You Most
Van Winkle, Joseph
  Happiness
  Mister Custer
Van Zandt, Steve
  I Don't Want to Go Home
Van Zandt, Townes
  Pancho and Lefty
Van Zant, Ronnie
  Free Bird
  Saturday Night Special
  Sweet Home Alabama
  What's Your Name
Vanadore, Lester
  Alone with You
  I'd Rather Loan You Out
  Too Much To Lose
Vance, Albert
  Disco Lady
Vance, Paul
  Can I Trust You?
  Catch a Falling Star
  Dommage, Dommage (Too bad, too bad)
  Gina
  Gone Is My Love
  Julie Knows
  King Size Papa
  Leader of the Laundromat
  One More Mountain (One More River)
  Playground in My Mind
  Run Joey Run
  Tar and Cement
  Tracy
  What Is Love?
  What Will My Mary Say?
  When Julie Comes Around

I'm Gonna Paper All My Walls with
Your Love Letters
Laughing on the Outside (Crying on
the Inside)
Miss America
Port-au-Prince
Rio Conchos
Sentimental Music
The Things That Mean So Much to
Me
Tropicana
Vanessa
Where Were You When I Needed
You?
You Walk By
You're So Understanding
Zsa Zsa
Wayne, Buddy
Something Pretty
Wayne, Curtis
Next in Line
Wayne, Don
The Belles of Southern Bell
Eight Years
If Teardrops Were Silver
The Nester
Saginaw, Michigan
Walk Tall (Walk Straight)
Wayne, Dottie
The Night Has a Thousand Eyes
Wayne, Edith
Crumbs off the Table
Mind, Body and Soul
Wayne, Edythe
Band of Gold
Give Me Just a Little More Time
You've Got Me Dangling on a String
Wayne, Lou
Sweethearts or Strangers
When a Soldier Knocks and Finds
Nobody Home
Wayne, Mabel
Chiquita
Don't Wake Me Up
A Dreamer's Holiday
I Understand
In a Little Spanish Town ('Twas on a
Night Like This)
It Happened in Monterey
Little Man, You've Had a Busy Day

My Angeline
On the Outgoing Tide
Ragamuffin Romeo
Ramona
The Right Kind of Love
Rose Ann of Charing Cross
So Madly in Love
Why Don't You Fall in Love with
Me
Wayne, Sid
Anything Can Happen-Mambo
Do the Clam
First Anniversary
I Need Your Love Tonight
I'm Gonna Knock on Your Door
It's Impossible
It's Only the Beginning
Mangos
Ninety Nine Years (Dead or Alive)
See You in September
Spinout
Stolen Moments
Two Different Worlds
A World of Love
Weatherly, Fred
Danny Boy
Weatherly, James
Where Do I Put Her Memory
You Are a Song
Weatherly, Jim
Midnight Train to Georgia
The Need to Be
Neither One of Us (Wants to Be the
First to Say Goodbye)
Where Peaceful Waters Flow
You're the Best Thing That Ever
Happened to Me
Weatherspoon, William
I've Passed This Way Before
What Becomes of the Brokenhearted?
Women's Love Rights
Weaver, Blue
(Our Love) Don't Throw It All
Away
Hold onto My Love
The Weavers, *see* Campbell, Paul
Webb, Bernard
Woman

Lyricists & Composers Index

Lyricists & Composers Index

2583

Lyricists & Composers Index

Lyricists & Composers Index

Lyricists & Composers Index

Wooden Heart
You, You, You Are the One
"A"—You're Adorable (The Alphabet
  Song)
Wiseman, Jack
  Cuban Mambo
Wiseman, Scott
  Have I Told You Lately That I Love
  You
  Remember Me (When the Candle
  Lights Are Gleaming)
Wisner, Jim
  Don't Throw Your Love Away
Withers, Bill
  Ain't No Sunshine
  Grandma's Hands
  Lean on Me
  Use Me
Withers, Tony
  Little Boy Lost
Wittstatt, Hans
  Pepe
Wizell, Murray
  I May Never Pass This Way Again
Wodehouse, P. G.
  Bill
  March of the Musketeers
  Oh Gee! Oh Joy!
  Say So!
Wohlman, Al
  You
Wolcott, Charles
  Ruby-Duby-Du
  Saludos Amigos
  Sooner or Later
  Two Silhouettes
Woldin, Judd
  Alaiyo
  Sweet Time
Wolf, Danny
  Sugar Moon
Wolf, Don
  Love Is All We Need
Wolf, Jack
  The Closing Credits
  The Ho Ho Song
  I'm a Fool To Want You
  In All My Wildest Dreams
Wolf, Peter
  Come Back

Give It to Me
Love Stinks
Must of Got Lost
One Last Kiss
You're the Only One
Wolf, Tommy
  The Ballad of the Sad Young Men
  I've Got a Lot To Learn about Life
  Laugh, I Thought I'd Die
  Little Bird
  Spring Can Really Hang You Up the
  Most
Wolfe, Jacques
  Short'nin' Bread
Wolfe, Shirley
  Lips of Wine
Wolfe, Steve
  It's a Heartache
Wolfert, Dave
  Songbird
Wolfert, David
  Heartbreaker
Wolff, Joe
  New Moon
Wolfolk, Carl
  Can I Change My Mind?
  Is It Something You've Got?
Wolfson, Mack
  C'est la Vie
  The Crazy Otto Rag
  Flowers Mean Forgiveness
  Happiness Street (Corner Sunshine
  Square)
Wolinski, David
  Do You Love What You Feel
Woloschuk, John
  Calling Occupants of Interplanetary
  Craft
Womack, Bobby
  Across 110th Street
  Breezin'
  I Found a True Love
  I'm a Midnight Mover
  I'm in Love
  Jealous Love
  Woman's Got to Have It
Womack, Friendly
  We Are the Future
Wonder, Stevie
  All in Love Is Fair

Music, Maestro, Please!
Now You're in My Arms
Pop! Goes Your Heart
Private Buckaroo
To Me
Try To See It My Way
Why Does It Get So Late So Early?
Why Don't We Do This More Often
Zip-a-Dee-Doo-Dah
Wyatt, Bennett
That's Me without You
Wyche, Sid
Alright, Okay, You Win
A Big Hunk o' Love
Talk That Talk
A Woman, a Lover, a Friend
Wyker, John
Motorcycle Mama
Wyker, Johnny, III
Let Love Come between Us
Wyle, George
The Ballad of Gilligan's Isle
Caramba! It's the Samba!
Doo Dee Doo on an Old Kazoo
I Didn't Slip, I Wasn't Pushed, I Fell
I Love the Way You Say Goodnight
I Said My Pajamas (And Put On My Pray'rs)
May Each Day
Noelle
Quicksilver
You Broke Your Promise
Wylie, Richard
With This Ring
Wyman, Bill
Play with Fire
Wynette, Tammy
Another Lonely Song
Singing My Song
(I'm a) Stand by My Woman Man
Stand By Your Man
Til I Can Make It on My Own
The Ways to Love a Man
We Sure Can Love Each Other
Wynn, Albert
That Creole Band
Wynn, Larry
Five Guys Named Moe
Wynn, Philippe
(Not Just) Knee Deep

Yakus, Herb
Chain Gang
Yakus, Milt
Old Cape Cod
Yakus, Milton
Go On with the Wedding
Yancy, Marvin
Here I Am (Come and Take Me)
Inseparable
I've Got Love on My Mind
The More You Do It, the More I Like It
Our Love
Sophisticated Lady (She's a Different Lady)
This Will Be (an Everlasting Love)
Yandell, Paul
I'll Repossess My Heart
Yankovic, Frank
Blue Bird Waltz
Yanovsky, Zal
Cocoanut Grove
Yarian, Christine
Do It Baby
Yarnall, Ernesto B.
Where Are You Now
Yarnall, Marion B.
Where Are You Now
Yarrow, Peter
Day Is Done
Man of Constant Sorrow
Puff (The Magic Dragon)
The Song Is Love
Torn Between Two Lovers
Weave Me the Sunshine
Yates, Carolyn Jean
I Won't Mention It Again
Yates, Steven
Ally, Ally Oxen Free
Yellen, Jack
According to the Moonlight
Ain't She Sweet
Are You Havin' Any Fun?
Bagdad
A Bench in the Park
Cheatin' on Me
Crazy Words—Crazy Tune (Vo-do-de-o)
Down by the O-HI-O (O-My!-O!)
Forever and Ever

Lyricists & Composers Index

Zambon, Fred
Suspicious Minds
Zamecnik, J. S.
Neapolitan Nights
Wings
Zanetis, Alex
As Long As I Live
As Usual
Back-Track
Big Wind
Guilty
I'm Saving My Love
Me
Snap Your Fingers
Zanetis, Alexander
I'm Gonna Change Everything
Zanin, Laura
Sole, Sole, Sole
Zany, King
All She'd Say Was "Umh Hum"
Coral Sea
When Buddha Smiles
Zappa, Frank
Dancin' Fool
Don't Eat the Yellow Snow
Zarate, Abel
Suavecito
Zaret, Hy
Dedicated to You
It All Comes Back to Me Now
My Sister and I
No Other Arms, No Other Lips
One Meat Ball
That's My Affair
There I Go
Unchained Melody
You Can't Hold a Memory in Your
Arms
You'll Never Get Away
Young and Warm and Wonderful
Zawinul, Joseph
Mercy, Mercy, Mercy
Zekley, Gary
Just Wait a Million Years
Sooner or Later
Yellow Balloon
Zeller, Phil
Hang 'Em High
I Can't Believe I'm Losing You
I'm Comin' Home, Cindy

Zeman, Vasek
Beer Barrel Polka (Roll Out the
Barrel)
Zerato, Lou
Beg, Borrow and Steal
Zero, Jack
Please No Squeeza Da Banana
Zesses, Nick
Hey Big Brother
Zevon, Warren
Carmelita
Desperados under the Eaves
Excitable Boy
Lawyers, Guns and Money
Mohammed's Radio
Poor Poor Pitiful Me
Werewolves of London
Zimbalist, Efrem
Believe Me, Beloved
Drop Me a Line
Oh, How I Long for Someone
Zimmerman, Leon
I'm Just a Vagabond Lover
Zoob, Dave
Sweet Lady
Zucker, Otto
Kum Ba Yah (Come By Here)
Sorry, I Ran All the Way Home

Important Performances Index

Songs are listed under the works in which they were introduced or given significant renditions. The index is organized into major sections by performance medium: Album, Movie, Musical, Opera, Operetta, Orchestra (for theme songs), Play, Radio Show, Revue, Television Show.

Album

Abbey Road
  Because
  Carry That Weight
  The End
  Golden Slumbers
  Here Comes the Sun
  I Want You (She's So Heavy)
  Maxwell's Silver Hammer
  Mean Mr. Mustard
  Octopus's Garden
  Oh! Darling
  Polythene Pam
  She Came In through the Bathroom
    Window
  Sun King
  You Never Give Me Your Money
Ace
  Playing in the Band
Aftermath
  Goin' Home
  It's Not Easy
  Stupid Girl
  Under My Thumb

AIA
  A Pirate Looks at Forty
Al Green Explores Your Mind
  Take Me to the River
Album III
  Needless to Say
  Red Guitar
Alice's Restaurant
  Alice's Restaurant
Alive on Arrival
  Goin Down to Laurel
  Grand Central Station March 18,
    1977
  Steve Forbert's Midsummer Night's
    Toast
  You Cannot Win If You Do Not
    Play
All-American Alien Boy
  All American Alien Boy
  God (Take 1)
American Beauty
  Friend of the Devil
American Gothic
  Montana Song
  Waiting for the Moving Van

American Stars and Bars
  Hurricane
Amigo
  Manzanillo Bay
Andy Pratt
  Give It All to Music
Animals
  Pigs on the Wing, Pt.1
Another Passenger
  Cow Town
  He Likes to Roll
Anthem of the Sun
  Alligator
Any Day Now
  Tears of Rage
  You Ain't Goin' Nowhere
Aoxomoxoa
  Doin' That Rag
  St. Stephen
The April Fools
  The April Fools
Are You Experienced?
  Are You Experienced?
  Fire
  Manic Depression
  Purple Haze
  The Wind Cries Mary
Argent
  Liar
Armed Forces
  Oliver's Army
  (What's So Funny 'Bout) Peace, Love
    and Understanding
Atlantic Crossing
  I Don't Want to Talk About It
  Sailing
  This Old Heart of Mine (Is Weak for
    You)
  Three Time Loser
Attempted Moustache
  Nocturnal Stumblebutt
  The Swimming Song
Aztec Two-Step
  The Persecution and Restoration of
    Dean Moriarity
The Band
  Across the Great Divide
  Jemima, Surrender
  King Harvest (Has Surely Come)

The Night They Drove Old Dixie
  Down
  Rag, Mama, Rag
Bare Trees
  Sentimental Lady
Bark
  Pretty as You Feel
  Third Week at the Chelsea
The Basement Tapes
  Million Dollar Bash
  Nothing Was Delivered
Beads and Feathers
  My House
The Beatles
  Back in the U.S.S.R.
  Birthday
  Blackbird
  The Continuing Story of Bungalow
    Bill
  Cry Baby Cry
  Dear Prudence
  Don't Pass Me By
  Everbody's Got Something to Hide
    except Me and My Monkey
  Glass Onion
  Good Night
  Happiness Is a Warm Gun
  Helter Skelter
  Honey Pie
  I Will
  I'm So Tired
  Julia
  Long, Long, Long
  Martha My Dear
  Mother Nature's Son
  Ob-La-Di, Ob-La-Da
  Piggies
  Revolution 9
  Rocky Racoon
  Savoy Truffle
  Sexy Sadie
  While My Guitar Gently Weeps
  Why Don't We Do It in the Road
  Wild Honey Pie
  Yer Blues
Beatles VI
  Tell Me What You See
  You Like Me Too Much
Beggars Banquet
  Dear Doctor

Jig-Saw Puzzle
No Expectations
Parachute Woman
The Salt of the Earth
Stray Cat
Sympathy for the Devil
Bein' Free
Stoney
The Bells
Disco Mystic
Stupid Man
Between the Buttons
Cool, Calm, and Collected
Something Happened to Me
Yesterday
Yesterday's Papers
Billy Joel
Captain Jack
Travelin' Prayer
You're My Home
Blessed Are. . .
The Night They Drove Old Dixie
Down
Blonde on Blonde
Absolutely Sweet Marie
Fourth Time Around
Most Likely You Go Your Way (and
I'll Go Mine)
Obviously Five Believers
One of Us Must Know (Sooner or
Later)
Pledging My Time
Sad-eyed Lady of the
Lowlands
Stuck inside of Mobile with the
Memphis Blues Again
Temporary Like Achilles
Visions of Johanna
Blood on the Tracks
Idiot Wind
Shelter from the Storm
Simple Twist of Fate
Tangled Up in Blue
Blood, Sweat and Tears
God Bless the Child
Smiling Phases
Blue
Blue

The Last Time I Saw Richard
Little Green
My Old Man
River
Blue Kentucky Girl
Hickory Wind
Blue River
Blue River
Is It Really Love at All
Time Run Like a Freight Train
Blue Valentine
Christmas Card from a Hooker in
Minneapolis
Romeo Is Bleeding
Wrong Side of the Road
Bob Dylan's Greatest Hits, Vol. II
Down in the Flood
I Shall Be Released
You Ain't Goin' Nowhere
Bob Dylan's Greatest Hits, Volume II
The Mighty Quinn (Quinn, the
Eskimo)
When I Paint My Masterpiece
Bookends
America
Punky's Dilemma
Born to Run
Backstreets
Jungleland
Thunder Road
Boys in the Trees
Tranquillo (Melt My Heart)
Brain Capers
Sweet Jane
Brave New World
Space Cowboy
Bread and Roses
Bread and Roses
Special Delivery
Breezy Stories
Angel Spread Your Wings
Magdalena
Bridge over Troubled Water
Cecilia
Bridges
The Bottle
We Almost Lost Detroit
Bringing It All Back Home
Bob Dylan's 115th Dream
Gates of Eden

It's All Over Now, Baby Blue
It's Alright, Ma (I'm Only Bleeding)
Love Minus Zero/No Limit
Maggie's Farm
On the Road Again
Outlaw Blues
She Belongs to Me
Bruised Orange
Bruised Orange (Chain of Sorrow)
Fish and Whistle
If You Don't Want My Love
That's the Way the World Goes
Round
Candy-O
Shoo Be Doo
Can't Buy a Thrill
Dirty Work
Carl and the Passions-So Tough/Pet
Sounds
Marcella
Cars
You're All I've Got Tonight
Catch a Fire
Four Hundred Years
Cheap Thrills
Ball and Chain
Combination of the Two
Chicago II
Make Me Smile
25 or 6 to 4
Chicago Transit Authority
Beginnings
Does Anybody Really Know What
Time It Is?
I'm a Man
Listen
Child Is Father to the Man
House in the Country
I Can't Quit Her
I Love You More Than You'll Ever
Know
Just One Smile
The Modern Adventures of Plato,
Diogenes, and Freud
Somethin' Goin' On
Without Her
Chords of Fame
Jim Dean of Indiana
Christmas and the Beads of Sweat
Been on a Train

Brown Earth
The Clash
Career Opportunities
White Riot
Close Up
We Had It All
Clouds
Both Sides Now
Chelsea Morning
Songs to Aging Children Come
That Song About the Midway
Coconut Gove
Rainbow Willie
Cold Spring Harbor
She's Got a Way
Collision Course
Texas Me and You
Comes a Time
Already One
Human Highway
Coney Island Baby
Charley's Girl
Coney Island Baby
The Confederacy
The Yellow Rose of Texas
Contribution
L Ballade
Man Hole Covered Wagon
Cool and Hot Sax
The Swingin' Shepherd Blues
Court and Spark
Car on a Hill
Down to You
Free Man in Paris
Same Situation
Crosby, Stills and Nash
Wooden Ships
Damn the Torpedoes
Even the Losers
Dancer with Bruised Knees
First Born
Walking Song
Darkness on the Edge of Town
Adam Raised a Cain
Darkness on the Edge of Town
Days of Future Passed
Nights in White Satin
Death of a Ladies Man
Iodine
True Love Leaves No Traces

Many a Mile
  Until It's Time for You to Go
Maria Muldaur
  Mad Mad Me
  My Tennessee Mountain Home
  Vaudeville Man
  The Work Song
Marquee Moon
  Friction
  Prove It
Mary
  Follow Me
Medley: I Can Sing a Rainbow/Love Is
    Blue
  Love Is Blue
Merrimack County
  Jamaica Say You Will
  Mother Earth
Miles of Aisles
  Jericho
Mink De Ville
  Cadillac Walk
  Mixed Up, Shook Up Girl
Mr. Fantasy
  Dear Mr. Fantasy
  Smiling Phases
Modern Love Songs
  Back in Your Life
More Than a New Discovery
  And When I Die
  Blowing Away
  Buy and Sell
  Flim Flam Man
  The Stony End
  Wedding Bell Blues
Music from Big Pink
  I Shall Be Released
  In a Station
  Tears of Rage
  This Wheel's On Fire
  To Kingdom Come
  We Can Talk
My Aim Is True
  Alison
  Watching the Detectives
My Name is Barbra
  Jenny Rebecca
Nashville
  This Wheel's On Fire

Nashville Skyline
  Country Pie
  Girl from the North Country
  Nashville Skyline Rag
  One More Night
  Peggy Day
  Tell Me That It Isn't True
  To Be Alone with You
Natty Dread
  Lively Up Yourself
Naturally
  Liar
Nested
  American Dreamer
  Child in a Universe
New Boots and Panties
  Sex and Drugs and Rock 'n' Roll
  Sweet Gene Vincent
New Morning
  Day of the Locusts
  If Not for You
  New Morning
  Sign on the Window
  Time Passes Slowly
  Went to See the Gypsy
New Skin for an Old Ceremony
  Take This Longing
New York Tendaberry
  Time and Love
  You Don't Love Me When I Cry
A Night at the Opera
  Death on Two Legs
A Night on the Town
  Pretty Flamingo
  The Wild Side of Life
Nighthawks at the Diner
  Big Joe and Phantom 309
Nothin' But the Blues
  Drinkin' Blues
  TV Mama
Now That Everything's Been Said
  Hi-De-Ho
  I Wasn't Born to Follow
Occasional Rain
  Ordinary Joe
  Trance on Sedgewick Street
Ogdens' Nut Gone Flake
  Lazy Sunday
O'Keefe
  The Road

2607

Small Change
  The Piano Has Been Drinking (Not
    Me)
  Step Right Up
Smile
  Stormy Love
Smiler
  Let Me Be Your Car
Some Girls
  Respectable
  Some Girls
Something New Under the Sun
  Maybe I'm Doing It Wrong
Son of a Son of a Sailor
  Cheeseburger in Paradise
Songs from a Room
  Bird on the Wire
  Story of Isaac
Songs in the Key of Life
  Black Man
  Isn't She Lovely
  Joy Inside My Tears
Songs of Leonard Cohen
  Hey, That's No Way to Say Goodbye
  Sisters of Mercy
  So Long, Marianne
  The Stranger Song
  Suzanne
  Winter Lady
Songs of Love and Hate
  Famous Blue Raincoat
Sounds of Silence
  Leaves That Are Green
Southbound
  Lion in the Winter
Spooky Two
  Better by You, Better Than Me
  Evil Woman
Stage Fright
  The Shape I'm In
  Stage Fright
Stand!
  Don't Call Me Nigger, Whitey
Station to Station
  Stay
Stick to Me
  Clear Head
  Soul on Ice
Sticky Fingers
  Moonlight Mile

Wild Horses
Still Crazy After All These Years
  I Do It for Your Love
Straight from the Heart
  I Feel Like Breaking Up Somebody's
    Home Tonight
  I'm Gonna Tear Your Playhouse
    Down
The Stranger
  Scenes from an Italian Restaurant
Stranger in Town
  Famous Final Scene
Street Hassle
  Dirt
  I Wanna Be Black
  Shooting Star
Streetlife Serenader
  The Entertainer
Streetlights
  Got You on My Mind
  That Song About the Midway
  What Is Success
Subway to the Country
  Subway to the Country
The Sutherland Brothers and Quiver
  Sailing
Sweet Baby James
  Country Road
  Steamroller Blues
  Sweet Baby James
Sweet Bird
  Dolphin's Lullabye
Sweet Forgiveness
  About to Make Me Leave Home
  Louise
Sweet Harmony
  Back by Fall
  Lying Song
  Wild Bird
Sweet Revenge
  Christmas in Prison
  Dear Abby
Sweetheart of the Rodeo
  Nothing Was Delivered
Taking My Time
  Guilty
Talking Heads '77
  Don't Worry 'bout the Government
  Psycho Killer

2610

However Much I Booze
Slip Kid
Who Came First
Pure and Easy
Who Knows Where the Time Goes
Bird on the Wire
Hello—Hooray
My Father
Story of Isaac
Who Knows Where the Time Goes?
Who's Next
Bargain
Goin' Mobile
The Song Is Over
Won't Get Fooled Again
Whose Garden Was This
Whose Garden Was This
The Wild, the Innocent, and the E Street Shuffle
4th of July, Asbury Park (Sandy)
Rosalita (Come Out Tonight)
Wild Billy's Circus Story
Wildflowers
Albatross
Hey, That's No Way to Say Goodbye
Michael from Mountains
Since You've Asked
Sisters of Mercy
Wish You Were Here
Have a Cigar
Shine on You, Crazy Diamond
Words & Music
P.F. Sloan
Words We Can Dance To
Banana Republic
Workingman's Dead
Casey Jones
The World's Greatest Lover
Ain't It Kinda Wonderful
Writer
Goin' Back
Wrong End of the Rainbow
Biloxi
Sweet Baby James
Year of the Cat
On the Border
Yellow Submarine
All Together Now
Hey Bulldog
It's All Too Much

Only a Northern Song
"Yesterday" . . .and Today
And Your Bird Can Sing
Doctor Robert
Drive My Car
I'm Only Sleeping
If I Needed Someone
Zuma
Cortez the Killer
Drive Back
Stupid Girl

Movie

Aaron Loves Angela
Aaron Loves Angela
Aaron Slick from Punkin Crick
I'd Like To Baby You
Life Is a Beautiful Thing
Marshmallow Moon
My Beloved
About Face
Spring Has Sprung
Accent on Youth
Accent on Youth
Across 110th Street
Across 110th Street
Ada
Ada
Adam's Rib
Farewell Amanda
Adorable
Adorable
Advance to the Rear
Today
The Adventures of Hajji Baba
Hajji Baba
Advise and Consent
Song from *Advise and Consent* (Heart of Mine)
An Affair To Remember
An Affair To Remember
The Affairs of Dobie Gillis
All I Do Is Dream of You
I'm Thru with Love
After the Thin Man
Smoke Dreams

Call of the Flesh
  Lonely
Cameo Kirby
  Romance
Can-Can
  Just One of Those Things
  Let's Do It (Let's Fall in Love)
  You Do Something to Me
Candy
  Child of the Universe
  Rock Me
Can't Help Singing
  Any Moment Now
  Californ-i-ay
  Can't Help Singing
  More and More
Canyon Passage
  Ole Buttermilk Sky
Captain Carey, U.S.A.
  Mona Lisa
Captain January
  At the Codfish Ball
  Early Bird
  The Right Somebody To Love
Captains of the Clouds
  Bless'em All
  Captains of the Clouds
Car Wash
  Car Wash
  I Want to Get Next to You
  Ooh Boy
Caravan
  Ha-cha-cha
  Happy, I Am Happy
The Cardinal
  Stay with Me
  Waltz from *The Cardinal*
Carefree
  Change Partners
  I Used To Be Color Blind
  The Night Is Filled with Music
  The Yam
Careless Lady
  All of Me
Carnegie Hall
  Beware My Heart
Carnival in Costa Rica
  Another Night Like This
Carolina Blues
  Poor Little Rhode Island

There Goes That Song Again
  You Make Me Dream Too Much
Carolina Moon
  Say Si Si
Carousel
  If I Loved You
  June Is Bustin' Out All Over
  Mister Snow
  A Real Nice Clambake
  Soliloquy
  What's the Use of Wond'rin'
  When the Children Are Asleep
  You'll Never Walk Alone
  You're a Queer One, Julie Jordan
The Carpetbaggers
  Monica
Casa Manana
  I Hear a Rhapsody
Casablanca
  As Time Goes By
Casbah
  For Every Man There's a Woman
  Hooray for Love
  It Was Written in the Stars
  What's Good about Goodbye?
Casey's Shadow
  Let Me Go Till I'm Gone
Casino Royale
  Casino Royale
  The Look of Love
The Cat and the Fiddle
  I Watch the Love Parade
  A New Love Is Old
  The Night Was Made for Love
  One Moment Alone
  Poor Pierrot
  She Didn't Say "Yes"
  Try To Forget
Cat Ballou
  The Ballad of Cat Ballou
Catch Us If You Can
  Catch Us If You Can
Celebration at Big Sur
  Red Eye Express
Centennial Summer
  All through the Day
  In Love in Vain
  Up with the Lark
A Certain Smile
  A Certain Smile

The Chalk Garden
  Madrigal
The Champ
  If You Remember Me
The Champagne Waltz
  The Champagne Waltz
Change of Habit
  Rubberneckin'
Charade
  Charade
Charlotte's Web
  Mother Earth and Father Time
Chasing Rainbows
  Happy Days Are Here Again
  Lucky Me—Lovable You
Chatterbox
  Mad about Him, Sad without Him,
    How Can I Be Glad without Him
    Blues
Check and Double Check
  Three Little Words
Cherokee Strip
  My Little Buckaroo
A Child Is Waiting
  Snowflakes
Children of Pleasure
  Dust
  Girl Trouble
  The Whole Darned Thing's for You
Children of the Ritz
  Some Sweet Day
China Gate
  China Gate
The China Syndrome
  Somewhere in Between
Chisum
  Turn Me Around
Chitty Chitty Bang Bang
  Chitty Chitty Bang Bang
  Hushabye Mountain
Christmas Holiday
  Always
  Spring Will Be a Little Late This
    Year
The Cincinnati Kid
  The Cincinnati Kid
Cinderella
  Bibbidi-Bobbidi-Boo (The Magic
    Song)
  Cinderella

A Dream Is a Wish Your Heart
    Makes
Cinderella Liberty
  Nice to Be Around
Cinderella Swings It
  I Heard You Cried Last Night (And
    So Did I)
Cinderfella
  Somebody
Circus of Horrors
  Look for a Star
Circus World
  Circus World
City Lights
  Who'll Buy My Violets? (La
    Violetera)
Clash by Night
  I Hear a Rhapsody
Claudine
  On and On
Cleo de 5 a 7
  You're Gone
Cleopatra
  Antony and Cleopatra Theme
  A World of Love
Cleopatra Jones
  Theme from *Cleopatra Jones*
Close Encounters of the Third Kind
  Theme from *Close Encounters of the
    Third Kind*
Coal Miner's Daughter
  Coal Miner's Daughter
Cocoanut Grove
  Cocoanut Grove
  Dreamy Hawaiian Moon
  Says My Heart
  You Leave Me Breathless
The Cocoanuts
  When My Dreams Come True
Cold Turkey
  He Gives Us All His Love
College Coach
  Lonely Lane
College Humor
  Down the Old Ox Road
  Learn To Croon
  Moonstruck
College Rhythm
  College Rhythm
  Stay As Sweet As You Are

The Five Pennies
   The Five Pennies
   Lullaby in Ragtime
   My Blue Heaven
Flame and the Flesh
   No One but You
Flap
   If Nobody Loves
The Fleet's In
   Arthur Murray Taught Me Dancing
      in a Hurry
   The Fleet's In
   I Remember You
   If You Build a Better Mousetrap
   Not Mine
   Somebody Else's Moon (Not Mine)
   Tangerine
   When You Hear the Time Signal
The Flight of the Phoenix
   The Phoenix Love Theme
Flipper's New Adventure
   Flipper
Flirtation Walk
   Flirtation Walk
   Mr. and Mrs. Is the Name
Flying Down to Rio
   Carioca
   Flying Down to Rio
   Music Makes Me
   Orchids in the Moonlight
F.M.
   F.M. (No Static at All)
   Livingston Saturday Night
   Poor Poor Pitiful Me
Folies Bergere
   I Was Lucky (C'etait Ecrit)
   Rhythm of the Rain
   You Took the Words Right Out of
      My Mouth
Follow the Band
   (Nobody Knows Better Than I) He's
      My Guy
Follow the Boys
   Beyond the Blue Horizon
   Follow the Boys
   I'll Walk Alone
   Is You Is, or Is You Ain't (Ma'
      Baby)
   Shoo-Shoo Baby

Follow the Fleet
   But Where Are You
   Get Thee behind Me Satan
   I'd Rather Lead a Band
   I'm Putting All My Eggs in One
      Basket
   Let Yourself Go
   Let's Face the Music and Dance
   We Saw the Sea
Follow the Leader
   Broadway
Follow Thru
   Button Up Your Overcoat!
   I Want To Be Bad
Follow Your Heart
   Follow Your Heart
   Magnolias in the Moonlight
   Who Minds about Me?
The Fool Killer
   The Fool Killer
Fools for Scandal
   There's a Boy in Harlem
Footlight Parade
   Ah, the Moon Is Here
   By a Waterfall
   Honeymoon Hotel
   Shanghai Lil
   Sittin' on a Backyard Fence
Footlights and Fools
   If I Can't Have You (If You Can't
      Have Me)
For Love of Ivy
   For Love of Ivy
For the Love of Benji
   Sunshine Smiles
For Whom the Bell Tolls
   A Love Like This
Force of Impulse
   The Blues I Got Comin'
      Tomorrow
   Strange Feeling
A Foreign Affair
   Black Market
The Forest Rangers
   Jingle Jangle Jingle
   Tall Grows the Timber
Forever Amber
   Forever Amber
Forever Darling
   Forever Darling

Night and Day
Gay Purr-ee
  Little Drops of Rain
  Mewsette
  Paris Is a Lonely Town
  Take My Hand, Paree
A Gay Ranchero
  A Gay Ranchero
Gentlemen Marry Brunettes
  Ain't Misbehavin'
  I've Got Five Dollars
  My Funny Valentine
Gentlemen Prefer Blondes
  Bye Bye Baby
  Diamonds Are a Girl's Best Friend
  A Little Girl from Little Rock
  When Love Goes Wrong
George White's 1935 Scandals
  According to the Moonlight
  It's an Old Southern Custom
  Nasty Man
George White's Scandals
  Liza (All the Clouds'll Roll Away)
Georgy Girl
  Georgy Girl
Get Hep to Love
  Siboney
Ghost Catchers
  These Foolish Things (Remind Me of You)
G.I. Blues
  Blue Suede Shoes
G.I. Joe
  Linda
Giant
  Giant
  There's Never Been Anyone Else but You
Gidget
  Gidget
Gidget Goes to Rome
  Gegetta
  Grande Luna Italiana (Gidget's Roman Moon)
The Gift of Love
  The Gift of Love
Gigi
  Gigi
  I Remember It Well
  I'm Glad I'm Not Young Anymore

The Night They Invented Champagne
  Thank Heaven for Little Girls
  Waltz at Maxim's
Gilda
  Put the Blame on Mame
Gimme Shelter
  Gimme Shelter
The Girl Can't Help It
  Blue Monday
Girl Crazy
  Bidin' My Time
  But Not for Me
  I Got Rhythm
  You've Got What Gets Me
The Girl Friend
  Two Together
Girl from Missouri
  A Hundred Years from Today
  Thank You for a Lovely Evening
Girl Happy
  Do the Clam
A Girl in Her Daddy's Bikini
  Attack
A Girl Named Tamiko
  A Girl Named Tamiko
Girl of the Golden West
  Who Are We To Say (Obey Your Heart)
The Girl Rush
  Birmin'ham
  An Occasional Man
Girls! Girls! Girls!
  Return to Sender
  Where Do You Come From?
Girlstown
  (I'm Just a) Lonely Boy
Give Me a Sailor
  Little Kiss at Twilight
  What Goes On Here in My Heart
Give Out Sisters
  Pennsylvania Polka
Give Us This Night
  Music in the Night (and Laughter in the Air)
The Glad Rag Doll
  Glad Rag Doll
The Glass Slipper
  Take My Love

I've Hitched My Wagon to a Star
   Silhouetted in the Moonlight
Hollywood Party
   Feelin' High
   I've Had My Moments
Hollywood Revue
   Blue Moon
Hollywood Revue of 1929
   Gotta Feelin' for You
   Low Down Rhythm
   Nobody but You
   Orange Blossom Time
   Singin' in the Rain
   You Were Meant for Me
   Your Mother and Mine
Holy Terror
   For You
   (I Am the Words), You Are the
     Melody
Home in Oklahoma
   The Everlasting Hills of Oklahoma
Home in Wyoming
   Tweedle-O-Twill
Honey
   Sing You Sinners
Honeymoon Lane
   The Little White House (at the End
     of Honeymoon Lane)
Honky Tonk
   He's a Good Man To Have Around
   I'm the Last of the Red Hot
     Mammas
Honolulu
   Honolulu
   This Night (Will Be My Souvenir)
Hooray for Love
   Hooray for Love
   I'm Livin' in a Great Big Way
   You're an Angel
Horse Feathers
   Ev'ryone Says "I Love You"
   Whatever It Is I'm Against It
Hot Heiress
   Like Ordinary People Do
Hound Dog Man
   Hound Dog Man
   This Friendly World
The House I Live In
   The House I Live In (That's America
     to Me)

Houseboat
   Almost in Your Arms
   Bing! Bang! Bong!
How Do I Love Thee
   How Do I Love Thee
How Green Was My Valley
   How Green Was My Valley
How the West Was Won
   How the West Was Won
How To Murder Your Wife
   How To Murder Your Wife
The Hucksters
   Don't Tell Me
Hullabaloo
   A Handful of Stars
   You Were Meant for Me
Humoresque
   Embraceable You
The Hurricane
   The Moon of Manakoora
Hush...Hush, Sweet Charlotte
   Hush...Hush, Sweet Charlotte
I Could Go On Singing
   By Myself
   I Could Go On Singing
   It Never Was You
I Cover the Waterfront
   I Cover the Waterfront
I Dood It
   Star Eyes
I Dream Too Much
   I Dream Too Much
   I Got Love
   I'm the Echo (You're the Song That
     I Sing)
   The Jockey on the Carousel
I Love Melvin
   A Lady Loves
I Married an Angel
   Did You Ever Get Stung?
   I Married an Angel
   I'll Tell the Man in the Street
   A Twinkle in Your Eyes
I Never Sang for My Father
   Strangers
I Surrender Dear
   I Surrender, Dear
I Walk Alone
   Don't Call It Love

Kansas City Bomber
  Kansas City Bomber
Kansas City Kitty
  Kansas City Kitty
Kathy-O
  Kathy-O
Keep 'em Flying
  You Don't Know What Love Is
Kein Mann zum Heiraten
  Banjo-Boy
Kelly's Heroes
  All for the Love of Sunshine
The Kentuckian
  The Kentuckian Song
Key Witness
  Ruby-Duby-Du
Kickin' the Moon Around
  Two Bouquets
The Kid from Brooklyn
  I Love an Old Fashioned Song
  You're the Cause of It All
The Kid from Spain
  What a Perfect Combination
Kid Millions
  An Earful of Music
  Okay Toots
  When My Ship Comes In
  Your Head on My Shoulder
Kid Nightingale
  Dancing with Tears in My Eyes
Killers Three
  Mama Tried
King Creole
  Don't Ask Me Why
  Hard Headed Woman
King of Burlesque
  I'm Shooting High
  I've Got My Fingers Crossed
  Lovely Lady
  Spreadin' Rhythm Around
  Whose Big Baby Are You
King of Jazz
  A Bench in the Park
  Happy Feet
  It Happened in Monterey
  Ragamuffin Romeo
The King of Jazz
  So the Bluebirds and the Blackbirds
    Got Together

King of Jazz
  Song of the Dawn
King of Kings
  King of Kings Theme
King of the Cowboys
  A Gay Ranchero
  I'm an Old Cow Hand (from the Rio
    Grande)
King Solomon of Broadway
  That's What You Think
The King Steps Out
  Stars in My Eyes
Kismet
  Stranger in Paradise
  Tell Me, Tell Me Evening Star
  Willow in the Wind
Kiss Me Deadly
  Blues from *Kiss Me Deadly*
Kiss Me Kate
  Always True to You (In My
    Fashion)
  Brush Up Your Shakespeare
  From This Moment On
  I Hate Men
  I've Come to Wive It Wealthily in
    Padua
  So in Love
  Tom, Dick or Harry
  Too Darn Hot
  We Open in Venice
  Were Thine That Special Face
  Where Is the Life That Late I Led?
  Why Can't You Behave
  Wunderbar
Kiss Me Stupid
  Wake Up, Brother, and Dance
Kiss the Boys Goodbye
  I'll Never Let a Day Pass By
  Kiss the Boys Goodbye
  Sand in My Shoes
Kiss Them for Me
  Kiss Them for Me
Kissin' Cousins
  Kissin' Cousins
The Kissing Bandit
  If I Steal a Kiss
  Love Is Where You Find It
  (I Offer You the Moon) Senorita
  Siesta
  What's Wrong with Me?

Klondike Annie
  Mister Deep Blue Sea
  Occidental Woman
Knickerbocker Holiday
  September Song
Knights of the Range
  Roll Along Covered Wagon
Knock on Wood
  Knock on Wood
Kotch
  Life Is What You Make It
La Cucaracha
  La Cucaracha
La Dolce Vita
  La Dolce Vita (The Sweet Life)
La Piscine
  Ask Yourself Why
  One at a Time
La Ronde
  La Ronde
La Strada
  Love Theme from *La Strada*
La Violetera
  Who'll Buy My Violets? (La
  Violetera)
Ladies' Man
  Cocktails for Two
  I Gotta Gal I Love (In North and
  South Dakota)
  What Am I Gonna Do about You?
Ladies They Talk About
  If I Could Be with You One Hour
  To-Night
The Lady and the Tramp
  He's a Tramp
  The Siamese Cat Song
Lady, Be Good
  Fascinating Rhythm
  The Last Time I Saw Paris
  Oh Lady, Be Good
Lady in the Dark
  Jenny
  My Ship
  Suddenly It's Spring
Lady Let's Dance
  Silver Shadows and Golden Dreams
The Lady Objects
  Mist over the Moon
  That Week in Paris

Lady of the Pavements
  Where Is the Song of Songs for Me?
Lady on a Train
  Gimme a Little Kiss, Will Ya Huh?
  Night and Day
Lady Sings the Blues
  Good Morning Heartache
  Happy (Love Theme from *Lady
  Sings the Blues*)
Land of the Pharaohs
  Land of the Pharaohs
Las Vegas Nights
  Dolores
The Las Vegas Story
  I Get Along without You Very Well
  (except Sometimes)
  My Resistance Is Low
The Last American Hero
  I Got a Name
The Last Round-Up
  An Apple for the Teacher
The Last Sunset
  Pretty Little Girl in the Yellow Dress
Last Tango in Paris
  Last Tango in Paris
The Last Tycoon
  You Have the Choice
The Late Show
  What Was
Laugh, Clown, Laugh
  Laugh! Clown! Laugh!
Laughing Irish Eyes
  All My Life
  Laughing Irish Eyes
Laura
  Laura
Lawrence of Arabia
  Theme from *Lawrence of Arabia*
Leave It to Lester
  I'm Yours
The Lemon Drop Kid
  Silver Bells
Les Demoiselles de Rochefort
  You Must Believe in Spring
Les Girls
  Ca, C'est l'Amour
Les Portes de la Nuit
  Autumn Leaves
Let Freedom Ring
  Dusty Road

2640

My Love Parade
  Paris, Stay the Same
Love Story
  Cornish Rhapsody
  Theme from *Love Story*
Love Thy Neighbor
  Dearest, Darest I
  Do You Know Why
  Isn't That Just Like Love
  My Heart Belongs to Daddy
Love with the Proper Stranger
  Love with the Proper Stranger
Lovely To Look At
  I Won't Dance
  Lovely To Look At
  Smoke Gets in Your Eyes
Lover, Come Back
  Just a Gigolo
Lover Come Back
  Lover Come Back
  Should I Surrender
Lovers and Other Strangers
  For All We Know
Loving You
  (Let Me Be Your) Teddy Bear
The Luck of Ginger Coffey
  The Luck of Ginger Coffey
    (Watching the World Go By)
Lucky Boy
  My Blackbirds Are Bluebirds Now
  My Mother's Eyes
Lucky Lady
  Lucky Lady
Lucky Me
  I Speak to the Stars
Lullaby of Broadway
  I Love the Way You Say Goodnight
  Just One of Those Things
  Lullaby of Broadway
  Please Don't Talk about Me When
    I'm Gone
  Zing Went the Strings of My Heart
Luxury Liner
  Yes! We Have No Bananas
The Mack
  Theme of *The Mack*
Mad about Music
  Chapel Bells
  I Love To Whistle
  A Serenade to the Stars

Madron
  Till Love Touches Your Life
The Magic Christian
  Come and Get It
The Magic Fountain
  The Magic Fountain
The Magic Garden of Stanley
    Sweetheart
  Nobody Knows
  Sweet Gingerbread Man
The Magnificent Seven
  The Magnificent Seven
Mahogany
  Do You Know Where You're Going
    To
The Main Event
  The Main Event/Fight
A Majority of One
  Theme from *A Majority of One*
Make a Wish
  Make a Wish
  Music in My Heart
Make Mine Music
  All the Cats Join In
  Casey at the Bat
  Johnny Fedora and Alice Blue
    Bonnet
  Without You
Malamondo
  Funny World
Malaya
  Blue Moon
  Paradise
Mammy
  Let Me Sing and I'm Happy
  Looking at You (across the Breakfast
    Table)
  My Mammy
  To My Mammy
Man about Town
  Figety Joe
  Strange Enchantment
  That Sentimental Sandwich
A Man and a Woman
  A Man and a Woman
A Man Could Get Killed
  Strangers in the Night
The Man from Laramie
  The Man from Laramie

Man from Music Mountain
  I'm Thinking Tonight of My Blue
    Eyes
The Man from the Diners' Club
  The Man from the Diners' Club
The Man I Love
  Body and Soul
Man of La Mancha
  The Impossible Dream (The Quest)
Man on Fire
  Man on Fire
The Man Who Knew Too Much
  Que Sera, Sera
The Man Who Shot Liberty Valance
  The Man Who Shot Liberty Valance
The Man with the Golden Arm
  The Man with the Golden Arm
  Molly-O
Mandalay
  When Tomorrow Comes
Manhattan Angel
  Candy Store Blues
Manhattan Melodrama
  Blue Moon
Mannequin
  Always and Always
Many Rivers To Cross
  The Berry Tree
Margie
  Margie
Marianne
  Blondy
  Just You, Just Me
Marine Raiders
  Bless'em All
Marjorie Morningstar
  A Very Precious Love
The Marriage-Go-Round
  The Marriage-Go-Round
Marriage on the Rocks
  Sinner Man
Married in Hollywood
  Dance Away the Night
Martin Block's Musical Merry-Go-
    Round
  Makin' Love, Mountain Style
Mary Poppins
  Chim Chim Cher-ee
  Feed the Birds (Tuppence a Bag)
  I Love To Laugh

Jolly Holiday
Let's Go Fly a Kite
The Life I Lead
The Perfect Nanny
Sister Suffragette
A Spoonful of Sugar
Stay Awake
Step in Time
Supercalifragilisticexpialidocious
M*A*S*H
  Song from M*A*S*H (Suicide Is
    Painless)
The Mating Game
  The Mating Game
The Mating Season
  When I Take My Sugar to Tea
A Matter of Innocence
  Pretty Polly
The Mayor of 44th Street
  When There's a Breeze on Lake
    Louise
Maytime
  Farewell to Dreams
McCabe and Mrs. Miller
  Sisters of Mercy
  The Stranger Song
  Winter Lady
McLintock!
  McLintock's Theme (Love in the
    Country)
Meatballs
  Meatballs
Medicine Ball Caravan
  Free the People
Meet Danny Wilson
  All of Me
  I've Got a Crush on You
  (I Got a Woman, Crazy for Me)
    She's Funny That Way
  That Old Black Magic
  You're a Sweetheart
Meet Me in St. Louis
  The Boy Next Door
  Boys and Girls Like You and Me
  Have Yourself a Merry Little
    Christmas
  Skip to My Lou
  The Trolley Song
  You and I

I'm an Indian
My Man (Mon Homme)
Second Hand Rose
My Own True Love
  My Own True Love
My Six Loves
  My Six Loves
My Weakness
  Gather Lip Rouge While You May
Nana
  That's Love
Nancy Goes to Rio
  Magic Is the Moonlight
Nashville
  Idaho Home
  I'm Easy
  It Don't Worry Me

Naughty but Nice
  Hooray for Spinach
  I'm Happy about the Whole Thing
  In a Moment of Weakness

Neptune's Daughter
  Baby, It's Cold Outside

Never a Dull Moment
  My Blue Heaven
  Sleepy Time Gal

Never on Sunday
  Never on Sunday

Never Say Goodbye
  Remember Me?

New Faces of 1937
  Love Is Never out of Season
  New Faces
  Our Penthouse on Third Avenue
  Peckin'

The New Interns
  Come On, Let Yourself Go

A New Kind of Love
  In the Park in Paree
  Mimi
  Paris Mist
  Theme from *A New Kind of Love*
  You Brought a New Kind of Love to
    Me

  The New Moon (1930)
    Lover, Come Back to Me

One Kiss
Stouthearted Men
Wanting You
The New Moon (1940)
  Lover, Come Back to Me
  Marianne
  One Kiss
  Softly, As in a Morning Sunrise
  Stouthearted Men
  Wanting You
New Orleans
  Do You Know What It Means To
    Miss New Orleans

  Where the Blues Were Born in New
    Orleans
New York, New York
  Happy Ending
  Theme from *New York, New York*

New York Nights
  A Year from Today

New York Town
  Love in Bloom
Night and Day
  Begin the Beguine
  Do I Love You?
  I Get a Kick out of You
  I'm in Love Again
  I've Got You Under My Skin
  Just One of Those Things
  Miss Otis Regrets (She's Unable To
    Lunch Today)
  My Heart Belongs to Daddy
  Night and Day
  What Is This Thing Called Love?
  You Do Something to Me
  You're the Top

A Night at the Opera
  Alone
  Cosi Cosa
  I'm in Love with My Car

The Night Has a Thousand Eyes
  The Night Has a Thousand Eyes

The Night Is Young
  When I Grow Too Old To Dream
Nitwits
  Music in My Heart

We Will Always Be Sweethearts
100 Men and a Girl
  It's Raining Sunbeams
One in a Million
  Who's Afraid of Love
One Minute to Zero
  When I Fall in Love
One More Tomorrow
  One More Tomorrow
One Night in the Tropics
  Remind Me
One Night of Love
  One Night of Love
One on One
  John Wayne
  My Fair Share
One Potato, Two Potato
  One Potato, Two Potato
One Touch of Venus
  (Don't Look Now, but) My Heart Is
    Showing
  My Week
  Speak Low
  That's Him
One, Two, Three
  The One, Two, Three Waltz
Operator 13
  Jungle Fever
  Once in a Lifetime
  Sleepy Head
The Opposite Sex
  Now! Baby, Now!
  The Young Man with a Horn
Orchestra Wives
  At Last
  I've Got a Gal in Kalamazoo
  People Like You and Me
  Serenade in Blue
  That's Sabotage
Other Side of the Mountain
  Richard's Window
The Other Side of the Mountain, Part
  Two
  The Other Side of the Mountain,
    Part Two
Our Dancing Daughters
  I Loved You Then As I Love You
    Now
Out of This World
  June Comes Around Every Year

Out of This World
Over the Trail
  Have I Told You Lately That I Love
    You
The Pagan
  Pagan Love Song
Pagan Love Song
  Pagan Love Song
  The Sea of the Moon
Page Miss Glory
  Page Miss Glory
Painting the Clouds with Sunshine
  Painting the Clouds with Sunshine
  Tip Toe through the Tulips with Me
Pal Joey
  Bewitched
  I Could Write a Book
  I Didn't Know What Time It Was
  The Lady Is a Tramp
  My Funny Valentine
  There's a Small Hotel
Paleface
  Buttons and Bows
Palm Beach Story
  Goodnight Sweetheart
Palm Springs
  I Don't Want To Make History (I
    Just Want To Make Love)
  I'm in the Mood for Love
Palmy Days
  Bend Down Sister
  There's Nothing Too Good for My
    Baby
Palooka
  Count Your Blessings
  Inka Dinka Doo
Pan-Americana
  Stars in Your Eyes
Pandora and the Flying Dutchman
  How Am I To Know?
Papa's Delicate Condition
  Call Me Irresponsible
Paper Tiger
  My Little Friend
Paradise Alley
  Too Close to Paradise
Paradise Isle
  Paradise Isle

Somebody Loves Me
Summertime
The Yankee Doodle Blues
Rhythm on the Range
Empty Saddles
The House Jack Built for Jill
I Can't Escape from You
I'm an Old Cow Hand (from the Rio Grande)
(If You Can't Sing It) You'll Have To Swing It
Rhythm on the River
Only Forever
Rhythm on the River
That's for Me
When the Moon Comes over Madison Square (The Love Lament of a Western Gent)
Rich, Young and Pretty
Dark Is the Night
I Can See You
There's Danger in Your Eyes, Cherie!
We Never Talk Much
Wonder Why

Ride 'em Cowboy
I'll Remember April
A-Tisket A-Tasket

Ride Tenderfoot Ride
Leanin' on the Ole Top Rail
The Woodpecker Song

Riders in the Sky
Riders in the Sky
Riders of the Whistling Pines
Toolie Oolie Doolie (The Yodel Polka)
Ridin' Down the Canyon
My Little Buckaroo
Ridin' on a Rainbow
Be Honest with Me

Riding High
The Horse Told Me
Sunshine Cake
(We've Got) A Sure Thing

Rio Bravo
Rio Bravo

Rio Conchos
Rio Conchos

Rio Rita
Long Before You Came Along
You're Always in My Arms (but Only in My Dreams)
Rio Rita (1929)
The Rangers' Song
Rio Rita
Rio Rita (1942)
The Rangers' Song
Rio Rita
Riptide
Riptide
The Ritz
Liberated Man
River of No Return
River of No Return
Road House
Again
Road to Bali
Chicago Style
The Road to Hong Kong
Let's Not Be Sensible
The Road to Hong Kong
Teamwork
Warmer Than a Whisper
Road to Morocco
Ain't Got a Dime to My Name (Ho Ho Ho Ho Hum)
Constantly
Moonlight Becomes You
Road to Morocco
Road to Rio
Apalachicola, Fla.
Be Beautiful
Experience
You Don't Have To Know the Language
Road to Singapore
Sweet Potato Piper
Too Romantic

Road to Utopia
It's Anybody's Spring
Personality
Put It There, Pal
Welcome to My Dream
Would You

Road to Zanzibar
Birds of a Feather
It's Always You

Poor You

Ship Cafe
 Change Your Mind
 Fatal Fascination

Shipmates Forever
 Abdul Abulbul Amir
 (Shipmates Forever) Don't Give Up
 the Ship
 I'd Rather Listen to Your Eyes

The Shocking Miss Pilgrim
 Back Bay Polka
 Changing My Tune
 For You, for Me, for Evermore

Shoot the Works
 Take a Lesson from the Lark
 Were Your Ears Burning, Baby?
 With My Eyes Wide Open, I'm
 Dreaming

Shopworn Angel
 A Precious Little Thing Called
 Love

Show Boat
 Here Comes the Show Boat
 I Have the Room Above
 I Still Suits Me
 The Lonesome Road

Show Boat (1929)
 Bill
 Can't Help Lovin' Dat Man
 Ol'Man River

Show Boat (1936)
 Bill
 Can't Help Lovin' Dat Man
 Make Believe
 Ol'Man River
 You Are Love

Show Boat (1951)
 Bill
 Can't Help Lovin' Dat Man
 I Might Fall Back on You
 Life upon the Wicked Stage
 Make Believe
 Ol'Man River

Why Do I Love You?
 You Are Love

Show Business
 Dinah

Show Girl in Hollywood
 My Sin

The Show of Shows
 If I Could Learn To Love (As Well
 As I Fight)
 Just an Hour of Love
 Lady Luck
 The Only Song I Know
 Singin' in the Bathtub
 You Were Meant for Me
 Your Love Is All That I Crave
 Your Mother and Mine

Sierra Sue
 Sierra Sue

Siete Mujeres
 Maria from Bahia

Silent Running
 Silent Running

Silver Spurs
 Tumbling Tumbleweeds

Since You Went Away
 Together

Sincerely Yours
 Sincerely Yours

Sing a Jingle
 Beautiful Love

Sing and Be Happy
 Travelin' Light
 What a Beautiful Beginning

Sing, Baby, Sing
 Love Will Tell

 The Music Goes 'Round and
 Around
 Sing, Baby, Sing
 Singing a Vagabond Song
 When Did You Leave Heaven
 When My Baby Smiles at Me
 You Turned the Tables on Me

Sing Me a Love Song
 Summer Night

Important Performances Index — Movie

Sweet Rosie O'Grady
  My Heart Tells Me (Should I Believe
    My Heart?)
Sweetheart of Sigma Chi
  And Then It's Heaven
  Five Minutes More
Sweetheart of the Fleet
  We Did It Before (And We Can Do
    It Again)
Sweetie
  He's So Unusual
  My Sweeter Than Sweet
Swing Fever
  Mississippi Dream Boat
Swing High, Swing Low
  Panamania
  Swing High, Swing Low
  (If It Isn't Pain) Then It Isn't Love
Swing in the Saddle
  When It's Harvest Time in Peaceful
    Valley
Swing Parade of 1946
  Just a Little Fond Affection
  Stormy Weather
Swing Symphony
  Cow-Cow Boogie (Cuma-Ti-Yi-Yi-
    Ay)
Swing Time
  Bojangles of Harlem
  A Fine Romance
  Never Gonna Dance
  Pick Yourself Up
  Waltz in Swingtime
  The Way You Look Tonight
Swing Your Lady
  Hillbilly from Tenth Avenue
Swiss Family Robinson
  Swiss Family Theme (My Heart Was
    an Island)
Sylvia
  Sylvia
Syncopation
  I'll Always Be in Love with You
  Jericho
Tabu
  Tabu
Tahiti Nights
  Cockeyed Mayor of Kaunakakai
Take a Chance
  Come Up and See Me Sometime

Eadie Was a Lady
  It's Only a Paper Moon
  New Deal Rhythm
  Night Owl
  Rise 'n Shine
  Should I Be Sweet?
Take Me Back to Oklahoma
  You Are My Sunshine
Take Me Out to the Ball Game
  Last Night When We Were Young
  The Right Girl for Me
  Strictly U.S.A.
Taking Off
  Goodbye, So Long
  Long Term Physical Effects
Tall, Dark and Handsome
  Wishful Thinking
Tammy and the Bachelor
  Tammy
Taras Bulba
  Theme from *Taras Bulba*
Tars and Spars
  I'm Glad I Waited for You
  Love Is a Merry-Go-Round
Tea for Two
  Charleston
  Crazy Rhythm
  Do Do Do
  I Know That You Know
  I Want To Be Happy
  No, No, Nanette
  Oh Me! Oh My!
  Tea for Two
Teacher's Pet
  Teacher's Pet
Tell It to the Judge
  Let's Fall in Love
Tell Me That You Love Me, Junie
  Moon
  Old Devil Time
10
  It's Easy to Say
10,000 Bedrooms
  Guaglioni
  Only Trust Your Heart
Tender Is the Night
  Tender Is the Night

The Tender Trap
  (Love Is) The Tender Trap
Tenderloin
  Lovely Laurie
The Texans
  Silver on the Sage
Thank God It's Friday
  Easy
  Last Dance
  Thank God Its Friday
  Too Hot ta Trot
Thank Your Lucky Stars
  The Dreamer
  How Sweet You Are
  I'm Ridin' for a Fall
  Thank Your Lucky Stars
  They're Either Too Young or Too
    Old
Thanks a Million
  Happy Days Are Here Again
  I'm Sitting High on a Hilltop
  I've Got a Pocketful of Sunshine
  New O'leans
  Sugar Plum
  Thanks a Million
Thanks for Everything
  Thanks for Ev'rything
Thanks for the Memory
  Two Sleepy People
That Certain Age
  Be a Good Scout
  My Own
  That Certain Age
  You're As Pretty As a Picture
That Certain Feeling
  That Certain Feeling
That Girl from Paris
  Seal It with a Kiss
That Lady in Ermine
  This Is the Moment
That Midnight Kiss
  Three o'Clock in the Morning
That Night in Rio
  Boa Noite
  Cae Cae
  Chica Chica Boom Chic
  I, Yi, Yi, Yi, Yi (I Like You Very
    Much)
  They Met in Rio (A Midnight
    Serenade)

That's Right—You're Wrong
  Scatterbrain
  The Little Red Fox (N'ya N'ya Ya
    Can't Catch Me)
Their Own Desire
  Blue Is the Night
There Was a Crooked Man
  There Was a Crooked Man
There's No Business Like Show
    Business
  After You Get What You Want, You
    Don't Want It
  Heat Wave
  Lazy
  Let's Have Another Cup of Coffee
  Remember
  There's No Business Like Show
    Business
They Call Me Mister Tibbs
  Soul Flower
They Came to Cordura
  They Came to Cordura
They Met in Argentina
  Amarillo
  Cutting the Cane
  Simpatica
  You've Got the Best of Me
36 Hours
  Theme from *36 Hours* (A Heart
    Must Learn To Cry)
This Earth Is Mine
  On the Sunny Side of the Street
  This Earth Is Mine
This Happy Feeling
  This Happy Feeling
This is Heaven
  This Is Heaven
This Is My Affair
  I Hum a Waltz
This Is the Life
  At Sundown
  L'Amour, Toujours, L'Amour—Love
    Everlasting
  With a Song in My Heart
This Is the Night
  This Is the Night
This Property Is Condemned
  Wish Me a Rainbow

Wake Up and Live
A Walk in the Spring Rain
  A Walk in the Spring Rain
Walk on the Wild Side
  Somewhere in the Used To Be
  Walk on the Wild Side
Walkin' My Baby Back Home
  Walkin' My Baby Back Home
Walking Tall
  Walking Tall
Walter Wanger's Vogues of 1938
  Lovely One
  That Old Feeling
War and Peace
  War and Peace
The Warriors
  In the City
  Last of an Ancient Breed
The Way We Were
  The Way We Were
Weary River
  Weary River
Week-End at the Waldorf
  And There You Are
Week-End in Havana
  Tropical Magic
  A Week-End in Havana
Welcome Stranger
  As Long As I'm Dreaming
  Country Style (Square Dance)
  My Heart Is a Hobo
  Smile Right Back at the Sun
Welcome to L. A.
  Welcome to L. A.
We're Not Dressing
  Good Night Lovely Little Lady
  It's the Animal in Me
  Love Thy Neighbor
  May I?
  Once in a Blue Moon
  (She Walks Like You—She Talks
    Like You) She Reminds Me of
    You
Westward Ho the Wagons!
  Wringle Wrangle
Wet Blanket Policy
  Woody Woodpecker
What a Way To Go
  Louisa's Theme

What a Way To Go!
  What a Way to Go
What a Widow!
  Love Is Like a Song
  You're the One
What Did You Do in the War, Daddy?
  In the Arms of Love
What Price Glory
  Charmaine
What's Buzzin' Cousin?
  Ain't That Just Like a Man
  Nevada
What's Cookin' Soldier
  Blue Flame
  What To Do
  You Can't Hold a Memory in Your
    Arms
What's Cooking?
  I'll Pray for You
What's New, Pussycat?
  Here I Am
  My Little Red Book (All I Do Is
    Talk about You)
  What's New, Pussycat?
The Wheeler Dealers
  The Wheeler Dealers
When Irish Eyes Are Smiling
  I'll Forget You
When Johnny Comes Marching Home
  We Must Be Vigilant
When Love Is Young
  When Love Is Young
When My Baby Smiles at Me
  By the Way
  What Did I Do?
When the Boys Meet the Girls
  Bidin' My Time
  But Not for Me
  Embraceable You
  Listen, People
When the Lights Go On Again
  When the Lights Go On Again (All
    over the World)
When You're in Love
  Our Song
  Siboney
  The Whistling Boy
Where Do We Go from Here?
  All at Once
  If Love Remains

Important Performances Index — Musical

Don't Think It Ain't Been Charming
I'd Know You Anywhere
I've Got a One Track Mind
Like the Fella Once Said
You've Got Me This Way (Whatta-
Ya-Gonna Do about It)
You'll Never Get Rich
Dream Dancing
Since I Kissed My Baby Goodbye
So Near and Yet So Far
Young As You Feel
The Cute Little Things You Do
Young at Heart
Hold Me in Your Arms
Just One of Those Things
Ready, Willing and Able
Someone To Watch over Me
Young at Heart
The Young Land
Strange Are the Ways of Love
Young Love
Young Love
Young Man with a Horn
Avalon
Can't We Be Friends?
I May Be Wrong (but I Think
You're Wonderful)
Lovin' Sam, the Sheik of Alabam'
The Man I Love
Melancholy Rhapsody
Moanin' Low
Tea for Two
The Very Thought of You
What Is This Thing Called Love?
With a Song in My Heart
The Young Ones
When the Boy in Your Arms Is the
Boy in Your Heart
The Young Ones
Young People
Tra-La-La
You're a Big Boy Now
Darling Be Home Soon
You're a Sweetheart
Broadway Jamboree
My Fine Feathered Friend
You're a Sweetheart
You're My Everything
I May Be Wrong (but I Think
You're Wonderful)

On the Good Ship Lollipop
You're My Everything
You're Never Too Young
Relax-Ay-Voo
You're the One
I Could Kiss You for That
You're the One (For Me)
Youth on Parade
I've Heard That Song Before
Ziegfeld Follies
The Babbitt and the Bromide
Limehouse Blues
Love
This Heart of Mine
Ziegfeld Girl
Minnie from Trinidad
Mister Gallagher and Mister Shean
Too Beautiful To Last
You Stepped Out of a Dream
Zorba the Greek
Theme from *Zorba the Greek*
Zwei Herzen im Dreivierteltakt
Two Hearts in Three-Quarter Time

Musical
Ace of Clubs
Sail Away
The Act
It's the Strangest Thing
My Own Space
Shine It On
Afgar
Caresses
Why Don't You?
Ain't Supposed to Die a Natural Death
Lily Done the Zampoughi Every
Time I Pulled Her Coattail
Tenth and Greenwich (Women's
House of Detention)
All American
Have a Dream
I Couldn't Have Done It Alone
I'm Fascinating
I've Just Seen Her
Nightlife
Once upon a Time
Our Children
What a Country!

Way Out West (on West End
  Avenue)
Where or When
Bajour
  I Can
  Living Simply
  Love Is a Chance
  Love-Line
  Must It Be Love?
Baker Street
  Finding Words for Spring
  I'd Do It Again
  A Married Man
  What a Night This Is Going To Be!
Ballroom
  Fifty Percent
Ballyhoo
  I'm One of God's Children (Who
    Hasn't Got Wings)
Banjo Eyes
  Nickel to My Name
  Not a Care in the World
  We Did It Before (And We Can Do
    It Again)
  We're Having a Baby
Barefoot Boy with Cheek
  After Graduation Day
Beggar's Holiday
  I've Got Me
  Maybe I Should Change My Ways
  On the Wrong Side of the Railroad
    Track
  Take Love Easy
  Tomorrow Mountain
  When I Walk with You
Bells Are Ringing
  Bells Are Ringing
  Independent (On My Own)
  Just in Time
  Long Before I Knew You
  Mu-Cha-Cha
  The Party's Over
Ben Franklin in Paris
  Half the Battle
  Look for Small Pleasures
  To Be Alone with You
Best Foot Forward
  Buckle Down, Winsocki
  Ev'ry Time
  I Know You by Heart

Just a Little Joint with a Juke Box
Shady Lady Bird
That's How I Love the Blues
The Three B's
What Do You Think I Am?
The Best Little Whorehouse in Texas
  Doatsy Mae
  Hard Candy Christmas
  No Lies
  24 Hours of Loving
Betsy
  Blue Skies
  Sing
  Stonewall Moskowitz March
  This Funny World
Between the Devil
  By Myself
  I See Your Face before Me
  Triplets
  Why Did You Do It?
  You Have Everything
Big Boy
  As Long As I've Got My Mammy
  Born and Bred in Old Kentucky
  Golden Gate
  Hello Tucky
  If You Knew Susie Like I Know
    Susie
  It All Depends on You
  Keep Smiling at Trouble
Billie
  Billie
  Where Were You-Where Was I?
Billy Rose's Jumbo
  The Circus on Parade
  Diavalo
  Little Girl Blue
  The Most Beautiful Girl in the
    World
  My Romance
  Over and Over Again
  There's a Small Hotel
Bloomer Girl
  The Eagle and Me
  Evelina
  I Got a Song
  Right As the Rain
  T'morra', T'morra'

Hello Daddy
  In a Great Big Way
  Let's Sit and Talk about You
  Out Where the Blues Begin
Hello, Dolly!
  Before the Parade Passes By
  Dancing
  Elegance
  Hello, Dolly!
  I Put My Hand In
  It Only Takes a Moment
  It Takes a Woman
  The Motherhood March
  Put On Your Sunday Clothes
  So Long, Dearie
Hello Yourself!!!
  I Want the World To Know
Her Family Tree
  Why Worry?
Here Goes the Bride
  Hello, My Lover, Good-bye
Here's Howe
  Crazy Rhythm
  Imagination
Here's Love
  Arm in Arm
  The Big Clown Balloons
  Expect Things To Happen
  Here's Love
  Look, Little Girl
  My State, My Kansas, My Home
  My Wish
  Pine Cones and Holly Berries
  That Man Over There
  You Don't Know
High Button Shoes
  Can't You Just See Yourself
  Get Away for a Day (In the
    Country)
  I Still Get Jealous
  On a Sunday by the Sea
  Papa, Won't You Dance with Me
  There's Nothing Like a Model "T"
  You're My Girl
High Spirits
  Forever and a Day
  I Know Your Heart
  If I Gave You. . .
  Something Tells Me

Was She Prettier Than I?
  You'd Better Love Me
Higher and Higher
  Ev'ry Sunday Afternoon
  From Another World
  It Never Entered My Mind
  Nothing but You
Hit the Deck
  Hallelujah!
  Sometimes I'm Happy
Hold Everything!
  Don't Hold Everything
  You're the Cream in My Coffee
Hold On to Your Hats
  Don't Let It Get You Down
  There's a Great Day Coming
    Manana
  The World Is in My Arms
Hold Your Horses
  If I Love Again
Honeydew
  Believe Me, Beloved
  Drop Me a Line
  Oh, How I Long for Someone
Honeymoon Lane
  Half a Moon
  Jersey Walk
  The Little White House (at the End
    of Honeymoon Lane)
  Mary Dear
Hooray for What!
  Buds Won't Bud
  Down with Love
  God's Country
  In the Shade of the New Apple Tree
  I've Gone Romantic on You
  Life's a Dance
  Moanin' in the Mornin'
Hot-cha!
  You Can Make My Life a Bed of
    Roses
House of Flowers
  House of Flowers
  I Never Has Seen Snow
  A Sleepin' Bee
  Smellin' of Vanilla
  Two Ladies in de Shade of de
    Banana Tree

Important Performances Index — Musical

Jo
  Brown Baby
Jubilee
  Begin the Beguine
  Just One of Those Things
  Me and Marie
  A Picture of Me without You
  Waltz down the Aisle
  When Love Comes Your Way
  Why Shouldn't I
Jump for Joy
  The Brown-Skin Gal in the Calico
    Gown
  Chocolate Shake
  I Got It Bad (And That Ain't Good)
  Jump for Joy
June Love
  Dear Love, My Love
Kean
  Chime In!
  Elena
  The Fog and the Grog
  Sweet Danger
  To Look upon My Love
  Willow, Willow, Willow
Keep Off the Grass
  Clear out of This World
  Crazy As a Loon
  A Latin Tune, a Manhattan Moon
    and You
  On the Old Park Bench
  Two in a Taxi
Kelly
  I'll Never Go There Anymore
Kid Boots
  Alabamy Bound
  Dinah
  I'm Goin' South
  Someone Loves You After All
The King and I
  Getting To Know You
  Hello, Young Lovers
  I Have Dreamed
  I Whistle a Happy Tune
  The March of the Siamese Children
  A Puzzlement
  Shall We Dance?
  Something Wonderful
  We Kiss in a Shadow

Kismet
  And This Is My Beloved
  Baubles, Bangles, and Beads
  Fate
  He's in Love
  Night of My Nights
  Not Since Nineveh
  Sands of Time
Kiss Me Kate
  Always True to You (In My
    Fashion)
  Another Op'nin', Another Show
  Bianca
  Brush Up Your Shakespeare
  I Am Ashamed That Women Are So
    Simple
  I Hate Men
  I've Come to Wive It Wealthily in
    Padua
  So in Love
  Tom, Dick or Harry
  Too Darn Hot
  We Open in Venice
  Were Thine That Special Face
  Where Is the Life That Late I Led?
  Why Can't You Behave
  Wunderbar
Knickerbocker Holiday
  How Can You Tell an American?
  It Never Was You
  September Song
  There's Nowhere To Go but Up
  Will You Remember Me?
Kwamina
  Another Time, Another Place
  Nothing More To Look Forward To
  Ordinary People
  Something Big
  What Happened to Me Tonight?
  What's Wrong with Me?
Lady, Be Good!
  Fascinating Rhythm
  The Half of It Dearie Blues
  Hang On to Me
  Little Jazz Bird
  The Man I Love
  Oh Lady, Be Good
  So Am I
  Swiss Miss

Important Performances Index - Musical

2683

Empty Pockets Filled with Love
The First Lady
Glad To Be Home
I'm Gonna Get Him
In Our Hide-Away
Is He the Only Man in the World
It Gets Lonely in the White House
I've Got To Be Around
Let's Go Back to the Waltz
Meat and Potatoes
The Only Dance I Know
Pigtails and Freckles
The Secret Service
They Love Me
The Washington Twist
Mr. Wonderful
I'm Available
Mr. Wonderful
Too Close for Comfort
Molly
If Everyone Got What They Wanted
In Your Eyes
More Than You Deserve
More Than You Deserve
What Became of the People We Were
The Most Happy Fella
Big D
Don't Cry
Happy To Make Your Acquaintance
Joey, Joey, Joey
The Most Happy Fella
My Heart Is So Full of You
Somebody, Somewhere
Standing on the Corner
Warm All Over
Murder at the Vanities
Sweet Madness
Music Box Revue of 1923
An Orange Grove in California
Music in the Air
And Love Was Born
I Am So Eager
I'm Alone
In Egern on the Tegern See
I've Told Every Little Star
One More Dance
The Song Is You
When the Spring Is in the Air
The Music Man
Goodnight My Someone

It's You
Lida Rose
Marian the Librarian
Seventy Six Trombones
Till There Was You
Will I Ever Tell You
My Fair Lady
Ascot Gavotte
Get Me to the Church on Time
I Could Have Danced All Night
I'm an Ordinary Man
I've Grown Accustomed to Her Face
Just You Wait
On the Street Where You Live
The Rain in Spain
Show Me
Why Can't the English
With a Little Bit of Luck
Wouldn't It Be Loverly?
Nellie Bly
Harmony
Just My Luck
The Nervous Set
The Ballad of the Sad Young Men
I've Got a Lot To Learn about Life
Laugh, I Thought I'd Die
Spring Can Really Hang You Up the
Most
New Girl in Town
Did You Close Your Eyes When We
Kissed
It's Good To Be Alive
Look at 'er
The New Yorkers
The Great Indoors
I Happen To Like New York
I'm Getting Myself Ready for You
Let's Fly Away
Love for Sale
Take Me Back to Manhattan
Where Have You Been?
The Night Boat
Left All Alone Again Blues
Whose Baby Are You?
A Night Out
Sometimes I'm Happy
Nina Rosa
Nina Rosa
Your Smiles, Your Tears

No, No, Nanette
  I Want To Be Happy
  No, No, Nanette
  Tea for Two
  Too Many Rings around Rosie
  You Can Dance with Any Girl At All
No Strings
  Be My Host
  Eager Beaver
  How Sad
  La La La
  Loads of Love
  Look No Further
  Love Makes the World Go
  Maine
  The Man Who Has Everything
  No Strings
  Nobody Told Me
  An Orthodox Fool
  The Sweetest Sounds
Nymph Errant
  Experiment
  How Could We Be Wrong
  The Physician
  Solomon
  When Love Comes Your Way
The O'Brien Girl
  Learn To Smile
Of Thee I Sing
  Because, Because
  The Illegitimate Daughter
  Love Is Sweeping the Country
  Of Thee I Sing
  Who Cares? (So Long As You Care for Me)
  Wintergreen for President
Oh Captain!
  All the Time
  Femininity
  Give It All You've Got
  The Morning Music of Montmartre
  Surprise
  We're Not Children
  You Don't Know Him
  You're So Right for Me
Oh, Kay!
  Clap Yo' Hands
  Dear Little Girl
  Do Do Do

Fidgety Feet
  Maybe
  Someone To Watch over Me
Oh, Please!
  I Know That You Know
  Like He Loves Me
Oklahoma!
  All er Nothin'
  Boys and Girls Like You and Me
  The Farmer and the Cowman
  I Cain't Say No
  Kansas City
  Many a New Day
  Oh, What a Beautiful Mornin'
  Oklahoma
  Out of My Dreams
  People Will Say We're In Love
  Pore Jud
  The Surrey with the Fringe on Top
Oliver!
  As Long As He Needs Me
  Consider Yourself
  Food, Glorious Food
  I'd Do Anything
  Where Is Love?
  Who Will Buy?
On a Clear Day You Can See Forever
  Come Back to Me
  Melinda
  On a Clear Day (You Can See Forever)
  She Wasn't You
  Wait Till We're Sixty-Five
On the Town
  Come Up to My Place
  I Can Cook Too
  I Get Carried Away
  Lonely Town
  Lucky To Be Me
  New York, New York
  Some Other Time
  Ya Got Me
On the Twentieth Century
  Five Zeros
  I Rise Again
  The Legacy
  Our Private World
On Your Toes
  Glad To Be Unhappy
  The Heart Is Quicker Than the Eye

Willa, Willa
Seesaw
  He's Good for Me
  It's Not Where You Start
Seventh Heaven
  C'est la Vie
  A Man with a Dream
  Where Is That Someone for Me
Shady Lady
  Swingy Little Thingy
She Loves Me
  Days Gone By
  Dear Friend
  Grand Knowing You
  Ilona
  She Loves Me
  Tonight at Eight
  Will He Like Me?
Shenandoah
  Next to Lovin' (I Like Fighting)
Sherry!
  Sherry!
She's My Baby
  A Baby's Best Friend
  Try Again Tomorrow
The Shocking Miss Pilgrim
  Aren't You Kind of Glad We Did?
Show Boat
  Bill
  Can't Help Lovin' Dat Man
  I Might Fall Back on You
  Life upon the Wicked Stage
  Make Believe
  Nobody Else but Me
  Ol'Man River
  Why Do I Love You?
  You Are Love
Show Girl
  Blah-Blah-Blah
  Can Broadway Do without Me?
  Do What You Do!
  I Ups to Him and He Ups to Me
  I'm Jimmy the Well Dressed Man
  Liza (All the Clouds'll Roll Away)
Shuffle Along
  Baltimore Buzz
  Bandana Days
  Gypsy Blues
  Honeysuckle Time
  I'm Craving for That Kind of Love

I'm Just Wild about Harry
Love Will Find a Way
Oriental Blues
Shuffle Along
Silk Stockings
  All of You
  It's a Chemical Reaction
  Josephine
  Paris Loves Lovers
  Satin and Silk
  Silk Stockings
  Too Bad
  Without Love
Silks and Satins
  My Little Bimbo Down on the
    Bamboo Isle
Simple Simon
  Dancing on the Ceiling
  Don't Tell Your Folks
  Happy Days and Lonely Nights
  He Was Too Good to Me
  I Must Love You
  I Still Believe in You
  I'm Yours
  Love Me or Leave Me
  Send for Me
  Ten Cents a Dance
Sinbad
  Avalon
  My Mammy
Sing Boy, Sing
  Sing Boy, Sing
Sky High
  Give Your Heart in June Time
Smiles
  I'm Glad I Waited
  More Than Ever
  Time on My Hands (You in My
    Arms)
  You're Driving Me Crazy (What Did
    I Do?)
Something for the Boys
  By the Mississinewah
  Could It Be You?
  Hey, Good-Lookin'
  Something for the Boys
Sons o' Guns
  Cross Your Fingers
  It's You I Love
  Why?

Golden Days
Just We Two
Serenade
Student Life
Students March Song
To the Inn We're Marching
The Three Graces
Gigolette
The Three Musketeers
Ma Belle
March of the Musketeers
The Vagabond King
Huguette Waltz
Love for Sale
Love Me Tonight
Only a Rose
Some Day
Song of the Vagabonds
Tomorrow
The White Eagle
Gather the Rose
Give Me One Hour
Regimental Song
The Yankee Princess
My Bajadere
Zigeunerliebe (Gypsy Love)
The White Dove

Orchestra

Abe Lyman and his Orchestra
California, Here I Come
Al Donahue and his Orchestra
Low Down Rhythm in a Top Hat
Alvino Ray and his Orchestra
Blue Rain
Art Kassel and his Orchestra
Doodle Doo Doo
Artie Shaw and his Orchestra
Nightmare
Ben Bernie and his Orchestra
Au Revoir, Pleasant Dreams
It's a Lonesome Old Town When
You're Not Around
Bennie Moten's Kansas City Orchestra
It's Hard To Laugh or Smile
Moten Stomp
Benny Goodman and his Orchestra
Good-bye

Let's Dance
Bert Lown and his Hotel Biltmore
Orchestra
Bye Bye Blues
Billy Butterfield and his Orchestra
What's New?
Blue Barron and his Orchestra
Sometimes I'm Happy
Bob Crosby Band
Summertime
Buddy Rogers and his Orchestra
My Buddy
Bunny Berigan and his Orchestra
I Can't Get Started
Casa Loma Orchestra
Was I To Blame for Falling in Love
with You
Charlie Barnet and his Orchestra
Clap Hands! Here Comes Charley!
Skyliner
Chick Webb and his Orchestra
Let's Get Together
Claude Hopkins and his Orchestra
(I Would Do) Anything for You
Claude Thornhill and his Orchestra
Snowfall
Count Basie and his Orchestra
One o'Clock Jump
Dean Hudson and his Orchestra
Moon over Miami
Del Courtney and his Orchestra
You're an Old Smoothie
Dick Jurgens and his Orchestra
Day Dreams Come True at Night
Don Redman and his Orchestra
Chant of the Weed
Dorsey Brothers Orchestra
Sandman
Duke Ellington and his Orchestra
Take the "A" Train
Things Ain't What They Used To Be
Earl Hines and his Orchestra
Deep Forest
Eddy Duchin and his Orchestra
My Twilight Dream
Ellington Orchestra
East St. Louis Toodle-o
Emery Deutsch and his Orchestra
Stardust on the Moon
When a Gypsy Makes His Violin Cry

Stan Kenton and his Orchestra
  Artistry in Rhythm
Ted Straeter and his Orchestra
  The Most Beautiful Girl in the
    World
Teddy Hill and his Orchestra
  Blue Rhythm Fantasy
Tex Beneke and his Orchestra
  Moonlight Serenade
Tommy Dorsey and his Orchestra
  I'm Gettin' Sentimental over You
Wayne King and his Orchestra
  The Waltz You Saved for Me
Will Hudson and his Orchestra
  Hobo on Park Avenue
Willie Bryant and his Orchestra
  It's Over Because We're Through
Willie Creager and his Orchestra
  The Parade of the Wooden Soldiers
Willie Lewis and his Orchestra
  Just a Mood
Woody Herman and his Orchestra
  Blue Flame
  Blue Prelude

Play
Cavalcade
  Mirabelle (Lover of My Dreams)
  Twentieth Century Blues
The French Doll
  Do It Again
The Great Magoo
  It's Only a Paper Moon
Happy Birthday
  I Haven't Got a Worry in the World
Happy End
  The Bilbao Song
Johnny Johnson
  Mon Ami, My Friend
  O, Heart of Love
  Oh, the Rio Grande
  To Love You and To Love You
June Moon
  June Moon
Kiki
  Someday I'll Find You
Kill That Story
  Two Cigarettes in the Dark

Little Miss Bluebeard
  I Won't Say I Will but I Won't Say I
    Won't
  So This Is Love
  Who'll Buy My Violets? (La
    Violetera)
Mamba's Daughters
  Lonesome Walls
Man in the Moon
  Worlds Apart
Naughty Cinderella
  Do I Love You? (When There's
    Nothing but Yes in My Eyes)
  That Means Nothing to Me!
Never Too Late
  Never Too Late
Nikki
  On Account of I Love You
  Taking Off
Paris
  Don't Look at Me That Way
  The Heaven Hop
  The Land of Going To Be
  Let's Do It (Let's Fall in Love)
  Let's Misbehave
  Two Little Babes in the Wood
Peter Pan
  Peter Pan, I Love You
Private Lives
  Someday I'll Find You
Processional
  The Yankee Doodle Blues
Shadow Play
  Play, Orchestra, Play
  Then
  You Were There
She Loves Me Not
  After All You're All I'm After
Singin' the Blues
  It's the Darndest Thing
  Singin' the Blues
The Social Register
  The Key to My Heart
Something Gay
  You Are So Lovely and I'm So
    Lonely
Son
  Come On-a My House
A Taste of Honey
  A Taste of Honey

Tonight at 8:30
  Play, Orchestra, Play
  Then
  You Were There

Radio Show
Arthur Godfrey Time
  It Seems Like Old Times
The Burns and Allen Radio Show
  The Love Nest
California Melodies Hour
  California Melodies
The Chase and Sanborn Hour
  Time on My Hands (You in My
  Arms)
Dr. Christian
  Rainbow on the River
Duffy's Tavern
  Leave Us Face It (We're in Love)
Easy Aces
  Manhattan Serenade
The First Nighter
  Neapolitan Nights
The Fitch Bandwagon
  Smile for Me
The Gibson Family
  If There Is Someone Lovelier Than
  You
Hollywood Hotel
  Blue Moon
Lady Esther Serenade
  The Waltz You Saved for Me
Lanny Ross' Campbell Soup Program
  I Kiss Your Hand, Madame
Major Bowes' Capitol Theatre Family
  With a Song in My Heart
Make Believe Ballroom
  It's Make Believe Ballroom Time
Make Mine Music
  Two Silhouettes
Manhattan Merry-Go-Round
  Manhattan Merry-Go-Round
Maxwell House Coffee-Time
  You and I
Maxwell House Show Boat
  Here Comes the Show Boat
  Let's Have Another Cup of Coffee
Milkman's Matinee
  The Milkmen's Matinee

Mr. Keene, Tracer of Lost Persons
  Someday I'll Find You
Pepper Young's Family
  Always
The Philco Hour
  Mem'ries
Pond's Vanity Fair
  My Love
Pursuit of Happiness
  Ballad for Americans
The Studebaker Champions
  Falling in Love with You
Tom Mix and His Straight-Shooters
  When the Bloom Is on the Sage

Revue
Africana
  I'm Coming Virginia
All Clear
  Have You Met Miss Jones?
  I'm So Weary of It All
All for Love
  Dreamer with a Penny
All in Fun
  It's a Big Wide Wonderful World
Along Fifth Avenue
  Skyscraper Blues
Americana
  Brother, Can You Spare a Dime?
  My Kinda Love
  Nobody Wants Me
  Red Apple
  Satan's L'il Lamb
Americana of 1926
  Sunny Disposish
  That Lost Barbershop Chord
  Why Do Ya Roll Those Eyes?
Andre Charlot's Revue of 1924
  Limehouse Blues
  Parisian Pierrot
  You Were Meant for Me
Andre Charlot's Revue of 1926
  A Cup of Coffee, a Sandwich, and
  You
  Gigolette
  Poor Little Rich Girl
  Russian Blues
Angel in the Wings
  Big Brass Band from Brazil
  Civilization (Bongo, Bongo, Bongo)

Doin' the Suzi-Q
Don't Worry 'bout Me
Frisco Flo
Happy As the Day Is Long
Here Goes (a Fool)
Ill Wind (You're Blowin' Me No
  Good)
I'm a Hundred Percent for You
I've Got the World on a String
Like a Bolt from the Blue
Minnie the Moocher's Wedding Day
Raisin' the Rent
Sidewalks of Cuba
Stormy Weather
That's What I Hate about Love
There's a House in Harlem for Sale
Truckin'
The Wail of the Reefer Man
Crazy with the Heat
Yes, My Darling Daughter
Cubanola
The Peanut Vendor
Dance Me a Song
I'm the Girl
Lilac Wine
Dixie to Broadway
I'm a Little Blackbird Looking for a
  Bluebird
Mandy, Make Up Your Mind
Earl Carroll Vanities
Climbing Up the Ladder of Love
Goodnight Sweetheart
Have a Heart
Hittin' the Bottle
I Gotta Right To Sing the Blues
Love Came into My Heart
The March of Time
My Darling
Earl Carroll Vanities of 1928
Blue Shadows
Once in a Lifetime
Earl Carroll Vanities of 1925
Rhythm of the Day
Earl Carroll's Vanities-12th Edition
Angel
The Ed Wynn Carnival
I Love the Land of Old Black Joe
Rose of Spain
Everybody's Welcome
As Time Goes By

Face the Music
Let's Have Another Cup of Coffee
On a Roof in Manhattan
Soft Lights and Sweet Music
Fifty-Fifty
The Gypsy in My Soul
I Live the Life I Love
Flying Colors
Alone Together
Louisiana Hayride
A Shine on Your Shoes
Smokin' Reefers
Flying Colours
Don't Let's Be Beastly to the
  Germans
The Garrick Gaieties
April Fool
I Am Only Human After All
Manhattan
Sentimental Me
The Garrick Gaieties of 1926
Mountain Greenery
What's the Use of Talking
Gay Paree
Collegiate
I Can't Believe That You're in Love
  with Me
Gay White Way
Beau Night in Hotchkiss Corners
George White's Music Hall Varieties
Fit As a Fiddle
Let's Put Out the Lights (and Go to
  Sleep)
George White's Scandals
The Girl Is You and the Boy Is
  Me
I've Got To Get Hot
Life Is Just a Bowl of Cherries
My Song
That's Why Darkies Were Born
This Is the Missus
The Thrill Is Gone
George White's Scandals of 1939
Are You Havin' Any Fun?
Something I Dreamed Last Night
George White's Scandals of 1920
Down by the O-HI-O (O-My!-O!)
On My Mind the Whole Night
  Long
Scandal Walk

The Texas Wheelers
  Flashback Blues
  Illegal Smile
That Was the Week That Was
  In the Summer of His Years
Three's Company
  Three's Company
Tonight
  Johnny's Theme
The Travels of Jaimie McPheeters
  Theme from *The Travels of Jaimie McPheeters*
12 O'Clock High
  12 O'Clock High
Twentieth Century
  So Long, Big Time
The Untouchables
  The Untouchables
USA Canteen
  I Believe
The Val Doonican Show
  I Believe My Love Loves Me
Valentine's Day
  Theme from *Valentine's Day*
Victory at Sea
  No Other Love
Voyage to the Bottom of the Sea
  Theme from *Voyage to the Bottom of the Sea*
Wagon Train
  Wagon Train
Welcome Back, Kotter
  Welcome Back
Where the Action Is
  Action
WKRP in Cincinnati
  Della and the Dealer
  WKRP in Cincinnati
The Young and the Restless
  The Young and the Restless Theme
Zorro
  Theme from *Zorro*

Awards Index

A year-by-year list of songs nominated for Academy Awards by the Academy of Motion Picture Arts and Sciences. Asterisks indicate the winners.

Grammy Awards from the National Academy of Recording Arts and Sciences have winners noted with asterisks from 1958, when the awards originated, and nominees from 1970 on.

1934
Academy Award
  Carioca
  The Continental*
  Love in Bloom

1935
Academy Award
  Lovely To Look At
  Lullaby of Broadway*

1936
Academy Award
  Did I Remember?
  I've Got You Under My Skin
  A Melody from the Sky
  Pennies from Heaven
  The Way You Look Tonight*
  When Did You Leave Heaven

1937
Academy Award
  Remember Me?
  Sweet Leilani*
  That Old Feeling

  They Can't Take That Away from Me
  Whispers in the Dark

1938
Academy Award
  Always and Always
  Change Partners
  The Cowboy and the Lady
  Dust
  Jeepers Creepers
  Merrily We Live
  Mist over the Moon
  My Own
  Now It Can Be Told
  Thanks for the Memory*

1939
Academy Award
  Faithful Forever
  I Poured My Heart into a Song
  Over the Rainbow*
  Wishing (Will Make It So)

1940

Academy Award
  Down Argentina Way
  I'd Know You Anywhere
  It's a Blue World
  Love of My Life
  Only Forever
  Our Love Affair
  Waltzing in the Clouds
  When You Wish upon a Star*
  Who Am I?

1941

Academy Award
  Baby Mine
  Be Honest with Me
  Blues in the Night (My Mama Done Tol' Me)
  Boogie Woogie Bugle Boy
  Chattanooga Choo Choo
  Dolores
  I Couldn't Sleep a Wink Last Night
  The Last Time I Saw Paris*
  Out of the Silence
  Since I Kissed My Baby Goodbye

1942

Academy Award
  Always in My Heart
  Dearly Beloved
  How about You?
  I've Got a Gal in Kalamazoo
  I've Heard That Song Before
  Love Is a Song
  Pig Foot Pete
  When There's a Breeze on Lake Louise
  White Christmas*

1943

Academy Award
  Change of Heart
  Happiness Is a Thing Called Joe
  My Shining Hour
  Saludos Amigos
  Say a Pray'r for the Boys over There
  That Old Black Magic
  They're Either Too Young or Too Old
  We Mustn't Say Goodbye

You'd Be So Nice To Come Home To
You'll Never Know*

1944

Academy Award
  I'll Walk Alone
  I'm Making Believe
  Long Ago (And Far Away)
  Now I Know
  Remember Me to Carolina
  Rio de Janeiro
  Silver Shadows and Golden Dreams
  Sweet Dreams, Sweetheart
  Swinging on a Star*
  Too Much in Love
  The Trolley Song

1945

Academy Award
  Ac-cent-tchu-ate the Positive (Mister In-Between)
  Anywhere
  Aren't You Glad You're You
  Cat and the Canary
  Endlessly
  I Fall in Love Too Easily
  I'll Buy That Dream
  It Might As Well Be Spring*
  Linda
  Love Letters
  More and More
  Sleighride in July
  So-o-o-o-o in Love
  Some Sunday Morning

1946

Academy Award
  All through the Day
  I Can't Begin To Tell You
  Ole Buttermilk Sky
  On the Atchison, Topeka and the Santa Fe*
  You Keep Coming Back Like a Song

1947

Academy Award
  A Gal in Calico
  I Wish I Didn't Love You So
  You Do
  Zip-a-Dee-Doo-Dah*

1948

Academy Award
  Buttons and Bows*
  For Every Man There's a Woman
  It's Magic
  This Is the Moment
  Woody Woodpecker

1949

Academy Award
  Baby, It's Cold Outside*
  It's a Great Feeling
  Lavender Blue (Dilly Dilly)
  My Foolish Heart
  Through a Long and Sleepless Night

1950

Academy Award
  Be My Love
  Bibbidi-Bobbidi-Boo (The Magic
    Song)
  Mona Lisa*
  Mule Train
  Wilhelmina

1951

Academy Award
  In the Cool, Cool, Cool of the
    Evening*
  Never
  A Place in the Sun*
  Too Late Now
  Wonder Why

1952

Academy Award
  Am I in Love
  Because You're Mine
  High Noon*
  Thumbelina
  Zing a Little Zong

1953

Academy Award
  The Moon Is Blue
  My Flaming Heart
  Sadie Thompson's Song
  Secret Love*
  That's Amore

1954

Academy Award
  Count Your Blessings Instead of
    Sheep
  The High and the Mighty
  Hold My Hand
  The Man That Got Away
  Three Coins in the Fountain*

1955

Academy Award
  Cheek to Cheek
  I'll Never Stop Loving You
  Love Is a Many-Splendored Thing*
  Something's Gotta Give
  (Love Is) The Tender Trap
  Unchained Melody

1956

Academy Award
  Friendly Persuasion
  Julie
  Que Sera, Sera*
  True Love
  Written on the Wind

1957

Academy Award
  An Affair To Remember
  All the Way*
  April Love
  Tammy
  Wild Is the Wind

1958

Academy Award
  Almost in Your Arms
  A Certain Smile
  Gigi*
  Song from *Some Came Running*
  A Very Precious Love

Grammy Award
  Volare*

1959

Academy Award
  The Best of Everything
  The Five Pennies
  The Hanging Tree
  High Hopes*

Strange Are the Ways of Love

1960

Academy Award
The Facts of Life
The Faraway Part of Town
The Green Leaves of Summer
Never on Sunday*
The Second Time Around

Grammy Award
Exodus*
Georgia on My Mind*
Let the Good Times Roll*
Mr. Lucky*

1961

Academy Award
Bachelor in Paradise
Love Theme from *El Cid* (The
Falcon and the Dove)
Moon River*
Pocketful of Miracles
Town without Pity

Grammy Award
The African Waltz*
Big Bad John*
Hit the Road, Jack*
Lazy River*
Let's Twist Again*
Lollipops and Roses*
Moon River*

1962

Academy Award
Days of Wine and Roses*
Love Song from *Mutiny on the
Bounty*
Song from *Two for the Seesaw* (A
Second Chance)
Tender Is the Night
Walk on the Wild Side

Grammy Award
Alley Cat*
Baby Elephant Walk*
Cast Your Fate to the Wind*
Desafinado (Slightly Out of Tune)*
Funny Way of Laughin'*

A Taste of Honey*
What Kind of Fool Am I?*

1963

Academy Award
Call Me Irresponsible*
Charade
It's a Mad, Mad, Mad, Mad World
More (Theme from *Mondo Cane*)
So Little Time

Grammy Award
Blowin' in the Wind*
Busted*
Days of Wine and Roses*
Deep Purple*
Detroit City*
Dominique*
Gravy Waltz*
Hello Mudduh, Hello Fadduh (A
Letter from Camp)*
More (Theme from *Mondo Cane*)*
Wives and Lovers*

1964

Academy Award
Chim Chim Cher-ee*
Dear Heart
Hush...Hush, Sweet Charlotte
My Kind of Town
Where Love Has Gone

Grammy Award
The Cat*
Dang Me*
Downtown*
The Girl from Ipanema*
A Hard Day's Night*
Hello, Dolly!*
Here Comes My Baby Back Again*
(You Don't Know) How Glad I Am*
People*
Pink Panther Theme*
We'll Sing in the Sunshine*

1965

Academy Award
The Ballad of Cat Ballou
I Will Wait for You
The Shadow of Your Smile*

The Sweetheart Tree
What's New, Pussycat?

Grammy Award
The "In" Crowd*
King of the Road*
The Shadow of Your Smile*
A Taste of Honey*

1966
Academy Award
Alfie
Born Free*
Georgy Girl
A Time for Love
The Wishing Doll

Grammy Award
Almost Persuaded*
Batman Theme*
It Was a Very Good Year*
Michelle*
Strangers in the Night*

1967
Academy Award
The Bare Necessities
The Eyes of Love (Carol's Theme)
The Look of Love
Talk to the Animals*
Thoroughly Modern Millie

Grammy Award
Gentle on My Mind*
Mission: Impossible*
Up-Up and Away*

1968
Academy Award
Chitty Chitty Bang Bang
For Love of Ivy
Funny Girl
Star!
The Windmills of Your Mind
(Theme from *The Thomas Crown Affair*)*

Grammy Award
Classical Gas*
(Sittin' on) The Dock of the Bay*

Little Green Apples*
Mrs. Robinson*

1969
Academy Award
Come Saturday Morning
Jean
Raindrops Keep Fallin' on My
Head*
True Grit
What Are You Doing the Rest of
Your Life?

Grammy Award
Aquarius*
A Boy Named Sue*
Color Him Father*
Games People Play*
Let the Sunshine In*
Midnight Cowboy*

1970
Academy Award
For All We Know*
Pieces of Dreams
Thank You Very Much
Till Love Touches Your Life
Whistling Away the Dark

Grammy Award
Bridge over Troubled Water*
(They Long to Be) Close to You
Didn't I (Blow Your Mind This
Time)
Everything Is Beautiful
The Fighting Side of Me
Groovy Situation
Hello, Darlin'
Is Anybody Goin' to San Antone
Let It Be
My Woman, My Woman, My Wife*
Patches (I'm Depending on You)*
Signed, Sealed, Delivered I'm Yours
Somebody's Been Sleeping in My Bed
We've Only Just Begun
Wonder Could I Live There
Anymore

1971

Academy Award
  Age of Not Believing
  All His Children
  Bless the Beasts and Children
  Life Is What You Make It
  Theme from *Shaft* (Who Shaft
    Where)*

Grammy Award
  Ain't No Sunshine*
  For the Good Times
  Help Me Make It Through the Night
  If I Were Your Woman
  It's Impossible
  It's Too Late*
  Joy to the World
  Me and Bobby McGee
  Mr. Big Stuff*
  My Sweet Lord
  My Way
  Never Can Say Goodbye
  (I Never Promised You a) Rose
    Garden
  Smiling Faces Sometimes
  Theme from *Shaft* (Who Shaft
    Where)
  You've Got a Friend*

1972

Academy Award
  Ben
  Come Follow, Follow Me
  Marmalade, Molasses and Honey
  The Morning After*
  Strange Are the Ways of Love

Grammy Award
  Alone Again (Naturally)
  American Pie
  Back Stabbers
  Delta Dawn
  Everybody Plays the Fool
  The First Time Ever I Saw Your
    Face*
  Freddy's Dead (Theme from
    Superfly)
  Funny Face
  Happiest Girl in the Whole U.S.A.

Kiss an Angel Good Morning*
Me and Mrs. Jones
Papa Was a Rollin' Stone*
Songs Sung Blue
Theme from *Summer of '42*
Without You
Woman (Sensuous Woman)

1973

Academy Award
  All That Love Went to Waste
  Live and Let Die
  Love
  Nice to Be Around
  The Way We Were*

Grammy Award
  Bad, Bad, Leroy Brown
  Behind Closed Doors*
  Cisco Kid
  Country Sunshine
  Family Affair
  Killing Me Softly with His Song*
  Love Train
  Midnight Train to Georgia
  The Most Beautiful Girl
  Old Dogs, Children and Watermelon
    Wine
  Superstition*
  Tie a Yellow Ribbon Round the Old
    Oak Tree
  Why Me
  You Are the Sunshine of My Life
  You're So Vain

1974

Academy Award
  Blazing Saddles
  I Feel Love
  The Little Prince
  We May Never Love Like This
    Again*
  Wherever Love Takes Me

Grammy Award
  Dancing Machine
  Don't Let the Sun Go Down on Me
  Fairytale
  Feel Like Makin' Love

For the Love of Money
Help Me
I Honestly Love You*
If We Make It Through December
I'm a Ramblin' Man
Living for the City*
Midnight at the Oasis
Paper Roses
Rock Your Baby
A Very Special Love Song
The Way We Were*
You and Me Against the World

1975

Academy Award
Do You Know Where You're Going
To
How Lucky Can You Get
I'm Easy*
Now That We're in Love

Grammy Award
At Seventeen
Blue Eyes Crying in the Rain
Feelings
Get Down Tonight
I'm Not Lisa
Love Will Keep Us Together*
Lyin' Eyes
Send in the Clowns*
That's the Way (I Like It)
Where Is the Love*

1976

Academy Award
Ave Satani
Evergreen*
Gonna Fly Now (Theme from
Rocky)

Grammy Award
Afternoon Delight
Broken Lady*
Disco Lady
The Door Is Always Open
Dropkick Me, Jesus
Every Time You Touch Me (I Get
High)
Fifty Ways to Leave Your Lover

Hank Williams, You Wrote My Life
I Write the Songs*
If You Leave Me Now
Love Hangover
Lowdown*
Misty Blue
(Shake, Shake, Shake) Shake Your
Booty
This Masquerade*
The Wreck of the Edmund Fitzgerald

1977

Academy Award
Candle on the Water
The Slipper and the Rose Waltz
Someone's Waiting for You
You Light Up My Life*

Grammy Award
Best of My Love
Blue Bayou
Brick House
Don't It Make My Brown Eyes
Blue*
Don't Leave Me This Way
Easy
Evergreen
Hotel California*
It Was Almost Like a Song
Lucille
Luckenbach, Texas (Back to the
Basics of Love)
Nobody Does It Better
Southern Nights
You Light Up My Life*
You Make Me Feel Like Dancing*

1978

Academy Award
Hopelessly Devoted to You
Last Dance*
The Last Time I Felt Like This
Ready to Take a Chance Again

Awards Index

Grammy Award
  Baker Street
  Boogie Oogie Oogie
  Dance, Dance, Dance (Yowsah,
    Yowsah, Yowsah)
  Every Time Two Fools Collide
  Fantasy
  Feels So Good
  The Gambler*
  Just the Way You Are*
  Last Dance*
  Let's Take the Long Way Around
    the World
  Mammas Don't Let Your Babies
    Grow Up to Be Cowboys
  Stayin' Alive
  Take This Job and Shove It
  Three Times a Lady
  Use ta Be My Girl
  You Don't Bring Me Flowers
  You Needed Me

1979

Academy Award
  It Goes Like It Goes*
  Looking Through the Eyes of Love

Grammy Award
  After the Love Has Gone*
  Ain't No Stopping Us Now
  All the Gold in California
  Blue Kentucky Girl
  Chuck E's in Love
  Deja Vu
  Every Which Way But Loose
  The Gambler
  Honesty
  I Will Survive
  If I Said You Had a Beautiful Body
    (Would You Hold It Against Me)
  Minute by Minute
  Reunited
  She Believes in Me
  We Are Family
  What a Fool Believes*
  You Decorated My Life*
  You Don't Bring Me Flowers

List of Publishers

A directory to publishers of the songs included in *Popular Music 1920-1979*. Publishers that are members of the American Society of Composers, Authors, and Publishers or whose catalogs are available under ASCAP license are indicated by the designation (ASCAP). Publishers that have granted performing rights to Broadcast Music, Inc., are designated by the notation (BMI). Publishers whose catalogs are represented by SESAC, Inc., are indicated by the designation (SESAC).

The addresses, which have been updated for this revised cumulation, were gleaned from a variety of sources, including ASCAP, BMI, SESAC, The Harry Fox Agency, Billboard Magazine, and The National Music Publishers' Association. As in any volatile industry, many of the addresses may become quickly outdated. In the interim between the book's completion and its subsequent publication, some publishers may have been consolidated into others or changed hands. This is a fact of life long endured by the music business and its constituents. The data collected here, and throughout the book, are as accurate as such circumstances allow.

A

A-H Music Corp. (ASCAP)
c/o Louis P. Randell
1140 Avenue of the Americas
New York, New York 10036

A-M Music Corp. (ASCAP)
609 Fifth Avenue
New York, New York 10017

Aba, Inc. (BMI)
c/o William E. Sheppard
16228 Keeler Drive
Granada Hills, California 91344

ABC Music Corp. (ASCAP)
437 Fifth Avenue
New York, New York 10019

Abekam Music (BMI)
c/o Sanford Ross Management
1700 Broadway
New York, New York 10019

List of Publishers

Aberbach, Inc. (BMI)
424 Madison Avenue
New York, New York 10017

Abigail Music Co. (BMI)
c/o Nancy Schimmel
1450 Sixth Street
Berkeley, California 94710

Abilene Music Inc. (ASCAP)
c/o David Chase
6 East 45th Street
New York, New York 10017

ABKCO Music Inc. (BMI)
1700 Broadway
New York, New York 10019

Abraham Music (ASCAP)
see Naked Snake Publishing

Acclaim Music, Inc. (BMI)
c/o Jim Reeves Enterprises, Inc.
Drawer 1
Madison, Tennessee 37115

Ace Publishing Co., Inc. (BMI)
Post Office Box 9341
Jackson, Mississippi 39206

Ackee Music Inc. (ASCAP)
see Island Music

Acme Music Publishing Co.
Address unknown

Acorn Music Corp. (BMI)
c/o The Richmond Organization
Suite 2160
10 Columbus Circle
New York, New York 10019

Acoustic Music Inc. (BMI)
Box 1546
Nashville, Tennessee 37202

Acuff-Rose Publications Inc. (BMI)
2510 Franklin Road
Nashville, Tennessee 37204

Adair Publishing Co. (BMI)
c/o Roland Wright
12302 Thaman Drive
Dickinson, Texas 77539

Stanley Adams Music, Inc. (BMI)
c/o Adams-Ethridge Publishing Co.
Kempner Street
Galveston, Texas 77550

Patrick Adams Productions Inc. (ASCAP)
142 West End Avenue
New York, New York 10023

Adams-Vee & Abbott, Inc. (BMI)
4th Floor
216 South Wabash Avenue
Chicago, Illinois 60604

Addax Music Co., Inc. (ASCAP)
see Famous Music Co.

Addison Street Music (ASCAP)
see Sterling Music Co.

Richard Adler Music (ASCAP)
c/o The Songwriters Guild
3rd Floor
276 Fifth Avenue
New York, New York 10001

Admiration Music, Inc. (BMI)
c/o Lee Silver
136 South Swall Drive
Beverly Hills, California 90211

A.D.T. Enterprises, Inc. (BMI)
c/o M. Warren Troob
4800 Gulf of Mexico Drive
Longboat Key, Florida 33548

Adult Music (BMI)
c/o Ken Adamany
315 West Gorham Street
Madison, Wisconsin 53703

Advanced Music Corp. (ASCAP)
488 Madison Avenue
New York, New York 10022

Affiliated Music Enterprises Inc.
Box 1929
Melbourne, Florida 32901

AGAC (ASCAP)
see Mercer K. #Ellington

Aguila Publishing Co. (BMI)
c/o Arthur Thomas
Box 1459
Nashville, Tennessee 37203

Ahab Music Co., Inc. (BMI)
1707 Grand Avenue
Nashville, Tennessee 37212

Ahlert-Burke Corp. (ASCAP)
c/o Fred Ahlert Music Corp.
8150 Beverly Boulevard
Los Angeles, California 90048

Fred Ahlert Music Corp.
8150 Beverly Boulevard
Beverly Hills, California 90048

Aimi Music (BMI)
see Broadcast Music Inc.

Airefield Music (BMI)
c/o Beechwood Music Corp.
6255 Sunset Boulevard
Hollywood, California 90028

Ajax Music (ASCAP)
c/o B. Phil Moore
Suite 202
8949 Sunset Boulevard
Los Angeles, California 90069

Akbestal Music, Inc. (BMI)
c/o Leonard Stogel & Associates,
Ltd.
9255 Sunset Boulevard
Los Angeles, California 90069

B. & G. Akst Publishing (ASCAP)
70 Niagara Street
Buffalo, New York 14202

Alamo Music, Inc. (ASCAP)
11th Floor
1619 Broadway
New York, New York 10019

Alarm Clock Music (ASCAP)
2854 Paraiso Way
La Crescenta, California 91014

Alchemy Music Inc. (ASCAP)
c/o D & M Business Management Inc.
22110 Clarendon Street
Suite 101
Woodland Hills, California 91367

Aldi Music (ASCAP)
see Notable Music Co., Inc.

Dick Alen Management, Inc. (BMI)
3633 Royal Meadow Road
Sherman Oaks, California 91403

Alexis Music Inc. (ASCAP)
c/o Lee Magid Inc.
Box 532
Malibu, California 90265

Alfred Music Co., Inc.
Address unknown

Algee Music Corp. (BMI)
see Notable Music Co., Inc.

Algonquin Music, Inc. (BMI)
1650 Broadway
New York, New York 10019

Algrace Music Co. (BMI)
c/o Larry Shayne Music, Inc.
6262 Hollywood Boulevard
Los Angeles, California 90028

Aliben Music (BMI)
c/o Zachary Glickman
6430 Sunset Boulevard
Suite 506
Los Angeles, California 90028

Alibri Music Co. (BMI)
93 East Alexandrine Street
Detroit, Michigan 48201

Alien Music (BMI)
c/o Pete Sears
2400 Fulton Street
San Francisco, California 94118

Alive Enterprises Inc. (BMI)
8600 Melrose Avenue
Los Angeles, California 90069

Aljarreau Music Co. (BMI)
c/o Patrick Rains
8752 Holloway Drive
Los Angeles, California 90069

Alkatraz Korner Music Co. (BMI)
Post Office Box 3316
San Francisco, California 94119

All By Myself Publishing Co. (BMI)
see Chappell & Co., Inc.

Allanwood Music (BMI)
c/o Gursey Schneider & Co.
Suite 2530
1900 Avenue of the Stars
Los Angeles, California 90067

Allied Music Corp. (ASCAP)
110 East 59th Street
New York, New York 10022

Allison's Music, Inc. (ASCAP)
c/o Robert Wrubel
6465 Regent Street
Oakland, California 94618

Almanac Music, Inc. (ASCAP)
c/o The Richmond Organization
10 Columbus Circle
New York, New York 10019

Almo Music Corp. (ASCAP)
1416 North La Brea Avenue
Hollywood, California 90028

Alstel Television Productions, Inc. (BMI)
c/o A. N. Albertini
145 Lakeview Drive
Media, Pennsylvania 19063

Altam Music Corp. (BMI)
see Al Gallico Music Corp.

Louis Alter Music Publications (ASCAP)
c/o The Sonwriters Guild
3rd Floor
276 Fifth Avenue
New York, New York 10001

American Metropolitan Enterprises of New
York, Inc. (BMI)
c/o Copyright Service Bureau, Ltd.
221 West 57th Street
New York, New York 10019

Amadeo-Brio Corp. (ASCAP)
c/o Funky but Music, Inc.
Post Office Box 1770
155 Sanders Ferry Road
Hendersonville, Tennessee 37075

A.M.C., Inc. (ASCAP)
250 West 54th Street
New York, New York 10019

Amelanie Music (ASCAP)
see The Hudson Bay Music Co.

American Academy of Music, Inc. (ASCAP)
1776 Broadway
New York, New York 10019

American Broadcasting Music Inc. (ASCAP)
4151 Prospect Avenue
Los Angeles, California 90027

American Cowboy Music Co. (BMI)
14 Music Circle East
Nashville, Tennessee 37203

American Dream Music Co. (ASCAP)
see The Hudson Bay Music Co.

American Gramophone
9130 Mormon Bridge Road
Omaha, Nebraska 68152

American Music, Inc. (BMI)
9109 Sunset Boulevard
Hollywood, California 90069

American Woolfsongs
c/o M. Shapiro, Esq.
315 South Beverly Drive
Suite 210
Beverly Hills, California 90212

American Wordways (ASCAP)
1780 Broadway
Room 1200
New York, New York 10019

Amestoy Music (BMI)
117 North Las Palmas
Los Angeles, California 90004

Amundo Music (ASCAP)
see Dangerous Music

Ananga-Ranga Music Corp. (BMI)
c/o Buddy Kaye
18531 Wells Drive
Tarzana, California 91356

Anaton Music (BMI)
c/o V. Montana, Jr.
203 Sixth Avenue
Cherry Hill, New Jersey 08034

Anchor Music (ASCAP)
see MCA Music

Andite Invasion (BMI)
c/o Hal Bynum
430 Third Avenue North
Nashville, Tennessee 37201

Andjun Publishing, Inc.
Address unknown

Andor Music Co. (ASCAP)
6381 Hollywood Boulevard
Hollywood, California 90028

Andustin Music Co. (ASCAP)
Box 669
Woodstock, New York 12498

Andval Music (BMI)
c/o Milt Grant
KTXA Channel 21 Inc.
1712 East Randol Mill Road
Arlington, Texas 76011

Angel Music, Inc. (BMI)
c/o Murray Sporn
Post Office Box 1276
Great Neck, New York 11024

Angel Wing Music (ASCAP)
c/o Southern Writers Group U.S.A.
Box 40764
Nashville, Tennessee 37204

Angle Music (USA) (BMI)
Address unknown

Anglo Rock Music
Address unknown

Annart Music Corp.
Address unknown

Anne-Rachel Music Corp. (ASCAP)
241 West 72nd Street
New York, New York 10023

Annie Over Music (ASCAP)
3422 Hopkins Lane
Nashville, Tennessee 37215

Antique Music (ASCAP)
see Chappell & Co., Inc.

Antisia Music Inc. (ASCAP)
1650 Broadway
Suite 1001
New York, New York 10019

Antlers Music (BMI)
c/o Kenneth G. Gist, Jr.
264 Wallace Road
Nashville, Tennessee 37211

Aphrodite Music (ASCAP)
c/o Eastman & Eastman
39 West 54th Street
New York, New York 10019

Appian Music Co. (ASCAP)
c/o Mitchell, Silberberg & Knupp
1800 Century Park East
Los Angeles, California 90067

Apple Cider Music (ASCAP)
28 Knollwood Drive
Cherry Hill, New Jersey 08034

Appleseed Music, Inc. (ASCAP)
c/o Sanga Music, Inc.
250 West 57th Street
New York, New York 10019

Appletree Music Co. (BMI)
see The Times Square Music Publications Co.

Appogiatura Music Inc. (BMI)
c/o Franklin, Weinrib, Rudell & Vasallo
950 Third Avenue
New York, New York 10022

Approximate Music (BMI)
c/o Ames & Associates
Post Office Box 5973-120
Sherman Oaks, California 91413

April Music Inc. (ASCAP)
1350 Avenue of the Americas
23rd Floor
New York, New York 10019

Aral Music Co. (ASCAP)
190 Waverly Place
New York, New York 10014

ARC Music (BMI)
110 East 59th Street
New York, New York 10022

Arc Music Corp. (BMI)
c/o The Goodman Group
110 East 59th Street
New York, New York 10022

Arch Music Co., Inc. (ASCAP)
c/o A. Schroeder International, Ltd.
1650 Broadway
New York, New York 10019

Argosy Music Corp.
Address unknown

Aria Music Co. (ASCAP)
c/o Sidney Lipman
2348 Linwood Avenue
Fort Lee, New Jersey 07024

Aries Music Co. (BMI)
Suite 4
5460 Edgewood Place
Los Angeles, California 90019

Arista Music Inc.
Attention: Ms. Carol King
8370 Wilshire Boulevard
Beverly Hills, California 90211

Ark-La-Tex Publishing Co. (BMI)
11th Floor
1619 Broadway
New York, New York 10019

Arko Music Corp. (ASCAP)
c/o Edwin H. Morris & Co., Inc.
39 West 54th Street
New York, New York 10019

Harold Arlen (ASCAP)
146 Central Park West
New York, New York 10023

Armo Music Corp. (BMI)
c/o Lois Publishing Co.
1540 Brewster Avenue
Cincinnati, Ohio 45207

Aroostook Music, Inc. (BMI)
c/o R. W. Curless
Box 1181
Bangor, Maine 04401

Arpege Music Corp. (ASCAP)
c/o Lyn Murray
3603 Westfall Drive
Encino, California 91436

Arriviste Ink Music (BMI)
c/o Mitchell, Silberberg & Knupp
1800 Century Park East
Suite 700
Los Angeles, California 90067

Arrow Music Co. (ASCAP)
2570 Superior Avenue
Cleveland, Ohio 44115

Artists Music Inc. (ASCAP)
see Interworld Music Group

Artophone Corp.
Address unknown

Arvee Music (BMI)
c/o Bernard C. Solomon
2020 Avenue of the Stars
Concourse Level
Los Angeles, California 90067

Asa Music Co. (ASCAP)
c/o United Artists Music
Publishing Group
729 Seventh Avenue
New York, New York 10019

Ascent Music Inc. (BMI)
c/o Logan H. Westbrooks
1902 Fifth Avenue
Los Angeles, California 90018

Emil Ascher Inc.
630 5th Avenue
New York, New York 10020

Asco Music
c/o Bing Crosby Productions
6311 Romaine Street
Hollywood, California 90038

ASG Music Co. (BMI)
see Butterfield Music Corp.

Ash Music (BMI)
c/o Harold K. Ashby
484 West 43rd Street
#7-K
New York, New York 10036

Ashna Music Corp. (BMI)
Post Office Box 701
Nashville, Tennessee 37202

Asleep at the Wheel Music (BMI)
see Bug Music

Assorted Music (BMI)
Attention: Earl Shelton
309 South Broad Street
Philadelphia, Pennsylvania 19107

Astaire Music (ASCAP)
c/o The Songwriters Guild
3rd Floor
276 Fifth Avenue
New York, New York 10001

Atlantic Music Corp. (BMI)
6124 Selma Avenue
Hollywood, California 90028

ATM Music (ASCAP)
see Portofino Music

Attache Music Publishers, Inc. (BMI)
6000 West Sunset Boulevard
Hollywood, California 90028

ATV Music Corp. (BMI)
c/o ATV Group
6255 Sunset Boulevard
Hollywood, California 90028

ATV Music Publishing of Canada, Ltd.
(BMI)
Suite 201
13 Balmuto Street
Toronto, Ontario M4Y 1W1
Canada

Audre Mae Music (BMI)
34 Dogwood Drive
Smithtown, New York 11787

Audubon Music, Inc. (ASCAP)
c/o Frank Music Corp.
39 West 54th Street
New York, New York 10019

Aunt Polly's Publishing Co. (BMI)
Post Office Box 120657
Nashville, Tennessee 37212

Aurelia Music (ASCAP)
see Aphrodite Music

Aurelius Music (ASCAP)
see Aphrodite Music

Avas Music Publishing Co., Inc. (ASCAP)
80 Central Park West
New York, New York 10023

Avco Music (ASCAP)
see Boca Music Inc.

Average Music (ASCAP)
197 East Avenue
Norwalk, Connecticut 06855

AVI Music Publishing Group, Inc. (ASCAP)
Suite 1212
7060 Hollywood Boulevard
Hollywood, California 90028

Avon Music, Inc. (BMI)
c/o Michael Langford
333 West 56th Street
New York, New York 10019

B

B-Flat Publishing Co. (BMI)
c/o Copyright Service Bureau
221 West 57th Street
New York, New York 10019

B. O. Cult Songs Inc. (ASCAP)
888 Seventh Avenue
New York, New York 10019

Ba-Dake (BMI)
c/o Super Songs Unlimited
200 West 51st Street
Suite 706
New York, New York 10019

Babb Music Publishers (BMI)
48th Avenue and Tennessee
Nashville, Tennessee 37209

Baby Chick Music Inc. (BMI)
see Vogue Music

Back Bay Music (BMI)
c/o Mietus Copyright Management
Post Office Box 432
2351 Laurana Road
Union, New Jersey 07083

Back to Mono Music Inc. (BMI)
c/o Phil Spector
Post Office Box 69529
Los Angeles, California 90069

Bacon Fat Music Co. (BMI)
see The EMP Co.

Badazz Music (ASCAP)
see Almo Music Corp.

Badco Music Inc. (ASCAP)
see WB Music Corp.

Abel Baer Music Corp. (ASCAP)
c/o The Songwriters Guild
3rd Floor
276 Fifth Avenue
New York, New York 10001

Bag of Tunes, Inc. (BMI)
c/o Richard M. Shelton
79 West Monroe Street
Chicago, Illinois 60603

Armen Bagdasarian (ASCAP)
411 South Burlingame Avenue
Los Angeles, California 90049

List of Publishers

Tom Bahler (ASCAP)
see Yellow Brick Road Music

Bais Music (BMI)
c/o East Publications
926 East McLemore Avenue
Memphis, Tennessee 38106

Balcones Publishing Co. (BMI)
c/o Lora Jane Richardson, Manager
1102 Upland Drive
Austin, Texas 78741

Bald Medusa Co. (ASCAP)
c/o Bob-Cor Music, Inc.
185 North Wabash Avenue
Chicago, Illinois 60601

Bamboo Music, Inc. (BMI)
Suite 308
7033 Sunset Boulevard
Hollywood, California 90028

Banana Music (BMI)
Attention: Charles Schneider
635 Madison Avenue
New York, New York 10022

Bantam Music Publishing Co. (ASCAP)
15639 Woodfield Place
Sherman Oaks, California 91403

Bar-Kay Music (BMI)
see WB Music Corp.

Baray Music Inc. (BMI)
49 Music Square East
Nashville, Tennessee 37203

Barcam Music (BMI)
c/o Camillo-Barker Enterprises
121 Meadowbrook Drive
Sommerville, New Jersey 08876

Barclay Music Corp. (ASCAP)
c/o Shapiro, Bernstein & Co., Inc.
10 East 53rd Street
New York, New York 10022

Barmour Music Corp. (BMI)
c/o Pickwick International, Inc.,
Records Division
7500 Excelsior Boulevard
Minneapolis, Minnesota 55426

Barnaby Music Corp. (ASCAP)
1500 North Vine Street
Hollywood, California 90028

Barnstorm Music (BMI)
c/o Jess S. Morgan and Co., Inc.
6420 Wilshire Boulevard
Nineteenth Floor
Los Angeles, California 90048

Baron Music Publishing Co. (BMI)
Attention: Copyright Department
1117 17th Avenue South
Nashville, Tennessee 37212

Barrere Music (ASCAP)
see Naked Snake Publishing

Paul Barrett Music, Inc. (BMI)
1450 Hackett Avenue
Long Beach, California 90815

Barricade Music Inc. (ASCAP)
see Almo Music Corp.

Jeff Barry Music (ASCAP)
c/o Jeff Barry
544 Bellagio Terrace
Los Angeles, California 90049

Barton Music Corp. (ASCAP)
Room 716
1619 Broadway
New York, New York 10019

Earl Barton Music, Inc. (BMI)
1121 South Glenstone Street
Springfield, Missouri 65804

Barwin Music (ASCAP)
c/o Edwin H. Morris & Co., Inc.
31 West 54th Street
New York, New York 10019

David Batteau Music (ASCAP)
see Dawnbreaker Music Co.

Stamps Baxter Music & Printing Co. (BMI)
see Affiliated Music Enterprises Inc.

Bay-Tone Music Co. (BMI)
c/o BMI
320 West 57th Street
New York, New York 10019

Bayes Music Corp. (BMI)
Post Office Box 2120
Toluca Lake
North Hollywood, California 91602

Beachhaven Music
Address unknown

Beaver Music Publishing Corp. (ASCAP)
c/o H. B. Webman & Co.
Suite 701
1650 Broadway
New York, New York 10019

Beckie Publishing Co., Inc. (BMI)
Post Office Box 14671
Memphis, Tennessee 38114

Beckin Music (BMI)
see MCA Music

Becks Music Co. (BMI)
c/o Patrick Ferraro
2834 Shillington Road
Sinking Spring, Pennsylvania 19608

Bee Cool Publishing Co. (BMI)
c/o Jamie Music Publishing Co.
919 North Broad Street
Philadelphia, Pennsylvania 19123

Bee Music Corp. (BMI)
c/o Aileen Colitz
578 Maitland Avenue
Teaneck, New Jersey 07666

Beechwood Music Corp. (BMI)
6255 Sunset Boulevard
Hollywood, California 90028

Begonia Melodies Inc. (BMI)
see Unichappell Music Inc.

Begorra Music (BMI)
c/o Mitchell, Silberberg & Knupp
1800 Century Park East
Los Angeles, California 90067

Belack Music (ASCAP)
157 West 57 Street
New York, New York 10019

Belfast Music (BMI)
see T A T Communications Co.

Bell Boy Music (BMI)
Attention: Earl Shelton
309 South Broad Street
Philadelphia, Pennsylvania 19107

Bellamy Brothers Music (ASCAP)
Route 2
Post Office Box 294
Dade City, Florida 33525

Belmar Music Publishing Co. (BMI)
c/o Aronstein & Aronstein
1650 Broadway
New York, New York 10019

Belwin, Inc. (ASCAP)
250 Maple Avenue
Rockville Centre, New York 11570

Belwin-Mills Publishing Corp. (ASCAP)
1776 Broadway
11th Floor
New York, New York 10019

Ben-Ghazi Enterprises, Inc. (BMI)
c/o Jack Pearl, Esq.
515 Madison Avenue
New York, New York 10022

Bencorp Publishing Inc. (ASCAP)
8025 Melrose Avenue
Los Angeles, California 90046

Benday Music Corp. (BMI)
c/o A. Halsey Conway, Esq.
1350 Avenue of the Americas
New York, New York 10019

Bendig Music Corp.
6290 Sunset Boulevard
Suite 916
Hollywood, California 90028

Benifield Music Co. (BMI)
c/o Tony Benifield
800 North Broad Street
Apartment 41
Building 10
Elizabeth, New Jersey 07208

Bennie Benjamin Music, Inc. (ASCAP)
1619 Broadway
New York, New York 10019

Benral Music Co. (BMI)
c/o Ben Raleigh
Apartment 416
1131 Alta Loma Road
West Hollywood, California 90069

Bentley Music Co. (BMI)
Post Office Box 1170
Chapel Hill, North Carolina 27514

Benton Music Co. (ASCAP)
896 Oneonta Drive
Los Angeles, California 90065

List of Publishers

Beresofsky/Hebb Ltd. (BMI)
c/o Walter R. Scott
4248 Laurel Canyon Boulevard
#206
Studio City, California 91604

Berkshire Music, Inc. (BMI)
c/o Copyright Service Bureau, Ltd.
221 West 57th Street
New York, New York 10019

Irving Berlin Music Corp. (ASCAP)
41st Floor
1290 Avenue of the Americas
New York, New York 10019

Bernhardt Music Co. (BMI)
c/o Larry Weiss Music, Ltd.
20523 Wells Drive
Woodland Hills, California 91364

Bernice Music, Inc. (BMI)
c/o Copyright Service Bureau, Ltd.
221 West 57th Street
New York, New York 10019

Bertam Music Co. (ASCAP)
see Jobete Music Co., Inc.

Berwill Publishing Co. (BMI)
Attention: Ken Mansfield
816 North La Cienaga Blvd.
Los Angeles, California 90069

Bess Music Co. (BMI)
c/o Robert H. Greenberg, Esq.
Suite 1850
2029 Century Park East
Los Angeles, California 90067

Betdolph Music (ASCAP)
see Notable Music Co., Inc.

Better Half Music Co. (ASCAP)
c/o Estate of Jacqueline Hilliard
Howard E. Guedalia, Executor
David's Way
Bedford Hills, New York 10507

Forrest Richard Betts Music (BMI)
c/o John Scher
412 Pleasant Valley
West Orange, New Jersey 07052

Paul Beuscher Editions (ASCAP)
Address unknown

Bewlay Brothers Music (BMI)
c/o Diamond & Wilson
2029 Century Park East
Suite 2500
Los Angeles, California 90067

Bexhill Music Corp. (ASCAP)
c/o Sidney G. Aron
10 East 40th Street
New York, New York 10016

Bible Belt Music (BMI)
c/o Mike Rosenfeld
270 North Cannon Drive
Beverly Hills, California 90025

Bibo Music Publishers (ASCAP)
see T. B. #Harms Co.

Freddy Bienstock Music Co. (BMI)
c/o Hudson Bay Music Co.
11th Floor
1619 Broadway
New York, New York 10019

Johnny Bienstock Music (BMI)
Apartment 27-G
1 Century City
Fort Lee, New Jersey 07024

Big Apple Music Co. (BMI)
see The EMP Co.

Big Ax Music (ASCAP)
see United Artists Music Co., Inc.

Big Billy Music, Co. (BMI)
c/o Bill Cook
171 Reynolds Street
Orange, New Jersey 07050

Big Bopper Music Co. (BMI)
Address unknown

Big "D" Music, Inc. (BMI)
Spartatorium Cadiz Industrial
Building
Dallas, Texas

Big Ears Music Inc. (ASCAP)
c/o Sy Miller
18 East 48th Street
Suite 1202
New York, New York 10017

Big Elk Music (ASCAP)
see Aphrodite Music

Big Four Music Corp. (ASCAP)
2323 West Third Street
Los Angeles, California 90057

Big Hawk Music (BMI)
74 Trieste Street
Iselin, New Jersey 08830

Big Hill Music Corp. (ASCAP)
41A East 74th Street
New York, New York 10021

Big Hurry Music, Inc. (ASCAP)
321 Commercial Avenue
Palisades Park, New York 07650

Big Kitty Music
see Walden Music Inc.

Big Leaf Music (ASCAP)
see Walden Music Inc.

Big Secret Music Inc. (ASCAP)
c/o Prager & Fenton
6363 Sunset Boulevard
Los Angeles, California 90028

Big Seven Music Corp. (BMI)
1790 Broadway
18th Floor
New York, New York 10019

Big Shot Music, Inc. (ASCAP)
6565 Sunset Boulevard
Hollywood, California 90028

Big Sky Music (ASCAP)
Box 860
Cooper Station
New York, New York 10276

Big Teeth Music Corp. (BMI)
c/o Millenium Entertainment Corp.
65 East 55th Street
New York, New York 10022

Big Three Music Corp.
729 Seventh Avenue
New York, New York 10019

Big Train Music Co. (ASCAP)
9110 Sunset Boulevard
Suite 200
Los Angeles, California 90069

Bill/Bob Publishing Co. (ASCAP)
c/o The Songwriters Guild
3rd Floor
276 Fifth Avenue
New York, New York 10001

Bill-Lee Music (BMI)
c/o Williams Nichols
233 West 99th Street
Apartment #5E
New York, New York 10025

Biltmore Music Corp. (ASCAP)
Suite 8A
345 West 58th Street
New York, New York 10019

Benny Bird Co., Inc. (BMI)
see Copyright Service Bureau Ltd.

Bishop Music Co. (ASCAP)
5101 Natilija
Sherman Oaks, California 91413

Stephen Bishop Music Publishing Co. (BMI)
c/o Ames & Associates
Post Office Box 5973-120
Sherman Oaks, California 91413

Bizarre Music Co. (BMI)
6430 Sunset Boulevard
Suite 1500
Los Angeles, California 90028

Black Bull Music (ASCAP)
see Jobete Music Co., Inc.

Black Byrd Music (BMI)
c/o Mason & Sloane
9200 Sunset Boulevard
Los Angeles, California 90069

Black Leather Music
c/o Don Sterling
260 South Beverly Drive
No. 310
Beverly Hills, California 90212

Black Sheep Music Inc. (BMI)
1009 17th Avenue South
Nashville, Tennessee 37212

Blackeye Music (ASCAP)
c/o Zolt & Loomis
211 South Beverly Drive
Suite 106
Beverly Hills, California 90212

Blackhawk Music Co. (BMI)
1420 Marron Circle Northeast
Albaquerque, New Mexico 87112

Milton Blackstone Music Corp. (ASCAP)
282 West End Avenue
New York, New York 10023

Blackstone Music, Inc. (ASCAP)
1841 Broadway
New York, New York 10023

Blackwood Music Inc. (BMI)
1350 Avenue of the Americas
23rd Floor
New York, New York 10019

Blen Music, Inc. (ASCAP)
Apartment 302
11670 Sunset Boulevard
Los Angeles, California 90049

Blendingwell Music (ASCAP)
94 Grand Avenue
Englewood, New Jersey 07631

Bleu Disque Music (ASCAP)
see WB Music Corp.

Blimp Music (ASCAP)
see Third Story Music Inc.

Blockbuster Music, Inc. (BMI)
c/o Harold B. Lipsius
919 North Broad Street
Philadelphia, Pennsylvania 19123

Ben Bloom Music Corp. (ASCAP)
1619 Broadway
New York, New York 10019

Bloor Music Publishers (BMI)
Box 2941
Escondido, California 92025

Blue Book Music (BMI)
1225 North Chester Avenue
Bakersfield, California 93308

Blue Crest Music, Inc. (BMI)
Post Office Box 162
Madison, Tennessee 37115

Blue Echo Music (ASCAP)
c/o Ray Griff Enterprises
1300 Division Street
Nashville, Tennessee 37202

Elijah Blue Music (BMI)
c/o Gus H. Small Jr.
1795 Peachtree Road Northeast
Atlanta, Georgia 30309

Blue Grass Music Co. (BMI)
Room 100
157 West 57th Street
New York, New York 10019

Blue Gum Music (ASCAP)
c/o Fischbach & Fischbach
2029 Century Park East
North Tower
Los Angeles, California 90067

Blue Harbor Music Co. (BMI)
see Dawnbreaker Music Co.

Blue Indigo Music Co. (BMI)
1328 South Del Mar
San Gabriel, California 91776

Blue Lake Music (BMI)
c/o Ovation Inc.
Richard Schory
1249 Waukegan Road
Glenview, Illinois 60025

Blue Midnight Music (ASCAP)
c/o Joseph F. Pascoff & Co.
666 5th Avenue
New York, New York 10019

Blue Monday Music (BMI)
6255 Sunset Boulevard
Suite 1019
Hollywood, California 90028

Blue Moon Music (ASCAP)
see April Music Inc.

Blue Network Music
see Interworld Music Group

Blue Network Music, Inc. (ASCAP)
c/o RCA Records
Attention: Dorothy A. Schwartz
1133 Avenue of the Americas
New York, New York 10036

Blue Peacock Music (BMI)
see Braintree Music

Blue Pearl Music Corp. (BMI)
Post Office Box 144
Deal, New Jersey 07723

Blue Quill Music (ASCAP)
see Cherry Lane Music Co., Inc.

Blue Ridge Publishing Co. (BMI)
c/o Bernard Pearlman
1540 Brewster Avenue
Cincinnati, Ohio 45207

Blue River Music, Inc. (BMI)
c/o Harry Bluestone
1626 North Vine Street
Hollywood, California 90028

Blue Seas Music Inc. (ASCAP)
c/o Braunstein & Chernin
50 East 42nd Street
New York, New York 10017

BNP Music Publishing Co. (ASCAP)
see T. B. #Harms Co.

Bob-Dan Music Co. (BMI)
29 West 125th Street
New York, New York 10027

Bobette Music (ASCAP)
c/o Shankman & De Blasio
185 Pier Avenue
Santa Monica, California 90405

Bobrich Music, Inc. (BMI)
263 Veterans Boulevard
Carlstadt, New Jersey 07072

Boca Music Inc. (ASCAP)
532 Sylvan Avenue
Englewood Cliffs, New Jersey 07632

Bocephus Music Inc. (BMI)
see Singletree Music Co., Inc.

Bonatemp Publishing Co. (BMI)
3141 North Robertson Street
New Orleans, Louisiana 70117

Bonnyview Music Corp. (ASCAP)
7120 West Sunset Boulevard
Los Angeles, California 90046

Boom Music, Inc. (BMI)
c/o Landsman & Frank
Suite 400
9595 Wilshire Boulevard
Beverly Hills, California 90212

Boosey & Hawkes Inc. (ASCAP)
24 West 57th Street
New York, New York 10019

Boston Music Co. (ASCAP)
116 Boylston Street
Boston, Massachusetts 02116

Boulder Music Corp. (ASCAP)
9 Rockefeller Plaza
New York, New York 10020

Bourne Co. (ASCAP)
437 Fifth Avenue
New York, New York 10016

Bovina Music (ASCAP)
see April Music Inc.

Bowling Green Music (BMI)
c/o Studio P/R, Inc.
224 South Lebanon Street
Lebanon, Indiana 46052

Roger Bowling Music (BMI)
Post Office Box 120537
Nashville, Tennessee 37212

Box & Cox Publications, Inc. (ASCAP)
c/o Abels, Clark & Osterberg
224 East 50th Street
New York, New York 10022

James Boy Publishing Co. (BMI)
Post Office Box 128
Worcester, Pennsylvania 19490

Perry Bradford Music Publishing Co.
104-49 165th Street
Jamaica, New York 11433

Patrick Bradley Music Corp. (BMI)
c/o Perception Ventures, Inc.
165 West 46th Street
New York, New York 10036

Bradshaw Music, Inc. (BMI)
8745 Sunset Boulevard
Hollywood, California 90046

Braintree Music (BMI)
c/o Segel & Goldman Inc.
9348 Santa Monica Boulevard
Number 304
Beverly Hills, California 90210

Brakenbury Music, Inc. (BMI)
c/o Daniel M. Sklar, Esq.
6399 Wilshire Boulevard
Los Angeles, California 90048

Bramble Music Publishing Co., Inc. (BMI)
1609 Roy Acuff Place
Nashville, Tennessee 37203

Bramsdene Music Corp. (BMI)
271 North Avenue
New Rochelle, New York 10802

Brandom Music Co. (ASCAP)
1323 South Michigan Avenue
Chicago, Illinois 60605

Brandwood Music Inc. (BMI)
c/o Ansley R. Fleetwood
4206 Lone Oak Road
Nashville, Tennessee 37215

Braun Music, Inc.
Address unknown

Brazos Valley Music, Inc. (BMI)
Box 78
Route 1
Sand Springs, Oklahoma 74063

Break of Dawn Music Inc. (BMI)
c/o Real Records Inc.
Post Office Box 958
434 Avenue U
Bogalvsa, Louisiana 70427

Breakfast Publishing Co., The (BMI)
c/o Donald C. Farber Esq., Lonboy,
Hewilt, O'Brien & Boardman
600 Madison Avenue
New York, New York 10022

Bregman, Vocco & Conn, Inc. (ASCAP)
1619 Broadway
New York, New York 10019

Brenner Music, Inc. (BMI)
11th Floor
1619 Broadway
New York, New York 10019

Bresnahan Music (BMI)
c/o Dan Dalton Productions
5241 Round Meadow Road
Calabasas, California 91302

Brew Music Co. (BMI)
c/o Drew Management Inc.
1995 Broadway
New York, New York 10023

Brewster Music Publishing, Inc. (BMI)
570 Seventh Avenue
New York, New York 10018

Bri-Deb Music Corp. (BMI)
c/o S. Shulman
Route 3
Oakvale Drive
Brentwood, Tennessee 37027

Briarpatch Music (BMI)
Box 140110
Donelson, Tennessee 37214

Bridgeport Music Inc. (BMI)
c/o Norman R. Kurtz
712 5th Avenue
New York, New York 10019

Bright Moments Music (BMI)
c/o Jesse Barish
2612 Pacific Avenue
Venice, California 90291

Bright Tunes Music Corp. (ASCAP)
2 Pennsylvania Plaza
New York, New York 10001

Brighton Music Co., Inc. (ASCAP)
Suite 804
1780 Broadway
New York, New York 10019

Brim Music Inc.
Post Office Box 120591
Nashville, Tennessee 37212

Bristol Music Corp. (ASCAP)
Suite 8A
345 West 58th Street
New York, New York 10019

Broadcast Music Inc. (BMI)
10 Music Square East
Nashville, Tennessee 37203

Broadside Music Inc. (BMI songs) (BMI)
c/o Jeff Barry Enterprises
9100 Sunset Boulevard
Suite #200
Los Angeles, California 90069

Broadway Music Corp. (ASCAP)
Suite 1920
135 West 50th Street
New York, New York 10020

Brockman Enterprises Inc. (ASCAP)
  Leibren Music Division
  c/o Jess S. Morgan & Co., Inc.
  6420 Wilshire Blvd.
  19th Floor
  Los Angeles, California 90048

Brojay Music (ASCAP)
  see Yellow Brick Road Music

Broken Bird Music (ASCAP)
  c/o Segel & Goldman Inc.
  9200 Sunset Boulevard
  Suite 1000
  Los Angeles, California 90069

Broken Moon
  Address unknown

Samuel Bronston Music Publishing, Inc.
(ASCAP)
  10 Columbus Circle
  New York, New York 10019

Bronze Music, Inc.
  c/o Surefire Music Co., Inc.
  60 Music Square West
  Nashville, Tennessee 37203

The Brooklyn Music Co. (ASCAP)
  Ms. Linda Laurie
  14660 Lacota Place
  Sherman Oaks, California 91403

Brother Publishing Co. (BMI)
  c/o Brother Records
  10880 Wilshire Boulevard
  Suite 306
  Los Angeles, California 90024

Brother Texas Music (BMI)
  6126 Selma Avenue
  Hollywood, California 90028

Brothers Two Music (ASCAP)
  c/o Harry Compton
  Route 1 Box 31
  Hurricane Hills, Tennessee 37078

Broude Brothers, Ltd. (ASCAP)
  170 Varick Street
  New York, New York 10013

Brouhaha Music (ASCAP)
  see Music Directions Associates Ltd.

Ray Brown Music (BMI)
  Post Office Box 1254
  Hollywood, California 90028

Bruin Music Co. (BMI)
  see Famous Music Co.

Bruised Oranges (ASCAP)
  see Big Ears Music Inc.

Bruiser Music, Div. of Scoop Enterprises
(BMI)
  see Blackwood Music Inc.

Albert E. Brumley & Sons
  Powell, Missouri 65730

Brunswick-Balke-Collender Co.
  Address unknown

Brut Music Publishing (ASCAP)
  Div. of Brut Productions Inc.
  1345 Avenue of the Americas
  New York, New York 10019

Bryden Music, Inc. (BMI)
  157 West 57th Street
  New York, New York 10019

Brynor Music, Inc. (BMI)
  c/o Ray Bryant
  179 Stoneway Lane
  Bala Cynwyd, Pennsylvania 19004

Buckaroo Music Publishing Co. (BMI)
  1921 Vista Del Mar
  Number 207
  Hollywood, California 90068

Buckeye Music, Inc. (ASCAP)
  c/o Carlson Music Co.
  4625 Northwest 44th Street
  Fort Lauderdale, Florida 33319

Buckeye Publishing Co. (BMI)
  204 West Eighth Street
  Cincinnati, Ohio 45202

Buckhorn Music Publishing Co., Inc. (BMI)
  Box 120547
  Nashville, Tennessee 37212

Budd Music Corp. (ASCAP)
  18531 Wells Drive
  Tarzana, California 19356

Buddah Music Inc. (ASCAP)
  see United Artists Music Co., Inc.

Buddy Music (BMI)
1046 Carol Drive
Los Angeles, California 90069

Bug Music (BMI)
Bug Music Group
6777 Hollywood Boulevard
9th Floor
Hollywood, California 90028

Buggerlugs Music Co. (BMI)
see Irving Music Inc.

Bull Fighter Music (BMI)
Box 435
Goodlettsville, Tennessee 37072

Bull Pen Music Co. (BMI)
11740 Ventura Boulevard
Studio City, California 91604

Bullet Proof Music Inc. (BMI)
c/o Gelfand, Breslauer, Macnaw,
Rennertt & Feldman
9134 Sunset Boulevard
Los Angeles, California 90069

Jim Bulliet Music Corp. (ASCAP)
Address unknown

Bulls-Eye Music, Inc. (ASCAP)
6526 Selma Avenue
Hollywood, California 90028

Buna Music Corp. (BMI)
Post Office Box 8
Santa Claus, Indiana 47579

Bungalow Music (ASCAP)
see Island Music

Fred Burch Music (BMI)
2805 Shauna Court
Nashville, Tennessee 37214

Burdette Music Co. (BMI)
c/o First American Marketing
Suite 411
1008 Western Avenue
Seattle, Washington 98104

Joe Burke Music Co. (ASCAP)
15 East 48th Street
New York, New York 10017

Burke-Van Heusen Co. (ASCAP)
A Division of Bourne Co.
437 Fifth Avenue
New York, New York 10016

Burlington Music Corp. (ASCAP)
539 West 25th Street
New York, New York 10001

Burnt Oak Publishing Co. (BMI)
Box 50
Route 3
Fairhope, Alabama 36532

Burthen Music Co., Inc. (ASCAP)
see Chappell & Co., Inc.

Bushka Music (ASCAP)
Manatt, Fellows, Rothenberg,
Manley & Tunney
1888 Century Park East
21st Floor
Los Angeles, California 90067

Butter Music (BMI)
Divison of Cream Records Inc.
8025 Helrose Avenue
Los Angeles, California 90046

Buttercup Music (BMI)
c/o Lorene Mann
399 Annex Avenue
Nashville, Tennessee 37209

Butterfield Music Corp. (BMI)
c/o Mr. Sidney Aron
Ten East 40th Street
New York, New York 10016

Butterfly Gong Music (BMI)
c/o Moultree Accountancy Corp.
Post Office Box 5270
Beverly Hills, California 90210

Red Buttons Music (ASCAP)
c/o Traubner & Flynn
No. 2500
2049 Century Park East
Los Angeles, California 90067

Buxton Hill Music Corp. (ASCAP)
609 Fifth Avenue
New York, New York 10017

Bygosh Music Corp. (ASCAP)
Rural Delivery One
Brookfield, Vermont 05036

C

C. C. Publishing Co., Inc. (ASCAP)
309 South Broad Street
Philadelphia, Pennsylvania 19107

C/Hear Services, Inc. (BMI)
c/o Emanuel S. Warshauer
460 Park Avenue
New York, New York 10022

Cachand Music Inc. (BMI)
see Copyright Service Bureau Ltd.

Irving Caesar Music Corp. (ASCAP)
850 Seventh Avenue
New York, New York 10019

Caesar's Music Library (ASCAP)
1022 North Palm Avenue
Los Angeles, California 90069

Cafe' Americana (ASCAP)

Cahn Music Co. (ASCAP)
Plymouth Music Co., Inc.
170 Northeast 33rd Street
Fort Lauderdale, Florida 33334

Caleb Music (ASCAP)
see Gypsy Boy Music Inc.

Caledonia Productions (ASCAP)
see WB Music Corp.

Caledonia Soul Music (ASCAP)
see WB Music Corp.

Caliber Music (ASCAP)
see Web 4 Music Inc.

Calico Records, Inc. (ASCAP)
490 Bakewell Building
Pittsburgh, Pennsylvania

CAM-USA Inc. (BMI)
420 Lexington Avenue
Suite 2820
New York, New York 10017

Cambrae Music (ASCAP)
see Brockman Enterprises Inc.

Camex Music Inc. (BMI)
489 Fifth Avenue
New York, New York 10017

Camp Songs Music (BMI)
c/o Gottlieb, Schiff, Ticktin,
Sternklar & Singer
Attention: Mark D. Sendroff
555 Fifth Avenue
New York, New York 10017

Campbell-Connelly, Inc. (ASCAP)
565 Fifth Avenue
New York, New York 10017

Canaan Music Inc. (ASCAP)
c/o Gelfand, Breslauer & Rennert
Box 2202
Palm Springs, California 92263

Canadiana-Begonia Melodies, Inc. (BMI)
c/o Chappell International-New York
810 Seventh Avenue
New York, New York 10019

Canadiana-Casserole (BMI)
c/o Chappell International-New York
810 Seventh Avenue
New York, New York 10019

Canadiana-Ensign (BMI)
c/o Chappell International-New York
810 Seventh Avenue
New York, New York 10019

Canadiana-Gibb Brothers (BMI)
c/o Chappell International-New York
810 Seventh Avenue
New York, New York 10019

Canadiana-Glaser (BMI)
c/o Chappell International-New York
810 Seventh Avenue
New York, New York 10019

Canadiana-Jadar (BMI)
c/o Chappell International-New York
810 Seventh Avenue
New York, New York 10019

Canadiana-Morris (BMI)
c/o Chappell International-New York
810 Seventh Avenue
New York, New York 10019

Canadiana-MRC (BMI)
c/o Chappell International-New York
810 Seventh Avenue
New York, New York 10019

Canadiana Music (BMI)
c/o Chappell International-New York
810 Seventh Avenue
New York, New York 10019

Canadiana-New Keys (BMI)
c/o Chappell International-New York
810 Seventh Avenue
New York, New York 10019

Canadiana-Six Continents (BMI)
c/o Chappell International-New York
810 Seventh Avenue
New York, New York 10019

Canadiana-Unichappell (BMI)
c/o Chappell International-New York
810 Seventh Avenue
New York, New York 10019

Canal Publishing Inc. (BMI)
6325 Guilford Avenue
Suite 4
Indianapolis, Indiana 46220

Candlewood Mountain Music Publishing Inc
(ASCAP)
see Almo Music Corp.

Cane Garden Music (ASCAP)
see Coral Reefer Music

Cannonball Music (BMI)
Address unknown

Canopy Music Inc. (ASCAP)
c/o Bruce V. Grakal
1427 7th Street
Santa Monica, California 90401

Can't Stop Music (BMI)
Division of Can't Productions Inc.
c/o Allen Grubman
65 East 55th Street
New York, New York 10022

Canterbury Music (BMI)
c/o David Rubinson
827 Folsom Street
San Francisco, California 94107

Capano Music (ASCAP)
A Division of Britone, Inc.
237 Chestnut Street
Westville, New Jersey 08093

Capizzi Music (BMI)
c/o Lenny Capizzi
Post Office Box 3576
Hollywood, California 90028

Capri Music Corp. (BMI)
c/o Alfred Publishing Co.
Post Office Box 5964
15335 Morrison Street
Sherman Oaks, California 91413

Captain Crystal Music (BMI)
7505 Jerez Court
Number E
Rancho La Costa, California 92008

Captive Music (BMI)
Div. of Aliases Inc.
2407 12th Avenue South
Nashville, Tennessee 37204

Caraljo Music Inc. (BMI)
c/o William Norman Jr.
332 Chartres Street
New Orleans, Louisiana 70130

Carbert Music Inc. (BMI)
1619 Broadway
Room 609
New York, New York 10019

Careers Music Inc. (ASCAP)
see Arista Music Inc.

Cares Music Co. (ASCAP)
14322 Califa Street
Van Nuys, California 91401

Roy J. Carew (ASCAP)
Apartment 51, 2-A
3380 Chiswick Court
Silver Spring, Maryland 20906

Carlot Music, Inc. (BMI)
c/o Fred Raphael
6758 Colgate Avenue
Los Angeles, California 90048

Carlyle Music Publishing Corp. (ASCAP)
1650 Broadway
New York, New York 10019

Carmichael Music Publications, Inc.
(ASCAP)
119 West 57th Street
New York, New York 10019

Carnegie Music Corp. (BMI)
c/o Massey Music Co., Inc.
60 West 68th Street
New York, New York 10023

Carney Music, Inc. (BMI)
2203 Spruce Street
Philadelphia, Pennsylvania 19103

Carolintone Music Co., Inc. (BMI)
3119 Kelton Avenue
Los Angeles, California 90034

Carreta Music, Inc. (BMI)
Post Office Box 3065
Brentwood, Tennessee 37027

Carrhorn Music Inc. (BMI)
809 Whipporwill Drive
Port Orange, Florida 32019

Carrie Music Co., Inc. (ASCAP)
c/o James Hendix Enterprises
Post Office Box 90639
902 42nd Avenue North
Nashville, Tennessee 37209

Alan Cartee Music (BMI)
22 Music Square East
Nashville, Tennessee 37203

Carthay Music Publishing Inc. (BMI)
One Carthay Plaza
Los Angeles, California 90048

Casa David (ASCAP)
see Jac Music Co., Inc.

Casa Latina, Inc. (ASCAP)
Suite 2P
345 West 58th Street
New York, New York 10019

Caseyem Music (BMI)
c/o Mike Curb Productions Inc.
3300 Warner Boulevard
Burbank, California 91510

Johnny Cash Music, Inc. (BMI)
11th Floor
1619 Broadway
New York, New York 10019

Buzz Cason Publications Inc. (ASCAP)
2804 Azalea Place
Nashville, Tennessee 37204

Cass County Music Co. (ASCAP)
Attention: Donald Henley
1800 Century Park East
Suite 900
Los Angeles, California 90067

Cassandra Music, Inc. (BMI)
c/o Stutz
Box 268
Glenwood Road
Ellington, Connecticut 06029

Casserole Music Inc. (BMI)
see Unichappell Music Inc.

Castle Hill Publishing Ltd. (ASCAP)
c/o Castle Music Productions
Duplex Suite
923 Fifth Avenue
New York, New York 10021

Castle Music (ASCAP)
see Sheepshead Bay Music

Castleridge Music (ASCAP)
Post Office Box 12723
Nashville, Tennessee 37212

Catalogue Music, Inc. (BMI)
Suite 348
870 Seventh Avenue
New York, New York 10019

Catch a Star Music Co. (BMI)
c/o Morningstar Enterprises Inc.
2229 Stradella Road
Los Angeles, California 90024

Cauldron Music (ASCAP)
see Walden Music Inc.

Cavalcade Music Corp. (ASCAP)
136 East 57th Street
New York, New York 10022

Cayman Music (ASCAP)
see Copyright Service Bureau Ltd.

Cebco Music (ASCAP)
c/o Charles E. Bloom
Oppenheim Appel Dixon & Co.
One New York Plaza
New York, New York 10004

Cecilia Music Publishing Co. (ASCAP)
c/o Peter F. O'Brien, S.J.
No. 4D
220 West 98th Street
New York, New York 10025

Cedarwood Publishing Co., Inc. (BMI)
39 Music Square East
Nashville, Tennessee 37203

Ceilidh Productions (ASCAP)
Attention: David Kranatt
350 West 51st Street
Apartment 3C
New York, New York 10019

Celann Music Co. (BMI)
1370 Avenue of the Americas
New York, New York 10019

Center City Music (ASCAP)
c/o Mitchell, Silberberg & Knupp
1800 Century Park East
Los Angeles, California 90067

Central Songs (BMI)
see Copyright Service Bureau Ltd.

Century Songs (BMI)
c/o Beechwood Music Corp.
6255 Sunset Boulevard
Holywood, California 90028

C'est Music (ASCAP)
see Quackenbush Music Ltd.

Cetra Music Corp. (BMI)
c/o Morton A. Kaplan
5828 South University Avenue
Chicago, Illinois 60637

Chambro Music Publishing Co. (BMI)
c/o E. S. Prager
1790 Broadway
New York, New York 10019

Champion Music Corp. (BMI)
c/o MCA Music
445 Park Avenue
New York, New York 10022

Chandos Music (ASCAP)
see Hillgreen Music

Channel Music Co. (ASCAP)
A Division of Music Associates
Suite A
1025 17th Avenue South
Nashville, Tennessee 37212

Chapin Music (ASCAP)
c/o Gelfand, Macnow, Rennert &
Feldman
489 Fifth Avenue
New York, New York 10017

Saul I. Chapin (ASCAP)
Address unknown

Chappell & Co., Inc. (ASCAP)
810 Seventh Avenue
New York, New York 10019

Chappell-Styne Music (ASCAP)
see Chappell & Co., Inc.

Chardon Music Inc. (BMI)
c/o Chardon Inc.
3189 Royal Lane
Dallas, Texas 75229

Ray Charles Enterprises (ASCAP)
see United Artists Music Co., Inc.

Charleville Music (BMI)
9885 Charleville Boulevard
Beverly Hills, California 90212

Charling Music Corp. (ASCAP)
31 West 54th Strret
New York, New York 10019

Chart Music Publishing House, Inc.
c/o Birch Tree Group, Ltd.
Post Office Box 2072
Princeton, New Jersey 08540

Chattahoochee Music (BMI)
4870 Lake Fjord Pass
Marietta, Georgia 30062

Cheap Thrills (ASCAP)
c/o Royalty Control Corp.
680 Beach Street
San Francisco, California 94109

Check Out Music (BMI)
280 South Beverly Drive
Suite 412
Beverly Hills, California 90212

Ched Music Co. (ASCAP)
c/o Charles Tobias
1650 Broadway
New York, New York 10019

Cheeks the Bird Music (BMI)
c/o Gelfand, Breslauer, Rennert &
Feldman
44 Montgomery Street
Suite 224
San Francisco, California 94104

Chenista Music (BMI)
see Regent Music

Cherio Corp. (BMI)
c/o Lee V. Eastman, Esq.
39 West 54th Street
New York, New York 10019

Cherritown Music Publishing Co. (BMI)
c/o George H. Brown Jr.
161 Jefferson Avenue
Memphis, Tennessee 38103

Cherry Lane Music Co., Inc. (ASCAP)
110 Midland Avenue
Port Chester, New York 10573

Cherry River Music Co. (BMI)
see Cherry Lane Music Co., Inc.

Cherrybell Music Co. (ASCAP)
Suite 201
1615 Westwood Boulevard
West Los Angeles, California 90025

Cheshire Music Inc. (BMI)
10 Columbus Circle
New York, New York 10019

Chesnick Music, Inc. (ASCAP)
c/o Norman Rosemont
The Plaza
Fifth Avenue and Central Park South
New York, New York 10019

Jerry Chesnut Music Inc. (BMI)
c/o Jerry Chestnut
40 Music Square East
Nashville, Tennessee 37203

Chester Music New York, Inc.
30 West 61st Street
New York, New York 10023

Chevis Publishing Corp. (BMI)
2527 Miami Avenue
Nashville, Tennessee 37214

Chic Music Inc. (BMI)
see WB Music Corp.

Chicken Flats Music Inc. (BMI)
c/o Eric Eisner
Mitchell, Silberberg, & Knupp
1800 Century Park East
Los Angeles, California 90067

Chicken Key Music Inc. (ASCAP)
see Cherry Lane Music Co., Inc.

Chimneyville Music Publishing Co. (BMI)
3538 Lee Drive
Jackson, Mississippi 39212

Chinnichap Publishing Inc. (BMI)
see Arista Music Inc.

Choice Music, Inc. (ASCAP)
9109 Sunset Boulevard
Hollywood, California 90046

Chorizo Music (BMI)
see Braintree Music

Chris-Marc Music
c/o Elmer Fox, Westheimer & Co.
1880 Century Park East
Suite 600
Los Angeles, California 90067

Christie-Max Music (ASCAP)
c/o The Songwriters Guild
3rd Floor
276 Fifth Avenue
New York, New York 10001

Chriswood Music (BMI)
1204 16th Avenue South
Nashville, Tennessee 37212

Chrome Willie Music (BMI)
c/o Don Bachrach, Esq.
Iglow & Bachrach
8601 Wilshire Boulevard
Suite 1001
Los Angeles, California 90211

Chrysalis Music Corp. (ASCAP)
Chrysalis Music Group
645 Madison Avenue
New York, New York 10022

List of Publishers

John Church Co. (ASCAP)
Bryn Mawr, Pennsylvania 19010

Cicada Music Inc. (BMI)
c/o Anthony Mazzone
30 Sherbrooke East Street
Apartment 2
Montreal, Quebec H2X 1C2
Canada

Cigar Music (ASCAP)
see Beechwood Music Corp.

Cinema 5 Publishing (ASCAP)
1500 Broadway
New York, New York 10036

Cinema Songs, Inc. (ASCAP)
c/o A. J. Silverman & Co.
12412 Ventura Boulevard
Studio City, California 91604

Cinerama Music (ASCAP)
141 South Robertson Boulevard
Los Angeles, California 90048

Cintom Music (ASCAP)
c/o Arnold Mills & Associates
Suite 201
8721 Sunset Boulevard
Los Angeles, California 90069

Cireco Music, Inc. (BMI)
10 & Parker Streets
Berkeley, California 94710

Claiborne Music (BMI)
Manor Club
4000 Montpelier Road
Rockville, Maryland 20853

Clamike Music (BMI)
c/o Mietus Copyright Management
Post Office Box 432
2351 Laurana Road
Union, New Jersey 07083

Clara Music Publishing Corp. (ASCAP)
see Sanga Music Inc.

Claremont Music, Inc. (ASCAP)
c/o Miller & Miller
32 Broadway
New York, New York 10004

Claridge Music (ASCAP)
see MPL Communications Inc.

Claude A. Music (ASCAP)
see Chappell & Co., Inc.

Clears Music (BMI)
c/o Segel & Goldman, Inc.
No. 304
9348 Santa Monica Boulevard
Beverly Hills, California 90210

Jack Clement Music, Inc. (BMI)
639 Madison Avenue
Memphis, Tennessee 38103

Cliffdweller Music (BMI)
c/o Anthem Music Productions
216 Carlton Street
Toronto, Ontario M5A 2L1
Canada

Clockus Music, Inc. (BMI)
c/o Ed Marmor
6017 Country Club Drive
Lake Shastina
Weed, California 96094

Coal Miner's Music Inc. (BMI)
7 Music Circle North
Nashville, Tennessee 37203

Coast Music (BMI)
see Amestoy Music

Coast to Coast Music Corp. (BMI)
Post Office Box 5339
FDR Station
New York, New York 10150

Cock & Trumpet Music Inc. (ASCAP)
see Arista Music Inc.

George M. Cohan Music Publishing Co.
(ASCAP)
c/o Freddy Bienstock Enterprises
1619 Broadway
New York, New York 10019

Colby Music, Inc. (ASCAP)
c/o Samuel Jesse Buzzell
460 Park Avenue
New York, New York 10022

Paul Colby Ltd. (ASCAP)
c/o Paul Colby
149 Bleecker Street
New York, New York 10012

Cold Zinc Music (BMI)
c/o John Ford Coley
Post Office Box 1030
Del Mar, California 92014

Cole Arama Music (BMI)
c/o Segel & Goldman Inc.
9348 Santa Monica Boulevard
2nd Floor
Beverly Hills, California 90210

Larry Coleman Music (BMI)
200 East 66th Street
New York, New York 10021

Colfam Music, Inc. (BMI)
c/o Melvin L. Collins
5622 South Maryland Avenue
Chicago, Illinois 60637

Colgems-EMI Music Inc. (ASCAP)
see Screen Gems-EMI Music Inc.

Colorado Music Inc. (ASCAP)
Attention: Kenneth Suddleson
c/o Loeb & Loeb
10100 Santa Monica Boulevard
Los Angeles, California 90067

Columbia Pictures Publications
16333 Northwest 54th Avenue
Hialeah, Florida 33014

Columbine Music Inc. (ASCAP)
see United Artists Music Co., Inc.

Com Music (ASCAP)
Attention: Lee Loughrane
c/o Kaufman, Eisenberg & Co.
9301 Wilshire Boulevard
Suite 212
Beverly Hills, California 90210

Combine Music Corp. (BMI)
35 Music Square East
Nashville, Tennessee 37203

Comet Music Corp. (ASCAP)
c/o ATV-Kirshner Music Corp.
6255 Sunset Boulevard
Hollywood, California 90028

Command Music Co., Inc. (BMI)
c/o William H. Peck
Post Office Box
Oyster Bay, New York 11771

Commander Publications (ASCAP)
1610 North Argyle Avenue
Hollywood, California 90028

Commodores Entertainment Publishing Corp (ASCAP)
c/o Benjamin Ashburn Associates
39 West 55th Street
New York, New York 10019

Complacent Toonz Inc. (BMI)
2029 Century Park East
Number 1370
Los Angeles, California 90067

Compton Music Corp. (ASCAP)
250 West 57th Street
New York, New York 10107

Concerto Music Corp. (ASCAP)
c/o Kathryn Fina
No. 101
4630 Willis Avenue
Sherman Oaks, California 91403

Concertone Songs, Inc. (ASCAP)
161 West 54th Street
New York, New York 10019

Conducive Music Inc. (BMI)
c/o Parks, Adams & Palmer
400 South Beverly Drive
Number 100
Beverly Hills, California 90212

Conestoga Music (BMI)
38 Yorkville Avenue
Toronto, Ontario M4W 165
Canada

Coney Island Whitefish Music (ASCAP)
Attention: Charles Shneider
635 Madison Avenue
New York, New York 10022

Congress Music Publications (ASCAP)
410 Northeast 17th Street
Miami, Florida 33132

Congressional Music Publications (ASCAP)
1224 Koko Head Avenue
Honolulu, Hawaii 96816

Conley Music, Inc. (ASCAP)
222 Rittenhouse Square
Philadelphia, Pennsylvania 19103

Curtain Call Productions, Inc. (ASCAP)
c/o Becker & London, Esq.
30 Lincoln Plaza
New York, New York 10023

Mann Curtis Music Co. (ASCAP)
122 Sequoia Glen Lane
Novato, California 94947

Curtis Music Enterprises, Inc. (ASCAP)
c/o Fred S. Kohler & Co.
171 Madison Avenue
New York, New York 10016

Dan Curtis Productions, Inc. (BMI)
5451 Marathon Street
Los Angeles, California 90038

Curtom Publishing Co., Inc. (BMI)
5915 North Lincoln Avenue
Chicago, Illinois 60645

CVY Music Publishing Co. (ASCAP)
390 West End Avenue
New York, New York 10024

D

Da Ann Music (ASCAP)
Attention: David Crawford
96 West Street
Englewood, New Jersey 07631

Dacapo Musik (ASCAP)
Address unknown

Daddy Sam Music Co. (BMI)
c/o Nino Tempo
19530 Superior Street
Northridge, California 91324

Ted Daffan Music (BMI)
1115 Thornton
Houston, Texas 77018

Daksel Music Corp. (BMI)
c/o Leber and Krebs Inc.
65 West 55th St.
New York, New York 10019

Dallas Music, Co., Inc. (BMI)
c/o Smokey Rogers
14011 Wembleton Drive
Victorsville, California 92392

Damian Music Publishing Co. (ASCAP)
Box 592
Blackhorse Pyke
Williamstown, New Jersey 08094

Damila Music, Inc. (ASCAP)
40 West 55th Street
New York, New York 10019

Dandelion Music Co. (BMI)
see Jamie Music Publishing Co.

Dandy Dittys (ASCAP)
see Jamie Music Publishing Co.

Dangerous Music (ASCAP)
Attention: William Rush
1512 Marion Street
Wall, New Jersey 07719

Daniel Music Ltd. (ASCAP)
c/o Zizzu, Marcus, Stein & Couture
Attention: Alan Stein
270 Madison Avenue
New York, New York 10016

Danielle Music Inc. (ASCAP)
Division of Hilton House, Inc.
Post Office Box 315
Cleveland, Ohio 44127

Charles N. Daniels, Inc. (ASCAP)
11th Floor
1619 Broadway
New York, New York 10019

Danor Music Inc. (BMI)
see Irving Music Inc.

Daphne Music Co. (BMI)
c/o Daniel E. Bellack
257 Kenilworth Avenue
Kenilworth, Illinois 60043

Dare Music Co. (BMI)
c/o Alvin Gladstone
Schultz Gladstone & Co.
98 Cutter Mill Road
Great Neck, New York 11021

Dark Cloud Music Inc. (BMI)
373 Walnut Street
Englewood, New Jersey 07631

Darkroom Music (BMI)
see WB Music Corp.

Darnoc Music (BMI)
2958 Beachwood Drive
Hollywood, California 90068

Dart Music Co. (BMI)
c/o Goddard Music Co.
1453 North Vine Street
Hollywood, California 90028

Dartmouth Music, Inc. (ASCAP)
Suite 2160
10 Columbus Circle
New York, New York 10019

Darwall Music Co. (BMI)
c/o Hadley Murrell
1777 North Vine
#222
Hollywood, California 90028

Davandou Music (ASCAP)
Address unknown

Joe Davis (ASCAP)
518 West 50th Street
New York, New York 10019

Benny Davis Music (ASCAP)
c/o The Songwriters Guild
3rd Floor
276 Fifth Avenue
New York, New York 10001

Davlin Music (ASCAP)
2308 Wellington Street
Salt Lake City, Utah 84107

Dawnbreaker Music Co. (BMI)
c/o Manatt, Phelps, Rothenberg &
Tunney
1888 Century Park East
21st Floor
Los Angeles, California 90067

Day Music Co. (ASCAP)
c/o Mort Garson
Apartment 1G
409 West 57th Street
New York, New York 10019

Dayben Music Corp. (ASCAP)
Room 405
39 West 55th Street
New York, New York 10019

Daywin Music, Inc. (BMI)
c/o Six Continents Music
Publishing, Inc.
8304 Beverly Boulevard
Los Angeles, California 90048

De Rose Music (ASCAP)
c/o The Songwriters Guild
3rd Floor
276 Fifth Avenue
New York, New York 10001

Debdave Music Inc. (BMI)
Post Office Box 140110
Donnelson, Tennessee 37214

Debmar Publishing Co., Inc. (ASCAP)
1320 Vine Street
Philadelphia, Pennsylvania 19107

DeCapo Music Inc. (BMI)
202 Adams Avenue
Memphis, Tennessee 38103

Decibel Publishing Co. (BMI)
c/o Cory Wade
4901 Southwest 71st Place
Miami, Florida 33155

Dee Dee (BMI)
318 West 78th Street
New York, New York 10024

Amy Dee Music Corp. (ASCAP)
c/o Milton Delugg
2740 Claray Drive
Los Angeles, California 90024

Dee Pam Publishing Co.
Address unknown

Deep Fork Music, Inc. (ASCAP)
15 East 48th Street
New York, New York 10017

Deer Patch Music (ASCAP)
see Sweet River Music Inc.

Deerhaven Music Corp. (ASCAP)
37 West 57th Street
New York, New York 10019

Deertrack Music (BMI)
7563 Delongpre Avenue
Los Angeles, California 90046

Dejamus Inc. (ASCAP)
see Dick James Music Inc.

Delbon Publishing Co. (BMI)
c/o Mason & Sloane
9200 Sunset Boulevard
Los Angeles, California 90069

Delicate Music Co. (ASCAP)
see Surrey Music Co.

Delightful Music Ltd. (BMI)
c/o Mr. Ted Eddy
200 West 57th Street
New York, New York 10019

Delmore Music Co. (ASCAP)
Post Office Box 2324
Menlo Park, California 94025

Richard Delvy Enterprises Inc. (ASCAP)
8127 Elrita Drive
Los Angeles, California 90046

Dena Music, Inc. (ASCAP)
6087 Sunset Boulevard
Hollywood, California 90028

Dennis Music Co., Inc. (BMI)
c/o Helen Blum
3900 Greystone Avenue
Riverdale, New York 10463

Denny Music, Inc. (ASCAP)
146 Seventh Avenue
Nashville, Tennessee 37203

Denslow Music, Inc. (ASCAP)
c/o Peggy Lee
2345 Kimridge Drive
Beverly Hills, California 90210

Denton & Haskins Corp. (ASCAP)
Post Office Box 340
Radio City Station
New York, New York 10101

Derglenn Publishing (BMI)
1006 Benedict Canon Drive
Beverly Hills, California 90210

Derringer Music Inc. (BMI)
c/o Borck & Mensch
350 Fifth Avenue
Room 5220
New York, New York 10001

Derry Music Co. (BMI)
Suite 800
601 Montgomery Street
San Francisco, California 94111

Desert Moon Songs Ltd. (ASCAP)
see Triple 'O' Songs Inc.

Desert Palms Publishing Co. (BMI)
3830 North Seventh Street
Phoenix, Arizona 85014

Desert Rain Music Ltd. (ASCAP)
see Triple 'O' Songs Inc.

Deshufflin' Inc.
c/o Michael Tannen, Esq.
36 East 61st Street
New York, New York 10021

Desiard Music Co., Inc. (BMI)
Room 2219
250 West 57th Street
New York, New York 10019

Desiderata Music Co., Inc. (BMI)
212 Old Short Hills Road
Short Hills, New Jersey 07078

Desilu Music Corp. (ASCAP)
see MPL Communications Inc.

Desmobile Music Co. (ASCAP)
Attention: Desmond Child
12 West 72nd Street
New York, New York 10023

Desmond Music Co. (BMI)
c/o Silverman & Shulman, P.C.
136 East 57th Street
New York, New York 10022

Despen Music Co. (BMI)
c/o Aloris
Burton-Despenza
4830 West Iowa Street
Chicago, Illinois 60651

DeSylva, Brown & Henderson, Inc.
(ASCAP)
609 Fifth Avenue
New York, New York 10017

Det Music, Inc. (BMI)
c/o David B. Cohen
Suite 600
9777 Wilshire Boulevard
Beverly Hills, California 90212

Detail Music, Inc. (BMI)
c/o Dave Armstrong
United Artists Music Co., Inc.
6753 Hollywood Boulevard
Los Angeles, California 90028

DeValbo Music
see WB Music Corp.

Devalex Music (ASCAP)
see Island Music

Devine's Music Ltd. (BMI)
see Unichappell Music Inc.

Devo Music (BMI)
c/o Neal Levin & Co.
9595 Wilshire Boulevard
Suite 505
Beverly Hills, California 90212

Devon Music, Inc. (BMI)
Suite 1406
10 Columbus Circle
New York, New York 10019

Al Dexter Songs (BMI)
Post Office Box 71
Denton, Texas 76201

Dialogue Music, Inc. (BMI)
A Division of Big Dwarf, Ltd.
c/o Weiss, Meiback & Shukat, Esq.
888 Seventh Avenue
New York, New York 10009

Diamond Touch Productions Ltd. (ASCAP)
see Columbia Pictures Publications

Diamondback Music Co. (BMI)
see Great Pyramid Music

Diana Music Corp. (BMI)
c/o GBRF
1880 Century Park East
Number 900
Los Angeles, California 90067

Dickiebird Music (BMI)
c/o Plant, Cohen and Company
9777 Wilshire Boulevard
Suite 600
Beverly Hills, California 90212

Dijon Music Publishing (BMI)
see Blackwood Music Inc.

Ding Dong Music Corp. (BMI)
c/o Barton Music Corp.
9220 Sunset Boulevard
Los Angeles, California 90069

Diogenes Music, Inc. (BMI)
c/o Stan Eisenberg & Co.
10680 West Pico Boulevard
Los Angeles, California 90064

Dirk Music (BMI)
c/o Amos Publications, Inc.
Suite 120
6565 Sunset Boulevard
Hollywood, California 90028

Walt Disney Music Co. (ASCAP)
350 South Buena Vista Street
Burbank, California 91521

Oliver Ditson Co. (ASCAP)
1712 Chestnut Street
Philadelphia, Pennsylvania 19103

Dixie Music Publishing Co. (BMI)
57 Third Avenue
New York, New York 10003

Django Music Inc. (ASCAP)
see Lonport Music Inc.

Dlief Music (BMI)
see Fourteenth Hour Music Inc.

Dog & Whistle Publishing (BMI)
c/o Tony Hendra
25 East 4th Street
New York, New York 10003

Dolfi Music, Inc. (ASCAP)
c/o Ross Jungnickel, Inc.
11th Floor
1619 Broadway
New York, New York 10019

Donaldson Publishing Co. (ASCAP)
c/o Edward Traubner & Co., Inc.
No 880
1901 Avenue of the Stars
Los Angeles, California 90067

Donka Music (ASCAP)
see Honey Bunny Music

Donna Music Publishing Co. (BMI)
c/o F. Pappalardi
P. O. Box 113
Woburn, Massachusetts 01801

Doors Music Co. (ASCAP)
c/o Greene & Reynolds
8200 Sunset Boulevard, No. 706
Los Angeles, California 90069

Doraflo Music, Inc. (BMI)
c/o Al Kohn
Warner Brothers Music
Suite 222
9200 Sunset Boulevard
Los Angeles, California 90069

Dorcam Music Corp. (BMI)
Address unknown

Dormie Music, Inc. (BMI)
Address unknown

Dorothy Publishing Co. (ASCAP)
Address unknown

Dorsey Brothers' Music, Inc. (ASCAP)
c/o Consolidated Music Sales, Inc.
799 Broadway
New York, New York 10003

Buster Doss Music (BMI)
113 South Kansas Street
Marceline, Missouri 64658

Double-A Music Corp. (ASCAP)
1 Dag Hammarskjold Plaza
New York, New York 10017

Double Diamond Music Co. (BMI)
205 South Broad Street
Philadelphia, Pennsylvania 19102

Double Exposure Music Inc. (ASCAP)
see WB Music Corp.

Double F Music (ASCAP)
see Delightful Music Ltd.

Double Jay Music (ASCAP)
see United Artists Music Co., Inc.

Double R Music Corp. (ASCAP)
see WB Music Corp.

Dovan Music (ASCAP)
c/o Lewis Khoury
1880 Century Park
Suite 1150
Los Angeles, California 90067

Downstairs Music, Inc. (BMI)
c/o Earl Shelton
309 South Broad Street
Philadelphia, Pennsylvania 19107

Downtown Music (ASCAP)
see The EMP Co.

Dragonwyck Music (BMI)
c/o David A. Gates
4373 Lemp Avenue
Studio City, California 91604

Drake Activities Corp. (ASCAP)
c/o Drake Music Group
809 18th Avenue South
Nashville, Tennessee 37203

Dream City Music (BMI)
44 Music Square West
Nashville, Tennessee 37203

Drive-In Music Co., Inc. (BMI)
7120 Sunset Boulevard
Hollywood, California 90046

Drolet Music
Address unknown

Drummer Boy Music Corp. (ASCAP)
see The EMP Co.

Drunk Monkey Music (ASCAP)
22713 Ventura Boulevard
Suite F
Woodland Hills, California 91364

Drunken Boat Music (ASCAP)
Mitchell, Silberberg & Knuff
1800 Century Park East
Los Angeles, California 90067

Duane Music, Inc. (BMI)
c/o Garne Thompson
Post Office Box 6174
Albany, California 94706

Al Dubin Music Co. (ASCAP)
c/o Warner Brothers Music
Penthouse
9000 Sunset Boulevard
Los Angeles, California 90069

Duce Music (ASCAP)
see T A T Communications Co.

Duchess Music Corp. (BMI)
see MCA Music

Vernon Duke Music Corp. (ASCAP)
c/o Larry Shayne Enterprises
6262 Hollywood Boulevard
Hollywood, California 90028

DuMonde Music (ASCAP)
see Almo Music Corp.

Dump Music Inc. (BMI)
2400 Fulton Street
San Francisco, California 94118

Dunbar-Golden West Melodies (BMI)
c/o Golden West Melodies
5858 Sunset Boulevard
Hollywood, California 90028

Dunbar-Ridgeway (BMI)
c/o Ridgeway Music Co., Inc.
5858 Sunset Boulevard
Post Office Box 710
Hollywood, California 90028

Dunbar-Singletree (BMI)
c/o Singletree Music Co., Inc.
815 18th Avenue South
Nashville, Tennessee 37213

Dundee Music (BMI)
c/o Nor Va Jak Music, Inc.
1321 West Seventh Street
Clovis, New Mexico 88101

Jimmy Durante Music Publishing Co., Inc
(ASCAP)
8710 Wilshire Boulevard
Beverly Hills, California 90211

Dwarf Music Co., Inc. (ASCAP)
see Big Sky Music

Dymor Productions, Inc. (ASCAP)
c/o Jerome B. Lurie, Esq.
1370 Avenue of the Americas
New York, New York 10019

Dynatone Publishing Co. (BMI)
see Unichappell Music Inc.

E

E & M Publishing Co. (BMI)
2674 Steele Street
Memphis, Tennessee 38127

E. Y. Harburg (ASCAP)
262 Central Park West
New York, New York 10024

Eager Music (BMI)
Post Office Box 287
Forest Park, Georgia 30050

Earbourne Music (BMI)
812 North McCadden Place
Los Angeles, California 90038

Earl Music Co. (ASCAP)
c/o Neverland Music Publishing Co.
225 East 57th Street
New York, New York 10022

Early Frost Music Corp. (BMI)
c/o TWM Management Services Ltd.
641 Lexington Avenue
14th Floor
New York, New York 10022

Early Morning Music (ASCAP)
Div. of EMP Ltd.
350 Davenport Road
Toronto, Ontario 180
Canada

Earmark Music Inc. (BMI)
see Fourth Floor Music Inc.

East Gate Music (ASCAP)
see Fourth Floor Music Inc.

East Hill Music Co. (ASCAP)
see Chappell & Co., Inc.

East/Memphis Music Corp. (BMI)
8025 Melrose Avenue
Los Angeles, California 90046

East Publications (BMI)
c/o Satellite Records
926 East McLemore Avenue
Memphis, Tennessee 38106

East-West Music, Inc. (ASCAP)
c/o The Goodman Group
110 East 59th Street
New York, New York 10022

Eastlake Music, Inc. (ASCAP)
Post Office Box 509
Montclair, New Jersey 07042

Eastwick Music Co. (BMI)
1314-24 South Howard Street
Philadelphia, Pennsylvania 19147

Easy Listening Music Corp. (ASCAP)
see Al Gallico Music Corp.

Easy Money Music (ASCAP)
c/o Gelfand, Rennert & Feldman
Attention: Babbie Green
1880 Century Park East
Number 900
Los Angeles, California 90067

Easy Nine Music (BMI)
c/o Johnny Christopher
Route 3, Barrel Springs
Hollow Road
Franklin, Tennessee 37064

Ebbett's Field Music (ASCAP)
c/o David Robinson
David Robinson & Friends, Inc.
827 Folsom Street
San Francisco, California 94107

Ecaroh Music, Inc. (ASCAP)
Suite 14L
400 Central Park West
New York, New York 10025

Ecnirp Music (BMI)
c/o Manatt, Phelps, Rothenberg &
Tunney
1888 Century Park East
Los Angeles, California 90034

Eden Music, Inc. (BMI)
Post Office Box 325
Englewood, New Jersey 07631

Edgevine Music Corp. (BMI)
c/o Paxwin Music Corp.
836 Riomar Drive
Vero Beach, Florida 32960

Editions Agel (ASCAP)
Address unknown

Edmark Productions Co. (BMI)
20802 Cedar Lane
Tomball, Texas 77375

Edobar Publishing Co. (BMI)
c/o William Doggett
120 West Bayberry Road
Islip, New York 11751

Edsel Music (BMI)
see Chappell & Co., Inc.

Edwardo Music Corp. (BMI)
3807 Lewis Lane
Amarillo, Texas 79109

Edwards Music Co., Inc. (ASCAP)
Room 1920
135 West 50th Street
New York, New York 10020

Eeegee Music (BMI)
c/o Copyright Service Bureau
221 West 57th Street
New York, New York 10019

Eeyor Music
825 Broadview Avenue
Toronto, Ontario M4K 2P9
Canada

Efsee Music, Inc. (BMI)
c/o George Scheck
161 West 54th Street
New York, New York 10019

E.G. Music Inc.

Egap Music, Inc. (BMI)
c/o Patti Page
Huntley House
314 Huntley Drive
Los Angeles, California 90048

Eighties Music
c/o Neil Levin & Associates
9595 Wilshire Boulevard
#505
Beverly Hills, California 90212

El Patricio Music (BMI)
see Unichappell Music Inc.

Elainea Music Publishing Co. (ASCAP)
Attention: Lalomie Washburn
715 South Normandie
Apartment 724
Los Angeles, California 90005

Elar Music Corp. (ASCAP)
c/o Chappell & Co., Inc.
810 Seventh Avenue
New York, New York 10019

Elbee Music Co.
c/o Lawrence H. Banks
14 Oakland Place
Brooklyn, New York 11226

Elbern Music Co. (ASCAP)
c/o Al Bart
6671 Sunset Boulevard
Suite 1574
Los Angeles, California 90028

Eldorado Music Co. (BMI)
1717 North Vine Street
Hollywood, California 90028

Elizabeth Music (BMI)
A Division of Script & Quill, Inc.
515 East Racquet Club Road
Palm Springs, California 92262

Elkhart Music
Address unknown

Mercer K. Ellington (ASCAP)
c/o AGAC
40 West 57th Street
New York, New York 10019

Elvis Music Inc. (BMI)
c/o Lester Boles
1619 Broadway
New York, New York 10019

Emanuel Music Corp. (ASCAP)
see WB Music Corp.

Embassy Music Corp. (BMI)
24 East 22nd Street
New York, New York 10010

Emerald City Music (ASCAP)
see Caesar's Music Library

Emerson Music Publications (BMI)
c/o Bernard Landes
725 Riverside Drive
New York, New York 10031

Emily Music Corp. (ASCAP)
160 West 73rd Street
New York, New York 10023

Emkay Music (BMI)
c/o Milton Kellem
Wildcat Music, Inc.
No. 114
2780 Northeast 183rd Street
North Miami Beach, Florida 33160

The EMP Co. (BMI)
The Entertainment Co.
40 West 57th Street
New York, New York 10019

Empress Music, Inc. (ASCAP)
119 West 57th Street
New York, New York 10019

Enchanted Music Co., Inc. (ASCAP)
c/o Alouette Productions, Inc.
315 West 57th Street
New York, New York 10019

Englewood Publications, Inc. (BMI)
c/o Baude Music
c/o Morris Rubenstein
6650 Sunset Boulevard
Hollywood, California 90028

Ennes Productions, Ltd. (ASCAP)
157 West 57th Street
New York, New York 10019

Ensign Music Corp. (BMI)
c/o Sidney Herman
1 Gulf & Western Plaza
New York, New York 10023

Epic III Ltd. (ASCAP)
see Rubicon Music

Equinox Music (BMI)
c/o Raymond Harris
Suite 1212
7060 Hollywood Boulevard
Hollywood, California 90028

Equitable Music Corp.
Address unknown

Josef Erickisson (ASCAP)
Address unknown

Erika Publishing (ASCAP)
c/o Elaine Wise
98 Willow Terrace Apartments
Willow Drive
Chapel Hill, North Carolina 27514

Erva Music Publishing Co., Inc. (BMI)
75 Brayton Street
Englewood, New Jersey 07631

Erwin-Howard Music Corp. (ASCAP)
c/o Mel Howard
Room 1108
501 Madison Avenue
New York, New York 10022

Escort Music Co. (BMI)
c/o Clifford L. Goldsmith
Post Office Box 78565
Los Angeles, California 90016

List of Publishers

Essential Music (BMI)
c/o Law Financial Services
No. 1, Gate 6, Suite E
Sausalito, California 94965

Essex International Inc. (ASCAP)
see TRO-Cromwell Music Inc.

Essex Music, Inc.
see TRO-Essex Music, Inc.

Redd Evans Music Co. (ASCAP)
c/o Vivian Evans
Suite 1400
545 Fifth Avenue
New York, New York 10017

Evansongs Ltd. (ASCAP)
c/o E.S.P. Management
1790 Broadway
New York, New York 10019

Everbright Music Co. (ASCAP)
c/o Belwin Mills Publishing Corp.
1776 Broadway
New York, New York 10019

Evie Music Inc. (ASCAP)
see Chappell & Co., Inc.

Evil Eye Music Inc. (BMI)
see Songways Service Inc.

Excellorec Music Co., Inc. (BMI)
1011 Woodland Street
Nashville, Tennessee 37206

Ezra Music Corp. (BMI)
8600 Melrose Avenue
Los Angeles, California 90069

F

Fabulous Music Ltd. (BMI)
Div. of Chancellor Records Inc.
c/o Ivan M. Hoffman
2040 Ave of the Stars
Suite 400
Los Angeles, California 90067

Fain Music Co. (ASCAP)
1640 San Ysidro Drive
Beverly Hills, California 90210

Fair Shake Music (BMI)
c/o Willie J. Barney
3234 West Roosevelt Road
Chicago, Illinois 60624

Fair Star Music (ASCAP)
1280 El Mirador Drive
Pasadena, California 91103

Fairlane Music Corp. (ASCAP)
8625 Santa Monica Boulevard
Los Angeles, California 90069

Fajob Music Publishing Co. (ASCAP)
Suite 1111
1420 Walnut Street
Philadelphia, Pennsylvania 19102

Fall River Music Inc. (BMI)
250 West 57th Street
Suite 2017
New York, New York 10019

Fame Publishing Co., Inc. (BMI)
603 East Avalon Avenue
Box 2527
Muscle Shoals, Alabama 35660

Famous Music Co. (ASCAP)
Gulf & Western Industries, Inc.
1 Gulf & Western Plaza
New York, New York 10023

Fanfare Music Co. (ASCAP)
1337 North Orange Drive
Hollywood, California 90028

Far Out Music (ASCAP)
7417 Sunset Boulevard
Hollywood, California 90046

Fargo House Inc. (ASCAP)
see Al Gallico Music Corp.

Farina Music (ASCAP)
c/o Bread & Roses
78 Throckmorton Avenue
Mill Valley, California 94941

John Farrar Music (BMI)
see Kidada Music Inc.

Fast Fade Music
Attention: James Thomas Wells
8818 Noble Avenue
Sepulveda, California 91343

Fat Zach Music, Inc. (BMI)
c/o Skinny Zach
Suite 1531
6430 Sunset Boulevard
Hollywood, California 90028

Fate Music (ASCAP)
see Buddy Music

Feather Music, Inc. (BMI)
c/o Paul Orland
Orland & Orland
Suite 415
9200 Sunset Boulevard
Los Angeles, California 90069

Featherbed Music Inc. (BMI)
see Unichappell Music Inc.

Fedora Music (BMI)
c/o Segel & Goldman Inc.
9368 Santa Monica Boulevard
Suite 304
Beverly Hills, California 90210

Fee Bee Music (BMI)
4517 Wainwright Avenue
Pittsburgh, Pennsylvania 15227

Leo Feist Inc. (ASCAP)
see MCA Music

B. Feldman & Co., Ltd. (ASCAP)
c/o Abels, Clark & Osterberg
224 East 50th Street
New York, New York 10022

Felicia Music Co., Inc. (BMI)
c/o Marshall Morris
Powell & Silfen
130 West 57th Street
New York, New York 10019

Felsted Music Corp. (ASCAP)
see Chappell & Co., Inc.

Fermata International Melodies Inc.
(ASCAP)
see Bendig Music Corp.

Festival Attractions Inc. (ASCAP)
c/o Kosmas & Messing
1841 Broadway
Suite 411
New York, New York 10023

Fez Music Co. (BMI)
c/o Cohen & Steinhart, Esq.
6430 Sunset Boulevard
Suite 1500
Los Angeles, California 90028

Fiction Music Inc. (BMI)
Post Office Box 135
Bearsville, New York 12409

Fiddleback Music Publishing Co., Inc.
(BMI)
1270 Avenue of the Americas
New York, New York 10020

Fidelity Music Co. (BMI)
c/o Jobete Music Co., Inc.
Suite 1600
6255 Sunset Boulevard
Hollywood, California 90028

Fideree Music Co. (ASCAP)
Address unknown

John Fields Music Co., Ltd. (ASCAP)
Address unknown

Fifth Floor Music Inc. (ASCAP)
see Third Story Music Inc.

Figure Music, Inc. (BMI)
c/o Jack Hooke
1631 Broadway
New York, New York 10019

Finchley Music Corp. (ASCAP)
c/o Arrow, Edelstein & Gross
919 Third Avenue
New York, New York 10022

Fingers Music (BMI)
see Cass County Music Co.

First Artists Music Co. (ASCAP)
9744 Wilshire Boulevard
Suite 600
Beverly Hills, California 90213

List of Publishers

First Generation Music Co. (BMI)
see Combine Music Corp.

First Lady Songs Inc. (BMI)
6 Music Circle North
Nashville, Tennessee 37203

Carl Fischer, Inc. (ASCAP)
62 Cooper Square
New York, New York 10003

Carey Fisher Music Co. (ASCAP)
c/o Bill Carey
292 Agate Street
Laguna Beach, California 92651

Fred Fisher Music Co. (ASCAP)
c/o Fisher Music Corp.
1619 Broadway
New York, New York 10019

Fisher Music Corp. (ASCAP)
1619 Broadway
New York, New York 10019

Doris Fisher Music Corp. (ASCAP)
1 Times Square Plaza
New York, New York 10036

Flagship Music Inc. (BMI)
1808 Division Street
Nashville, Tennessee 37203

Flair Publishing Co. (BMI)
5810 South Normandie Avenue
Los Angeles, California 90044

Flamm Music Inc. (BMI)
see Chappell & Co., Inc.

Harold Flammer, Inc. (ASCAP)
c/o Shawnee Press
Waring Enterprises
Delaware Water Gap, Pennsylvania 18327

Flanka Music Corp. (ASCAP)
119 West 57th Street
New York, New York 10019

Flatt and Scruggs Publishing Co. (BMI)
201 Donna Drive
Madison, Tennessee 37115

Fleetwood Mac Music Ltd. (BMI)
315 South Beverly Drive
Suite 210
Beverly Hills, California 90212

Fleur Music (ASCAP)
see Columbia Pictures Publications

Fling Music, Inc. (BMI)
c/o Don Costa
1491 Carla Ridge
Beverly Hills, California 90210

Flojan Music Publishing Co. (ASCAP)
42 Lafayette Place
Woodmere, New York 11598

Flonan Publishing Co. (ASCAP)
R.F.D. 2
Osyka, Mississippi 39657

Florence Music Co., Inc. (ASCAP)
609 Fifth Avenue
New York, New York 10017

Flying Addrisi Music (BMI)
c/o Dick Addrisi
3374 Canton Way
Studio City, California 91604

Folk-Legacy Records, Inc. (BMI)
Sharon Moutain Road
Sharon, Connecticut 06069

Folkways Music Publishers, Inc.
see TRO-Folkways Music Publishers, Inc.

Fool's Gold (ASCAP)
c/o Segel & Goldman, Inc.
9348 Santa Monica Boulevard
Beverly Hills, California 90210

Forrest Hills Music Inc. (BMI)
1609 Hawkins Street
Nashville, Tennessee 37203

Forshay Music (BMI)
250 Tryon Avenue
Teaneck, New Jersey 07666

Forster Music Publishers, Inc. (ASCAP)
216 South Wabash Avenue
Chicago, Illinois 60604

Fort Knox Music Co. (BMI)
see The Hudson Bay Music Co.

Four Jays Music Co. (ASCAP)
9425 Sunset Boulevard
Beverly Hills, California 90210

Four Knights Music Co. (BMI)
8467 Beverly Boulevard, No. 109
Los Angeles, California 90048

Four Score Music Corp. (BMI)
c/o Brown, Kraft & Co.
11940 San Vincente Boulevard
Los Angeles, California 90049

Four Star Music Co., Inc. (BMI)
Suite 312
9220 Sunset Boulevard
Los Angeles, California 90069

Fourteenth Hour Music Inc. (ASCAP)
17187 Wyoming Avenue
Detroit, Michigan 48221

Fourth Floor Music Inc. (ASCAP)
Box 135
Bearsville, New York 12409

Fox Fanfare Music Inc.
see Twentieth Century Fox Music Corp.

Fox-Gimbel Productions (BMI)
c/o Mr. Sidney Aron
10 East 40th Street
New York, New York 10016

Sam Fox Publishing Co., Inc. (ASCAP)
73-941 Highway 111
Suite 11
Palm Desert, California 92260

Foy Lee Publishing Co. (BMI)
Post Office Box 779
Conroe, Texas 77301

Frabjous Music (BMI)
c/o Ames & Associates
Post Office Box 5973-120
Sherman Oaks, California 91413

France Music Co. (BMI)
c/o Orenstein, Arrow, Silverman
& Parcher
1370 Avenue of the Americas
New York, New York 10019

Francis, Day & Hunter, Inc. (ASCAP)
c/o The Big 3
7165 Sunset Boulevard
Hollywood, California 90046

Francis Lemargue Ste Ave (ASCAP)
Address unknown

Francon Music Corp. (ASCAP)
c/o George Scheck
161 West 54th Street
New York, New York 10019

Frank Music Co. (ASCAP)
see MPL Communications Inc.

Frederick Music Co. (BMI)
5710 North Broadway
Chicago, Illinois 60660

Free Breez Music (BMI)
c/o Tom Lazaros
7681 Heyden
Detroit, Michigan 48228

Arthur Freed Music (ASCAP)
c/o The Songwriters Guild
3rd Floor
276 Fifth Avenue
New York, New York 10001

Bobby Freeman Music (BMI)
c/o Cooper, Epstein & Hurewitz,
P.C.
9465 Wilshire Boulevard
Beverly Hills, California 90212

Foster Frees Music Inc. (BMI)
c/o Shankman De Blasio
185 Pier Avenue
Santa Monica, California 90405

Freeway Music Corp. (BMI)
c/o Beechwood Music Corp.
6255 Sunset Boulevard
Hollywood, California 90028

Fremart Music Co. (BMI)
1467 North Vine Street
Hollywood, California 90028

Friday's Child Music (BMI)
2203 Spruce Street
Philadelphia, Pennsylvania 19103

Hugo W. Friedhofer
2840 Woodstock Road
Los Angeles, California 90046

Frost Music Corp. (BMI)
c/o Big Seven Music Corp.
18th Floor
1790 Broadway
New York, New York 10019

List of Publishers

Fullness Music Co. (BMI)
see Blackwood Music Inc.

Funt Music (BMI)
c/o Wayne Richard Parker
1855 Pepper Tree Court
Thousand Oaks, California 91360

G

G & H Music Publishing House, Inc. (BMI)
c/o H. Golder
No. 303
7690 Northwest 18th Street
Margate, Florida 33063

G Q Publishing (ASCAP)
see Arista Music Inc.

Galahad Music Inc. (BMI)
250 W. 57th St.
New York, New York 10019

Gale & Gayles, Inc. (BMI)
1930 Renee Circle
Palm Springs, California 92262

Galeneye Music (BMI)
see Unichappell Music Inc.

Galleon Music Inc. (ASCAP)
see Al Gallico Music Corp.

Al Gallico Music Corp. (BMI)
344 East 49th Street
New York, New York 10017

Gambi Music Inc. (BMI)
see Copyright Service Bureau Ltd.

Gang Music Ltd. (BMI)
c/o TWM Management Services, Ltd.
641 Lexington Avenue
New York, New York 10022

Ganga Publishing Co. (BMI)
see Screen Gems-EMI Music Inc.

Gannon & Kent Music Co. (ASCAP)
c/o Edward Traubner & Co., Inc.
132 South Rodeo Drive
Beverly Hills, California 90212

Gar Publishing Co. (BMI)
c/o Anthony J. Garrio
1927 Williamsbridge Road
Bronx, New York 10461

Garden Court Music Co. (ASCAP)
Box 1132
Plattsburgh, New York 12901

Garden Rake Music Inc. (BMI)
c/o Shankman De Blasio
185 Pier Avenue
Main Street at Pier
Santa Monica, California 90405

Garland Music, Inc. (ASCAP)
c/o Copyright Service Bureau
221 West 57th Street
New York, New York 10022

Gates Music Inc. (BMI)
c/o Chuck Mangione
1845 Clinton Avenue
Rochester, New York 14621

Larry Gatlin Music (BMI)
see Combine Music Corp.

Gaucho Music (BMI)
Div. of Guardian Productions Inc.
161 West 54th Street
New York, New York 10019

Gavadima Music Inc. (ASCAP)
Peter C. Bennett, Esq.
9060 Santa Monica Boulevard
Suite 300
Los Angeles, California 90069

Gay Noel Music Co., Ltd. (ASCAP)
Address unknown

Gear Publishing (ASCAP)
Div. of Hideout Productions
567 Purdy
Birmingham, Michigan 48009

Geld Music (ASCAP)
see Plymouth Music Co., Inc.

Gemrod Music, Inc. (BMI)
Copyright Service Bureau, Ltd.
221 West 57th Street
New York, New York 10019

General Motors Corp., Chev. Motor Di'
Detroit, Michigan

General Music Publishing Co., Inc.
(ASCAP)
145 Palisade Street
Dobbs Ferry, New York 10522

Genius Music Corp. (ASCAP)
c/o Saturday Music, Inc.
37 West 57th Street
New York, New York 10019

Gentleman Jim Music Corp. (ASCAP)
440 Riverside Drive
New York, New York 10027

Gentoo Music Inc. (BMI)
see Screen Gems-EMI Music Inc.

Geoff & Eddie Music Co., Inc. (BMI)
see Blackwood Music Inc.

Gershwin Publishing Corp. (ASCAP)
609 Fifth Avenue
New York, New York 10017

Get Loose Music Inc. (BMI)
Post Office Box 1198
Jacksonville, Florida 32201

Gianni Music (BMI)
Fischbach & Fischbach
2029 Century Park East
Number 1370
Los Angeles, California 90067

Giant Enterprises Music (BMI)
see Strong Songs

Gibb Brothers Music (BMI)
see Unichappell Music Inc.

Hugh & Barbara Gibb Music (BMI)
c/o Prager & Fenton
444 Madison Avenue
New York, New York 10022

Andy Gibb Music (BMI)
c/o Prager and Fenton
444 Madison Avenue
New York, New York 10022

Gil Music Corp. (BMI)
c/o George Pincus
Room 806
1650 Broadway
New York, New York 10019

Gillam Publishing Co. (ASCAP)
Address unknown

Giovanni Music, Inc. (ASCAP)
157 West 57th Street
New York, New York 10019

Giving Music (ASCAP)
see Broken Bird Music

Giving Room Music, Inc. (BMI)
c/o Warner Bros. Music
Suite 704
900 Sunset Boulevard
Los Angeles, California 90069

Glad Music Co. (BMI)
c/o H.W. Daily Sr.
3409 Brinkman Street
Houston, Texas 77018

Gladstone Music, Inc. (ASCAP)
c/o Vee Jay Records, Inc.
1449 South Michigan Avenue
Chicago, Illinois 60605

Gladys Music (ASCAP)
see Chappell & Co., Inc.

Glamorous Music, Inc. (ASCAP)
c/o Helios Music Corp.
Post Office Box 1182
Radio City Station
New York, New York 10101

Glasco Music (ASCAP)
see United Artists Music Co., Inc.

Glaser Publications, Inc. (BMI)
c/o Sidney Herman
1 Gulf & Western Plaza
New York, New York 10023

Glenwood Music Corp. (ASCAP)
see Beechwood Music Corp.

Glorste, Inc. (ASCAP)
175 South Mapleton Drive
Los Angeles, California 90024

Gnossos Music (ASCAP)
c/o Segel & Goldman, Inc.
9126 Sunset Boulevard
Los Angeles, California 90069

Gobbler's Knob Publishing Co. (BMI)
c/o Hamblen Music Co.
3100 Torreyson Place
Los Angeles, California 90046

Bella Godiva Music (ASCAP)
see Chappell & Co., Inc.

Gold Forever Music Inc. (BMI)
see Blackwood Music Inc.

Gold Hill Music Inc. (ASCAP)
5032 Lankershim Boulevard
North Hollywood, California 91601

Gold Horizon Music Corp. (BMI)
Columbia Plaza East
Suite 215
Administered by Screen Gems-EMI
Music, Inc.
Burbank, California 91505

Golden Bell Songs (ASCAP)
c/o Becker & Co.
40 Galesi Drive
Wayne, New Jersey 07470

Golden Clover Music (ASCAP)
see Chappell & Co., Inc.

Golden Mountain Music Inc. (ASCAP)
c/o Freedman Snow & Co.
1092 Mount Pleasant Road
Toronto, Ontario M4P 2M6
Canada

Golden Torch Music Corp. (ASCAP)
see Gold Horizon Music Corp.

Golden Unlimited Music (BMI)
c/o Super Songs Unlimited
Suite 706
700 West 51st Street
New York, New York 10019

Golden West Melodies, Inc. (BMI)
5858 Sunset Boulevard
Hollywood, California 90028

Golden World (ASCAP)
c/o Eden Ahbez
Post Office Box 162
Sunland, California 91040

Goldline Music Inc. (ASCAP)
see Silverline Music Inc.

Bobby Goldsboro Music (ASCAP)
see House of Gold Music Inc.

Michael H. Goldsen, Inc. (ASCAP)
6124 Selma Avenue
Hollywood, California 90028

Jerry Goldstein Music, Inc. (BMI)
c/o Mason & Co.
75 Rockerfeller Plaza
New York, New York 10019

Golo Publishing Co. (BMI)
c/o Unichappell Music, Inc.
32nd Floor
810 Seventh Avenue
New York, New York 10019

Gomace Music, Inc. (BMI)
1000 North Doheny Drive
Los Angeles, California 90069

Good Friends Music (ASCAP)
see WB Music Corp.

Good High Music (ASCAP)
c/o Gelfand, Breslauer, Rennert &
Feldman
1880 Century Park East
Suite 900
Los Angeles, California 90067

Good Sam Music (BMI)
c/o Rondor Music, Inc.
1358 North La Brea Avenue
Los Angeles, California 90028

Good Time Acre Music Publishing Co.
(BMI)
15609 Damon Avenue
Cleveland, Ohio 44110

Goodman Music Co., Inc. (ASCAP)
Apartment 9A
825 West End Avenue
New York, New York 10025

Goombay Music, Inc. (ASCAP)
c/o Rondor Music, Inc.
1358 North La Brea Avenue
Hollywood, California 90028

Gordon Enterprises (ASCAP)
5362 Cahuenga Boulevard
North Hollywood, California 91605

Gordon Music Co., Inc. (ASCAP)
No. 103
12111 Strathern Street
Hollywood, California 91605

Gouda Music (ASCAP)
c/o Don Bachrach
1515 North Crescent Heights
Boulevard
Los Angeles, California 90046

Gower Music, Inc. (BMI)
  Post Office Box 80699
  World Way Postal Center
  Los Angeles, California 90080

Grajonca Music
  c/o Bill Graham Presents
  201 11th Street
  San Francisco, California 94103

Grand Canyon Music, Inc. (BMI)
  c/o Mason & Co.
  75 Rockerfeller Plaza
  New York, New York 10019

Grandma Annie Music (BMI)
  c/o Sy Miller, Esq.
  18 East 48th Street
  Suite 1202
  New York, New York 10017

Granite Music Corp. (ASCAP)
  c/o Criterion Music Corp.
  6124 Selma Avenue
  Hollywood, California 90028

Granson Music Co. (BMI)
  c/o Jose E. Granson
  12156 Blix Street
  Hollywood, California 91607

Grass Root Productions (BMI)
  c/o Arthur T. Lee
  4717 Don Lorenzo Drive
  Los Angeles, California 90008

Grean Music Co. (ASCAP)
  Address unknown

Greasy King Music Inc. (BMI)
  c/o Mr. Fogerty
  Box 9245
  Berkeley, California 94709

Greasy Shift Music (BMI)
  see Bug Music

Great Foreign Songs, Inc. (ASCAP)
  c/o Kermit Goell
  No. 112
  7 West 96th Street
  New York, New York 10025

Great Honesty Music Inc.
  Box 547
  Larkspur, California 94939

Great Pyramid Music (BMI)
  10 Waterville Street
  San Francisco, California 94124

Al Green Music Inc. (BMI)
  3208 Winchester Road
  Memphis, Tennessee 38118

Green Apple Music Co. (BMI)
  see Musicways Inc.

Steve Greenberg Music (ASCAP)
  see Chappell & Co., Inc.

Mort Greene Music Co. (ASCAP)
  72-890 Deer Grass Drive
  Palm Desert, California 92260

Greenlee Music (BMI)
  c/o Tri-City Records
  1003 Bingham Street
  Pittsburgh, Pennsylvania 15203

Greenwood Music Co. (BMI)
  c/o C. Carson Parks
  6001 Kenwood Drive
  Nashville, Tennessee 37215

Gregory Music Corp.
  Address unknown

Greta Music Corp. (BMI)
  c/o Jack Gold
  4001 Royal Oak Place
  Encino, California 91436

Grey Dog Music (ASCAP)
  c/o Pryor, Cashman & Sherman
  410 Park Avenue
  New York, New York 10022

Grey Fox Music, Inc. (BMI)
  c/o Wallace Magaziner
  15th Floor
  1776 Broadway
  New York, New York 10019

Grimora Music (ASCAP)
  see April Music Inc.

Groovesville Music Inc. (BMI)
  15855 Wyoming Avenue
  Detroit, Michigan 48238

Groton Music, Inc. (BMI)
  c/o MCA Records
  10 East 53rd Street
  New York, New York 10025

Guaranty Music (BMI)
c/o Jim Buchanan
Route Number 1
Box 698
Ashland City, Tennessee 37015

Guerrilla Music (BMI)
c/o Warner Brothers Music
9000 Sunset Boulevard
Los Angeles, California 90069

Guild Music Co. (BMI)
c/o Mrs. Dorinda Morgan
1600 East Ogden Avenue
Las Vegas, Nevada 98101

Gulf Stream Music (BMI)
c/o Carolyn McCord
Fisherman's Wharf
5005 Dauphin Island Parkway
Mobile, Alabama 33605

Gunston Music, Inc. (ASCAP)
c/o Arnold Roseman
Suite 302
9350 Wilshire Boulevard
Beverly Hills, California 90212

Gypsy Boy Music Inc. (ASCAP)
Mitchell, Silberberg & Knupp
1800 Century Park East
Los Angeles, California 90067

H

Haliburton Music Publishing (ASCAP)
see Summer Camp Publishing Co.

Hall Music (BMI)
Div. of Open End Music
7720 Sunset Boulevard
Los Angeles, California 90046

Hallenbeck Music Co. (BMI)
c/o Greene & Reynolds
Attention: Bob Greene
1900 Avenue of the Stars
Suite 1424
Los Angeles, California 90067

Hallmark Music Co.
626 North Rodeo Drive
Beverly Hills, California 90210

Hallnote Music (BMI)
Post Office Box 40209
Nashville, Tennessee 37204

Hamblen Music Co., Inc. (BMI)
7740 Mulholland Drive
Los Angeles, California 90046

Hammer & Nails Music (ASCAP)
see Almo Music Corp.

Hampshire House Publishing Corp.
(ASCAP)
see TRO-Cromwell Music Inc.

Hamstein Music (BMI)
c/o Bill Ham
Box 19647
Houston, Texas 77024

Hancock Music Co. (BMI)
c/o David Rubinson & Friends, Inc.
827 Folsom Street
San Francisco, California 94107

Handy Brothers Music Co., Inc. (ASCAP)
200 West 72nd Street
New York, New York 10023

Hanks Music, Inc. (BMI)
c/o Unichappel Music, Inc.
810 Seventh Avenue
New York, New York 10019

Hanna Music (ASCAP)
see Brockman Enterprises Inc.

Hanover Music Corp. (ASCAP)
545 Muskingum Place
Pacific Palisades, California 90272

Charles H. Hansen Music Corp. (ASCAP)
1860 Broadway
New York, New York 10023

Happiness Music Corp. (ASCAP)
9428 Manor Road
Leawood, Kansas 66206

Happy Sack Music Ltd. (ASCAP)
Chillynipple Music Division
Attention: Brian Ahern
2200 Younge Street
Suite 502
Toronto, Ontario M4S 2C6
Canada

Harbor Hills Music (BMI)
Attention: Bill Johnson
2175 June Drive
Nashville, Tennessee 37214

Harborn Music, Inc. (BMI)
c/o S. H. Bourne
437 Fifth Avenue
New York, New York 10016

Harbot Music
2 Music Circle South
Nashville, Tennessee 37203

Hargrove Music Corp. (BMI)
Suite 5C
10 West 66th Street
New York, New York 10023

Harlem Music (BMI)
c/o Lynn Boehringer
355 Harlem Road
West Seneca, New York 14224

Harmony Music Corp. (ASCAP)
Braunstein & Chernin
50 East 42nd Street
New York, New York 10017

T. B. Harms Co. (ASCAP)
100 Wilshire Boulevard
Suite 700
Santa Monica, California 90401

Harms, Inc. (ASCAP)
488 Madison Avenue
New York, New York 10022

Chess Music Inc. (ASCAP)
see T. B. #Harms Co.

Harold and Dimple Publishing Co. (BMI)
2616 West 73rd Street
Los Angeles, California 90043

Harrick Music Inc. (BMI)
7764 N.W. 71st Street
Miami, Florida 33166

Charles K. Harris Music Publishing Co.
(ASCAP)
1740 Broadway
New York, New York 10019

Harrison Music Corp. (ASCAP)
6253 Hollywood Boulevard
Hollywood, California 90028

Harvard Music, Inc. (BMI)
625 Madison Avenue
New York, New York 10022

Harwin Music Corp. (ASCAP)
31 West 54th Street
New York, New York 10019

Hastings Music Corp. (BMI)
see United Artists Music Co., Inc.

Hat Band Music (BMI)
The Sound Seventy Suite
210 25th Avenue North
Nashville, Tennessee 37203

Edwin R. Hawkins Music Co. (ASCAP)
1971 Hoover Avenue
Oakland, California 94602

Haymarket (ASCAP)
see Interworld Music Group

Lee Hazlewood Music Corp. (ASCAP)
30th Floor
1501 Broadway
New York, New York 10036

Heart's Delight Music (BMI)
c/o Manatt, Phelphs, Rothenberg,
Manley, & Tunney
1888 Century Park East
21st Floor
Los Angeles, California 90067

Neal Hefti Music, Inc. (ASCAP)
c/o International Korwin Corp.
211 West 56th Street
New York, New York 10019

Helena Music Corp. (ASCAP)
c/o Joe Darion
Box 216
Pinnacle Road
Lyme, New hampshire 03768

Helios Music Corp. (BMI)
Post Office Box 1182
Radio City Station
New York, New York 10101

Hello Darlin'
see Columbia Pictures Publications

Hello There Music Publishing (ASCAP)
see Fred Ahlert Music Corp.

2763

List of Publishers

Hendricks Music, Inc. (ASCAP)
90 State Street
Brooklyn, New York 11201

Herald Square Music Co. (ASCAP)
see The Hudson Bay Music Co.

Herbert Music Co., Inc. (ASCAP)
c/o Robert R. Kaufman
51 Chambers Street
New York, New York 10007

Hermosa Music Corp. (BMI)
c/o Robert A. Blackwell
5656 Cleon Avenue
North Hollywood, California 91601

HG Music Inc. (ASCAP)
232 East 61st Street
New York, New York 10021

Hi-Lo Music Inc. (BMI)
639 Madison
Memphis, Tennessee 38103

Hi-Ti Music Co. (ASCAP)
c/o Gillin Scott Alberstew
Suite 350
14651 Ventura Boulevard
Sherman Oaks, California 91403

Hickory Grove Music (ASCAP)
see April Music Inc.

Hidden Music (BMI)
c/o Machat & Machat
1501 Broadway
30th Floor
New York, New York 10036

Hideout Records/Distributing Co. (ASCAP)
see Gear Publishing

Hidle Music (BMI)
1607 North El Centro Avenue
Hollywood, California 90028

Hierophant Inc. (BMI)
c/o Brock & Mensch
350 Fifth Avenue
Room 5220
New York, New York 10001

High Society Music Publishers (BMI)
1230 South Wilton Place
Los Angeles, California 90019

High Wave Music (ASCAP)
see WB Music Corp.

Hightone Publishers (BMI)
1443 North Hudson Avenue
Chicago, Illinois 60610

Hill & Range Songs Inc. (BMI)
see Unichappell Music Inc.

Hillary Music, Inc. (BMI)
1608 Argyle
Hollywood, California 90028

Hillgreen Music (BMI)
c/o Folklore Productions Inc.
1671 Appian Way
Santa Monica, California 90401

Hilmer Music Publishing Co. (ASCAP)
see Almo Music Corp.

Catherine Hinen (ASCAP)
c/o Abraham Marcus
Suite 324
9171 Wilshire Boulevard
Beverly Hills, California 90210

Hip Hill Music Publishing Co. (BMI)
c/o Mira A. Smith
Box 17365
Nashville, Tennessee 37217

Hip Trip Music Co. (BMI)
c/o Melvin Katten
4100 Mid Continental Plaza
55 East Monroe Street
Chicago, Illinois 60603

Hiriam Music (BMI)
c/o Rightsong Music
810 Seventh Avenue
New York, New York 10019

Hobby Horse Music (BMI)
Div. of Garrett Enterprises
6255 Sunset Boulevard
Suite 1019
Hollywood, California 90028

Hobsong (BMI)
see Twentieth Century Fox Music Corp.

Hoedown Music (BMI)
Post Office Box 9194
Richmond, Virginia 23227

Al Hoffman Songs, Inc. (ASCAP)
c/o Music Sales Corp.
Attention Michael B. Bieber
799 Broadway
New York, New York 10003

Holicanthus Music (ASCAP)
see MCA Music

Hollenbeck Music Co. (BMI)
c/o Ernst & Whinney
1875 Century Park East
Los Angeles, California 90067

Holliday Publications (ASCAP)
319 Lee Avenue
Yonkers, New York 10705

Hollis Music, Inc.
see TRO-Hollis Music, Inc.

Holly Bee Music Co. (BMI)
2741 Cove Circle Northeast
Atlanta, Georgia 30319

Hollyland Music Co. (BMI)
c/o Phil Zeller
Post Office Box 12714
East Las Vegas, Nevada 89112

Holmby Music Corp. (ASCAP)
see Chappell & Co., Inc.

Holmes Line of Music (ASCAP)
see WB Music Corp.

Home Folks Music, Inc. (BMI)
11th Floor
1619 Broadway
New York, New York 10019

Home Grown Music Inc. (BMI)
4852 Laurel Canyon Boulevard
North Hollywood, California 91607

Homewood House Music (BMI)
c/o James Golden
3128 Cavendish Drive
Los Angeles, California 90064

Honest John Music (ASCAP)
Suite 202
15300 Ventura Boulevard
Sherman Oaks, California 91403

Honest Music (ASCAP)
Attention: Craig Wasson
4133 Kraft Avenue
Studio City, California 91604

Honey Bunny Music (BMI)
Attention: Dick Monda
17800 Lanark Street
Reseda, California 91335

John Lee Hooker
c/o Jim Lewis
7451 Third Avenue
Detroit, Michigan 48202

Hot Buns Publishing Co. (BMI)
c/o Jeffrey Graubart
Suite D402
Chocolate Building, Ghirardelli Sq.
900 North Point
San Francisco, California 94109

Hot Cha Music Co. (BMI)
see Six Continents Music Publishing Inc.

Hot Chocolate Music Co., Ltd.
Address unknown

Hot Kitchen Music (ASCAP)
Attention: James Jesse Winchester
53 Ballantyne North
Montreal West, Quebec H4X 2B7
Canada

Hot Red Music (BMI)
Div. of Red Hot Enterprises Inc.
c/o Weiss, Meibach & Shukat
888 Seventh Street
New York, New York 10019

Hotshot Music, Inc. (BMI)
c/o Big Shot Music, Inc.
6565 Sunset Boulevard
Hollywood, California 90028

House of Bryant Publications (BMI)
c/o Nona Thomas
Post Office Box 570
Gatlinburg, Tennessee 37736

House of Cash Inc. (BMI)
Box 508
Hendersonville, Tennessee 37075

House of Cash-Southwind Music (ASCAP)
Post Office Box 508
Hendersonville, Tennessee 37075

House of Gold Music Inc.
P.O. 120967
Acklyn Station
Nashville, Tennessee 37212

House of Weiss Co. (ASCAP)
see Twentieth Century Fox Music Corp.

Harlan Howard Songs (BMI)
59 Music Square West
Nashville, Tennessee 37203

Paul Howard (ASCAP)
Address unknown

HRH Television Features Corp.
Address unknown

Hub Music Co. (ASCAP)
Edward Traubner
132 South Rodeo Drive
Beverly Hills, California 90035

Hudmar Publishing Co. (ASCAP)
c/o Schlesinger & Dave
6255 Sunset Boulevard
Suite 1214
Hollywood, California 90028

The Hudson Bay Music Co. (BMI)
1619 Broadway
Suite 906
New York, New York 10019

Hummable Music Co. (ASCAP)
Address unknown

Don Hunt (ASCAP)
Address unknown

Ian Hunter Music (ASCAP)
see April Music Inc.

R. L. Huntzinger, Inc.
Lawson Court
Post Office Box 854
Cincinnati, Ohio 45201

Hurdon Music Publishers

Husky Music Co., Inc. (BMI)
38 Music Square East
Nashville, Tennessee 37203

Hustlers Inc. (BMI)
c/o Alan Walden
5722 Kentucky Downs
Macon, Georgia 31210

Mamie Hutton Music (ASCAP)
c/o Calvin Rhodes
5439 Gilmore Avenue
St. Louis, Missouri 63120

I

I Love Music (BMI)
c/o Joyce Records Corp.
3277 Malcolm Avenue
Los Angeles, California 90034

Ice Age Music (ASCAP)
c/o Segel & Goldman
9348 Santa Monica Boulevard
Beverly Hills, California 90210

Ice Nine Publishing Co., Inc. (ASCAP)
Box 1073
San Rafael, California 94915

Icebag Corp. (BMI)
2400 Fulton Street
San Francisco, California 94118

Iceman Music Corp. (BMI)
see Unichappell Music Inc.

Impulsive Music (ASCAP)
see April Music Inc.

Imusic Inc. (ASCAP)
c/o Schlanger, Blumenthal & Lynne,
Esqs.
488 Madison Avenue
New York, New York 10022

In Music Co. (ASCAP)
2101 Ivar Avenue
Hollywood, California 90028

In-the-Pocket Music Co. (BMI)
c/o Cholly Bassoline
Apartment 5
620 East Lincoln Street
Royal Oak, Michigan 48067

Indano Music Co. (ASCAP)
625 Madison Avenue
New York, New York 10002

Inevitable Music (BMI)
6117 Glen Holly Avenue
Hollywood, California 90028

Integrity Music Corp. (ASCAP)
Apartment 14A
1050 Fifth Avenue
New York, New York 10028

Interior Music Corp. (BMI)
see Irving Music Inc.

International Korwin Corp. (ASCAP)
60 West 57th Street
Suite 14F
New York, New York 10019

International Music, Inc. (ASCAP)
c/o Oscar Cohen
18th Floor
445 Park Avenue
New York, New York 10022

International Pauline Corp. (ASCAP)
45 West 56th Street
New York, New York 10019

Intersong, USA Inc.
see Chappell & Co., Inc.

Interval Music (BMI)
Alan Lorber Productions Inc.
c/o Alan Lorber
414 East 52nd Street
Apartment 4A
New York, New York 10022

Interworld Music Group
8304 Beverly Blvd.
Los Angeles, California 90048

Intune Inc. (BMI)
see Dick James Music Inc.

Ipanema Music Co. (ASCAP)
1700 Rising Glen Road
Los Angeles, California 90069

Maurice Irby Music (BMI)
325 Ruthland Road
Freeport, New York 11520

Ireneadele Publishing (ASCAP)
8150 Beverly Boulevard
Los Angeles, California 90048

Iris-Trojan Music Corp. (BMI)
37 West 57th Street
New York, New York 10019

Ironside Music (ASCAP)
Box 564
Hollister, Missouri 65672

IRP Music, Inc. (BMI)
1619 Broadway
New York, New York 10019

Irving Music Cordell Russell (BMI)
1358 North La Brea
Hollywood, California 90028

Irving Music Inc. (BMI)
1358 North La Brea
Hollywood, California 90028

Irving Music Inc.-East Memphis (BMI)
1358 North La Brea
Hollywood, California 90028

Isalee Music Publishing Co. (BMI)
Berry Park
Buckner Road
Wentzville, Missouri 63385

Island Music (BMI)
c/o Mr. Lionel Conway
6525 Sunset Boulevard
Hollywood, California 90028

Islip Music Publishing Co. (BMI)
c/o Angelyn Doggett
120 West Bayberry Road
Islip, New York 11751

Itasca Music (BMI)
c/o ATM Music
Suite 600
8732 Sunset Boulevard
Los Angeles, California 90069

Ivanhoe Music, Inc. (ASCAP)
415 East 52nd Street
New York, New York 10022

Izzylumoe Music
c/o Financial Management
International
9200 Sunset Boulevard
Suite 931
Los Angeles, California 90069

J

J & H Publishing Co.
see Johi Music Publishing Co., Inc.

Jac Music Co., Inc. (ASCAP)
5253 Lankershin Boulevard
North Hollywood, California 91601

Jack & Bill Music Co. (ASCAP)
see T. B. #Harms Co.

Jack Music Inc. (BMI)
Post Office Box 120477
Nashville, Tennessee 37210

List of Publishers

Jack o' Diamonds Publications, Inc. (BMI)
4200 Central Pike
Hermitage, Tennessee 37076

Teddy Jack Music (BMI)
Post Office Box 1006
Hendersonville, Tennessee 37075

Jackelope Publishing (BMI)
see Blackwood Music Inc.

Jacktone Music Corp.
see MCA Music

Jacon Music (BMI)
2958 North Beachwood Drive
Hollywood, California 90068

Jadar Music Corp. (BMI)
see Unichappell Music Inc.

Jaep Music, Inc. (BMI)
c/o Copyright Service Bureau, Ltd.
221 West 57th Street
New York, New York 10019

Jaglea Music Co. (BMI)
Apartment 406
1009 North Ocean Boulevard
Pompano Beach, Florida 33062

Jalynne Corp. (BMI)
c/o Irving Nahan
2203 Spruce Street
Philadelphia, Pennsylvania 19103

Jamersonian Music (ASCAP)
Attention: James Jamerson
4807 Beck Avenue
#6
North Hollywood, California 91601

Dick James Music Inc. (BMI)
24 Music Square East
Nashville, Tennessee 37203

Tommy James Music Inc. (BMI)
30 Woodlawn Avenue
Clifton, New Jersey 07013

Jamie Music Publishing Co.
c/o A. Schroder International Ltd.
919 North Broad Street
Philadelphia, Pennsylvania 19123

Jamil Music (BMI)
413 North Parkerson Avenue
Post Office Box 1345
Crowley, Louisiana 70526

Jando Music Inc. (ASCAP)
see Jack Music Inc.

Janeiro Music Co. (ASCAP)
1700 Rising Glen Road
Los Angeles, California 90069

Jarest Music Co. (ASCAP)
4516 Lennox Avenue
Sherman Oaks, California 91423

Jaspar Music (BMI)
c/o J. Parks Associates
852 Elm Street
Manchester, New hampshire 03101

Jasperilla Music Co. (ASCAP)
c/o Mitchell, Silberberg & Knupp
1800 Century Park East
Los Angeles, California 90067

Jastone Publications (BMI)
Post Office Box 4351
Takoma Park, Maryland 20912

Jat Music, Inc. (BMI)
c/o Irwin A. Deutscher, Trustee
5th Floor
St. Cloud Corner
500 Church Street
Nashville, Tennessee 37219

Jatap Publishing Co., Inc. (BMI)
c/o Irving Mills Music
408 North Palm Drive
Beverly Hills, California 90210

Jay-Boy Music Corp. (BMI)
c/o Danny Kessler
Suite 1920
135 West 50th Street
New York, New York 10020

Fred Jay
Address unknown

Jay Love Music Corp. (ASCAP)
c/o Sport N Dress
Attention: Miriam Jerome
747 White Plains Road
Scarsdale, New York 10583

Jay Music (ASCAP)
6654 Allott Avenue
Van Nuys, California 91401

Jaymar Music Publishing Co., Inc. (ASCAP)
c/o Martin Mills Enterprises, Inc.
1619 Broadway
New York, New York 10019

Jay's Enterprises (ASCAP)
see Chappell & Co., Inc.

Jazz Bird Music (ASCAP)
see WB Music Corp.

JC Music Co. (ASCAP)
see Jac Music Co., Inc.

JEC Publishing (BMI)
8025 Melrose Avenue
Los Angeles, California 90046

Jeddrah Music (ASCAP)
c/o Front Line Management
9044 Melrose Avenue
3rd Floor
Los Angeles, California 90069

Jeff-Mar Music Co., Inc. (BMI)
c/o Michael F. Sukin Esq.
919 Third Avenue
38th Floor
New York, New York 10022

Jefferson Music Co., Inc. (ASCAP)
1619 Broadway
New York, New York 10019

Garland Jeffreys Music (ASCAP)
c/o Levine & Thall, PC
485 Madison Avenue
New York, New York 10022

Gordon Jenkins, Inc. (ASCAP)
c/o Braunstein, Chernin & Plant
449 South Beverly Drive
Beverly Hills, California 90212

Waylon Jennings Music (BMI)
1117 17th Avenue South
Nashville, Tennessee 37212

Jenny Music, Inc. (ASCAP)
c/o Robert W. Scott
126 Greenway North
Forest Hills, New York 11375

Jericho Music Corp. (ASCAP)
1 Tobin Avenue
Great Neck, New York 11021

Jerryco Music Co. (ASCAP)
c/o Edwin H. Morris & Co., Inc.
39 West 54th Street
New York, New York 10019

Jet Music Inc. (BMI)
see Blackwood Music Inc.

Jetstar Publishers, Inc. (BMI)
c/o Abnak Music Enterprises, Inc.
825 Olive Street
Dallas, Texas 75201

Jewel Music Publishing Co., Inc. (ASCAP)
c/o The Goodman Group
110 East 59th Street
New York, New York 10022

Jim-Edd Music (BMI)
Post Office Box 78681
Los Angeles, California 90016

Jimi-Lane Music (BMI)
Box 5295
Ocean Park Station
Santa Monica, California 90405

Jimpire Music Inc. (BMI)
c/o Martin Itzler
110 East 59th Street
New York, New York 10022

Jimskip Music, Inc. (BMI)
c/o Larry Taylor
No. 301
910 South Holt Avenue
Los Angeles, California 90035

Jiru Music (ASCAP)
201 West 77th Street
Suite 3C
New York, New York 10024

Jo Ro Music Corp. (ASCAP)
c/o Larry Spier, Inc.
401 Fifth Avenue
New York, New York 10016

Joachim Music Inc. (BMI)
c/o Paul H. Wolfowitz
59 East 54th Street
Suite 22
New York, New York 10022

Jobete Music Co., Inc. (ASCAP)
6255 Sunset Boulevard
Hollywood, California 90028

List of Publishers

Jodrell Music Inc. (ASCAP)
c/o Michael Lippman Inc.
9669 Oak Pass Road
Beverly Hills, California 90210

Johi Music Publishing Co., Inc. (BMI)
Satin, Tenenbaum, Eichler & Zimmer
1776 Broadway
New York, New York 10019

Johnsongs Inc. (ASCAP)
see MCA Music

Johnstone-Montei, Inc. (BMI)
Suite 7201
6255 Sunset Boulevard
Hollywood, California 90028

Joli Tinker Publishing Co. (ASCAP)
Post Office Box 932
Radio City Station
New York, New York 10019

Jolly Cheeks Music (BMI)
c/o Griesdorf, Chertkoff, Levitt, &
Associates
2200 Younge St.
Suite 502
Toronto, Ontario M4S 2O6
Canada

Jondora Music (BMI)
10 & Parker Street
Berkeley, California 94710

Jones Music Co.
c/o Dorothy Mae Rice Jones
1916 Portman Avenue
Cincinnati, Ohio 45237

Jonico Music Inc. (ASCAP)
see Chappell & Co., Inc.

Jonware Music Corp. (BMI)
c/o Aleen Colitz, Esq.
578 Maitland Avenue
Teaneck, New Jersey 07666

Jot Music Co. (BMI)
2203 Spruce Street
Philadelphia, Pennsylvania 19103

Joy Music, Inc. (ASCAP)
1790 Broadway
New York, New York 10019

Joy U.S.A. Music Co. (BMI)
c/o Peter Shukat
111 West 57th Street
New York, New York 10019

Joyful Wisdom Publishing Co. (BMI)
c/o Alkatraz Korner Music
Post Office 3316
San Francisco, California 94119

Joyfully Sad Music (BMI)
c/o Copyright Service Bureau, Ltd.
221 West 57th Street
New York, New York 10019

Jubilee Music Inc. (ASCAP)
see Chappell & Co., Inc.

Ross Jungnickel, Inc. (ASCAP)
11th Floor
1619 Broadway
New York, New York 10019

Junik Music, Inc. (BMI)
28 North Belmont Avenue
Arlington Heights, Illinois 60004

Just Music, Inc. (BMI)
20-F Robert Pitt Drive
Monsey, New York 10952

Justunes Inc. (ASCAP)
see WB Music Corp.

K

Kags Music Corp. (BMI)
c/o Abkco Music, Inc.
1700 Broadway
New York, New York 10019

Irving Kahal Music, Inc. (ASCAP)
c/o A. Halsey Cowan, Esq.
1350 Avenue of the Americas
New York, New York 10019

Gus Kahn Music Co. (ASCAP)
6223 Selma Avenue
Hollywood, California 90028

Kahoona Tunes, Inc.
Address unknown

Kaiser Music Co. (ASCAP)
see Sanphil Music Co.

Kalimba Music (ASCAP)
see Columbia Pictures Publications

Charles Emmerich Kalman, Inc. (ASCAP)
241 West 72nd Street
New York, New York 10023

Kalmann Music, Inc. (ASCAP)
300 Farwood Road
Philadelphia, Pennsylvania 19151

Kama Rippa Music (ASCAP)
see Buddah Music Inc.

Kama Sutra Music Inc. (BMI)
see United Artists Music Co., Inc.

Kamakara Music (ASCAP)
c/o Helen S. Darion
Box 216
Pinnacle Road
Lyme, New hampshire 03768

Kamakazi Music Corp. (BMI)
c/o Miles J. Lource
314 West 71st Street
New York, New York 10023

Kander & Ebb Inc. (BMI)
see Unichappell Music Inc.

Kangaroo Music, Inc. (BMI)
Suite 1H
2310 Ocean Parkway
Brooklyn, New York 11223

Les Kangas Music Publishing Co. (BMI)
7902 Dewey Street
San Gabriel, California 91776

Kaskat Music, Inc. (BMI)
323 East Shore Road
Great Neck, New York 11023

Edward Kassner Music Co., Inc. (ASCAP)
756 Seventh Avenue
New York, New York 10019

Kavelin Music (BMI)
No. 121
8670 Burton Way
Los Angeles, California 90048

K.C.M. Music (ASCAP)
c/o Mike Curb Productions
111 North Hollywood Way
Burbank, California 91505

Keca Music Inc. (ASCAP)
c/o The Creative Music Group
6430 Sunset Boulevard
Suite 716
Hollywood, California 90028

Keetch, Caesar & Dino Music, Inc. (BMI)
Room 1006
1841 Broadway
New York, New York 10023

Milton Kellem Music Co., Inc. (ASCAP)
No. 114
2780 Northeast 183rd Street
North Miami Beach, Florida 33160

Kemo Music Co. (BMI)
c/o Beechwood Music Corp.
6255 Sunset Boulevard
Hollywood, California 90028

Kensho Music (ASCAP)
c/o Dave Kogan
350 5th Avenue
New York, New York 10001

Arthur Kent Music Co. (ASCAP)
1412 Golfview Drive
North Myrtle Beach, South Carolina 29582

Walter Kent Music Co. (ASCAP)
55 Edgecomb Avenue
New York, New York 10030

Kentucky Music, Inc. (BMI)
11th Floor
1619 Broadway
New York, New York 10019

Keva Music Co. (BMI)
c/o Richard Becker
Post Office Box 144
7 Queen Anne Drive
Deal, New Jersey 07723

Gilbert Keyes Music Co. (ASCAP)
6223 Selma Avenue
Hollywood, California 90028

Keymen Music (BMI)
c/o Copyright Service Bureau, Ltd.
221 West 57th Street
New York, New York 10019

Keystone Music Co. of California (ASCAP)
9615 Helen Avenue
Sunland, California 91040

Kichele Music (ASCAP)
see Interworld Music Group

Kicking Bear Music (ASCAP)
see WB Music Corp.

Kicks Music (BMI)
see E. B. Marks Music Corp.

Kidada Music Inc. (BMI)
7250 Beverly Boulevard
Suite 206
Los Angeles, California 90036

Kiddio Music Co. (BMI)
c/o Martin Poll
919 Third Avenue
New York, New York 10022

Kilynn Music Publishing, Inc. (BMI)
c/o Mietus Copyright Management
Post Office Box 432
2351 Laurana Road
Union, New Jersey 07083

Kimlyn Music Co., Inc. (ASCAP)
see Sherlyn Publishing Co., Inc.

Charles E. King (ASCAP)
Post Office Box 2691
Pompano Beach, Florida 33062

King Guitar Inc. (ASCAP)
see MCA Music

Kingsley Music, Inc. (ASCAP)
Room 501
1619 Broadway
New York, New York 10019

Kipahulu Music Co. (ASCAP)
see Colgems-EMI Music Inc.

Kipeth Music Publishing Co. (BMI)
c/o Hardee, Barovick, Konecky
& Braun
Attention: Schoefield
One Dag Hammarskjold Plaza
New York, New York 10022

Charles Kipps Music Inc. (BMI)
One Lincoln Plaza
Suite 330
New York, New York 10023

Don Kirshner Music Inc. (BMI)
see Blackwood Music Inc.

Kirshner Songs Inc. (ASCAP)
see Blackwood Music Inc.

Kiss
Glickman & Marks Management Co.
655 Madison Ave
New York, New York 10021

Kiss Music Co. (ASCAP)
2916 East Great Smokey Court
Westlake Village, California 91362

Kitty Anne Music Co., Inc.
see International Korwin Corp.

Kling Klang Music Inc. (ASCAP)
see Famous Music Co.

Klondike Enterprises Ltd. (BMI)
see Mietus Copyright Management

Knee Trembler Music (ASCAP)
see Fourth Floor Music Inc.

Knollwood Music Corp. (ASCAP)
c/o Fred Albert Music Corp.
Suite 202
8150 Beverly Boulevard
Los Angeles, California 90048

Know Music (ASCAP)
6300 Southcenter Boulevard
Suite 200
Seattle, Washington 98188

Knox Music, Inc. (BMI)
639 Madison Avenue
Memphis, Tennessee 38103

Kooper Music Co. (BMI)
see Mietus Copyright Management

Koppelman-Bandier Music Corp. (BMI)
c/o Martin Bandier
The Entertainment Co.
40 West 57th Street
Number 1510
New York, New York 10019

Korchmar Music (ASCAP)
c/o Nick Ben-Meir
144 South Beverly Drive
Suite 500
Beverly Hills, California 90212

Korwin Music, Inc. (ASCAP)
57 West 56th Street
New York, New York 10019

Kramer-Whitney, Inc. (ASCAP)
1650 Broadway
New York, New York 10019

Kuptillo Music (ASCAP)
Box 1010
Lakspur, California 94939

L

La Brea Music (ASCAP)
see Almo Music Corp.

La Salle Music Publishers, Inc. (ASCAP)
1740 Broadway
New York, New York 10019

Lady Jane Music (BMI)
Box 614
Tahoe City, California 95730

Ladysmith Music Inc. (ASCAP)
see Arista Music Inc.

Lair Music Publishing Co. (BMI)
c/o Lonzo & Oscar Music
Publishing Co.
Post Office Box 208
Goodlettsville, Tennessee 37072

Lakeview Music Corp. (BMI)
1631 Broadway
New York, New York 10019

Laminations Music (ASCAP)
Attention: Robert Lamm
c/o Kaufman, Eisenberg & Co.
9301 Wilshire Boulevard
Suite 212
Beverly Hills, California 90210

Lancaster Music Publications, Inc. (BMI)
806 16th Avenue South
Nashville, Tennessee 37203

Landers-Roberts Music (ASCAP)
see Chappell & Co., Inc.

John Lange Music Co. (ASCAP)
320 Riverside Drive
New York, New York 10024

Lansdale Music Corp. (BMI)
c/o Nicholas A. Busillo
1023 North 67th Street
Philadelphia, Pennsylvania 19151

Lansdowne Music Publishing (ASCAP)
see Bloor Music Publishers

Lar-Bell Music Corp. (BMI)
Suite 140
9110 Sunset Boulevard
Los Angeles, California 90069

Largo Music, Inc. (ASCAP)
425 Park Avenue
New York, New York 10022

Lark Music, Inc. (BMI)
Music Administration Service Co.
c/o SAS, Inc.
1414 Avenue of the Americas
New York, New York 10019

Larrabee Music, Inc. (BMI)
c/o Maurice M. Kahn
6381 Hollywood Boulevard
Hollywood, California 90028

Larrick Music Co. (BMI)
c/o Marvin Hughes
2513 Lincoya Court
Nashville, Tennessee 37214

Last Minute Music (BMI)
c/o Toni Kathrin Stern
688 Orchard Avenue
Santa Barbara, California 93108

Laughing Willow Co., Inc., The (ASCAP)
c/o Arnold Liebman
159 West 53rd Street
New York, New York 10019

Laurel Canyon Music Ltd. (ASCAP)
see Bruce Springsteen Publishing

Laurel Music Corp. (ASCAP)
22 West 48th Street
New York, New York 10036

Laurie Productions, Inc. (ASCAP)
Laurie Publishing Group
20-F Robert Pitt Drive
Monsey, New York 10952

Laursteed Music, Inc. (ASCAP)
c/o Edward Traubner & Co. Inc.
Suite 501
132 South Rodeo Drive
Beverly Hills, California 90212

Jason Lawrence Music, Inc. (ASCAP)
c/o Sanford Green
Suite 1006
1841 Broadway
New York, New York 10023

Lazy Day Music (BMI)
c/o Lyons
No. 11B
677 West End
New York, New York 10025

LDJN Music Corp. (ASCAP)
c/o Leeds Music Corp.
445 Park Avenue
New York, New York 10022

Le Bill Music, Inc. (BMI)
Post Office Box 11152
Forth Worth, Texas 76109

Le-Mor Music Co. (ASCAP)
251 East Grand Street
Chicago, Illinois 60605

Lear Music, Inc. (ASCAP)
314 Huntley Drive
Los Angeles, California 90048

Leeds Music Corp. (ASCAP)
see MCA Music

Legacy Music, Inc. (BMI)
c/o Screen Gems-EMI Music, Inc.
Attention: Jerry Isaacson
6255 Sunset Boulevard
Hollywood, California 90028

Legibus Music Co. (BMI)
c/o Peter Bennett, Esq.
9060 Santa Monica Boulevard
Suite 300
Los Angeles, California 90069

Legs Music, Inc. (ASCAP)
c/o Abkco Music
1700 Broadway
New York, New York 10019

Leidasnow Music (ASCAP)
Attention: Leida Snow
118 Riverside Drive
New York, New York 10024

Lemon Tree Music, Inc. (ASCAP)
c/o Will Holt
Apartment 8W
45 East 66th Street
New York, New York 10021

Lena Music, Inc. (BMI)
Suite 507
1619 Broadway
New York, New York 10019

Lencal Music Co. (BMI)
2012 Cambridge Place
South Pasadena, California 91030

Lennon Music (BMI)
c/o Oppenheim, Appel, Dixon & Co.
1 New York Plaza
New York, New York 10004

Leon Music (ASCAP)
c/o The Songwriters Guild
3rd Floor
276 Fifth Avenue
New York, New York 10001

Leonard-Worth Songs (ASCAP)
Address unknown

Samuel M. Lerner Publications (ASCAP)
7650 Hollywood Boulevard
Los Angeles, California 90046

Edgar Leslie (ASCAP)
59 West 46th Street
New York, New York 10036

Let There Be Music Inc. (ASCAP)
see Buzz Cason Publications Inc.

Levine & Brown Music Inc. (BMI)
c/o Arrow, Edelstein & Gross
Attention: John Gross, Esq.
919 Third Avenue
New York, New York 10022

Adam R. Levy & Father Enterprises Inc.
(BMI)
see Big Seven Music Corp.

Lou Levy Music Co., Inc. (ASCAP)
26 East 63rd Street
Apartment 12-A
New York, New York 10021

Lewin Schuster Music Co. (ASCAP)
c/o Phoebe Lewin
Apartment 19S
301 East 79th Street
New York, New York 10021

Lewis Music Publishing Co., Inc. (ASCAP)
Ashley Dealer's Inc.
263 Veteran's Boulevard
Carlstadt, New Jersey 07072

Lexicon Music Inc. (ASCAP)
Box 296
Woodland Hills, California 91365

Libijon Music, Inc. (BMI)
Address unknown

Liccianetti Music International (ASCAP)
Address unknown

Lida Enterprises, Inc. (ASCAP)
c/o Notable Music Co., Inc.
200 West 54th Street
New York, New York 10019

Lido Music Inc. (BMI)
c/o Segel & Goldman Inc.
9348 Santa Monica Boulevard
Beverly Hills, California 90210

Lily Pond Music (BMI)
c/o Irving Markowitz
30 Park Place
East Hampton, New York 11937

Limax Music, Inc. (BMI)
Barington Plaza
Apartment A 1310
111740 Wilshire Boulevard
Los Angeles, California 90025

Limerick Music Corp. (ASCAP)
c/o The Songwriters Guild
3rd Floor
276 Fifth Avenue
New York, New York 10001

Lincoln Music Corp. (ASCAP)
c/o Abner Silver
Suite 203
160 Central Park South
New York, New York 10019

Lindabet Music Inc. (ASCAP)
see Jericho Music Corp.

Lindseyanne Music Co., Inc. (BMI)
c/o Steve Alaimo
495 South East 10th Court
Hialeah, Florida 33010

Linduane Corp. (BMI)
c/o Al Wilde
25 Central Park West
New York, New York 10023

Lion Music Corp. (ASCAP)
1540 Broadway
New York, New York 10036

Lion Publishing Co., Inc. (BMI)
c/o Don D. Robey
2809 Erastus Street
Houston, Texas 77026

Little Dickens Music Publishers (ASCAP)
c/o Segel & Goldman Inc.
9348 Santa Monica Boulevard
#304
Beverly Hills, California 90210

Little Dipper Music Corp. (BMI)
c/o Big Seven Music Corp.
18th Floor
1790 Broadway
New York, New York 10019

Little Hurry Music, Inc. (BMI)
c/o Mietus Copyright Management
Post Office Box 432
2351 Laurana Road
Union, New Jersey 07083

Little Kitty Music (ASCAP)
c/o Craig Hull
6995 Trolleyway
Playa Del Rey, California 90291

Little Max Music Co. (BMI)
see Blackwood Music Inc.

Little River Publishing Co. (BMI)
131 North Porter
Norman, Oklahoma 73069

Livingston & Evans, Inc. (ASCAP)
c/o Larry Shayne Enterprises
6362 Hollywood Boulevard
Hollywood, California 90028

Liza Music Corp. (ASCAP)
1700 Broadway
New York, New York 10019

Llee Corp. (BMI)
c/o Lee V. Eastman
39 West 54th Street
New York, New York 10019

Lloyd and Logan, Inc. (BMI)
c/o Copyright Service Bureau, Ltd.
221 West 57th Street
New York, New York 10019

Loaves and Fishes Music Co., Inc. (BMI)
c/o Bicycle Music Co.
8075 West Third Street, Suite 400
Los Angeles, California 90048

John Jacob Loeb Co. (ASCAP)
42 Lafayette Place
Woodmere, New York 11598

Lois Publishing Co. (BMI)
1540 Brewster Avenue
Cincinnati, Ohio 45207

Lola Publishing Corp. (BMI)
70-72 Bridge Avenue
Bay Head, New Jersey 08742

Lollipop Music Corp. (BMI)
Penthouse C
132 East 45th Street
New York, New York 10017

Lombardo Music, Inc. (ASCAP)
1619 Broadway
New York, New York 10019

Londontown Music, Inc. (ASCAP)
c/o Garrett Music Enterprises
Suite 1019
6255 Sunset Boulevard
Hollywood, California 90028

E. M. Long Publishing Co., Inc. (BMI)
840 South Highland Street
Memphis, Tennessee 38111

Longhorn Music Co. (BMI)
c/o United Record Distributors
1613 St. Emanuel Street
Houston, Texas 38127

Lonport Music Inc. (BMI)
c/o Sidney A. Seidenberg
1414 Avenue of the Americas
New York, New York 10017

Loresta Music (ASCAP)
c/o Jeffrey Graubart
4th Floor - Chocolate Building
Suite D402 - Ghirardelli Square
900 North Point
San Francisco, California 94109

Lorijoy Music Inc. (BMI)
39 West 55th Street
Suite 405
New York, New York 10019

Loring Music Co. (BMI)
Division of Loring Productions, Inc.
1048 North Carol Drive
Los Angeles, California 90069

Lorlimar Music Publishing Co. (BMI)
Post Office Box 1340
Studio City, California 91604

Lornhole Music (BMI)
1427 Seventh Street
Santa Monica, California 90406

Lorville Music Co., A (ASCAP)
see Terrace Music

Lost Cabin Music (BMI)
c/o Gregory E. Fishbach
1 Century Plaza
2029 Century Park East
Suite 1370
Los Angeles, California 90067

Lovelane Music Publishing (BMI)
c/o Samuel S. Kaplan
Apartment E
12801 Woodbridge
Studio City, California 91604

Low-AB Music (BMI)
3051 Clairmont Road Northeast
Atlanta, Georgia 30329

Low-Sal, Inc. (BMI)
3051 Clairmont Road North East
Atlanta, Georgia 30329

Low-Twi Music, Inc. (BMI)
3051 Clairmont Road
Atlanta, Georgia 30329

Lowe Music Publishing Corp. (ASCAP)
c/o David J. Steinberg
20th Floor
121 South Broad Street
Philadelphia, Pennsylvania 19107

Lowery Music Co., Inc. (BMI)
3051 Clairmont Road North East
Atlanta, Georgia 30329

LT Music Co. (ASCAP)
31-Fresh Pond Parkway
Cambridge, Massachusetts 02138

LTD Inc. (ASCAP)
Attention: Ron Nadel
114 North Swall Drive
Los Angeles, California 90048

Lucid Music (BMI)
c/o Fidlon & Barkan
122 East 55th Street
New York, New York 10022

Lucky Pork Music (ASCAP)
c/o Ron Nagle
222 Montcalm Street
San Francisco, California 94110

Lucky Three Music Publishing Co. (BMI)
Div. of Salsoul Record Corp.
c/o Larry Spier
401 Fifth Avenue
New York, New York 10016

Luckyu Music (BMI)
c/o Jess S. Morgan and Co., Inc.
6420 Wilshire Boulevard
Nineteenth Floor
Los Angeles, California 90048

Ludix Publishing Co., Inc. (BMI)
c/o Irving Music, Inc.
1358 North La Brea
Hollywood, California 90028

Ludlow Music Inc. (BMI)
10 Columbus Circle
Suite 1406
New York, New York 10019

Lunatunes Music (BMI)
2400 Fulton Street
San Francisco, California 94118

Lupercalia Music Publishing Co. (ASCAP)
c/o Purcell
210 East 53rd Street
New York, New York 10022

Lupine Music (BMI)
Post Office Box 4404
Las Vegas, Nevada 89106

Luvlin Music Inc. (BMI)
c/o Copyright Service Bureau, Ltd.
221 West 57th Street
New York, New York 10019

Lyle Music, Inc. (ASCAP)
120 East 34th Street
New York, New York 10016

Lyn-Lou Music, Inc. (BMI)
1518 Chelsea Avenue
Memphis, Tennessee 38108

Lyresong Publishing Co. (BMI)
c/o B. H. Richardson
1227 Spring Street Northwest
Atlanta, Georgia 30309

Lyvia Music
Address unknown

M

M & M Music Co. (BMI)
c/o Monument Music
Attention Larry Uttal
141 East 88th Street
New York, New York 10028

Mabs Music Co. (ASCAP)
8721 Sunset Boulevard
Los Angeles, California 90069

John D. MacArthur Music Corp. (BMI)
1631 Broadway
New York, New York 10019

Macaulay Music Ltd. (ASCAP)
see Almo Music Corp.

Macawrite Music (ASCAP)
see Brockman Enterprises Inc.

Maclen Music Inc. (BMI)
see ATV Music Corp.

List of Publishers

Maclen Music of Canada (BMI)
c/o ATV Group
6255 Sunset Boulevard
Hollywood, California 90028

Macmillan Performing Arts Music Inc.
(ASCAP)
see G. Schirmer Inc.

Mad Hatter Music Corp. (BMI)
Address unknown

Mad Vincent Music (BMI)
c/o Satin, Tenenbaum, Eichler &
Zimmerman
1776 Broadway
New York, New York 10019

Madison Music (BMI)
c/o Samberg
80 Murray Drive
Westbury, New York 11590

Maestro Music, Inc. (BMI)
9060 Santa Monica Boulevard
West Hollywood, California 90069

Maggie Music Co., Inc. (BMI)
Room 715
1650 Broadway
New York, New York 10019

Magicland Music (ASCAP)
c/o Leber-Krebs Inc.
65 West 55th Street
New York, New York 10019

Magidson Music Co., Inc. (ASCAP)
10464 Lindbrook Drive
Los Angeles, California 90024

Magnolia Publishing Co. (BMI)
14155 Magnolia Boulevard
Van Nuys, California 93001

Mainman Music (ASCAP)
200 Central Park South
Suite 31A
New York, New York 10019

Mainstay Music Inc. (BMI)
see Al Gallico Music Corp.

Major Oak Music (ASCAP)
c/o Harold Sanford Kant
232 Wilshire Boulevard
#450
Santa Monica, California 90401

Major Songs Co. (ASCAP)
c/o The Songwriters Guild
3rd Floor
276 Fifth Avenue
New York, New York 10001

Make Me Smile Music (ASCAP)
Attention: James Pankow
c/o Kaufman, Eisenberg & Co.
93-1 Wilshire Boulevard
Suite 212
Beverly Hills, California 90210

Malaco Music Co. (BMI)
Box 9287
Jackson, Mississippi 39206

Malapi Music (BMI)
Post Office Box 1103
Grand Canyon, Arizona 86023

Malbiz Publishing (BMI)
see Blackwood Music Inc.

Malkyle Music Co. (BMI)
c/o Kaufman & Bernstein
1900 Avenue of the Stars
Number 2270
Los Angeles, California 90067

Mallory Music Publications (BMI)
c/o Woodhaven Farms
Route 1
Little New York Road
Alexander City, Alabama 35010

Malneck Music (ASCAP)
508 North Elm Drive
Beverly Hills, California 90210

Malvern Music Co. (ASCAP)
Chester County
Malvern, Pennsylvania 19355

M.A.M. (Music Publishing Corp.) (ASCAP)
see Management Agency & Music
Publishing

Man-Ken Music Ltd. (BMI)
34 Pheasant Run
Old Westbury, New York 11568

Management Agency & Music Publishing
(BMI)
Attention: Jon Devirian
10100 Santa Monica Boulevard
Suite 205
Los Angeles, California 90067

Management Three Music (BMI)
9744 Wilshire Boulevard
Fourth Floor
Beverly Hills, California 90212

Henry Mancini Enterprises (ASCAP)
see Chappell & Co., Inc.

Mandy Music (ASCAP)
c/o Johnny Beinstock
1619 Broadway
Penthouse
New York, New York 10019

Manitou-Champion (BMI)
c/o MCA, Inc.
445 Park Avenue
New York, New York 10022

Manitou-Duchess (BMI)
Manitou-Duchess Music Corp.
c/o MCA Music
445 Park Avenue
New York, New York 10022

Manitou-Management Music Publishing
(BMI)
Management Agency and Music
Publishing, Inc.
Attention: Jon Devirian
10100 Santa Monica Boulevard
Los Angeles, California 90067

Manitou-Music Corp. of America (BMI)
c/o MCA Music
445 Park Avenue
New York, New York 10022

Mann & Weil Songs Inc. (BMI)
see ATV Music Corp.

David Mann Music Co. (ASCAP)
3 Daniel Lane
Kinnelon, New Jersey 07405

Herbie Mann Music Corp. (ASCAP)
c/o Mietus Copyright Management
Post Office Box 432
2351 Laurana Road
Union, New Jersey 07083

Mansion Music Corp. (ASCAP)
136 West 52nd Street
New York, New York 10019

Manticore Music (ASCAP)
c/o Arrow, Edelstein, Gross
& Margolis
919 Third Avenue
New York, New York 10022

Maple Leaf Music Publishing Co., Inc.
(BMI)
1650 Broadway
New York, New York 10019

Mara-Lane Music Corp. (ASCAP)
609 Fifth Avenue
New York, New York 10017

Maravilla Music, Inc. (BMI)
Post Office Box 1898
Studio City, California 91604

Maraville Music Corp. (ASCAP)
1619 Broadway
New York, New York 10019

Marbill Music (BMI)
Post Office Box 11152
Fort Worth, Texas 76110

Marchar Music, Inc. (BMI)
Post Office Box 24396
Nashville, Tennessee 37202

Ricci Mareno Music
3706 D Hillsboro Road
Nashville, Tennessee 37215

Ernie Maresca, Inc. (ASCAP)
c/o Schwartz Music Co., Inc.
Laurie Publishing Group
20-F Robert Pitt Drive
Monsey, New York 10952

Maribus Music Inc. (BMI)
119 West 57th Street
New York, New York 10019

Marilor Lorimar (ASCAP)
see Lorlimar Music Publishing Co.

Marimba Music Corp. (ASCAP)
c/o Orland, Chase & Mucci
48 West 48th Street
New York, New York 10036

Mariposa Music Inc. (BMI)
713 18th Avenue South
Nashville, Tennessee 37204

Marizona Music (BMI)
713 18th Avenue South
Nashville, Tennessee 37203

Mark Three Music (BMI)
c/o Jerry Allison
Route 1
Box 222
Lyles, Tennessee 37098

Mark VII Music (ASCAP)
4024 Radford Avenue
North Hollywood, California 91604

Marke Music Publishing Co., Inc. (ASCAP)
c/o The Songwriters Guild
3rd Floor
276 Fifth Avenue
New York, New York 10001

E. B. Marks Music Corp. (BMI)
1790 Broadway
New York, New York 10019

Edward B. Marks Music Corp. (BMI)
1790 Broadway
New York, New York 10019

Bob Marley Music Ltd. (ASCAP)
see Almo Music Corp.

Marlin Enterprises
Address unknown

Marlo Music Corp. (ASCAP)
c/o David W. Katz
Attention: P. Plumer
10 East 40th Street
New York, New York 10016

Marlong Music Corp. (ASCAP)
1650 Broadway
New York, New York 10019

Kenny Marlow (BMI)
c/o Grille Music
107 Parkway Towers
Nashville, Tennessee 37219

Marsaint Music Inc. (BMI)
Attention: Marshall E. Sehorn
3809 Clematis Avenue
New Orleans, Louisiana 70122

Marson Inc. (BMI)
c/o Jimmie Loden
3833 Cleghorn Avenue
Suite 400
Nashville, Tennessee 37215

Martin Music (ASCAP)
13455 Ventura Boulevard
Sherman Oaks, California 91400

Mack Martin Music Co. (BMI)
Brevoort Hotel
6326 Lexington
Hollywood, California 90038

Marty's Music Corp. (BMI)
713 18th Avenue South
Nashville, Tennessee 37203

Marvin Music Co. (ASCAP)
1 Times Square Plaza
New York, New York 10036

Marwood Music (BMI)
17 McNab Boulevard
Scarborough, Ontario M1M 2W3
Canada

Marybeth Music (BMI)
c/o Mary Glen Music
14 East 23rd Street
Spray Beach, New Jersey 08008

Matamoros Music (BMI)
c/o Billy Walker
Post Office Box 618
Hendersonville, Tennessee 37075

Matragun Music Inc. (BMI)
c/o Jess S. Morgan & Company
6420 Wilshire Boulevard
19th Floor
Los Angeles, California 90048

Maureen Music, Inc. (BMI)
c/o A. R. Weiss
27 Fairbanks Boulevard
Woodbury, New York 11797

Peter Maurice Music Co., Ltd. (ASCAP)
1619 Broadway
New York, New York 10019

Mauve Music Inc. (ASCAP)
Spensley, Horn, Jubas & Lubitz
1880 Century Park East
Suite 500
Los Angeles, California 90067

Maxana Music Corp. (ASCAP)
729 Seventh Avenue
New York, New York 10019

Maxim Music (ASCAP)
c/o Robert Colby
37 West 57th Street
New York, New York 10019

Maxwell Music Corp. (ASCAP)
1 Washington Square
Larchmont, New York 10538

Ray Maxwell Music Publishing Co. (BMI)
Post Office Box 5973
Sherman Oaks, California 91413

May 12th Music Inc. (BMI)
Div. of Whitfield Records Inc.
901 Westbourne Drive
Los Angeles, California 90069

Maya Productions (ASCAP)
c/o David J. Cogan Management
350 5th Avenue
New York, New York 10001

Mayday Music (BMI)
Div. of Mediarts Inc.
c/o Larry Reynolds
1900 Avenue of the Stars
Los Angeles, California 90067

Mayfair Music Corp. (ASCAP)
31 West 54th Street
New York, New York 10019

Maygar Publishing Co. (BMI)
c/o Garry Sherman
27 Independence Court
Clifton, New Jersey 07013

Maypole Music, Inc. (ASCAP)
200 West 57th Street
New York, New York 10019

Mburu Music (ASCAP)
see Columbia Pictures Publications

MCA, Inc. (ASCAP)
445 Park Avenue
New York, New York 10022

MCA Music (ASCAP)
Div. of MCA Inc.
445 Park Avenue
New York, New York 10022

Joseph Allen McCartly (ASCAP)
Address unknown

Van McCoy Music Inc. (BMI)
see WB Music Corp.

McCullough Pigott, Ltd. (ASCAP)
Address unknown

McDonald Music Co. (BMI)
Box 3316
San Francisco, California 94116

McDorsbov Music (ASCAP)
see Almo Music Corp.

McHugh & Adamson Music, Inc. (ASCAP)
609 Fifth Avenue
New York, New York 10017

Jimmy McHugh Music, Inc. (ASCAP)
Suite 400
9301 Wilshire Boulevard
Beverly Hills, California 90210

McLaughlin Publishing Co. (BMI)
c/o Mietus Copyright Management
Post Office Box 432
2351 Laurana Road
Union, New Jersey 07083

Meadowlark Music (ASCAP)
1608 Argyle
Hollywood, California 90028

Mee Moo Music (BMI)
c/o Irwin A. Deutscher
First American Center
18th Floor
Nashville, Tennessee 37338

Melder Publishing Co., Inc. (BMI)
c/o Joe Jones
10556 Arnwood Road
Lake View Terrace, California 91342

Mellin Music, Inc. (BMI)
1650 Broadway
New York, New York 10019

Robert Mellin Music Publishing Corp. (BMI)
1841 Broadway
Room 100
New York, New York 10023

Mellow Music Publishing Co. (BMI)
Suite 305
1650 Broadway
New York, New York 10019

Melody Lane, Inc. (BMI)
1740 Broadway
New York, New York 10019

Melody Music Co. (ASCAP)
Post Office Box 751
Evanston, Illinois 60204

Melody Trails Inc. (BMI)
10 Columbus Circle
Suite 1406
New York, New York 10019

Melomega Music Ltd. (ASCAP)
Box 2
Wayne, Pennsylvania 19087

Melrose Music Corp. (ASCAP)
31 West 54th Street
New York, New York 10019

Mentally Incompetent Music (BMI)
c/o Front Line Management
9044 Melrose Avenue
3rd Floor
Los Angeles, California 90069

Mercedes Music Co. (BMI)
c/o Robert Davenport
Post Office Box 4581
North Hollywood, California 91607

Mercer Music (ASCAP)
see WB Music Corp.

Merjoda Music, Inc. (BMI)
c/o Unichappel
810 Seventh Avenue
New York, New York 10019

Merrill Music Corp. (ASCAP)
see Golden Bell Songs

Merrimac Music Corp. (BMI)
c/o The Goodman Group
110 East 59th Street
New York, New York 10036

Mesquite Music Corp. (ASCAP)
31 West 54th Street
New York, New York 10019

Metorion Music Corp. (BMI)
210 Fifth Avenue
New York, New York 10010

Metro Goldwyn Mayer Inc. (BMI)
10202 West Washington Boulevard
Culver City, California 90230

Mews Music Ltd. (ASCAP)
see MCA Music

Mexican Music Centre, Inc. (ASCAP)
Suite 2P
345 West 58th Street
New York, New York 10019

Joseph Meyer (ASCAP)
Address unknown

Michael Reine Music Co., Ltd.
Address unknown

Michele Publishing Co. (BMI)
6724 Allott Avenue
Van Nuys, California 91401

Mickey Rooney Publishing Co. (ASCAP)
c/o Ruth Webb Enterprises
7500 Devista Drive
Los Angeles, California 90046

Midday Music Co. (BMI)
233 East Erie Street
Chicago, Illinois 60611

Midsong Music Inc. (ASCAP)
see Reno-Metz Music Inc.

Mietus Copyright Management (BMI)
Post Office Box 432
2351 Laurana Road
Union, New Jersey 07083

Mighty Three Music (BMI)
c/o Earl Shelton
309 South Broad Street
Philadelphia, Pennsylvania 19107

Milber Enterprises Corp.
Address unknown

Milene Music Co. (ASCAP)
see Acuff-Rose Publications Inc.

Milk Money Music (ASCAP)
c/o Segel & Goldman Inc.
9126 Sunset Boulevard
Los Angeles, California 90069

Miller Music Corp. (ASCAP)
  see United Artists Music Co., Inc.

Mills Music Inc. (ASCAP)
  see Belwin-Mills Publishing Corp.

Mimosa Publishing Co. (BMI)
  c/o Bobby L. Moore
  507 Graycroft Avenue
  Madison, Tennessee 37115

Miraleste Music (BMI)
  A Division of Richard Delvy
  Enterprises
  8127 Elrita Drive
  Los Angeles, California 90046

Miran Publishing Inc. (BMI)
  c/o Michael Mesnick
  9100 Wilshire Boulevard
  Suite 440
  Beverly Hills, California 90212

Misirlou Music, Inc. (BMI)
  625 Madison Avenue
  New York, New York 10022

Mister T. Music (BMI)
  2112 South Michigan Avenue
  Chicago, Illinois 60616

Joni Mitchell Publishing Corp. (BMI)
  c/o Segel & Goldman Inc.
  9200 Sunset Boulevard
  Suite 1000
  Los Angeles, California 90069

Mixed Bag Music, Inc. (BMI)
  c/o P. Lawrence
  355 East 72nd Street
  New York, New York 10021

Mixer Music (BMI)
  c/o George John Morris
  Post Office Box 1746
  Covina, California 91722

M.J.Q. Music, Inc. (BMI)
  Room 1100
  1697 Broadway
  New York, New York 10019

Mocrisp Music (ASCAP)
  c/o Gavin C. Wright
  3708 Palos Verdes Way
  South San Francisco, California 94080

Modern Age Music Co. (BMI)
  13833 Riverside Drive
  Sherman Oaks, California 91423

Modern Music Publishing Co., Inc. (BMI)
  5810 South Normandie Avenue
  Los Angeles, California 90044

Ivan Mogull Music Corp. (ASCAP)
  625 Madison Avenue
  New York, New York 10022

Mojave Music, Inc. (BMI)
  c/o Jones E. Former
  713 18th Avenue South
  Nashville, Tennessee 37204

Mole Hole Music (BMI)
  c/o Bug Music Group
  9th Floor
  6777 Hollywood Boulevard
  Hollywood, California 90028

James V. Monaco, Inc. (ASCAP)
  c/o Mrs. James V. Monaco
  Box 126
  Route 5
  Hot Springs Nat Park, Arkansas 71901

Monarch Music Corp. (ASCAP)
  Penthouse Suite
  10622 Commerce Avenue
  Tujunga, California 91042

Mongo Music (BMI)
  c/o Copyright Service Bureau, Ltd.
  221 West 57th Street
  New York, New York 10019

Monmar Music, Inc. (ASCAP)
  Address unknown

Montauk Music, Inc. (BMI)
  c/o Belle Nardone
  H. B. Webman & Co.
  Suite 701
  1650 Broadway
  New York, New York 10019

Montclare Music Corp. (BMI)
  Suite 407
  1800 North Argyle Avenue
  Hollywood, California 90028

Montvale Music
c/o Oriolo Film Studio
50 E. 42nd St.
Rm. 511
New York, New York 10022

Monument Music, Inc. (BMI)
225 East 57th Street
New York, New York 10022

Mood Music Co., Inc. (ASCAP)
666 Fifth Avenue
New York, New York 10019

Moogy Music (BMI)
c/o Mark Klingman
73 East Second Street
New York, New York 10003

Moon & Stars Music (BMI)
see Cotillion Music Inc.

Moonlight & Magnolias Music Publishing
(BMI)
c/o Cooper, Epstein & Hurewitz
9465 Wilshire Boulevard
Suite 800
Beverly Hills, California 90069

Moonlight Music, Inc. (BMI)
9288 Kinglet Drive
Hollywood, California 90069

Moorpark Music Corp. (ASCAP)
c/o Marielle Music Publishing Corp.
Post Office Box 842
Radio City Station
New York, New York 10019

Moose Music Ltd. (ASCAP)
see Early Morning Music

Morgan Manor Music Co. (ASCAP)
2283 Bridlewood Drive
Las Vegas, Nevada 89109

Morkay Music (ASCAP)
c/o Mary Louise Glover
6253 Hollywood Boulevard
Suite 1122
Los Angeles, California 90027

Morley Music Co., Inc. (ASCAP)
c/o Eastman & Eastman
39 West 54th Street
New York, New York 10019

Morning Music, Ltd. (BMI)
Post Office Box 120478
Nashville, Tennessee 37212

Edwin H. Morris Co. (ASCAP)
see MPL Communications Inc.

Morris Music, Inc. (BMI)
c/o Unichappell Music, Inc.
32nd Floor
810 Seventh Avenue
New York, New York 10019

Bryan Morrison Music (ASCAP)
c/o Roemer & Nadler
437 Madison Avenue
New York, New York 10016

Morro Music Corp. (BMI)
Suite 1531-2
250 West 57th Street
New York, New York 10019

Moth Music Ltd. (BMI)
see Chrysalis Music Corp.

Mother Bertha Music, Inc. (BMI)
c/o Phil Spector International Inc.
Post Office Box 69529
Los Angeles, California 90069

Mother Fortune Inc. (BMI)
641 Lexington Avenue
New York, New York 10022

Mother Tongue Music (ASCAP)
see Roger Cook Music

Mountain City Publishing Co. (BMI)
c/o H. H. Schleif
Post Office Box 294
Darsy, Tennessee 37317

Mourbar Music Co. (ASCAP)
see Plymouth Music Co., Inc.

Movietone Music Corp. (ASCAP)
c/o Sam Fox Publishing Co., Inc.
Suite 11
73-941 Hwy. 111
Palm Desert, California 92260

MPL Communications Inc. (ASCAP)
c/o Lee Eastman
39 West 54th Street
New York, New York 10019

MRC Music Corp. (BMI)
see Management Agency & Music
Publishing

Ms Foundation for Women
370 Lexington Avenue
New York, New York 10017

MTM Enterprises Inc. (ASCAP)
see Reno-Metz Music Inc.

Muhon Music
see Chappell & Co., Inc.

Mulberry Square Publishing Co.
Suite 120
10300 North Central Expressway
Dallas, Texas 75230

Mulj Music Co. (BMI)
Post Office Box 264
Brentwood, Tennessee 37027

Munchkin Music (ASCAP)
Open End Music Inc.
7720 Sunset Boulevard
Los Angeles, California 90046

Murbo Music Publishing Inc. (BMI)
c/o Bonnie Bourne
437 Fifth Avenue
New York, New York 10016

Mured Publishing Co. (BMI)
8008 Rodgers Road
Elkins Park, Pennsylvania 19117

Murfeezongs (ASCAP)
see Roger Cook Music

Murray-Callendar Productions (ASCAP)
230 West 55th Street
Suite 17D
New York, New York 10019

Murray Productions (ASCAP)
1775 Broadway
New York, New York 10019

Muscle Shoals Sound Publishing Co., Inc.
(BMI)
Post Office Box 915
Sheffield, Alabama 35660

Music by Shay (ASCAP)
2201 Channel Road
Balboa, California 92661

Music City Music Inc. (ASCAP)
see Combine Music Corp.

Music Corp. of America (BMI)
see MCA, Inc.

Music Directions Associates Ltd.
156 Fifth Avenue
Suite 1120
New York, New York 10010

Music For Unicef
see Unichappell Music Inc.

Music Maximus
1650 Broadway
New York, New York 10019

Music Mill Publishing (BMI)
see Carrhorn Music Inc.

Music, Music, Music, Inc. (ASCAP)
157 West 57th Street
New York, New York 10019

Music of the Times Publishing Corp.

Music Productions (ASCAP)
c/o Wayne Shanklin, Jr.
Suite 202
6515 Sunset Boulevard
Hollywood, California 90028

Music Products, Inc. (BMI)
Attention: Clyde Otis
345 West 58th Street
New York, New York 10019

Music Sales Corp. (ASCAP)
24 East 22nd Street
New York, New York 10010

Music Workshop (ASCAP)
c/o Don Henri Orchestra
8100 South West 23rd Court
Pompano Beach, Florida 33068

Music World Corp. (BMI)
808 North Crescent Drive
Beverly Hills, California 90210

Musical Comedy Productions Inc. (BMI)
10 Columbus Circle
New York, New York 10019

Musical Works (ASCAP)
77 West Washington Street
Chicago, Illinois 60602

Musicways Inc. (BMI)
2049 Century Park East
Los Angeles, California 90067

Mutual Music Society, Inc. (ASCAP)
609 Fifth Avenue
New York, New York 10017

My Baby's Music (ASCAP)
see Carrhorn Music Inc.

Myers Music (ASCAP)
1920 Chestnut Street
Philadelphia, Pennsylvania 19103

Myownah Music Inc. (BMI)
Post Office Box 11546
Nashville, Tennessee 37211

Myra Music Co. (BMI)
c/o Paul Landersman
201 Edwin Avenue
Harrisburg, Pennsylvania 17110

Mysterians Music, Ltd. (BMI)
c/o BMI
320 West 57th Street
New York, New York 10019

Mystery Music Inc. (BMI)
c/o Pink L. Murphey
2520 Cedar Elm Lane
Plano, Texas 75075

N

N. S. Beaujolais Music, Inc. (ASCAP)
c/o United Artists Music
Publishing Group
729 Seventh Avenue
New York, New York 10019

Naked Snake Publishing (ASCAP)
21800 Saddle Creek Road
Topanga, California 90290

Nancy Music Co. (ASCAP)
24 Chandler Drive
Emerson, New Jersey 07630

National Lampoon Music (ASCAP)
Attention: Charles Schneider
635 Madison Avenue
New York, New York 10022

Nattahnam Music (BMI)
c/o Hermine Hanlin
51 West 86th Street
New York, New York 10024

Nebraska Music (ASCAP)
c/o Bradshaw & Thomas
1145 Sunset Vale Avenue
Los Angeles, California 90069

Al J. Neiburg, Music Publisher (ASCAP)
2801 Northwest 60th Avenue
C-253
Sunrise, Florida 33313

Neighborhood Music (ASCAP)
see April Music Inc.

Joe Neil Music Co. (ASCAP)
20 East 22nd Street
New York, New York 10003

Neil Music, Inc. (BMI)
Suite 4A
8400 Sunset Boulevard
Los Angeles, California 90069

Neillrae Music (BMI)
7760 La Cosa Drive
Dallas, Texas 75248

Ed. G. Nelson (ASCAP)
Address unknown

Nelson Music Publishing Co. (ASCAP)
Suite 307
1717 North Highland Avenue
Hollywood, California 90028

Steve Nelson (ASCAP)
Address unknown

Willie Nelson Music Inc. (BMI)
225 Main Street
Danbury, Connecticut 06810

Nelton Corp. (BMI)
c/o Sidney Aron, C.P.A.
Suite 1910
10 East 40th Street
New York, New York 10016

Nep Music, Inc. (ASCAP)
Post Office Box 926
1321 West Seventh Street
Clovis, New Mexico 88101

Neverland Music Publishing Co. (BMI)
c/o Indursky & Schindler, P.C.
225 East 57th Street
New York, New York 10022

New Cadenza Music Corp. (ASCAP)
see Catch a Star Music Co.

New Christy Music Publishing Co. (BMI)
c/o Randy Sparks
Sparks Ranch
11047 Gregory Road
Linden, California 95236

New Dawn Music Corp. (ASCAP)
609 Fifth Avenue
New York, New York 10017

New Era Music Corp. (BMI)
322 West 48th Street
New York, New York 10036

New Executive Music (BMI)
c/o Ziffren, Brithenham, Gullen
Attention: John G. Branca
Suite 2350
2049 Century Park East
Los Angeles, California 90067

New Hidden Valley Music Co. (ASCAP)
see Blue Seas Music Inc.

New Keys Music Inc. (BMI)
11 Music Square South
Nashville, Tennessee 37203

New Leaf Music (BMI)
c/o Henry Prichard
5524 Candlelight Drive
La Jolla, California 92037

New Research Publishing Co. (BMI)
c/o Dora A. Pukish
37 Club Grounds North
Florissant, Missouri 63033

New Tandem Music Co. (ASCAP)
c/o Tandem Productions
1901 Avenue of the Stars
Los Angeles, California 90067

New World Music Corp. (ASCAP)
c/o Warner Brothers Music
9000 Sunset Boulevard
Los Angeles, California 90069

New World Music Corp. (ASCAP)
75 Rockefeller Plaza
New York, New York 10020

New York American, Inc.
Address unknown

Charles Newman Publications (ASCAP)
328 South McCarty Drive
Beverly Hills, California 90210

Roger Nichols Music Inc.
Address unknown

Nick-O-Val Music (ASCAP)
332 West 71st Street
New York, New York 10023

Nickel Shoe Music Co., Inc. (BMI)
1422 Chestnut Street
Philadelphia, Pennsylvania 19102

Nicolet Music (BMI)
c/o Richard Pegue
9831 South Ingleside
Chicago, Illinois 60628

Ninandy Music Co. (BMI)
c/o Copyright Service Bureau, Ltd.
221 West 57th Street
New York, New York 10019

Ninja Music Co. (ASCAP)
Weiss, Meibach & Bomser
888 Seventh Avenue
New York, New York 10106

Ninny Publishing Co. (BMI)
c/o Paul Winley
Post Office Box 1214
New York, New York 10027

Ninth Music (BMI)
c/o Lawrence N. Rogers
2323 Curinth Avenue
Los Angeles, California 90064

Nite Stalk Music (ASCAP)
see WB Music Corp.

List of Publishers

No Thought Music (ASCAP)
c/o Jon Waxman, Esq.
291 Broadway
New York, New York 10007

Kenny Nolan Publishing Co. (ASCAP)
c/o Peter C. Bennett
9060 Santa Monica Boulevard
Suite 300
Los Angeles, California 90069

Nom Music, Inc. (BMI)
c/o Big Seven Music Corp.
18th Floor
1790 Broadway
New York, New York 10023

Noma Music, Inc. (BMI)
241 West 72nd Street
New York, New York 10023

Nootrac Music, Ltd. (ASCAP)
c/o Steingarten & Barash
488 Madison Avenue
New York, New York 10022

Nor Va Jak Music, Inc. (BMI)
1321 West Seventh Street
Clovis, New Mexico 88101

Norbay Music, Inc. (BMI)
c/o Arthur Talmadge
Suite 348
870 Seventh Avenue
New York, New York 10019

Norbud (BMI)
see New Tandem Music Co.

North & Son Music, Inc. (ASCAP)
666 Fifth Avenue
New York, New York 10019

North State Music (ASCAP)
Post Office Box 6038
Raleigh, North Carolina 26708

North State Musical Productions, Inc.
(ASCAP)
Post Office Box 183
Goldsboro, North Carolina 27530

Northern Music Co.
Address unknown

Northern Music Corp. (ASCAP)
c/o MCA Music
445 Park Avenue
New York, New York 10022

Northridge Music Co. (ASCAP)
see Interworld Music Group

Northridge Music, Inc. (ASCAP)
8370 Wilshire Boulevard
Beverly Hills, California 90211

Robert Norton Co.
Address unknown

Noskag Music (BMI)
c/o June Jackson
1217 North 33rd Street
San Diego, California 92102

Noslen Music Co. (BMI)
c/o Audre & Nyles Nelson
No. 5
313 East Hazel Street
Inglewood, California 90302

Notable Music Co., Inc. (ASCAP)
Cy Coleman Enterprises
200 West 54th St.
New York, New York 10019

Nothing Music Co. (ASCAP)
c/o The Songwriters Guild
3rd Floor
276 Fifth Avenue
New York, New York 10001

Nouveaux Music Co. (BMI)
1810 Calvert Street North West
Washington, District of Columbia 20009

Novalene Music (BMI)
c/o Pat Vegas
Box 1129
Studio City, California 91604

Now Sounds Music (BMI)
c/o Gelfand, Breslauer, Rennert &
Feldman
1880 Century Park East
Ninth Floor
Los Angeles, California 90067

Nuages Artists Music Ltd. (ASCAP)
see Almo Music Corp.

O

Oakfield Avenue Music Ltd. (BMI)
c/o David Gotterer
Mason & Co.
Suite 1800
75 Rockefeller Plaza
New York, New York 10019

Oakland Music Co. (ASCAP)
622 North Palm Drive
Beverly Hills, California 90210

Obie Music, Inc. (BMI)
c/o Copyright Service Bureau
221 West 57th Street
New York, New York 10019

Obscure Music Inc. (ASCAP)
190 Waverly Place
New York, New York 10014

Oceans Blue Music (BMI)
c/o Copyright Service Bureau Ltd.
221 West 57th Street
New York, New York 10019

Octave Music Publishing Corp. (ASCAP)
520 Fifth Avenue
New York, New York 10036

Ode Records Inc.
Greene & Reynolds
1900 Avenue of the Stars
Suite 1424
Los Angeles, California 90067

Odette Music Corp. (ASCAP)
c/o Helene Blum
3900 Greystone Avenue
Riverdale, New York 10463

Odin Music, Co. (ASCAP)
Suite C
1708 Pandora Avenue
Los Angeles, California 90024

Odom & Neiburg Publishing Co. (BMI)
2536 North Broad Street
Philadelphia, Pennsylvania 19132

Of the Roses (ASCAP)
Post Office Box 66558
Seattle, Washington 98166

Off the Wall Music (BMI)
12228 Arbor Place
Los Angeles, California 90044

Oh Boy Music Co. (ASCAP)
see Great Honesty Music Inc.

Milton Okun Publishing Co. (BMI)
Post Office Box 4247
Greenwich, Connecticut 06830

Old Brompton Road Pub (ASCAP)
see Jobete Music Co., Inc.

Old Fashion Music (ASCAP)
see Brockman Enterprises Inc.

Old Lyne Music (BMI)
Room 1100
1650 Broadway
New York, New York 10019

Old St. Paul Publishing (ASCAP)
Attention: Fred Werner
Box 49441
Los Angeles, California 90049

Olde Clover Leaf Music (ASCAP)
c/o The Songwriters Guild
3rd Floor
276 Fifth Avenue
New York, New York 10001

List of Publishers

Olga Music (BMI)
c/o Delores Jabara
135 79th Street
Brooklyn, New York 11209

Olimac Music, Inc. (BMI)
130 Belmont Street
Englewood, New Jersey 07631

Sy Oliver Music Corp. (BMI)
c/o Sy Oliver
Apartment 13A
865 West End Avenue
New York, New York 10025

Oliver Music Publishing Co. (ASCAP)
Address unknown

Olrap Publishing Co., Inc. (BMI)
c/o George R. Davis, Jr.
206 Vanderbilt Avenue
Brooklyn, New York 11205

On Time Music, Inc. (BMI)
c/o Diamond & Wilson
2029 Century Park East
25th Floor
Los Angeles, California 90067

One Song Publishing (BMI)
c/o Dave White
No. 205
7777 Hollywood Boulevard
Los Angeles, California 90046

Open Curtain Publishing Co. (BMI)
c/o Sheila Lane Reed
211 South Beverley Drive
Suite 106
Beverly Hills, California 90212

Open Road Music, Inc. (BMI)
c/o Jim Reeves Enterprises, Inc.
Drawer 1
Madison, Tennessee 37115

Open Window Music Co. (BMI)
see WB Music Corp.

Oracle Music Productions, Inc. (BMI)
c/o Warner-Tamerlane Publishing Co.
Suite 222
9200 Sunset Boulevard
Los Angeles, California 90069

Walter Orange Music (ASCAP)
see Brockman Enterprises Inc.

Ordena Music (BMI)
Div. of Ordena Enterprises Inc.
Box 1686
Jackson, Tennessee 38301

Orellia Publishing Co. (BMI)
c/o Copyright Service Bureau, Ltd.
221 West 57th Street
New York, New York 10019

Orleansongs (ASCAP)
Pryor, Cashman, Sherman & Flynn
Attention: Howard Siegel, Esq.
410 Park Avenue
New York, New York 10022

Orpheum Music (BMI)
70 Parker Avenue
San Francisco, California 94118

Osmusic Publishing Co. (BMI)
1420 East 800 North
Orem, Utah 84057

Otis Rene Publications (ASCAP)
5048 Valley Ridge Avenue
Los Angeles, California 90043

Out of Business (ASCAP)
c/o Monitor Music Service Corp.
1780 Broadway
Suite 1200
New York, New York 10019

Outer Banks Music (BMI)
1100 17th Street South
Nashville, Tennessee 37212

Overdue Music (ASCAP)
Attention: David Walinski
7250 Beverly Boulevard
Suite 200
Los Angeles, California 90036

Owen Publications (BMI)
Post Office Box 842
Bakersfield, California 93302

Owens-Kemp Music Co. (ASCAP)
c/o Helen Owens
1304 Hexem Avenue
Santa Rosa, California 95404

Don Owens Music, Inc. (BMI)
c/o Robert Buckalew
219 Adams Avenue
Memphis, Tennessee 38103

List of Publishers

Owlofus Music (ASCAP)
see Myownah Music Inc.

Oyster Music (ASCAP)
see Walden Music Inc.

P

Pacific Gas & Electric Music (BMI)
c/o Tom Marshall
3315 West Washington Boulevard
Los Angeles, California 90018

Page Boy Publications
c/o Warner McPherson
Route 2
Lyles, Tennessee 37098

Painless Music (BMI)
c/o M.P.M.
518 North La Cienega Boulevard
Los Angeles, California 90048

Painted Desert Music Corp. (BMI)
10 East 53rd Street
New York, New York 10022

Palopic Music Corp. (BMI)
see Music Maximus

Pam-Bar Music, Ltd. (BMI)
c/o Mark Barkan
150 West 55th Street
New York, New York 10019

Pambill Music, Inc. (ASCAP)
c/o Carlton Record Corp.
345 West 58th Street
New York, New York 10019

Pamco Music, Inc. (BMI)
c/o ABC Contemporary Music
Publishing
8255 Beverly Boulevard
Los Angeles, California 90048

Pamelarosa Music, Inc. (ASCAP)
c/o Famous Music Corp.
1 Gulf & Western Plaza
New York, New York 10023

Pamper Music, Inc. (BMI)
Post Office Box 96
119 Two Mile Pike
Goodlettsville, Tennessee 37072

Pamscene Music (BMI)
Address unknown

Panther Music Corp. (ASCAP)
c/o Hudson Bay Music Co.
11th Floor
1619 Broadway
New York, New York 10019

Paperwaite Music (BMI)
c/o TWM Management Services, Ltd.
641 Lexington Avenue
New York, New York 10022

Para-Thumb Music Corp. (BMI)
c/o Sidney Herman
1 Gulf & Western Plaza
New York, New York 10023

Parabut Music Corp. (BMI)
c/o Sid Herman
1 Gulf & Western Plaza
New York, New York 10023

Paradise Valley Music Co. (ASCAP)
Address unknown

Paramount Music Corp. (ASCAP)
c/o Famous Music Corp.
1 Gulf & Western Plaza
New York, New York 10023

Paris Music Co., Inc. (ASCAP)
Room 1115
1650 Broadway
New York, New York 10019

Park Lane Music Co., Ltd. (ASCAP)
see Castle Hill Publishing Ltd.

Parker Music (BMI)
10th & Parker Street
Berkeley, California 94710

Barry Parker Music (BMI)
1555 East 19th Street
Brooklyn, New York 11230

Parkwood Music Co. (BMI)
Suite 432
25900 Greenfield Road
Oak Park, Michigan 48237

Parody Publishing (BMI)
c/o Mr. Don Bowman
1538 North Grand Oaks
Pasadena, California 91104

List of Publishers

O. Z. Parris Co.
Address unknown

Participation Music Inc. (ASCAP)
1348 Lexington Avenue
New York, New York 10028

Partner Music (BMI)
1518 Chelsea Avenue
Memphis, Tennessee 38108

Passkey Music Inc. (BMI)
c/o Jerry Chesnut
40 Music Square East
Nashville, Tennessee 37203

Patcheal Music (BMI)
Div. of War Inc.
c/o Troy Shondell
901 St. Felix Drive
Huntington, Indiana 46750

Patin Music (BMI)
see Blackwood Music Inc.

Patramani Music (BMI)
Post Office Box 44459
Panorama City, California 91412

Patricia Ed. Mus. (ASCAP)
Address unknown

Patricia Music Publishing Corp. (BMI)
c/o Big Seven Music Corp.
18th Floor
1790 Broadway
New York, New York 10023

Patsy Ann Music (BMI)
Suite 411
Forrest Hotel
224 West 49th Street
New York, New York 10019

Pattern Music, Inc. (ASCAP)
c/o Creative Music Group
Suite 1502
6430 Sunset Boulevard
Hollywood, California 90028

Patti Enterprises, Inc. (ASCAP)
c/o Jerry Lewis
Suite 1
3305 West Spring Mountain Road
Las Vegas, Nevada 89102

Paulanne Music Inc. (BMI)
c/o Feinman & Krasilovsky
Attention: Andrew J. Feinman, Esq.
424 Madison Avenue
New York, New York 10017

George Paxton Corp. (ASCAP)
c/o Paxwin House
836 Riomor Drive
Vero Beach, Florida 32960

Paxton Music, Inc. (ASCAP)
1619 Broadway
New York, New York 10019

Gary S. Paxton Publications, Inc. (BMI)
Post Office Box 40986
Nashville, Tennessee 37204

Paxwin Music Corp. (BMI)
c/o George Paxton
836 Riomar Drive
Vero Beach, Florida 32960

Peaceable Kingdom Publishing (ASCAP)
Attention: C. Randolph Navert
3525 Encinal Canyon Road
Malibu, California 90265

Peach Music
806 17th Avenue South
Nashville, Tennessee 37203

Peacock Music Publishing (BMI)
20th Century Music
8544 Sunset Boulevard
Los Angeles, California 90069

Peanut-Butter Publishing, Inc. (BMI)
c/o Kelli Ross
203 West 80th Street
New York, New York 10024

Pearl Dee Publishing Co. (BMI)
Route 1
Franklin, Tennessee 37064

Pedal Point Music (BMI)
c/o Nicholas Grillo
6363 Sunset Blvd
Suite 900
Los Angeles, California 90028

Pedro Music Corp. (BMI)
c/o Mr. Cyril Shane
1724 Bowcliff Terrace
Westlake Village, California 91361

Peejay Music Co. (ASCAP)
c/o Jay Ellington Lee
8 Tyler Street
Norwell, Massachusetts 02061

Peer-Donovan, Ltd. S. A. (BMI)
c/o Peer-Southern Organization
6777 Hollywood Boulevard
Hollywood, California 90028

Peer International (Canada) (BMI)
180 Bloor Street, West
Toronto, Ontario M5S 2V6
Canada

Peer International Corp. (BMI)
see Peer-Southern Org.

Peer-Southern Org.
1740 Broadway
New York, New York 10019

Peg Music Co. (BMI)
c/o Earl S. Shuman
111 East 88th Street
New York, New York 10028

P.E.M. Associates (ASCAP)
c/o David Gotterer
Suite 1800
75 Rockefeller Plaza
New York, New York 10019

Pemora Music Co., Inc. (BMI)
251 Broadway
Lynbrook, New York 11563

Pencil Mark Music, Inc. (ASCAP)
6 Eaton Lane
Scarsdale, New York 10583

Penn Music Co. (ASCAP)
c/o George Mysels
1315 North Orange Drive
Hollywood, California 90028

Penny Music Co. (BMI)
130 South Fourth Street
Las Vegas, Nevada 89101

Penron Music Publications (BMI)
c/o Ronald J. Hargrove
1923 Foothill Drive
Glendale, California 90912

Penumbra Music Co. (BMI)
c/o Trascott, Alyson, Craig Inc.
222 Cedar Lane
Box 278
Teaneck, New Jersey 07666

Pepamar Music Corp. (ASCAP)
see WB Music Corp.

Perkins Publishing Co.
c/o Mrs. C. Thomason
1209 Saunders Avenue
Madison, Tennessee 37115

Perren Vibes Music Inc. (ASCAP)
c/o Mr. Lennie Hodes
11704 Ventura Boulevard
Studio City, California 91604

Perv's Music (BMI)
c/o Pervis Staples
8125 South Cottage Grove Avenue
Chicago, Illinois 60619

Peso Music (BMI)
6255 Sunset Boulevard
Suite 1019
Hollywood, California 90028

Ben Peters Music (BMI)
900 Old Hickory Boulevard
Route 6
Brentwood, Tennessee 37027

Petra Music (BMI)
c/o Donald Seiler & Co.
44 Montgomery
Suite 4211
San Francisco, California 94104

Dave Peyton Music Co.
Address unknown

Philanda Music, Inc. (BMI)
9000 Sunset Boulevard
Los Angeles, California 90069

Photo Play Music Co., Inc. (ASCAP)
143-66 Beech Avenue
Flushing, New York 11355

Phylmar Music Inc. (ASCAP)
Attention: Stan Hoffman
200 West 57th Street
New York, New York 10019

Pic Music Corp. (ASCAP)
39 West 54th Street
New York, New York 10019

Piccadilly Music Corp. (BMI)
c/o Copyright Services Bureau, Ltd.
221 West 57th Street
New York, New York 10019

Pick A Hit Music Inc. (BMI)
816 19th Avenue South
Nashville, Tennessee 37203

Pickwick Music Corp. (ASCAP)
445 Park Avenue
New York, New York 10022

Piedmont Music Co., Inc. (ASCAP)
136 West 52nd Street
New York, New York 10019

Pierreco Music (BMI)
c/o Pierre Cossette
8899 Beverly Boulevard
Los Angeles, California 90048

Pigfoot Music (ASCAP)
P. O. Box 130
Point Reyes, California 94956

Pimpernel Music Co. (BMI)
c/o BMI
320 West 57th Street
New York, New York 10019

George Pincus & Sons Music Corp.
(ASCAP)
1650 Broadway
New York, New York 10019

Pinelawn Music Publishing Co., Inc. (BMI)
c/o Copyright Service Bureau, Ltd.
221 West 57th Street
New York, New York 10019

Pioneer Publishing Co. (BMI)
8665 Wilshire Boulevard
Beverly Hills, California 90211

Pirooting Publishing (ASCAP)
c/o Segel & Goldman Inc.
9348 Santa Monica Boulevard
#304
Beverly Hills, California 90210

Pixruss Music (ASCAP)
Attention: Ms. Rose Cason
Route 1
Springfield, Tennessee 37172

Placid Music Corp.
Attention: G.H. Cowan
2 Glenbrook Dr.
New Rochelle, New York 10804

Plain & Simple Music Corp. (ASCAP)
see The Hudson Bay Music Co.

Plainview Music, Inc. (BMI)
c/o Jimmy Dean Companies
1341 West Mockingbird
Dallas, Texas 75247

Plan Two Music, Inc. (ASCAP)
1619 Broadway
New York, New York 10019

Planemar Music Co. (BMI)
56 Ferry Street
Newark, New Jersey 07105

Planetary Music Publishing Corp. (ASCAP)
1790 Broadway
18th Floor
New York, New York 10019

Platinum Music Publishing (ASCAP)
c/o The Music Factory, Inc.
567 Northwest 27th Street
Miami, Florida 33127

Play Music, Inc. (BMI)
Suite 802
1697 Broadway
New York, New York 10019

Play My Music (BMI)
see Know Music

Players Music Corp. (ASCAP)
609 Fifth Avenue
New York, New York 10017

Plus Two Music
c/o Jordan-Herman-Holmes
Attention: Stan Herman
1014 4th Street
Santa Monica, California 90403

Plymouth Music Co., Inc. (ASCAP)
170 Northeast 33rd Street
Fort Lauderdale, Florida 33334

Pocono Publishing Co., Inc. (BMI)
c/o Copyright Service Bureau, Ltd.
221 West 57th Street
New York, New York 10019

Polish Prince Music (ASCAP)
c/o Kaufman, Eisenberg & Co.
9301 Wilshire Boulevard
Suite 212
Beverly Hills, California 90210

Polite Music (ASCAP)
Attention: Crystal Zevon
6420 Wilshire Boulevard
19th Floor
Los Angeles, California 90048

Lew Pollack Music (ASCAP)
9330 Hazen Drive
Beverly Hills, California 90210

Polo Grounds Music (BMI)
Div. of David Rubinson & Friends
827 Folsom Street
San Francisco, California 94107

Pommard Publishing Co. (BMI)
c/o Dick K. Withers
Box 53
Nashville, Tennessee 37221

Pomona Music Corp. (BMI)
c/o Painted Desert Music
10 East 53rd Street
New York, New York 10022

Ponderosa Music Co., Inc. (BMI)
c/o Shapiro, Bernstein & Co., Inc.
10 East 53rd Street
New York, New York 10022

Pontra Music Corp. (BMI)
3703 North Seventh Street
Phoenix, Arizona 85014

Poo Poo Publishing Co. (BMI)
c/o Vinny Barrett
428 Peabody Street Northwest
Washington, District of Columbia 20011

Pop 'N' Roll Music (ASCAP)
114 West 7th Street
Suite 717
Austin, Texas 78701

Popular Music Co. (ASCAP)
49 West 45th Street
New York, New York 10036

Porchester Music Inc. (ASCAP)
see Braintree Music

Porgie Music Corp. (BMI)
1619 Broadway
New York, New York 10019

Porpete Music (BMI)
Box 777
Hollywood, California 90028

Portable Music Co., Inc. (BMI)
200 West 54th Street
New York, New York 10019

Portent Music (ASCAP)
Attention: Robie Porter
9825 Melinda Drive
Beverly Hills, California 90210

Cole Porter Music, Inc. (ASCAP)
c/o Florence Leeds
27th Floor
345 Park Avenue
New York, New York 10022

Portofino Music (BMI)
1025 North Roxbury Drive
Beverly Hills, California 90210

Post Music, Inc. (ASCAP)
1556 North La Brea Avenue
Hollywood, California 90028

PPI Music (ASCAP)
see Music Maximus

Premier Music Publishing Co. (BMI)
Post Office Box 338
East Pasadena, California 91107

Elvis Presley Music, Inc. (BMI)
c/o Chappell & Co.
810 Seventh Avenue
New York, New York 10019

Theodore Presser Co. (ASCAP)
Presser Place
Bryn Mawr, Pennsylvania 19010

Prestige Music Co., Inc. (BMI)
c/o Parker Music
10th & Parker Street
Berkeley, California 94710

Preston Songs (ASCAP)
see Almo Music Corp.

Prigan Music Corp. (BMI)
c/o Lloyd Price
39 West 55th Street
New York, New York 10019

Prima Donna Music Co. (BMI)
see Al Gallico Music Corp.

Primary Music Corp. (BMI)
c/o Fred Anisfield
100 Bennett Avenue
New York, New York 10033

Prince Street Music (ASCAP)
Attention: John Frankenheimer, Esq.
Loeb & Loeb
10100 Santa Monica Boulevard
Suite 2200
Los Angeles, California 90046

Princess Music Publishing Corp. (ASCAP)
c/o H. B. Webman
Suite 701
1650 Broadway
New York, New York 10019

Print Music Co., Inc. (ASCAP)
c/o Jepalana Productions
723 Seventh Avenue
New York, New York 10019

Henry Pritchard
1543 Sunset Plaza Drive
Hollywood, California 90069

Prize Music, Inc. (ASCAP)
3106 Belmont Boulevard
Nashville, Tennessee 37212

Producers Music Publishing Co., Inc.
(ASCAP)
c/o Chappell & Co.
810 Seventh Avenue
New York, New York 10019

Progressive Music Publishing Co., Inc.
(BMI)
11th Floor
1619 Braodway
New York, New York 10019

Project Seven Music (BMI)
Division of Continental Total
Media Project, Inc.
120 Charles Street
New York, New York 10014

Pronto Music, Inc. (BMI)
c/o Warner-Tamerland Publishing
Corp.
75 Rockerfeller Plaza
New York, New York 10019

Prophecy Publishing Inc. (ASCAP)
3201 Guadulupe
Austin, Texas 78705

Prophet Music Inc. (ASCAP)
Bicycle Music Co., The
8756 Holloway Drive
Los Angeles, California 90069

Public Domain Foundation (ASCAP)
c/o Gelfand, Macnow, Rennert
& Feldman
Box 2202
Palm Springs, California 92263

Pulleybone Music (ASCAP)
see Aunt Polly's Publishing Co.

Pure Songs (ASCAP)
see Screen Gems-EMI Music Inc.

Pure Soul Music Corp. (BMI)
Address unknown

Q

Quackenbush Music Ltd. (ASCAP)
Box 2202
Palm Springs, California 92263

Quality-Slow Dancing (BMI)
38 Birchmount Road
Scarborough, Ontario M1K 1M7
Canada

Quartet Music, Inc. (ASCAP)
1619 Broadway
New York, New York 10019

Queen Music Ltd. (BMI)
see Beechwood Music Corp.

Quickit Publishing Co. (BMI)
Box 2001
Muscle Shoals, Alabama 35660

Quintet Music, Inc. (BMI)
c/o Hudson Bay Music Co.
11th Floor
1619 Broadway
New York, New York 10019

Quinvy Music Publishing Co. (BMI)
Post Office Box 215
Sheffield, Alabama 35660

Quixotic Music Corp. (ASCAP)
see Edwardo Music Corp.

R

R & M Music Productions Inc. (ASCAP)
Attention: Martin Machat
1501 Broadway
30th Floor
New York, New York 10036

R. C. Jay Publishing
Address unknown

R S O Publishing Inc. (ASCAP)
1775 Broadway
New York, New York 10019

R-T Publishing Co. (BMI)
c/o Lois Publishing Co.
1540 Brewster Avenue
Cincinnati, Ohio 45207

Rabbit's Foot Music Corp. (BMI)
c/o Big Seven Music Corp.
18th Floor
1790 Broadway
New York, New York 10023

Racer Music Corp. (ASCAP)
see Tangerine Music Corp.

Rada Dara Music (BMI)
c/o Donald Rubin
29775 Pacific Coast Highway
Zuma Beach, California 90265

Radio Telemusic (ASCAP)
see Tangerine Music Corp.

Radmus Publishing Inc. (ASCAP)
c/o Larry Shayne Enterprises
6362 Hollywood Boulevard
Hollywood, California 90028

Ragged Island Music Publishers (BMI)
4307 Saundersville Road
Old Hickory, Tennessee 37138

Ragtime Music Corp. (ASCAP)
c/o Al Greiner
1697 Broadway
New York, New York 10019

Rainy Wednesday Music (BMI)
see Unichappell Music Inc.

Raisin Music (ASCAP)
see April Music Inc.

Raleigh Music, Inc. (BMI)
817 16th Avenue South
Nashville, Tennessee 37203

Ralph's Radio Music (BMI)
Post Office Box 127
Demorest, Georgia 30535

Ram Music (ASCAP)
see Management Agency & Music
Publishing

Rambed Publishing Co., Inc. (BMI)
c/o Copyright Service Bureau, Ltd.
221 West 57th Street
New York, New York 10019

Ramrod Music (ASCAP)
c/o Michael Tannen, Esq.
36 East 61st Street
New York, New York 10021

Ram's Horn Music Co., Inc. (ASCAP)
see Big Sky Music

Ramsel Publishing Co. (BMI)
c/o Hill-Taylor, Inc.
180 North La Salle Street
Chicago, Illinois 60601

Ranbach Music (BMI)
see Screen Gems-EMI Music Inc.

Randy-Smith Music Corp. (ASCAP)
3941 Woodlawn Drive
Nashville, Tennessee 37205

Fred Raphael Music, Inc. (ASCAP)
6758 Colgate Avenue
Los Angeles, California 90048

Rare Blue Music Inc. (ASCAP)
see Chrysalis Music Corp.

Rathvon Music (ASCAP)
991 Highland Avenue
Pelham Manor, New York 10801

Raton Songs, Inc. (BMI)
532 Sylvan Avenue
Englewood Cliffs, New Jersey 07632

Rawlou Music (BMI)
c/o Segel & Goldman, Inc.
No. 304
9348 Santa Monica Boulevard
Beverly Hills, California 90210

Raydiola Music (ASCAP)
Post Office Box 5270
Beverly Hills, California 90210

Don Raye (ASCAP)
Address unknown

Rayven Music Co., Inc. (BMI)
c/o Duke Niles
155 East 47th Street
New York, New York 10017

Razaf Music (ASCAP)
c/o The Songwriters Guild
3rd Floor
276 Fifth Avenue
New York, New York 10001

Razor Sharp Music, Inc. (BMI)
c/o Earl Shelton
309 South Broad Street
Philadelphia, Pennsylvania 19107

Razzle Dazzle Music Inc. (BMI)
c/o Hermie Hanlin
51 West 86th Street
New York, New York 10024

Walter Reade-Sterling Music Corp.
(ASCAP)
c/o Fred Ahlert Music Corp.
Suite 202
8150 Beverly Boulevard
Los Angeles, California 90048

Rear Exit Music (ASCAP)
Attention: Phil Walden
Box 5127
Macon, Georgia 31208

Recco Corp. (BMI)
c/o Irving Siders
180 East End Avenue
New York, New York 10028

Record Music Publishing Co. (ASCAP)
Room 605
1650 Broadway
New York, New York 10019

Recording Dynamics (ASCAP)
see Terrace Music

Recordo Music Publishers (BMI)
c/o Leon Rene
2124 West 24th Street
Los Angeles, California 90018

Red Admiral Music Inc. (BMI)
see Chrysalis Music Corp.

Red Bridge Publishing Corp. (ASCAP)
c/o Herman Edel
Post Office Box 3929
Aspen, Colorado 81611

Red Bullet Music (ASCAP)
see Chappell & Co., Inc.

Red Cloud Music Co. (ASCAP)
c/o Breslauer, Jacobsen & Rutman
10880 Wilshire Boulevard
Suite 210
Los Angeles, California 90024

Red Cow Music Inc. (ASCAP)
see Chappell & Co., Inc.

Red Giant Inc. (ASCAP)
c/o Vance
130 Beach 137th Street
Belle Harbor, New York 11693

Red Hook Music Corp. (ASCAP)
33 West 60th Street
New York, New York 10019

Red Pajamas Music (ASCAP)
c/o Sy Miller
18 East 48th Street
Suite 1202
New York, New York 10017

Red River Songs, Inc. (BMI)
1001 North Lincoln Street
Burbank, California 91506

Red Shift Music (BMI)
c/o R. J. Hippard
2069 linnington Avenue
Los Angeles, California 90025

Rumanian Pickleworks Co. (BMI)
c/o Satin, Tennenbaum, Eichlert &
Zimmerman
Attention: Mr. S. Tennenbaum
1776 Broadway
New York, New York 10019

Rumbalero Music, Inc. (BMI)
11th Floor
1619 Broadway
New York, New York 10019

Russell Ballard Ltd. (ASCAP)
see April Music Inc.

Rust Enterprises, Inc. (ASCAP)
c/o Laurie Publishing Group
20-F Robert Pitt Drive
Monsey, New York 10952

R.W.P. Inc. (ASCAP)
156 West 77th Street
Apartment 4B
New York, New York 10024

Rydal Music Co., Inc. (BMI)
c/o Louis Silvestri
Valley and Middletown Roads
Glen Mills, Pennsylvania 19342

Rylan Music Corp. (ASCAP)
c/o Philip Becker, C.P.A.
40 Galesi Drive
Wayne, New Jersey 07470

Rytvoc, Inc. (ASCAP)
39 West 54th Street
New York, New York 10019

S

S & J Music Publishing Corp. (ASCAP)
c/o Laurie Publishing Group
20-F Robert Pitt Drive
Monsey, New York 10952

S. J. W. Music, Inc. (BMI)
7224 Hillside Avenue
Hollywood, California 90046

Sa-Vette Music (BMI)
see Six Continents Music Publishing Inc.

Sabal Music (ASCAP)
see Sawgrass Music Publishing Inc.

Sage and Sand Music Publishers
c/o Merit Music Corp.
815 18th Avenue South
Nashville, Tennessee 37203

Saggifire Music (ASCAP)
see Columbia Pictures Publications

Sahara Music, Inc. (ASCAP)
609 Fifth Avenue
New York, New York 10017

Sailmaker Music (ASCAP)
see Chappell & Co., Inc.

Sailor Music (ASCAP)
c/o Gregory Fischbach
2029 Century Park East
North Tower Suite 1370
Los Angeles, California 90067

St. Louis Music Corp. (BMI)
11th Floor
1619 Broadway
New York, New York 10019

St. Nathanson Music (ASCAP)
see United Artists Music Co., Inc.

St. Nicholas Music, Inc. (ASCAP)
11th Floor
1619 Broadway
New York, New York 10019

Salaam Music Co. (BMI)
642 West Athens
Los Angeles, California 90000

Salmon Music (ASCAP)
c/o Sanford & Townsend
10507 Tennessee Avenue
Los Angeles, California 90064

Saloon Songs, Inc. (BMI)
c/o Nathan Golden & Associates
Suite 508
9601 Wilshire Boulevard
Beverly Hills, California 90210

Sammy Gallop Music (ASCAP)
c/o Sylvia Gallop
3742 Sapphire Drive
Encino, California 91436

Sanborn Publishing Co. (BMI)
Address unknown

Sandbox Music, Inc. (ASCAP)
160 West 54th Street
New York, New York 10019

Sands Music Corp. (ASCAP)
116 Central Park South
New York, New York 10019

Sanga Music Inc. (BMI)
250 West 57th Street
Suite 2017
New York, New York 10019

Sanphil Music Co. (BMI)
c/o Cooper, Epstein & Hurrwitz
9465 Wilshire Boulevard
Suite 800
Beverly Hills, California 90212

Saran Music Co. (BMI)
Post Office Box 17667
Dallas, Texas 75217

Sark Music (BMI)
A Division of Record Music, Inc.
8419 63rd Avenue
Middle Village, New York 11379

Sashay Music Inc. (ASCAP)
see Chappell & Co., Inc.

Sattwa Music (ASCAP)
c/o Lee Michaels
22541A Pacific Coast Highway
#62
Malibu, California 90265

Saturday Music Inc. (BMI)
see Screen Gems-EMI Music Inc.

Saunders Publications, Inc. (ASCAP)
119 West 57th Street
New York, New York 10019

Savoy Music Co. (BMI)
56 Ferry Street
Newark, New Jersey 07105

Sawandi Music (BMI)
Address unknown

Sawgrass Music Publishing Inc. (BMI)
1520 Demonbruen
Nashville, Tennessee 37203

Saxon Music Corp. (BMI)
c/o Walter Hofer, Esq.
Copyright Service Bureau
221 West 57th Street
New York, New York 10020

Boz Scaggs Music (ASCAP)
c/o Front Line Management
9044 Melrose Avenue
Third Floor
Los Angeles, California 90069

Scarab Publishing Corp. (BMI)
see Ensign Music Corp.

Scarsdale Music Corp. (ASCAP)
666 Fifth Avenue
New York, New York 10019

Peter Schaeffers Music Corp. (BMI)
Room 1920
135 West 50th Street
New York, New York 10020

Scheffel Music Corp. (ASCAP)
c/o Lawrence J. Greene
Suite 9-D
150 West 55th Street
New York, New York 10019

Schine Music (ASCAP)
c/o David Schine & Co., Inc.
626 South Hudson Avenue
Los Angeles, California 90005

G. Schirmer Inc. (ASCAP)
866 Third Avenue
New York, New York 10022

Schroder Music Co. (ASCAP)
1450 Sixth Street
Berkeley, California 94710

Edward Schuberth & Co., Inc.
263 Veterans Boulevard
Carlstadt, New Jersey 07072

Arthur Schwartz Music (ASCAP)
R.D. 1, Box 80
Kintnersville, Pennsylvania 18930

Schwartz Music Co., Inc. (ASCAP)
Laurie Publishing Group
20-F Robert Pitt Drive
Monsey, New York 10952

Scopat Music Co. (BMI)
Address unknown

Scorpio Music (ASCAP)
see Can't Stop Music

Andrew Scott Inc. (ASCAP)
see MCA Music

Scott-Tone Music (ASCAP)
Attention: Tony Scotti
2114 Pico Boulevard
Santa Monica, California 90405

SCP Music Corp. (ASCAP)
c/o Carl Prager
525 East 86th Street
New York, New York 10028

Screen Gems-EMI Music Inc. (BMI)
6255 Sunset Boulevard
12th Floor
Hollywood, California 90028

Sea-Lark Enterprises, Inc.
c/o A. Schroeder International,
Ltd.
25 West 56th Street
New York, New York 10019

Seagrape Music Inc. (BMI)
c/o Wallace D. Franson
Jess Morgan & Co.
19th Floor
6420 Wilshire Boulevard
Los Angeles, California 90048

Seasons Four Music Corp. (BMI)
see Gavadima Music Inc.

Seasons Music Co. (ASCAP)
c/o Peter Bennett
9060 Santa Monica Boulevard
Suite 300
Los Angeles, California 90069

Seaview Music Inc. (BMI)
5719 Knob Road
Nashville, Tennessee 37209

John Sebastian Music (BMI)
c/o Mitchell, Silberberg & Knupp
1800 Century Park East
Los Angeles, California 90067

Second Decade Music (BMI)
c/o TWM Management
641 Lexington Avenue
New York, New York 10022

See This House Music (ASCAP)
c/o Edward Traubner
Traubner & Flynn
2049 Century Park East
Suite 2500
Los Angeles, California 90067

Seldak Music Corp. (ASCAP)
see Daksel Music Corp.

Selma Music Corp. (BMI)
c/o Morty Croft
345 West 58th Street
New York, New York 10019

Seneca Music Co. (ASCAP)
c/o Ellis L. Walsh
1042 West 81st Street
Los Angeles, California 90044

Senor Music (ASCAP)
Garrett Music Enterprises
6255 Sunset Boulevard
Suite 1019
Hollywood, California 90028

Serendipity Publishing Corp. (BMI)
c/o Free Flow Productions
1209 Baylor
Austin, Texas 78703

Sergeant Music Co. (ASCAP)
c/o Sinatra Enterprises
1041 No. Formosa Avenue
Hollywood, California 90046

Seven Eight Nine Music Assoc. (ASCAP)
c/o M. C. Leary
224 East 50th Street
New York, New York 10022

Shada Music Inc. (ASCAP)
see Chevis Publishing Corp.

Shade Tree Music Inc. (BMI)
c/o Merle Haggard
Box 500
Bella Vista, California 96008

Shag Publications (BMI)
1861 West Adams Boulevard
Los Angeles, California 90018

Shakewell Music, Inc. (BMI)
c/o George Scheck
161 West 54th Street
New York, New York 10019

Shamley Music (ASCAP)
see MCA Music

Shapiro, Bernstein & Co., Inc. (ASCAP)
10 East 53rd Street
New York, New York 10022

Shari Music Publishing Corp. (ASCAP)
c/o Sanga Music, Inc.
Suite 2017
250 West 57th Street
New York, New York 10107

Sharina Music Co. (BMI)
c/o Sharri Paullus
6938 Amberly Road
Memphis, Tennessee 38138

Eddie Shaw Music Co. (ASCAP)
9128 Sunset Boulevard
Los Angeles, California 90069

Shawnee Press, Inc. (ASCAP)
Division of Waring Enterprises,
Inc.
Delaware Water Gap, Pennsylvania 18327

Larry Shayne Enterprises
6362 Hollywood Boulevard
Suite 222
Hollywood, California 90028

American Compass Music Corp. (ASCAP)
see Larry Shayne Enterprises

Larry Shayne Music Inc. (ASCAP)
see Six Continents Music Publishing Inc.

Sheepshead Bay Music (ASCAP)
Peter M. Thall
485 Madison Avenue
New York, New York 10022

Shelby Music
Address unknown

David Shelley Publishing Co. (ASCAP)
6124 Selma Avenue
Hollywood, California 90028

Shenandoah Music (ASCAP)
Terrace Music
803 18th Avenue South
Nashville, Tennessee 37203

Sherlyn Publishing Co., Inc. (BMI)
see Big Seven Music Corp.

Al Sherman Music Co. (ASCAP)
Apartment 305
700 South Hobart Boulevard
Los Angeles, California 90005

Shermley Music Co. (ASCAP)
c/o Filmation Studios
18107 Sherman Way
Reseda, California 91335

Sherwin Music, Inc. (ASCAP)
c/o Robert Mellin
1841 Broadway
New York, New York 10023

Nathaniel Shilkret Music Co., Inc. (ASCAP)
Post Office Box 38
Malverne, New York 11565

Shillelagh Music Co. (BMI)
c/o Mitchell, Silberberg & Knupp
1800 Century Park East
Los Angeles, California 90067

Shirley's Music Co. (BMI)
c/o Sound of America
3531 Baronne Street
New Orleans, Louisiana 70115

Shoals Music Mill Publishing Co. (ASCAP)
see Alan Cartee Music

Show Biz Music (BMI)
Div. of Show Biz Inc.
1006 Baker Building
Nashville, Tennessee 37203

Shubert Music Publishing Corp. (ASCAP)
c/o Syd Goldberg
488 Madison Avenue
New York, New York 10022

Shukat Co., Ltd. (ASCAP)
see Shukat Productions

Shukat Productions (ASCAP)
Attention: Scott Shukat
340 West 55th Street
New York, New York 10019

Sido Music Establishment (BMI)
Address unknown

Sigma Music, Inc. (ASCAP)
11th Floor
1619 Broadway
New York, New York 10019

Silhouette Music Corp. (ASCAP)
1842 West Avenue
Miami Beach, Florida 33139

Silk Stockings Music (BMI)
c/o Gregory Fishbach
2029 Century Park East
Suite 1370
Los Angeles, California 90067

Silkie Music Publishers (BMI)
71 West 23rd Street
New York, New York 10010

Silver Blue Music (ASCAP)
see Columbia Pictures Publications

Silver Cloud Music Inc. (ASCAP)
c/o Mr. Eddie Biscoe
Post Office Box 5292
Beverly Hills, California 90210

Silver Dawn Music (BMI)
see Muscle Shoals Sound Publishing Co.,
Inc.

Silver Fiddle (ASCAP)
c/o Segel & Goldman Inc.
9200 Sunset Boulevard
Suite 1000
Los Angeles, California 90069

Silver Star Music Publishing Co., Inc. (BMI)
c/o Unichappel Music, Inc.
810 Seventh Avenue
New York, New York 10019

Silver Steed Music Inc. (BMI)
c/o Borck and Mensch
350 Fifth Avenue
Room 5220
New York, New York 10001

Silver Wing Songs (BMI)
c/o Chris Crosby
2364 Hermits Glen
Los Angeles, California 90046

Silverline Music Inc. (BMI)
329 Rockland Road
Hendersonville, Tennessee 37075

Silvertown Music Corp. (ASCAP)
11th Floor
1619 Broadway
New York, New York 10019

Simon House, Inc. (BMI)
11th Floor
1619 Broadway
New York, New York 10019

George Simon, Inc. (ASCAP)
c/o George Simon, Inc.
2147 Sunshine Circle
Palm Springs, California 92262

List of Publishers

Paul Simon Music (BMI)
1619 Broadway
New York, New York 10019

Singing River Publishing Co., Inc. (BMI)
c/o Marion Carpenter
205 Acacia Street
Biloxi, Mississippi 39530

Singing Wire Music Inc. (BMI)
Box 2446
Muscle Shoals, Alabama 35660

Shelby Singleton Music Inc. (BMI)
3106 Belmont Boulevard
Nashville, Tennessee 37212

Singletree Music Co., Inc. (BMI)
815 18th Avenue South
Nashville, Tennessee 37213

Singular Music Publishing Co., Inc. (BMI)
c/o Artie Singer
2016 Walnut Street
Philadelphia, Pennsylvania 19103

Siquomb Publishing Corp. (BMI)
c/o Segel & Goldman Inc.
9348 Santa Monica Boulevard
Beverly Hills, California 90210

Siren Songs (BMI)
c/o Gelfand, Rennert & Feldman
Attention: Babbie Green
1880 Century Park East
Number 900
Los Angeles, California 90067

Six Continents Music Publishing Inc.
8304 Beverly Blvd.
Los Angeles, California 90048

Six Pictures Music (BMI)
c/o Gelfand, Rennert & Feldman
1880 Century Park East
Number 900
Los Angeles, California 90067

Six Strings Music (BMI)
c/o David Steinberg, Esq.
818 Widener Building
1339 Chestnut Street
Philadelphia, Pennsylvania 19107

62 Revue Publishers, Inc. (ASCAP)
240 West 55th Street
New York, New York 10019

Sixuvus Revival Music Co. (BMI)
Box J
Aliquppa, Pennsylvania 15001

Skidmore Music Co., Inc. (ASCAP)
10 East 53rd Street
New York, New York 10022

Skinner Music Co., Inc. (ASCAP)
14455 Riata Circle
Reno, Nevada 89511

Skinners Pond-Jack O. Diamonds (BMI)
c/o Jack O'Diamonds Publications
4200 Central Pike
Hermitage, Tennessee 37212

Skinny Zach Music Inc. (ASCAP)
19301 Ventura Boulevard
Suite 205
Tarzana, California 91356

Skol Music (BMI)
c/o Sonny Curtis
Box 58
Route 2
Dickson, Texas 37055

Sky Harbor Music (BMI)
c/o Jess S. Morgan & Co., Inc.
6420 Wilshire Boulevard
Nineteenth Floor
Los Angeles, California 90048

Skyforest Music Co., Inc.
Music Admin. Service Company
c/o S A S Inc.
1414 Avenue of the Americas
New York, New York 10019

Skyhill Publishing Co., Inc. (BMI)
see Island Music

Sleeping Son Music Inc. (BMI)
c/o Stan Vincent
311 East 83rd Street
New York, New York 10028

Sleepy Hollow Music (ASCAP)
Post Office Box 7
Swannanda, South Carolina 28778

Slow Dancing Music Inc. (BMI)
c/o Murray Deutch
515 Madison Avenue
Suite 808
New York, New York 10022

Small Hill Music (ASCAP)
c/o Neil Levin & Co.
9595 Wilshire Boulevard
Number 505
Beverly Hills, California 90212

Patti Smith Music (ASCAP)
see Ninja Music Co.

Paul J. Smith (ASCAP)
1349 Lexington Avenue
New York, New York 10028

Snow Music
c/o Jess Morgan & Co., Inc.
6420 Wilshire Boulevard
Nineteenth Floor
Los Angeles, California 90048

Hank Snow Music, Inc. (BMI)
c/o Unichopped Music, Inc.
810 Seventh Avenue
New York, New York 10019

Snowden Music (ASCAP)
344 West 12th Street
New York, New York 10014

Snug Music (ASCAP)
c/o The Doobro Corp.
Attention: Kathy Nelson
Post Office Box 359
Sonoma, California 95476

Ted Snyder Music Publishing Co. (ASCAP)
Post Office Box 2327
Palm Desert, California 92260

Solitaire Music (ASCAP)
see Interworld Music Group

Somerset Songs Publishing Inc. (ASCAP)
see Evansongs Ltd.

Sommersongs (BMI)
c/o Bert Sommer
4412 Whitsett Avenue
Studio City, California 91604

Song and Dance Music Co. (ASCAP)
see Daksel Music Corp.

Song of Cash Inc. (ASCAP)
see House of Cash Inc.

Song Painter Music (BMI)
see Screen Gems-EMI Music Inc.

Song Tailors Music Co. (ASCAP)
Box 2631
Muscle Shoals, Alabama 35660

Song Yard Music (ASCAP)
c/o Segel & Goldman, Inc.
9348 Santa Monica Boulevard
Beverly Hills, California 90210

Songfest Music Corp. (ASCAP)
c/o Gill Music Corp.
1650 Broadway
New York, New York 10019

Songs Music, Inc. (ASCAP)
Post Office Box 102
Scarborough, New York 10582

Songways Service Inc.
10 Columbus Circle
Suite 1406
New York, New York 10019

Sonkay Publishing Co. (BMI)
c/o Melvin A. Friedman
9 Fawnridge Court
St. Louis, Missouri 63141

Sook Music (ASCAP)
Arrow, Silverman, Parcher &
Margolis
9200 Sunset Boulevard
Los Angeles, California 90069

Sophisticate Music, Inc. (BMI)
41 Algonquin Road
Yonkers, New York 10710

Soquel Songs (ASCAP)
c/o Bruce Cohn Music
Attention: Pat Simmons
Post Office Box 878
Sonoma, California 95476

Soultown Music Inc. (BMI)
c/o C. Prager
15 Columbus Circle
New York, New York 10023

Sound of Nolan Music (BMI)
c/o Peter C. Bennett, Esq.
9060 Santa Monica Boulevard
Suite 300
Los Angeles, California 90069

Sounds Music Co. (ASCAP)
301 East 47th Street
New York, New York 10017

Sounds of Lucille Inc. (BMI)
Music Administration Service Co.
c/o S A S, Inc.
1414 Avenue of the Americas
New York, New York 10019

Sour Grapes Music (ASCAP)
see Walden Music Inc.

South Fifth Avenue Publishing (ASCAP)
c/o Prince in New York Corp.
Feinman & Krasilousky
424 Madison Avenue
New York, New York 10017

South Memphis Music (BMI)
5050 Poplar
Suite 517
Memphis, Tennessee 38157

South Mountain Music Corp. (BMI)
2nd Floor
1631 Broadway
New York, New York 10019

Southern Belle Music Publishers (BMI)
3516 Gillespie Avenue
Nashville, Tennessee 37205

Southern Love Music Co. (BMI)
c/o Unichappell
810 Seventh Avenue
New York, New York 10019

Southern Music Publishing Co., Inc.
(ASCAP)
1740 Broadway
New York, New York 10019

Southern Nights Music (ASCAP)
see Combine Music Corp.

Southside Music Corp. (BMI)
Post Office Box 809
Westport, Connecticut 06880

Southtown Music, Inc. (BMI)
c/o Pickwick International
Suite 603
1370 Avenue of the Americas
New York, New York 10019

Sovereign Music Corp. (ASCAP)
c/o Al Lewis
22 East 49th Street
New York, New York 10017

Space Potato Music Ltd. (ASCAP)
1290 Avenue of the Americas
#3230
New York, New York 10019

Spanish Music Ltd.
Address unknown

Special Rider Music (ASCAP)
see Big Sky Music

Spectorius Music Corp. (BMI)
c/o Leonard Hodes
5477-24 Nestle Avenue
Tarzana, California 91356

Spellgold Music (BMI)
20th Century Fox Studios
Box 900
Beverly Hills, California 90213

Aaron Spelling Productions (BMI)
Post Office Box 900
Beverly Hills, California 90213

Spielman Music Co. (ASCAP)
Apartment 16B
710 West End Avenue
New York, New York 10025

Larry Spier, Inc. (ASCAP)
401 Fifth Avenue
New York, New York 10016

Spike's Music (BMI)
c/o Jeffrey Berger
2131 Capitol Avenue
Suite 300
Sacramento, California 95816

Spina Music (ASCAP)
2232 Vista Del Mar Place
Hollywood, California 90028

Spinnaker Music Co. (BMI)
c/o John A. Doley
825 Las Palmas Road
Pasadena, California 91105

Spitfire Music Inc. (BMI)
c/o Mr. Joel Cohen
10043 Hillgrove Drive
Beverly Hills, California 90210

Spitzer Songs, Inc. (BMI)
c/o Braunstein and Chernin
50 East 42nd Street
New York, New York 10017

Spoone Music Corp. (ASCAP)
Suite 706
9255 Sunset Boulevard
Los Angeles, California 90069

Spring Creek Music (ASCAP)
2804 Azalea Place
Nashville, Tennessee 37204

Springalo Toones (BMI)
Suite 200
7715 Sunset Boulevard
Los Angeles, California 90046

Bruce Springsteen Publishing (ASCAP)
36 East 61st Street
New York, New York 10021

Springtime Music Inc. (BMI)
c/o Andrew Feinman
424 Madison Avenue
New York, New York 10017

Spruce Run Music Co. (ASCAP)
see Chappell & Co., Inc.

Harry D. Squires, Inc.
Address unknown

Stafree Publishing Co. (BMI)
c/o Estelle Axton
3114 Radford Road
Memphis, Tennessee 38111

Stage & Screen Music Inc. (BMI)
see Unichappell Music Inc.

Stage Door Music Publishing (BMI)
c/o Bob Archibald
567 Northwest 27th Street
Miami, Florida 33127

Stallion Music Inc. (BMI)
see Tree Publishing Co., Inc.

Stallman Records Inc. (BMI)
1697 Broadway
Suite 401
New York, New York 10019

Stance Music Co. (BMI)
c/o Calvin Carter
2219 East 70th Street
Chicago, Illinois 60649

Standard Music (BMI)
see Emil Ascher Inc.

Staple Music Co. (BMI)
c/o Copyright Service Bureau, Ltd.
221 West 57th Street
New York, New York 10019

Star Spangled Music (ASCAP)
Attention: Rod McBrien
349 East 49th Street
New York, New York 10017

Starday Music (BMI)
c/o Don Pierce
Post Office Box 115
Madison, Tennessee 37115

List of Publishers

Starrite Publishing Co. (BMI)
3409 Brinkman
Houston, Texas 77018

Stasny Music Corp. (ASCAP)
1619 Broadway
New York, New York 10019

State of the Arts Music (ASCAP)
see Yellow Brick Road Music

Steamed Clam Music (BMI)
Attention: Richard I. Leher, Esq.
c/o Mitchell, Silberberg and Knupp
1800 Century Park East
Suite 700
Los Angeles, California 90067

Julian Stearns Arena Music, Inc. (ASCAP)
c/o Elizabeth Stearns Stutt
Apartment 16P
25 Sutton Place South
New York, New York 10022

Steel Chest Music Inc. (ASCAP)
see Skinny Zach Music Inc.

Stein & Van Stock, Inc. (ASCAP)
c/o Jobete Music Co., Inc.
Suite 1600
6255 Sunset Boulevard
Hollywood, California 90028

Billy Steinberg Music (ASCAP)
c/o Manatt, Phelps, Rothenberg &
Tunney
1888 Century Park East
21st Floor
Los Angeles, California 90067

Sterling Music Co. (ASCAP)
c/o Fred Ahlert Music Corp.
8150 Beverly Boulevard, Suite 202
Los Angeles, California 90048

Ray Stevens Music (BMI)
1707 Grand Avenue
Nashville, Tennessee 37212

Dorothy Stewart (ASCAP)
Address unknown

Stigwood Music Inc. (BMI)
see Unichappell Music Inc.

Stillman Song Co., Inc. (ASCAP)
c/o Paul Stillman
Apartment 36F
15 West 72nd Street
New York, New York 10023

Stephen Stills Music (BMI)
Div. of Gold Hill Music, Inc.
5032 Lankershim Boulevard
Suite Number 2
North Hollywood, California 91601

Larry Stock Music, Inc. (ASCAP)
46B Sterling Street
Lakehurst, New Jersey 08733

Stone Agate Music Corp. (BMI)
6255 Sunset Boulevard
Hollywood, California 90028

Stone Diamond Music Corp. (BMI)
6255 Sunset Boulevard
Suite 1600-Department 4-7566
Los Angeles, California 90028

Stonebridge Music (ASCAP)
The Bicycle Music Co.
8075 West Third Street, Suite 400
Los Angeles, California 90048

Storm King Music Inc. (BMI)
250 West 57th Street
Suite 2017
New York, New York 10019

Story Songs Ltd. (ASCAP)
Marshall, Morris, Powell & Silfen
130 West 57th Street
New York, New York 10019

Storybook Music Co. (BMI)
Post Office Box 37
Saugatuck Station
Westport, Connecticut 06880

Strada Music Co. (ASCAP)
c/o Linden & Deutsch
110 East 59th St.
New York, New York 10022

Strange Euphoria (ASCAP)
Post Office Box 66558
Seattle, Washington 98166

Stranger Music Inc. (BMI)
c/o Machat & Kronfeld
1501 Broadway
30th Floor
New York, New York 10036

Stratford Music Corp. (ASCAP)
see Chappell & Co., Inc.

Straw Hat Music Inc. (ASCAP)
see Bygosh Music Corp.

Street Sense Music (ASCAP)
c/o Mitchell, Silberberg & Knupp
1800 Century Park East
Suite 700
Los Angeles, California 90067

Stringberg Music Co. (BMI)
2641 Pulley Road
Nashville, Tennessee 37214

Stripe Music (BMI)
c/o Tom Nixon
Redondo Beach, California

Strong Arm Music (ASCAP)
c/o Fourth Floor Music, Inc.
Post Office Box 135
Bearsville, New York 12409

Strong Songs (BMI)
750 Park Avenue
New York, New York 10021

Charles Strouse Music (ASCAP)
see Big Three Music Corp.

Stuckey Publishing Co. (BMI)
5009 Ashby Drive
Brentwood, Tennessee 37027

Stygian Songs (ASCAP)
see Almo Music Corp.

Su-Ma Publishing Co., Inc. (BMI)
Post Office Box 1125
Shreveport, Louisiana 71163

Henry SueMay Publishing Inc. (BMI)
c/o Lloyd Remick, Esq.
1529 Walnut Street
6th Floor
Philadelphia, Pennsylvania 19102

Sugarplum Music Co. (BMI)
c/o Patsy Bruce
1022 16th Avenue South
Nashville, Tennessee 37212

Summer Camp Publishing Co.
c/o Andre Link-Cinpix, Inc.
8275 Mayrand
Montreal, Quebec H4P 2C8
Canada

Summerhill Songs Inc. (BMI)
c/o Mason & Company
75 Rockefeller Plaza
New York, New York 10019

Summit Music Corp. (ASCAP)
c/o Herb Reis
1619 Broadway
New York, New York 10019

Sunbeam Music Corp. (BMI)
c/o Sunbeam/Valando Music
1700 Broadway
New York, New York 10019

Sundown Music Co. (BMI)
c/o Violet Muszynski
Post Office Box 127
Mason, Illinois 62443

Sunshine Music Co. (BMI)
c/o Jeffrey E. Gorden
No. 108
12111 Strathern Street
North Hollywood, California 91605

Suolubaf Music (BMI)
see Towser Tunes Inc.

Super Songs Unlimited-Sealark (BMI)
Suite 706
200 West 51st Street
New York, New York 10019

Superhype Publishing (ASCAP)
see Walden Music Inc.

Supreme Music Corp. (ASCAP)
1619 Broadway
New York, New York 10019

Sure Fire Music Co., Inc.
60 Music Square West
Nashville, Tennessee 37203

Surrey Music Co. (ASCAP)
  c/o Mr. Frank Stanton
  2315 Foxhaven Drive
  Franklin, Tennessee 37064

Swallow Turn Music (ASCAP)
  see WB Music Corp.

Wilbur Sweatman Music Publishing Co.
(ASCAP)
  c/o Robert Sweeney
  2821 Highland Avenue
  Kansas City, Missouri 64109

Sweet City Records Inc. (ASCAP)
  Attention: Carl Maduri
  28001 Chagrin Boulevard
  Suite 205
  Cleveland, Ohio 44122

Sweet Glory Music Inc. (BMI)
  c/o Martin Itzler
  110 East 59th Street
  New York, New York 10022

Sweet Harmony Music Inc. (ASCAP)
  see WB Music Corp.

Sweet Publishing Ltd. (ASCAP)
  see WB Music Corp.

Sweet River Music Inc. (ASCAP)
  c/o Ampex Corp.
  2201 Lunt Avenue
  Elk Grove Village, Illinois 60007

Sweet Summer Night Music (ASCAP)
  1224 North Vine Street
  Los Angeles, California 90038

Swell Sounds (ASCAP)
  see April Music Inc.

Swing & Tempo Music Publishing Co., Inc.
(BMI)
  c/o Lionel Hampton Enterprises,
  Inc.
  1995 Broadway
  New York, New York 10023

Keith Sykes Music (BMI)
  c/o Keith Sykes
  3974 Hawkins Mill Road
  Memphis, Tennessee 38128

Syl-Zel Music Co. (BMI)
  c/o BMI
  320 West 57th Street
  New York, New York 10019

Sylvia Moy
  Address Unknown

Sylvia Music Publishing Co., Inc. (BMI)
  128-05 161st Street
  Jamaica, New York 11434

T

T A T Communications Co. (BMI)
1901 Avenue of the Stars
Suite 600
Los Angeles, California 90067

Taco Tunes Inc. (ASCAP)
c/o Overland Productions
1775 Broadway
New York, New York 10019

Tadzio Music Co. (ASCAP)
360 East 55th Street
New York, New York 10022

Takya Music, Inc. (ASCAP)
Post Office Box 667
Stroudsburg, Pennsylvania 18360

Talking Beaver (BMI)
Mike Brewer
Route 5
Box 168-A
Claremore, Oklahoma 74107

Tallyrand Music (ASCAP)
see Stonebridge Music

Talmont Music Co. (BMI)
c/o Pickwick International
Suite 603
1370 Avenue of the Americas
New York, New York 10019

Talsil Music Co. (BMI)
c/o Tallu Rosen
Sutton Terrace Apartments
50 Belmont Avenue
Bala-Cynwyd, Pennsylvania 19004

Tamir Music (ASCAP)
c/o Philip Springer
Post Office Box 1174
Pacific Palisades, California 90272

Tammi Music Ltd. (BMI)
c/o Zolt and Loomis
60 East 42nd Street
Suite f1442
New York, New York 10017

Tangerine Music Corp. (BMI)
Attention: Joe Adams
2107 West Washington Boulevard
Los Angeles, California 90018

Tannen Music Enterprises (BMI)
c/o Paul Tannen
38 Laurel Ledge Court
Stamford, Connecticut 06903

Tapier Music Corp. (BMI)
c/o BMI
320 West 57th Street
New York, New York 10019

Taradam Music Inc. (BMI)
1427 Seventh Street
Santa Monica, California 90401

Tarantula Music (ASCAP)
c/o Segel & Goldman, Inc.
9348 Santa Monica Boulevard
Number 304
Beverly Hills, California 90210

Tarka Music Co. (ASCAP)
see Island Music

Tauripin Tunes (ASCAP)
c/o The Doobro Corp.
Attention: Kathy Nelson
Post Office Box 359
Sonoma, California 95476

Larry Taylor Music Corp. (ASCAP)
136 West 52nd Street
New York, New York 10019

Tee and Wink Music Inc. (BMI)
Box 22635
Nashville, Tennessee 37202

Tee Pee Music Co., Inc. (ASCAP)
Room 715
1650 Broadway
New York, New York 10019

Teena Music Corp. (ASCAP)
142 East 34th Street
New York, New York 10016

Temanja Music (BMI)
1111 Ophir Drive
Los Angeles, California 90024

Tembo Music (ASCAP)
2300 Sherbrooke Street East
Montreal, Quebec H2K 1E5
Canada

List of Publishers

Templeton Publishing Co., Inc. (ASCAP)
 Shawnee Press, a Division of
 Waring Enterprises, Inc.
 Delaware Water Gap, Pennsylvania
 18327

Tempo Music (ASCAP)
 c/o Alexandria House
 Post Office Box 300
 Alexandria, Indiana 46001

Ten-East Music (BMI)
 c/o L. Lee Phillips
 Mitchell, Silberberg & Knupp
 1800 Century Park East
 Los Angeles, California 90067

Tender Tunes Music Co., Inc. (BMI)
 c/o Werner Hintzen
 United Artists Music Co., Inc.
 6753 Hollywood Boulevard
 Los Angeles, California 90028

Tennessee Music, Inc. (BMI)
 2001 June Drive
 Nashville, Tennessee 37214

Terrace Music (ASCAP)
 see Blue Lake Music

Terraform Music (ASCAP)
 see Fourth Floor Music Inc.

Terran Music, Inc. (BMI)
 6036 Mayflower Street
 Maywood, California 90270

Texoma Music Corp. (ASCAP)
 Box 74A
 Route 1
 Park Hill, Oklahoma 74451

Thelonious Music (BMI)
 c/o Morris Zuckermen, C.P.A.
 303 West 42nd Street
 New York, New York 10036

Thin Ice Music (ASCAP)
 c/o Segel & Goldman, Inc.
 9348 Santa Monica Boulevard
 Beverly Hills, California 90210

Third Story Music Inc. (BMI)
 6430 Sunset Boulevard
 Suite 1500
 Los Angeles, California 90028

Thirteen Productions, Inc.
 Address unknown

Thirty-Four Music (ASCAP)
 4329 Colfax Avenue
 Studio City, California 91604

Gordon V. Thompson, Ltd. (ASCAP)
 29 Birch Avenue
 Toronto, Ontario M4V 1E2
 Canada

Kay Thompson Music, Inc. (ASCAP)
 9527 Glenwood Road
 Brooklyn, New York 11236

Thorkus Publishing Co. (BMI)
 2525 Horseshoe Canyon Road
 Los Angeles, California 90040

Three Bridges Music Corp. (ASCAP)
 see Chappell & Co., Inc.

Threesome Music
 1801 Avenue of the Stars
 Suite 911
 Los Angeles, California 90067

Threshold Music (BMI)
 c/o Thomas L. Hilliard
 372 Provident Avenue
 Winnetka, Illinois 60093

Thrush Music Publishing Co. (BMI)
 c/o Brian Ross Productions
 3884 Franklin Avenue
 Los Angeles, California 90027

Thunderbird Music, Inc. (ASCAP)
 6515 Sunset Boulevard
 Hollywood, California 90028

Thursday Music Corp. (BMI)
 c/o Fred Ahlert, Jr.
 Suite 202
 8150 Beverly Boulevard
 Los Angeles, California 90048

Tic-Toc Music
 see ATV Music Corp.

Tickson Music (BMI)
 c/o Fischbach, Fischbach & Weiner
 2029 Century Park East
 Suite 1370
 Los Angeles, California 90028

Tideland Music Publishing Corp. (BMI)
Room 501
756 Seventh Avenue
New York, New York 10019

Tidewater Music Co. (BMI)
10880 Wilshire Boulevard
19th Floor
Los Angeles, California 90024

Tiger Music, Inc. (BMI)
241 West 72nd Street
New York, New York 10023

Timana Music (ASCAP)
c/o Tim Saunders
315 West 86th Street
New York, New York 10024

Time Being Music Co. (BMI)
c/o Jury Krytiuk
1343 Matheson Boulevard
Mississauga, Ontario L4W 1R1
Canada

Times-Co. Music (ASCAP)
Address unknown

The Times Square Music Publications Co.
(BMI)
1619 Broadway
11th Floor
New York, New York 10019

Timtobe Music Ltd. (ASCAP)
see Chappell & Co., Inc.

Tinkle Tunes (BMI)
c/o Jean Millington
1427 Union Drive
Davis, California 95616

Tiny Tiger Music (ASCAP)
see Screen Gems-EMI Music Inc.

TNT Music, Inc. (BMI)
3110 Climbing Rose
San Antonio, Texas 78230

Tobac Music (BMI)
c/o Gil Cabot Associates, Inc.
Post Office Box 3901
Hollywood, California 90028

Tobago Music Co.
Address unknown

Tobey Music Corp. (ASCAP)
1650 Broadway
New York, New York 10019

Tobias & Lewis Music Publishers (ASCAP)
Room 604
1650 Broadway
New York, New York 10019

Harry Tobias Music
Address unknown

Toccoa Industries, Inc. (BMI)
c/o Mietus Copyright Management
Post Office Box 432
2351 Laurana Road
Union, New Jersey 07083

Tod Music, Inc. (ASCAP)
632 Winchester Avenue
Union, New Jersey 07083

Tonopah Music Co. (BMI)
10880 Wilshire Boulevard
19th Floor
Los Angeles, California 90024

Top of the Town Music Co. (BMI)
see The EMP Co.

Top Pop Music Co. (BMI)
see Kiddio Music Co.

Top Soil Music (BMI)
c/o Zissu Marcus, Stein & Couture
270 Madison Avenue
New York, New York 10016

Top Talent Inc. (ASCAP)
Strawberry Hill Music Division
Attention: E. E. Siman, Jr.
1121 South Glenstone
Springfield, Missouri 65804

Topper Music Publishing Corp. (ASCAP)
225 East 47th Street
New York, New York 10017

Toter Back Music (ASCAP)
see Sherlyn Publishing Co., Inc.

List of Publishers

Touch Music (ASCAP)
see Sweet River Music Inc.

Touch of Gold Music (BMI)
15625 Vandorf Place
Encino, California 91436

Town and Country Music, Inc. (BMI)
c/o Copyright Service Bureau, Ltd.
221 West 57th Street
New York, New York 10019

Towser Tunes Inc. (BMI)
c/o Weiss and Meibach
888 7th Avenue
New York, New York 10019

Tracebob Music (BMI)
Suite 1225
6430 Sunset Boulevard
Hollywood, California 90028

Trane Music (ASCAP)
Manatt, Phelps, Rothenberg,
Manley & Tunney
1888 Century Park East
21st Floor
L ; Angeles, California 90067

Tredlow Music, Inc. (BMI)
200 West 57th Street
New York, New York 10019

Tree Publishing Co., Inc. (BMI)
Box 1273
Nashville, Tennessee 37203

Tree-Twitty Bird (BMI)
Post Office Box 1273
Nashville, Tennessee 37203

Tri-Chappell Music Inc. (ASCAP)
see Chappell & Co., Inc.

Tri-Parte Music, Inc. (BMI)
Room 701
1650 Broadway
New York, New York 10019

Triangle Music Corp. (ASCAP)
11th Floor
1619 Broadway
New York, New York 10019

Trident Music (ASCAP)
see B. Feldman & Co., Ltd.

Trillion Music, Inc. (BMI)
51 West 86th Street
New York, New York 10024

Trillium Music (ASCAP)
see Chappell & Co., Inc.

Trio Music Co., Inc. (BMI)
1619 Broadway
New York, New York 10019

Triple 'O' Songs Inc. (BMI)
Attention: Nancy Ruehs
425 East 58th Street
Suite 35 A
New York, New York 10022

Triple Three Music, Inc. (BMI)
Suite 1401
1650 Broadway
New York, New York 10019

TRO-Andover Music, Inc. (ASCAP)
Suite 1460
10 Columbus Circle
New York, New York 10019

TRO-Cromwell Music Inc. (ASCAP)
10 Columbus Circle
New York, New York 10019

TRO-Essex Music, Inc. (ASCAP)
Suite 1460
10 Columbus Circle
New York, New York 10019

TRO-Folkways Music Publishers, Inc. (BMI)
Suite 1460
10 Columbus Circle
New York, New York 10019

TRO-Hampshire House Publishing Corp.
(ASCAP)
Suite 1460
10 Columbus Circle
New York, New York 10019

TRO-Hollis Music, Inc. (BMI)
Suite 1460
10 Columbus Circle
New York, New York 10019

TRO-Melody Trails, Inc. (BMI)
Suite 1460
10 Columbus Circle
New York, New York 10019

TRO-Total Music, Inc. (BMI)
Suite 1460
10 Columbus Circle
New York, New York 10019

Trolley Group Inc., The (ASCAP)
c/o Jim Healy
3340 Peachtree Road
Suite 2930 - Tower Place
Atlanta, Georgia 30326

Trousdale Music Publishers, Inc. (BMI)
c/o ABC Contemporary Music
Publishing
8255 Beverly Boulevard
Los Angeles, California 90048

Troy Martin Music, Inc. (BMI)
Post Office Box 58
Nashville, Tennessee 37202

Trumar Music Inc. (BMI)
c/o Prelude Records
200 West 57th Street
New York, New York 10019

Ernest Tubb Music, Inc. (BMI)
c/o Drake Music Group
809 18th Avenue South
Nashville, Tennessee 37203

Tuckahoe Music, Inc. (BMI)
c/o Jim Reeves Enterprises, Inc.
Post Office Drawer 1
Madison, Tennessee 37115

Marshall Tucker Publishing Co. (BMI)
c/o Ronald Taft
18 West 55th Street
New York, New York 10019

Tumble Weed Publishing Co. (BMI)
c/o Van J. Ray
2818 Remond
Dallas, Texas 75211

Tuna Fish Music Inc. (BMI)
see Blackwood Music Inc.

June S. Tune (ASCAP)
Address unknown

Tune Publishers Inc. (BMI)
123 East Alabama Street
Florence, Alabama 35630

Tune Towne Tunes, Inc. (BMI)
c/o Dolores A. & Ralph I. Olsen
9218 Fifteenth Northwest
Seattle, Washington 98117

Tunetime Music, Inc. (BMI)
c/o George Pincus
Room 402
1650 Broadway
New York, New York 10019

Tuneville Music, Inc. (BMI)
c/o Walter A. Smith
Post Office Box 24206
Nashville, Tennessee 37202

Tupper Publishing Co. (BMI)
c/o Laurence Lighter, Esq.
1414 Avenue of the Americas
New York, New York 10019

Turkey Tunes of Santa Cruz (BMI)
236 Sixth Avenue
Santa Cruz, California 95062

Turnpike Tom Music (ASCAP)
see United Artists Music Co., Inc.

Turp Tunes, Ltd. (BMI)
c/o Stonewall Jackson
Lake Waterloo
Brentwood, Tennessee 37207

TV Music Co. (ASCAP)
1650 Broadway
New York, New York 10019

Tweed Music Co. (ASCAP)
Apartment 8D
10 West 74th Street
New York, New York 10023

Twentieth Century Fox Music Corp.
(ASCAP)
10201 West Pico Boulevard
Los Angeles, California 90035

Twentieth Century Music Corp. (ASCAP)
1619 Broadway
New York, New York 10019

Twin Forks Music, Inc. (BMI)
c/o Five Sisters Music, Inc.
3rd Floor
964 Second Avenue
New York, New York 10022

List of Publishers

Twitty Bird Music Publishing Co. (BMI)
c/o Harrianne Condra
Box 1273
Nashville, Tennessee 37202

Two Dees Music (ASCAP)
4445 Northwest 11th Terrace
Oklahoma City, Oklahoma 73107

Two Knight Publishing Co. (BMI)
c/o Copyright Service Bureau Ltd.
221 West 57th Street
New York, New York 10019

Tyler Publishing Co. (BMI)
Post Office Box 231
325 South Bois d'Arc Avenue
Tyler, Texas 75701

Tylerson Music Co. (ASCAP)
1270 Avenue of the Americas
New York, New York 10020

U

Ubiquitous Music Publisher (BMI)
312 S. Mansfield
Los Angeles, California 90036

Udell Music (ASCAP)
see Plymouth Music Co., Inc.

Uganda Music, Inc. (BMI)
c/o Publishers Licensing Corp.
94 Grand Avenue
Englewood, New Jersey 07631

Ultra Music (BMI)
8268 Sunset Boulevard
Los Angeles, California 90046

Unart-Hastings (BMI)
c/o Werner Hintzen
United Artists Music Co., Inc.
6753 Hollywood Boulevard
Los Angeles, California 90028

Unart Music Corp. (BMI)
see United Artists Music Co., Inc.

Unart-Tender Tunes (BMI)
c/o Werner Hintzen
United Artists Music Co., Inc.
6753 Hollywood Boulevard
Los Angeles, California 90028

Unart-Unart (BMI)
c/o Werner Hintzen
United Artists Music Co., Inc.
6753 Hollywood Boulevard
Los Angeles, California 90028

Unbelievable Publishing Corp. (BMI)
105 Midwood Street
Brooklyn, New York 11225

Under Cut Music Publishing Co., Inc.
(BMI)
c/o Robert Casper
1780 Broadway
New York, New York 10019

Unearthly Music Inc. (BMI)
see Fiction Music Inc.

Unichappell Music Inc. (BMI)
810 Seventh Ave.
32nd Floor
New York, New York 10019

Unichappell Music-Six Continents (BMI)
32nd Floor
810 Seventh Avenue
New York, New York 10019

Unichappell-Newkeys (BMI)
32nd Floor
810 Seventh Avenue
New York, New York 10019

Unison Music Co. (ASCAP)
c/o Vic Mizzy
Post Office Box 1792
Beverly Hills, California 90213

United Artists Music Co., Inc.
6753 Hollywood Boulevard
Los Angeles, California 90028

United International Copyright (ASCAP)
Post Office Box 168
New York, New York 10018

United Music Corp. (ASCAP)
101 West 55th Street
New York, New York 10019

United Publishing Co.
Address unknown

Universal Music Corp. (ASCAP)
732 Broadway
New York, New York 10003

Universal Songs Ltd. (ASCAP)
see Ensign Music Corp.

Up the Block Music (ASCAP)
4329 Colfax Avenue
Studio City, California 91604

Upam Music Co. (BMI)
c/o Gopam Enterprises, Inc.
No. 13C-W
11 Riverside Drive
New York, New York 10023

Upfall Music Corp. (ASCAP)
see Chrysalis Music Corp.

Upward Spiral Music (ASCAP)
see WB Music Corp.

U.S. Songs (ASCAP)
see The Hudson Bay Music Co.

V

Vadim Music
Address unknown.

Val-ie Joe Music (BMI)
c/o Shelton, Kalcheim and Cotnoir
79 West Monroe Street
Suite 1305
Chicago, Illinois 60603

Valando Music, Inc. (ASCAP)
c/o Sunbeam/Valando Music
No. 2110
1270 Avenue of the Americas
New York, New York 10020

Valiant Music Co., Inc. (ASCAP)
1619 Broadway
New York, New York 10019

Valley Entertainment Enterprises, Inc.
(ASCAP)
2357 Edelweiss Drive
Beverly Hills, California 90210

Valley Music Ltd.
Address unknown

Valley Publishers, Inc. (BMI)
c/o Hudson Bay Music Co.
11th Floor
1619 Broadway
New York, New York 10019

Valley Spring Music Corp. (BMI)
c/o A. Halsey Cowan
1350 Avenue of the Americas
30th Floor
New York, New York 10019

Valyr Music Corp. (ASCAP)
c/o Philip Becker
40 Galesi Drive
Wayne, New Jersey 07470

Van Halen Music (ASCAP)
Attention: Gail Liss
6525 Sunset Boulevard
Seventh Floor
Hollywood, California 90028

Van Heusen Music Corp. (ASCAP)
301 East 69th Street
Apartment 15B
New York, New York 10021

Van-Lee Music Corp. (ASCAP)
see Paul J. Vance Publishing Co.

Paul J. Vance Publishing Co. (ASCAP)
523 Post Avenue
Westbury, New York 11590

Vanderbuilt Music Corp. (ASCAP)
120 East 34th Street
New York, New York 10001

Ross Vanelli Publishing (BMI)
99 June Court
Thousand Oaks, California 91360

Vanguard Songs (BMI)
6255 Sunset Boulevard
Hollywood, California 90028

Vanjo Music (BMI)
827 Meridian Street
Nashville, Tennessee 37207

Vantim Music (BMI)
c/o Timothy Alvarado
4929 Morse Avenue
Sherman Oaks, California 91403

Vapac Music, Inc. (BMI)
1829 South Micigan Avenue
Chicago, Illinois 60616

List of Publishers

Varia Publishing Co. (BMI)
Taylor-Gardner Enterprises Inc.
c/o Bill Taylor
258 Sailfish
Antioch, Tennessee 37013

Variety Music Inc. (BMI)
c/o Metro-Goldwyn-Mayer, Inc.
10202 West Washington Boulevard
Culver City, California 90230

Vaudeville Music Ltd. (BMI)
c/o Prior, Braun, Cashman
and Sherman
410 Park Avenue
New York, New York 10022

Vector Music (BMI)
c/o Jerry Reed Enterprises
1107 18th Avenue South
Nashville, Tennessee 37212

Vee Ve Music Corp. (BMI)
c/o Mietus Copyright Management
Post Offfice Box 432
2351 Laurana Road
Union, New Jersey 07083

Velvet Apple Music (BMI)
Three International
8 Music Square West
Nashville, Tennessee 37212

Venice Music, Inc. (BMI)
c/o ATV Group
6255 Sunset Boulevard
Hollywood, California 90028

Venus Music Corp. (ASCAP)
1841 Broadway
New York, New York 10023

Vernon Music Corp. (ASCAP)
1619 Broadway
New York, New York 10019

Very Important Publications, Inc. (BMI)
c/o George Greif
Suite 200
8467 Beverly Boulevard
Los Angeles, California 90048

Very Own Music (BMI)
c/o Super Songs
Suite 706
200 West 51st Street
New York, New York 10019

Veytig Music (BMI)
Post Office Box 4094F
San Francisco, California 94110

Victoria Publishing Co. (ASCAP)
c/o George Lee
488 Madison Avenue
New York, New York 10022

Victory Music Co. (BMI)
Post Office Box 432
2351 Laurana Road
Union, New Jersey 07083

Vidor Publications, Inc. (BMI)
1001 North Lincoln Street
Burbank, California 91506

Vigilance Music (BMI)
Post Office Box 1750
Altadena, California 91001

Villa Moret, Inc. (ASCAP)
785 Market Street
San Francisco, California 94103

Village Music Co. (BMI)
c/o Sid Prosen
37-11 87th Street
Jackson Heights, New York 11372

Vincent Music Co., Inc. (BMI)
5710 North Broadway
Chicago, Illinois 60660

Vindaloo Productions Inc. (BMI)
Attention: Robert L. Casper
Casper and Epstein P.C.
1780 Broadway
New York, New York 10019

Vintage Music, Inc. (BMI)
c/o Combine Music Corp.
21 Music Square East
Nashville, Tennessee 37203

Virgin Music Ltd. (ASCAP)
see Chappell & Co., Inc.

Vogel & Clarence Williams
Address unknown

Jerry Vogel Music Co., Inc. (ASCAP)
58 West 45th Street
New York, New York 10036

Volkwein Brothers, Inc. (ASCAP)
632-634 Liberty Avenue
Pittsburgh, Pennsylvania 15222

Harry Von Tilzer Music Publishing Co.
see T. B. Harms Co.

Vonglo Music Co. (BMI)
Post Office Box 2
Cambria Heights, New York 11411

W

W & K Publishing Corp. (BMI)
100-19 Alcott Place
Bronx, New York 10475

Wabash Music Co. (BMI)
c/o Blanche Melrose
5650 Kalmia Drive
Orlando, Florida 32807

Walden Music Inc. (ASCAP)
75 Rockefeller Plaza
New York, New York 10019

Walnut Music Corp. (BMI)
c/o Kenny's Record Shop
148 West 125th Street
New York, New York 10027

Wanessa Music, Inc. (BMI)
Post Office Box 4
Cresskill, New Jersey 07626

Billy Ward Music Co. (BMI)
Suite 205
8913 West Olympic Boulevard
Beverly Hills, California 90211

Warden Music Co., Inc. (BMI)
Post Office Box 3065
Brentwood, Tennessee 37027

Warner Brothers, Inc. (ASCAP)
9000 Sunset Boulevard
Los Angeles, California 90069

Warner Brothers-Seven Arts Music
(ASCAP)
9000 Sunset Boulevard
Los Angeles, California 90069

Warner-Tamerlane Publishing Corp. (BMI)
see WB Music Corp.

Warock Music, Inc. (ASCAP)
400 Madison Avenue
New York, New York 10017

Bernie Wayne Music Co. (BMI)
c/o AGAC
40 West 57th Street
New York, New York 10019

Wayne Music Publishing Co. (BMI)
c/o Arnett Cobb
2411 Wheeler Street
Houston, Texas 77004

WB Music Corp. (ASCAP)
Warner Brothers, Inc.
9000 Sunset Boulevard
Los Angeles, California 90069

We Three Music, Inc. (BMI)
c/o Hal Wesmon
1650 Broadway
New York, New York 10019

Web 4 Music Inc. (BMI)
2107 Faulkner Road Northeast
Atlanta, Georgia 30324

Webster Music Corp. (ASCAP)
c/o Traubner & Flynn
2049 Century Park East
#2500
Los Angeles, California 90067

Wedge Music (BMI)
see Skinny Zach Music Inc.

Wednesday Morning Music Co. (BMI)
c/o Alan Klein
No. 212C
4672 Walford Road
Warrensville Heights, Ohio 44128

Weed High Nightmare Music (BMI)
see Screen Gems-EMI Music Inc.

Weill-Brecht-Harms Co., Inc. (ASCAP)
75 Rockefeller Plaza
New York, New York 10020

Weiss & Barry, Inc. (BMI)
c/o Pickwick International, Inc.
7500 Excelsior Boulevard
Minneapolis, Minnesota 55426

George Weiss
Address unknown

Sam Weiss Music, Inc. (ASCAP)
6253 Hollywood Boulevard
Hollywood, California 90028

Welbeck Music
  see Cherry Lane Music Co., Inc.

Welbeck Music Corp. (ASCAP)
  see ATV Music Corp.

Bruce Welch Music Inc. (ASCAP)
  see April Music Inc.

The Welk Music Group
  1299 Ocean Avenue
  Suite 800
  Santa Monica, California 90401

Wells Music, Inc.
  Address unknown

Welsh Witch Publishing (BMI)
  c/o Gelfand, Breslauer, Rennert &
  Feldman
  1880 Century Park East
  Suite 900
  Los Angeles, California 90067

Wemar Music Corp. (BMI)
  Suite 201
  6515 Sunset Boulevard
  Hollywood, California 90028

Wendell Hall Music Maker (ASCAP)
  c/o The Songwriters Guild
  3rd Floor
  276 Fifth Avenue
  New York, New York 10001

Wesaline Music
  Address unknown

C. & B. West Publishing Co. (BMI)
  Post Office Box 4404
  Las Vegas, Nevada 89106

Western Music Publishing Co. (ASCAP)
  Suite 8
  10000 Riverside Drive
  North Hollywood, California 91602

Westminster Music, Ltd. (ASCAP)
  Address unknown

Wests, Ltd. (ASCAP)
  Address unknown

Westside Music, Inc. (BMI)
  c/o Becker & London
  Gulf & Western Building
  15 Columbus Circle
  New York, New York 10023

Whiskey Drinkin' Music (BMI)
  see Bug Music

Leonard Whitcup, Inc. (ASCAP)
  215 East 68th Street
  New York, New York 10021

White Oak Songs (ASCAP)
  see Canopy Music Inc.

Whiting Music Corp. (ASCAP)
  Room 509
  1619 Broadway
  New York, New York 10019

Whitney Blake Music Publishers (ASCAP)
  Address unknown

Whitney-Kramer-Zaret Music Co. (ASCAP)
  1650 Broadway
  New York, New York 10019

Wildcat Music, Inc. (BMI)
  c/o Milton Kellem
  No. 114
  2780 Northeast 183rd Street
  North Miami Beach, Florida 33160

Wilderness Music Publishing Co. (BMI)
  c/o Tree Publishing Co., Inc.
  Post Office Box 1273
  Nashville, Tennessee 37207

The Wildflowers Co. (ASCAP)
  see Rocky Mountain National Park Music
  Co.

Slim Willet Songs (BMI)
  Post Office Box 997
  Abilene, Texas 79604

Dootsie Williams, Inc. (BMI)
  Suite 334
  121 South Hope Street
  Los Angeles, California 90012

Jerry Williams Music Inc. (BMI)
  see ATV Music Corp.

List of Publishers

Williamson Music Inc. (ASCAP)
see Chappell & Co., Inc.

Chuck Willis Music Co.
Address unknown

Willong Music, Inc. (BMI)
2660A East Medicine Lake Boulevard
Minneapolis, Minnesota 55427

Willow Girl Music (BMI)
c/o Arrow, Edelstein and Gross P.C.
919 Third Avenue
New York, New York 10022

Willow Way Music Co. (BMI)
see United Artists Music Co., Inc.

Bob Wills Music, Inc. (BMI)
11th Floor
1619 Broadway
New York, New York 10019

Wimot Music Publishing (BMI)
c/o Alan Rubens
1307 Vine St.
Philadelphia, Pennsylvania 19107

Win or Lose Publishing (BMI)
see Walden Music Inc.

Wind and Sand Music (ASCAP)
Box 324
Bearsville, New York 12409

Wind Chime Music (BMI)
see House of Gold Music Inc.

Windfall Music Enterprises Inc. (BMI)
1790 Broadway
Penthouse
New York, New York 10019

Window Music Publishing Inc. (BMI)
809 18th Avenue South
Nashville, Tennessee 37203

Windsong Music (BMI)
2811 Wilton Road
West Columbia, South Carolina 29169

Wingate Music Corp. (ASCAP)
c/o ABC Contemporary Music
Publishing
8255 Beverly Boulevard
Los Angeles, California 90048

Winlyn Music, Inc. (BMI)
Attention: Lester Boles
11th Floor
1619 Broadway
New York, New York 10019

Winter Blues Music Inc. (BMI)
c/o Borck and Mensch
350 Fifth Avenue
Room 5220
New York, New York 10001

Wintergreen Music, Inc. (ASCAP)
162 East 55th Street
New York, New York 10022

Wishbone Music Inc. (BMI)
c/o Don Williams Music Group
1888 Century Park East
Suite 1222
Los Angeles, California 90067

Witch Music (ASCAP)
see WB Music Corp.

M. Witmark & Sons (ASCAP)
488 Madison Avenue
New York, New York 10022

Wolf-Mills Music, Inc. (ASCAP)
8814 Trask Avenue
Playa del Rey, California 90291

Wonder Music, Inc. (BMI)
3051 Clairmont Road Northeast
Atlanta, Georgia 30329

Wonderland Music Co., Inc. (BMI)
c/o Vic Guder-Director of
Music Publishing
350 South Buena Vista Street
Burbank, California 91521

B. F. Wood Music Co., Inc. (ASCAP)
11th Floor
1619 Broadway
New York, New York 10019

Woodcrest Music, Inc. (BMI)
Hilltop Road
Birchrunville, Pennsylvania 19421

Wooden Nickel Music Inc. (ASCAP)
c/o Cooper, Epstein & Hurewitz
9465 Wilshire Boulevard
Suite 800
Beverly Hills, California 90212

List of Publishers

Woodmere Music (BMI)
c/o Douglas Horn, Esq.
730 Bunker Road
North Woodmere, New York 11598

Woodrow Music, Inc. (ASCAP)
Address unknown

Woodsongs Music (BMI)
Attention: Woodrow Wilson
Fee Records
16116 Bentley Avenue
Detroit, Michigan 48219

Woolnough Music Inc. (BMI)
1550 Neptune
Leucadia, California 92024

Words & Music, Inc. (ASCAP)
8th Floor
17 West 60th Street
New York, New York 10023

World Artist Music Co., Inc.
Box 4247
Greenwich, Connecticut 06830

World Music, Inc. (ASCAP)
1619 Broadway
New York, New York 10019

World Song Publishing
see Interworld Music Group

World War Three Music (BMI)
Attn: Earl Shelton
309 South Broad Street
Philadelphia, Pennsylvania 19107

World Wide Music Co., Ltd.
Ash Street, Route 2, Box 466-B
Central City, Kentucky 42330

Wormwood Publishing Co. (BMI)
c/o Wayne Moss
1108 Cinderella Street
Madison, Tennessee 37115

Wow and Flutter Music Publishing
(ASCAP)
c/o Jess S. Morgan & Co., Inc.
6420 Wilshire Boulevard
19th Floor
Los Angeles, California 90048

Vernon Wray Music (BMI)
c/o Kenneth L. Allen, P.C.
Suite 705
177 North Church Avenue
Tucson, Arizona 85701

Wren Music Co., Inc. (BMI)
c/o MPL Communications, Inc.
39 West 54th Street
New York, New York 10019

Wright-Gerstl Productions (BMI)
c/o Gerstl & Gorman Inc.,
Attorneys at Law
33 Soledad Drive
Box 3024
Monterey, California 93940

L. Wright Music Co., Ltd. (ASCAP)
Address unknown

Wrights Music Co. (ASCAP)
636 Lou Ann Street
Salem, Virginia 24153

Wrist Music Co. (BMI)
c/o Joseph Sarauno
Post Office Box 1537
Hollywood, California 90028

Writers Night Music (ASCAP)
Post Office Box 22635
Nashville, Tennessee 38202

Wynwood Music Co. (BMI)
Post Office Box 101
Broad Run, Virginia 22014

X

X-Ray Music (BMI)
12328 Deer Brook Lane
Los Angeles, California 90049

XIV Music Co., Inc.
c/o Nat Schnaph
10 Swirl Lane
Levittown, New York 11756

Y

Yameta Co., Ltd. (BMI)
Address unknown

Yeah Inc. (ASCAP)
  Mr. Melvin Van Peebles
  850 7th Avenue
  New York, New York 10019

Yellen & Fain (ASCAP)
  The Jack Yellen Farm
  Springville, New York 14141

Jack Yellen Music (ASCAP)
  300 East 40th Street
  New York, New York 10022

Yellow Brick Road Music (ASCAP)
  7250 Beverly Boulevard
  Los Angeles, California 90036

Yellow Dog Music Inc. (ASCAP)
  see The Hudson Bay Music Co.

Yessongs (ASCAP)
  see Walden Music Inc.

Yo-Ho Publishing Co. (BMI)
  c/o Mietus Copyright Management
  Post Office Box 432
  2351 Laurana Road
  Union, New Jersey 07083

Yolk Music Co. (ASCAP)
  see Six Continents Music Publishing Inc.

Vincent Youmans Co., Inc. (ASCAP)
  390 West End Avenue
  New York, New York 10024

Young City Music (BMI)
  see Screen Gems-EMI Music Inc.

Victor Young Publications, Inc. (ASCAP)
  c/o Chappell Music Co.
  810 Seventh Avenue
  New York, New York 10019

Yuggoth Music (BMI)
  c/o James Golden
  3128 Cavandish Drive
  Los Angeles, California 90064

Yvonne Publishing Co. (BMI)
  Apartment 11
  11425 Rochester Avenue
  Los Angeles, California 90025

Z

Zawinul Music (BMI)
  c/o Gopam Enterprises, Inc.
  No. 13C-W
  11 Riverside Drive
  New York, New York 10023

Zeitgeist Music Co. (BMI)
  c/o Gretchen Cryer
  885 West End Avenue
  New York, New York 10025

Zerlad Music Enterprises, Ltd. (BMI)
  c/o Management Three Music
  4th Floor
  9744 Wilshire Boulevard
  Beverly Hills, California 90212

Zero Productions (BMI)
  c/o Clog Holdings
  3300 Warner Boulevard
  Burbank, California 91501

Zevon Music (BMI)
  c/o Jess Morgan & Co., Inc.
  6420 Wilshire Boulevard
  Nineteenth Floor
  Los Angeles, California 90048

Zipf Music Publishing Co.
  Address unknown

Zira Music Publishing Co. (BMI)
  c/o Isaac Harper, Jr.
  c/o Top Ten Record Shop
  202 East 170th Street
  Bronx, New York 10456

Zodiac Music Corp. (BMI)
  c/o Harold Orenstein
  110 West 57th Street
  New York, New York 10019

Zomba Enterprises Inc. (BMI)
  1348 Lexington Avenue
  New York, New York 10028